Introduction to

PSYCHOLOGY

Introduction to PSYCHOLOGY

Patricia M. Wallace
University of Maryland

Jeffrey H. Goldstein
Temple University

Peter Nathan
*Rutgers, The State University
of New Jersey*

wcb
Wm. C. Brown Publishers
Dubuque, Iowa

Book Team
Editor *James M. McNeil*
Developmental Editor *Sandra E. Schmidt*
Production Editor *Diane Clemens*
Designer *Kay Dolby*
Permissions Editor *Carla D. Arnold*
Photo Research Editor *Michelle Oberhoffer*

wcb group
Wm. C. Brown *Chairman of the Board*
Mark C. Falb *President and Chief Executive Officer*

wcb
Wm. C. Brown Publishers, College Division
G. Franklin Lewis *Executive Vice-President, General Manager*
E. F. Jogerst *Vice-President, Cost Analyst*
George Wm. Bergquist *Editor in Chief*
John Stout *Executive Editor*
Beverly Kolz *Director of Production*
Chris C. Guzzardo *Vice-President, Director of Sales and Marketing*
Bob McLaughlin *National Sales Manager*
Julie A. Kennedy *Production Editorial Manager*
Marilyn A. Phelps *Manager of Design*
Faye M. Schilling *Photo Research Manager*

CONTENTS

list of boxes

preface

*I*n taking a close look at today's introductory psychology students, a psychology professor would notice many important differences between them and the students of a decade or more ago. Both the characteristics of the students and the field of psychology have changed in some fundamental ways.

The current college population is far more varied than the average population of a decade ago. Although there are many students who have followed the traditional pattern of moving directly from high school into college, today's freshman class is likely to be made up of older students as well. These older students may be full-time students who postponed college for a few years or more after high school or who interrupted their college studies to work for a short time. There are also an increasing number of adult part-time students who continue to hold down jobs while attending classes or who attend college part-time because of family or other responsibilities. These changing enrollment patterns mean that a typical introductory class today is going to be far more heterogeneous than the introductory psychology class of a decade ago.

Concern with career plans is a common thread in the motivations of today's college student of any age. This generation of "traditional" college students who enter college shortly after graduating from high school are far more goal-oriented and career-oriented than their counterparts of a decade ago, and more interested in the relevance of their studies to their future endeavors. At the same time, older students may seek to integrate the world of work with the world of learning, applying what they acquire in college at their current jobs; or, they may be returning to school to improve their employment potential or to upgrade their skills.

As the needs of the students are changing, so is the field of psychology. Now psychologists study human behavior from many different perspectives, using several levels of analysis. From the standpoint of putting together introductory psychology materials for the student of the 1980's, the most important trends are in the expansion of psychology's subject fields and the sophisticated application of psychological knowledge.

Both applied research and the process of applying psychological information to real world problems are gaining momentum, and more psychologists are becoming involved in such applications. Examples cover a broad spectrum: techniques to help astronauts avoid space sickness; treatments for epilepsy; design of hospitals; steps to avoid panic in crowds; training techniques for people whose offices are computerizing; software for computer-assisted instruction; career counseling for job-changers; recovery procedures after a stroke; approaches to help managers avoid racial discrimination; strategies to minimize sleeping problems in shift workers; memory aids; methods to avoid temporary blindness in night combat; counseling approaches for dying patients. The list of applications continues to grow.

These changes in the composition of the introductory psychology class and in the field of psychology create a need for a new, forward-looking introductory text. The new directions in psychology and the characteristics and motives of the students taking psychology have come together in that they both are more problem-centered. Students would like to see how psychology can contribute to solving their personal problems and the problems of the world in general. And psychology can contribute a great deal. Students are more practical, career-oriented, and consumer-oriented, and may be more mature, and they want a high quality course. They do not want a "watered down" version of psychology, but many, especially those who have been out of school for some time, will want and need a variety of pedagogical aids.

We wrote this text with a heterogeneous audience in mind. The book contains all the core material one would expect in any mid-level introductory psychology text. There is considerable emphasis on experimental methods and research; each chapter contains detailed descriptions of specific research studies as well as highlighted research boxes. The material is not reduced in scope or in complexity, but is presented in a way that is appropriate for the new composition of students.

We have paid special attention to the growing field of applied research and psychological applications, describing how principles worked out in the laboratory are transferred to real world settings. The attention devoted to applications is partly due to the phenomenal growth in this area of psychology. It also coincides with the changing needs and interests of the student population. The text incorporates many examples of applied research in each chapter, highlighted boxes on applications, and a chapter that is devoted exclusively to applied areas, including information on industrial and organizational psychology, human factors, and environmental psychology. This chapter in particular was included to acknowledge how psychology is pushing out its boundaries and expanding into more and more areas. In addition, computer applications of psychology are covered in a special appendix.

What else is special about this text? To accommodate and encourage a wide range of students, we've provided a built-in study reinforcement system that actively involves your students in learning. The built-in study system leads to mastery of text material without the need for a separate study guide. These learning aids have been carefully designed to enhance student learning. Each chapter begins with an **Outline,** which shows the overall organizational framework of the chapter, and with a list of **Learning Objectives,** page-referenced to help your students focus their studying and check their learning. Within the chapter, every important new **key term** is boldfaced; its definition follows

in italic type. A fill-in-the-blank **Guided Review,** referenced to learning objective, follows each major section of the chapter. A complete, page-referenced outline **Summary** appears at the conclusion of the chapter. It is followed by a page-referenced **Action Glossary** which asks students to match key terms and definitions to create their own glossary. Finally, twenty multiple-choice questions appear in a **Self-Test.** These questions are referenced to both learning objectives and text pages, allowing students to check their learning and refer back to chapter material that may require further study for mastery. A list of **Suggested Readings** concludes the chapter.

The applications orientation is further reinforced by the boxes that appear in each chapter. **Career Boxes** in each chapter discuss how psychology might be used on the job, or describe specific careers related to the area of psychology discussed in the chapter. **Application Boxes** present an interesting application of chapter content. And **Research Boxes** focus in depth on an exciting new research study and are designed to help your students understand the research process.

Along with comprehensive psychology, applications and career orientation, and a built-in study system, Wm. C. Brown Publishers can offer you more: a unique *value* to you and your students. As a publisher, **wcb** has eliminated many of the unnecessary frills to keep the price of this text very low. Unnecessary color photos and white space have been eliminated. Your students do not have to pay the extra cost of a hard-cover binding and of an additional **Study Guide.** Students get a solid, comprehensive, well-balanced presentation of all the major areas of psychology at about half the price of similar texts.

To supplement the built-in study system in the text, **wcb** is offering a unique learning aid to your students, the **wcb Study Tapes.** Two ninety-minute cassette tapes include chapter and key term reviews for each of the sixteen chapters in this text. These tapes reinforce study of the text for even more effective learning.

A complete instructional package also accompanies this text. An **Instructor's Manual** with **Test Item File** of over 2,000 test questions is available, prepared by Frank Calabrese of Community College of Philadelphia. The Instructor's Manual includes chapter summaries, chapter outlines, key terms, discussion questions, essay questions, lecture suggestions, and film suggestions. The Test Item File includes more than 2,000 multiple-choice questions and 300 fill-in-the-blank and true/false questions. Each multiple-choice item is page-referenced to the text and identified as factual, conceptual, or applied.

Another instructional aid available to adopters of this text is **Psycom, Psychology on Computer: Simulations, Experiments and Projects.** Psycom is the interactive software package for introductory psychology that provides twelve high-interest simulations for the microcomputer. Psycom helps the student to learn how to collect data and to analyze and discuss the results within the context of scientific study. The Psycom package includes a set of program diskettes, an instructor's package, and a student workbook.

All test questions are available on **wcb TestPak,** a free computerized testing service available to adopters of INTRODUCTION TO PSYCHOLOGY. The call-in/mail-in service offers a test master, a student answer sheet, and an answer key within two working days of receipt of the instructor's request.

TestPak is also available for instructors who want to use their Apple IIe, Apple IIc, or IBM PC microcomputer system to create their own tests. Upon adoption of INTRODUCTION TO PSYCHOLOGY and upon request, the instructor will receive program diskettes and the user's guide. With these, the instructor will be able to create tests, answer sheets, and answer keys. The program allows for adding, deleting, or modifying test questions. No programming experience is necessary.

Also free to adopters of INTRODUCTION TO PSYCHOLOGY is **wcb QuizPak,** the interactive self-testing, self-scoring quiz program. Your students can review text material from any chapter by testing themselves on an Apple IIe, IIc, or IBM PC. Adopters will receive the QuizPak program, question disks, and an easy-to-follow User's Guide. You may modify or delete the questions we provide or add your own. No programming experience is necessary.

wcb GradePak is a computerized grading program available free to qualified adopters. It makes calculating and reporting your students' grades an easy task! Each disk holds data for classes of up to 500 students and 60 scores per student, calculates class averages on all scores and overall class averages, provides a grade profile report, and allows numeric input as well as letter grades. GradePak runs on the Apple IIe, IIc, and on the IBM PC. (Apple is a registered trademark of Apple Computer, Inc.)

part

I

INTRODUCTION TO PSYCHOLOGY

c h a p t e r

1

Psychology: With Applications

LEARNING OBJECTIVES

After reading this chapter, the student should be able to

1. define psychology, and provide descriptive examples of the kind of subject matter psychologists investigate. **(p. 4)**

2. provide examples of the kind of work psychologists do in academic settings, government, business, and private practice. **(p. 5)**

3. explain the fundamental elements of the scientific approach to the study of behavior. **(p. 6)**

4. describe and provide examples of descriptive and experimental research in psychology, and state the advantages and disadvantages of each. **(p. 11)**

5. describe historical approaches to the study of psychology, and identify the founders of these schools of thought. **(p. 17)**

6. describe four modern perspectives in psychology, each of which emphasizes different aspects and causes of human behavior. **(p. 19)**

7. define and provide examples of applied and basic research in psychology. **(p. 23)**

Psychology: A Subject for and about People

Studying human behavior can be rather simple; many of us do it every day:

I noticed you aren't laughing at my jokes these days.

Cheryl is such a bore. She never wants to go anywhere. I think she's afraid of crowds or something.

If we want to sell this toothpaste, we've got to design ads with plenty of sex, sex, sex!

It can also be an extremely complicated endeavor. Psychologists can design elaborate studies, using hundreds of subjects and electronic measuring equipment that resembles the console of a space shuttle. Still, when they have gathered all their data and then report the conclusions they have drawn, psychologists seldom say anything very decisive about human behavior. Their reports often include tentative phrases like "The data *suggest* that . . ." or "*Sometimes* people *tend* to . . ."

We all work with, play with, and observe other people all the time. Why are they so hard to understand? In fact, why are *we* so hard to understand? What is it about the subject of psychology that tongue-ties even the most experienced scientists?

Psychology: What Is It?

Psychology is *the study of behavior.* Although this definition seems simple, the range of behavior in which psychologists are interested is enormous, from the behavior of a tiny cell in the brain to the behavior of large groups of people. Furthermore, psychology is not limited to the study of human behavior; it also includes the behavior of animals. One goal of research on animal behavior is to learn more about human beings. Another, however, is simply to learn more about the other species that share our planet.

Not all psychologists agree completely with the definition of psychology that is given here. Many psychologists prefer to limit the science to the study of easily observable, overt behavior. Others, however, think the definition of psychology should be expanded to "the study of behavior and mental processes" to make it clear that thoughts, dreams, images, and other mental activities are an important part of what psychology is all about, even though they are not readily observable. As we will see later in this chapter, defining the term psychology is a controversial issue.

Who Are Psychologists?

A psychologist is a specialist in psychology. The term is usually used to refer only to people with advanced degrees in the subject: a Ph.D. or a newer, more clinical type of degree called Doctor of Psychology (Psy.D.). (See Career Box: Training in Psychology.)

Types of Psychologists. Because the subject matter of psychology is so diverse, psychologists have become specialized within the field. Some have specialized in **physiological psychology,** *the study of the relationship between physiology and behavior.* Others have specialized in **social psychology,** *which is the study of the way humans behave in groups.* Table 1.1 lists several specialties within psychology and gives a brief description of each. The table also gives the percentage of doctoral-level psychologists in each field (Stapp, Tucker, and VandenBos, 1985).

Clinical psychology, *which involves the diagnosis and treatment of behavioral disorders,* has always been the most popular specialty within psychology. But, as the table shows, psychologists are involved in a great deal more than the study and treatment of abnormal behavior. Psychologists, particularly those involved with clinical work, often are confused with **psychiatrists,** *who are medical doctors specializing in behavioral disorders.* Although a clinical psychologist and a psychiatrist might use very similar techniques to treat a patient who is afraid of the dark, their training and orientation may be quite different. Also, a psychiatrist can prescribe drugs.

Table 1.1 Specialties in psychology

Specialty	Description	Percent of doctoral-level psychologists
Clinical	Diagnosis and treatment of emotional and behavioral disorders.	44
Counseling and guidance	Deals with personal problems not classified as illnesses, such as vocational and social problems of college students.	11
Developmental	Studies behavioral changes that occur during growth and development of an organism.	4
Educational	Studies ways to apply psychological principles to the educational setting.	6
School	Does testing, guidance, and research in the schools.	5
Experimental	Usually does research on topics such as perception, sensation, or memory, using either human or animal subjects. (Since many kinds of psychologists perform experiments, this category is not well named.)	3
Comparative	Studies the behavior of animals, often in natural settings.	0.3
Physiological	Studies the relationship between behavior and physiology.	1
Industrial/organizational	Does research on human behavior in work settings, and applies psychological principles to business and management problems.	6
Personality	Studies the individual characteristics that account for each person's unique adjustments to the environment.	0.8
Psychometrics	Does research and development work on psychological tests and measurements, including IQ tests, vocational interest tests, and personality measures.	0.8
Social	Studies social interactions and the ways that human beings influence one another's behavior in group settings.	3
Psychology, general		2

From J. Stapp, A. M. Tucker, and G. R. VandenBos, "Census of Psychological Personnel: 1983," in American Psychologist, 40, 1317–1351. Copyright © 1985 by the American Psychological Association. Reprinted by permission of the publisher and the author.

What Do Psychologists Do?

Most people seem to think that psychologists are usually engaged in private practice, seeing patients as do physicians and dentists. Actually, only about five percent of psychologists work full-time in an independent practice. The settings in which psychologists work are almost as diverse as the topics that interest them. Table 1.2 shows the results of a survey of psychologists (Stapp, Tucker, and VandenBos, 1985) who listed their major employment.

The largest proportion of doctoral-level psychologists are employed by academic institutions (30.1 percent). Usually, they teach undergraduate and graduate students, do research, and do some writing. An academic psychologist whose specialty is physiological psychology, for example, might teach one or two introductory-level psychology courses, one advanced course on the biological basis of behavior, and perhaps one graduate seminar on a specialized topic like drugs and the nervous system. In addition, this psychologist might run an animal laboratory with hundreds of rats and

Table 1.2 Employment settings of psychologists

Setting	Percent
University settings	18.3
Four-year college	4.7
Other academic settings (two year colleges, medical schools, etc.)	6.3
Schools and other educational settings	14.9
Independent practice	17.5
Hospitals	8.9
Clinics	9.6
Other human services (counseling centers, rape centers, child abuse centers, hot lines, etc.)	8.1
Business and government (consulting firms, government research organizations, criminal justice system, government agencies, private research, etc.)	12.2

From J. Stapp, A. M. Tucker, and G. R. VandenBos, "Census of Psychological Personnel: 1983," in American Psychologist, 40, 1317–1351. Copyright © 1985 by the American Psychological Association. Reprinted by permission of the publisher and the author.

conduct research on the effects of maternal nutrition on the brain development and later behavior of the pups.

A social psychologist who works in a government research organization may have very different responsibilities. Her work might take her to a Marine combat-training area in Virginia. She may study, for example, how the relationship between five Marines who are locked up together for four days (to simulate prisoner-of-war conditions) begins to change and deteriorate. The government often has questions that can be answered by psychological research, and it usually hires psychologists to carry out that research.

A psychologist employed by another government agency, the Department of the Interior, might work on completely different projects. With a background in comparative psychology, this person might report to a prairie-dog town, instead of a downtown office, each morning at 8:00. His research might focus on the communication signals used by prairie dogs to warn one another of approaching predators.

Another psychologist might treat patients at a veteran's hospital. This individual probably would be trained in clinical psychology. He or she could spend the day giving patients psychological tests and trying to learn more about their behavioral disorders. This person might run group therapy sessions or treat patients on a one-to-one basis.

It should be clear from this discussion that psychologists do many fascinating things. What they share is their interest in behavior. The Research Box: The Psychology of Psychology shows that psychologists are even interested in their own behavior.

GUIDED REVIEW

Learning Objectives 1 and 2

1. Psychology is the study of _____ , both of human beings and other animals. Many psychologists add the words "and mental processes" to the definition of psychology to emphasize that mental activities are also appropriate topics for psychological investigation.

2. The term _____ refers to specialists in psychology who have advanced graduate degrees in the field.

3. Psychologists usually specialize in subfields such as _____ (which deals with the relationship between physiology and behavior), or _____ (which deals with the diagnosis and treatment of behavioral disorders). Other subfields include social psychology, developmental psychology, or comparative psychology.

ANSWERS

1. behavior 2. psychologist 3. physiological psychology; clinical psychology

The Psychological Approach to Behavior

Psychology is a science, and psychologists studying behavior follow all the rules of the scientific method. As a tool for acquiring knowledge about our world, the scientific approach has proven invaluable. In order for the method to work, scientists must make three important assumptions about the nature of the world. These assumptions are **order, determinism,** and **discoverability.**

CAREER BOX

Training in Psychology

The term "psychologist" usually refers to people who have successfully completed a doctoral degree based in part on a dissertation related to the field of psychology. This is usually a requirement for becoming a member of the American Psychological Association (A.P.A.). The training a psychologist receives varies, depending on his or her choice of a specialty. For example, a person who wants to become a licensed clinical psychologist would first earn a bachelor's degree and then enter an APA-approved graduate clinical training program. Such programs are offered at many universities in the country. This requires substantial coursework in fields such as abnormal psychology and psychological testing, as well as an internship in which the graduate student works under supervision in some clinical setting, such as a mental health clinic, a V.A. hospital, or a center for the treatment of drug abusers.

Although the title of psychologist is usually reserved for people with a doctorate degree, individuals with master's or bachelor's degrees often work in psychological settings. People with master's degrees in some area of behavioral science can provide clinical services under the supervision of a psychologist, and the *Monitor* (the A.P.A.'s monthly newspaper) often announces these kinds of openings. For example,

a recent issue contained the following announcements:

Substance abuse counselor: Progressive community mental health center has opening for an experienced substance abuse counselor. Master's degree and experience in direct service is required. . . .

Victimology specialist: MA in psychology or related field preferred. Concentration areas of spouse abuse, rape counseling, and crisis intervention. Duties include counseling, outreach, consultation and education. Writing skills necessary. . . .

There are also opportunities for people with a bachelor's degree in psychology to work in psychology-related settings. Various agencies of the federal government, for example, employ individuals with undergraduate training in psychology to work as psychology aides, psychology technicians, researchers, trainers, and other occupations. In the private sector, psychology graduates are hired as research assistants, therapist trainees, learning disabilities teachers, lab assistants, psychometrics workers, mental health counselors, residential counselors, childcare workers, and probation counselors. As we shall see in the Career Boxes in other chapters, training in psychology is also useful in other employment settings.

First, they assume that the world is orderly and that events do not occur in a random, chaotic way. It would be impossible to make any generalizations about human behavior if this assumption were not true. *Second, the* *scientific approach assumes that some events determine the occurrence of other events—that there is a cause-and-effect chain of determinism.* It may not always be possible to identify all the causes of an event,

RESEARCH BOX

The Psychology of Psychology

One of the most interesting research topics in psychology is the field of psychology itself: how it is changing, who is entering it, who is succeeding in it (and who is failing), why people choose it, and where it is going next. Psychologists have an intense interest in human behavior including their own.

Ray Over, for example, a psychologist at LaTrobe University in Australia, has conducted some interesting studies of the publications in psychological journals. In one study he found that since 1949, the number of papers published with more than one author has been growing considerably (Over, 1982). This could mean that the pursuit of knowledge in psychology is becoming less and less a "lone-wolf" occupation. Research studies are more likely to involve teams of researchers, often with different specializations and complimentary expertise. He also found that psychologists rarely list their names in alphabetical order on their published papers. Instead, they tend to list the authors according to how much each contributed to the research project. This is sometimes very difficult to do, especially when there are more than two or three people involved.

Several researchers have examined publication patterns to determine how men and women fare and whether there might be any differences in either the productivity or recognition of men and women. One study, for example, measured research productivity by the number of papers published per year (Over, 1982).

Women publish significantly fewer papers than men, but the quality of those papers appeared to be the same, judging from the number of times each paper was cited in other articles. Nevertheless, the top awards in most disciplines usually go to the prolific scientists, and psychology is no exception. The barriers and difficulties women face in a career in psychology seem to parallel those in other fields. They have more trouble finding jobs, they are promoted more slowly, and they are paid less than men with comparable qualifications.

On a humorous note, J. T. Dillon (1981) argues that the primary correlate of scholarship in psychology is not gender or productivity; it is the colon (:). He noted that most of the titles of papers in psychological journals were long, difficult to read, and awkward, partly because they contained a colon. Examples are numerous. Even the authors of this text have used the device (Complex environments: effects on brain development [Wallace, 1974]; Outcomes in professional team sports: chance, skill, and situational factors [Goldstein, 1979]). An analysis of the titles of articles appearing in a variety of scholarly and nonscholarly publications showed that more than two-thirds of the published scholarly articles contained colons. In contrast, a majority of the unpublished research titles, and the published nonresearch titles, were without colons. Dillon calls the phenomenon "titular colonicity" (which may sound more like a glandular disease than a correlate of scholarship).

but scientists assume that they exist. *Last, scientists assume that the causes for any particular events are discoverable, at least theoretically.* They do not allow words like "magic" or "unknowable" to creep into their explanations.

The goals of the scientific approach are important ones for psychology. First, the method seeks to obtain understanding by describing events accurately and tracing the sequence of causes that led to them. A second goal is prediction. Once scientists understand a particular behavior, such as human violence, then it becomes possible to predict who will show violence and when they will show it. Being able to predict the occurrence of an event is an important step in being able to control it, which is the last goal of science. With respect to violence, it would be important for scientists to know not only when it is going to occur but what might be done to lessen it or eliminate it completely. The key to this approach is **objectivity;** *events in the environment must be observed as dispassionately as possible, without our usual human prejudices and emotional distortions.* We must try to observe human behavior without biases and without preconceived notions of how and why we do things. This may not be completely possible since our thinking is so closely linked to our culture, our period of history, our politics, and many other factors (Kennedy, et al., 1984; Krasner and Houts, 1984; Scarr, 1985). Nevertheless, it is an important goal.

Observing Behavior

The first step in the psychological approach is to objectively observe behavior. This is not as easy as it seems because we have so many expectations and preconceived ideas about how people behave. For example, the toddlers in figure 1.1 might be fighting over access to a slide, a type of behavior that is familiar to parents of two-year-olds. But one child might be trying to help the other, or they might both be nervously clinging to the bars because of a sudden earthquake tremor.

Figure 1.1 It is difficult to make an objective observation about these children because of preconceived ideas about how children behave

An objective description of an event should simply describe the people, their clothing, their postures and positions relative to one another, their facial expressions, their movements, their voices and words, and the environment. The description might offer hypotheses about the motives or emotions of the people, but it should make it clear that these are inferences and not objective observations. When the information about an event is limited, the observer tends to draw inferences in order to complete the picture and put together a coherent and understandable happening. Often these inferences are inaccurate or biased due to faulty memory, prejudices, and stereotypes.

Figure 1.2 *Behavior can be described on many levels, ranging from the physiological to the social and political*

Levels of Analysis.   The two standing boys in figure 1.2 both have their fists up, and the boy on the ground appears distressed. We might infer that they have been fighting and that the boy on the ground was knocked down. While this description is accurate and objective, it is limited to only one level of analysis. Behavior can be described on many levels, ranging from the physiological to the social and political.

On the physiological level, we might have discussed the heart rate or blood pressure of the boy in the football shirt, or perhaps the amount of hormones circulating in his body. Emotional behavior, including aggression, is related to a number of physiological changes, and we could easily have mentioned some of them in the description.

Any description and explanation of the boys' behavior would be more complete if it included a discussion of previous experience. For instance, the father of the boy in the football shirt might have rewarded his son for being a bully from the time he started interacting with other children.

A social explanation of the incident might be that the boy on the right is copying the aggressor's behavior because of social pressure. On a political level of analysis, we might describe the aggressive scene in terms of the American culture. Boys are often encouraged to be fairly aggressive in the United States.

Which explanation is correct? They all are. Any human behavior can be described and explained on many levels: a complete explanation should include reference to several levels. Human behavior is so complex that it rarely has a single cause on a single level. When we try to predict a behavior like aggression, for example, it becomes apparent that single-level explanations fall short. Aggression, cannot be completely explained by hormones or particular kinds of brain activity. Nor can we explain it entirely in terms of upbringing, neighborhood experiences, or cultural expectations. People who come from violent neighborhoods are not necessarily violent themselves.

Hypotheses and Theories.   Once scientists have made some objective observations of behavior on one or more levels of analysis, they might form a **hypothesis.** *A hypothesis is a tentative statement, not yet tested, about the relationship between two or more events.* For example, a scientist might formulate a hypothesis after watching several episodes in a restaurant in which patrons attacked waiters who took too long to serve them: "If people are frustrated by long waits, they behave aggressively toward the source of their frustration."

After testing this hypothesis (using methods described in the next section), the scientists may form other, related hypotheses: "If hungry people are frustrated by being denied access to food, they will behave aggressively toward the source of their frustration." "If people are frustrated by having to suddenly change their plans, they will behave aggressively toward the source of their frustration." After testing several related hypotheses, the researchers may formulate a **theory,** or *a general statement about human behavior.* For example, they may propose a theory that links frustration of all kinds to aggressive behavior. This theory may stimulate people to deduce more new hypotheses, which, if tested and confirmed, would make the theory more convincing. If some hypotheses deduced from the theory cannot be confirmed, scientists may conclude that frustration only results in aggression in certain limited circumstances. The theory is then modified and refined to describe the conditions under which frustration can be expected to result either in aggression or some other behavior.

Research Strategies

The rules that govern what evidence can be used to confirm or contradict a hypothesis are very strict. First, the evidence must be objective, as we discussed earlier. Second, it must be public; it has to be there for everyone to see. For example, in a study of mental telepathy a subject might describe a city park he has never been to but in which an experimenter is now sitting. Another experimenter, who knows the place, might write down the description and be amazed at how accurate it is: "It's grayish, with many people who seem very busy and anxious. There are a few plants nearby, and I hear the noises of the city in the background." At first this description might seem uncannily accurate. However, a person who doesn't know it is a city park could apply the description to hundreds of places. It might be a shopping plaza, a crowded office building, a school yard, or almost any place.

Finally, the evidence must be repeatable. Provided the sequence of causes really leads to the event, the experimenters should be able to set up the sequence a second, third, or fourth time and observe the same events.

Meeting these requirements means doing carefully controlled research. The two major kinds of research are descriptive and experimental.

Descriptive Research. **Descriptive research** is vital to the scientific approach. This kind of research is basically observation, but the kind of observations that are conducted can sometimes become very sophisticated. *In descriptive research, the scientist observes and describes what is happening in a situation, without actually trying to control the forces that might be causing the individuals under observation to behave in certain ways.* There are many kinds of descriptive research: three of them are field studies, case studies, and correlational studies.

A **field study** *is one in which the scientist goes to the environment in which the behavior of interest normally takes place.* Jane Goodall (1963), for example, spent many years studying the behavior of wild chimpanzees near Lake Tanganyika in Africa. She actually lived on the site, taking notes and recording the day-to-day activities of the chimps.

In another example of a field study, a scientist spent a day observing children in a nursery school (Fawl, 1963). The investigator did not try to interfere in any way with what the children were doing; he just observed their behavior in their natural environment. Among other things, he noted that the children experienced an average of sixteen frustrating events during the day. Although laboratory studies had shown that children often show aggression in response to frustration, the nursery-school children in this field study did not demonstrate the expected high levels of aggression. Thus, one important function of field studies is to confirm (or disconfirm) the findings that scientists obtain from the more controlled conditions of the laboratory.

The **case study** *involves repeated observations of the same individual over a long period of time, rather than the observation of groups.* For example, one might observe the progress of a person who is trying to quit smoking. First she might switch to low-tar cigarettes but find, after several days, that she smokes twice as many as her usual brand. Then she may try smoking only one cigarette per hour in an effort to maintain more conscious control over her habit. If this doesn't work, she might try completely stopping all at once. If she managed to not smoke for several months, we could conclude that "cold turkey" can be an effective way for some people to quit smoking.

The case study method is frequently used by clinical psychologists to provide more detailed and precise descriptions of behavioral disorders. Consider, for example, the case of a person with multiple personalities (Ludwig, et al., 1972). Jonah came to the hospital complaining of headaches followed by memory loss. The attendants at the hospital noticed that his personality changed from day to day. On one day he might be shy, retiring, passive, and very polite; on another, he was cold and nasty. Psychiatrists found that Jonah had four distinct personalities: one primary one and three secondary ones. On tests of intelligence, all four "people" scored essentially alike, but on tests designed to measure emotionality they were vastly different. Later in this book we will see an interesting case study of a person who was able to listen to more than eighty single-digit numbers and repeat them all in the exact order.

Correlational studies *observe and measure events, trying to find associations between them.* For example, one might measure personality traits in a group of children and find that those who tend to be more anxious also tend to bite their nails more. Or a researcher might find that people living in noisy environments are less likely to persist at a difficult task than people living in quiet areas. Associations between two **variables,** or *things that vary,* are often expressed in terms of a statistic called the **correlation coefficient,** *a measure of association that can range between −1 and +1.* For example, if the relationship between nail biting and anxiety levels is very strong, the correlation might be high, perhaps around +.75. If the relationship between noise levels and persistence is also strong, the coefficient would be high again. However, the value would be negative, because as one variable increases (noise), the other decreases (persistence). As the relationship between two variables becomes weaker, the value of the coefficient approaches zero. (See Appendix A for details.)

Descriptive research has a number of advantages and limitations. It provides a basis for forming hypotheses about behavior: a scientist must observe and describe behavior in order to obtain ideas about what causes people to behave in certain ways. Also, descriptive research provides a means to study behavior in the natural environment. The events in a laboratory experiment are carefully controlled, as we shall see in the next section. But it sometimes happens that people and animals behave differently in the real world and in the experimental laboratory. Field studies in particular enable scientists to see whether the conclusions they have drawn from their experimental studies apply in the uncontrolled real world. An important limitation of descriptive research concerns the ability to draw conclusions about causes and effects. For example, one might be tempted to conclude that the association between anxiety and nail biting meant that high anxiety levels were *causing* children to bite their nails. However, this conclusion cannot be drawn from such a study. It could be that the children were noticing the terrible condition of their nails and became anxious because they were afraid their parents would notice too. Or perhaps some of the children were anxious and biting their nails more frequently because they were doing poorly in school. The best way to draw firm conclusions about causes and effects is to perform experimental research.

Experimental Studies. A great deal of psychological knowledge has been acquired from **experimental research,** mostly in laboratories, but sometimes in the field as well. *In experimental research, the scientist seeks to control or manipulate some events in an effort to determine precise cause-and-effect relationships.*

A team of researchers noticed that people are able to remember what happened at an event much more accurately when they are aware of some of the common errors in observation. The researchers began to think that training might improve the accuracy of the observers, so they formulated the hypothesis that the more training a person receives in avoiding observational errors, the more accurate his or her observations will be.

In any experiment, one of the variables will be manipulated by the researchers. This **independent variable** *is the one that is the presumed cause of changes in the other variable.* In our example, the investigators hypothesized that an increase in the amount of training would produce an increase in observer accuracy. Thus the "amount of training to avoid observational errors" is the variable that will be manipulated. The other variable, observer accuracy, is called the **dependent variable:** *the researcher will measure this variable, and changes in it depend on changes in the independent variable.*

The first step in any experiment is to create **operational definitions** for the variables. *The researchers must state the procedures, or operations, that they intend to use to measure the dependent variable and experimentally manipulate the independent variable.* For example, if the researchers want to measure appetite, perhaps because they think some drug might affect it, they need to indicate how they intend to do it. Will they offer each subject a bowl of pretzels and count how many each eats? Will they ask each subject to rate himself or herself from one to ten on a "hunger scale"? Any psychological variable can be measured in a number of ways.

The researcher must also operationally define the independent variable by stating how it will be manipulated. If the study concerns drugs, the amount of drug might be manipulated by giving some subjects no drug and other subjects some quantity, say 1 mg, of drug. If the study is about the effects of high and low self-esteem, the researcher might try to manipulate this variable by calling some subjects "stupid and dirty" and others "smart and well-groomed."

In the study on observer accuracy, the researchers wanted to manipulate "amount of training" and measure "the accuracy of the observer." The simplest way to manipulate the amount of training a person receives is to train some subjects and not the others. The subjects who receive training would be called the **experimental group.** *This group receives the independent variable treatment.* The subjects who do not receive

training are the **control group.** In an experiment, *members of the control group do not receive the independent variable treatment.* To measure observer accuracy the researchers could ask the subjects to relate as much as possible about the events that took place within the first hour after a lecture was over. They could also show all the subjects a slide and ask them some questions about it, scoring their answers. There are many possible operational definitions for psychological variables, each with advantages and limitations. For example, asking subjects to describe what happened after the lecture would be realistic to some extent, but the researchers would have a difficult time deciding whether the observations were accurate since each subject would have had different experiences.

The researchers in the study of observer accuracy chose to measure the dependent variable, observer accuracy, by showing all the subjects a videotape of a group discussion between several industrial managers. Afterwards, the subjects had to answer seventy-five objective questions concerning the videotape (Thornton and Zorich, 1980). The researchers manipulated the independent variable by giving different instructions to the different groups. Before the videotape, the subjects in the experimental group were lectured on observational skills. They learned about the common mistakes observers make, such as losing detail through simplification, making "snap" judgments, allowing stereotypes to affect perceptions, and being influenced too strongly by a single characteristic of a person, such as good looks. The subjects in the control group did not receive this kind of training: they were simply told to watch the tape, take notes, and be prepared to answer questions on it later.

An absolutely critical feature of the design of any experiment is **experimental control:** *the experimental group and the control group should be as similar as possible in terms of how they are treated, their IQs, their goals, their interests, and their personalities.* The only systematic difference between the two groups should be in the amount of training they received in avoiding observational errors. Experimental controls would ensure that the two groups do not differ in other ways. For example, all the subjects should watch the same videotape under the same conditions. If the subjects who receive observational training watch a different tape, any difference between their scores on the follow-up test, and the scores of the subjects who receive no training, might be related to the tapes rather than to the amount of training.

The choice of subjects for an experiment is also an important element. This **sample** should be *a representative subset of the group whose behavior you are actually interested in.* For example, if you are interested in the effects of alcohol on teenagers, your sample should be representative of teenagers.

The subjects in your sample must be **randomly assigned** to the two groups. *This means that the experimenter arbitrarily places subjects into either the control or the experimental group, perhaps by tossing a coin.* This ensures that one group will not have all the geniuses, or most of the athletes, or all the females, for example. Randomization is an important means of experimental control.

The final steps of an experimental study are to collect the data and analyze the results. Psychologists use statistics for the data analysis, a mathematical tool that allows conclusions to be drawn from data that may not be entirely clear-cut. (See Appendix A for more information.) In the experiment on observer accuracy, for example, most of the experimental subjects had higher scores on the follow-up test than did the controls. The average number correct for the experimental subjects was fifty-two; for the controls, it was forty-five. However, some experimental subjects had lower scores than controls, perhaps because they did not watch the tape carefully despite their training. A statistical analysis demonstrated that even though some experimental subjects scored lower than some controls, the experimental group scored higher overall. The difference between their average scores was great enough that it was highly unlikely to have occurred by chance.

More Advanced Experimental Designs. A more complicated experiment might involve three or more groups and more than one independent variable. One researcher, for example, developed a hypothesis involving the way people search out and identify objects visually. When you are looking for a friend in a crowd, runway lights from an aircraft, or a typographical error on a page, many things affect how long the search takes. According to the hypothesis, an important factor is the number of similar items in the area. The number of total items in the area may be very high, but if there are few that are similar to the target, the search time should be short. If there are many similar ones, the search time should be proportionately longer.

In an actual experiment, people looked for a particular three-digit number of a specific color on a screen filled with thirty three-digit numbers. For the control group, only the target was the specified color. For one experimental group, ten items were the same color as the target, and for a second experimental group, thirty were the same color (Carter, 1982). Before they began the search, the subjects were told only the first two digits of the target number. None of the other items in the field began with these two numbers. The dependent variable for this experiment was the amount of time it took the subjects to find the target number and identify its third digit. The independent variable in this experiment was the number of similar targets in the search field; the three groups had zero, ten, and thirty similar targets, respectively.

To make the experiment even more complicated and permit it to provide more information, a second independent variable was added. Each of the three groups of subjects performed a second series of searches. This time, the screen contained sixty instead of thirty items, making the display much more crowded and dense. As before, the control group's target was the only one in the field with the designated color. The two experimental groups had either ten or thirty similarly colored items. The second independent variable, then, was the total number of items on the screen, or the density of the display.

The results of the experiment showed that regardless of whether the screen contained a total of thirty or sixty items, a search took longer when there were more items that were the same color as the target. Also, it took longer to search a screen containing sixty items than one containing only thirty. The results also show an **interaction** between the two independent variables. *This means that the effects of one independent variable depend on the level of the other.* When there was only one target and no other items of the same color, the difference between the search times for the thirty-item screen and the sixty-item screen was very small (.97 seconds vs. 1.02 seconds). But when there were some similar targets in the field, the effect of the density of the display was greater.

Most of the experiments reported in psychology journals are like this one in the sense that they incorporate more than two groups, more than one independent variable, and often more than one dependent variable. The advantage to such complicated designs is that they permit researchers to draw conclusions about several hypotheses at once, without having to perform several separate experiments. They also provide a means to determine the combined effects of variables, something that is not possible with simple designs.

Experimental Studies in the Field. An example of how an experiment might be conducted in a natural setting involves Texas Instruments Incorporated (Gomersall and Myers, 1966). On the basis of interviews with more than 400 employees of the company, the managers suspected that new hires were extremely anxious. Their anxieties seemed to be getting in the way of their ability to learn during those critical first weeks of training.

The management designed a study to determine whether an initial orientation that included some procedures to reduce anxieties might improve the workers' performance during their training. A sample of new hires was assigned to the experimental group; these people received the regular orientation and a one-day "anxiety reduction" workshop. The workshop leaders encouraged the new employees, for example, by emphasizing that their opportunity for success was very good and that they should try to get to know their supervisors personally. They also asked the new employees to disregard all the "hall talk," a kind of hazing of the new hires in which the older employees exaggerated the strictness of work rules, standards, and discipline. The independent variable in this study was the type of orientation, and the dependent variable was the performance of the new employees during the training period.

Figure 1.3 shows the results of the experiment. Especially during the first months of employment, the employees given special training to reduce anxiety performed much better. In terms of dollars and cents, the improvement was about fifty percent. For each 100 new hires in the department, the company had a first-year savings of $50,000 and additional savings because of reductions in turnover and absenteeism.

Performing experiments in a field setting is difficult because it is harder to control the variables. It was impossible for Texas Instruments to be sure that the experimental and control groups received exactly the same regular orientation, the same "hazing," and the same directions from supervisors. Nevertheless, experiments in the field can provide a great deal of information, particularly when they are used in conjunction with lab studies.

Experiments Using Animals. Psychologists often use animal subjects in their research although they really are concerned with human behavior. An important question is whether the behavior of animals is the same as the behavior of humans. The answer is "sometimes."

Depending on the problem, animal research can be very valuable. If researchers are investigating the activity of a single cell in the brain in response to the presence of a particular drug, it would be appropriate to use animal subjects. First, it would be unethical in most cases to place electrodes inside the brain of a human subject. Second, the effects of a drug on a single brain cell in the cat, for example, are likely to be very

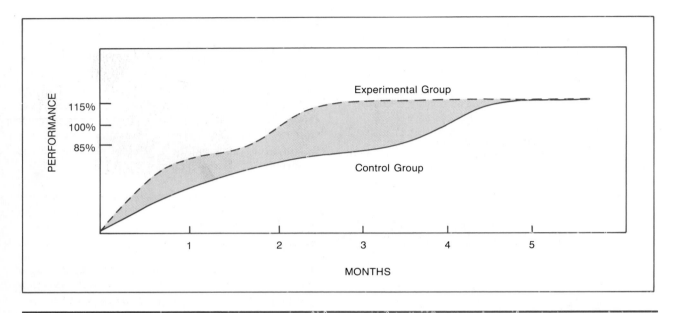

Figure 1.3 *The performance of a control group of new hires who were given conventional job training and orientation and of an experimental group who were given an additional day of anxiety-reduction training. (Reprinted by permission of the Harvard Business Review. An exhibit from "Breakthrough in on-the-job training," by E. A. Gommersall and M. S. Myers (July/August 1966). Copyright © 1966 by the President and Fellows of Harvard College. All Rights Reserved.)*

similar to the drug's effects on human brain cells. If the researchers are investigating a problem that is mainly confined to humans, it makes no sense to use animal subjects. For example, studies of love, panic in theaters, group decision making, or jury behavior, require human volunteers acting as subjects.

There is a wide "gray" area in which the behavior of animals is probably similar to humans but not identical. The learning process is a good example. Are the principles that govern the way a rat learns to run a maze the same as the principles governing human learning? Researchers often use animal models to study learning and other psychological phenomena, but they are very cautious about generalizing their conclusions to humans. They prefer to have some kind of corroboration from human studies to confirm their findings in animal subjects.

Regardless of whether psychologists study humans or animals, or choose the descriptive or experimental approach, they must perform their research in an ethical manner, being careful to consider the dignity and welfare of the subjects. The Application Box: Ethical Principles of Psychologists describes the approach of the American Psychological Association with regard to ethics.

GUIDED REVIEW

Learning Objectives 3 and 4

1. Psychology is a _____ and uses the scientific method, an approach to acquiring knowledge that assumes _____ , _____ , and _____ . The three main goals of science are understanding, prediction, and control. A key component of observation is _____ .

2. After observing behavior objectively, scientists formulate _____ and develop general frameworks, or _____ , about the causes of behavior.

3. Many research strategies are used to test hypotheses. The two major categories are _____ and _____ .

4. Descriptive research relies on observation of behavior. Examples include _____ , _____ , and _____ .

5. Experimental studies, which use careful _____ _____ , can usually provide clear-cut answers about causes and effects. The experimenter manipulates the _____ and measures the effects of the manipulation on the _____ . To perform an experiment, variables must have _____ that state how the variable will be manipulated or measured.

ANSWERS

definitions
controls; independent variable; dependent variable; operational
4. field studies, case studies, correlational studies 5. experimental
2. hypotheses; theories 3. descriptive research, experimental research
1. science; order, determinism, discoverability; objectivity

Perspectives in Psychology

Different groups of psychologists interested in behavior and mental processes have chosen to emphasize different levels of analysis. They have also followed somewhat different clues and leads in formulating hypotheses and constructing theories. As a result, there are several different major perspectives within the field of psychology, each one emphasizing different aspects and causes of behavior. Each perspective, or school of thought, has attracted many followers over the years and has waxed and waned in popularity. No single perspective is completely correct; nor is it completely wrong. Each one has contributed greatly to our understanding of behavior. Two historical schools of thought that formed the foundations for later theories were *structuralism* and *functionalism*. Contemporary perspectives include *psychoanalysis,* originally developed by Sigmund Freud; *behaviorism,* a perspective that was particularly favored by American psychologists such as John B. Watson and B. F. Skinner; *cognitive psychology,* an approach that emphasizes the importance of studying mental activities in addition to overt behavior; and *humanistic psychology.*

Figure 1.4   Wilhelm Wundt (1832–1920)

Historical Schools of Thought

The study of behavior has its roots in the writings of the Greek philosophers Plato and Aristotle, but most historians date the origin of modern scientific psychology to the middle of the nineteenth century. During that time a German professor in Leipzig and an American professor in Cambridge were opening up laboratories of psychology and beginning to train students in the science of human behavior.

The German, Wilhelm Wundt (fig. 1.4), originally received a medical degree from the University of Heidelberg. At Leipzig he was appointed to a chair in philosophy, but he pursued an experimental and physiologically oriented study of behavior. (His electic career illustrates the diverse origins of the science of psychology itself. The discipline has borrowed ideas and theories from medicine, physiology, philosophy, and many other subjects.)

Wundt was the founder of a school of thought known as **structuralism.** *This school considered the major task of psychology to be the study of the structure, or content, of mental processes.* Wundt used a variety of techniques in his laboratory to achieve this goal. For example, he carefully controlled the mental processes required by a subject in a particular task, and he then measured the subject's reaction time. By subtraction, he was able to deduce the amount of time required for

APPLICATION BOX

Ethical Principles of Psychologists

Any scientist who conducts research should be concerned with ethics. Scientists do not operate in a vacuum, and they need to be concerned with how their research might affect human beings, animals, plant life, or the environment. Because of the nature of research in psychology, psychologists must be especially cognizant of ethical principles and guidelines. Many experiments in psychology, for example, ask for volunteers to act as subjects, and often the subjects do not know exactly what kind of experiment they are volunteering for. The American Psychological Association has adopted a formal statement of ethical principles, and acceptance of membership in the APA commits the member to them. The following is the Preamble to the most recent version of these ethical principles:

Preamble

Psychologists respect the dignity and worth of the individual and strive for the preservation and protection of fundamental human rights. They are committed to increasing knowledge of human behavior and of people's understanding of themselves and others and to the utilization of such knowledge for the promotion of human welfare. While pursuing these objectives, they make every effort to protect the welfare of those who seek their services and of the research participants that may be the object of study.

They use their skills only for purposes consistent with these values and do not knowingly permit their misuse by others. While demanding for themselves freedom of inquiry and communication, psychologists accept the responsibility this freedom requires: competence, objectivity in the application of skills, and concern for the best interests of clients, colleagues, students, research participants, and society. In the pursuit of these ideals, psychologists subscribe to principles in the following areas: 1. Responsibility, 2. Competence, 3. Moral and Legal Standards, 4. Public Statements, 5. Confidentiality, 6. Welfare of the Consumer, 7. Professional Relationships, 8. Assessment Techniques, 9. Research With Human Participants, and 10. Care and Use of Animals.

Acceptance of membership in the American Psychological Association commits the member to adherence to these principles.

Psychologists cooperate with duly constituted committees of the American Psychological Association, in particular, the Committee on Scientific and Professional Ethics and Conduct, by responding to inquiries promptly and completely. Members also respond promptly and completely to inquiries from duly constituted state association ethics committees and professional standards review committees.

Figure 1.5 William James (1842–1910)

Figure 1.6 Sigmund Freud (1856–1939)

a particular mental process to occur. The best-known tool used by Wundt and his students was called **introspection,** *a rigorous and highly disciplined technique that allowed the individual to analyze conscious experience in terms of elementary sensations and feelings.* Not all students were able to master it; those who could not were encouraged to pursue careers in something other than psychology (Fancher, 1979).

About the same time Wundt founded his laboratory in Leipzig, William James (fig. 1.5) was opening one at Harvard University. James was a superb teacher, but his most important contribution to psychology was his *Principles of Psychology,* a massive two-volume work published in 1890. It contained chapters on brain function, habit, sensation, perception, attention, memory, imagination, emotions, hypnotism, and many other topics familiar to modern psychologists. Throughout the work James emphasized that which was practical and "functional," partly as a reaction against Wundt's structural approach, which he perceived as excessively disjointed and mainly descriptive. The chapter on emotions in *Principles of Psychology* provides a good example of James's interest in the "how" and "why" of behavior, rather than in the "what." He points out that a person's actions have a significant effect on the emotions the person feels. (See chapter 8 for a more detailed description of James's views on emotions.)

Whistling to keep up courage is no mere figure of speech. On the other hand, sit all day in a moping posture, sigh, and reply to everything with a dismal voice, and your melancholy lingers . . . (James, 1890).

The school of thought that James inspired became known as **functionalism.** *It emphasized the purpose and utility of behavior, particularly within the framework of evolution. It was also interested in individual differences between people because these differences shed light on why some people adapt well to their environment and others adapt poorly.* SELF ESTEEM, PRIDE SELF CONCEPT,

We know of no psychologists today who call themselves structuralists or functionalists, but Wundt, James, and their students made enormous contributions to the field of psychology, and contemporary psychologists are still influenced by their thinking.

Psychoanalysis

The ideas of Sigmund Freud (fig. 1.6) are so pervasive in twentieth-century Western thought that even students who have never had a course in psychology are familiar with terms like Oedipal complex, libido, and repression. **Psychoanalysis** *is both a school of thought and a system of therapy developed by Freud and expanded and modified by his students and followers. The approach emphasizes the importance of unconscious processes in personality, especially unconscious* *memories of childhood events*. While Wundt was studying conscious processes, Freud was postulating the existence and influence of the unconscious mind, a realm that was unreachable through introspection. The well-known "Freudian slip" is an example of how unconscious thoughts can express themselves in overt behavior. A mother unconsciously worried over her young son's ability to cross streets might send him off to the store saying, "Don't forget the blood" instead of "Don't forget the bread." These hidden concerns might also reveal themselves in dreams. Freud made ample use of a variety of techniques, including dream analysis and hypnosis, to reach and understand the workings of the unconscious mind.

In addition to its emphasis on the unconscious, the psychoanalytic approach also addresses the importance of instincts that compel people to behave in certain ways and the means that people use to control these instinctual pressures. Attempts to control sexual instincts, for example, result in behaviors like repression, in which a motive is deliberately repressed or "forgotten."

Under Freud's guidance, psychoanalysis became an enormously influential school of psychology, and Freud inspired a large number of students. Some students adhered strictly to his point of view; others, however, proposed slight or sometimes drastic modifications to his theories about human behavior. Carl Jung, for example, believed that Freud overemphasized the importance of sexuality and underrated social and cultural factors. The psychoanalytic perspective is certainly not without its critics; a number of psychologists argue that much of Freud's theory was based on the case histories of only a few Viennese patients. Much of it is also extremely difficult to test in the laboratory, making it a theory that no one can prove or disprove. Nevertheless, the influence of psychoanalytic thought in art, literature, and particularly in abnormal psychology and psychotherapy, is unmistakable.

Figure 1.7 *John B. Watson (1878–1958)*

Behaviorism

The school of thought known as **behaviorism** *proposed that only overt behavior should be the subject matter of psychology and that the inner workings of the mind should be ignored.* It developed during the early 1900s, primarily as a reaction against the technique of introspection. It has its roots in functionalism, which, as we mentioned, also rejected introspection. The American psychologist John B. Watson (fig. 1.7) argued that Wundt's technique was a futile approach and that its results did not meet the criteria for scientific evidence. The data of psychology should be observable and measurable; hence the emphasis on overt behavior. As editor of the *Psychological Review,* Watson published an important paper describing the behaviorist position:

> Psychology as the behaviorist views it is a purely objective natural science. Its theoretical goal is the prediction and control of behavior. Introspection forms no essential part of its methods, nor is the scientific value of its data dependent upon the readiness with which they lend themselves to interpretation in terms of consciousness . . . (Watson, 1913).

The school of behaviorism had a large following in the United States and in particular became associated with learning. B. F. Skinner (fig. 1.8), a prominent American psychologist, developed theories about the roles of rewards and punishments in learning, excluding mental processes such as thought and imagery. An important tenet of the behaviorist viewpoint is that

How we →
Percieve
The world
→

Figure 1.8 B. F. Skinner (1904–   )

psychologists should be just as interested in the behavior of animals and children as they are in adult behavior. Thus, rat and pigeon cages became typical sights in the laboratories of psychologists; indeed, most of Skinner's theories of learning were based on studies of rats and pigeons.

The behaviorist perspective is sometimes called "black box" psychology because it is not concerned with what goes on inside the mind. It is only concerned with the effects of the environment (input) on behavior (output). Mental processes take place inside the "black box" and are not considered appropriate for objective psychological analysis.

Behaviorism provided the impetus to change the definition of psychology from the study of conscious experience, as Wundt defined it, to the study of behavior. Now, this definition is still the one that is most frequently used. Throughout this book you will notice references to the behavioristic point of view, and in Chapter 5 we will discuss the approach in more detail.

Cognitive Psychology

Area of study
not a theory

Cognitive psychology *emphasizes that the mind is an active, thinking organ that processes information it receives. It is not just a "black box." According to cognitive psychology, explanations of behavior cannot be complete if they include only references to overt behavior and the effects of the environment. They must*

also include an analysis of mental activities. Psychologists who favor the cognitive perspective usually like to define their subject matter as "the study of behavior *and* mental processes."

Cognitive psychology grew out of the work of a group of scientists in Germany, known as the **Gestalt psychologists,** during the early part of the twentieth century (Mandler, 1985). *The word "gestalt" means "form, or pattern," and these researchers emphasized not just how the human mind receives information from the environment but also how it processes and interprets that information.* Perception was one of their most frequent research topics, and they demonstrated that the mind organizes pieces of visual input into meaningful wholes. They insisted that behavior was not just dependent on the fragmented pieces of visual input; it depended on the way the mind organized and interpreted those perceptual fragments.

Researchers in cognitive psychology utilize a number of different techniques to infer how human beings process and store information. For example, they might compare how long it takes an individual to respond to questions like, "Is a canary a bird?" and "Is a fish an animal?" to make inferences about how knowledge is stored and processed in the human brain. They also take advantage of advanced techniques in electrical recording of brain activity.

Some cognitive psychologists make use of **protocol analysis,** *a technique in which a subject provides verbal reports on his own mental activities while working on a task* (Ericsson and Simon, 1984). In many ways, protocol analysis is very similar to introspection, but it is used in a more limited and standardized way. Efforts are made to avoid the pitfalls of the older technique, such as the fact that talking about a task while you are doing it tends to interfere with doing the task.

The cognitive perspective gained an enormous following in the seventies and early eighties, partly because it has expanded the boundaries of psychological investigation beyond the narrow strictures of behaviorism. The approach is particularly attractive to researchers who study memory processes.

Humanistic Psychology

Humanistic psychology *takes an approach that emphasizes the uniqueness of human beings; it focuses heavily on human values and subjective experience* (Guilford, 1984). Psychologists who prefer this perspective consider the individual's interpretations of events as most important in the understanding of human behavior. They believe that other perspectives—behaviorism and psychoanalysis in particular—are excessively mechanistic in that they view behavior as primarily controlled by the environment. Humanistic psychologists place greater importance on an individual's own will.

Humanistic psychology is more of a philosophical orientation toward human behavior. It does not rely on the scientific method but on understanding the inner life of each person. It has been closely associated with a variety of consciousness-expanding techniques designed to reach this inner life, such as encounter groups, sensitivity sessions, and mystical experiences. Many humanistic theories propose that the major motivational force of human beings is **self-actualization,** *or developing the human potential to its fullest.*

The humanistic perspective reminds psychologists that one of their tasks is to help solve issues relating to human welfare. The cares and concerns of individual people can sometimes become lost amidst the reaction-time experiments, the rats learning to run mazes, and the analysis of dreams.

GUIDED REVIEW

Learning Objectives 5 and 6

1. Historical perspectives that have been taken by psychologists include _____ and _____ . Structuralism, founded by Wilhelm Wundt, emphasized studies of conscious experience through introspection. Functionalism, inspired by William James, focused on the purpose and utility of behavior, particularly as it permitted adaptation to the environment.

2. More contemporary perspectives include _____ , _____ , _____ , and _____ .

3. _____ , proposed by Sigmund Freud, emphasizes the importance of unconscious processes, instincts, and early experience in behavior.

4. _____ , founded by John B. Watson, stresses observation of overt behavior and the role of environmental factors, particularly rewards and punishments, in the control of behavior.

5. Cognitive psychology, with its origins in _____ , investigates both overt behavior and private mental activities, using a variety of techniques to make inferences about how we store and process information.

6. The more philosophical perspective, known as _____ , emphasizes the inner conscious experiences of each individual person, using techniques such as encounter groups, sensitivity sessions, and mystical experiences. Humanistically oriented psychologists downplay the importance of the scientific method in the study of behavior.

ANSWERS

1. structuralism, functionalism 2. psychoanalysis, behaviorism, cognitive psychology, humanistic psychology 3. Psychoanalysis 4. Behaviorism 5. Gestalt psychology 6. humanism

Applying Psychology

One of the most important goals of psychology is to help solve some of the problems we face (e.g. Spence, 1985; Bevan, 1982). This is a tall order, considering that the behavior and mental processes of human beings are so complex. Terrorism, drug abuse, senility, violence, crime, suicide, and war are only a few of these problems. Psychologists have learned a great deal about human behavior, however, and many psychologists see it as their responsibility to address these important issues.

Applied Research, Basic Research, and Applications of Psychological Knowledge

The continuum of psychological research ranges from the very basic kinds of research to the very applied. Basic research is not conducted because a particular social issue is in dire need of solutions; it is conducted because scientists are curious about the nature of human and animal behavior and want to learn more about it. For instance, the physiological psychologist who is studying the role of maternal nutrition in the brain development of rat pups is doing purely basic research. This research would be conducted primarily to learn more about the world, not because anyone is particularly interested in how they might create "super-smart" rats by feeding their mothers high-protein diets.

Even though basic research is not conducted to provide solutions to pressing problems in our society, it can often have many practical applications. The studies on brain development in rats, for example, might offer valuable information to people who are trying to improve the diets of impoverished people. Political leaders might be particularly interested in prenatal nutrition programs to insure that pregnant women, at least, have adequate nutrition. Such applications of psychological knowledge are becoming more and more common as psychologists acquire more information about behavior.

At the other end of the research continuum are studies in applied psychology. Applied research is often specially designed to answer a specific question and address a pressing problem. The study of the behavior of hostages during a simulated kidnapping is a good example. Another is an investigation of the relationship between behavior patterns and heart disease. A third might be a study conducted for the highway department to determine human reaction times to different colors. Applied research on this topic led policymakers to the decision to use red for "stop" and green for "go" in traffic lights. Some applied research is designed not so much to solve societal problems but to contribute to the capitalistic endeavor. For instance, an applied research project might determine how much television advertising is required to increase the sales of a product.

The distinction between basic and applied research is not always very clear; they do not constitute two separate categories but rather are two ends of a continuum. Much research contains elements of both. When universities first began establishing departments of psychology in the late nineteenth and early twentieth centuries, most staff members concentrated almost exclusively on basic research. This was appropriate, because such a young discipline really did not have enough basic knowledge about behavior and mental processes to contribute very much in the way of applications and specific answers to real-world questions. Psychologists who were just beginning to learn how people developed prejudice, for example, could hardly be expected to design applied research studies that would help create public policy or to suggest legislation that would eliminate prejudice.

As knowledge in the field of psychology grew, applications and applied research became much more common. Now, as you can see from table 1.2, large numbers of psychologists are engaged in either applied research or in applying what has already been learned about behavior, rather than in basic research endeavors. Clinical psychologists, who comprise the largest proportion of psychologists, apply what has been learned about abnormal behavior to people in hospitals, outpatient clinics, community mental health centers, and many other settings. Psychologists working in business apply what has been learned about the psychology of large organizations. The ways in which our knowledge of psychology can be applied is almost endless.

A large number of psychologists engaged in research focus on applied issues rather than, or in addition to, basic ones. This applied research is carried out in government agencies, hospitals, universities, businesses, and just about anywhere psychologists are employed. Shifts in government funding policies have contributed to the trend toward more applied research. As money for research became scarce, government funding agencies like the National Institute of Mental Health and the National Science Foundation tended to emphasize investigations that might yield answers to important problems facing the American people. But

part of the trend is also due to the maturation of psychology as a scientific discipline. We have the expertise and theoretical frameworks to perform intelligent applied research, and we can be confident in applying what we've learned about behavior thus far.

GUIDED REVIEW

Learning Objective 7

1. An important goal of psychology is solving the problems facing our world. Toward this end, psychologists conduct _____ , which uses the scientific method to find answers to specific, practical questions. They also apply the knowledge they have gained from basic research to real world problems.

2. _____ is conducted primarily to learn more about the world, although many psychological applications may arise from it.

ANSWERS
1. applied research 2. Basic research

SUMMARY

I. Psychology is a subject for and about people. (p. 4)

   A. Psychology is usually defined as the study of behavior, although many psychologists add the phrase "and mental processes" to the definition to emphasize that psychology also includes the study of mental activity.   (p. 4)

   B. The subfields of psychology include clinical psychology, social psychology, physiological psychology, developmental psychology, comparative psychology, and many others. (p. 4)

   C. Psychologists work in many settings, including academia, government, business, and private practice.   (p. 5)

II. Psychology uses the scientific method in its approach to the study of behavior, an approach that assumes order, determinism, and discoverability. A key feature of the scientific approach is objectivity. (p. 6)

   A. The first step in studying behavior is to perform objective observations.   (p. 9)

      1. Behavior can be analyzed on many levels, from the physiological to the social and political. Most behaviors are influenced by factors operating at many levels.   (p. 10)

      2. After observing behavior, scientists formulate hypotheses and develop general theoretical frameworks to explain behavior. (p. 10)

   B. Research strategies generally fall into two categories: descriptive research and experimental research.   (p. 11)

1. Descriptive research relies on observation. Examples include field studies, case studies, and correlational studies.   (p. 11)

2. Experimental research involves the manipulation of the independent variable by the experimenter and observation of its effects on the dependent variable. Experimental controls are used to ensure that the experimental and control groups are different only with respect to the independent variable. The independent and dependent variables in an experiment must have operational definitions.   (p. 12)

3. More advanced and complicated experimental studies may involve two or more independent variables operating simultaneously and the measure of several dependent variables. Complex experimental designs enable researchers to identify interactions between independent variables.   (p. 14)

4. Field studies are important in psychology because they investigate the effects of variables in real settings, rather than in the laboratory. It is more difficult to control extraneous variables in the field, however. (p. 15)

5. Experiments using animals are conducted to learn more about the behavior of animals and to acquire information that might generalize to human behavior. (p. 15)

III. Psychologists have emphasized different approaches in the study of behavior and have taken different perspectives.   (p. 17)

A. Two historical perspectives, or schools of thought, were structuralism and functionalism. (p. 17)

B. Modern perspectives include psychoanalysis, behaviorism, cognitive psychology, and humanistic psychology. Psychoanalysis emphasizes the importance of unconscious processes, instincts, and early childhood experiences.   (p. 19)

C. Behaviorism stresses the observation of overt behavior and the role of environmental factors, particularly rewards and punishments, in behavior.   (p. 20)

D. Cognitive psychology investigates both overt behavior and private mental activities, using techniques such as reaction time, electrical recordings of the brain, and protocol analysis to learn how the human being processes information.   (p. 21)

E. The humanistic perspective emphasizes the inner conscious experiences of individuals, stressing the importance of the uniqueness of human beings and focusing on human values and subjective experience.   (p. 22)

IV. The application of psychological knowledge to problems in the real world is an important goal of psychology.   (p. 23)

A. Whereas basic psychological research is conducted to learn more about human behavior in general, applied psychological research usually involves using the scientific method to obtain answers to specific, practical questions. The two kinds of research overlap considerably, however.   (p. 23)

B. As more basic psychological knowledge accumulates, more applications of psychological knowledge become possible. Psychology as a field has become mature enough to offer a great deal of useful information toward the solution of practical problems.   (p. 24)

ACTION GLOSSARY

Match the terms in the left column with the definitions in the right column.

C   1. Psychology (p. 4)
E   2. Physiological psychology (p. 4)
F   3. Clinical psychology (p. 4)
A   4. Psychiatrist (p. 4)
D   5. Order (p. 6)
B   6. Determinism (p. 6)

A. *A physician whose specialty is the diagnosis and treatment of individuals with behavioral disorders.*

B. *One of the assumptions of the scientific method. Refers to the assumption that cause-and-effect relationships exist in the world and that some events can be said to cause other events.*

C. *Usually defined as the science of behavior, although many psychologists prefer to broaden the definition by including the study of mental activity or processes.*

D. *One of the assumptions of the scientific method. Refers to the assumption that events do not occur in a random, chaotic way.*

E. *A branch of psychology that is concerned with the relationship between biological processes and behavior.*

F. *A branch of psychology concerned with the study, diagnosis, and treatment of individuals with behavioral disorders.*

D   7. Discoverability (p. 6)
F   8. Objectivity (p. 9)
B   9. Hypothesis (p. 10)
E 10. Theory (p. 11)
C 11. Descriptive research (p. 11)
A 12. Field study (p. 11)

A. *A type of descriptive research that usually takes place outside the laboratory, in a setting in which the behavior being observed normally occurs.*

B. *A tentative statement about the relationship between two or more variables that may be proved or disproved by the scientific method.*

C. *A type of research in which events are observed and described, but not manipulated in any way.*

D. *One of the assumptions of the scientific method. Refers to the assumption that it is possible to discover causes and effects, at least theoretically.*

E. *A set of statements of propositions that attempt to explain a body of facts.*

F. *The component of the scientific method in which scientists observe events without preconceived notions, prejudice or bias.*

F 13. Case Study (p. 11)
A 14. Correlational study (p. 12)
D 15. Variable (p. 12)
B 16. Correlation coefficient (p. 12)
E 17. Experimental research (p. 12)
C 18. Independent variable (p. 13)

A. *A type of descriptive research in which the characteristics and behavior of individuals are observed and measured, and attempts are made to find relationships between two or more variables.*

B. *A numerical value between -1 and $+1$ that indicates the degree of relationship between two variables in terms of both strength (the absolute value of the coefficient), and direction (the sign of the coefficient).*

C. *In an experiment, the variable that is actively manipulated and controlled by the scientist. Changes in this variable are presumed to cause changes in the other variable.*

D. *Anything that can vary, either in discrete steps or along some continuum.*

E. *A type of research designed to determine cause-and-effect relationships between variables by controlling the conditions under which observations are made. The independent variable(s) of the experiment are controlled and manipulated systematically in order to observe any resulting changes in the measurements of the dependent variable(s).*

F. *A type of descriptive research that involves repeated observations of the same individual over a long period of time.*

B 19. **Dependent variable** (p. 13)
F 20. **Operational definition** (p. 13)
A 21. **Experimental group** (p. 13)
C 22. **Control group** (p. 13)
E B 23. **Experimental control** (p. 13)
D 24. **Sample** (p. 14)

A. *In an experiment, the group that receives the level of the independent variable that is not zero and receives the treatment that is under investigation.*

B. *In an experiment, the variable that will be measured by the scientist rather than actively manipulated. Changes in this variable are hypothesized to depend on changes in the other variable.*

C. *In an experiment contrasting two or more groups, the group that is given no treatment, a placebo, or a zero level of the independent variable. Measurements on this group provide a means to assess the effects of a treatment given to a different group.*

D. *A subgroup of a population that is generally representative of that population. In research, conclusions drawn from the behavior of this subgroup can be generalized to the population from which the sample was drawn only if the subgroup is a representative one.*

E. *Refers to the experimenter's arrangement of extraneous variables, or those other than the independent and dependent variables. Ensures that all groups are affected equally by extraneous variables, so that any changes in the dependent variable can be attributed to the independent variable.*

F. *Explains how a variable or phenomenon will be manipulated, produced, or measured for the purposes of research.*

C 25. **Randomly assigned** (p. 14)
D 26. **Interaction** (p. 15)
F 27. **Structuralism** (p. 17)
B 28. **Introspection** (p. 19)
A 29. **Functionalism** (p. 19)
E 30. **Psychoanalysis** (p. 19)

A. *A school of psychology associated with the ideas of William James. Emphasized the purpose and utility of behavior, particularly within the framework of evolution.*

B. *A technique in which trained individuals studied, analyzed, and reported on their own conscious experience in terms of elementary sensations and feelings, and in which the interpretation of experience and feeling were avoided.*

C. *A means of experimental control in which subjects are placed into groups by chance, such as by tossing a coin. Provided the sample is large, the technique ensures that the average characteristics of each group are approximately equal before the administration of the independent variable.*

D. *Occurs when the effects of one independent variable depend on the level of the other independent variable.*

E. *A school of psychology founded by Sigmund Freud. Emphasized the role of unconscious processes in behavior. Also refers to a body of techniques used to investigate the mind and to treat certain kinds of behavior disorders.*

F. *A school of psychology associated with the ideas of Wilhelm Wundt. Proposed that the major task of psychology was the study of the structure, or content, of mental processes.*

D 31. **Behaviorism** (p. 20)
C 32. **Cognitive psychology** (p. 21)
B 33. **Gestalt psychology** (p. 21)
E 34. **Humanistic psychology** (p. 22)
A 35. **Self-actualization** (p. 22)

A. *An individual's motivation to develop his or her potential to its fullest.*

B. *A school of psychology that emphasizes patterns, forms, and wholes in perception, rather than individual elements.*

C. *A school of psychology that stresses the role of such processes as thinking, knowing, decision making, and perceiving, in behavior.*

D. *A school of psychology associated with the ideas of John B. Watson. Proposes that the only legitimate subject matter for psychology is overt behavior, rather than the inner workings of the mind. One of the goals is to increase the objectivity of psychological inquiry.*

E. *An approach in psychology that emphasizes subjective experience and the uniqueness of human beings.*

ANSWERS

34. E; 35. A

18. C; 19. B; 20. F; 21. A; 22. C; 23. E; 24. D; 25. C; 26. D; 27. F; 28. B; 29. A; 30. E; 31. D; 32. C; 33. B;

1. C; 2. E; 3. F; 4. A; 5. D; 6. B; 7. D; 8. F; 9. B; 10. E; 11. C; 12. A; 13. F; 14. A; 15. D; 16. B; 17. E;

SELF-TEST

1. The area or specialization in psychology that deals with the diagnosis and treatment of behavioral or mental disorders is
   - (a) psychiatry.
   - (b) clinical psychology.
   - (c) social psychology.
   - (d) personality.
   (LO 1; p. 4)

2. The largest number of psychologists are employed by
   - (a) mental hospitals and similar institutions.
   - (b) colleges and universities.
   - (c) federal and state agencies (other than *b* above).
   - (d) business and corporations.
   (LO 2; p. 5)

3. Order in the world, determinism, and discoverability are three assumptions of
   - (a) science.
   - (b) psychology.
   - (c) understanding.
   - (d) both a and b.
   (LO 3; p. 6)

4. The goals of the scientific approach are
   - (a) determinism, predictions, and treatment.
   - (b) order, understanding, and control.
   - (c) description, prediction, and control.
   - (d) description, prediction, and understanding.
   (LO 3; p. 9)

5. A tentative statement about the possible relationship among two events is a(n)
   - (a) explanation.
   - (b) hypothesis.
   - (c) description.
   - (d) correlation.
   (LO 4; p. 10)

6. A theory is
   - (a) a statement about the causes of behavior that may involve many observations.
   - (b) a complex hypothesis.
   - (c) proof about an explanation of behavior.
   - (d) not related to hypotheses.
   (LO 4; p. 11)

7. Scientific evidence must be
   - (a) public.
   - (b) objective.
   - (c) repeatable.
   - (d) all of the above.
   (LO 4; p. 11)

8. A professor found that the students in her class who were doing well had also done relatively well in high school and that those doing poorly had done less well in high school. This represents a
   - (a) high negative correlation.
   - (b) high positive correlation.
   - (c) low correlation.
   - (d) causal relationship.
   (LO 4; p. 12)

9. In a study, a psychologist makes one group of animals hungry and leaves the other group well fed.
   - (a) Hunger is the dependent variable.
   - (b) This may be the result of the study.
   - (c) Hunger is the independent variable in this study.
   - (d) This case study is examining the results of hunger on some variable.
   (LO 4; p. 13)

10. An educational psychologist is interested in the effect of teaching technique on learning. She designs an experiment in which she teaches two nearly identical classes with different teaching methods and gives them the same examination at the end of the semester.
    - (a) The result on the examination is the independent variable.
    - (b) The result on the examination is the dependent variable.
    - (c) This is only a study of correlation.
    - (d) This is a case study of educational practice.
    (LO 4; p. 13)

11. An operational definition of intelligence might be
    - (a) a person's score on an IQ test.
    - (b) a person's problem-solving ability.
    - (c) the amount of knowledge that a person has.
    - (d) the theoretical genetic basis of intelligence.
    (LO 4; p. 13)

12. If the experimental and control groups are exactly the same (or as similar as possible), except with respect to the independent variable, which of the following is true?
    (a) No experiment is possible because there is no difference between the groups.
    (b) A case study is the study of choice.
    (c) Only a correlation would be appropriate.
    (d) Experimental control has been exercised.
    (LO 4; p. 13)

13. Randomized assignment of subjects to groups in an experiment is
    (a) a way of assuring that the sample is representative of the population from which it was drawn.
    (b) a control procedure.
    (c) a way of operationally defining the independent variable.
    (d) necessary in a study that is looking at a correlational.
    (LO 4; p. 14)

14. A study investigating the effects of the level of hunger and the level of fatigue on reaction time, measured in seconds, obtained the following average reaction times for four groups of subjects:

| | *Level of hunger* | |
Level of fatigue	low	high
low	1.0	.5
high	.5	1.0

    These data suggest that
    (a) higher levels of fatigue result in shorter reaction times.
    (b) higher levels of hunger result in shorter reaction times.
    (c) neither hunger level nor level of fatigue affect reaction time.
    (d) there may be an interaction between hunger and fatigue with respect to their influence on reaction time.
    (LO 4; p. 15)

15. Why are lower animals sometimes used to study problems of interest to psychologists?
    (a) Animal psychological processes are all exactly the same as human psychological processes.
    (b) Some experiments are not ethically possible with human subjects.

(c) Some studies, on the brain for example, are possible to do with animals, and the results are likely to be the same in the animal as in a human.
    (d) Both b and c are true.
    (LO 4; p. 15)

16. The school of thought known as structuralism
    (a) was started by William James.
    (b) was started by Wilhelm Wundt.
    (c) is aimed at understanding the content of consciousness or mental processes.
    (d) Both b and c are true.
    (LO 5; p. 17)

17. A school of thought that was based upon the existence of an unconscious mind was
    (a) Freud's psychoanalysis.
    (b) James' functionalism.
    (c) cognitive psychology.
    (d) humanistic psychology.
    (LO 5; p. 19)

18. A school of thought in psychology that admitted only to the importance of overt observable events and actions was
    (a) Freud's psychoanalysis.
    (b) James' functionalism.
    (c) Watson's behaviorism.
    (d) experimental psychology.
    (LO 5; p. 20)

19. Cognitive psychology grew out of
    (a) psychoanalysis.
    (b) functionalism.
    (c) behaviorism.
    (d) Gestalt psychology.
    (LO 6; p. 21)

20. A study aimed at finding out how to make first-year college students learn more of the work they are assigned would be an example of
    (a) pure basic research.
    (b) applied research.
    (c) experimental research.
    (d) correlational research.
    (LO 7; p. 23)

ANSWERS

1. b, 2. b, 3. d, 4. c, 5. b, 6. a, 7. d, 8. b, 9. c, 10. b, 11. a, 12. d, 13. b, 14. d, 15. d, 16. a, 17. a, 18. c, 19. d, 20. b

SUGGESTED READINGS

Borchardt, D. H., and R. D. Francis. How to find out in psychology: a guide to the literature and methods of research. New York: Pergamon, 1984. An annotated guide that describes how to search the published literature in psychology.

Corsini, R. J., ed. *Encyclopedia of psychology.* New York: Wiley, 1984. An excellent though costly four-volume reference set for psychology students.

Ellis, J. *The social history of the machine gun.* New York: Random House, 1975. A fascinating account of the human element in the technology of warfare, one that offers insights about how human values were changed by technological advances.

Fancher, R. E. *Pioneers of psychology.* New York: W. W. Norton, 1979. A small book providing short biographies and descriptions of theories of some eminent psychologists.

Martin, D. W. *Doing psychology experiments.* 2d ed. Monterey, CA: Brooks/Cole, 1985. An easy-to-read introduction to research methodology that is very appropriate for lower-level students in psychology.

Miller, S. *Experimental design and statistics.* 2d ed. London: Methuen, 1984. This is a small handbook that covers basic experimental design, descriptive statistics, and various kinds of inferential statistical techniques that can be used in simple experiments.

Schultz, D. *A history of modern psychology.* 3d ed. New York: Academic Press, 1981. An examination of the historical roots of psychology.

Skinner, B. F. *Science and human behavior.* New York: Macmillan, 1953. A classic on the subject of behaviorism.

Woods, P. J., ed. *The psychology major: training and employment strategies.* Washington, D.C.: American Psychological Association, 1979. A collection of articles covering topics such as the job prospects for psychology majors, training for careers in mental health and community service, and the status of the undergraduate psychology curriculum.

p a r t

II

BASICS OF BEHAVIOR

c h a p t e r

2

Biological Basis of Behavior

LEARNING OBJECTIVES

After reading this chapter, the student should be able to

1. describe the neuron's structure. **(p. 34)**
2. explain how the neuron moves information from one end to the other. **(p. 37)**
3. explain how neurons communicate with one another. **(p. 39)**
4. describe the methods used to study the nervous system. **(p. 42)**
5. outline the main structures of the brain and the spinal cord. **(p. 44)**
6. explain the role of the peripheral nervous system in the control of movement, the transmission of sensory signals, and the preparation of the body for an emergency. **(p. 50)**
7. describe the major endocrine glands and their hormones, and give examples of how some of them affect behavior. **(p. 54)**
8. define the neural disorders called epilepsy and stroke, and explain how studying these disorders can help scientists learn more about brain function. **(p. 57)**
9. explain the specializations of the right and left hemispheres of the brain. **(p. 60)**
10. describe how studies of split-brain patients have led to insights regarding the nature of the mind and consciousness in human beings. **(p. 65)**

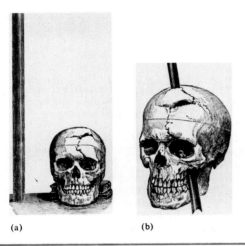

(a)   (b)

Figure 2.1 Drawings to illustrate the injury to Phineas P. Gage. (a) Relative size of the tamping iron and Gage's skull. (b) Route of passage through the victim's skull

On the afternoon of September 13, 1848, Phineas T. Gage was working with blasting powder and an iron bar, and an accidental spark caused an explosion that drove the bar through his head. The bar entered below his left jaw, emerged near the midline of the top of his skull, and landed several feet away (fig. 2.1).

Miraculously, Mr. Gage did not die from this wound. His fellow railroad workers drove him to his hotel in an oxcart, and he walked up the flight of stairs to his room by himself. A physician dressed the wound, and within a few weeks Gage was back on his feet, apparently recovered.

He was not the same, however. Before the accident Gage was well-liked by all who knew him and was very efficient at his foreman's job. After his accident he became irresponsible, obstinate, and generally incapable of holding a job. He moved frequently and eventually became an exhibit in a circus. He lived for thirteen years drifting from job to job (Harlow, 1848; 1868).

The fact that Gage survived at all is amazing, but his changed personality is even more remarkable. Gage's unusual case makes it clear that biology and behavior are inextricably interwoven. They are interdependent, and changes in one produce changes in the other. We cannot truly understand one without studying the other. For example, recent studies have found that events in the body affect behavior. Certain drugs, by changing biological events, can produce hallucinations; changes in brain chemicals can influence mood; and damage in certain parts of the brain can produce changes in aggressiveness, speech, remembering, and many other behaviors. Also, behavior can affect biological events. Constant worrying about deadlines appears to be related to heart disease; an active and enriched environment can alter brain development; and some people are able to lower their blood pressure just by thinking about it. A study of the biological basis of human behavior lays the groundwork for understanding how your body and behavior interact.

The Neuron: Building Block of the Nervous System

Living organisms are made up of cells, each with its own nucleus, cell membrane, and other structures. Some living things, like the amoeba, consist of only one cell. Others, like algae, contain many cells that are very similar to one another. A living organism as complex as a human being contains an enormous number of cells, which are organized into specialized groups to perform certain functions. Muscle cells are designed to contract, red blood cells to carry oxygen, and bone cells to provide a sturdy skeleton for the body.

The **neuron** *is another kind of cell, specialized to process information. One of its tasks is to move information from place to place in the body. Another is to collect input from other neurons, process it, and pass along the information to other neurons.* (See fig. 2.2.)

The Neuron's Structure

Although all living cells have many common features, they also show important differences that relate to their specialized functions. For example, a muscle cell is long and narrow, a shape that facilitates contraction. The neuron's structure enables it to process information. Neurons are not all alike, since they perform somewhat

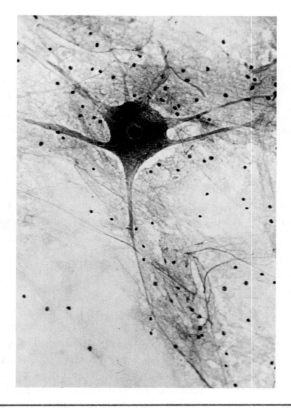

Figure 2.2 *The neuron is a cell that specializes in processing information*

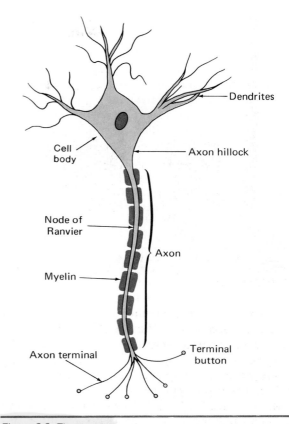

Figure 2.3 *The neuron*

different functions depending on where they are located in the nervous system. However, all neurons share a number of characteristics. A neuron has four main parts, shown in figure 2.3.

1. The *dendrites,* or input end.
2. The *cell body,* where the nucleus is located.
3. The *axon,* a long projection that carries information from the cell body to the ends of the axon.
4. The *axon terminals,* or output end.

The Dendrites. The **dendrites** *of a neuron look somewhat like a tree, and in fact they are often called the "dendritic tree." They are the portion of the cell that receives most of the input.* Each of the tiny knobs on the tree receives a message from a nearby neuron.

While some neurons in the nervous system receive input from only a few other neurons, others have an enormous dendritic tree with thousands of knobs.

Psychologists are interested in dendritic trees because they point to a remarkable potential for intercellular communication. It is tempting to assume that the degree of branching is at least partly related to the degree of behavioral flexibility. Although this connection has not yet been clearly demonstrated, certain findings lead in that direction. For example, patients with **Alzheimer's disease,** *a form of presenile dementia,* show reduced branching in their dendritic trees, suggesting deterioration or elimination of some branches (Scheibel and Scheibel, 1975). Also, the environment in which a growing organism develops can affect many aspects of brain development (Bennett, Diamond, Krech and Rosenzweig, 1964; Rosenzweig, 1984) including dendritic branching.

In one set of experiments (Greenough, 1975), some rats were reared in standard laboratory cages by themselves, with only food, water, and nesting material. Others were reared in a more complex environment, one that might even be called "enriched." They lived with other rats in larger cages and were given many toys, such as dolls, tin cans, and blocks, to play with. When all the rats were grown, the researchers compared their brains and found, among many differences, that the brains of the enriched rats had larger dendritic trees. Neurons with more extensive dendritic trees receive more input and might make more connections with other neurons.

No one knows whether rats from an enriched environment are actually more intelligent than rats reared in impoverished lab cages, but they do have more flexible behavior. For example, they seem to be less emotional when psychologists test them in mazes, and they perform better on complex problems (Brown, 1968). Rats reared in standard cages usually hide in the corner the first time they are confronted with a new environment, and they lose control of their bladder and bowels.

It is clear that an enriched environment can have substantial effects on the brains of rats and other animals. Similar changes probably occur in growing children. For example, children reared in the relatively unstimulating environments characteristic of some institutions are often sluggish, even retarded, suggesting possible brain abnormalities. Enriching intervention programs are known to be helpful (Hayden and Haring, 1985). Psychologists have known that the way infants are reared could affect their behavior. Now it seems possible that the way they are reared may affect their brain development as well.

The Cell Body.   The **cell body** *is the part of the neuron that contains the nucleus, the structure containing the cell's genetic information, and many of the structures that maintain the life of the cell, manufacture proteins, dispose of waste, and produce energy.* It acts as the factory of the cell, receiving directions from the DNA in the nucleus to synthesize the required cellular components, acquiring the raw materials from the bloodstream in the form of sugars and proteins, and finally assembling them.

The size of the cell bodies of neurons varies considerably. Some are as tiny as four or five microns in diameter. (A micron is 1/1000 millimeter.) Others range up to 50 or 100 microns in diameter and are almost visible to the naked eye.

The Axon.   The long thin tube that carries information from the cell body to the axon terminals is the **axon.** *Most axons in the human nervous system are surrounded by* **myelin,** *a whitish, fatty substance that provides insulation.* The membrane of the axon only comes into contact with the surrounding fluid at the **nodes of Ranvier** *which are locations along the axon where the insulating myelin is absent.*

The reason why most axons are surrounded by myelin is simple: the substance acts like an electrical insulator and makes it possible for axons to transmit signals from one end to the other much faster. Ordinarily, the speed at which a message moves along an axon is proportional to the axon's diameter—the larger the diameter, the faster the transmission speed. Myelination makes it possible for messages to "skip" from one node of Ranvier to the next. In some myelinated neurons the velocity of conduction is as high as 120 meters per second (268 mph).

The loss of myelin in the human nervous system produces tragic results; it is the primary cause of a disease called **multiple sclerosis.** The disease affects about 250,000 people in the United States, and it usually is first diagnosed in young adults between the ages of twenty and forty. For unknown reasons, it is more common in women. Symptoms include vision problems, muscle weakness, lack of coordination, and spastic motions. The cause of the breakdown of myelin is unknown, but one possibility is a virus infection and an immune reaction against the virus (Morell and Norton, 1980).

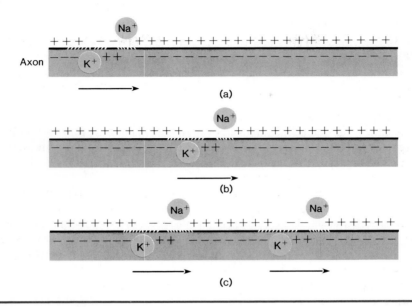

Figure 2.4 Transmission of neural messages

The Axon Terminals. When the axon reaches its destination, it branches. *At the ends of all the branches are the output ends of the cell, called the* **axon terminals.** These swollen endings contain **neurotransmitters,** *which are special chemicals that enable neurons to pass messages to one another.*

Moving Information down the Axon

ELECTRICAL

The process of moving messages from one end of the axon to the other is called **axonal conduction.** It is basically an electrical process and involves the movement of charged particles through pores in the axon's membrane. These particles are ions; the most important ones for understanding axonal conduction are sodium ($Na+$), potassium ($K+$), and chloride ($Cl-$), as well as large protein molecules with negative charges. These ions are not distributed evenly across the axon's membrane when the neuron is at rest, and their concentrations on either side of the membrane change dramatically when the neuron is moving a message.

Most of the principles of axonal conduction were deduced from experiments on a surprisingly large axon in the giant squid. (See Research Box: Studying the Squid's Axon.)

The Resting Potential. When the axon is at rest, there are more negative ions in the fluid inside the cell than in the fluid surrounding the cell. This is because the membrane of the axon will not allow some of the larger ions, like sodium, to move back and forth freely. Sodium, which has a positive charge, is kept outside, and there is a buildup of negative charges inside. For most resting neurons, the difference between the charges on the outside and the inside of the axon is about -70 millivolts (1/1000 volt). *The charge difference across the axon's membrane is called the cell's* **resting potential.**

The Action Potential. When the neuron is about to move a message, the resting potential changes drastically (fig. 2.4). The membrane at the beginning of the

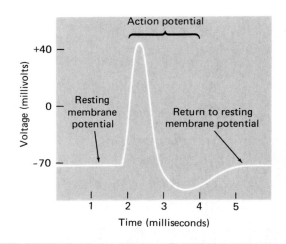

Figure 2.5 *The action potential, or "spike"*

Figure 2.6 *Example of a patterned sequence of spikes produced by a neuron across the span of a second*

axon suddenly becomes more permeable as certain channels in the membrane open rapidly. This allows the positively charged sodium ions to rush in. Just as abruptly, the membrane becomes almost impermeable to sodium again, closing the channels, and the inrush of sodium stops. At the same time the membrane closes its doors to sodium, it opens its doors to potassium, a positively charged ion, which begins to leave the cell. It is pushed out because the sodium ions have increased the concentration of positive ions inside the cell. Since positive charges repel one another, the potassium ions leak out toward the extracellular fluid where the concentration of positive ions is much lower. The loss of the positive potassium ions from inside the cell causes the axon to return to its original negative potential. *The brief moment when the inside of the axon has an overabundance of positive charges is called the* **action potential.** *This electrical burst of activity constitutes the neural message within the axon.* It is often called a "spike." The graph showing the changes in voltage (fig. 2.5) makes the reason for the nickname clear.

Since some sodium ions enter and some potassium ions leave the cell each time the neuron fires, it would seem that the cell would eventually overflow with sodium ions and make it impossible to produce any more

action potentials. However, neurons have a **sodium-potassium pump** to prevent this from occurring. *The pump is not completely understood, but we do know that it forces sodium out of the cell and potassium back in.* It is also clear that the pump is very costly in terms of energy. Each neuron spends about forty percent of its energy on this pump.

The spike travels down the length of the axon as an action potential in one part of the membrane triggers another one in the part of the membrane next to it. In myelinated axons, the spike skips from one node of Ranvier to the next because the tight insulation prevents any movement of ions except at the exposed nodes. The action potential does not travel like a ripple in a pond; it does not fade away. When it reaches the axon terminals, it is the same size and strength as it was when it started. This is called the **all-or-none principle** of axonal conduction. *Either a full-sized spike is triggered and travels all the way down the axon, or it isn't; there is no such thing as a weak, half-sized spike.*

It is true that at any given time a single neuron's message is either an action potential or a resting potential. But the rate with which action potentials occur in a neuron can vary enormously; they can also appear in specific patterns, making it possible for a single neuron to move more complicated messages. In one second, for example, one neuron might produce a patterned sequence of spikes like the one shown in figure 2.6. Even more important, though, is the fact that the human brain contains at least ten billion neurons arranged in specific structures and pathways. It is this vast network of cells and the ever-changing patterns of action potentials in different areas that provide us with the biological underpinnings of being human.

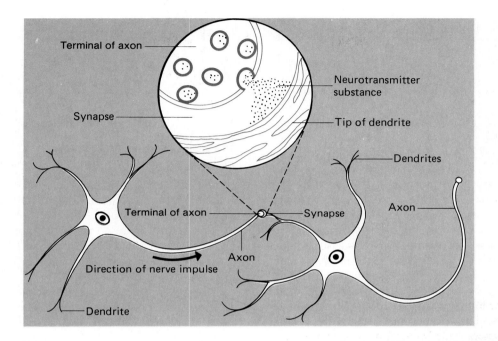

Figure 2.7 *The synapse*

Moving Information from One Neuron to Another

Although the neuron uses an electrical process to move information down its own axon, it uses a chemical process to move it to the next neuron. *The process whereby information is passed from one neuron to the next is called* **synaptic transmission.** It occurs at *the junction between two neurons, called the* **synapse** (fig. 2.7).

The synapse between two neurons is usually located between the axon terminal of one neuron and the dendritic knob of another. (Earlier we mentioned that a terminal is the output end of the neuron and the dendrite is the input end.) The information moves in only one direction: from the terminal of the first neuron to the dendrite of the second. (In recent years, scientists have found that neurons are able to receive incoming information at many places besides the dendrites, such as along the cell body's membrane and even on the axon [Schmitt, et al., 1976]; however, most synapses link one cell's axon terminal with another's dendrite.)

The axon terminal contains little pockets, or **vesicles,** *filled with neurotransmitter.* Researchers have identified several different kinds of neurotransmitters, and there may be many more. But a single neuron apparently uses only one kind at all of its terminals.

Neurotransmitters fascinate psychologists. One reason is that many of the psychoactive drugs affect neurotransmitter activity in various ways, thereby affecting the activity of the nervous system. An example is reserpine, a drug that has been used in India for hundreds of years to treat snakebite, circulatory disorders, and behavioral problems. It is also used as a treatment for high blood pressure, but up to fifteen percent of the people who take it become quite depressed (Sachar and Baron, 1979). Reserpine has an interesting effect on the vesicles that store **catecholamines,** *a class of neurotransmitter substances:* it makes the membranes of these vesicles "leaky." The vesicles lose

RESEARCH BOX

Studying the Squid's Axon

The details of axonal conduction were worked out many years ago in some classic experiments that took advantage of the enormous axon of the giant squid (Hodgkin and Katz, 1949; Keynes, 1958; Hodgkin, 1964). This unmyelinated axon is very durable and has become a favorite of neuroscientists. It can be removed from the animal, placed in a petri dish, and kept alive for long periods of time. One reason for its popularity is its incredible size. It's diameter is about 500 times larger than unmyelinated fibers in the cat's nervous system. Obviously, it is much easier to insert electrodes into the squid's axon, and fortunately, the neurons of the squid and the mammal work in very much the same way.

In an experiment designed to find which ions were most important in the axon's resting potential, the axon was placed in a bath, and an electrode inside the axon recorded its potential.

When the concentration of sodium or chloride ions in the bath was changed, the resting potential of the axon did not change very much. But if the concentration of potassium ions was altered, the resting potential changed considerably. This study demonstrated that the axon's resting potential is due to the different concentrations of potassium on the outside and inside of the axon, and also to the fact that the membrane (at rest) is selectively permeable to potassium.

The squid's axon can even be squeezed, and the axoplasm inside can be pushed out with a roller. Then it can be filled with a fluid with specified ion concentrations to further investigate the electrical properties of the axon. When the inside of the axon and the bath in which it is floating have the same ion concentrations, the membrane potential is zero. But if the experi-

---

some of their neurotransmitter, and it is destroyed by enzymes inside the cell, thereby depleting the brain's supply of this important substance (Dunn and Bondy, 1974). The effects of drugs like reserpine on neurotransmitter activity and on behavior have led many scientists to the conclusion that synapses that use catecholamines are somehow involved in mood. (The effects of drugs on brain and behavior is discussed further in Chapter 3.)

When a spike courses down the axon, it arrives very quickly at the neuron's axon terminals. This causes a vesicle of neurotransmitter to fuse with the terminal's membrane and release its chemical contents into the outside fluid (fig. 2.6). When the molecules of neurotransmitter reach the dendrite of the next neuron, they

attach to specific receptor sites on the membrane and produce a disturbance in the membrane's permeability to ions.

The distribution of positive and negative ions is uneven across the dendrite's membrane, just as it was across the axon's membrane. This means that any change in the permeability of the membrane will produce some movement of ions from one side to the other. The details concerning which ions move and why are rather complicated and not completely understood, but it is clear there is no sudden inrush of sodium ions as there is during a spike. Instead, the movement of ions is gradual, producing a less dramatic change in the potential at the dendrite. Nevertheless, this change is how the second neuron "knows" the first showed a spike.

menters add potassium ions to the outside bath and inject the axon with a solution that is low in potassium, then the recorded membrane potential is reversed. Instead of the usual -70 mv, the potential is $+70$ mv. Studies like these also show that the potassium level is an important factor in the resting potential.

The squid axon has also been important in studies of the action potential, especially in demonstrating that the axon's membrane opens up sodium channels and sodium ions rush into the cell. In one experiment, the axon was placed in different baths containing varying concentrations of sodium ions, and the size of the artificially generated action potentials was recorded. When the bath had a normal amount of sodium, the action potential was its usual size, reaching about $+40$ mv. But when the bath was diluted and contained a lower concentration of sodium,

the action potentials' peaks were lower. This and other studies demonstrated that sodium is the key ion involved in generating an action potential.

The reason the squid's axon is so large is that the invertebrates do not have myelination in their nervous systems, and so the speed of conduction depends on the diameter of the axon. If information must be moved rapidly, the axon must be fairly large in diameter. The squid's axon conducts impulses at about 25 meters per second, a figure that compares well with myelinated axons in the mammalian nervous system (10 to 100 meters/second). This particular axon is wider in the squid because of its function. It controls the muscles that the squid uses to suddenly change course and dart away by squirting a jet of water, or "jet propulsion."

Ions do not always move in the same direction. *Some synapses are called* **excitatory** *because the membrane allows positive ions to seep in, thereby "exciting" the next neuron and making it more likely to spike.* Others are called **inhibitory** *because positive ions leave the dendrite, making it more negative than usual and therefore less likely to spike.*

The message that travels down the axon is in the form of an action potential, which is basically an electrical signal. When that message is moved to the next neuron, it is changed to a chemical signal through the release of neurotransmitter by the axon terminal. The message is transformed back into an electrical signal at the next neuron's dendrite. It is as if the nervous system uses two different languages—one for moving information *within* a neuron, and another for moving information *between* neurons.

To Spike or Not to Spike

What makes a neuron trigger a spike in the first place? We mentioned earlier that a single neuron might be receiving inputs from hundreds or even thousands of other neurons through its dendrites, and it would be impossible for the neuron to trigger a spike every time any of those other neurons triggered one. Instead, the neuron integrates and summarizes all those incoming signals. This is how the neuron processes information.

The neuron does its own summarizing electrically—it adds up all the electrical changes occurring in all its dendrites. If these changes are large enough and in the right direction at any moment, the neuron triggers its own action potential. If the changes continue to be large, the neuron triggers many spikes in rapid succession, even up to 100 per second. *The place at which incoming electrical activity from the dendrites is integrated and summarized is called the* **axon hillock,** and it is *located in the cell body just at the point where the axon protrudes.*

The tiny cells called neurons form the building blocks of the nervous system. The human brain contains ten to fifteen billion of them, and each one synapses with hundreds or thousands of its neighbors. Throughout our lives, but particularly when our bodies are young and growing, neurons are changing. They sprout axons, form new synapses, and lose old ones. Their activity is the basis for our behavior and our thoughts.

GUIDED REVIEW

Learning Objectives 1, 2, and 3

1. The neuron is specialized to process information. Its four main parts are the _____ , the _____ , the _____ , and the _____ .

2. Axons are tubelike cables protruding from the cell body, usually surrounded by _____ , a fatty insulating substance. Myelin is absent only at the _____ . Myelination allows neural messages to skip from node to node. Loss of myelin is the primary cause of _____ .

3. _____ is the electrical process by which a neural message moves from one end of the axon to the other. The _____ is the difference between the charges inside and outside of the axon when it is at rest. The _____ or spike is the neural message itself. It travels down the axon using the _____ principle of conduction.

4. The _____ is the junction between two neurons. _____ is a chemical process involving the release of _____ from the axon terminal when a spike courses down the axon. Neurotransmitter causes either an _____ or _____ electrical disturbance in the dendrite's membrane.

5. A neuron receives inputs from many other neurons all over its dendritic tree. These are integrated and summarized at the _____ , and the resulting summary determines whether the neuron will trigger its own spike.

ANSWERS

neurotransmitter; excitatory, inhibitory 5. axon hillock.
action potential; all-or-none 4. synapse; Synaptic transmission;
Ranvier; multiple sclerosis 3. Axonal conduction; resting potential;
1. dendrites, cell body, axon, axon terminals 2. myelin; nodes of

The Central Nervous System

The billions of neurons in the human body are part of the nervous system. Together, they provide the basis for our thoughts, actions, feelings, desires, and emotions; they give us the ability to move, breathe, digest food, and pace our hearts. The pattern of spiking in these neurons changes constantly, even while we sleep. When they are disrupted or altered by drugs, brain damage, lack of sleep, sensory deprivation, or other events, our behavior is changed.

The nervous system is usually divided into two main parts called the **central nervous system (CNS),** *which includes the brain and spinal cord,* and the **peripheral nervous system (PNS),** *which includes all the neurons that lie outside the brain and spinal cord.* One of the differences between the two is that axons in the PNS regenerate if they are damaged; but for reasons that are not well understood, axons in the CNS generally do not, although much progress is being made to promote their growth and recovery of function (Freed, Medinaceli, and Wyatt, 1985). In this section we will explore the CNS, focusing on the activities of the human brain, which is so important in our behavior.

Studying the Central Nervous System

Studying the CNS may sound like a pursuit that is only possible with the sophisticated equipment and high technology found in large research centers. In fact, much of what we know about the brain was learned with little more than a sharp eye and keen observation. A sharp knife and a microscope were the first important research tools, and once the electrical nature of the brain was understood, voltmeters and microelectrodes could be added to the tool box.

The four most common methods used to study the relationship between brain function and behavior are (1) anatomical techniques, (2) electrical recording, (3) electrical stimulation of the brain (ESB), and (4) brain lesions. Each has advantages and disadvantages, and it is usually necessary to use more than one method to definitely relate brain function to a particular behavior.

Anatomical Techniques. In anatomical studies, neuroanatomists examine brain tissue and pathways and note any correlations between the appearance of the tissue and the behavior of the animal or human. The experiment that found increased dendritic branching in enriched rats is a good example of an anatomical study. Specific changes in the anatomy of the rats' brains were related to the characteristics of the rearing environment and also to later changes in behavior.

Anatomical methods do not just consist of sectioning the tissue and looking at its structure. Neuroanatomists make extensive use of stains and dyes to highlight different parts of the neuron; they may also inject radioactive substances and follow their course. For example, one very powerful technique involves the injection of radioactively labeled glucose. Since active neurons need nutrition, they pick up the glucose from the bloodstream before the less active ones do. Later examination of the brain tissue reveals which areas were most active at the time, since they will have the highest concentrations of radioactivity.

With the development of noninvasive techniques like X rays, it has become possible to examine the neuroanatomy of living human beings more closely. *A type of X ray called* **computerized axial tomography,** *or* **CAT scan,** *uses a computer and multiple X rays to obtain detailed pictures of the brain.* (See fig. 2.8.)

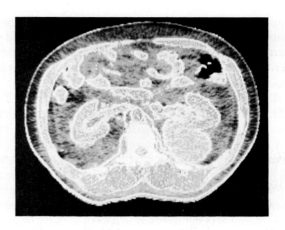

Figure 2.8   *An example of a CAT scan*

Electrical Recording. The fact that neurons transmit messages using potentials means that a great deal of brain activity is electrical. *The electrical activity of the brain can be measured and recorded using an* **electroencephalograph,** *or* **EEG.** *Electrodes are placed on the scalp, and the rapidly changing electrical events occurring between them are recorded as waves on moving chart paper.* The wave patterns are different depending on the location of the electrodes and on the person's state of consciousness. Chapter 3 explores this phenomenon in more detail.

In medicine, the EEG is used to monitor patients with epilepsy, head injuries, or infections. In an EEG from a patient who recently had a stroke, the patterns from the electrodes on the left side of the brain were slower than those on the right, indicating the stroke primarily affected the left side. This was particularly true for the pair of electrodes that had been placed directly over the language areas of the brain. This patient showed severe speech problems after his stroke (Dahlberg and Jaffe, 1977).

The signals on the EEG are also used in most states to determine whether a person is legally dead. We used to consider a person legally dead when the heart stopped. Now, with advances in technology, a patient can be maintained on life-support equipment, even though he or she may have no hope of ever regaining consciousness. The concept of brain death emerged as a result of many legal battles over whether it was moral, ethical, and legal to disconnect a patient's life-support equipment.

Brain death is now defined by several events. The EEG must be flat for several days, showing that the brain is producing little or no electrical activity. The patient must also be unresponsive or in a coma. If two doctors agree that brain death has occurred, it is usually possible to remove the patient from the equipment.

While the EEG is used to record a kind of summarized electrical activity in large parts of the brain, microelectrodes can be used to record activity in small groups of neurons, and even in individual cells. A tiny hole is drilled through the skull. The microelectrode is then inserted into the brain and placed next to or into the axon of a neuron, where it detects the changes in voltage that accompany spikes. This technique has been used very successfully in animal studies of vision. One experiment demonstrated that one neuron in a monkey's brain changed its rate of spiking only when the monkey was looking at a picture of another monkey's hand (Gross, et al., 1972). This cell was in the brain area that processes visual input and memories. Perhaps this neuron, and others that respond to different shapes, form the basis of what we understand as "perception."

Electrical Stimulation of the Brain (ESB). Electrical stimulation of the brain (ESB) is a technique used to relate activity in particular brain regions to behavior. An electrode is inserted into a specific brain region, and current is passed through. This causes rapid spiking in the surrounding neurons. During some kinds of brain surgery in which this technique is used, the patient is wide awake. The surgeon electrically stimulates some brain area and notes any reactions in the patient. (The patient does not experience any pain from the electric current, however; the brain feels no pain. This operation requires only a local anesthetic on the scalp.) The use of this technique has revealed a great deal about the functions of various brain areas, which we will discuss later in this section.

Brain Lesions and Brain Damage. Though the changes in behavior that people undergo after brain damage can often be tragic, they provide scientists with insights into how particular areas of the brain are involved in specific behaviors. Our understanding of the brain processes, especially those underlying language, has advanced considerably because of studies of patients with brain damage. In animal experiments, portions of the brain are destroyed by a lesion, which is produced either by cutting away sections of brain tissue or by administering large jolts of electrical current. Then the behavior of the animal is observed. Any changes might be due to the damage in that brain area.

Brain damage in some areas of the brain occasionally produces rather remarkable changes. In one case, a patient called H. M. underwent an operation designed to relieve severe epilepsy. The operation included the removal of a small part of the brain. After surgery, H. M. had fewer epileptic seizures, but he also showed an astounding memory deficit. Minutes after reading a magazine article, he could read it again as though he had never seen it before. Apparently, his ability to remember new information for more than a few seconds was completely lost (Milner, 1970). H. M.'s case suggested that the area that was removed, a structure called the **hippocampus,** might be *an area of the brain that has some role in long-term memory* (Isaacson and Proram, 1975; Gray and McNaughton, 1983).

The Brain's Structure

The human brain is actually very large, but it is folded and contorted a great deal inside the skull. The working parts of the brain are the neurons, but the brain also contains **glial cells.** *These cells perform many chores, such as filtering substances from the bloodstream and preventing important chemicals from leaving the brain. Glial cells also provide a supporting matrix.*

The brain is shaped somewhat like a mushroom (fig. 2.9). The stem contains the structures that take care of basic and somewhat mechanical functions like breathing and heart action. *The huge overhanging top*

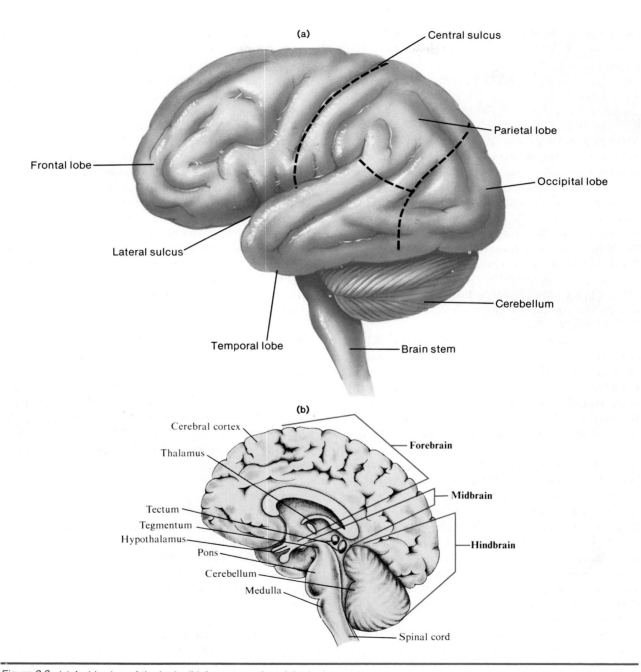

Figure 2.9 *(a) A side view of the brain. (b) A cross section of the brain.*

part of the brain is "newer;" that is, it evolved later, and its structures and pathways perform the functions related to human intelligence. This brain area is the massive **cerebral hemispheres.** *The left hemisphere controls activities on the right side of the body, and the right hemisphere controls the left side.* The **corpus callosum** *is a bundle of fibers that links the two hemispheres so they communicate all the time.* (Usually, the left hand does indeed know what the right hand is doing. In a special case we discuss at the end of this chapter, the communication between the two hemispheres is broken, and the person has "two brains in one.")

During the Middle Ages, the idea arose that different areas of the brain were involved in different behaviors. This concept was carried to an extreme during the eighteenth and nineteenth centuries by a group called the **phrenologists.** *They believed you could understand a person's behavior by feeling for bumps and depressions on the skull.* For instance, one person might have an enlargement in the area of the skull labeled 149, which was believed to be involved in responsibility. Some phrenologists even tried to mold the behavior of children by putting caps on their head to produce bumps in certain places.

Today, most people would agree that the phrenologists carried things a bit far. Their initial idea did have an important grain of truth; it is clear that certain brain areas are indeed involved in particular behaviors. However, brain areas are usually involved in more than one behavior, and each behavior involves many brain areas. Pathways in the brain that span several structures seem to be more related to particular behaviors than individual structures or discrete areas. Nevertheless, it is important to keep in mind how quaint and naive scientific ideas may sound 100 years after they have been proposed. We can only wonder which of our ideas will sound absurd to people in the twenty-first century.

Anatomists mapped the brain and named its structures long before anyone was able to relate activity in particular areas to brain function. They named brain areas based on how they looked rather than on what they did. Although hundreds of structures have been identified, named, and renamed, we will only examine a few of the major ones, especially those involved in interesting behaviors.

The Cerebral Cortex.   The outer layer of the cerebral hemispheres, with all the folds and crevices, is the **cerebral cortex.** The word "cortex" comes from the Latin word meaning "bark;" the cerebral cortex is literally the bark of the brain. The huge size of the cerebral hemispheres in humans and in other primates is due partly to the enormous development of cortical tissue. This tissue does most of the higher-order information processing, and you are using it right now to read and understand this sentence.

The Lobes.   The cerebral hemispheres include four major subareas called lobes. These are the frontal lobe, the parietal lobe, the temporal lobe, and the occipital lobe. The **frontal lobe** *is very large in human beings, compared to other animals, and is involved in memory, reasoning, thinking, and movement. The* **occipital lobe,** *in the back of the brain, processes visual information.*

Across the top of the brain is the **parietal lobe,** *an area that processes sensory information from the skin.* The amount of brain tissue devoted to each body part is not proportional to the size of that part. Those body parts that perform fine movements and are more sensitive are the ones that have the largest brain area devoted to them, both in the parietal lobe and in the areas of the frontal lobe that control movement. Figure 2.10 shows a drawing of the body parts in proportion to the amount of brain tissue. The fingers need a lot of brain area, and so do the mouth and tongue (for speaking). But the huge torso really requires very little.

The **temporal lobes** *process auditory information and, apparently, auditory memories as well.* Electrical stimulation of this area in a person sometimes provokes

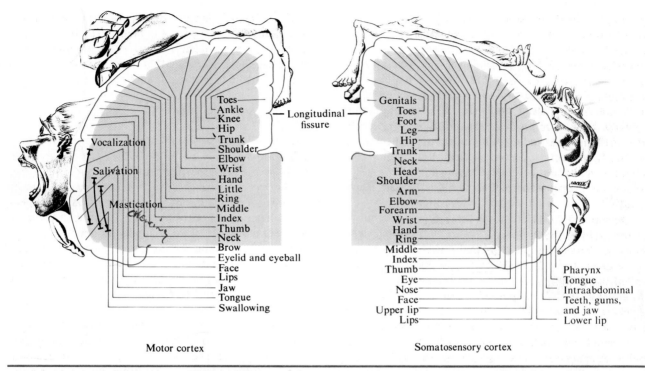

Figure 2.10 *The amount of motor and somatosensory cortex that serves each area of the body is proportional to the sensitivity of the area, or its need for fine motor control, rather than its size.*

Labels (Motor cortex): Vocalization, Salivation, Mastication, Toes, Ankle, Knee, Hip, Trunk, Shoulder, Elbow, Wrist, Hand, Little, Ring, Middle, Index, Thumb, Neck, Brow, Eyelid and eyeball, Face, Lips, Jaw, Tongue, Swallowing

Longitudinal fissure

Labels (Somatosensory cortex): Genitals, Toes, Foot, Leg, Hip, Trunk, Neck, Head, Shoulder, Arm, Elbow, Forearm, Wrist, Hand, Ring, Middle, Index, Thumb, Eye, Nose, Face, Upper lip, Lips, Pharynx, Tongue, Intraabdominal, Teeth, gums, and jaw, Lower lip

a vivid memory. Following are two examples of what patients have said when they were stimulated in various places on the temporal cortex during neurosurgery (Penfield, 1975):

> I think I heard a mother calling her little boy somewhere. It seemed to be something that happened years ago. . . . It was somebody in the neighborhood where I live.

> Yes . . . I heard voices down along the river somewhere . . . a man's voice and a woman's calling . . . I think I saw the river.

The Limbic System

Below the cortex are a group of structures that form the **limbic system.** *These brain areas appear to be involved in emotional behavior.* Brain damage in one section can cause a peaceful, calm animal to become extremely aggressive and dangerous. Damage in another part might cause an animal to show no fear at all. For example, a monkey might pick up a live snake, showing no emotion other than curiosity. No normal monkey would ever do that.

The **hypothalamus** *is an important part of the limbic system. Despite its tiny size, this structure and the pathways that run through it play major roles in some of our most fascinating behaviors, including sex, aggression, eating (and overeating), drinking, and control of body temperature.* It is not surprising that damage in this area can have many different effects, depending on where the damage occurs. A lesion in the central portion, for example, causes a rat to overeat and become grossly obese within a few weeks.

In the early days of electrical-stimulation experiments, a group of psychologists was studying the effects of tiny electrical stimulations in the brains of rats (Olds and Milner, 1954). When they inserted an electrode into a rat's brain, their aim was sometimes not very good. They were aiming for a lower region of the brain, but they accidentally hit the hypothalamus. When the rat recovered from the operation, they turned on the current. Strangely, the rat did not eat, fight, or even look frightened. It just kept returning to the corner of the box where it received the shock.

James Olds and his colleagues designed a "do it yourself" stimulation box with a lever that the rat could use to stimulate its own brain. Very quickly the animal learned to press the lever. It pressed and pressed, thousands of times an hour, until it dropped from exhaustion. It would barely stop to eat or sleep. The area that was being stimulated in the brain clearly had something to do with reward or pleasure. At the time, the area was dubbed the "pleasure center." Later experiments showed that rather than a "center," it is actually pathways that are related to reward and run through the hypothalamus. So it could be called the "pleasure pathway" (Olds and Fobes, 1981).

Electrical stimulation in this location is also very pleasurable for humans. Patients who receive this treatment continue to stimulate their own brains, sometimes until they go into convulsions. Afterwards, the patients lie relaxed, smiling happily, and seem to have enjoyed the experience.

The Cerebellum.   Located behind and partly underneath the cerebral hemispheres is the **cerebellum,** *a large structure involved in coordination and movement.* This brain area regulates the rate, force, and coordination of every move, working with both the spinal cord and the areas of the frontal lobes involved in the control of movement.

The Medulla.   A large area of the lower part of the brain, called the **medulla,** *controls many of the maintenance functions of the body, for example, heart action, breathing, and digestion.* Part of it also plays an important role in waking and sleeping.

The Spinal Cord

The **spinal cord** *is a long mass of nervous tissue carrying sensory information from the arms, legs, and trunk to the brain. The spinal cord also contains neurons that carry information in the opposite direction, from the brain to the body.* These neurons carry signals that produce contraction or relaxation in the muscles of the body. If you damaged your spinal cord, you might lose all feeling in the parts of your body that are located below the damaged area; the sensations would not be able to pass by the injury and reach your brain. Also, your brain would not be able to send signals to your muscles to make them contract, so the parts of your body below the injury would be paralyzed.

Although the brain is the master information processor, the spinal cord is able to do some simple processing. Some reflexes can occur without any help from the motor areas of the brain. The knee jerk is a good example. When you strike the hollow of your knee, your leg kicks. The information travels from the tendon in your knee to your spinal cord. Neurons traveling from the cord to the muscles in your leg are then excited, causing your leg to jerk. The information from your knee also traveled to your brain, and you feel the sensations, but the jerk would have occurred even if it had not reached the brain.

Another good example of a spinal reflex shows how important they can be (fig. 2.11). If you touch your finger to a hotplate, you pull it away *before* you ever feel the pain. The reason is that the action potentials from your finger traveled first to your spinal cord and then immediately back to the muscles in your finger without going to the brain first. You only feel the pain when the messages finally reach the brain. Fortunately,

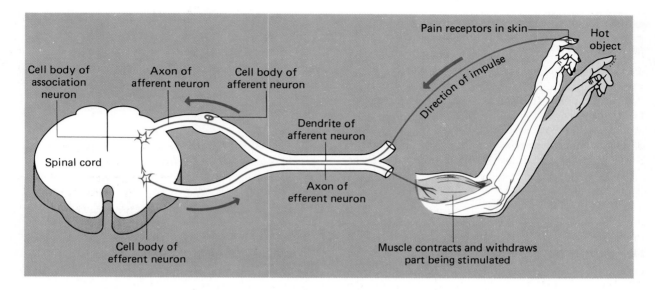

Figure 2.11 An example of a spinal reflex: the reflexive withdrawal of the hand from a hot object

the route from your finger to your spinal cord and back is much shorter than the route from your finger to your brain.

Animal Brains. The most obvious difference between animal brains and the human brain is the amount of cortex in proportion to body size. The lower mammals have less cortex than humans but much more than birds or reptiles. The amount of cortex an animal has is a rough index of its capacity for learning.

The cortex in an animal also functions differently. For example, a large amount of the human parietal lobe is devoted to processing information from the fingers. This arrangement would not be very useful to a cat, for instance. Instead, much of a cat's cortex processes input from its whiskers, from which the cat learns a great deal about its environment. In pigs, large brain areas are devoted to the snout.

Other structures in the brains of animals also vary in size or function, according to the habits of the species. You might have guessed that a dog has enormous

olfactory bulbs, *which are brain structures that process smells.* The cerebellum of a bird is very large in proportion to its body size, mostly because of its need for precise motor coordination and balance during flight.

The brains of fish and reptiles do not have very much cortex. This does not mean they are unintelligent, but it does suggest that behavioral flexibility and learning do not play very large roles in their survival. Most of them can find their own food and take care of themselves soon after birth; they do not need to learn very much from the environment to survive. In contrast, human beings are almost completely helpless at birth; they need to interact with and learn from their environments so they can eventually take care of themselves.

GUIDED REVIEW

Learning Objectives 4 and 5

1. The two parts of the nervous system are the _____ and the _____ .

2. Four methods of studying the relationship between brain and behavior are _____ , _____ , _____ , and _____ .

3. Major brain areas include the _____ , divided into left and right _____ , and also into lobes, called _____ , _____ , _____ , and _____ .

4. The _____ performs some simple information processing and controls certain reflexes, such as the knee jerk.

5. One way that animal brains differ from human brains is in the size of particular brain areas, especially the _____ . The amount of cortex is a rough index of the importance of behavioral flexibility in the species.

ANSWERS

1. central nervous system, peripheral nervous system 2. anatomical techniques, electrical recording, electrical stimulation of the brain, brain lesions 3. cerebral cortex; hemispheres; frontal, temporal, parietal, occipital 4. spinal cord 5. cerebral cortex

The Peripheral Nervous System

All the neurons that lie outside the brain and spinal cord belong to the peripheral nervous system (PNS). This includes the neurons leading from the spinal cord to the muscles, and also the sensory neurons that bring information about touch, pain, and temperature from the skin to the spinal cord.

The reflexes we discussed in connection with the spinal cord involved neurons in the PNS. In the example of the knee-jerk reflex, a sensory neuron in the knee joint triggered action potentials in response to a blow on the knee, and it sent this message to the spinal cord, where the axon terminals of the sensory neuron are located. The terminals transferred the message through a synapse to the dendrites of a motor neuron, which then passed the information along its axon back to the muscles of the leg.

Sensory and Motor Neurons

Sensory neurons bring information from all over the body to the spinal cord, where it is relayed up to the parietal lobe of the brain. *Neurons carrying information toward the central nervous system are called* **afferent.** These sensory neurons do not receive input from the terminals of other neurons but from muscle fibers, tendons, joints, and special structures in the skin. These neurons can provide information about the position of your knee joint, the location of a mosquito on your back, or the discomfort of a tight-fitting shoe.

When you want to initiate a movement of the big toe, for example, the signal originates in the cortex (although no one understands quite how). It is relayed back down through the spinal cord to the motor neurons in the leg through the **efferent** *pathways, which carry information away from the central nervous system.* The message is then passed along these neurons, whose axon terminals synapse onto muscle fibers in the toe, rather than onto dendrites of other neurons.

When the message reaches the axon terminals, the neurons release neurotransmitter that causes the muscle cells to contract, moving your big toe. The whole process takes only a fraction of a second.

The Autonomic Nervous System *HAS BECOME AN ENEMY TO US.*

Another set of neurons, most of which lie in the PNS, is the **autonomic nervous system** *(ANS). It connects the brain and spinal cord to the stomach, intestines, heart, blood vessels, bladder, lungs, and the other body organs.* This network was named "autonomic" because at one time everyone believed it operated automatically, without any voluntary control. Recently, though, scientists have found that some people are able to learn some control over its functions, provided they receive the proper training. This special kind of learning will be discussed further in Chapter 5.

One function of the ANS is to help the body cope with emergencies and then help it relax when the crisis has passed. To perform these two activities, the ANS has two parts: the sympathetic division and the parasympathetic division (fig. 2.12).

Suppose you are sitting calmly in a hotel room in Mexico reading a travel guide. Out of the corner of your eye you spot a fist-sized dark shape on the floor. You get up to move a little closer and discover it is a tarantula. Your heart races, your blood pressure rises, you breathe faster, your mouth gets dry, and you desperately try to remember the word for "help" in Spanish. *Physiological changes such as increased heart rate, blood pressure, and respiration are produced by the activation of the* **sympathetic division;** *they are all designed to help your body cope with an emergency* (fig. 2.13). *ON SWITCH*

The purpose of these changes is to slow down bodily processes that are not terribly important during an emergency (like digestion) and to speed up those that will help you run faster or fight harder. For example, the increase in blood pressure brings more oxygen to the muscles so they can contract very tightly. The sympathetic nervous system also triggers hormonal reactions that assist in putting the body on "emergency status;" these reactions are discussed in the next section. *The entire spectrum of changes produced by sympathetic activation is called the* **fright-fight-flight response.**

You have probably read stories in the newspapers about people who are able to perform amazing feats of strength and endurance during a crisis. A woman can lift a car off an injured child after an accident. A seriously wounded soldier can carry an unconscious friend away from the battle. Soldiers often say they can't even feel the pain of their wounds until they get back to the medical aid station. Boxers sometimes say the same thing about the injuries they suffer in a boxing match. These types of responses are made possible by the sympathetic division of the ANS.

When the emergency is over, it is the job of the **parasympathetic division** *to return the body to normal. These neurons slow the heart rate and breathing and decrease the blood pressure. Generally, the neurons of the parasympathetic division reach the same body organs as do those of the sympathetic division, but they have the opposite effect.* *OFF SWITCH*

There does not need to be a tarantula in your room for your sympathetic division to activate. This system is active, on and off, all day long: when the phone rings; when the boss calls you in; when you are worrying about the children playing in the street; and when it is examination time. The long-term effects of chronic sympathetic activation can have serious consequences. Some people have high blood pressure, others develop ulcers, and still others find they suffer from insomnia, nervous tics, depression, or a drinking problem. (We will discuss the effects of too much stress in Chapter 13.)

SYMPATHETIC DIVISION

PARASYMPATHETIC DIVISION

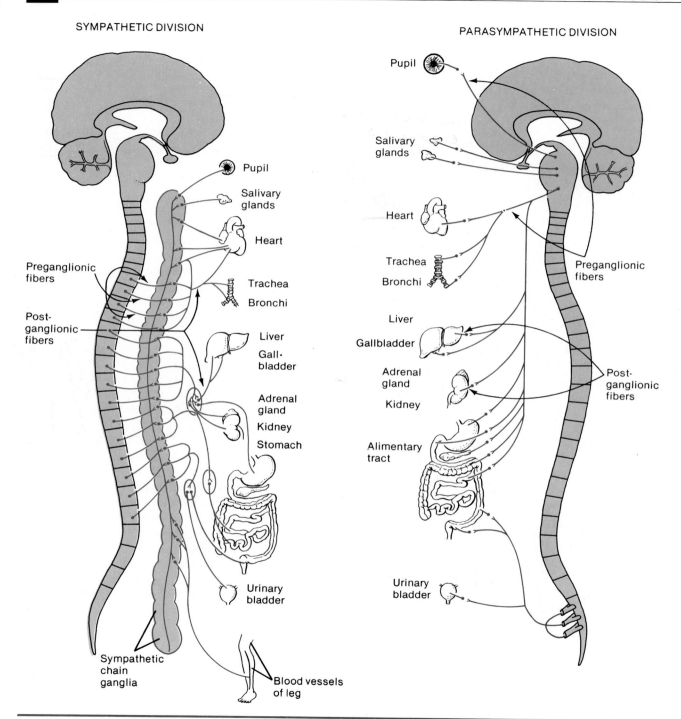

Pupil

Salivary glands

Heart

Trachea
Bronchi

Preganglionic fibers

Post-ganglionic fibers

Liver

Gall-bladder

Adrenal gland

Kidney

Stomach

Sympathetic chain ganglia

Urinary bladder

Blood vessels of leg

Pupil

Salivary glands

Heart

Trachea
Bronchi

Preganglionic fibers

Liver

Gallbladder

Adrenal gland

Kidney

Alimentary tract

Post-ganglionic fibers

Urinary bladder

Figure 2.12 The sympathetic and parasympathetic divisions of the nervous system

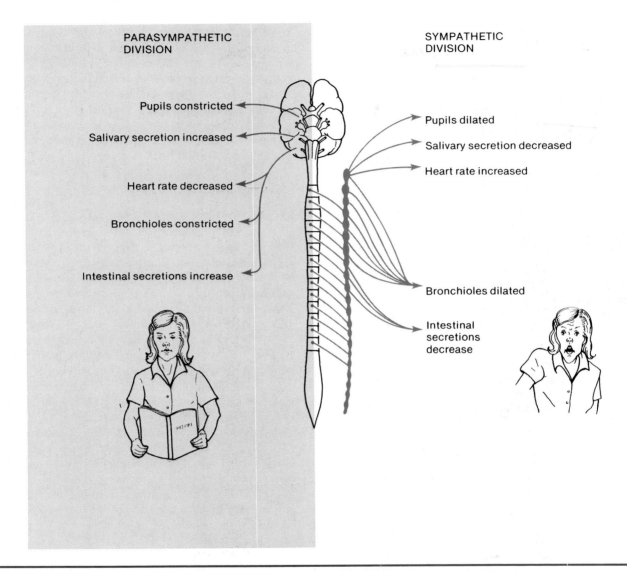

Figure 2.13   Physiological changes produced by the activation of the sympathetic division of the nervous system

GUIDED REVIEW

Learning Objective 6

1. The _____ includes all the neurons outside the brain and spinal cord.

2. _____ carry information from the body to the spinal cord; _____ carry information from the spinal cord to the muscles.

3. The _____ includes the _____ , which prepares the body for emergencies by increasing heart rate, breathing rate, and blood pressure, and by decreasing responses such as digestion, and the _____ , which helps return the body to normal afterwards.

4. The spectrum of changes produced by sympathetic activation is called the _____ .

ANSWERS

1. peripheral nervous system (PNS) 2. Sensory neurons; motor neurons 3. autonomic nervous system (ANS); sympathetic division; parasympathetic division 4. fright-fight-flight response

The Endocrine System

The **endocrine system** *includes a number of glands that release important substances near capillaries carrying blood so the substances reach all parts of the body through the circulatory system. These substances, or* **hormones,** *are special chemical messengers that regulate physiological processes in the body.* Most are designed to affect a specific target organ some distance away; but some have more general effects throughout the body.

Hormones and Glands

The major endocrine glands in the body are shown in figure 2.14. Table 2.1 lists some of the glands, the hormones produced by them, and their chief functions. The glands vary a good deal, both in the hormones they produce and in their functions. *The ovary, for example, produces the hormones* **estrogen** *and* **progesterone,** *which affect female sex characteristics such as breast development and the arrangement of fat in the body.*

Part of the adrenal gland produces the hormone norepinephrine, which also acts as a neurotransmitter in the nervous system. This hormone is important in the fright-fight-flight response discussed earlier. Its release is triggered by the sympathetic nervous system when the body is under stress, and many of its effects on the body duplicate the effects of sympathetic activation. For example, the hormone causes blood pressure to rise and heart and respiration rates to increase.

The **pituitary gland,** *located at the base of the brain just under the hypothalamus, is called the master gland. It produces several different hormones, most of which act on other endocrine glands* (table 2.1). One of its products, for example, is a hormone that stimulates the thyroid gland and triggers the production of the thyroid's hormone. The pituitary also produces *adrenocorticotrophic hormone,* which is usually called *ACTH.* When this substance is released by the pituitary, it triggers the adrenal gland to release some of its hormones.

Another reason the pituitary is called the master gland is that it acts as the intermediary between the brain and the endocrine system. The activity of the pituitary is actually controlled by the hypothalamus, the structure located just above the gland. *Neurons in the hypothalamus produce* **releasing factors,** *substances that trigger hormone release by the pituitary gland.* For example, *when a person is under great stress, the hypothalamus will release* **corticotropin releasing factor,** *which then stimulates the pituitary to release ACTH.* This is a complicated system but one that permits a finely tuned integration of the two major physiological systems involved in behavior.

Hormones and Behavior

Hormones have important effects on quite a variety of emotions and behaviors in animals, including aggression, courtship and sexual behavior, learning and memory, maternal behavior, hoarding (in rodents), scent marking (in several species of mammals), and even migration (in fish and birds). Maternal behavior

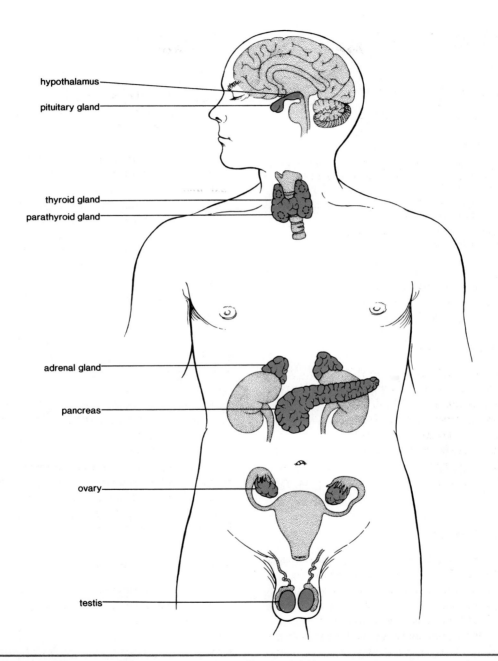

Figure 2.14   *The major endocrine glands. Note that the ovaries are found only in females and the testes only in males.*

Table 2.1 The principal endocrine glands and their hormones

Gland	Principal hormones	Chief functions
Pituitary gland	Thyroid stimulating (TSH, thyrotropin) Adrenocorticotropic (ACTH)	Stimulates thyroid Stimulates adrenal gland
	Follicle stimulating (FSH) Leuteinizing (LH)	Reproductive functions
	Prolactin Growth (GH)	Milk production Growth
	Antidiuretic (ADH, vasopressin) Oxytocin	Water retention by kidneys Uterine contraction
Thyroid	Thyroxin	Increases metabolic rate
Adrenal gland	Cortisol Mineralocorticoids	Formation of glucose Sodium retention; potassium excretion by kidneys
	Norepinephrine	Fright-fight-flight
Testes	Androgens (testosterone)	Secondary male characteristics
Ovary	Estrogen Progesterone	Secondary female characteristics

in rodents is a good illustration of how hormones influence behavior. Nonpregnant female mice will build nests if they receive small doses of the ovarian hormone progesterone (Lisk, Pretlow, and Friedman, 1969). Several hormones in rats, especially ones from the ovaries, influence behavior like retrieving and caring for pups after they are born. (Moltz, Lubin, Leon, and Numan, 1970). Injections of these hormones in a sequence that mimics the hormonal events of pregnancy caused virgin female rats to begin caring for the young.

In human beings, the link between hormones and behavior is less direct. For example, adoptive parents can provide wonderful care for babies without receiving hormone therapy. Nevertheless, hormones do seem to have important effects on several behaviors in human beings. In men *the sex hormone* **testosterone,** *released from the testes, is involved in sex drive,* as we will see in Chapter 8. Large reductions of this hormone, especially if they occur before puberty, usually

result in lowered sex drive and lower aggressiveness (Rubin, Reinisch, and Haskett 1981). The effects of castration on prepubertal boys have been known for 2000 years. Such boys, who were called eunuchs, had little sexual appetite and were therefore employed to attend the harems of wealthy men in ancient Rome.

The connection between hormones and behavior is not one-way. Behavior can affect the endocrine system just as hormones can affect behavior. For example, as an individual begins to worry, get angry, or become emotionally excited, several events happen. First, the sympathetic nervous system is activated, as we mentioned earlier. This triggers the fright-fight-flight response and the release of certain hormones from the adrenal gland. At the same time, the hypothalamus directs the pituitary to release ACTH, which then triggers the release of different hormones, like **cortisol,** from another part of the adrenals. **Cortisol** *is an adrenal hormone that helps the body return to normal when a* *stressful experience is over. It supplies the cells with nutrients that are vital in repairing injured tissues.* Thus, the hormonal response to stress is quite complex, involving responses that help the body cope with the emergency and help it resist the harmful effects of stress.

GUIDED REVIEW

Learning Objective 7

1. The endocrine system includes glands that release _____ , special chemical messengers that regulate bodily processes.

2. Most hormones are released into the _____ by a gland and trigger activity in a target organ some distance away.

3. The _____ is the master gland because it releases hormones that control the activities of other endocrine glands and provides the link between the brain and the endocrine system.

4. The brain controls the endocrine system through the hypothalamus. Neurons produce _____ that affect the release of hormones by the pituitary.

5. Hormones affect a variety of behaviors in mammals, including sex, aggression, migration, and emotional behavior. Maternal behavior in rodents is under the control of several hormones, including _____ and _____ . In humans, the effects of hormones on behavior are less direct.

6. Behavior also affects the endocrine system. Emotional behavior, for example, triggers the hormonal events associated with stress, including the release of hormones by the _____ glands.

ANSWERS

1. hormones 2. bloodstream 3. pituitary gland 4. releasing factors 5. estrogen, progesterone 6. adrenal

When Things Go Wrong: Malfunctions in the Nervous System

Although the human brain is well protected, it can be harmed by many events. Brain damage may occur at birth because of lack of oxygen, or it may be the result of accidental injuries suffered in a car accident, for example. Occasionally there are cases in which the reasons for brain damage are unknown. The genes could contain an error, and the brain could develop abnormally from conception. This section explores only two of the many kinds of brain malfunctions: epilepsy and stroke.

Epilepsy

One of the most frightening and misunderstood disorders of the brain is called **epilepsy,** *a name coming from the Greek word for "seizure." The main symptom of epilepsy is the occurrence of seizures.* Researchers estimate that more than four million Americans have the disease, and some think the number is much higher. Friends, neighbors, and especially employers often discriminate against epileptics, and many "go underground," keeping their secret to themselves.

If you were walking and talking with an epileptic and he or she had a very short seizure ("petit mal"), you might not even notice it. The longer "grand mal" seizures that involve convulsions can be terrifying—not for the epileptic but for the people watching. The epileptic does not remember the episode (Penfield, 1975).

The EEG is particularly useful in showing what happens in the brain during a seizure. EEG records show that the brain waves clearly become abnormal when a seizure begins. Most scientists hypothesize that a group of neurons in one part of the brain, a part that is damaged in some way, begins firing very rapidly and in unison. If it is going to be a major seizure, the abnormal firing pattern spreads to other parts of the brain.

In some people the epileptic seizures begin soon after a head injury. In these cases, the head injury clearly produced the damage that resulted in the disorder. For most other victims, the cause of epilepsy is unknown. Scientists agree that damage in the brain could be caused by a birth injury, poor nutrition, fevers, infections, or perhaps environmental poisons. Furthermore, a person can develop epilepsy at any age. Well over half of those in whom it develops, however, begin having seizures before they are out of elementary school.

Historically, treatments for epilepsy have included visits to hot-springs resorts, diets of barley water and porridge, and even electrical shocks. Ben Franklin treated a 24-year-old epileptic with shocks to the head over a two-week period in 1752. The patient claimed that the bizarre treatment worked. The most common modern treatment for epilepsy is anticonvulsant drug therapy. About half the patients can be completely free of seizures when they take these drugs; another thirty percent gain some control over their seizures.

Despite the availability of effective drugs to control seizures, epileptics are often the victims of outdated laws and suspicions. Until recently, some states permitted epileptics to be sterilized, and some had strict rules about marriage. The McCarran-Walter Immigration Act lumped epileptics with lepers, alcoholics, paupers, and prostitutes and refused them entry into the United States. Most of these laws have now been repealed, but the superstitions and fears surrounding the disease remain.

Stroke

Clay Dahlberg had just come home from teaching a night class. He picked up the newspaper and sat down to enjoy a pleasant but uneventful dinner. On the first bite he choked, and his vision became hazy. The vision cleared up a few minutes later, but he began coughing and choking again and felt very weak. He wanted to call for help; the words wouldn't come out. He tried to remove the last bite of food from his mouth, but his right hand was hanging limply, and he could not move it. A psychiatrist, Clay Dahlberg knew what his symptoms meant: he was having a stroke (Dahlberg and Jaffe, 1977). A **stroke** *is a rupture or blockage of a blood vessel in the brain.*

The onset of a stroke is usually sudden, and the behavioral changes that follow it are often very dramatic. However, they vary from person to person. One victim might be unable to speak, even though he knows what he wants to say. Another might find that she is no longer able to move her left leg. Still another might find himself totally unable to understand what other people are saying, even though he can still hear. The results of a stroke depend not only on how much brain tissue is damaged but on where in the brain the damage occurs. Dahlberg's stroke was produced by a blocked blood vessel on the left side in the areas of the brain that are involved in movement and speech. The brain tissue surrounding the blockage was without oxygen for a time, and it was damaged.

As we discussed earlier, the left side of the body is controlled by the right side of the brain, and vice versa. This means that a stroke on the left side of the brain will usually result in weakness or paralysis of some of the muscles on the right side of the body. For right-handed people this is very inconvenient. But the location of a stroke can mean much more than inconvenience. If the stroke is on the left side, the areas of the brain that are important for language are in danger.

Figure 2.15 shows the locations of several major brain areas important for language. *Two critical structures for language processing are* **Wernicke's area** *and* **Broca's area.** The messages from these areas reach the motor areas in the frontal lobes controlling the mouth and tongue. These areas are also connected to the visual and auditory parts of the brain as well. In order for a person to read, messages from the visual area must reach the language areas of the brain. And in order for a person to understand spoken language, connections must exist between the language areas and the parts of the temporal lobe that process auditory information.

A stroke can damage any of the language areas or any of the connections between the language areas and other critical brain structures. This would result in **aphasia,** *or language difficulty due to brain damage.* Depending on the location of the stroke, the victim might lose the ability to read, to speak, or perhaps to understand spoken language.

Victims of a stroke sometimes are unable to name familiar objects. Try listing all the fifty states. You probably missed a few, but you would recognize them quickly if someone mentioned them. Now imagine what it would be like if all the objects in the world were like the states you left out; you couldn't think of their names, but you could recognize them.

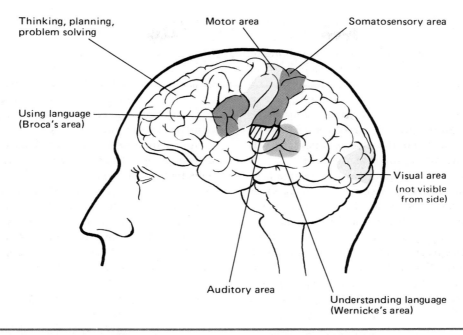

Figure 2.15 The left cerebral hemisphere, showing the main areas involved in language processing

The inability to read your own language is also difficult to comprehend. It would be as if these sentences were in a foreign language that uses our own alphabet:

"Bostika no vetsopridai bor 'striniwa' eo pa naiba."

Clay Dahlberg was fortunate because his stroke did not damage the most important language areas. It injured the pathways that make connections between the language areas and the motor areas controlling his mouth and tongue. He could still understand other people, and he could still think of what he wanted to say, but he could not make his mouth say it.

Recovering from a stroke is an arduous task involving many long months of hard work and therapy. Often the help of specialists is needed. (See Career Box: Speech Pathologist.) The functions previously performed by the damaged neurons must be assumed by healthy ones. It is like going back to school and relearning everything all over again. Sometimes the relearning is not complete, perhaps because the damage

was too extensive, and the victim never completely regains what was lost. We can learn and form new synapses at any age, but it is easiest while we are young and growing.

Clay Dahlberg regained the ability to say simple sentences within weeks after the stroke, although he became confused if there was more than one other person present. He had problems with naming, memory, and arithmetic—skills that healthy people take for granted. He and his wife Jane took a trip to Scandinavia for a few months after the stroke. He found he had trouble telling right from left: "I would look at the maps and ascertain that a right turn was in order and then say, 'Turn left.' Jane followed my instructions. 'I said left.' Jane: 'I turned left.' Clay: 'No, I said left.' Jane: 'It is left.' Then the car stalled . . . I had not heard myself say 'left' when I meant 'right.' "

Twenty months after the stroke, Clay Dahlberg returned to work. Except for a slight droop on the right side of his face and occasional difficulty finding the right words, he has recovered. During his recuperation he

---

CAREER BOX

Speech Pathologist

Speech pathologists work with the millions of individuals who have speech problems caused by strokes, mental retardation, cleft palates, emotional problems, and even speakers of other languages. The speech pathologist evaluates their disorders and provides treatment, often in cooperation with physicians, psychologists, physical therapists, counselors, or schoolteachers. Employment opportunities exist in schools, clinics, research centers, hospitals, government agencies, industry, and private practice. Training for a career in speech pathology usually requires a bachelor's degree, and many states are beginning to require a master's degree for certification in the field.

Understanding the biological basis of language production is critical for the speech pathologist. (Many of the topics we discuss in this chapter are directly applicable.) Part of the speech pathologist's job is to administer a lengthy series of tests to recent stroke victims. The tests are designed to determine exactly which speech functions are affected and which might improve. An understanding of biological psychology is, therefore, important for the speech pathologist, but knowledge of other psychological principles are also necessary. For example, patients may feel frustrated and depressed if their progress is slow, and it is helpful if the speech pathologist is familiar with the concept of motivation.

A great deal of patience and understanding is required to help a stroke victim recover language function, and the speech pathologist may have to work with the patient through weeks or even months of recovery.

---

never gave up. The recovery process is very much an individual matter, and willpower plays a big role. If the patient stays depressed and quits trying, recovery is much slower. As Dahlberg put it, he "opted for life."

GUIDED REVIEW

Learning Objective 8

1. The major symptom of _____ is the occurrence of seizures. The cause is often known, and treatment usually involves anticonvulsant drugs.

2. _____ is due to a ruptured or blocked blood vessel in the brain. If it occurs on the left side, it usually results in some type of _____ , or difficulty with language. The major language areas of the brain, called _____ and _____ , are on the left side of the brain.

Two Brains in One

Clay Dahlberg's language problems were a result of damage to the left side of the brain. People with damage to the right side usually have some weakness or paralysis on the left side of the body, but it is very unusual for them to show any aphasia. Problems with arithmetic, naming, and even memory are less frequent.

The left side of the brain came to be known as the "major" hemisphere and the right side as the "minor" one; some psychologists concluded that consciousness, as well as language, was located on the left side. The function of the right side was unclear. A type of surgery that is sometimes used for patients with epilepsy has given scientists a way to find out what the right side of the brain does.

ANSWERS

1. epilepsy 2. Stroke; aphasia; Wernicke's area, Broca's area

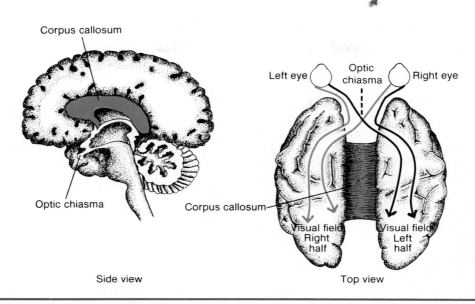

Corpus callosum

Optic chiasma

Side view

Left eye   Optic chiasma   Right eye

Corpus callosum

Visual field Right half

Visual field Left half

Top view

Figure 2.16   A diagram showing the pathways traveled by information from the left and right visual fields of the eyes to the left and right hemispheres

The Split Brain

In some very rare cases of severe epilepsy, drugs do not help, and the damaged brain tissue cannot be safely removed. One treatment, however, involves cutting the corpus callosum, the bundle of fibers connecting the right and left hemispheres. This surgery prevents a seizure that begins on one side of the brain from spreading to the other side. After the surgery the patient's seizures are less severe and less frequent, but the person is left with a "split brain." The person talks and acts normally; he or she does not have a "split personality" as far as friends can tell. Yet despite the apparent normalcy of these people, some researchers, such as Roger Sperry (who was awarded a Nobel prize for his work), were convinced that a person with a split brain must be different in some way. Eventually they developed some tests that showed some very remarkable differences (Sperry, 1974, 1982; Gazzaniga, 1967).

If you are blindfolded and an object is placed in your left hand, the messages from your fingers will tell your brain what the object is. These messages will first reach the right side of your brain, but they would quickly travel to the left along the corpus callosum. In a person with a split brain, the messages from the left hand only reach the right side of the brain. The left brain literally has no idea what the left hand is doing.

Also, these patients can receive visual signals on only one side of the brain. If we show a picture in the left side of a person's visual field for a brief moment, that information would only reach the person's right brain. Pictures or words flashed to the right visual field only reach the left brain, as shown in figure 2.16, provided the subject focuses on a central point.

Normally, of course, a person with a split brain does not walk around blindfolded. It is also a simple matter to move the eyes so that both sides of the brain can "see" the picture. But by using tests that send messages to only one side of the brain, scientists have found that the two brains have different strengths and weaknesses.

The Left Hemisphere—Master of Language and Arithmetic. Whenever the researchers flashed a written word to the left brain the person could read it easily. But when they showed a word to the right brain, the person said there was nothing there. It looked as though the left hemisphere did all the reading. Actually it does most of the reading, but it does *all* the talking.

When arithmetic problems were presented to the left hemisphere, the person could solve them. The same problems presented to the right hemisphere elicited only blank stares, unless the problems were simple additions with sums of less than twenty.

Many people began to think that the left hemisphere used a kind of analytical approach to the world. It controlled everything the person said, it could understand written words, and it could do arithmetic. Since the right hemisphere did not control verbal skills, scientists could not determine its function.

Soon techniques were designed to allow the right hemisphere to be heard; scientists discovered that although the right hemisphere does not control speech, it does control the left hand. Instead of asking for a verbal answer, they could ask a person to point to answers, using the left hand. They found that the right hemisphere has some strengths that the left hemisphere lacked.

The Right Hemisphere—Master of Space. When the researchers showed the word "fork" to a person's right hemisphere, the person had no trouble pointing to a fork with the left hand. The right side can "read" simple nouns like "fork" or "brush" reasonably well, but it cannot read verbs or long sentences. Also, the right hemisphere cannot "talk about" what it reads.

The right brain also seems to need to look at words for a longer period of time before demonstrating its linguistic abilities. In one experiment, split-brain patients wore a patch over one eye and a special contact lens over the other. This allowed visual input to reach only one side of the brain, regardless of how much the patient moved the eye. The experimenters could then present the same visual stimulus for as long as half an hour, rather than just a fraction of a second, giving the patient a chance to ponder the words (Zaidel, 1975). Using their right hemispheres, the patients were able to read nouns and verbs much better, and on one test they demonstrated a mental age only two years lower than when they were using their left hemispheres. Even using this technique, however, the patients were unable to read and comprehend sentences when using the right hemisphere.

The right brain does deal with space and patterns extremely well, though, and much better than the left. When the researchers asked a patient to copy some simple drawings, he could do it much better with the left hand even though he was right handed.

A person is also much better at copying a pattern of shapes with colored blocks when using the left hand (right hemisphere). On one test a patient was asked to try using his right hand for this task, but he performed poorly. He kept trying to use his left hand to "help." He finally had to sit on his left hand to keep it from interfering (Gazzaniga, 1967).

The superiority of the right brain in dealing with space has been demonstrated in other ways as well. In one study, subjects were shown a group of geometric forms and were asked to pick out the matching one from among several forms hidden from view behind a screen (Franco and Sperry, 1977). The patients were consistently able to do better on this task using their left hands, showing that their right brains are more adept at dealing with shapes and patterns, both visually and by touch. It appears the right brain shows superiority on tasks that require the subject to capture the holistic characteristics of a situation. Other studies have suggested that the right brain is also superior at recognizing faces and at musical perception (Sidtis, 1984), supporting the view that the right brain takes a more "holistic" approach, whereas the left is more analytical.

The right brain has a sense of humor, and may be more emotional than the left. On one occasion a psychologist presented a picture of a nude to a patient's right brain. She started to laugh, and the testers asked why. Her left hemisphere had not "seen" the picture, and did not know why she was laughing. She said, "Oh, I don't know . . . nothing . . . oh that funny machine."

Although most of our information about specializations of the two hemispheres has come from studies of split-brain patients and victims of brain damage, studies of normal people have confirmed most of the findings. For example, experiments show that when people listen to one list of words or numbers with one ear and another list, simultaneously, with the other ear, they tend to recall better the words presented to the right. (Kimura, 1961; Bryden, 1982). *This experimental technique, in which different auditory stimuli are simultaneously presented to each ear, is called* **dichotic listening.** Information input from each ear is competing for the person's attention, and for most right-handed people, the input from the right ear is attended to a little better. Since messages from the right ear reach the left hemisphere first, these studies support the conclusion that the left hemisphere is heavily involved in language abilities.

The dichotic listening experiments also support the view that the right brain has its own set of specializations. A left ear advantage is reported in studies in which the auditory stimuli are musical (Bartholomeus, 1974; Gordon, 1980), or other nonverbal sounds, such as laughing, crying, and sighing (King and Kimura, 1972). Environmental sounds, such as a car starting or a toilet flushing, also result in a left ear advantage when they are presented dichotically (Curry, 1967).

In one study (Bartholomeus, 1974), the researcher had eight different singers sing sequences of letters, so the stimuli were a combination of verbal material (the letters) and musical material. The "songs" were presented dichotically, and the subjects were asked to recall either the melodies, the singers, or the specific letter sequences. The researcher found a left ear advantage when the subjects tried to recognize the melody, a right ear advantage when they tried to recall the letter sequences, and no ear advantage when they tried to remember the different voices of the singers. This study suggests that the components of a complex stimulus are processed differently and that both hemispheres are involved.

What about the Lefties?

His name is Babe Ruth. He is built like a bale of cotton and pitches left handed for the Boston Red Sox. All left-handers are peculiar and Babe is no exception, because he can also bat. (Anonymous New York Sportswriter)

Throughout history, left-handed people have been thought of as being peculiar. Proportionally more "lefties" have been rumored to be neurotic, homosexual, artistic, epileptic, mentally retarded, stubborn, and inclined to lives of crime. Some research has suggested that left-handers have lower intelligence, poorer reading ability, impaired spatial ability, a greater tendency to alcoholism, and a higher incidence of mental retardation (Corballis and Beale, 1976; Hardyck and Petrinovitch, 1977; Hecaen and Ajuriaguerra, 1964; Bakan, 1973; Satz, 1972). Although there may be some differences between right- and left-handers, a major study found that left-handers show no cognitive deficit (Hardyck, Petrinovitch, and Goldman, 1976).

One important difference between right- and left-handed people is in the organization of brain functions. The brains of some left-handers are organized like those of right-handed people, with language abilities on the left and spatial abilities on the right. But other left-handers have language abilities primarily in the right hemisphere, and still others have a more symmetrical distribution. Perhaps because their brain functions are distributed more evenly, left-handed people tend to have a larger corpus callosum, the neural bridge between the hemispheres (Witelson, 1985).

This conclusion has been reached through a variety of means (Bryden, 1982; Herron, 1980). For example, left-handers are more likely to suffer from aphasia after brain damage to only one side of the brain, indicating that many of them have speech functions on the right side or both sides (Satz, 1980). Dichotic-listening studies show that some left-handers show a small, left ear advantage, and others, particularly the people who prefer to use their left hands for most tasks, show a *right* ear advantage (Dee, 1971).

No one is quite sure why some people prefer to use the left hand for writing, ball throwing, holding a tennis racket, and other tasks. (See Application Box: Are You

---

APPLICATION BOX

Are You Right-Handed or Left-Handed?

The research on the specializations of the right and left hemispheres of the brain suggests that right-handed and left-handed people have different brain organizations. Usually, most of the language functions of right-handed people are located primarily in the left hemisphere. Left-handed people are much more variable. One reason that they may be more variable is that "right-handed" and "left-handed" are not two separate and distinct categories; many people fall somewhere in between. A test to determine an individual's degree of left-handedness includes the following questions. (Circle L if you usually use your left hand, R if you usually use your right, and B if you use either hand.)

Right-handed people usually answer most question with "R." But, not surprisingly, left-handed people typically vary in the number of "L" answers they give. "Extreme" left-handers may answer as many as 16 items or more with "L." "Moderately" left-handed people may answer with several Bs and only twelve or fewer Ls. Most left-handed people answer some of the questions with one or two Rs as well, and some give as many as eight Rs (Raczkowski, Kalat, and Nebes, 1973).

With which hand do you:

1. draw?   L   R   B
2. write?   L   R   B
3. remove the top card of a deck of cards (i.e., dealing)?   L   R   B
4. use a bottle opener?   L   R   B
5. throw a baseball to hit a target?   L   R   B

Reprinted with permission from Neuropsychologia, 12, D. Raczkowski, J. W. Kalat, and R. Nebes, "Reliability and validity of some handedness questionnaire items," Copyright © 1974, Pergamon Press, Ltd.

Right-Handed or Left-Handed?) Some hypothesize that hand preference is partly predisposed by inheritance. For example, adopted children resemble their biological parents more than their adoptive parents in terms of handedness (Carter-Saltzman, 1980). This suggests that some genetic predisposition for hand preference may exist.

Hand preference is clearly influenced by environmental factors as well, especially the attitudes of parents and teachers. The incidence of left-handedness rose from about five percent to eleven percent during the twentieth century (Chamberlain, 1928; Rife, 1940), probably because of social pressures from the "experts." John B. Watson, a leading psychologist of the early twentieth century, thought that a child who showed some preference for the left hand should be taught to prefer the right. Schools followed his advice, and the incidence of left-handedness declined dramatically. Unfortunately, however, it became clear that the effort to change hand preference in children appeared to cause other problems, such as stuttering or thumb-sucking. Now most psychologists advise allowing children to use whichever hand they choose.

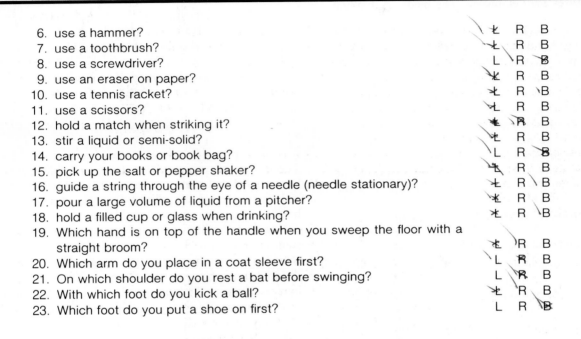

6. use a hammer?   L R B
7. use a toothbrush?   L R B
8. use a screwdriver?   L R B
9. use an eraser on paper?   L R B
10. use a tennis racket?   L R B
11. use a scissors?   L R B
12. hold a match when striking it?   L R B
13. stir a liquid or semi-solid?   L R B
14. carry your books or book bag?   L R B
15. pick up the salt or pepper shaker?   L R B
16. guide a string through the eye of a needle (needle stationary)?   L R B
17. pour a large volume of liquid from a pitcher?   L R B
18. hold a filled cup or glass when drinking?   L R B
19. Which hand is on top of the handle when you sweep the floor with a straight broom?   L R B
20. Which arm do you place in a coat sleeve first?   L R B
21. On which shoulder do you rest a bat before swinging?   L R B
22. With which foot do you kick a ball?   L R B
23. Which foot do you put a shoe on first?   L R B

Although lefties are probably not more stubborn or retarded, they are different. They can remember musical notes better than right-handers (Deutsch, 1980), and they are more likely to choose careers in artistic fields (Mebert and Michel, 1980). Of the children who score highest on the Scholastic Aptitude Test, more than twenty percent are left-handed or ambidextrous, a rate that is twice as high as that found in the general population (Benbow, 1985).

The reasons why left-handed people are different in some ways is not known. Many scientists suspect that their "peculiarities" are related to their brain organization. Or perhaps functions that are served by the right hemisphere in right-handers, like spatial abilities and music perception, become more developed in left-handers.

Right and Left, East and West

The findings about the specializations of the right and left hemispheres have led to many controversial hypotheses about the human mind, and even about human cultures. One hypothesis is that humans have two ways of thinking. One way is more rational and considers events in sequence. This mode would be controlled by the left hemisphere (in most people). The other mode is more emotional and considers events as a whole rather than in sequence. This "right-brain approach" is somewhat freer and probably more creative (Bogen, 1969).

Another controversial proposal is the notion that whole cultures may emphasize one mode of thinking more than another. Some psychologists view the science and technology of the Western world as evidence of left-brain dominance. The very high verbal and written skills in the West, and the advanced math, certainly require the ability to think in sequence. You cannot understand the words on this page if you look at the page as a whole; you must read the words in sequence. In contrast, some Eastern cultures seem to emphasize the more holistic, right-brain approach. Zen Buddhist philosophy emphasizes the "here and now" and a kind of holistic acceptance of just being. It attempts to avoid the analytical reasoning typical of the left brain.

Whether there are basic differences between the brains of people from different cultures is unknown. Recent research in Japan suggests that the language a person learns in childhood may influence hemispheric specializations (Tsunoda, 1971; Sibatini, 1980). According to these preliminary studies, speakers of Japanese, even if they are Caucasians, process most sounds in their left hemispheres, while native speakers of other languages, such as Korean, English, and Chinese, process sounds on both sides.

Some people have criticized the emphasis on left-brain abilities and have encouraged the development of more right-brain skills. But the distinction between left-brain skills and right-brain skills has probably been exaggerated. Normal people use both sides of their brains, and they have an intact corpus callosum to connect the two sides. The two sides of the brain have somewhat different specializations, but they also share many common functions.

Mind, Consciousness, and the Brain

The people with a split brain seem to have two separate minds, or different consciousnesses. They can do two tasks as quickly and easily as normal people can do one. The two minds learn clever ways of communicating with one another, but they do not always agree. Remember the patient who had to sit on his left hand to keep it from interfering while he worked on a block problem with his right hand.

Perhaps these studies, more than any others on the brain, show that what we call "mind" or "consciousness" is really brain. They shed light on an age-old controversy called the **mind-body problem,** *which debates the question of whether the mind is nonphysical and the body physical, or whether both are physical.* Throughout history many scientists and philosophers have argued that mind and body are separate elements and that the mind that thinks, feels, decides, remembers, and understands, is something nonphysical. Psychologists and other scientists have not taken a unified stand on this issue, probably because there is still no clear-cut answer to it. However, studies like those on the split-brain patients, and other more recent experiments exploring the biological basis of consciousness, are leading many scientists to the conclusion that mind and body are one and the same. When the brain is split in half, the mind is also split in half, creating two minds in one. Mind does not appear to be something separate and apart from the neurons and chemicals that make up our brains. When a person's brain is damaged, his or her mind will be altered, even if ever so slightly. If the brain is damaged too much, as in the case of Phineas T. Gage, the person may change so much that we can no longer recognize him. Carl Sagan (1977), a scientist and philosopher, states this point of view very forcefully:

> My fundamental premise about the brain is that its workings—what we sometimes call 'mind'—are a consequence of its anatomy and physiology, and nothing more.

Not all scientists agree with this idea, but the evidence is compelling. If it is true, and if human beings gradually come to accept it, it will have profound implications. It will mean that we must change the way we view ourselves. The idea attacks many fundamental human philosophies and conflicts with our beliefs about religion, free will, and the concept of the human soul.

It is humbling to think of the billions of neurons and chemicals in our brains—and then to realize that *they* are doing the thinking. What else can think about its own workings? What else can invent ways to improve and repair itself? What else lasts for seventy-five years or more, operating on a huge assortment of fuel and requiring little or no maintenance? As little as we may know about the brain, we know enough to appreciate how remarkable it is.

GUIDED REVIEW

Learning Objectives 9 and 10

1. In the split-brain operation, the _____ is severed, dividing the brain into right and left halves.

2. The _____ is specialized for language, arithmetic and analytical skills. The _____ is superior in spatial abilities.

3. The brains of _____ people show variable hemispheric specializations. In some, the right brain is specialized for language, and in others, language abilities are more symmetrical.

4. A person with a split brain has two "minds," suggesting that the mind is the same as the brain and is made up of chemicals and neurons. The question of whether the mind is nonphysical whereas the body is physical, or whether they are both physical, is the

_____ .

ANSWERS

1. corpus callosum 2. left hemisphere; right hemisphere 3. left-handed 4. mind-body problem

SUMMARY

I. The neuron is the building block of the nervous system. It is specialized to process information. (p. 34)

  A. The four main parts of the neuron are the dendrites, the cell body, the axon, and the axon terminals.   (p. 35)

    1. The dendrites are the input portion of the neuron.   (p. 35)

    2. The cell body contains the nucleus and many other structures that help to maintain the life of the neuron.   (p. 36)

    3. The axon is the long thin tube that carries information from the cell body to the axon terminals.   (p. 36)

    4. The axon terminals are the output ends of the cell.   (p. 37)

  B. Axonal conduction is the electrical process whereby information is moved from one end of the axon to the other.   (p. 37)

    1. At rest, a neuron shows a resting potential, which is the difference in charge across the axon's membrane.   (p. 37)

    2. When a neural impulse is generated, an action potential is produced. The action potential travels down the axon using the all-or-none principle of axonal conduction. (p. 38)

  C. Synaptic transmission is the process whereby information is moved from one neuron to another. It is a chemical process involving the release of neurotransmitter from the axon terminals as a result of the arrival of an action potential. The neurotransmitters affect the electrical properties of the next neuron's dendrites. The neurotransmitter produces either an excitatory or an inhibitory disturbance in the dendrite's membrane. (p. 39)

D. A neuron receives inputs from many other neurons all over its dendritic tree. The incoming messages are summarized and integrated at the axon hillock. If the resulting summary is large enough, the neuron will trigger an action potential.   (p. 41)

II. The human nervous system is divided into the central nervous system and the peripheral nervous system. The central nervous system consists of the brain and spinal cord, and the peripheral nervous system includes all the neurons lying outside the brain and spinal cord.   (p. 42)

A. There are four methods that are most commonly used to investigate the relationship between the brain and behavior.   (p. 43)

1. Anatomical studies compare the appearance of brain tissue and note correlations between its appearance and the behavior of the organism.   (p. 43)

2. Electrical recording techniques can record the activity of groups of brain cells, as in the EEG, or the activity of individual brain cells.   (p. 43)

3. Electrical stimulation of the brain is used to activate specific neural pathways or areas and to observe any changes in behavior.   (p. 44)

4. Studies of animals or people with brain lesions or brain damage can lead to some insights about the possible role of the damaged portions of the brain.   (p. 44)

B. The human brain is shaped somewhat like a mushroom, with the older, more primitive areas in the "stem" part and the more recently evolved areas in the "cap."   (p. 44)

1. The cerebral cortex is the outer layer of the cerebral hemispheres.   (p. 46)

2. The cerebral hemispheres include four major subareas, called lobes.   (p. 46)

3. The limbic system includes a group of structures lying below the cortex, which seem to be involved in emotional behavior.   (p. 47)

4. The cerebellum is located behind and partly underneath the cerebral hemispheres; it is involved in coordination and movement.   (p. 48)

5. The medulla is a large area in the lower part of the brain that controls maintenance activities such as breathing, heart rate, and digestion.   (p. 48)

C. The spinal cord performs simple information processing and controls certain reflexes, such as the knee jerk.   (p. 48)

D. The brains of lower animals differ from those of humans in the size of certain brain areas, especially the cerebral cortex. The amount of cortex relative to body size is a general estimate of the importance of behavioral flexibility in the species.   (p. 49)

III. The peripheral nervous system (PNS) includes all the neurons lying outside the brain and spinal cord. (p. 50)

A. Sensory and motor neurons form a large part of the PNS. They carry information from the body to the spinal cord, and vice versa. (p. 50)

B. The autonomic nervous system, part of which lies in the PNS, includes the sympathetic division, which prepares the body for emergencies by raising heart rate, breathing rate, and blood pressure and by moderating other physiological responses. The autonomic nervous system also includes the parasympathetic division, which helps return the body to normal after sympathetic activation. The entire spectrum of physiological responses produced by sympathetic activation is the fright-fight-flight response.   (p. 51)

IV. The endocrine system includes several glands in the body that release hormones.   (p. 54)

A. Hormones are special chemical messengers that can regulate bodily processes in distant target organs. They are released into the bloodstream by endocrine glands. The pituitary gland is the master endocrine gland; it provides a link between the brain and the endocrine system. The hypothalamus controls the activity of the pituitary gland; it releases substances called releasing factors, which affect the release of hormones by the pituitary.   (p. 54)

B. Hormones affect a variety of behaviors in many mammals, including sex, aggression, migration, emotional behavior, and maternal behavior. In human beings, the effects of hormones are less direct than in other mammals. The relationship between hormones and behavior is complex. Hormones can affect behavior, and behavior can affect the activity of the endocrine system. (p. 54)

V. Studies of brain disorders can help researchers better understand brain function.   (p. 57)

A. Epilepsy is a disease that involves the occurrence of seizures. The causes of the disease are varied, and treatment usually involves the administration of anticonvulsant drugs.   (p. 57)

B. Stroke is a rupture or blockage of a blood vessel in the brain. The behavioral changes that follow a stroke are varied, depending on where the brain damage occurred and how much brain tissue was damaged. Stroke victims sometimes suffer some type of aphasia. (p. 58)

VI. Studies of people with brain damage or a split brain suggest that the right and left hemispheres have somewhat different specializations.   (p. 60)

A. An operation called the "split-brain" technique severs the corpus callosum and is performed only in cases of extreme epilepsy. The split-brain patients have been tested to determine the hemispheric specializations.   (p. 61)

1. In right-handed people, the left side of the brain is superior in the performance of language, arithmetic, and analytical tasks. (p. 62)

2. The right hemisphere appears to be superior at tasks involving spatial abilities. (p. 62)

B. The hemispheric specializations of left-handed people are more varied than those of right-handed people. The causes of hand preference are unknown, although some studies implicate genetic factors.   (p. 63)

C. Some psychologists have hypothesized that cultural emphases on right- or left-brain modes of thinking exist.   (p. 65)

D. The mind-body problem debates whether the mind is nonphysical whereas the body is physical or whether they are both physical. (p. 66)

ACTION GLOSSARY

Match the terms in the left column with the definitions in the right column.

___ **1. Neuron (p. 34)**
___ **2. Dendrite (p. 35)**
___ **3. Alzheimer's disease (p. 35)**
___ **4. Cell body (p. 36)**
___ **5. Axon (p. 36)**
___ **6. Myelin (p. 36)**
___ **7. Multiple sclerosis (p. 36)**
___ **8. Axon terminal (p. 37)**
___ **9. Neurotransmitter (p. 37)**

A. *The whitish fatty substance that provides insulation along the length of the axon.*
B. *A form of presenile dementia that is related to neural degeneration. Symptoms include forgetfulness, confusion and irritability, and speech difficulties.*
C. *The basic structural and functional unit of the nervous system, specialized to process information.*
D. *Chemicals that are contained in the vesicles of the axon terminal and are involved in synaptic transmission between neurons.*
E. *The input end of the neuron that receives messages from other neurons. It is usually shaped like a tree, with branches covered with knobs.*
F. *The long thin part of the neuron that carries information from the cell body to the axon terminals.*
G. *The output ends of the neuron, located on the tips of the branches of the axon.*
H. *The part of the neuron containing the nucleus and other structures responsible for maintaining the life of the cell.*
I. *A disease caused by the loss of myelin in the nervous system. Symptoms include vision problems, muscle weakness, lack of coordination, and spastic motions.*

____ 10. **Axonal conduction** (p. 37)
____ 11. **Resting potential** (p. 37)
____ 12. **Action potential** (p. 37)
____ 13. **Sodium-potassium pump** (p. 38)
____ 14. **All-or-none principle** (p. 38)
____ 15. **Synaptic transmission** (p. 39)
____ 16. **Synapse** (p. 39)
____ 17. **Vesicle** (p. 39)
____ 18. **Catecholamine** (p. 39)

A. *The difference in charge across the axon's membrane when the neuron is at rest.*
B. *A class of neurotransmitter substances that includes dopamine, norepinephrine, and epinephrine.*
C. *The process by which a neural message is moved from one neuron to another at their junction.*
D. *The process by which neural messages are moved from one end of the axon to the other by means of the movement of ions across the axon's membrane.*
E. *Refers to the property of axonal conduction in which an action potential is conducted along the axon without a reduction in its size.*
F. *A transient change in the potential across the membrane of an axon that is propagated along the axon. It is the neural message traveling down the axon, and is sometimes called a "spike."*
G. *A saclike structure in the axon terminal that contains neurotransmitter.*
H. *A metabolic mechanism that forces sodium ions out of the cell and potassium ions back in, in order to prevent the eventual loss of the potential across the axon's membrane as the positive sodium ions accumulate with each action potential.*
I. *The junction between two neurons, usually between the axon terminal of one neuron and the dendrite of the next.*

____ 19. **Excitatory synapse** (p. 41)
____ 20. **Inhibitory synapse** (p. 41)
____ 21. **Axon hillock** (p. 42)
____ 22. **Central nervous system (CNS)** (p. 42)
____ 23. **Peripheral nervous system (PNS)** (p. 42)
____ 24. **Computerized axial tomography (CAT scan)** (p. 43)
____ 25. **Electroencephalograph (EEG)** (p. 43)
____ 26. **Hippocampus** (p. 44)
____ 27. **Glial cells** (p. 44)

A. *The area of the cell body where the axon protrudes. Is involved in the summarization of the incoming electrical messages from all the neuron's dendrites.*
B. *A device used to measure and record the electrical activity of the brain by means of electrodes placed on the scalp.*
C. *A part of the limbic system of the brain that may play a role in long-term memory.*
D. *A technique for visualizing the brain that utilizes the computer and multiple X rays.*
E. *The part of the nervous system that includes the brain and spinal cord.*
F. *A type of synapse in which the release of neurotransmitter by the first neuron produces inhibition in the next neuron, making it less likely that the second neuron will spike.*
G. *A type of synapse in which the release of neurotransmitter by the first neuron produces excitation in the next, with a greater likelihood that the second neuron will spike.*
H. *Supporting cells within the brain.*
I. *All the neurons that lie outside the brain and the spinal cord.*

____ 28. **Cerebral hemispheres** (p. 46)
____ 29. **Corpus callosum** (p. 46)
____ 30. **Phrenologist** (p. 46)
____ 31. **Cerebral cortex** (p. 46)
____ 32. **Frontal lobe** (p. 46)
____ 33. **Parietal lobe** (p. 46)
____ 34. **Temporal lobe** (p. 46)
____ 35. **Limbic system** (p. 47)
____ 36. **Hypothalamus** (p. 47)

A. *A group of brain structures that appear to be involved in emotional behavior. Located below the cerebral cortex.*
B. *A bundle of fibers that connects the left and right cerebral hemispheres.*
C. *The large outer layer of brain tissue of the cerebral hemispheres.*
D. *A person who believed in the now obsolete theory that attempted to link behavioral traits to bumps and depressions on the skull.*
E. *A brain structure that is involved in sex, aggression, hunger, thirst, and other motivated behaviors, as well as autonomic and endocrine functions. Located just above the pituitary gland near the base of the brain.*
F. *The lobe of the cerebral cortex that is involved in the processing of sensory information from the skin. Located between the occipital and frontal lobes.*
G. *A lobe of the cerebral cortex involved in memory, reasoning, thinking, and movement.*
H. *A lobe of the cerebral cortex involved in processing auditory information. Located on the sides of the brain.*
I. *The two symmetrical halves of the top part of the brain that are connected by a bundle of fibers.*

_____ 37. **Cerebellum** (p. 48)
_____ 38. **Medulla** (p. 48)
_____ 39. **Spinal cord** (p. 48)
_____ 40. **Olfactory bulbs** (p. 49)
_____ 41. **Afferent pathway** (p. 50)
_____ 42. **Efferent pathway** (p. 50)
_____ 43. **Autonomic nervous system** (p. 51)
_____ 44. **Sympathetic division** (p. 51)
_____ 45. **Fright-fight-flight response** (p. 51)

A. *The entire spectrum of physiological changes that prepares an organism for an emergency. Produced by activation of the sympathetic division of the autonomic nervous system.*
B. *Pathway that carries information toward the central nervous system.*
C. *The large spherical brain structure involved in motor coordination. Located beneath the occipital lobe.*
D. *A component of the autonomic nervous system whose activation during stressful situations results in such effects as increased heart rate, blood pressure, and respiration, and inhibition of digestive activities.*
E. *The part of the nervous system that connects the brain and spinal cord to body organs such as the stomach, intestines, and heart.*
F. *Structures in the front of the brain that process information about smell.*
G. *The mass of nervous tissue carrying information between parts of the body—such as the arms, legs, and trunk—and the brain.*
H. *Pathway that carries information away from the central nervous system.*
I. *A lower part of the brain involved in maintenance functions of the body, such as heart action, sleeping and waking, breathing and digestion.*

_____ 46. **Parasympathetic division** (p. 51)
_____ 47. **Endocrine system** (p. 54)
_____ 48. **Hormone** (p. 54)
_____ 49. **Estrogen** (p. 54)
_____ 50. **Progesterone** (p. 54)
_____ 51. **Pituitary gland** (p. 54)
_____ 52. **Releasing factors** (p. 54)
_____ 53. **Corticotropin releasing factor** (p. 54)
_____ 54. **Testosterone** (p. 56)

A. *A substance released by an endocrine gland into the bloodstream or body fluids that acts as a special chemical messenger to regulate physiological processes in the body.*
B. *A component of the autonomic nervous system that returns the body to normal after a stressful situation. Its activation decreases heart rate, blood pressure, and respiration rate.*
C. *Substances released from the neurons of the hypothalamus that control and direct the activity of the pituitary gland.*
D. *A system of glands that release hormones into the bloodstream.*
E. *A substance released by the neurons of the hypothalamus that causes the pituitary gland to release ACTH.*
F. *A hormone secreted by the ovaries.*
G. *Male sex hormone released from the testes.*
H. *The master endocrine gland located at the base of the brain beneath the hypothalamus. Produces several hormones, most of which stimulate other endocrine glands to release their own hormones.*
I. *A hormone released by the ovaries.*

_____ 55. **Cortisol** (p. 56)
_____ 56. **Epilepsy** (p. 57)
_____ 57. **Stroke** (p. 58)
_____ 58. **Wernicke's area and Broca's area** (p. 58)
_____ 59. **Aphasia** (p. 58)
_____ 60. **Dichotic listening** (p. 63)
_____ 61. **Mind-body problem** (p. 66)

A. *Areas of the brain important for language.*
B. *Language difficulty due to brain damage.*
C. *A rupture or blockage of a blood vessel in the brain.*
D. *A controversy that debates whether the mind is separate and distinct from, or a part of, the body.*
E. *A hormone released by the outer part of the adrenal gland that participates in the body's response to stress.*
F. *A disorder associated with changes in the electrical activity of the brain. The major symptom is the occurrence of major or minor seizures.*
G. *An experimental technique in which separate messages are presented to each ear simultaneously through headphones. The technique is useful in studies of functional lateralization of the brain.*

ANSWERS

1. C. 2. E. 3. B. 4. F. 5. H. 6. A. 7. I. 8. G. 9. D. 11. A. 12. F. 13. H. 14. E. 15. C. 16. I. 17. G.
18. B. 19. G. 20. F. 21. A. 22. E. 23. I. 24. D. 25. B. 26. C. 27. H. 28. I. 29. B. 30. D. 31. C. 32. C. 33. F.
34. H. 35. A. 36. E. 37. C. 38. I. 39. G. 40. F. 41. B. 42. H. 43. E. 44. D. 45. A. 46. B. 47. D. 48. A. 49. I.
50. F. 51. H. 52. C. 53. E. 54. G. 55. E. 56. F. 57. C. 58. A. 59. B. 60. G. 61. D

SELF-TEST

1. The cell in the human body that contains an axon, dendrite, and cell body is called
   (a) nerve.
   (b) neuron.
   (c) synapse.
   (d) vesicle.
   (LO 1; p. 35)

2. Dendritic trees
   (a) carry neuronal information towards the cell body.
   (b) carry neuronal information away from the cell body.
   (c) are only structurally important.
   (d) contain neurotransmitters.
   (LO 1; p. 35)

3. The frequently myelinated part of the neuron is called the
   (a) axonal terminal.
   (b) cell body.
   (c) dendrite.
   (d) axon.
   (LO 1; p. 36)

4. An axon that has a higher concentration of negative ions inside, compared to outside of its membranes, is
   (a) displaying an action potential.
   (b) displaying a dendritic potential.
   (c) displaying a resting potential (at rest).
   (d) has an excess of sodium ions inside the cell relative to normal.
   (LO 2; p. 37)

5. The low concentration of sodium ions inside the axon is maintained in the face of continued axonal firing or action potentials. The mechanism
   (a) depends upon the existence of myelin.
   (b) depends upon the existence of potassium ions.
   (c) is entirely passive (i.e., requires no energy).
   (d) is the sodium-potassium pump.
   (LO 2; p. 38)

6. Synaptic transmission
   (a) is mediated by the release of a chemical messenger.
   (b) produces a spike on the receiving dendrite.
   (c) depends upon actual contact between neurons.
   (d) occurs only in the central nervous system.
   (LO 3; p. 39)

7. The place in the cell at which electrical activity (neuronal information) is integrated and summarized is
   (a) the node of Ranvier.
   (b) the synapse.
   (c) the point at which the axon connects to the cell body.
   (d) the point at which the dendrite connects to the cell body.
   (LO 3; p. 41)

8. The electroencephalograph (EEG)
   (a) is an electrical recording technique.
   (b) is an electrical stimulation technique.
   (c) is an anatomical technique.
   (d) must be used to declare a patient legally dead.
   (LO 4; p. 43)

9. During an experiment on brain function, a part of the hypothalamus of a rat is painlessly destroyed with a small lesion. The rat is allowed to recover and is observed for three months. The rat is observed to become obese during this time, whereas other rats without brain lesions in other areas of the brain do not. A reasonable interpretation of this result is that
   (a) the lesion stimulated the rat's appetite.
   (b) the hypothalamus affected eating behavior in some way, although the precise mechanism is unknown.
   (c) The hypothalamus is involved in taste.
   (d) Rats usually get obese if allowed access to sufficient food.
   (LO 4; p. 44)

10. The parts of the cerebral cortex that have visual functions are the
    (a) frontal lobes.   (c) temporal lobes.
    (b) parietal lobes.   (d) occipital lobes.
    (LO 5; p. 46)

11. The part of the brain that appears involved in the processing of emotional information is the
    (a) cerebral cortex.   (c) limbic system.
    (b) medulla.   (d) cerebellum.
    (LO 5; p. 47)

12. The part of the brain that appears to play major roles in behaviors such as sex and aggression is the
    (a) hypothalamus.   (c) medulla.
    (b) cerebral cortex.   (d) limbic system.
    (LO 5; p. 47)

13. The spinal cord, usually thought of as only carrying information between the brain and the body, actually processes neuronal information. The specific behaviors involved are called
    (a) motivations.   (c) reflexes.
    (b) feelings.   (d) sensations.
                              (LO 5; p. 48)

14. Motor pathways are _____ with respect to the brain.
    (a) afferent   (c) neutral
    (b) efferent   (d) dominant
                              (LO 6; p. 50)

15. Sympathetic nervous system activity involves
    (a) a decrease in blood pressure.
    (b) an increase in the activity of the stomach and intestine.
    (c) an increase in heart rate and respiration.
    (d) salivation.
                              (LO 6; p 51)

16. The pituitary gland controls the _____ and is in turn controlled by the _____ .
    (a) stress response; ACTH
    (b) hypothalamus; endocrine glands
    (c) endocrine glands; master gland
    (d) endocrine glands; hypothalamus
                              (LO 7; p. 54)

17. The dominant male sex hormone is
    (a) estrogen.   (c) cortisol.
    (b) testosterone.   (d) progesterone.
                              (LO 7; p. 56)

18. A brain disorder in which cells in a part of the brain begin firing very rapidly and in unison or synchrony and affect large areas of the brain is called
    (a) aphasia.   (c) multiple sclerosis.
    (b) epilepsy.   (d) Wernicke's disorder.
                              (LO 8; p. 57)

19. A stroke that damages Broca's area in the left frontal lobe may result in a condition known as
    (a) aphasia.   (c) paralysis.
    (b) obesity.   (d) epilepsy.
                              (LO 9; p. 58)

20. Some psychologists have suggested that the split-brain operation actually
    (a) can cause epilepsy.
    (b) causes too much brain damage to be used as a treatment for anything.
    (c) decreases intelligence.
    (d) creates two minds in the same person.
                              (LO 9; p. 61)

ANSWERS

1. b, 2. a, 3. d, 4. c, 5. d, 6. a, 7. c, 8. a, 9. b, 10. d, 11. c, 12. a, 13. c, 14. b, 15. c, 16. d, 17. b, 18. b, 19. a, 20. d

SUGGESTED READINGS

Bloom, F. E., A. Lazerson, and L. Hofstadter. *Brain, mind, and behavior.* New York: Freeman, 1985. An introductory textbook, dealing with the neurosciences, which is coordinated with the PBS series called "The Brain."

Bryden, M. P. *Laterality: functional asymmetry in the intact brain.* New York: Academic Press, 1982. A readable book that discusses the techniques and findings of research on cerebral lateralization of function.

Churchland, P. M. *Matter and consciousness.* Cambridge, MA: MIT Press, 1984. A fascinating discussion of the mind-body problem, behaviorism, and other topics that affect our understanding of ourselves.

Eccles, Sir John, and D. N. Robinson. *The wonder of being human: our brain and our mind.* New York: Free Press, 1984. A short book that describes the humanistic approach of these two neuroscientists.

Kolb, B., and I. Q. Whishaw. *Fundamentals of human neuropsychology.* 2d ed. New York: Freeman, 1985. An advanced text on neuropsychology that also includes thought-provoking essays on the nature of mind.

Reinvang, I. *Aphasia and brain organization.* New York: Plenum, 1985. Examines the relationship between language disorders and brain organization in human beings.

Springer, S. P., and G. Deutsch. *Left brain, right brain.* Revised edition San Francisco: W. H. Freeman, 1985. A good introduction to the research on cerebral lateralization, including chapters on history, split-brain studies, sex and asymmetry, and the development of asymmetry.

c   h   a   p   t   e   r

3

The Psychology of Consciousness

Consciousness is not an easy subject to explore, because the word means so many things. Webster's dictionary defines it as "awareness, especially of something within oneself," and this is a good starting point. To be conscious is to be aware of one's internal and external environments and to sense and perceive what is going on there. Consciousness can also refer to less passive mental activities than simply awareness, however; it can refer to planning, making choices, and decision making.

Many psychologists believe that the study of consciousness is one of the most important aspects of psychology. For reasons that we will discuss later, that task was almost ignored for many years. But now the perplexing questions about human consciousness are stimulating much research, and we are likely to know more about it in the future.

The Study of Normal Consciousness

Your state of consciousness as you are reading this sentence is probably the one that is normal for you. You are alert (we hope), awake, thinking, and aware of your surroundings. If you start to daydream, your state of consciousness changes slightly. No longer are you aware of the meaning of the words on this page. In fact, you may find yourself reading a whole paragraph without understanding a single word of it. Instead of focusing your consciousness on the book, you might daydream about last night's party, tomorrow's meeting with the boss, your psychology class, or something else.

What Is Consciousness?

Consciousness *is difficult to define, but a workable definition is that it is your state of awareness of external and internal events.* This definition incorporates quite a wide range of mental activity that can be categorized in many different ways. For example, mental activity might be passive or active (Deikman, 1971). In a passive state, you simply "take in" your environment rather than plan or make decisions. You might listen to music, look at a landscape, or lie on a beach feeling the sun

warm your skin. In a more active mode you might plan tomorrow's picnic, solve a crossword puzzle, or decide whether to open your own restaurant.

The normal state of consciousness can be distinguished from several alternate states, as we shall see later in this chapter. This distinction usually refers to a qualitatively different state of awareness. For example, during a dream you are aware of events, but they are certainly not the same ones that you would be aware of if you were awake. Nevertheless, you are still aware, even though the awareness is of a different nature.

Some processes are characterized by a much lower level of awareness than the ones that take place during your normal state. Much of the neural activity that takes place in your brain has very little to do with consciousness. It might be controlling heart rate, body temperature, or the secretion of hormones. The nervous system is responsible for coordinating and controlling many activities, most of which never reach awareness.

The definition of consciousness that is most useful, that of the awareness of internal and external events, covers a broad range of mental phenomena, including sensation. This is the process by which information in the environment is translated into neural messages through activity in the sense organs, such as the eye, ear, nose, taste buds, or skin. Information about the external world cannot reach a person's consciousness without first being experienced through the senses. It also is very much related to the process of perception, in which information from the senses is integrated and understood. (Sensation and perception are discussed in Chapter 4.) The process of attention is important in consciousness, too, since it controls what we focus on. The study of consciousness also involves learning, memory, motivation, and emotion, since these too affect our mental activity.

Psychologists ordinarily study each of these processes separately, even though they are not separate at all. In order to avoid the illusion of separateness, many psychologists adopt the term "information processing" and use it as a theoretical framework to investigate human behavior. **The information-processing approach** *concerns how people attend to, select, and integrate information and how they later use it to make decisions and guide their behavior* (Kantowitz, 1984). The approach emphasizes the analogy of the movement of information through a computer, using terms borrowed from computer science (such as input, output, and processing) to describe behavior.

The many different terms used in the study of consciousness can be very confusing because they are not clearly defined. Some terms include references to a particular aspect of the theory of one psychologist and a slightly different feature in the theory of another. One reason for this confusion is that the study of consciousness has a turbulent history. In fact, consciousness was almost completely ignored for more than forty years.

The History of Consciousness in Psychology

Early definitions of psychology emphasized consciousness and "mental life" very heavily. For example, in 1890, the American psychologist William James defined the discipline of psychology as "the science of mental life, both of its phenomena and their conditions." Another early definition (Ladd, 1887) called psychology "the description and explanation of states of consciousness as such."

Perhaps the most important tool of the early psychologists who were studying consciousness was introspection, the technique developed by Wilhelm Wundt. Introspection involved trained observers who noted their own thoughts and feelings and avoided the intrusion of any meaning. For example, an observer might perceive the color red, reporting the reactions without reference to the possible meaning of red (in stop lights, in blood, in a flag, for example). These introspectionists were trying to be objective in the sense that they wanted their descriptions of experiences to be free of personal biases. But objectivity requires more: it insists that independent observers arrive at the same conclusions about events. Since independent observers could not observe what was going on in the introspectionist's mind, the technique could not pass a critical test of objectivity.

Trends in the other sciences during the late nineteenth century were further emphasizing the importance of objectivity. Biologists were discovering evolutionary theory and turning away from earlier, more mystical views about the nature of life. The emphasis on objectivity was not lost on psychologists, particularly John B. Watson at the University of Chicago. He and many of his contemporaries were frustrated with introspection because it limited psychology in important ways. For example, you could not obtain or rely on introspection reports from infants, animals, or emotionally disturbed people. Watson urged psychologists to focus their attention on objective observations of behavior rather than on subjective reports. Most psychologists were very receptive to this view and consequently abandoned the study of consciousness. The objective observation of behavior very soon developed into "behaviorism," an approach to psychology that accepted only observable behavior as its subject matter.

The behaviorist approach was dominant in psychology for many years and was espoused by several very famous researchers, most notably B. F. Skinner (Skinner, 1938, 1953, 1974). However, during the seventies and eighties, psychologists began turning once more to the study of consciousness, trying to broaden the scope of their subject (Hilgard, 1980). Topics that had been ignored because they required the investigation of private mental experience, rather than observable behavior, began receiving more attention. Imagery is a good example. The mental "gymnastics" an individual uses when imagining a scene cannot be directly studied by watching the person's behavior.

Electrical Signs of Consciousness

Your state of consciousness is related to the activity of neurons in your brain. Although that activity is incredibly complex, involving innumerable tiny changes in electrical and chemical reactions, we are beginning to understand how to monitor it.

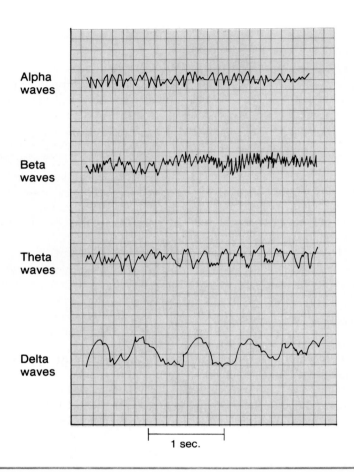

Alpha
waves

Beta
waves

Theta
waves

Delta
waves

|← 1 sec. →|

Figure 3.1   EEG brain waves

The EEG.   In Chapter 2 we briefly discussed the electroencephalograph (EEG). Electrodes placed on the scalp can detect very slight changes in the electrical activity of the brain. Because the movement of charged particles plays such an important role in the neuron's messages, the electrical charge in any brain area is constantly changing, depending on the activity of the neurons in that area. At one moment, the charge over the visual area of the brain might be slightly negative, relative to the charge over another part of the brain. The EEG records these differences in charges for parts of the brain, producing a chart record of their changes over time. Most researchers agree that what contributes the most to the EEG record (fig. 3.1) is the excitatory and inhibitory potentials originating particularly from the dendrites of cells within the range of the recording electrodes.

An individual's EEG is extremely complex, and the waveforms vary depending upon the part of the brain from which they originate, what kind of task the individual is performing, and even the person's emotional state. For example, activity in the parietal lobes shows

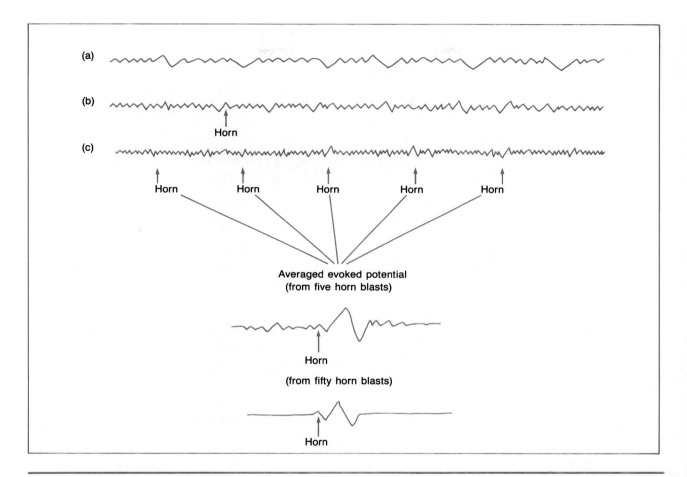

Figure 3.2 **The evoked potential**

distinct patterns when a subject is performing tasks that vary in their attentional demands. A task that requires the person to pay attention to visual cues is associated with different waveforms than one that involves more internal information processing, such as mental arithmetic. Also, emotional factors appear to influence the EEG. The patterns are distinguishable depending on whether a subject is viewing scenes evoking positive or negative feelings (Ray and Cole, 1985). We will see in a later section the ways in which the EEG has been very useful in the study of sleep and dreams.

The Evoked Potential. Computers have made the EEG even more useful as a tool for studying conscious processes. If we are recording from the auditory area of your brain while you are awake, the EEG pattern might look like figure 3.2a. If we suddenly sounded a loud horn, the EEG pattern would probably look like figure 3.2b. There seems to be no difference. But the electrical activity in the auditory area of the brain does show some response to a loud noise, however, proportionately very few neurons actually respond, and the activity in the others "drown out" their response.

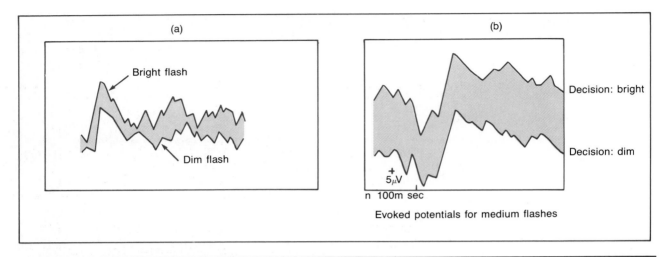

(a)

Bright flash

Dim flash

(b)

Decision: bright

Decision: dim

+
5μV

n 100m sec

Evoked potentials for medium flashes

Figure 3.3 Evoked potentials recorded for bright and dim flashes

If we present the loud noise over and over and average the EEG waveforms that were recorded just before, during, and just after the noise, we see the electrical response to the noise much more clearly. Figure 3.2c shows how this works. The neurons that responded to the noise continue to show a response each time the noise is presented. But those that were just firing in random patterns eventually cancel each other out, leaving a flat, averaged EEG. The waveform is called the **evoked potential;** *it is the neural response to a stimulus, such as a sound, obtained by averaging many EEG patterns recorded during repeated presentations of the stimulus.*

The evoked potential has become a major tool in the study of conscious processes and has made it possible to obtain observable recordings of private mental activities. In one study, for example, it was used to investigate decision making (Begleiter and Porjesz, 1975). Subjects were told that a series of flashes would be presented on a screen in front of them and that some would be dim and others bright. The subjects merely had to press one button for a dim flash and another for a bright one. Figure 3.3a shows the evoked potentials for the

dim and bright flashes. As the researchers expected, they were quite different because the flashes were different. Part of the waveform is produced by the properties of the stimulus, so bright and dim flashes produced different evoked potentials.

Next, the task was made a little more interesting. The subjects were told that for every correct response they would get a nickel, but for every mistake, twenty cents would be deducted from their winnings. (It is important to keep the subjects interested since you need so many trials to get a good averaged evoked potential.) Instead of just dim and bright flashes, the researchers presented a few medium flashes as well. Sometimes the subjects thought the medium flash was dim, and at other times they thought it was bright. The researchers averaged the EEG records for the medium flashes depending on what decision the subject had made about it.

Figure 3.3b shows the evoked potentials for the medium flashes that the subjects decided were dim, and also for those that they thought were bright. The waveforms are very different. Since the flashes were the same, the difference in the brain's electrical activity must be related to the decisions the subjects made. You can even guess which decision they made by looking at the waveform.

Recordings of evoked potentials are not exactly the same as mind reading, but they are some of the first observable signs of conscious processes, events that previously were very private.

GUIDED REVIEW

Learning Objectives 1 and 2

1. _____ is the state of awareness of internal and external events.

2. The term _____ is frequently used to refer to many of the events involved in consciousness collectively, such as sensation, perception, and cognition, to avoid the illusion that they are separate processes.

3. Consciousness was first studied using _____ , but many felt the technique was not objective enough. _____ , on the other hand, emphasized the observation of behavior rather than studies of private mental activity. Now the study of consciousness is an important part of psychology.

4. Advances in electronics have permitted scientists to study consciousness more directly, using the _____ . The _____ , which averages many EEG records obtained during repeated stimulus presentations, is another important tool in the study of consciousness.

ANSWERS

Behaviorism 4. EEG; evoked potential
1. Consciousness 2. information processing 3. introspection;

Biological Rhythms, Sleep and Dreams

Every night when you drift off to sleep, you enter an alternate state of consciousness. When you begin to dream, you enter still another alternate state of consciousness. These states are perfectly normal modes of consciousness, though very different from your normal waking state.

Sleep is part of a biological rhythm of shifts of consciousness, one that repeats itself every twenty-four hours. It is not only part of a rhythm; it contains

Figure 3.4 *The most pronounced biological rhythm is the circadian cycle, that moves in synchrony with the day-night cycle.*

rhythms of its own. The dreams we experience several times each night are part of the normal sleep pattern of human beings.

Biological Rhythms

We live on a planet that has daily, monthly, and yearly rhythms, and some of these have important influences on our behavior and physiology. The yearly cycle, for example, appears to result in behavioral fluctuations, though this is not well understood in humans. Some people experience a "winter depression," for example. A few researchers who have studied this phenomenon have found that the depression can be relieved by bright light in the morning and evening (Rosenthal, 1985).

The best understood cycle is the **circadian rhythm,** *the twenty-four-hour rhythm that corresponds to the earth's daily rotation* (fig. 3.4). For most people on regular schedules, body temperature usually peaks around 2:00 P.M. and is at its lowest point between 2:00

RESEARCH BOX

The Biological Clock

P ractically all living things show circadian rhythms. Some animals are active in the daytime and sleep at night; others are nocturnal. Many come out of their burrows only at dawn or dusk and remain inside at other times. But all seem to synchronize their cycles, one way or another, to the alternating periods of light and dark. The cyclical nature of living things is so familiar and pervasive that many scientists assumed it was simply a response to the alternation of light and dark. However, experiments revealed that circadian rhythms are at least partly "built in." Many living things seem to have a self-winding biological clock that produces circadian rhythms, even in the absence of alternating day-and-night cycles.

A courageous man who volunteered to live underground, by himself, without any cues to tell him what time of day it was (Aschoff, 1969) helped scientists learn more about the sleep/waking cycle. For the first six days of the experiment the man lived under normal conditions, waking in the morning and going to sleep at night. On the seventh day, he went under-

ground and began "free-running"—waking up and going to sleep whenever he wanted to, without knowing what time it was. Each day that he was underground he began to wake up later and later; by the seventeenth day he was waking up around midnight and going to sleep in the early afternoon. In the absence of time cues, this man's biological clock was free-running at a period of 25.4 hours per cycle, instead of the usual 24. When he returned to a normal light/dark schedule on the 24th day, his rhythm again synchronized to the 24-hour day.

Studies like this one suggest that living things have a biological clock, probably somewhere in their nervous systems. Ordinarily the clock is synchronized to the 24-hour day/night cycle. But if no cues are available, the clock will run on its own, producing a "circadian" rhythm that is close to, but not identical to, the 24-hour cycle.

Recent experiments on animals have provided very important clues to the location of this biological clock. In rodents, at least, the clock appears to be in a section of the hypothalamus called the suprachiasmatic nucleus (SCN). Le-

and 4:00 A.M. Weight shows a circadian rhythm as well, peaking in the late afternoon or early evening. Heart rate peaks in the early afternoon and blood pressure in the early evening. Some systems peak in the middle of the night, such as the content of sodium in the plasma. Practically every physiological system shows a circadian rhythm, although they don't all necessarily peak at the same time of day (Luce, 1970). The Research Box: The Biological Clock describes hypotheses about the mechanisms underlying the circadian rhythm.

The pronounced rhythmicity of these physiological systems has some important implications. For example, people are more susceptible to the effects of drugs at different times of day. One study of cancer patients found marked differences in the response to chemotherapy depending on the time of day at which the drugs were administered (Hrushesky, 1985).

Behavior is also affected by the day/night cycle. People usually perform best in the early afternoon and worst in the early morning hours. Individuals show

sions of this brain area disrupt several circadian rhythms in hamsters, especially their wheel-running cycles (Zucker, et al., 1976). Hamsters are ordinarily nocturnal creatures that do most of their wheel running at night. Lesioned animals, however, show erratic cycles. Their activity patterns are not only very irregular when there are no time cues, but they also have great difficulty in synchronizing their activity to a normal day/night cycle.

In birds, a different structure appears to play the role of the circadian pacemaker (Gaston and Menaker, 1968). This is the pineal gland, located near the thalamus. Lesions of this area disrupt a variety of circadian rhythms in birds, just as lesions in the hypothalamus disrupt them in mammals.

Both "clocks" must receive information about the light in the environment in order to synchronize to the day/night cycle. The rodent's hypothalamus gets this information from the rodent's eyes. But the bird's pineal gland does not depend on input from the bird's eyes. Instead, this tissue is directly sensitive to light. The light can pass through the feathers, skin, and skull of the bird's head and reach the pineal gland, synchronizing its activity to the day/night cycle.

The suprachiasmatic nucleus in mammals and the pineal gland in birds are clearly biological clocks, but they may not be the only ones. In some mammals, lesions of the SCN abolish some circadian rhythms, but not all of them. A primate, for example, will continue to show body temperature rhythms even after its suprachiasmatic nucleus has been lesioned. This suggests that the primate has one or more clocks in addition to the one in the SCN. The locations of these other clocks are not yet known. (See Takahashi and Zatz [1982] for a review of this topic.)

variation in their peak performance times, however; there are clearly "early birds" and "night owls" (Horne and Ostberg, 1977).

The circadian rhythm in behavior affects the performance of people who work at night. Even if they have a chance to sleep during the day, they make more mistakes at night. For example, a group of researchers in Sweden determined the accuracy of three shifts of gas-meter readers who were responsible for recording number entries in a factory ledger (Bjerner, Holm, and Swensson, 1955). The factory operated twenty-four hours a day, and they were able to determine the number of errors made each hour of every day between the years 1912 and 1931. The workers showed the worst performance around 2:00 in the morning.

Shift Work. A growing number of businesses and factories are operating around the clock, and many are resorting to shift work to staff their operations. Many

CAREER BOX

Air Traffic Controller

People who are interested in air transportation might be interested in a career as an air traffic controller. Working at computer terminals in airport towers, controllers coordinate flights to prevent accidents and minimize delays. Before giving instructions to pilots, they must consider such factors as weather, traffic density, and size of planes in the area. Applicants for controller jobs must be in excellent physical health and must be able to demonstrate a potential for learning and performing ATC work. Successful applicants receive formal and on-the-job training for several years before becoming qualified controllers.

The rotating shifts of the typical air traffic controller often create problems. The controller may work during the daytime for several days in a row, switch to evenings for another several days, and then work the "graveyard" shift for one or two days. The controller's circadian rhythms are disrupted almost constantly. One way that many controllers try to adapt to such a demanding schedule is to maintain the usual rhythm of sleeping at night. For most of the time the ATC works either at the beginning or end of the waking period. Then for a couple of days per week the controller stays up all night to work. Thus, fatigue (and perhaps errors as well) are concentrated in the night shift.

companies ask their workers to change to a new shift every seven days, moving from the day shift to the evening shift to the "graveyard" shift. A strategy favored in Europe is to move workers to a new shift every day or two. Regardless of the actual schedule, shift workers have difficulty establishing a regular twenty-four hour biological rhythm.

Scientists at the Civil Aeromedical Institute conducted a study on the effects of a twelve-hour shift rotation (Higgins, et al., 1975). They measured a variety of physiological and behavioral activities in fifteen men, first during their normal waking hours, and then after a "shift" when they began sleeping between 10:30 A.M. and 6:00 P.M. Some men adjusted easily to the new working hours, and their physiological systems began peaking around 4:00 A.M. instead of 4:00 P.M. A few never adjusted at all. It took most of the men several days, however, to modify their cycles in accordance with

the new day/night cycle. For example, the subjects took an average of five days to begin showing a peak body temperature at the right time of "day." For most subjects, several physiological systems were "out of synch" for a few days.

The subjects' performance on the behavioral test after the shift was dismal, and it was still not quite normal even nine days after the shift. Again, some subjects adapted better than others, but it is clear that shift rotations can present a serious problem both to worker's health and to performance on the job.

Apparently, some shift-work schedules are less taxing than others. Studies of humans living under conditions without time cues show that they tend to adopt a longer "day," usually about twenty-five hours, suggesting that our natural rhythm is slightly longer than an earth day. Researchers who were assisting the managers of a chemical plant in Utah experimented with a new shift schedule that took advantage of the

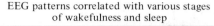

EEG patterns correlated with various stages of wakefulness and sleep

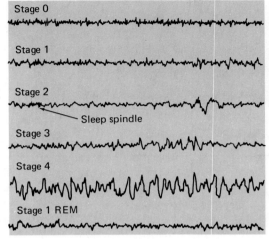

EEG patterns corresponding to various behavioral states

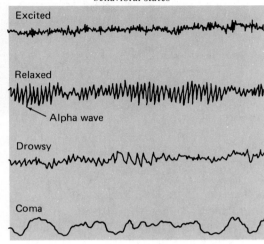

Figure 3.5 EEG patterns typical of wakefulness (0) and various stages of sleep. (After A Manual of Standardized Terminology, Techniques, and Scoring System for Sleep Stages of Human Subjects, *by A. Rechtschaffen and A. Kales [Eds.], National Institutes of Health, No. 204, 1968.)*

longer human rhythms, and also respected the length of time most people take to resynchronize after a phase shift. The workers, who formerly changed shifts weekly, were asked to change every twenty-one days to a new shift that required staying up later rather than going to bed earlier. Staying up later is easier for humans because of our longer natural "day." These workers were very pleased with the new schedule; turnover dropped, and production rose (Czeisler, Moore-Ede, and Coleman, 1985). (See Career Box: Air Traffic Controller.)

The Stages of Sleep

The alternate state of consciousness known as sleep has rhythms of its own that exist within the twenty-four-hour circadian rhythm. The seven or eight hours you spend sleeping are actually very active ones. You go through several stages of deeper and deeper sleep, then into a dream, then back again to lighter sleep, repeating four or five cycles per night. The EEG has always been a favorite tool of sleep researchers because the patterns for each stage are distinguishable.

As you drift off to sleep, the patterns on the EEG gradually show fewer and fewer beta waves, which are high frequency, low amplitude waveforms characteristic of the alert state (fig. 3.5). **Alpha waves,** *which are lower frequency and higher amplitude waves occurring about 8 to 12 per second, are characteristic of the relaxed state.* **Delta waves,** *very low frequency (1 to 4 per second) and high amplitude waves, are characteristic of the EEG pattern of people in the deeper stages of sleep, especially Stages 3 and 4, as shown in figure 3.5.* **Slow-wave sleep** *is the term used to describe the four stages of sleep in which delta waves become more and more predominant.*

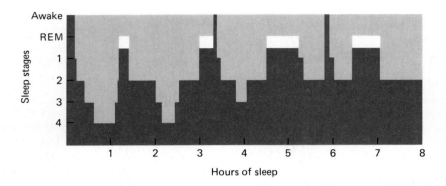

Figure 3.6 The cycles within sleep during a typical night

About every ninety minutes or so, and after the person has drifted to Stage 4, then back to a lighter sleep stage, the EEG shows some unusual patterns. Very rapid beta waves begin appearing even though the person seems to be quite asleep. The person has entered **REM,** *a period of sleep associated with dreaming and characterized by rapid eye movements, beta waves on the EEG, and a loss of tonus in the muscles of the neck.*

As the night continues, the person goes through about four or five episodes of REM sleep that grow longer and longer. Figure 3.6 shows the cycles of sleep during a typical night.

Dreaming

The content of dreams has interested people since the earliest times. One of the first books about dreams is an Egyptian papyrus dating back to 1350 B.C.

One view of dreams is that they are a different reality, one in which the dreamer leaves the physical body behind. Another popular theory is that dreams are omens and predict the future. Most psychologists, however, view dreams as reflections of people's waking lives. Instead of omens or out-of-body experiences, they represent the individual's present anxieties and concerns. These concerns are often expressed symbolically, and sometimes the symbols are indeed obscure.

Jerry, a boy from a farm in the midwest, participated in a study on dreams in a sleep laboratory at the University of Illinois (Cartwright, 1977). On the first night he was able to recall several dreams. In the first dream he was playing with the leads from the electrodes, pulling out plugs, and trying to put them back in the correct order. The second dream involved his confusion about whether to stop at a stop sign.

In the third dream he was going to the Chicago Public Library to return a book, but he felt terribly confused about where the book should go. The library looked like the one at the University of Illinois, but Jerry thought it was at the same place as Cook County Hospital. The fourth and fifth dreams of the evening were much less realistic:

> I was making mudpies. I remember sitting there on the ground . . . having to add water. . . . I had one person helping me. . . . some girl. . . .

> My mother was giving me a bath. . . . I was getting my ear washed. I remember seeing the sink on the wall and Mom had water in it and she was rinsing out the washrag. . . .

Rosalind Cartwright (1977) interpreted the content of Jerry's dreams by referring to aspects of his waking life. The first dream, for example, apparently reflected concern over sleeping in the laboratory. It is not a fanciful dream at all but a quite realistic one. The first three dreams all contain a common theme. In each,

Jerry is trying to do something on his own but is unsure of himself and feeling anxious about it. In the last two dreams, the content reflects a period when Jerry's life was simpler. Several weeks after the experiment Jerry summed up his interpretation of the dreams himself:

> They all followed from that first one about trying to figure things out for myself and not being sure I can do it right. This place [medical school] really has me working to keep up. I'm just a country boy, and I've never lived in a big city before. Guess I've always been like that, though. My father always gave me impossible jobs to do, like keeping a second-hand car running for him . . . I thought I left that frustration all behind me with the hicks and the turkey farmers, but I guess I haven't because I still get mad talking about it and I guess that's what made me dream about it.

The interpretations of Jerry's dream were very personal, and it would not be possible to guess what the dreams meant without hearing several of them and without knowing something about Jerry's life. Symbols and events in dreams vary considerably among people. Just because a woman dreams of a snake (which is often regarded as a phallic symbol) does not mean she is over-concerned about sex. Many alternate symbolic meanings may be assigned to the dream; perhaps it simply indicates an interest in reptiles.

The Functions of Sleep and Dreaming

Anyone who has had to stay awake all night knows how insistent the urge to sleep can be. The incredible strength of the urge suggests that sleep serves some very important function. But what is it? Why do we sleep? The intuitive answer is "to rest." Perhaps our nervous systems become worn down during the day and need time to recuperate.

The trouble with that hypothesis, though, is that neurons do not rest at night. In fact, during REM sleep they are at least as active as they are during the waking hours. One way to determine why we sleep is to conduct sleep deprivation experiments, in which subjects are deprived of all or parts of their sleep for long periods of time. If, for example, people who are deprived of sleep for two or three days begin to lose their memories, we might suppose that sleep is important for some process involved in memory. In some ways, however, the approach has the same flaws as the lesion experiments discussed in Chapter 2. Even if a certain behavior is affected when a process (or brain area) is eliminated, it does not necessarily mean that that process (or brain area) is directly involved in the behavior under normal conditions. Nevertheless, combined with other kinds of experiments, the sleep deprivation study is a useful tool in attempting to determine why we sleep.

It is not easy to keep people awake for two or three days straight. In one series of experiments (Webb, 1975), the subjects became very grouchy, grim, and apathetic, as well as very sleepy. They also showed slight hand tremors, difficulty in focusing their eyes, drooping eyelids, and an increased sensitivity to pain. They were especially sleepy at night, when they would ordinarily be sleeping. After three days of sleep deprivation, many showed moments of confusion, although they could still manage to perform a task if they wanted to. In a very few instances, and only after prolonged sleep loss, a subject may show some extreme abnormal behavior. In this particular experiment, one subject had hallucinations about a gorilla and fell to the floor screaming in terror during one of the psychological tests. Instances like these are quite rare, however. Wilse Webb and Rosalind Cartwright (1978) summarized the sleep deprivation literature by saying that the main effect of sleep loss is simply sleepiness.

Not all scientists agree that sleep deprivation has so little effect, however. Deprivation of REM sleep in particular appears to have some important, though subtle, effects on memory. In one study, subjects were asked to memorize a ghost story before they went to sleep wearing EEG recording electrodes. Some subjects were then deprived of Stage 4 slow-wave sleep by being awakened each time their EEG indicated Stage 4. The others were deprived of REM sleep by the same technique. The REM-deprived subjects were much less able to recall the story in the morning (Tilley and Empson,

1978). Studies like this one suggest that REM sleep is somehow involved in the storage of memories, particularly of emotionally charged events that took place during the day.

Other theories about why we sleep and dream have also been proposed. One suggests that sleep evolved as a way of keeping humans out of danger for part of the day, especially that part when they would be most vulnerable to predators (Webb, 1975). If this were the main function of sleep, then it really would have very little function at all anymore. Other proposals emphasize the importance of dreams as "safety valves;" they allow the gratification of wishes that could not be fulfilled during the day.

Another theory suggests that dreaming gives our nervous systems a chance to practice coordinated motor sequences while we are not moving. Young animals and humans spend considerable time in REM sleep. Perhaps this provides their nervous systems with stimulation during a period of life when stimulation from the environment is not very abundant (Roffwarg, et al., 1966). The REM sleep may also allow key sensory and motor areas of the nervous system to "practice" during this important period of maturation.

One kind of practice that REM sleep may be providing involves the ability to coordinate the eye movements necessary to see depth in the visual field (Berger, 1969). The rapid eye movements may be stimulating the motor system responsible for the coordination of the two eyes. In fact, one study found that depth perception is better immediately following REM sleep than it is right before it (Lewis, et al., 1978).

Sleep and dreaming may serve more than one function. It is quite possible that several of these hypotheses are correct.

GUIDED REVIEW

Learning Objectives 3, 4, 5, and 6

1. The most pronounced biological rhythm is the _____ , which repeats every twenty-four hours. Human beings show dramatic physiological and behavioral changes within this cycle.

2. Sleep constitutes a large part of the circadian cycle, and it has rhythms of its own. Periods of _____ , in which the EEG records show increasingly slower and larger _____ waves, alternate with periods of _____ , in which rapid eye movements appear and the brain shows _____ waves, patterns that are also characteristic of waking.

3. _____ sleep is associated with dreaming. Dream content usually reflects a person's anxieties and concerns, although the symbols may not be obvious.

4. Since the nervous system is as active during sleep as it is during waking, resting is not the main reason we sleep. _____ have found that two or three days of sleep loss is not very damaging, although some people may show marked behavioral changes. REM sleep may be the most important component of sleep. It appears to be important in _____ , particularly of emotional events.

ANSWERS

1. circadian rhythm 2. slow-wave sleep; delta; REM; beta 3. REM 4. Sleep deprivation studies; memory storage

Hypnosis

The word "hypnotism" was not used until the middle of the nineteenth century, but hypnotic phenomena have been observed since ancient times. Few topics in psychology are surrounded by as many misunderstandings, myths, mysteries, or rumors, perhaps because much of what the public knows about hypnosis comes from watching stage acts. The modern study of hypnosis developed from **mesmerism,** *a body of knowledge and superstition named after one of its eighteenth-century proponents, Anton Mesmer.*

Mesmer was an Austrian physician who used what he thought was magnetism to treat his wealthy Parisian patients. The patients sat around a large tub of water filled with iron filings, and they held onto metal rods through which the "magnetic fluid" was supposed to flow. Making a theatrical appearance in flowing silk robes, Mesmer made passes over each patient with his hands and muttered impressive-sounding jargon to aid the magnetic transfer. Mesmer's unorthodox treatments received a less-than-friendly reception from the medical community, and they were eventually discredited completely by a team sent by the French king to investigate mesmerism. This group of scientists, which included Benjamin Franklin, attributed the cures that Mesmer and his followers achieved not to the power of magnetism but to the power of the imagination.

Mesmer's flamboyant technique did not intentionally include hypnosis. But as his followers dropped the more bizarre elements of the treatments, they began to focus on the production of "magnetic somnambulism" (sleeplike state), still insisting that magnetism rather than imagination was of primary importance. Eventually some physicians discovered they could use mesmerism to relieve pain, even during surgery. Dr. William Curtis wrote "On Tuesday, Feb. 4th (1837), before a numerous company assembled to witness the operation, I extracted a large molar tooth without the knowledge of the patient whilst in a magnetic sleep. The patient is a girl . . . only mesmerized a few times . . ." (from Gibson, 1977).

The medical community did not welcome this novel approach to surgery, despite the fact that chemical anesthetics were still unknown and many surgical patients died from the shock of the pain. Mesmerism was still linked too closely to magic and superstition for people to take it seriously. It did not acquire any scientific respectability until the middle of the nineteenth century, when James Braid, a Scottish physician, (fig.

Figure 3.7 James Braid, Scottish physician who studied hypnotism

3.7) renamed it "hypnotism" and attributed the phenomenon to mechanical changes in the nervous system rather than to "magnetic fluids." Braid's physiological notions were still quite innacurate, but at least he added credibility to the study of hypnosis.

Hypnosis became a popular tool of psychiatrists during the late nineteenth century, particularly those treating patients with physical symptoms that had no apparent organic cause. For example, a patient who was paralyzed for no obvious physical reason, and who probably became that way because of a psychological trauma, would be a prime candidate for therapy with hypnosis. Sigmund Freud made some use of the technique during his career. Yet despite the new scientific credibility of the technique, it again fell out of favor. This time physicians probably lost interest because it was unreliable. As we shall see, the degree to which people can be hypnotized varies considerably, and it is impossible to predict in advance who can be hypnotized. A physician who tried to hypnotize a patient and failed miserably would certainly lose some prestige and might hesitate to use the technique again. In the United States, psychologists lost interest in hypnosis also because of the rise of behaviorism and the general tendency toward studying only observable behavior rather than states of consciousness. Today, however, there is renewed interest in the phenomenon, interest that has accompanied the general resurgence of investigations into consciousness.

What Is Hypnosis?

Hypnosis is another psychological term that is defined differently by different psychologists, depending on their theoretical point of view. One group sees hypnosis merely as a state of heightened suggestibility, not anything unusual and not very different from an ordinary state of consciousness (Barber, 1969). Others, particularly Ernest Hilgard (1977), view the phenomenon as an example of divided consciousness. These psychologists use a metaphor of a "hidden observer" to explain how part of a person can be aware of some things while another part seems unaware of the same things. For example, when a person is told that she will not be able to hear anything, part of her responds as if she were indeed deaf. But under appropriate circumstances she may be able to report the sounds that were present in the room. Her "hidden observer" was listening.

Perhaps the best way to define **hypnosis** *is as a state of consciousness in which the individual typically displays the following characteristics:*

1. *Attention is highly focused.* Most people pay very close attention to the hypnotist's voice and may ignore other voices or noises in the room.
2. *The subject is more suggestible and prefers to let the hypnotist tell him or her what to do.* For example, when the hypnotist says "Your body feels very relaxed," the subject readily relaxes.
3. *The subject willingly and uncritically accepts many illogical situations,* and might, for example, pet an imaginary rabbit.

The suggestibility of the subject during hypnosis can be extended beyond the session itself by means of **posthypnotic suggestions.** *A hypnotized person is told that he will perform in a certain way, often in response to a certain signal, when no longer hypnotized.* Often the person will comply with the suggestion even though he is unaware of its origin. A subject might be told that after she wakes up, she will not be able to find her keys. Later, she will absentmindedly search for the keys unsuccessfully.

A special posthypnotic suggestion is **posthypnotic amnesia,** *in which the subject appears to forget everything that transpired during the hypnosis session because the hypnotist suggested that he do so.* These memories are not lost forever, however, since they can be retrieved at a signal from the hypnotist.

A rather controversial aspect of hypnosis is **age regression:** *when a hypnotized person is told to relive an experience of childhood, he sometimes seems to do it with remarkable vividness.* One subject who had a very refined British accent began speaking in the Cockney accent she used as a youngster (Gibson, 1977). Another began speaking fluent Japanese, which he had not used since childhood and had almost completely forgotten (Fromm, 1970).

In an early experiment to test the accuracy of subjects' recollections during age regression, fifty college students were hypnotized and told to regress back to their birthdays and to Christmas Day at the ages of four, seven, and ten (True, 1949). At each age, the subject was asked "What day of the week is it?" The reply was checked against a calendar. Their accuracy was truly amazing—eighty-one percent were correct. Unfortunately, attempts to repeat this experiment have met with failure, increasing the controversy over age regression under hypnosis. Many scientists suspect that age regression is simply the result of the person's increased suggestibility and increased willingness to act out a role. Whether long-forgotten memories or childhood abilities can be retrieved in this way is still a matter of dispute.

Who Can Be Hypnotized?

The fact that not everyone can be hypnotized is one of the most perplexing characteristics of hypnosis. Hypnotic susceptibility does not seem to be related in any straightforward way to personality traits, and so far, it is not possible to predict who can be hypnotized and who can not. If a person is gullible, it does not necessarily mean she is suggestible in the hypnotic sense. Hilgard (1970) suggests that susceptibility to hypnosis may be related to a capacity for imagination, one that develops and is nurtured during childhood.

Standard procedures for testing hypnotic susceptibility have been developed by Hilgard and his associates (Hilgard and Hilgard, 1975). First the hypnotist tells the subject to relax and to listen carefully to the hypnotist's voice. Then the hypnotist counts backward from twenty, telling the subject to relax more deeply and to accept whatever instructions the hypnotist offers. This first part of the session is called **hypnotic induction;** *it is a series of suggestions designed to put the person into a light hypnotic trance if the subject is susceptible and willing.* In the second part, the subject is scored on five items, all designed to determine how imaginative the subject is and how willing he or she is to accept the suggestions of the hypnotist (see table 3.1).

Hypnosis and Law Enforcement

The use of hypnosis by police has created a great deal of controversy. Scientists who work with hypnosis are fully aware that hypnotized people can exaggerate, make up stories, and even deliberately lie. They wonder whether police should rely on any information obtained by this technique. Nevertheless, police are enthusiastic about its use, not as a tool to interrogate suspects about their involvement in a crime but as a means to help witnesses retrieve memories that might otherwise be deeply buried.

Laboratory simulations of crimes provide some support for using hypnosis to help eyewitnesses remember. In one experiment, the investigator let sixty-five subjects watch movies of crimes and later compared their

Table 3.1 A portion of the Stanford Hypnotic Clinical Scale (SHCS)	
Item	Score
1. Moving hands together (or 1a. Hand lowering) Describe movement:	
(At end of session, probe for type of experience if movement is very fast:)	
Score (+) if movement is slow and hands are not more than six inches apart by end of 10 seconds.	(1) _____
* * *	
3. Age regression (school)	
Selected grade: _____	
Where are you? _____	
What are you doing? _____	
_____	
Who is your teacher? _____	
How old are you? _____	
What are you wearing? _____	
Who is with you? _____	
a. Hypnotist's rating:	
_____ : _____ : _____	
No Good Fair	
regression	

Reprinted, with permission, from "Hypnosis in the Relief of Pain," by E. R. Hilgard and J. R. Hilgard. Copyright © 1975, 1983 by William Kaufmann, Inc., Los Altos, CA 94022. All Rights Reserved.

memories about details while under hypnosis and in an ordinary state of consciousness (Griffin, 1980). Most subjects were able to relate more details under hypnosis, provided they were susceptible to the procedure in the first place.

However, other studies have found that hypnosis actually hinders accurate recall (Sanders and Simmons, 1983). A large group of college students were shown a twenty-second videotape depicting a pickpocket stealing a wallet. A week later, all the subjects returned to the lab. Half were hypnotized, and the other half were simply given instructions to "replay" the incident on an internal, mental TV screen. Then all subjects viewed a videotaped lineup that included the perpetrator, and they answered ten specific questions about the theft.

Only seventeen percent of the hypnotized subjects correctly identified the pickpocket in the lineup, compared to forty percent of control subjects. The hypnotized subjects also made more errors on the questions. They were particularly susceptible to so-called "leading" questions. For example, one question was "Did you notice it when the victim looked at his pocketwatch?" The question implied that the victim actually did look at his watch when in fact he did not. The researchers concluded that hypnosis is a hindrance to accurate recall because it makes the person too susceptible to suggestions. They felt it should only be used as a last resort in legal cases, and then the results should be considered more as anonymous tips rather than valid testimony.

Many psychologists are critical of the use of hypnosis by the police because hypnotized subjects do not seem to remember events very accurately. One psychiatrist even thinks that witnesses previously hypnotized by the police should not be allowed to testify in court at all because their memories might have been altered during the trance.

Despite the controversies, the number of police departments that use hypnosis is rapidly growing. More than ten thousand police officers have received training in hypnosis, and many police departments have behavioral science units that routinely use hypnosis.

GUIDED REVIEW

Learning Objectives 7, 8, and 9

1. Hypnosis developed from a body of knowledge and superstition called _____ . It was particularly useful in treating patients with sensory or motor difficulties that were produced by psychological traumas rather than organic damage.

2. The state of consciousness an individual is in during hypnosis is still controversial. Some view it simply as a state of _____ . Others see it as a state of _____ . Characteristics of the hypnotized subject include highly focused attention, increased suggestibility, willingness to act out roles, and uncritical acceptance of illogical situations.

3. A hypnotized subject may also be susceptible to _____ , which means that the subject carries out a suggestion after awakening. _____ is a special kind of posthypnotic suggestion in which the subject forgets what happened during the session. Some hypnotized subjects can show _____ , in which they appear to relive past events.

4. Susceptibility to hypnosis varies considerably between people and can be measured by a _____ .

ANSWERS

1. mesmerism 2. heightened suggestibility; divided consciousness
3. posthypnotic suggestion; Posthypnotic amnesia; age regression
4. hypnotic susceptibility test

Chemical Alterations in Consciousness

If the cocaine business were legal and listed by Fortune 500, it would rank seventh in domestic sales volume, somewhere between Ford Motor Company and Gulf Oil (Van Dyke and Byck, 1982). Cocaine sales comprise only part of the total drug business in the United States, a business that includes underground traffic in marijuana, heroin, psychedelic drugs, tranquilizers, and a bewildering array of other mind altering substances, as well as legal trade in alcohol, barbiturates, tobacco, caffeine, and prescribed mood elevators and tranquilizers.

The range of drugs capable of producing changes in behavior and in consciousness is very wide. Even aspirin might be included, since it relieves pain. **Psychoactive drugs** *are those whose main effect is supposed to be an alteration in consciousness.* These drugs can be grouped into five main categories, as shown in table 3.2.

Table 3.2 Classification and examples of psychoactive drugs

I. General depressants
   Barbiturates (pentobarbital, secobarbital, pentathol)
   Nonbarbiturate sedatives (Quaalude)
   Antianxiety agents (Valium, Librium, Miltown, Equanil)
   Others (alcohol, chloral hydrate, ether)

II. Stimulants
   Amphetamines (Benzedrine, Dexedrine)
   Clinical antidepressants (Elavil, Parnate)
   Cocaine
   Caffeine
   Nicotine

III. Opiates
   Opium
   Morphine
   Codeine
   Heroin

IV. Hallucinogenic drugs
   LSD
   Mescaline
   Psilocybin
   PCP
   Cannabis, marijuana, hashish

V. Antipsychotic agents
   Phenothiazines (chlorpromazine)
   Reserpine
   Haloperidol
   Lithium

The **general depressants** *act in various ways to reduce activity in the nervous system.* The **stimulants** *have an excitatory effect on activity in the central nervous system; hence the term "stimulant." The* **opiates** *include any natural or synthetic drug that exerts actions on the body similar to those induced by morphine, a major pain-relieving agent that is obtained from the opium poppy. The* **hallucinogenic drugs** *are a heterogeneous group of compounds that can produce visual, auditory, or other hallucinations and can separate the individual from reality by inducing distortions in cognition and perception. The psychoactive drugs used for therapeutic purposes are sometimes called* **antipsychotic agents,** *but their actions can vary widely.* Phenothiazines, for example, are often used to treat psychotic symptoms; the drug appears to affect activity

at certain neurotransmitter sites in the brain. Marijuana is not included in this table because there is a great deal of controversy about whether it is a depressant or a hallucinogen. *The psychoactive ingredient in marijuana is* **tetrahydrocannibinol (THC).** *This substance produces a range of physiological effects, including slight drying of the mouth, occasional dizziness, and nausea. Psychological alterations at low doses are generally mild and may include changes in mood, daydreaming, or sleepiness. At higher doses, the psychological alterations can include sensory distortions and mild hallucinations.*

How Do Drugs Work?

Despite the widespread use of drugs and the intensive research into their mechanisms of action, it is still not clear how most drugs produce their behavioral effects. Furthermore, even though two drugs produce similar behavioral changes, they might do it in different ways. For example, both marijuana and alcohol can cause a person to feel euphoric, but the two drugs work very differently.

The effect of a drug depends on a number of factors, including the way the drug is taken, how much is taken, how rapidly the drug reaches the bloodstream, how much of the drug reaches the nervous system, and how quickly the drug is broken down and excreted from the body. Drugs that are injected into a vein affect a person much more rapidly than those taken orally. The injected drug enters the bloodstream immediately and reaches all parts of the body within minutes; the drug taken by mouth must be broken down by digestive enzymes in the stomach before it is absorbed into the bloodstream. Because the effects of an injected drug are so rapid, there is usually no time for anyone to counteract an overdose, but there is with drugs that are taken by mouth.

The dose of a drug also helps determine its effects. Sometimes there is a simple relationship between dose and response: the greater the dose, the greater the behavioral change. But very often a larger dose of a drug produces completely different responses. For example, low doses of cocaine usually produce euphoria and a sense of well being in the user, but higher doses can lead to extreme anxiety and suspiciousness.

Even if we know exactly how a drug was taken, how much of it was taken, and all the other factors surrounding the use of the drug, we still might not be able to predict how that drug will affect a specific person. Different people can respond very differently to the same drug. For example, several cups of coffee produce nervousness in most people, but it can produce severe panic in certain susceptible people (Charney, Heninger, and Jatlow, 1985).

Tolerance and Dependence.   Some psychoactive drugs produce a phenomenon called **tolerance,** *a term that refers to the fact that after taking repeated doses of a drug, the person requires a larger dose to achieve the same behavioral or physiological effect.* A person's tolerance to a drug is a very complicated matter. It depends only partly on how often and how much of a drug has been used. It also depends on psychological factors, such as where the drug is taken. In a fascinating study that demonstrated the importance of psychological factors in the development of tolerance, rats were injected with glucose and increasing doses of heroin on alternate days for one month. Some rats were injected with heroin while they were next to their home cage and injected with glucose in a separate room. Others were given the glucose near their home and the heroin in a strange room. Then all the rats were injected with very large doses of heroin, either in the same environment in which they had been receiving their heroin injections or in the other room. This large dose was lethal to many rats, but particularly to those that were injected in the room where they had been getting only glucose. In other words, they were more vulnerable to the large dose if they were in a room where they were not "expecting" heroin. The researchers speculate that many deaths due to so-called "overdoses" may really

be due to a temporary drop in tolerance because of psychological factors. The user dies even though the dose is the same as one injected only days earlier. Perhaps the victim injected the drug while in a novel environment (Siegel, Hinson, Krank, and McCully, 1982).

Because psychoactive drugs within the same class are often chemically very similar, they sometimes produce **cross-tolerance,** *a phenomenon in which tolerance to one drug has the effect of causing tolerance to another, even when the person had never used the other drug.* For example, a person who has developed tolerance to alcohol will also show tolerance to other drugs in the general depressant category.

Several of the psychoactive drugs also have the ability to produce **physical dependence.** *By the usual definition, a person has become dependent upon a drug if tolerance has developed, if the drug is needed for the person to function normally, and if continued doses are required to prevent the onset of withdrawal symptoms.* By this definition, virtually all of the drugs in the depressant category may result in dependence. In fact, a person who has developed a tolerance for the barbiturates and suddenly stops taking the drug might die from convulsions. All of the opiates can produce physical dependence as well.

Many of the psychoactive drugs produce psychological dependence even if they do not produce physical dependence. **Psychological dependence** *occurs when a person learns to use a drug habitually to relieve stress or to relax, thereby becoming quite dependent on the substance. This is true even if little or no physical dependence has developed and no physical withdrawal symptoms would appear if the person stopped taking the drug.* Psychological dependence on a drug can be an extremely powerful force. For example, people who smoke cocaine (rather than "snort" it) often show a pattern of behavior that is clearly self-destructive; they may spend most of their waking hours taking the drug or finding means to obtain it. (See Application Box: Cocaine.)

APPLICATION BOX

Cocaine

I felt like I could handle just about anything that came up. . . . I never felt so confident.
What's the big deal? I couldn't notice much of a difference.
You really feel like you're flying. . . . It tickles my nose though.

According to the reports of cocaine users, this very popular drug produces quite a range of experiences. Most users feel euphoria and elation, and perhaps a sense of clear and powerful thinking. These sensations usually disappear within an hour, and some users become depressed and begin to crave more cocaine.

The use of cocaine dates back at least 5,000 years, according to archaeological evidence in Ecuador. To the Incas, the coca plant, from which cocaine is derived, was divine and was treated as a symbol of high social and political rank. The Inca leaders controlled the use of coca, confining it mostly to the ruling classes. Unauthorized chewing of the coca leaves was considered a sacrilege.

The cocaine in use today in the United States and Europe is usually finely chopped cocaine hydrocholoride, extracted from the plant. The powdery substance is placed in a mound on a smooth surface, such as a mirror, and users inhale it through a rolled dollar bill or a straw. It is easily absorbed into the bloodstream through the mucous membranes in the nose. Cocaine can also be injected directly into a vein or smoked and absorbed through the lungs. Many users like to take repeated small doses of the substance in order to maintain the feelings of euphoria over a longer period of time.

Cocaine acts like a local anesthetic when it is applied topically, much like procaine and lidocaine, which are chemically quite similar. A local anesthetic blocks axonal conduction when it is applied to the nerve, probably by altering the nature of the axon's membrane. When an axon conducts an impulse, its membrane becomes very permeable to sodium ions; these ions rush through the axon's membrane into the

Psychosocial Drug Effects. The fact that people react differently to the same drug is partly due to personality and to social factors surrounding the use of the drug. For instance, people who take the hallucinogen PCP, or "angel dust," sometimes show violent and self-destructive behavior; but some suspect that these reactions are more common in people who have a latent mental disorder. The social milieu in which a user takes a drug can also have an important influence on the drug's effects. A person who smokes marijuana while alone may experience drowsiness and daydreaming. In the company of other people, and with the same drug dose, the same person might show garrulousness and hilarity.

A fascinating study that examined muscle tension after withdrawal from caffeine (White, et al., 1980) demonstrated how complex drug effects can be. Two groups of subjects—one that rarely drank coffee and one consisting of heavy coffee drinkers—avoided caffeine for three hours. The researchers then measured

cell. Immediately afterward, the membrane suddenly becomes impermeable to sodium ions once again, stopping the flow of ions. As the impulse travels down the axon, segments of the axon's membrane become permeable and impermeable in sequence, until the message reaches the axon terminals. Local anesthetics such as cocaine appear to interfere with the channels in the axon's membrane, making it difficult for sodium ions to pass through. The presence of the anesthetic makes it difficult or impossible for a neuron to conduct impulses along its axon.

When cocaine gets into the bloodstream, it acts like a stimulant rather than an anesthetic. It increases heart rate, raises blood pressure, and in large doses it raises body temperature. It is called a "sympathomimetic" because it mimics many of the effects of activation of the sympathetic nervous system.

In the brain, cocaine interferes with the process of synaptic transmission. Ordinarily, when an impulse travels down the axon, the axon's terminals release some neurotransmitter into the synaptic space. These neurotransmitter molecules affect the dendrites of the next neuron and then are deactivated, either by enzymes or by the process called reuptake. Some neurotransmitter molecules are taken back up into the terminal to be used again in synaptic transmission. Cocaine blocks this reuptake mechanism, leaving the neurotransmitter in the synaptic space where it can continue to affect the dendrite of the next neuron. Cocaine's action at important synapses in the brain that are involved in mood and emotion are probably the main reason the drug produces euphoria and elation (Van Dyke and Byck, 1982).

muscle tension in their forearms using **electromyography (EMG),** *a technique that records electrical signals from muscle tissue.* Half of each group then drank straight grapefruit juice whereas the other half drank juice laced with a heavy dose of caffeine. (The juice masked the taste of the caffeine, so no one could tell whether the drink contained caffeine.)

The EMG measurements showed that the heavy caffeine users had more muscle tension after caffeine withdrawal than did the light users, showing the importance of tolerance and dependence on the effects of a drug. However, heavy caffeine users all showed a decrease in muscle tension after drinking their grapefruit juice, regardless of whether the juice contained any caffeine. Low caffeine users showed a slight increase in tension. This study suggests that both the light and heavy coffee drinkers all behaved in accordance with their expectations of how caffeine would affect them after a long abstinence. And their expectations affected their behavior even if their drink contained no caffeine.

The Effects of Drugs on the Brain. Most of the psychoactive drugs seem to produce alternate states of consciousness by acting on the brain, particularly at the synapse. They appear to change the way neurons in the brain communicate with one another.

The hallucinogenic drug mescaline, for example, is structurally very similar to one of the neurotransmitters used in the brain to pass messages from one neuron to the next. Scientists hypothesize that the receptor sites in the brain that normally respond to the neurotransmitter probably respond to mescaline just as well. The mescaline molecule "mimics" the real neurotransmitter.

Cocaine molecules act on the synapse in a different way. Normally, the neurotransmitter molecules are released by one neuron, diffuse across a tiny gap between the neurons, and attach to receptor sites on the membrane of the next neuron. The neurotransmitter must be removed from this gap quickly to make room for the next release of neurotransmitter. One way the neurons accomplish this rapid removal is by taking the neurotransmitter molecules back up. This is an efficient process since the same molecule can be used again when the neuron sends another chemical signal to its neighbor. Cocaine seems to interfere with this process by preventing the reuptake of the neurotransmitter. Too much neurotransmitter is left in the gap, confusing the neuron that is receiving the chemical signal (Van Dyke and Byck, 1982).

The brain produces many neurotransmitters, but one that appears to be particularly affected by psychoactive drugs like cocaine is **norepinephrine.** *Norepinephrine is a neurotransmitter used by the brain and also by the autonomic nervous system (discussed in the last chapter).* It plays an important role in some of the brain areas involved in mood, a fact that may help explain why many psychoactive drugs can produce euphoria or depression.

Table 3.3 The behavioral effects of depressant drugs

Normal behavior

Relief from anxiety

Disinhibition, euphoria

Drowsiness

Sleep

General anesthesia

Coma

Death

Closeup of the General Depressants

The general depressants represent the largest drug problem in the United States. More than nine million people are alcoholics, and millions more are physically dependent on other drugs in this category, such as sleeping pills and tranquilizers. These drugs produce tolerance (some very quickly), and all are capable of producing physical dependence.

Barbiturates, the **nonbarbiturate hypnotics,** and a variety of **antianxiety agents,** as well as structurally unrelated chemicals such as alcohol and drugs used for anesthesia, *are all examples of general depressants.* These substances produce a similar sequence of behavioral effects with increasing dose, shown in table 3.3. In fact, any general depressant might be called a tranquilizer, a sleeping pill, or even an anesthetic, depending on the dose given.

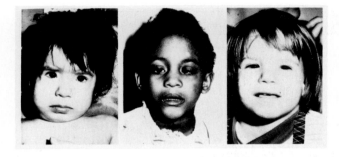

Figure 3.8   Children afflicted with fetal alcohol syndrome

Alcohol. The most widely used general depressant is ethyl alcohol. For the light social drinker, alcohol provides an occasional pleasure, but for many people alcohol is the cause of behavior problems as well as health problems. For instance, about one in four mental patients is an alcoholic, although some are recovered. Drunken driving either directly causes or contributes to 25,000 deaths on the highway every year. Alcohol is the root cause of cirrhosis of the liver, which ranks as the sixth leading cause of death. Some researchers estimate that in more than sixty percent of violent homicides, the killer had been drinking. Alcohol is also an important factor in sex crimes.

The most recently discovered hazard associated with alcohol is **fetal alcohol syndrome (FAS),** *a condition that affects some babies born to mothers who drank during their pregnancies. Symptoms include mental retardation, growth deficiencies, hyperactivity, poor attention span, and unusual facial characteristics such as drooping eyelids and crossed eyes.* The photographs in figure 3.8 show children afflicted with the disorder (Streissguth, et al., 1980). Because so little is known about FAS and how much alcohol can cause it, many obstetricians are recommending that their pregnant patients avoid alcohol altogether.

The effects of alcohol on the brain are not well understood, but researchers have found that alcohol depresses activity in brain cells in several areas, particularly the cerebellum, the structure involved in coordination and fine motor control (Bloom, 1985).

Alcohol produces the range of behavioral changes shown in table 3.3. In the body, alcohol dilates the blood vessels of the skin, producing a warm flush. Using alcohol to keep warm in winter is pointless, since the initial warm flush is followed by a decrease in body temperature; the peripheral dilation of the vessels causes a loss of body heat.

Why one individual becomes an alcoholic and another, who drinks just as much, does not, is one of the most perplexing problems in drug research. Clearly the development of physical dependence to alcohol is not simply related to how much or how often a person drinks. Most alcoholics appear to be anxious people and use alcohol to relieve their anxiety. They think the drug will improve their self-esteem and confidence. Alcoholics also tend to show some common features in their childhoods and in their relationships with their parents, features that distinguish them from nonalcoholics. For instance, in an early study of samples of male alcoholics and nonalcoholic controls, a larger percentage of the alcoholics came from families in which the father figure was very weak or absent. Forty-eight percent of alcoholics, compared to seventeen percent of controls, reported the absence of a father figure during the early part of childhood. Table 3.4 lists some other aspects of family background in which there were large differences between alcoholics and nonalcoholic controls (Chein, Gerard, Lee, and Rosenfeld, 1964).

A recent study, however, suggests that personality disorder and childhood problems may not be as important as other factors (Vaillant and Milofsky, 1982). This thirty-three-year investigation followed the lives of 456 inner-city white men, collecting data on childhood adjustment, family problems, drinking behavior, and other variables. The two variables that were most closely related to the drinking patterns of the men were ethnic background and family history of alcohol abuse. Childhood problems played less of a role.

The role of family history may also be important because of genetic or prenatal factors. Researchers in Denmark interviewed the now grown-up children of alcoholic parents, some of whom had been given up for

Table 3.4 Selected items on which the family backgrounds of alcoholics and nonalcoholics were very different

Item	Percentages	
	Alcoholics	Controls
1. Boy experienced an extremely weak father-son relationship	80	45
2. For a significant part of early childhood, boy did not have a father figure in his life	48	17
3. Some father figure was cool or hostile to boy	52	13
4. Father had unrealistically low aspirations for the boy (late childhood and early adolescence)	44	0
5. Some father figure was an immoral model (early childhood)	23	0
6. Marked impulse orientation in father figure	26	0
7. Father had unstable work history during boy's early childhood	43	14
8. Father was unrealistically pessimistic or felt that life is a gamble	47	11
9. Lack of warmth or overtly discordant relations between parents	97	41
10. Mother figure was more important parent in boy's life during late childhood period	73	45
11. Some mother figure cool or hostile to boy (early childhood)	23	0
12. Some mother figure cool or hostile to boy (late childhood)	37	3
13. Boy experienced extremely weak mother-son relationship	40	7
14. Mother did not trust authority figures	38	10
15. Mother had unrealistically low aspirations for boy (late childhood and early adolescence)	31	0
16. Mother was unrealistically pessimistic or felt that life is a gamble	31	7
17. No clear pattern of parental roles in formation of disciplinary policy (adolescence)	23	0
18. Parental standards for boy were vague or inconsistent (early childhood)	55	4
19. Parental standards for boy were vague or inconsistent (adolescence)	63	3
20. Boy was overindulged, frustrated in his wishes, or both	70	10

From Chein, L., Gerard, D., Lee, R., and E. Rosenfeld, Narcotics, Delinquency and Social Policy. *Copyright © 1964 by Tavistock Publications, Ltd. Reprinted by permission.*

adoption early in life and reared by nonalcoholic parents (Goodwin, 1979). The children of the alcoholic parents were more prone to develop alcoholism in adulthood, regardless of whether they were reared by their own alcoholic parents or by their nonalcoholic adoptive parents. The sons of alcoholic parents were particularly vulnerable—they were four times more likely to become victims of the disease than were the sons of nonalcoholic parents, even if they were reared in normal homes. Strangely, the children of alcoholic parents were not more likely to develop any other behavioral problems—only alcoholism.

Studies like these are leading scientists to search for biological factors that might be inherited and that might predispose a person to become alcoholic. For example, enzymes that break down alcohol in the body are known to be more or less effective in different people, a difference that may be due to heredity.

Other General Depressants. Insomnia is a common complaint for which general depressants may be prescribed as an adjunct therapy since the drugs appear to act on specific pathways in the brain involved in wakefulness (Kales and Kales, 1984). Barbiturates were once frequently used for this purpose, but all of the general depressants can induce sleep if they are given in an appropriate dose. Although they may be helpful for a short time, they quickly begin to cause more problems than they solve.

After a person takes **flurazepam,** a *kind of sleeping pill* (Feinberg, et al., 1977), the amount of REM drops off dramatically while the amount of Stage 2 sleep increases, in terms of the percent of total sleep time. The person may be sleeping more but dreaming less. REM sleep is probably the most critical portion of the night's sleep, so this loss reduces the quality of the person's sleep time. When the drug is withdrawn, the amount of REM sleep increases dramatically in a rebound effect. In severely dependent users the rebound can be drastic indeed, causing nightmares, vivid dreaming, and very disturbed sleep. Many people believe that they can't sleep without their pills; in fact, the pills are causing their insomnia.

When the so-called "minor tranquilizers" were first introduced, physicians thought they could safely prescribe them to relieve anxiety and also to aid sleep. But research eventually revealed that drugs such as Valium, Librium, or Quaalude posed as many dangers as the barbiturates. They also induce tolerance and physical dependence. General depressants have a variety of names, for example, sleeping pills, sedatives, barbiturates, minor tranquilizers, and antianxiety agents. Each category differs chemically, but the human brain seems to react very similarly to all of them.

GUIDED REVIEW

Learning Objectives 10, 11, and 12

1. Drugs whose main effect is to produce an alteration in consciousness are called _____ .

2. Psychoactive drugs are grouped into five categories: _____ , _____ , _____ , _____ , and _____ .

3. Some psychoactive drugs produce _____ , which means that the dose of drug must be increased in order to achieve the same effect. Some also produce _____ or addiction. Because the effects of some of the drugs are so pleasurable, they can also produce _____ .

4. The effects of a drug depend in part on _____ factors, such as the personality or expectations of the user, and also on the social circumstances in which the drug is ingested.

5. Many psychoactive drugs produce their effects on behavior and consciousness by acting on the brain, particularly at the _____ .

6. _____ produce a sequence of changes, including relief from anxiety and euphoria; sleep; coma; and eventually death, at high doses. Sleeping pills are a widely used depressant, though they produce more problems for insomniacs than they solve because they interfere with REM sleep. Alcohol is another depressant drug. It is dangerous to pregnant women because it may produce the _____ in babies. The causes of alcoholism are unclear, but they may include genetic factors and family history, childhood problems, and personality disorders.

ANSWERS

1. psychoactive 2. depressants, stimulants, opiates, hallucinogens, antipsychotic agents 3. tolerance; physical dependence; psychological dependence 4. psychosocial 5. synapse 6. Depressants; fetal alcohol syndrome

SUMMARY

I. Consciousness is the state of mind that shifts slightly from moment to moment.   (p. 76)

   A. A working definition of consciousness is the awareness of internal and external events. (p. 76)

   B. Early studies of conscious processes used introspection; behaviorists rejected this tool and instead favored the study of overt behavior. Recently, conscious processes has become an important focus of many psychological studies. (p. 77)

   C. Your state of consciousness is related to the activity of neurons in your brain. This activity can be measured in various ways.   (p. 77)

     1. The EEG records electrical activity in large areas of the brain. Certain waveforms are known to be related to particular states of consciousness. (p. 78)

     2. The responses of brain cells to specific stimuli can be measured using evoked potentials, which average EEG patterns recorded after repeated presentations of the same stimulus.   (p. 79)

II. Sleep and dreaming constitute alternate states of consciousness.   (p. 81)

   A. Sleeping is part of a twenty-four-hour circadian rhythm, during which people show cyclic physiological and behavioral changes.   (p. 81)

     1. Disruptions in the circadian rhythm, produced by shift work, cause the physiological cycles to become desynchronized; resynchronization can take several days.   (p. 83)

   B. Sleep can be divided into two stages. In slow-wave sleep, the EEG patterns show alpha and delta waves; in REM, the patterns show faster beta waves.   (p. 85)

   C. REM appears to be associated with dreaming; the content of dreams often reflects a person's anxieties and concerns, although the symbols may not be obvious.   (p. 86)

   D. The functions of sleep are not well understood, but REM appears to be important in memory storage, particularly for emotional events. (p. 87)

III. The modern study of hypnosis developed from mesmerism, a body of knowledge and superstition popular in the eighteenth century.   (p. 88)

   A. The exact nature of hypnosis is controversial. It appears to be a state of consciousness characterized by highly focused attention, increased suggestibility, willingness to act out roles, and uncritical acceptance of illogical situations. Some view it as simply a state of increased suggestibility; others view it as a state of "divided consciousness."   (p. 90)

   B. For reasons that are not well understood, people vary dramatically in their susceptibility to hypnosis.   (p. 91)

   C. The use of hypnosis to help eyewitnesses recall events concerning crimes is growing, but many psychologists are concerned about the practice because of the studies showing that hypnosis does not necessarily produce accurate recall. (p. 91)

IV. Chemical alterations in consciousness can be produced by a wide range of psychoactive drugs, including general depressants, stimulants, opiates, hallucinogens, and antipsychotic agents.   (p. 92)

   A. The effects of a drug depend on a variety of factors, including the dose, the route of administration, the amount that reaches the bloodstream, and the rate of excretion. (p. 93)

1. Some drugs, such as depressants, can produce tolerance and physical dependence and/or psychological dependence. (p. 94)

2. Psychosocial factors are important influences on the behavioral effects of psychoactive drugs. (p. 95)

3. Psychoactive drugs generally produce their effects on behavior by altering the activity in certain synapses in the brain. (p. 97)

B. Depressants produce a wide range of behavioral effects, such as relief from anxiety, euphoria, and coma or death, depending on the dose that reaches the brain. Drugs in this category produce tolerance and dependence. (p. 97)

1. The most widely used general depressant is alcohol. (p. 98)

2. Sleeping pills are another example of general depressants. (p. 99)

ACTION GLOSSARY

Match the terms in the left column with the definitions in the right column.

____ 1. **Consciousness** (p. 76)
____ 2. **Information processing** (p. 77)
____ 3. **Evoked potential** (p. 79)
____ 4. **Circadian rhythms** (p. 81)
____ 5. **Alpha waves** (p. 85)
____ 6. **Delta waves** (p. 85)
____ 7. **Slow-wave sleep** (p. 85)
____ 8. **REM sleep** (p. 86)

A. *High amplitude, low frequency brain-wave patterns of one to four cycles per second recorded by means of an EEG. The appearance of these patterns in the EEG usually signifies slow-wave sleep.*

B. *Regular brain wave patterns from eight to twelve cycles per second recorded by means of an EEG. Usually accompanies behavioral relaxation.*

C. *A state of awareness of internal and external events; includes perceptions, private thoughts, dreams, and other mental activities that are only accessible to others through verbal report.*

D. *The stage of sleep characterized by high amplitude, low frequency wave patterns on the EEG, including delta waves. Can be divided into four stages, depending on its depth.*

E. *A waveform obtained by averaging many EEG patterns recorded during a series of repeated presentations of a sensory stimulus.*

F. *The stage of sleep characterized by rapid eye movements and high frequency, low amplitude beta waves on the EEG. Most dreaming appears to occur during this stage.*

G. *An approach to the study of human behavior that emphasizes the integration of sensation, perception, cognition, memory, and other processes. The approach uses many analogies from computer science, such as the concept of the flow of information through a system.*

H. *Changes in physiology or behavior that go through a complete cycle in twenty-four hours.*

____ 9. **Mesmerism** (p. 88)
____ 10. **Hypnosis** (p. 90)
____ 11. **Posthypnotic suggestion** (p. 90)
____ 12. **Posthypnotic amnesia** (p. 90)
____ 13. **Age regression** (p. 90)
____ 14. **Hypnotic induction** (p. 91)
____ 15. **Psychoactive drug** (p. 92)
____ 16. **General depressant** (p. 93)

A. *The subject appears to forget what happened during the hypnosis session until signaled to remember.*

B. *An altered state of consciousness in which the person seems very suggestible.*

C. *A technique in which the hypnotist suggests that a hypnotized subject relive, through fantasy, earlier experiences and memories, perhaps from childhood.*

D. *A hypnotized subject is told that he or she will perform some activity after the hypnotic trance is ended, perhaps on some signal from the hypnotist. The subject is often unaware of the suggestion or of the reason for his or her activity.*

E. *A psychoactive drug whose main effect is the decrease of central nervous system activity.*

F. *A drug whose main effect is designed to be an alteration in consciousness.*

G. *A procedure that is used to produce a hypnotic trance in a susceptible person, usually involving relaxation and suggestions.*

H. *An early version of hypnotism, named after one of its eighteenth-century proponents. The technique was thought to operate through "magnetic fluids."*

___ 17. **Stimulant** (p. 93)
___ 18. **Opiate** (p. 93)
___ 19. **Hallucinogenics** (p. 93)
___ 20. **Antipsychotic agents** (p. 93)
___ 21. **Tetrahydrocannibinol** (p. 93)
___ 22. **Tolerance** (p. 94)
___ 23. **Cross-tolerance** (p. 94)
___ 24. **Physical dependence** (p. 94)

A. *A state in which an individual has developed tolerance to a particular drug, needs it in order to function normally, and experiences withdrawal symptoms when it is no longer administered.*
B. *A phenomenon produced by certain drugs in which increasing doses are required to achieve the same behavioral or physiological effect of the drug the longer the drug is used.*
C. *Psychoactive drugs used to treat mental disorders.*
D. *A phenomenon in which tolerance to one drug develops because of continued use of another chemically similar drug, even though the individual never used the first drug.*
E. *A psychoactive drug whose main effect is to increase activity in the central nervous system.*
F. *A natural or synthetic drug that exerts actions on the body similar to those induced by morphine.*
G. *The psychoactive ingredient in marijuana.*
H. *Various psychoactive drugs that can produce distortions in cognition and perception.*

___ 25. **Psychological dependence** (p. 94)
___ 26. **Electromyograph (EMG)** (p. 96)
___ 27. **Norepinephrine** (p. 97)
___ 28. **Barbiturates** (p. 97)
___ 29. **Nonbarbiturate hypnotics** (p. 97)
___ 30. **Antianxiety agents** (p. 97)
___ 31. **Fetal alcohol syndrome (FAS)** (p. 98)
___ 32. **Flurazepam** (p. 100)

A. *An apparatus that records electrical signals from muscle tissue.*
B. *A group of symptoms characteristic of some babies born to women who drink a great deal of alcohol during pregnancy. Symptoms include drooping eyelids, crossed eyes, growth deficiencies, hyperactivity, and mental retardation.*
C. *A neurotransmitter used by the nervous system, especially by the sympathetic division of the autonomic nervous system, and in pathways of the brain involved in mood.*
D. *An example of a depressant drug.*
E. *An example of a depressant drug.*
F. *A state in which a person comes to rely on a drug habitually for the relief of stress, for euphoria, or for other effects.*
G. *A depressant drug used as a sedative.*
H. *An example of a depressant drug.*

ANSWERS

18. F, 19. H, 20. C, 21. G, 22. B, 23. D, 24. A, 25. F, 26. A, 27. C, 28. E, 29. H, 30. H, 31. B, 32. G

1. C, 2. G, 3. E, 4. H, 5. B, 6. A, 7. D, 8. F, 9. H, 10. B, 11. D, 12. A, 13. C, 14. G, 15. F, 16. E, 17. E.

SELF-TEST

1. The focusing of consciousness is called
   (a) attention.
   (b) perception.
   (c) sensation.
   (d) thinking.
   (LO 1; p. 76)

2. Wundt studied consciousness using the technique called
   (a) psychoanalysis.
   (b) introspection.
   (c) hypnosis.
   (d) mesmerism.
   (LO 1; p. 77)

3. An electrical recording technique that averages the brain's response to many presentations of a specific stimulus is called the
   (a) electroencephalograph.
   (b) electromyograph.
   (c) evoked potential.
   (d) CAT scan.
   (LO 2; p. 80)

4. A circadian rhythm is based upon a cycle of about
   (a) an hour.
   (b) a day.
   (c) a lunar month.
   (d) a year.
   (LO 3; p. 81)

5. The timing of the circadian rhythm is controlled by
   (a) the lunar cycle.
   (b) prenatal factors.
   (c) the changes in noise usually found in the day and night.
   (d) the day-and-night light cycle.
   (LO 3; p. 81)

6. If locked away in a deep cave or other continuously dark place, a person's sleep/waking cycle
   (a) runs freely and averages about 25 hours.
   (b) stays the same as it was above ground.
   (c) becomes shorter so that the person ends up waking at midnight.
   (d) breaks down so that the person does not have long periods of sleep and waking.
   (LO 3; p. 82)

7. In one study of the distribution of people's errors during the circadian cycle the worst performance was
   (a) at about 8 A.M.
   (b) at about 10 P.M.
   (c) at mealtime.
   (d) at about 2 A.M.
   (LO 3; p. 83)

8. During slow-wave sleep, the predominant wave form of the EEG
   (a) shifts from the delta wave to the beta wave.
   (b) shifts from the beta wave to the alpha wave.
   (c) shifts from the beta wave to the alpha wave to a predominance of delta waves.
   (d) is the alpha wave.
   (LO 4; p. 85)

9. The stage of sleep during which most dreaming is thought to take place is
   (a) the stage of REM sleep.
   (b) the stage of alpha waves.
   (c) slow-wave sleep.
   (d) when delta waves predominate.
   (LO 5; p. 86)

10. The main result of a single night of sleep loss appears to be
    (a) hallucinations.
    (b) paranoia.
    (c) sleepiness.
    (d) heart problems.
    (LO 6; p. 87)

11. The discovery of hypnotism is attributed to
    (a) Benjamin Franklin.
    (b) Mesmer.
    (c) Freud.
    (d) William Curtis.
    (LO 7; p. 88)

12. Hypnotism involves
    (a) attention and suggestibility.
    (b) a kind of magnetism.
    (c) an involuntary compulsion.
    (d) age regression.
    (LO 7; p. 90)

13. Testimony received under hypnosis
    (a) is widely used by the police and welcomed in court.
    (b) is rarely used by police and welcome in court when it is.
    (c) is absolutely prohibited for court use.
    (d) is controversial.
    (LO 9; p. 91)

14. The general depressants
    (a) include alcohol.
    (b) reduce activity in the nervous system.
    (c) are not addictive.
    (d) both a and b.
    (LO 10; p. 93)

15. Sondra was addicted to heroin. After a car accident in which she broke her arm, she was taken to a hospital, and a physician gave her the standard-size injection of morphine to relieve the pain. It did not relieve her pain, and she requested a higher dose. This illustrates
    (a) tolerance.
    (b) cross tolerance.
    (c) dependence.
    (d) addiction.
    (LO 11; p. 94)

16. The development of tolerance is usually associated with the use of
    (a) alcohol.
    (b) opiates.
    (c) barbiturates.
    (d) all of the above.
    (LO 11; p. 94)

17. Cocaine has its effect by
    (a) causing more neurotransmitter to be released at the synapse.
    (b) stimulating the dendrites that cause euphoria.
    (c) acting as a mild depressant.
    (d) blocking reuptake of neurotransmitter at the synapse.
    (LO 11; p. 95)

18. The fetal alcohol syndrome
    (a) is a major cause of alcoholism.
    (b) is found only in the babies of very heavy drinkers.
    (c) may result from relative modest drinking in susceptible fetuses.
    (d) is actually a drug interaction between alcohol and other general depressants.
    (LO 12; p. 98)

19. The general depressants prescribed for insomnia
    (a) provide natural and restful sleep if not used more than a couple of times a week.
    (b) stimulate REM and provide good relief from insomnia.
    (c) cannot result in dependence if used only for inducing sleep.
    (d) depress the amount of REM sleep and reduce the quality of the person's sleep time.
    (LO 12; p. 99)

20. The most serious drug problem in the United States from the perspective of the number of people affected (and damaged) is from
    (a) the opiates.
    (b) cocaine.
    (c) alcohol.
    (d) hallucinogens.
    (LO 12; p. 98)

ANSWERS

1. a, 2. b, 3. c, 4. b, 5. d, 6. a, 7. d, 8. c, 9. a, 10. c, 11. b, 12. a,
13. d, 14. d, 15. b, 16. d, 17. d, 18. c, 19. d, 20. c

SUGGESTED READINGS

Hilgard, E. R. Consciousness in contemporary psychology. *Annual Review of Psychology* 31 (1980): 1–26. An excellent article that explains the history of the study of consciousness in psychology and portends future trends.

Julien, R. M. *A primer of drug action.* San Francisco: W. H. Freeman, 1975. A small paperback that describes in clear language the basic psychological and physiological effects of the major psychoactive drugs.

Moore-Ede, M. C., F. M. Sulzman, and C. A. Fuller. *The clocks that time us: Physiology of the circadian timing system.* Cambridge, MA: Harvard University Press, 1982. An introduction to the role of circadian rhythms in physiology and behavior.

Rosett, H. L., and L. Weiner. *Alcohol and the fetus: a clinical perspective.* New York: Oxford University Press, 1984. A readable book that covers the problem of fetal alcohol syndrome.

Udolf, R. *Forensic hypnosis: Psychological and legal aspects.* Lexington, MA: Lexington Books, 1983. The author is trained in both psychology and law, and he presents his view of the use of hypnosis to memory enhancements in criminal cases.

Webb, W. B. *Sleep: the gentle tyrant.* Englewood Cliffs, NJ: Prentice-Hall, 1975. An old but still very readable and interesting popular account of sleep.

c h a p t e r

4

Sensation and Perception

LEARNING OBJECTIVES

After reading this chapter, the student should be able to

1. define sensation and perception, and explain why they are difficult to separate from one another. **(p. 108)**
2. describe the main components of a sensory system, and explain how scientists investigate their properties. **(p. 108)**
3. diagram the structure of the eye, and label its main parts. **(p. 110)**
4. explain how the visual system processes color information, pattern information, and information about the distance of objects. **(p. 115)**
5. describe the three main parts of the human ear. **(p. 121)**
6. explain the nature of sound and how the human ear is able to transform sound information into neural messages. **(p. 123)**
7. name and describe two types of deafness. **(p. 123)**
8. describe the nature of the skin, and explain what kind of information the receptors in the skin are able to process. **(p. 127)**
9. explain some of the factors that influence our perception of pain and some of the treatments that are used to control pain. **(p. 129)**
10. describe the chemical senses, and show how they are important in communication and in the choice of food. **(p. 132)**
11. describe the general principles of perception first recognized by Gestalt psychologists. **(p. 135)**
12. explain how individual factors, such as previous experience and culture, can influence our perceptions. **(p. 138)**
13. show how the processes of perception and attention are related. **(p. 140)**
14. define ESP, and list several different categories of the phenomenon. **(p. 141)**
15. explain a study that appears to demonstrate the existence of ESP. **(p. 142)**
16. describe some of the reasons why scientists are skeptical about the existence of ESP. **(p. 143)**

The sensory systems are the means by which we receive information about the external and internal environments. There are five basic senses with which most people are familiar: vision, audition, touch, smell, and taste. There are also less widely known sensory systems, such as the vestibular system, which is so important in balance, and some that exist only in a few animals as far as we know, such as the ability of some snakes to detect infrared radiation or the recently discovered ability of some frogs to detect seismic vibrations (Lewis and Narens, 1985).

Vision

The visual system is the means by which we receive information about the patterns of light in our environment. It is the most well-researched sensory system of human beings, and probably the most important. The human visual system shares a number of features with all kinds of sensory systems, whether they exist in frogs, monkeys, or other animals.

Common Features of Vision and Other Sensory Systems

Sensation *refers to the transmission of information about the environment to the brain.* All sensory systems, including vision, are designed to perform this function. Most psychologists view sensation as the events taking place in the eyes, the ears, or the other structures that receive environmental information, including the pathways to the brain. Once the information arrives in the brain, sensation begins to blend with **perception,** *a process that involves the interpretation and integration of incoming sensory information.* Sensation and perception are very closely related events, and there is only an arbitrary distinction between them.

For example, when a black cat crosses the road, the visual system senses a dark object of a certain shape moving in the distance. The neural activity providing this information quickly blends into all the activity that defines and interprets the information, by identifying it as a cat, by attending to its movement into the traffic flow, and perhaps by recalling the association of black cats and bad luck.

The structures of sensory systems all have certain basic features. Each has a **sense organ,** *such as the eye or the ear, that performs the first steps in transforming environmental energy into neural activity.* One of the functions of the ear, for example, is to collect sound waves in the air. *All the sensory systems have* **receptors,** *or specialized neurons that actually perform the transformation of physical energy into neural messages.* **Transduction** *refers to the process by which physical energy originating in the environment is converted to neural signals.* It differs from one sensory system to the next because the nature of the stimulus varies. In vision, the stimulus is light; in the skin senses, the stimulus might be pressure on the skin. Each system also has an afferent pathway of neurons that leads to the appropriate brain areas.

The Sensitivity of Sensory Systems.

One of the characteristics of all sensory systems is their sensitivity, a property that can be measured by **absolute threshold.** *This term refers to the point at which a stimulus becomes too weak for the sensory system to detect it.* At what point does a light, twenty feet away, become too dim for a person to see it? Or, when is a sound too quiet for a bat's ears to detect it? Table 4.1 gives some approximate absolute thresholds for human sensory systems. However, it is important to remember that thresholds vary considerably from one person to the next.

Table 4.1 Some approximate values for absolute thresholds	
Sense	Threshold
Vision	A candle flame seen at 30 miles on a dark, clear night
Hearing	The tick of a watch under quiet conditions at 20 feet
Taste	One teaspoon of sugar in two gallons of water
Smell	One drop of perfume diffused into the entire volume of a six-room apartment
Touch	The wing of a fly falling on your cheek from a distance of one centimeter

From E. Galanter, "Contemporary Psychophysics," in New Directions in Psychology, *by R. Brown, et al. Reprinted by permission.*

In theory, it may seem easy to determine when a person stops seeing a dim light at twenty feet and thus determine the absolute threshold. The experimenter would simply turn on a light, making it dimmer and dimmer for each trial, and ask the subject whether he saw it. In practice, though, there is a range of light intensities of which people are not really sure. Some people who don't mind ambiguity will say that they did see the light even when it is extremely dim. Others want to be very sure, so they say they don't see any light even when they thought they might have. The former would seem to have a much more sensitive visual system than the latter. The difference between the two, however, is not in visual sensitivity; it is in personality, judgment, or other nonsensory variables. *A technique called* **signal detection** *circumvents the problem of individual differences in "willingness to guess" in studies of absolute thresholds. The experimenter occasionally includes a trial in which no signal is presented. Frequent "false alarms," in which the subject says "Yes, I saw the light" when no light appeared, are taken into account in the calculation of sensitivity* (Egan, 1975; Ludel, 1978).

Another measure of sensitivity in a sensory system is the **just noticeable difference,** or **j.n.d.** *This represents how finely tuned a system is, in the sense of how much of a change in the environment is required for the system to detect it.* For example, can a person detect the difference between one and two teaspoons of sugar in a gallon of water? Between a spot of light at 450 nanometers and one at 460 nanometers? Between a 100–gram weight in the hand and a 120–gram weight?

A remarkable feature of the j.n.d. is that it follows **Weber's Law.** *This principle states that the j.n.d. is a constant fraction of stimulus intensity, at least within the intermediate range of intensities for the sensory system.* For example, the j.n.d. for a 100–gram weight might be 2 grams, meaning that a subject holding a 100–gram weight could not reliably distinguish it from weights of 99 grams, 101 grams, or even 101.5 grams. The comparison weight must differ by at least 2 grams. A subject holding a 200–gram weight would have a j.n.d. of 4 grams, so the other weight must be at least 204 grams. And a person holding an 800–gram weight would have a j.n.d. of 8 grams. The constant fraction for weight lifting is 1/50. Other sensory abilities, such as detecting changes in the pitch of a sound, the taste of a sugar solution, the loudness of a tone, or the brightness of a light, have their own fractions.

In practice, Weber's Law means it is easy, for example, to feel the difference when someone adds a can of soda to your day pack, but not to your big backpack. Further, on a three-way light bulb the change from 50 to 100 watts is much more noticeable than the change from 100 to 150.

The Visual Stimulus—Light

Light waves are thought to be a form of electromagnetic radiation, but even physicists do not completely understand them. They travel at a speed of 186,000

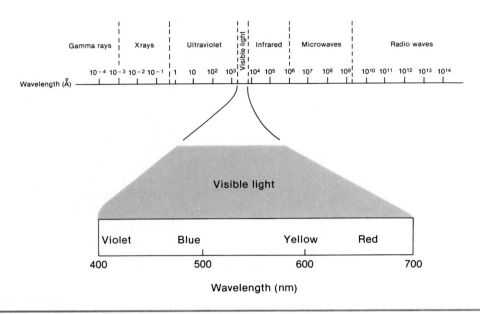

Figure 4.1 *The electromagnetic energy spectrum, with enlargement of the visible portion*

miles per second (300,000 km/sec) and exist in an enormous range of **wavelengths,** *or distance from the peak of one wave to the peak of the next.* Human beings can see only a very small fraction of the electromagnetic radiation present in the environment, including X rays and gamma rays, which have very short wavelengths; infrared rays; radar; and radio waves, which have wavelengths that range to hundreds of meters (fig. 4.1). *The* **visible spectrum** *is the tiny portion of the electromagnetic spectrum visible to the human visual system; it ranges from 380 nanometers (one-billionth of a meter) to 760 nanometers.* Babies and many animals can see almost, but not quite, the same range of wavelengths as adult humans. The visible spectra varies for different organisms. A bee, for example, cannot see red, but it can see ultraviolet wavelengths. And the pit viper has a sensory system that can detect infrared radiation ("see" is probably not the right word). (See Research Box: Infrared "Vision" in Pit Vipers.)

Within the visible spectrum, different wavelengths of light are seen as different colors by animals that have color vision. The shorter light waves appear purple or blue to us, and the longer ones are red. We can only guess what the bee "sees" when it looks at ultraviolet light.

The Structure of the Eye

The eye is the sense organ for vision (fig. 4.2). Most of the structures shown in this diagram are designed to focus or otherwise modify the light waves coming into the eye before they reach the receptors in the back of the eyeball. The **cornea,** for example, *is the transparent protective covering on the front of the eye; it helps to focus the light. The* **iris** *is the part of the eye that has color, and it is a muscle that opens wide or contracts around the pupil, thereby regulating the amount of light that reaches the inside.* The **lens,** *which is the transparent elastic tissue located behind the iris,*

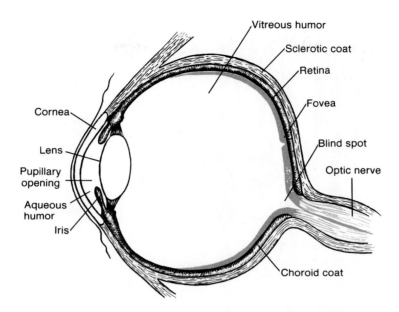

Figure 4.2   A side view of the eye

refracts light rays so they are properly focused on the receptors in the back of the eyeball. The lens can become thicker or thinner and thus "fine tune" the focusing process. Using the process called **accommodation,** *the elastic lens can adjust its shape to focus on nearby or distant objects.* As you get older, lens tissue becomes more brittle and less able to thicken, making it more difficult for you to focus on nearby objects. The lens also has a yellow tint to screen out some of the blue and ultraviolet light, a tint which becomes more dense with age.

Changes in the lens are usually responsible for **cataracts,** *a condition in which the lens tissue becomes cloudy, eventually resulting in blindness.* Cataracts are caused by aging, X rays, and even heat. They are common in glassblowers, for example. The treatment for cataracts is surgical removal of the lens. Before this type of surgery was developed, people with cataracts became permanently blind.

The Retina.   The **vitreous humor** *is a jellylike substance that fills the inside of the eyeball.* It is usually clear, but occasionally it may contain shreds of debris that create shadows in the field of vision. Behind the vitreous humor is the **retina:** *this is the paper-thin layer of receptors and other cells covering the inside back of the eyeball.* You can actually see the retina by shining a flashlight on a person's pupil. Although the pupil looks dark, it is actually almost transparent and only appears dark because there is no source of light inside the eye. Since the retina contains many blood vessels, it will look reddish-pink under the light. If you have ever taken a photograph with a flash camera and found that your subjects had red eyes, you have taken a picture of their retinas. Sometimes the flash attachment on a camera is right next to the camera lens. When you photograph people who are looking directly at the camera, you light

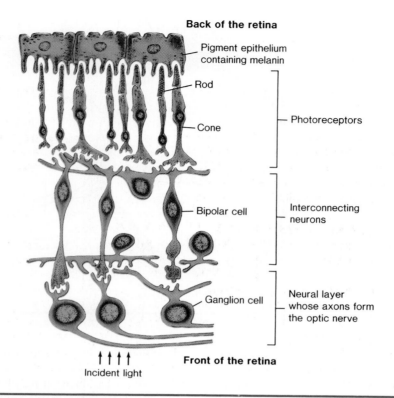

Back of the retina

Pigment epithelium
containing melanin

Rod

Cone ⎤
      ⎬ Photoreceptors
      ⎦

Bipolar cell ⎤
             ⎬ Interconnecting
             ⎦ neurons

Ganglion cell ⎤
              ⎬ Neural layer
              ⎦ whose axons form
                the optic nerve

↑ ↑ ↑ ↑
Incident light   **Front of the retina**

Figure 4.3 A schematic diagram of the human retina

up the portion of the retina that is directly in line with the lens. To avoid this problem, you can buy an extension that moves the flash a few inches further from the lens. Then the flash still goes through the pupil and lights up part of the reddish retina, but not the same part you are photographing.

Rods and Cones.   The retina contains two types of receptors: the rods and the cones (fig. 4.3). At first glance, the diagram may seem odd because the rods and cones appear to be facing away from the direction in which the light is coming. The receptors are inverted, however, because of their heavy requirement for oxygen. They must be close to the bloodstream, and the

blood vessels would block some of the light if the retina were turned over. It is relatively easier for light to pass through the retinal layers, however.

The **rods** *are receptor cells, most of which are located on the periphery of the retina; they are specialized to respond at very low light intensities, though they cannot discriminate between the different wavelengths (colors).* The cones are concentrated in the **fovea,** *or the center of the retina.* **Cones** *are receptor cells that process color information and information about very fine-grained patterns.* When you look at this sentence you are using the cones in your fovea to see the print. Despite its enormous importance to the human visual system, foveal vision covers only a very small part of the visual field—about the diameter of a quarter held at arm's length.

RESEARCH BOX

Infrared "Vision" in Pit Vipers

One of the most unusual sensory systems in the animal kingdom belongs to the pit vipers, which includes rattlesnakes, water moccasins, copperheads, and pythons. These snakes have the ability to detect infrared radiation, or heat, and they use their ability to find and strike at living prey.

Just beneath each eye in the rattlesnake is a pit organ, a small cavity containing a suspended membrane with thousands of tiny temperature-sensitive receptors. Infrared radiation activates these receptors, which pass along the message to the brain. These pit organs apparently evolved from the skin senses, since the receptors appear to be very similar to the temperature-sensitive receptors present in human skin. However, the snake uses them in a way that resembles vision more than touch. The pit organs provide the snake with detailed information about the presence and location of objects in space that are giving off infrared radiation.

Research on rattlesnakes has demonstrated that the information the snake gets from the pit organs is almost unbelievably accurate. The snakes were placed on a pedestal and given small electric shocks to encourage them to strike at the warmed tip of a soldering iron. A videotape camera recorded the strike so its accuracy could be measured. The strikes were usually accurate to within five degrees of the center of the target, even when the snakes' eyes were completely covered. This kind of accuracy is deadly for a mouse, daytime *or* night.

By electrically recording the impulses from the receptors, researchers have been able to determine how sensitive a snake's pit organs actually are. The neurons show a noticeable increase in firing to a human hand located about half a meter away. When water of different temperatures flows directly over the pit organs, the receptors show even greater sensitivity. Changes of only .003 degrees Celsius produce a detectable change in firing rates.

In accordance with their different functions, rods and cones differ in both their quantity and in their distribution in the human eye. There are many more rods than cones in the eye, although rods are totally absent in the fovea. As you leave the foveal region, the density of rods increases rapidly, reaching a peak at about twenty degrees away from the foveal central point. Thereafter, the density of rods diminishes gradually (Osterberg, 1935).

Cones can resolve finely detailed patterns better than rods because of the way in which each receptor passes on its messages to the brain (fig. 4.3). Through their connections with several kinds of intermediate neurons in the retina, information from the 130 million rods and cones eventually converges onto one of the approximately one million **ganglion cells,** *neurons which lead out of the retina toward the brain.* The input from a great many rods converges onto a single ganglion cell. This means that the brain receives only a summary about the activity of individual rods, so the picture it gets is "grainy." In contrast, the brain receives much more detailed information from the cones. One ganglion cell might receive input from only a few cones.

The relationship between the snake's visual system and this infrared detecting system extends beyond analogy. Both visual information and information from the pit organs is transmitted to the same area of the brain, the tectum. This area appears to integrate information coming from various sensory systems to provide a coherent picture of the animal's spatial environment. In mammals, the main sensory organs involved are vision and audition, because these two senses are most important in locating objects in space. But for the snake, the pit organs play a major role in this task. Electrical recording studies of single neurons in the rattlesnake's tectum have shown that this brain area contains several categories of cells, each of which is sensitive to particular kinds of stimulation. One type of cell, for example, responds only when both the eyes *and* the pit organs are stimulated at the same time. Another will respond when either one is stimulated. A third responds to a warm object when the room is lighted, but not when it is dark, and not when the object is thermally neutral.

The tectum seems to be involved in the perception and integration of information related to the spatial environment. In mammals, this brain area contains cells that integrate auditory and visual information. In snakes, there are cells that integrate information from the eyes and the pit organs. Based on what we know about how the tectum integrates sensory information in the snake, the animal's perception of the world must be an odd mixture of "sights" (Newman and Hartline, 1982).

In addition, there are clustered in the fovea a small number of cones (perhaps fifty thousand) that have their very own ganglion cell "pipeline" to the brain.

Transduction in the Receptors

Each time light strikes a rod or a cone, chemical changes take place that result in the release of neurotransmitter by the receptor cell. These events are the most important part of the transduction process in the visual system.

The chemical reactions were first observed by Franz Boll in 1876, when he isolated a brilliant red substance inside the receptor of a frog. This substance was **photopigment,** *a remarkable light-sensitive chemical that loses its color in the light but regains it in the dark because the chemical changes are reversed.* Depending on the animal and the kind of receptor, the nature of the pigment varies. For example, **rhodopsin,** *the photopigment in the human rod,* is transformed into one unstable chemical after another when light strikes the rod. It finally breaks apart into **retinal and opsin,** *which are rhodopsin's two principal components.* It is this chemical breakdown of rhodopsin that causes electrical disturbances in the membrane of the receptor and triggers a change in the neuron's release of neurotransmitter. Light energy is thus transformed into a neural message.

In the dark, the retinal and opsin are synthesized back into rhodopsin, provided enough Vitamin A is present. People whose diets are deficient in this vital chemical sometimes suffer from **night-blindness,** *a condition in which the rods do not function properly* (Wald, 1968).

The process of transduction in cones is not quite so well understood. The pigments of the cones contain retinal and one of three different opsins. Each of the three kinds of opsin is sensitive to light at different wavelengths, making it possible for cones to respond differently depending on the color of the light, as we shall discuss in a later section.

Dark Adaptation. **Dark adaptation** *refers to the time during which the receptors are resynthesizing their pigments and becoming sensitive to light once again.* The process occurs at different rates in rods and cones, again showing the distinction between these two types of receptors. When you look at a bright light and then go into a dark room, your ability to see a dim spot of light gradually improves. During the first ten minutes the cones adapt as much as they can, but the rods continue to adapt. You can no longer tell the color of the dim light, but you can see dimmer and dimmer lights as your rods adapt to the dark. It usually takes about thirty minutes for the rods to recover completely. If the eyes are exposed to a bright light again, both the rods and cones will become much less sensitive to dim light. The curves in figure 4.4 have distinct components—one that represents the dark adaptation of the cones, and another that represents the rods.

Soldiers are trained to make sure both their rods and cones remain dark adapted (though they may not realize it). When they throw a grenade at night, they cover one eye and watch with the other. Then the bright

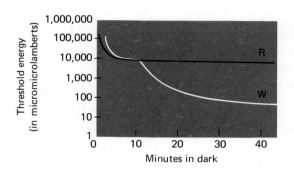

Figure 4.4 Dark adaptation curves

light of the explosion only causes the breakdown of the photopigment in the rods and cones of one eye while the pigment in the other remains dark adapted.

Seeing Patterns

Seeing patterns, such as the words on this page, involves the activity of neurons all along the visual pathway to the brain. As the information from the rods and cones travels from the receptors to the ganglion cells and then to the brain, it is summarized, modified, enhanced, exaggerated, and deleted. Because of all the changes, what you actually perceive is not quite the same as what was originally sensed at the level of the receptor. A great deal of information processing occurs throughout the pathway from the receptor to the brain.

Receptive Fields. The visual system, and other sensory systems as well, organizes the incoming information by using receptive fields. **The receptive field** *of a cell in a sensory pathway is the area in the environment in which the presentation of a stimulus will cause a change in the cell's firing rate.* For example, the receptive field of a ganglion cell is a specific area in the visual field. When a light stimulus appears in that area, the ganglion cell will change its firing rate. Since a ganglion cell receives input from a great many receptors, it acts as a kind of clearinghouse for information from a particular zone on the retina.

Some pioneering studies on cats (Kuffler, 1953) demonstrated how the receptive field organization leads to an enhancement of contrast. An electrode was inserted directly into the ganglion cell of an anesthetized cat, and records of that cell's firing pattern were made as the cat's eye was stimulated with light. When a tiny spot of light appeared in most places on a screen in front of the cat, the ganglion cell did not change its firing rate. But when the light appeared in a small area where the spot was hitting the ganglion cell's receptive field, the cell made three different kinds of responses.

When the light appeared directly in the center of the field, the response was an immediate burst of spikes followed by a return to normal when the light was turned off. When the light appeared in the outer portion of the field, or surround, the cell showed no response until the light was turned off; then it showed a rapid burst of firing. In a small ring between the center of the field and the outer portion, both the onset and the offset of a light caused a short burst of firing. This pattern of response became known as "center-on, surround-off". Later studies found that if a light appeared in the center and the surround at the same time, the cell showed no response (Rodieck and Stone, 1965). This kind of organization means that the ganglion cell is comparing the brightness of the center spot to the brightness of the surround. When the contrast between the two is maximal, the cell will give the greatest response.

Feature Detectors.   The work of Nobel prizewinners David Hubel and Torsten Wiesel has led to many exciting discoveries about how neurons in the brain process visual patterns. Using single-cell recordings, they demonstrated the presence of **feature detectors,** *a term used to describe cells in the visual cortex that change their firing rates in response to specific stimuli located in their receptive fields* (Hubel and Wiesel, 1959, 1962, 1965). **Simple cells** *were one type of feature detector; these cells increased their firing rates most vigorously when a straight line or bar was shown in the cell's receptive field.* As the bar was turned, the cell's response diminished. Hubel and Wiesel hypothesized that simple cells were receiving input from groups of cells in the brain that had overlapping circular receptive fields, arranged in a line.

Complex cells *comprised another group of feature detectors; these visual cortical cells responded best when the stimulus was a line that was turned in a certain orientation and moving in a specific direction.* Some cells even showed "preferences" for bars of a specific length. These might be receiving their input from groups of simple cells with overlapping receptive fields.

The visual area of the brain seems to be mapped in a very logical and hierarchical way, with neurons that respond to adjacent receptive fields right next to one another. In a remarkable study that demonstrated the orderliness of the brain, a monkey was injected with a **2-DG,** *a radioactive form of glucose that is taken up in great quantities by active neurons.* Since the substance cannot get out of the cells once it gets in, a search for radioactivity in the brain tissue will reveal which neurons were active and which ones were not. After the injection, the retina was stimulated with a pattern of vertical lines. A picture of the brain tissue showed radioactive "columns" in the visual area of the monkey's brain, indicating that the columns of neurons were the ones responding to the vertical lines (Hubel, Wiesel, and Stryker, 1978).

Feature detectors are designed to detect specific features in the environment, hence their name. Later in this chapter we will see that the nature of feature detectors can be changed by the environment. The work involving feature detectors is extremely important because it is the first step in bridging the gap between sensation and perception.

Seeing in Color

The ability to see in color is not unique to humans. Many birds, fish, other primates, insects, some snakes, and even the octopus can see color, although their eyes are not necessarily like the human eye. The way humans see color was for a long time a source of controversy, generating two major theories. One was called the trichromatic theory, and the other was the opponent process theory. As it turned out, both were correct. Color vision in human beings is based on two different processes—one that works in the retina and another that codes color in the brain.

Trichromatic Theory.   Cones come in three different types, each of which is most sensitive to a particular range of wavelengths. There are cones that are most sensitive to light in the blue range, in the green range, and in the red range (Marks, et al., 1964). For example, when blue light reaches the retina, the blue-sensitive cones react the most and produce changes in the firing rates of the neurons they are connected to. The **trichromatic theory** *predicted the existence of three classes of cones in the retina, and their selective activation by red, blue, and green, as a means to transform color information in the environment into neural signals.* Colors other than red, blue, or green are produced by mixtures of those three and by activity in more than one kind of cone. Purple light produces a response in both blue- and red-sensitive cones, for example.

This very elegant system of color vision was first proposed in 1802 by Thomas Young and later modified by Hermann von Helmholtz. But its verification had to wait for the invention of **microspectrophotometry,** *a technique that could measure light absorption in individual cones.* A tiny beam of light is shone on a single cone, and the amount of light reflected back is measured. Whatever wavelengths are not reflected back are absorbed. Tests of many cones demonstrated that they tended to fall into one of three categories, each most sensitive to a different color (Marks, et al., 1964).

Opponent Process Theory.   Another new technology involving single-cell electrical recording from visual areas of the monkey brain demonstrated the way the brain codes color (DeValois, et al., 1966). Four different kinds of cells were found, each of which responded to not one, but two colors, by a change in firing rate. One kind increased its firing rate when the animal was looking at green but slowed down when it was looking at red. Another increased for red but slowed down for green. The third and fourth kinds responded to blue and yellow by speeding up or slowing down. The **opponent process theory** *had originally predicted that individual cells could code information about two separate colors by slowing their firing rates for one color and speeding up for the other.* Both the trichromatic and the opponent process theories were correct, but for different parts of the visual system.

The opponent process theory explains the occurrence of **negative afterimages** very well. *These are afterimages that appear a different color than the original stimulus.* If you looked at a red square for about thirty seconds, then looked at a white space, you would see a green square about the same size. The green square, of course, would not be on the paper but in your brain. It is produced by the sudden increase (or decrease) in the firing rate of those brain cells that had changed their firing rate for red. The sudden change in the opposite direction signals green, so you "see" a green square.

The way the visual system moves from a trichromatic coding system to an opponent process system is complicated. One theory proposes a special kind of neural wiring diagram in which an opponent process cell in the brain would receive input from all three kinds of cones, but some of the input is inhibitory and some is excitatory (Hurvich and Jameson, 1974). For example, a red-green opponent process cell might receive excitatory input from blue and red cones and inhibitory input from green cones.

The engineers who designed color television used a similar "wiring diagram" (Coren, Porac, and Ward, 1979). The color in the TV studio is first broken down into three components (red, green, and blue) by the camera. Then it is transformed into two "opponent process" signals instead of three. When it reaches your TV set, it is transformed back into the red, green, and blue signals.

Most people who are color-blind see some color, but they have difficulty distinguishing certain colors. The most common form of color blindness is a result of the absence of normal red-sensitive cones (Frome, et al., 1982). People with this type of color blindness have trouble distinguishing red from green. A much rarer variety of color blindness occurs when only one type of cone functions; these people see the world entirely in black, white, and shades of gray.

Seeing Depth and Distance

Although the retina has only two dimensions, human beings process information in three. *We use two different kinds of cues to see depth:* **monocular cues,** *based on the cues available to one eye, and* **binocular cues,** *which take advantage of the fact that we have two eyes spaced slightly apart.*

The monocular cues are based primarily on experience, a topic we will discuss again later in this chapter. For example, we learn that people are larger than cats, so when we see them together, we can judge their distance by making some unconscious calculations. If the image of the cat is very large on the retina, relative to the image of the person, we assume that the cat is closer. Another monocular cue involves the perception of detail. Objects we perceive as clear and detailed are probably closer than objects that seem fuzzy.

The most important cues for depth, however, come from the use of two eyes. Aircraft pilots are medically grounded if they lose sight in one eye, even temporarily, because of their urgent need for extremely precise depth perception. Monocular cues are simply not enough.

Convergence *is a kind of binocular cue for depth that uses information supplied by the muscles that move the eyes.* When you look at an object close to the end of your nose, you can feel the contraction of the muscles that pull your eyes toward the nose. The muscles that pull your eyes outward, toward the temples, are contracted when you view an object in the distance. These muscles send signals to the brain, thereby providing important information about the distance of the object.

The most important cue for judging distance comes from **stereoscopic vision,** *which refers to the fact that the two eyes see overlapping but slightly different views of the world.* The closer the object is, the more different are the views that the two eyes see. If you hold your finger about five inches from your nose and then alternately close one eye then the other, you can appreciate stereoscopic vision. Although the cue is processed unconsciously, it is a vital one for judging distance.

The 3-D viewers that children play with create stereoscopic vision artificially. The cameras that take the pictures that you use 3-D viewers to look at are built so that they can simultaneously take two pictures of the same scene; the pictures are taken from slightly different angles. The picture displaced to the left appears only to the left eye in the viewer, and the right eye sees only the one displaced to the right. The visual cortex fuses the two images, creating the illusion of depth. Thus, it is just as though the person were really seeing the image with his or her own two (slightly separated) eyes.

The visual cortex appears to contain cells designed to process the stereoscopic information coming in from the two eyes. Most of the simple cells that Hubel and Wiesel investigated in monkeys responded only to a stimulus in one eye. The complex cells showed more preference. Some responded to input from one eye only, others to the other eye, and some to both, although most showed a preference for one eye or the other. There are also, however, some cells that apparently play an important role in depth perception. These are strictly binocular, in the sense that they will only respond when both eyes are stimulated simultaneously (Clarke and Whitteridge, 1978). Significantly, they tend to respond best when a stimulus is almost, but not quite, in the same location of the visual field of both eyes, a feature that suggests they are responding to stereoscopic information. Various studies have demonstrated that such cells exist in humans as well (Hitchcock and Hickey, 1980; Sloane and Blake, 1984).

Visual Problems

Even the federal government recognizes the importance of vision; blindness is the only sensory handicap that earns an extra tax exemption. Although total blindness is not very common, more than six percent of the people in the United States have a visual impairment that limits their activities in some way.

One of the most common visual disorders is nearsightedness. People who are nearsighted cannot focus properly on objects in the distance because their eyeballs are elongated. The image is focused just in front of the retina. Farsightedness in young people is usually caused by the opposite problem—short eyeballs. In older people it may be caused by changes in the lens. Eyeglasses correct both problems.

Glassblower's cataract is not the only occupational hazard related to vision. Staring at video display terminals (VDTs) can cause various visual disorders. Complaints about VDTs have increased steadily over the past few years, and government agencies are studying the possible health risks. People who work with the computer displays report more visual fatigue, headaches, blurry vision, eye strain, and burning sensations in the eyes than do other people (Dainoff, et al., 1981), and some say their color vision is affected after watching the screen for long periods of time. No one is quite certain why VDTs should produce these visual problems, but it may be partly due to the dot matrix letters. The eye may continually try to focus the letters better in a futile attempt to produce a clear image. It may also be a result of the stress associated with computerizing an office.

GUIDED REVIEW

Learning Objectives 1, 2, 3, and 4

1. Sensory systems are the means by which information about the environment is transmitted to the brain, a process called _____ . Sensory systems include _____ , the specialized cells that change physical energy into changes in neural firing rates; a _____ , which modifies the physical energy before it reaches the receptors; and a pathway of neurons that lead from the sense organ to the brain.

2. The sensitivity of a sensory system can be measured by _____ , a value that refers to the weakest or least intense stimulus that can be detected. Absolute thresholds are not single numbers but a range in which the subject is not sure that the stimulus has been presented.

3. _____ is a technique used to measure sensitivity. It takes into account the fact that people vary in their willingness to guess about the presence of a stimulus when they are not sure.

4. Sensitivity of sensory systems is also characterized by the _____ , which represents the amount of change in the environmental stimulus that is required for the individual to notice the change. _____ states that the j.n.d. is a constant fraction of stimulus intensity.

5. The stimulus for the visual system is light. Light waves have different _____ , and human beings can only see certain wavelengths of light, called the _____ . Different wavelengths of light are seen as different colors.

6. The eye is the sense organ for vision; some important structures include the _____ , the _____ , the _____ , and the _____ .

7. The _____ is the layer of receptor cells in the back of the eyeball. There are two types of receptors: the _____ , which are specialized for night vision, and the _____ , which see color and finely detailed patterns.

8. The receptors are connected to the _____ , which lead out of the optic nerve to the brain.

9. The process of transduction in the rods involves the breakdown of the _____ , which, in human rods, is _____ . When the molecule of rhodopsin breaks into _____ and _____ , the receptor's release of neurotransmitter is altered. Rhodopsin is resynthesized in the dark.

10. The process of _____ involves the recovery of the photopigment molecules. It is faster for rods than for cones, and the difference can be measured through behavioral tests of visual sensitivity.

11. The _____ organization of cells in the visual system enhances contour and contrast by special sensitivity to light onsets and offsets and to differences in brightness between adjacent areas on the retina. Receptive fields of ganglion cells are circular, with a center region and a surround.

12. Cells in the cortex, sometimes called _____ , have preferred stimuli, such as bars, moving bars, or lines in specific orientations.

13. Color vision in human beings is explained by two different theories: the _____ and the _____ theory. The trichromatic theory predicts that there are three types of receptors, each sensitive to a different wavelength of light. The opponent process theory

predicts that each cell is responsive to a pair of colors (red-green, blue-yellow). The trichromatic theory is correct for the retina, and the opponent process theory is correct for cells in the brain that process color.

14. The ability of humans to perceive depth and distance is due to _____ and _____ cues, which involve the use of one eye and both eyes, respectively. Monocular cues include the use of knowledge about the size of objects. Binocular cues include _____ , in which the brain receives signals from the eye muscles. Organisms with two eyes having overlapping fields of vision have _____ , and the disparity between the two views provides an important cue to distance.

15. Some common visual problems include color blindness, usually caused by an absence of functional red-sensitive cones; nearsightedness and farsightedness, caused by eyeballs that are too long or too short, respectively; and _____ , or clouding of the lens tissue. Frequent use of video display terminals (VDT's) may also produce visual problems.

ANSWERS

1. sensation; receptors; sense organ 2. absolute thresholds 3. Signal detection 4. just noticeable difference (j.n.d.); Weber's law 5. wavelengths; visible spectrum 6. cornea, iris, pupil, lens 7. retina; rods; cones 8. ganglion cells 9. photopigment; rhodopsin; retinal, opsin 10. dark adaptation 11. receptive field 12. feature detectors 13. trichromatic theory, opponent process 14. monocular, binocular; convergence; stereoscopic vision 15. cataract

Audition

Audition *is the sense of hearing.* The human auditory system is very efficient at some tasks and less so at others, just like our other sensory systems. Human ears are able to detect rapid changes in sounds, though the range of sounds they can hear is limited, compared to animals like dogs or bats. To understand language, we need to be able to hear rapid changes, so our hearing abilities are just right for us. Our ears are also able to locate the source of a sound, though again they are not the best in the animal kingdom. The barn owl is much better at this than we are (Knudsen, 1981). Imagine a barn owl hunting for mice at night and then diving for

its prey. You can see why it needs a keen ability to locate sound. A small error in judgment could mean simply a missed meal, or it could mean a suicidal dive into the ground at top speed.

Sound

Sound *is the physical energy in the environment that is transformed by the auditory system.* Sound waves are produced when things vibrate in air or water (for example, vocal cords, gongs, or clarinet reeds). When something vibrates, it causes the molecules around it to collide with one another, pushing molecules forward in wavelike motions. *Sound waves consist of alternate*

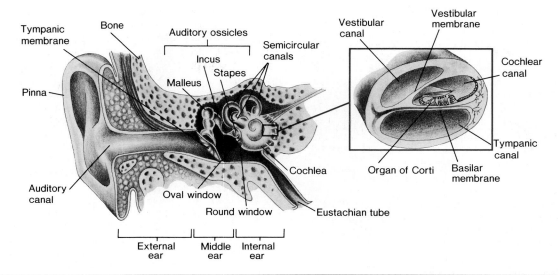

Figure 4.5   The human ear

compressions, *in which the air molecules are pushed closer together, followed by* **rarefactions,** *in which the molecules spread out.* Just as waves move through water for long distances without actually moving the molecules of water themselves for more than a few inches, sound waves travel through air or other media. The air molecules themselves only move back and forth over very short distances, but the alternations of compressions and rarefactions may travel for miles. Sound waves cannot travel in a vacuum because there are no molecules.

The **frequency** *of a simple sound wave represents the number of alternating compressions and rarefactions passing through a given point over a period of time.* It is usually measured in **Hertz,** *or cycles per second.* **Pitch** *refers to the way the physical stimulus is experienced by human beings, and it roughly equates to the sound's frequency.* High pitches are associated with rapid vibrations, and lower base notes are associated with slower vibrations. The spoken voice is usually around 1000 Hz. If you think that a 20,000 Hz

tone is high, imagine what the bat hears when it is listening to a sound at 150,000 Hz. Although the barn owl can locate sounds very well, it can only hear sounds ranging from about 100 to 12,000 Hz. (Superior abilities in one area are usually offset by inferior abilities in another.)

Most of the sounds we hear every day are complex mixtures of many sound waves with varying frequencies and other characteristics. The sound of speech, for example, is not a single sound wave at 1000 Hz; it is an intricate blend of many sound waves.

The Ear

The sense organ for hearing is the ear, shown in figure 4.5. The ear has three main parts: (a) the **outer ear,** *which is the exterior part that collects the sound waves;* (b) the **middle ear,** *which contains several important bones that amplify and transmit the sound waves;* and (c) the **inner ear,** *which contains the sensory receptors for audition.*

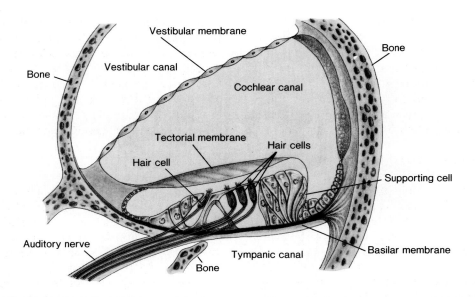

Bone

Vestibular membrane

Vestibular canal

Cochlear canal

Bone

Tectorial membrane

Hair cells

Hair cell

Supporting cell

Auditory nerve

Tympanic canal

Basilar membrane

Bone

Figure 4.6   A cross section of part of the cochlea, showing the basiliar membrane and the hair cells

Sound waves follow a path from the outer ear through the **auditory canal,** *the long passageway leading from the outer ear to the middle ear.* The **tympanic membrane** *is located at the end of the auditory canal; it is set into vibratory motion by the incoming sound wave.* The motion of the tympanic membrane sets the **malleus, incus,** and **stapes** into motion. *These are the three bones of the middle ear that transmit the vibrations from the tympanic membrane to the fluid of the inner ear.*

When you have a cold, you may have trouble hearing because the tissue in the middle ear becomes inflamed from the infection and blocks the passage of air. For the eardrum to vibrate normally, the pressure of the air on both sides of the drum must be equal. Since the inflamed tissue interferes with the movement of air in this area, it also prevents the eardrum from vibrating properly. The hearing difficulty that most people experience when they are flying on an airplane is also due to pressure differences on either side of the eardrum.

The stapes (from the Latin word meaning "stirrup"), rests its footplate on the **oval window,** *a membrane of the inner ear that receives the sound vibrations coming from the middle ear.* The vibration in the stapes sets the oval window into motion, which then sets the fluid of the coiled cochlea into motion. The snail-shaped **cochlea** *forms the inner ear and contains the receptor cells for hearing.* The receptor cells are located along the **basilar membrane,** *a long membrane inside the cochlea which follows its curvature.* When the fluid inside the cochlea begins to vibrate, it sets the basilar membrane into motion; it is this motion and the deformation of the membrane that causes the receptor cells to release neurotransmitter. **Hair cells** *are the receptors for hearing; they are located along the basilar membrane in the cochlea* (fig. 4.6).

The inner ear contains the receptors for another sensory system besides audition: the **vestibular system.** *The main functions of this system are to provide information about head orientation and movement, which* *is useful in maintaining upright posture and controlling eye movements.* It is not well known because the sensations arising from it rarely reach the level of consciousness, although they do appear to cause motion sickness in some circumstances. For example, the astronauts have become painfully aware of this sensory system, since they sometimes suffer from the disorder described in the Application Box: Space Motion Sickness.

The **semicircular canals** and the **vestibule** *are the two main components of the vestibular system,* shown in figure 4.5. The canals are oriented in three different planes; when you rotate your head in one of the planes, such as by shaking your head "no," you cause movement in the fluid of the canal oriented in that direction. The fluid movement stimulates the receptor cells located inside the canals. The sacs inside the vestibule have receptors that are embedded in a gelatinous mass. When the orientation of the head shifts, the mass shifts with it and stimulates the receptors.

The Coding of Sound

Nobel prize winner Georg von Bekesy worked out the details of how the basilar membrane responds to sounds of different frequencies (Bekesy, 1949). He discovered a fairly close relationship between the frequency of a sound and the place on the basilar membrane that was most deformed in response to that sound. Low-frequency sounds produce the most deformation of the membrane near the stapes, whereas high-frequency sounds deform the membrane further away. Thus, the frequency of a sound is coded at the level of the receptors; different receptors respond to sounds of different frequencies.

The way organisms are able to determine where a sound is coming from involves the distance between the two ears. If someone snaps his fingers while standing at your left side, the sound wave will reach the left ear first. If the finger snapper is standing in front of you, the sound wave will reach both ears at the same time.

If the sound comes from the right, the wave will reach your right ear first. The brain relies on these time differences to determine where in space the sound originated (Licklider, 1959). In fact, the human brain can detect differences down to a fraction of a millisecond, making it possible to identify with incredible accuracy the direction from which the sound wave is coming. (Wallach, Newman, and Rosenzweig, 1949).

Hearing Problems

You can get some idea what it might be like to be blind by covering your eyes. To understand what a profound hearing loss might be like, imagine sitting in on a conversation with friends and being able to see their lips moving and see them laughing but being unable to hear them.

There are two general kinds of deafness. One is **conduction deafness:** *it results when the receptor cells for audition are intact but there is a problem somewhere along the route from the eardrum to the cochlea.* A person with this kind of deafness would not be able to hear sounds conducted in air but would be able to hear a tuning fork vibrating against his or her skull. The sound waves can be transmitted through the bones of the skull and set the cochlear fluid in motion. The hearing difficulty associated with a common cold falls into this category. **Nerve deafness** is *due to damage to the receptors in the cochlea or to the auditory nerve.* The sound waves arrive at the cochlea, but for some reason the hair cells of the basilar membrane fail to send messages to the brain. The progressive degeneration of the hair cells would cause nerve deafness. Usually, the receptors responsive to the higher-frequency sounds (furthest away from the stapes) are the first to begin degenerating.

The stress and isolation of deafness is severe and sometimes even leads to mental illness. Particularly when a person starts to lose his hearing later in life and is not aware of it, he may begin to think people are deliberately whispering to prevent him from hearing.

APPLICATION BOX

Space Motion Sickness

On December 21, 1968, the Apollo 8 spacecraft was launched from Cape Canaveral on a Saturn V. It was the first time human beings tried to orbit the moon, and the three man crew successfully reached lunar orbit on Christmas Eve. The historic mission was commanded by Frank Borman. One of the first things he did after the spacecraft left earth was throw up.

This embarrassing malady was not limited to the Apollo 8 commander. Space motion sickness, as it is called, has afflicted almost half of the astronauts and cosmonauts in one form or another. The Soviets have had as much trouble with this problem as the Americans. Titov experienced nausea and vomiting on the Soviet Vostok mission in 1962. Symptoms usually begin the first day in space and sometimes last as long as a week. Although the condition does not seem to be serious, it can certainly be disabling to an astronaut who has important work to accomplish.

On longer missions, such as those of Skylab or Soyuz, when the astronauts and cosmonauts stay in space for months at a time, space motion sickness does not present too much of a problem. Missing two or three days of work at the beginning of the mission is inefficient, but it doesn't threaten the success of the entire mission. For the Space Shuttle crew, however, space motion sickness is a much more serious hazard. This spaceship was designed to make short, busy missions lasting about a week. If half the crew is debilitated by nausea and vomiting for two or three days, the mission's goals will be in jeopardy. NASA is focusing considerable attention on learning more about the disorder, especially on finding ways to predict it, treat it, and prevent it.

This kind of motion sickness appears to be only remotely related to seasickness. Astronauts who are totally immune to motion sickness in normal gravity sometimes show extreme susceptibility to space sickness in zero gravity, making it extremely difficult to predict who the next victim will be. Therefore, NASA can't easily solve the problem by testing astronauts on the

---

Symptoms of paranoia may result. This mental illness makes people more hostile, suspicious, and arrogant (see Chapter 13).

Philip Zimbardo and his colleagues demonstrated the relationship between hearing loss and paranoia experimentally (Zimbardo, et al., 1981). Three groups of college men with normal hearing were hypnotized and given posthypnotic suggestions. One group (the control) was told they would have itchy ears. A second group (the experimental) was told they would have a partial hearing loss. Hearing loss was also suggested to the third group, but they were aware of the suggestion.

The subjects in the experimental group became more irritated, hostile, and unfriendly, compared to the subjects in either control group, demonstrating that hearing loss can very quickly produce personality problems, particularly if the person is unaware of the sensory deficit.

ground and eliminating those who are susceptible to motion sickness in boats, cars, or airplanes.

Treating space-sick astronauts has not been very successful either. The remedy that has been used is called ScopeDex, a combination of scopolamine and Dexedrine. The scopolamine helps eliminate the nausea, and the Dexedrine counteracts the drowsiness and lethargy that are side effects of the scopolamine. Unfortunately, this drug helps only some of the astronauts.

Another promising technique is **biofeedback,** a procedure that has been successful in treating motion sickness in air crews. Subjects learn to control their autonomic responses, including stomach queasiness, as they are gradually exposed to more and more provocative stimulation. While sitting in a rotating chair, they receive feedback about some of their ongoing biological processes and attempt to voluntarily modify them. (See Chapter 5 for a more complete description of biofeedback.)

Much of NASA's interest is very practical; the agency would like to have either effective countermeasures for the disorder or successful predictive tests. But some of their research is devoted to understanding the basic nature of the phenomenon. Many scientists now think that the problem is due to the unusual barrage of sensory signals that the brain receives in a weightless environment. Two sensory systems seem to be involved—the visual system, which normally receives input in a "head up" orientation but which receives input in all directions in space; and the vestibular system in the inner ear, the sense organ that detects gravity on earth and tells the brain which way is "up." In the weightless environment of space, both of these systems are receiving strange and unfamiliar information, and probably more important, their signals conflict with one another. The result, for reasons no one understands, is uncomfortable feelings in the stomach, nausea, and vomiting.

Loss of hearing in older adults is an extremely difficult handicap and may cause personality problems. But in children, hearing problems are even more tragic because they interfere with language development. Psychologists know very little about what the best methods are for training deaf children to communicate. Some believe that they should not learn sign language because it might lessen their motivation for the incredibly difficult task of learning to speak. They argue that learning to speak offers the deaf child the best hope of becoming part of normal society. Others, who are equally adamant, believe that deaf children should learn "total communication," which includes both sign language and oral speech. (See fig. 4.7.) They feel that sign language allows a child to communicate better at home (if, of course, the rest of the family uses it), and at an earlier age. Because it becomes more and more difficult to learn language as a child gets older, the

Figure 4.7 *Communicating with the deaf using sign language*

ability to communicate early is crucial. Unfortunately, factual information on the success of each method is scarce (Benderly, 1980).

The structures of the ear can be damaged by a staggering variety of microbes, mishaps, and mistreatments. Genetic defects account for a large number of hearing losses. Infections in a pregnant woman are a leading cause of deafness in infants. From 1963 to 1965 there was an epidemic of German measles in the United States; the number of deaf children born during those years doubled. Furthermore, certain drugs, such as streptomycin, taken during pregnancy may produce nerve deafness by causing degeneration of the hair-cell receptors, thereby affecting hearing in babies. After birth, children and young adults can suffer hearing loss from meningitis, drugs such as streptomycin, and even the common cold with ear infections.

Noise pollution is another leading cause of hearing loss. Soldiers, police officers, riveters, rock stars, airplane mechanics, and anyone who works with frequent loud noise usually has at least some hearing loss. Once it became clear that noise could damage the receptor cells in the ear, Congress passed the Walsh-Healey Public Contracts Act in 1970. This law specifies how loud the noise in factories, offices, and apartment buildings can be. The **decibel** *is the unit used to measure noise intensity levels, and table 4.2 gives some examples of how loud various noises are in decibels (dB).*

No law can prevent people from willingly exposing themselves to loud noises, though, and amplified music is one of the major causes of noise-induced hearing loss. It is probably not an exaggeration to say that many twenty-year-olds who listen to rock music have hearing equivalent to that of a person who is fifty years old. The Walsh-Healey Act allows exposure to 110 dB for no longer than thirty minutes per day, but rock music fans often expose themselves to louder noises for much longer periods. Once the receptor cells for hearing are destroyed, they cannot be replaced. The hearing losses produced by noise are permanent.

Table 4.2 The decibel levels for some common sounds		
Decibel	Type of sound	Times as loud as 0 dB
0	The least sound heard by a normal human ear	—
10	The rustle of leaves in a light breeze	10
20	An average whisper four feet away from hearer	100
50	Average residence	100,000
60	Normal conversation at three feet	1,000,000
90	A moderate discotheque	1,000,000,000
110	A pneumatic drill	100,000,000,000
120	A jet engine	1,000,000,000,000

From B. Tannenbaum and M. Stillman, Understanding Sound. *Copyright* © *1973 McGraw-Hill Book Company. Reprinted by permission.*

GUIDED REVIEW

Learning Objectives 5, 6, and 7

1. The auditory system transforms _____ in the environment into neural messages. Frequency of sound waves is measured in _____ and roughly equates to our sensation of _____ .

2. The sense organ for hearing is the ear. Sound waves set the _____ into motion, and the vibrating membrane sets the bones of the middle ear—the _____ , _____ , and _____ —into motion. These bones produce wavelike motion in the fluid in the _____ and set the _____ into motion along the length of the cochlea.

3. The receptor cells for hearing are _____ cells, located on the basilar membrane. Movement of the membrane and of the fluid in the cochlea causes the receptor cells to release neurotransmitter, thereby changing the sound waves into neural messages.

4. The portion of the basilar membrane near the _____ is deformed most in response to low-frequency sounds; higher-frequency sounds cause deformation of the membrane progressively further away from the stapes.

5. Deafness is classified into two types: _____ , in which sound waves do not reach the receptors, and _____ , in which the abnormality is in the receptors or auditory nerve.

6. Hearing loss may be caused by genetic problems, prenatal infections, reactions to drugs, and noise pollution. Noise levels are measured in _____ .

ANSWERS

1. sound waves; Hertz; pitch 2. tympanic membrane; malleus, incus, stapes; cochlea; basilar membrane 3. hair 4. stapes 5. conduction deafness; nerve deafness 6. decibels

Touch, Smell, and Taste

The senses of touch, smell, and taste are not as well-understood as vision and audition, although they also play vital roles in our lives. Imagine being unable to feel temperature changes in your hands and getting frostbitten every winter.

The Skin Senses

The part of the skin you can feel on the outside of your body is really only a fraction of your skin. The **epidermis,** *or outer layer of skin,* covers the **dermis,** *which is the inner layer of skin that contains most of the receptors for touch, temperature, and pain* (fig. 4.8).

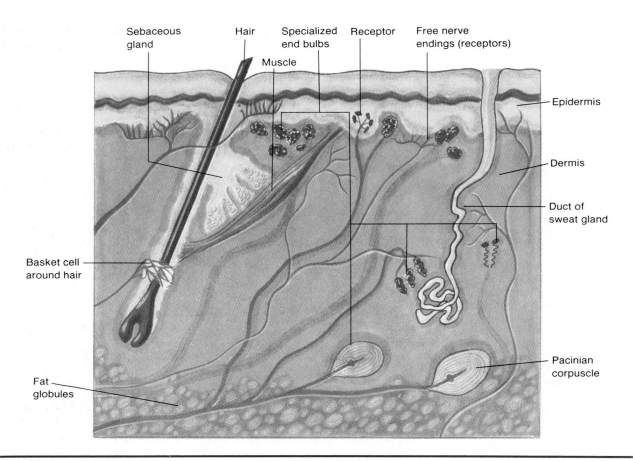

Figure 4.8 *A cross section of skin*

Skin contains an enormous variety of structures, and many of these are receptors. It would be convenient if touch, temperature, and pain information were each handled by a different receptor, but this is not the case. *One kind of receptor in the skin, called the* **Pacinian corpuscle,** *seems to transform changes in mechanical pressure on the skin into neural information.* But the other receptors do not appear to be related to a single kind of sensation; they seem to respond to more than one kind of stimulation.

Information from the skin receptors is organized very logically by the nervous system. For instance, sensations from the right leg are kept separate from those coming from the left, and those are kept separate from information coming from the right arm. The brain receives the information according to where it comes from on the body and processes it in the parietal lobes. Even in the brain, though, the information from different parts of the body is kept together. As we saw in Chapter 2, the amount of brain tissue devoted to processing sensations from a particular body area is related to the sensitivity of that area, rather than its size. For example, the amount of parietal lobe tissue that processes information from the fingers is proportionately quite large compared to the amount devoted to processing information from the torso.

The Special Sense of Pain

A young woman in Canada could take a bath in ice water or in water that was almost boiling. Electric shocks didn't bother her. Neither pinches, punches, burns, needles, nor dental drills produced any response from her. For as long as she could remember, she had never felt any pain.

As a child, she bit off the tip of her tongue; she also suffered third-degree burns on her legs when she knelt on a radiator to gaze out a window. She had severe problems in her joints because she rarely shifted her weight from one foot to another. She only lived to the age of twenty-nine (Melzack and Wall, 1965).

Pain is the body's way of telling us something is wrong. It is an extremely important warning system that helps to prevent further damage by triggering some appropriate behavior. For example, when you feel pain in your joints, you shift your position—this action prevents you from stressing those joints to the point of permanent damage.

Although it is clear why we need pain to survive, it is not clear what pain is. The sensation of pain depends in part on the nature of the stimulus. Damage to the tissues apparently activates pain receptors; but pain is not always proportional to the extent of tissue damage. The same stimulus can produce very different reactions in different people, and also in the same person at different times.

For example, on a hiking trip in the Himalayas, the responses of the Nepalese porters to electric shocks was compared to the responses of the Western hikers (Clark and Clark, 1980). The abilities of the Nepalese and the Westerners to detect the low-current shocks did not differ, but it took much higher voltage levels for the Nepalese to describe the shocks as "faint pain" or "very painful." The Nepalese interpreted the sensations differently, perhaps because they lived under harsher conditions.

Stress can affect the perception of pain as well. A phenomenon called **stress-induced analgesia,** *in which an organism's sensitivity to painful stimulation appears to decrease during stressful situations,* demonstrates quite clearly that the perception of pain varies in the same individual depending on the circumstances (Amir, et al., 1980; Ross and Randich, 1984).

Gate Control Theory of Pain. The **gate control theory of pain,** *proposed many years ago, suggests that a kind of "gate" exists in the spinal cord and that it controls whether information about painful stimulation will reach the brain* (Melzack and Wall, 1965). Neural signals carrying information about pain are carried along the very thin nerve fibers leading to the spinal cord. When they reach the "gate," the amount of stimulation coming in from the larger nerve fibers, is compared to information about nonpainful stimuli on the skin. If there is relatively more input from the pain fibers, the gate "opens," and the pain messages are sent to the brain. If the larger fibers are carrying more input, the gate "closes," and the pain messages never reach the brain.

The gate control theory also predicted that the brain plays an important role in controlling the gate in the spinal cord: it could send messages *down* the cord and open or close the gate independently. This part of the theory was proposed to explain why a person's emotions, culture, and personality can have so much effect on the way pain is perceived. The brain's role in controlling the gate was presumed to be primarily unconscious. For example, a person under severe stress would not consciously be sending messages to close the gate, although that person would probably experience an inhibition of pain for a short time. There may be ways for an individual to gain some conscious control over these efferent messages, however, as we discuss later.

Since the gate control theory was first proposed, much has been learned about pain. Although the theory has weaknesses, it has helped us to better understand some of the mysteries surrounding this sensory system, and it has offered some clues to how chronic pain might be treated.

Treatments for Pain

Three methods used to treat pain include morphine, electrical stimulation, and acupuncture. These are not the only treatments, but they are particularly interesting because they all seem to relieve pain by a common underlying mechanism.

Morphine. This extremely potent pain-relieving drug is the active ingredient in opium, obtained from the opium poppy. Opium has been used for medicinal purposes since at least 300 B.C., and references to the drug date back thousands of years. In addition to its well-known use as a pain reliever, it has been employed to treat coughing, diarrhea, insomnia, snake bite, asthma, epilepsy, and even deafness. It does cause constipation, inhibit coughing, and promote sleepiness, but it probably is not useful for the other ailments. The drug also produces tolerance and physical dependence.

Why morphine is so effective at relieving pain was a complete mystery until very recently. A series of startling scientific discoveries in the 1970s, resulting from some work on drug dependence, solved this mystery and gave us a much better understanding of the whole subject of pain.

Researchers reasoned that if morphine controls pain, it must be acting on the nervous system, probably the brain. They concluded that the brain must contain receptors for the drug. Experiments using radioactively labeled opiates proved that the brain does indeed contain such receptors. When radioactively labeled opiates were injected, they became particularly concentrated in the pituitary gland, the hypothalamus, and the limbic system, apparently because these brain areas have specific receptor sites for opiate molecules. But the researchers did not know why the human brain contained receptors for a plant, especially one that is not even edible.

Finding the answer did not take long. If the brain contained opiate receptors, it probably also contained its *own* opiatelike substance. Brain tissue from the areas where the receptors were found was tested, and a chemical that acted like morphine was discovered (Hughes, 1975). Therefore, the human brain's opiate receptors are really not designed for the plant. They are designed to work with *the brain's own pain relievers, called* **endorphins.** *These are a group of opiatelike substances released by the lower part of the brain.* The fact that the opium plant's molecules fit the receptors is just a curious accident.

Since these original discoveries, scientists have found that the brain contains not just one opiatelike compound, now called endorphins, but a "whole zoo" of them, as one pain researcher put it. Although they solved one mystery, they created many more. Endorphins are not just involved in pain; they are implicated in mental illness, memory, temperature regulation, and motivation, and they appear to be partly responsible for stess-induced analgesia (Bolles and Fanselow, 1982).

Electrical Stimulation. Another exciting development in pain research is the use of electrical stimulation of the brain. Electrodes are implanted in specific brain sites, and a tiny current is passed through. Usually the patient controls the stimulation, and most find it remarkably effective in relieving pain. This procedure does have its drawbacks, however; it requires surgery, and if the patient uses it too much, it seems to lose its effectiveness. Apparently it produces tolerance and dependence, as do many drugs (Hosobuchi, et al., 1977).

The brain sites that are most effectively stimulated are near the hypothalamus; these are the same ones that are most responsive to endorphins. In addition, drugs that interfere with the brain's response to endorphins also inhibit the pain-relieving effects of brain stimulation. These drugs probably "lock up" the receptor sites to which the endorphin molecules attach themselves. It is possible that brain stimulation works by activating the patient's own endorphin system, but much more research is needed to confirm this (Liebeskind and Paul, 1977).

Acupuncture. One of the most controversial topics in American medicine is acupuncture, a system of pain control developed by the Chinese. Long thin needles are inserted into the skin at specific sites, and (in modern acupuncture) an electric current is passed through the needles for about twenty minutes. (See fig. 4.9.) The sites vary, depending on the location of the pain, but oddly, the needles are usually inserted in a location quite distant from the injury. For example, a man undergoing surgery for stomach ulcers had acupuncture needles inserted in his ears (Dimond, 1971).

There appears to be no doubt that acupuncture works; it clearly relieves pain in many people (Ulett, 1981). For as many as ninety percent of the surgery patients in China, the acupuncture procedure is used. *Why* it works is still very much a mystery. The Chinese, relying on the oldest healing tradition in the world, believe that the procedure improves the internal balance between yin and yang, the two opposing elements in the universe. Western scientists, though, prefer a more scientific explanation.

One hypothesis accounting for the pain relieving effects of acupuncture involves the gate control theory. The needles stimulate the larger touch fibers rather than the pain fibers, and when these signals reach the gate in the spinal cord, they cancel out the pain messages that are arriving by way of the thinner nerve fibers, closing the gate. Another hypothesis is that the needles somehow activate the patient's endorphins, and these substances relieve pain all over the body.

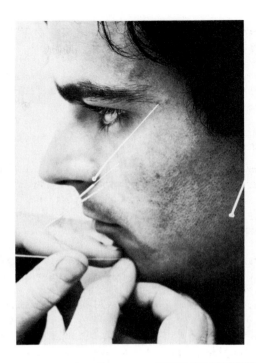

Figure 4.9 A man undergoing acupuncture treatment

A third explanation of the potent effects of this ancient tradition is that it acts as a **placebo,** *an inert or innocuous (harmless) medication given especially to satisfy the patient.* (The familiar "sugar pill" is the classic example.) If the patient believes the placebo will help, it often does. Scientists estimate that at least one-third of the patients who are suffering from pain will report relief if they are treated with a placebo. In a study comparing the effects of placebos to those of morphine, the innocuous placebo was able to relieve pain in dental patients about as well as 8 mg of morphine (Levine and Gordon, 1984). How placebos work is still unclear, but many scientists think they enable the patient to activate the brain's endorphin system.

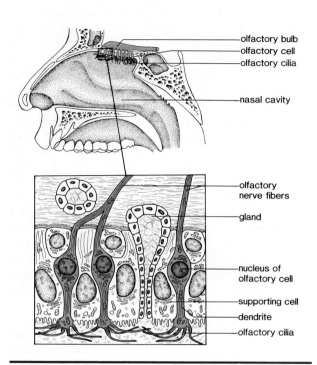

Figure 4.10   *The receptors for olfaction, or smell*

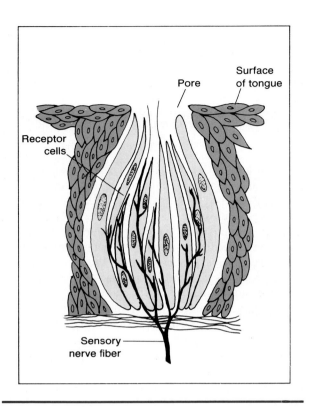

Figure 4.11   *The receptors for gustation, or taste*

Acupuncture may prove to be useful in studying placebo effects. In China the procedure is being used in a culture in which everyone believes in its usefulness, much as we believe in the effectiveness of prescribed drugs. Even if the placebo effect plays a substantial role in acupuncture, the procedure might also affect the patient's perception of pain in other ways as well, such as through endorphin release. We clearly have a great deal more to learn about the sense of pain.

Smell and Taste: The Chemical Senses

Human beings have an extraordinary range of senses. Not only can they see, hear, and touch their environment, they can smell it and taste it. **Olfaction,** or *the sense of smell,* and **gustation,** *the sense of taste,* are usually grouped together as the chemical senses because the physical stimulus to which they respond is a chemical, rather than a light wave, sound wave, or pressure.

The receptors for smell (fig. 4.10) and taste (fig. 4.11) are able to transform information about a molecule, either in the air or in a liquid, into neural messages. Most scientists agree that the tiny hairlike projections of the receptors have sites that can interact with molecules. Presumably, the shape of the molecule affects *how* it interacts with the receptor, and it perhaps affects to which receptors it adheres.

Tastes are generally divided into four basic categories: salty, sweet, bitter, and sour. Odors are usually categorized as well, using identifiers such as minty, floral, and musky. One might suppose that there are different chemical receptor sites for each category of taste or smell, but research on this issue has not provided any clear answers. In the gustatory system, for example, some neurons act like **labeled lines,** *a term used to describe sensory neurons with highly specific responses to particular stimuli.* Nevertheless, many neurons in the gustatory system respond to several tastes but with different firing patterns, suggesting that a particular stimulus might be coded by patterns of firing in several receptors rather than activation in a single type of receptor. Perhaps the chemical senses use a combination of methods to code different tastes and odors into neural signals (Pfaffman, 1955; Frank and Norgren, 1979; Pfaff, 1985).

The Importance of the Chemical Senses.   It is easy to see how humans rely on their senses of sight, hearing, or touch. But why do we need smell or taste? What do they have to do with our survival?

The answer to that question is better understood if we look at smell and taste from an evolutionary perspective, comparing our abilities and preferences with those of other animals. The chemical senses are crucially important in the choice of foods and in communication.

The sense of taste and taste preferences of a species are closely connected to the species' eating habits. For example, humans can taste, and usually prefer, sweet foods. This is not accidental; it is because we have relied heavily on ripe fruits for food during our evolution. It was also important to avoid rotten fruits, so we developed a dislike for and an ability to detect sour and bitter flavors. The flavors themselves are not "in" the foods. They exist on our tongues and in our brains only, and they have evolved differently in other animals. Animals that rely on rotten fruit (e.g., insects) probably find them to be quite sweet. And the cat, for example, does not prefer the same foods we do. It does not eat fruits, has never relied on them, and has consequently not developed the same sense of "sweet." Instead, it prefers salty tastes like those of fresh meat.

The sense of smell plays a significant role in communication between mammals. A mouse, for example, can tell a great deal about another mouse from a single sniff. It can tell whether the other mouse is male or female, whether it is a member of the group or a stranger, whether it is in heat (if it is female), whether it is a dominant or subordinate male, and whether the other mouse is frightened. **Pheromones** are *the odors that the mice and other animals use in communication,* and for mice, many of these odors are in the urine (Whitten and Bronson, 1970). These pheromones can have intriguing effects. For example, a recently impregnated female mouse will abort her pregnancy if she smells the urine from a strange male, come into heat again, and mate with the stranger. From the male stranger's point of view, the chemical is quite useful.

A pheromone appears to be the reason pigs are so enthusiastic about their search for truffles. The French have always used the animal to find the highly prized delicacy, which is a fungus that smells like a combination of musk, nuts, and ozone. Truffles contain a substance that is also present in the testes of the boar—one that plays a role in the animal's mating behavior (Claus, et al., 1981).

Whether odors are also used in human communication is not known, but our sense of smell is certainly refined. For example, human beings can tell two people apart by smell, unless the two people are identical twins on the same diet (Wallace, 1977). There are also several fascinating studies that seem to suggest that odors play a role in our sex lives. For instance, the substance in truffles that attracts the pig is also produced by the testes of men. Students at the University of Birmingham in England were shown pictures of normally dressed women and were asked to score the pictures for beauty. Some of the subjects had been exposed to the chemical during the viewing, and these subjects rated the pictures "more beautiful" than did the other subjects (Kirk-Smith, et al., 1978). Considering how much money we spend on perfumes, deodorants, scented candles, and other artificial stimulation for our chemical senses, it would not be too outlandish to suppose that odors play a much larger role in our lives than we suspect.

CAREER BOX

Wine Taster

A few lucky people in the world are able to make their living entirely by tasting and evaluating wines. Some of these work for wineries, others for magazines dedicated to fine foods and travel. Many write books, articles, or columns on wine appreciation. Whether you are tasting wine as a professional or as as interested layperson, some knowledge of the principles of sensation and perception will make the experience more enjoyable.

Fine wine should appeal to more than just the sense of taste. The sense of smell is important because wine usually has an interesting aroma that can stimulate the olfactory receptors. Also, the sense of taste is very much affected by olfactory sensations. (Try offering a piece of potato and a piece of apple to a blindfolded subject who is holding his nose. He probably won't be able to tell the difference.) Wine tasters also value their sense of touch, which tells them about the oiliness or viscosity of the wine they are drinking. And finally, vision is also important. Seeing the clarity and color of a wine should be part of the whole wine-tasting experience.

The categories by which wines are judged demonstrates the weight each kind of sensation is given by the professionals. Following is a scorecard used by the enology (wine) department at the University of California at Davis in judging wines. The maximum score is 20.

Factor	Points
Clarity and freedom from sediment	2
Color (depth and tint and appropriateness, for type)	2
Aroma and bouquet	4
Freedom from acetic odor	2
Total acid to the taste	2
Tannin (astringency)	2
Extract (body)	1
Sugar	1
General taste (the mouth's impression of flavor)	2
Overall impression	2

To taste and evaluate wines under ideal situations requires some understanding of the psychology of sensation and perception. For example, the wine should be spat out, not drunk, because alcohol will dull the senses. To provide optimal conditions for the sense of vision, the wine should be viewed on a clean white surface with good side illumination. Also, the room should be as odorless as possible. Wine tasters also take ample consideration of the principles of social psychology: they insist that no one is to make comments about any of the wines until everyone has tasted and made notes because they know that perception is only partly a function of sensation. Other factors, including the influence of other people's opinions, can influence perception as well.

GUIDED REVIEW

Learning Objectives 8, 9, and 10

1. The skin senses are made up of a collection of overlapping senses that detect touch, temperature changes, and painful stimulation on the skin. The skin has an outer layer, or _____ , and an inner layer, or _____ .

2. Our experience of pain is determined not only by the actual stimulation, but also by personality and emotional and cultural factors. Stress reduces sensitivity to pain, a phenomenon called _____ .

3. The _____ of pain predicts the existence of a "gate" in the spinal cord that controls whether information about pain reaches the brain. The gate is affected by the relative amount of stimulation from large and small fibers, and by messages coming from the brain.

4. Three treatments for pain include morphine, electrical stimulation of the brain, and acupuncture. The effectiveness of all three treatments may be related to the brain's own opiatelike substances, called _____ . Placebos may also be effective in relieving pain in some cases for the same reason.

5. The chemical senses, which include _____ (smell) and _____ (taste), can detect the presence of certain molecules in the air or on the tongue. The receptors in the nose and on the tongue probably have sites that interact with the molecules that produce taste or odor sensations.

6. The sense of taste is important in the choice of food. Different animals have different taste preferences depending on their eating habits. Smell is important for communication in mammals. Communication odors are called _____ .

ANSWERS

1. epidermis; dermis 2. stress-induced analgesia 3. gate control theory 4. endorphins 5. olfaction; gustation 6. pheromones

Perception

The distinction between sensation and perception is not a clear one; the two phenomena tend to merge into one another. In each of the previous sections, we discussed not only sensation but certain aspects of perception as well. For example, we discussed how the brain perceives patterns in the visual world. The sensation of an object is more or less a function of the properties of the object, given the limits of the sensory system. Our perception of that object is influenced by more than that, especially by a need to make order out of a constant barrage of stimulation.

The importance of pattern and organization as perceptual principles was first recognized during the early twentieth century by the proponents of Gestalt psychology, described in Chapter 1. The word "gestalt" means "pattern" or "form" in German, and these scientists emphasized that perception involved more than the mere addition of the total number of sensations impinging on the sensory systems. In other words, the whole (perception) is more than the sum of its parts (sensations).

General Principles of Perception

The image in figure 4.12a is extremely complicated, although it may not seem so. Because of the way our brains are organized, and because of our experiences, we can look at such complex images and sort them out easily. We use several methods to accomplish this: (1) perceptual constancies; (2) figure-ground relationships; and (3) perceptual organizing principles.

Perceptual Constancies. Is the coin in the foreground much larger than the one in the background? Their images on your retina would tell you that it is,

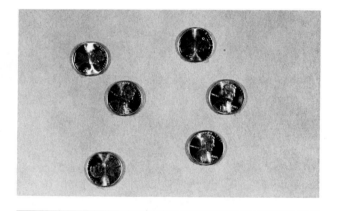

Figure 4.12 *Coins are different sized ovals because of perspective*

and a ruler would tell you the same thing. But your perception of the two coins tells you they are the same size, the same circular shape, and about the same color. (Check figure 4.12b to see the actual characteristics of the images.)

Perceptual constancy refers to *the ability to perceive an object as constant, despite changes in size, color, or shape at the retina*. It probably develops from infancy as our experience with objects grows. Colin Turnbull, an anthropologist, described a case in which an African pygmy, who had lived in the forest all his life, had no chance to see objects at a long distance.

The pygmy had not developed some aspects of perceptual constancy of size.

. . . Kenge looked over the plains and down to where a herd of about a hundred buffalo were grazing some miles away. He asked me what kind of insects they were, and I told him they were buffalo, twice as big as the forest buffalo known to him. He laughed loudly and told me not to tell such stupid stories. . . . We got into the car and drove down to where the animals were grazing. He watched them getting larger and larger, and though he was as courageous as any pygmy, he moved over and sat close to me and muttered that it was witchcraft. . . . Finally, when he realized that they were real buffalo he was no longer afraid, but what puzzled him was why they had been so small, and whether they really had been small and suddenly grown larger, or whether it had been some kind of trickery. (Turnbull, 1961)

A characteristic of perceptual constancy probably also explains why it is difficult to estimate the lengths of the lines in the Müller-Lyer illusion, shown in figure 4.13. Although you may not be aware of it, you tend to perceive depth in any two-dimensional picture. Seeing depth in the "arrow" results in an image like an outside corner of a building, or the binder of a book. Depth in the "feather" produces an image more like an inside corner or an open book. Your brain automatically processes the distance of those two corners and decides that the outside corner is a little closer. If the retinal images of two vertical lines are the same size, their actual size is also the same only if they are the same distance away from you. Since your brain has decided otherwise, you perceive that the one that appears to be further away is longer.

Figure-Ground Relationships. Another general principle of visual perception is that we tend to perceive some images as figures and others as grounds. Figures usually have certain properties that grounds do not. They are closer, more like "things," more easily remembered, and they seem to have a shape. In contrast, the grounds are relatively formless and further away. The fact that figures stand out in our perception may be due to the way our visual system is organized.

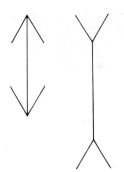

Length: The vertical lines are the
same length.

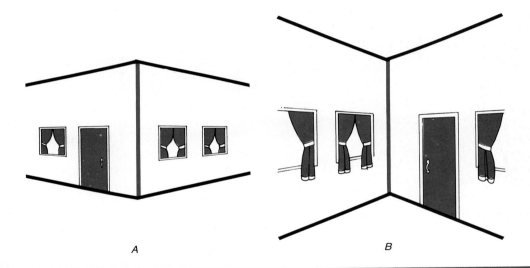

A

B

Figure 4.13   The Müller-Lyon illusion

For example, the enhancement of contour and contrast is an important element in the neurophysiology of vision, as we discussed earlier in this chapter. The drawing in figure 4.14 shows a visual illusion with reversible figure and ground. Most people first see the black shapes as the figures and the white as the formless background. But keep looking . . . .

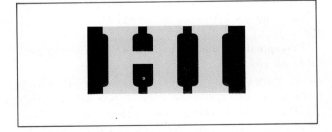

Figure 4.14   Reversible figure-ground illusion

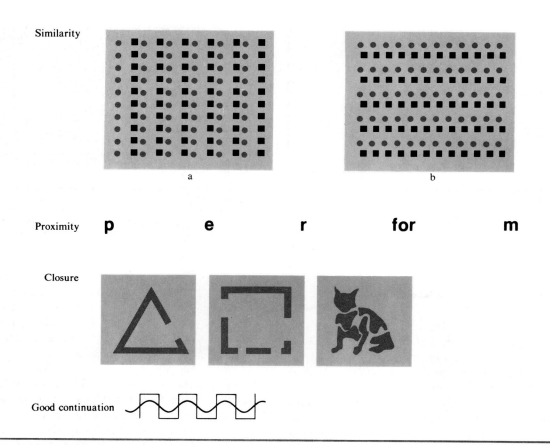

Figure 4.15   *The organizing principles of perception*

Organizing Principles.   We bring more order to the complex visual patterns striking the retina by using several organizing principles. Figure 4.15 shows how each of these works. Using the **principle of similarity,** *we perceive images that resemble one another as a group, even though they may be further apart.* **The principle of proximity** *predicts that we will perceive objects that are close together as a group.*

A third important organizing principle is the **principle of closure.** *When a shape is enclosed by lines, even if incompletely, it tends to form a figure,* especially if it is a familiar shape, such as the cat in figure 4.13. The last set of drawings demonstrates the **principle of good continuation,** *which means that images that appear to follow in the same direction, for example in a regular sine-wave pattern, will be perceived as part of the same figure.*

Individual Factors in Perception

The process of perception is similar in all of us, but that does not mean we all see the same event in exactly the same way. The images on the retina are modified, reorganized, distorted, ignored, and given meaning at all levels of processing, from the sense organ to the brain.

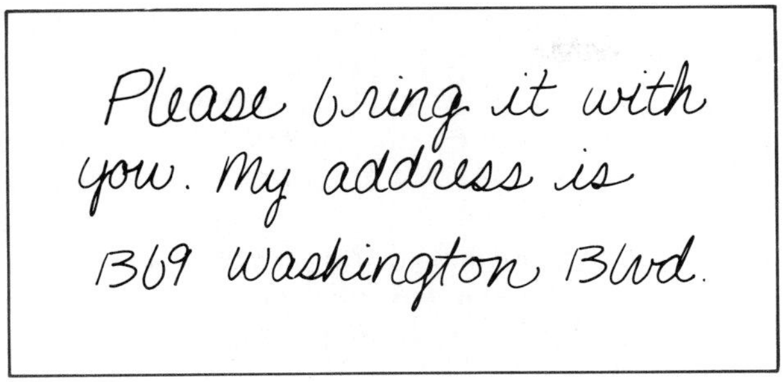

Please bring it with
you. My address is
1369 Washington Blvd.

Figure 4.16 Perceptual set

Figure 4.17 *The perception of a scene depends partly on the interests of the perceiver, which can direct his or her attention. A politician might perceive the messages on the signs; a pickpocket might focus on the location of accessible wallets.*

The way they are changed, and the resulting perception, may be quite different in each of us. Some of the factors that can affect perception include previous experience, personality and interests, and culture.

Previous Experience.   Read the message in figure 4.16. You probably had no problem reading the 13 and the B (in Blvd.), or the b in bring and the 6 in 1369, despite the fact that the image on your retina was identical in both cases. The words that preceded the ambiguous images established a context and created a **perceptual set** *or expectation about what you would see.* This set, made up of your recent experience, influenced how you perceived the image.

Very early previous experiences may affect how the brain processes visual information in a much more fundamental way. Studies of the responses of single cells in the visual system of cats, discussed earlier, found that individual cells respond to a certain class of stimuli, such as a horizontal bar in the receptive field. These preferences are determined to some extent by the images the cat saw while it was growing up. Kittens that were reared wearing goggles that permitted them to see only horizontal lines had many more cells with preferences for horizontal bars and fewer with preferences for vertical bars (Hirsch and Spinelli, 1971). This amazing series of experiments suggested that early experiences could affect our later perceptions in a very fundamental way—by modifying the "preferences" of the brain cells involved in sensory processing. Although

later experiments have questioned whether Hubel and Wiesel's feature detectors were specialized to respond to bars or some other characteristic of the visual environment (DeValois and DeValois, 1980), it seems that early experiences can have subtle effects on the way the brain processes visual information.

Personality and Interests.   The personality and interests of the individual perceiver are other factors that can determine how a scene is perceived by influencing what the person pays attention to. One person in figure 4.17 would probably pay attention to the signs. A pickpocket may perceive quite different things because he might attend to where the wallets are.

In one attempt to link perception to personality traits, people were classified as being either extroverts or introverts based on their answers to a questionnaire (Eysenck, 1967). Several experiments found that the outgoing and sociable extroverts tended to have less sensitive sensory systems than did the more withdrawn introverts. For example, one study found that introverts have lower average thresholds for vision (Siddle, Morrish, White, and Mangen, 1969), hearing (Stelmack and Campbell, 1974), and touch (Coles, Gale, and Kline, 1971). It is possible that extroverts have a neural system that is slower to respond and more weakly aroused. These studies were particularly interesting because the extroverts were more likely to say they saw a stimulus when they were not sure. However, the signal-detection technique confirms that the introverts have greater sensitivity. The introverts just preferred to say they saw the stimulus only when they were certain.

Culture. The pygmy's experience with the buffalo is a good example of how culture can influence the way a person perceives. Another example involves our experience with the "carpentered" world. From infancy, people who live in Western cultures are exposed to rectangular rooms, squared corners, and right angles. But people who live in some other cultures are not. For instance, the Zulus of Africa are surrounded by circular architecture—they live in round huts with circular doors. These people are less susceptible to certain visual illusions, such as the one in figure 4.11 (Segall, Campbell, and Herskovitz, 1966).

Perception and Attention

The process of perception is very much affected by **attention,** *a phenomenon that involves filtering of incoming stimuli.* Human beings do not pay attention to everything in their environments; nor do they attend to all the stimuli impinging on their sense organs. We attend to some stimuli and do not notice others. William James (1890) recognized the importance of attention very early: "A thing may be presented to a man a hundred times, but if he persistently fails to notice it, it cannot be said to enter his experience."

Selective Attention. Human beings have a great deal of control over which stimuli they attend to and which they do not. The process of attention is a selective one. At a cocktail party, one might pay strict attention to a conversation with the boss while "tuning out" nearby chatter. Yet even though the person's attention is given to a certain category of incoming information (the conversation with the boss), she can still monitor other

events, such as the arrival of new refreshments at the bar, the entrance of new guests, or the music on the stereo. The person's attention can also shift very suddenly because of this monitoring process. For example, if another guest mentions the person's name, her attention is likely to shift from the conversation with the boss to the dialogue in which her name was mentioned.

Studies of attention have found that people have a limited ability to process incoming information. If they are not attending to it, they usually cannot recall very much of it. *In an experimental technique called* **shadowing,** *subjects listen to one set of stimuli through one sensory channel and another set through a different channel. They try to repeat aloud, or shadow, the messages coming in through one of the two channels* (Cherry, 1953). Typically, they can recall very little or nothing of the message coming in through the other channel, even if the same stimuli are repeated over and over to the unattended sensory channel. For example, subjects who shadow one set of words entering one ear, while another set is presented dichotically to the other ear, usually cannot recall anything from the unattended list of words (Moray, 1959).

It might seem as though the person became functionally deaf in one ear. But apparently the words are heard; they just do not remain very long in the person's memory. If the experimenter interrupts the shadowing task and quickly asks the subject to recall as many words as possible from the unattended channel, the person can often remember the last five or six words (Glucksberg and Cowen, 1970; Norman, 1969).

The Bottleneck Model of Attention. *An interesting theory of attention, called the* **bottleneck model,** *suggests that there is a biological limitation on the amount of information that can be processed at one time* (Deutsch and Deutsch, 1963; Norman, 1968; Schneider and Shiffrin, 1977, Pashler, 1984). If the task is not too difficult, the person can devote part of his information processing capacity to the main task and some of the "leftover" capacity to a secondary task. For example, one can read a book and listen to the radio, provided the material in the book is not too taxing. Well-practiced and fairly automatic tasks require very little mental effort, so the individual need not devote very much information processing capacity to them.

Attention seems to play an important role in controlling what stimuli can pass through the bottleneck and which ones cannot. Some recent studies on the visual cortex of monkeys suggest how this filtering process is related to the way cells respond to stimuli that appear within their receptive fields. As we discussed earlier, visual cortical cells have preferred stimuli to which they respond with increased firing rates. But when the monkeys were trained to ignore that stimulus and attend to a different stimulus in the same receptive field, the cell's response to the formerly preferred stimulus was much reduced. Thus, the cells in the cortex were not just automatically reacting to the patterns in the environment like a camera. They appeared to be filtering out irrelevant information based on what the animal was attending to (Moran and Desimone, 1985).

GUIDED REVIEW

Learning Objectives 11, 12, and 13

1. The process of perception is influenced by general principles that operate in everyone and by individual factors. It is closely related to the process of _____ , in which incoming stimuli are filtered.

2. _____ refers to the tendency to perceive objects as constant, despite changes in size, shape, or color on the retina. Some images are perceived as figures, usually those that are closer and have shape.

3. Several organizing principles predict how we will sort images into groups or patterns. The _____ , for example, states that objects that are closer together will be seen as part of a group.

4. Previous experience affects perception by establishing a _____ . The context of a particular image creates a set of expectations and therefore influences the way we perceive the image.

5. Very early visual experiences can affect the properties of cells in the _____ of the brain by altering their preferred stimuli.

6. The _____ suggests that there are biological limitations on the amount of information that can be processed at one time. Attentional processes affect what information passes through the bottleneck; attention also affects the responses of visual cortical cells to stimuli in their receptive fields.

ANSWERS

1. attention 2. Perceptual constancy 3. principle of proximity 4. perceptual set 5. visual cortex 6. bottleneck model of attention

Extrasensory Perception

What I'm looking at is a little boat jetty or little boat dock along the bay. It is in a direction about like that from here. Yeah, I see the little boats, some motor launches, some little sailing ships, sails all furled, some with the masts stepped and others are up. Little jetty or little dock there. . . . Funny thing—this flashed in kinda looks like a Chinese or Japanese pagoda effect. . . .

Pat Price was describing the Redwood City Marina. He had never been to the marina, and he was not there when he described it, although an experimenter was. Price was in a laboratory at the Stanford Research Institute, miles away, participating in an experiment on remote viewing.

What Is ESP?

Extrasensory perception (ESP) *is perception that does not require stimulation of a sense organ.* Researchers usually break it down into three main categories:

1. **telepathy**—*the transference of one person's thoughts to another, as in remote viewing;*
2. **clairvoyance**—*the ability to perceive objects or events not present or affecting the person's senses; and*
3. **precognition**—*the ability to perceive future events.*

Another phenomenon that is usually grouped with ESP is **psychokinesis,** *or the ability to move objects without touching them in any way.* The field of psychology called **parapsychology** *investigates ESP or psychokinesis using the scientific method.*

Does ESP Exist?

Surveys of the general public have found that a large majority of people believe that ESP exists. In one survey, ten percent of the sample reported having a psychic experience of their own. Yet the subject is controversial among scientists; most are skeptical, partly because ESP experiences usually do not take place in a laboratory, where scientists can observe them. Rather, they are usually the anecdotal reports of people who are involved in some major life crisis; very often the psychic experience is about a close family member.

For example, the sinking of the ocean liner *Titanic* in 1912 elicited many reports of psychic experiences. On the night of the disaster a woman in New York had a dream in which she saw her mother in a small boat tossing about on the waves. The woman did not even know her mother was on the ill-fated ship until she saw her mother's name on the passenger list in the newspaper. The mother survived and later confirmed the accuracy of her daughter's dream (Pratt, 1973).

Stories like this one are not difficult to find, though they may be very difficult to explain. However, anecdotes do not satisfy the scientist's strict criteria for demonstrating the existence of a phenomenon. Repeatable and carefully controlled experiments, conducted under the critical eyes of unbiased observers, are required.

Experiments in Parapsychology. Research in this topic has been going on for more than fifty years in this country. Courses in the subject are offered at major universities, doctorate degrees are awarded, and the U.S. Government provides money for research. There is a division of parapsychology in the American Psychological Association and also in the American Association for the Advancement of Science. One of the most convincing of the hundreds of experiments that have been conducted is the study on "remote viewing," with ex-police commissioner Pat Price.

Price was invited to participate as a subject because he told the experimenters he used parapsychology all the time in his everyday life. During an experiment, Price remained in the laboratory with one experimenter, while another went to a locked safe, picked up a randomly selected set of "traveling orders" that told him where to go, and then followed the orders. Price, still in the lab, began to describe the "view" into a tape recorder after the experimenter had time to reach the site (Targ and Puthoff, 1977).

This procedure was used nine times, and the traveling experimenter went to an arts-and-crafts plaza, a swimming pool, a nature preserve, and other visually distinct places. A judge compared the taped descriptions to the actual sites and was able to match seven to the correct locations. This is a remarkable number of "hits;" if Pat were merely guessing, the judges may have matched only one site to the taped description.

Skepticism

The experiments appeared to be well controlled, and there did not seem to be any way for the subject to cheat. However, a short time after the results were published, two scientists found a very significant flaw (Marks and Kamman, 1978). Pat's taped descriptions contained important cues that could reveal to the judges which site was being described. For example, the experimenter with Price said "nothing like having three successes behind you." This statement, and others like it, gave away the *order* in which Pat was describing the sites. Since the judge already knew the order in which the travelers visited the sites, the job of matching the site to the description became much easier. One of the scientists criticizing the study was able to match the five sites to five taped descriptions without even visiting the sites! When those little cues were deleted from the transcript, judges could not match them up.

Flaws like this one, and even outright trickery, have been found in many supposedly "conclusive" experiments on ESP (Hansel, 1980). Most scientists question whether parapsychologists have come up with even a single reliable result, one that can withstand rigorous experimental conditions and one that can be repeated. People on both sides of the controversy have strong feelings. Parapsychologists compare themselves to stoned prophets and burned witches, blaming the priggishness of contemporary science for their lack of acceptance. Many scientists feel they have "bent over backwards" in giving parapsychologists a chance to demonstrate their claims.

It is true that we have much to learn about how human beings sense and perceive their environment. The results of many experiments remain unexplained, and the history of science is filled with examples of how yesterday's impossibility became today's fact. Certainly no scientists want to look ridiculous 100 years from now because they scoffed at parapsychology. Yet as each new and "incontrovertible" finding in the field is disputed—invalidated as outright trickery or flawed by sloppy experimental procedures—one begins to wonder whether ESP exists or whether we simply want it to exist. The only answer we have right now is that we just don't know.

GUIDED REVIEW

Learning Objectives 14, 15, and 16

1. Three types of extrasensory perception, or ESP, are _____ , _____ , and _____ . _____ , which refers to the ability to move objects without touching them, is also usually grouped with ESP. The scientific investigation of ESP is called _____ .

2. Recent experimental results suggesting that some form of ESP exists includes studies demonstrating _____ _____ , a variety of telepathy. The subject remains in the laboratory and describes a scene, perhaps miles away, visited by an experimenter.

Most experimental demonstrations of ESP phenomena, including remote viewing, have been shown to involve trickery or to have serious experimental flaws. This would suggest that either ESP does not exist or is a very elusive phenomenon that is extremely difficult to demonstrate under laboratory conditions.

ANSWERS

1. telepathy, clairvoyance, precognition; Psychokinesis; parapsychology 2. remote viewing

SUMMARY

I. The visual system is the means by which we receive information about the patterns of light in the environment.   (p. 108)

 A. All sensory systems share many characteristics, including their involvement in the tasks of sensation and perception, their general structures, and their ability to transduce physical energy to neural signals.   (p. 108)

  1. The sensitivity of sensory systems can be described by their absolute thresholds or by their j.n.d.'s.   (p. 108)

 B. Light is the environmental stimulus for the visual system.   (p. 109)

 C. The eye is the sense organ for vision, and it consists of several specialized structures, such as the cornea, the iris, the lens, and the retina. (p. 110)

  1. The receptors for vision are located in the retina.   (p. 111)

  2. The retina contains two types of receptors: rods and cones. Rods are specialized for vision in low-light intensities, and cones process color and pattern information. (p. 112)

 D. The transduction process involves the breakdown of photopigment in the presence of light, which causes electrical disturbances in the membrane of the receptors.   (p. 114)

  1. The process of dark adaptation involves the recovery of the photopigment molecules. (p. 115)

 E. Seeing patterns in the visual field requires the activity of neurons all along the visual pathway to the brain.   (p. 115)

  1. The visual system organizes patterns in the visual field using receptive fields. (p. 115)

  2. Single-cell recordings in the cat visual cortex led to the discovery of feature detectors, cells that respond only to certain stimuli in their receptive fields.   (p. 116)

 F. Two theories have been proposed to explain how humans can process color information. (p. 117)

  1. The trichromatic theory proposes the existence of three kinds of cells with sensitivities to different ranges of wavelengths.   (p. 117)

  2. The opponent process theory suggests that individual cells are sensitive to pairs of colors and that they respond to each member of the pair by increasing or decreasing their firing rates.   (p. 117)

 G. The visual system processes depth information using both monocular and binocular cues. (p. 118)

 H. Visual problems include color blindness, nearsightedness, farsightedness, and cataract. (p. 119)

II. Audition is the sense of hearing.   (p. 120)

 A. Sound is the physical stimulus in the environment that stimulates the auditory system and is transformed into neural energy. (p. 120)

 B. The ear is the sense organ for audition; it consists of the outer ear, the middle ear, and the inner ear. The receptors for audition are hair cells on the basilar membrane of the cochlea in the inner ear.   (p. 121)

 C. Sound waves of different frequencies cause different parts of the basilar membrane to vibrate in resonance, thereby providing a mechanism for the coding of sound.   (p. 123)

 D. Two types of deafness are conduction deafness and nerve deafness. Deafness can cause personality problems and is particularly detrimental in young children who have not yet acquired language.   (p. 123)

III. The senses of touch, smell, and taste play important roles in our lives.   (p. 127)

 A. The skin senses include a group of overlapping senses that detect touch, temperature changes, and painful stimulation on the skin.   (p. 127)

 B. The experience of pain is partly determined by the actual stimulation and partly by other factors, including personality, emotions, culture, and stress.   (p. 129)

1. The gate control theory of pain predicts the existence of a "gate" in the spinal cord that controls whether neural messages carrying information about pain will reach the brain.   (p. 129)

C. Several treatments are available for pain, and some of them seem to share common underlying mechanisms.   (p. 130)

1. Morphine appears to relieve pain by mimicking the activity of natural opiatelike chemicals produced by the brain, called endorphins.   (p. 130)

2. Electrical stimulation of the brain may relieve pain by activating areas that produce endorphins.   (p. 130)

3. Acupuncture is a controversial technique that relieves pain in some patients. (p. 131)

D. The chemical senses, which include olfaction and gustation, detect the presence of certain molecules in the air or on the tongue. (p. 132)

1. Chemical senses play important roles in communication and in the choice of food in some animals.   (p. 133)

IV. Perception is not easily distinguished from sensation; it involves the integration and interpretation of sensory information.   (p. 135)

A. A number of general principles of perception help human beings organize their perceptual worlds.   (p. 135)

1. Perceptual constancies refer to the ability to perceive an object as constant, despite changes in size, color, or shape at the retina.   (p. 135)

2. "Figures" are perceptually distinct from "grounds" partly because of their contrast and contours, their form, and their nearness.   (p. 136)

3. Organizing principles of perception include the principle of proximity, the principle of similarity, the principle of good continuation, and the principle of closure. (p. 138)

B. Individual factors affect the perception of objects and events.   (p. 138)

1. Previous experience affects perception because of the effects of perceptual sets. (p. 139)

2. Personality and interests affect what people pay attention to and thus what they perceive.   (p. 139)

3. Culture influences perception partly by controlling people's perceptual experiences. (p. 140)

C. The process of perception is affected by attention, in which incoming information is filtered.   (p. 140)

1. People demonstrate selective attention, in which the filtering process is under the control of the individual.   (p. 140)

2. The bottleneck model of attention suggests that there is a biological limitation on the amount of information that can be processed at one time. Attentional processes affect how cells in the visual cortex respond to their preferred stimuli. (p. 140)

V. Extrasensory perception (ESP) refers to perception that does not require stimulation of a sense organ. (p. 141)

A. Categories of ESP include telepathy, clairvoyance, and precognition. Psychokinesis is also considered a form of ESP.   (p. 142)

B. The question of whether ESP exists is controversial.   (p. 142)

1. Some experiments, such as those on "remote viewing," appear to demonstrate the existence of some forms of ESP. (p. 142)

C. Many scientists are skeptical of the existence of ESP because the experiments on them are usually flawed in some way.   (p. 143)

ACTION GLOSSARY

Match the terms in the left column with the definitions in the right column.

____ 1. Sensation (p. 108)
____ 2. Perception (p. 108)
____ 3. Sense organ (p. 108)
____ 4. Receptors (p. 108)
____ 5. Transduction (p. 108)
____ 6. Absolute threshold (p. 108)
____ 7. Signal detection (p. 109)
____ 8. Just noticeable difference (j.n.d.) (p. 109)
____ 9. Weber's Law (p. 109)
____ 10. Wavelength (p. 110)

A. *Specialized neurons located in sense organs that transduce parts of the physical energy in the environment, such as visible light, into neural messages.*
B. *The j.n.d. of a particular characteristic of a sensory system is a constant fraction of the stimulus intensity.*
C. *A technique to measure absolute thresholds that takes into account the fact that threshold measurements depend on the sensitivity of the individual's sensory system and on the person's willingness to say he sensed a stimulus when he was not quite sure.*
D. *The process by which incoming sensory information is integrated and interpreted by the brain.*
E. *The point at which a stimulus becomes too weak for an individual's sensory system to detect it.*
F. *The process by which information in the form of physical energy in the environment is transmitted to the brain through the sensory systems.*
G. *The distance from the peak of one light wave to the peak of the next.*
H. *A measure of sensory-system sensitivity that represents how well an individual can detect a very slight change in a stimulus in one characteristic, such as weight, intensity, or color. The measure indicates how "finely tuned" the sensory system is.*
I. *A structure designed to receive environmental energy, such as light or sound, and perform the first steps in transforming the energy into neural messages.*
J. *The process by which receptors in the sense organs transform parts of the physical energy in the environment into neural messages.*

____ 11. Visible spectrum (p. 110)
____ 12. Cornea (p. 110)
____ 13. Iris (p. 110)
____ 14. Lens (p. 110)
____ 15. Accommodation (p. 111)
____ 16. Cataract (p. 111)
____ 17. Vitreous humor (p. 111)
____ 18. Retina (p. 111)
____ 19. Rods (p. 112)
____ 20. Fovea (p. 112)

A. *A type of receptor primarily located in the periphery of the retina. Is responsive in dim light but does not discriminate between different colors.*
B. *The process by which the lens of the eye changes shape in order to focus light images on the retina, depending on the distance of the object.*
C. *The portion of the electromagnetic spectrum that humans can see; from 380 nanometers to 760 nanometers.*
D. *A small depression in the center of the retina, with a high density of cones and very clear pattern and color vision.*
E. *The transparent protective covering over the front of the eye.*
F. *The tissue behind the iris that can change shape, or accommodate, in order to focus the images of objects on the retina, depending on the distance of the object.*
G. *The jelly-like substance filling the inside of the eyeball.*
H. *Colored muscular portion of the eye that surrounds the pupil and regulates the amount of light that enters it.*
I. *The layer of receptors and other cells in the back of the eyeball.*
J. *Clouding of the lens tissue that can eventually result in blindness.*

____ 21. Cones (p. 112)
____ 22. Ganglion cells (p. 113)
____ 23. Photopigment (p. 114)
____ 24. Rhodopsin (p. 114)
____ 25. Retinal (p. 114)
____ 26. Retinal and opsin (p. 114)
____ 27. Night blindness (p. 115)
____ 28. Dark adaptation (p. 115)
____ 29. Receptive field (p. 115)
____ 30. Feature detectors (p. 116)

A. *One of the two components of the photopigment contained in receptors of the retina.*
B. *One of the two components of the photopigment contained in receptors of the retina. Similar in structure to Vitamin A.*
C. *The substance in the receptors of the retina that undergoes a chemical transformation when it is struck by light. The chemical change causes the receptor to adjust its release of neurotransmitter, thereby transducing light energy into neural energy.*
D. *A condition in which the rods do not function properly due to a deficiency of Vitamin A; the person has difficulty seeing in dim light.*
E. *A type of receptor located mainly in the center of the retina. Transmits detailed pattern and color information.*

F. *The photopigment contained in rods, made up of two parts: retinal and opsin.*
G. *Cells in the brain that are designed to detect specific features of the environment, such as a dark bar that is oriented vertically.*
H. *Neurons in the retina in the afferent visual pathway.*
I. *That portion of the visual field in which the presentation of a visual stimulus will produce an alteration in the firing rate of a neuron.*
J. *The process by which the eye becomes sensitive to images in dim light, dependent on the resynthesis of photopigment in the receptors.*

___ **31. Simple cell (p. 116)**
___ **32. Complex cells (p. 116)**
___ **33. Trichromatic theory (p. 117)**
___ **34. Microspectrophotometry (p. 117)**
___ **35. Opponent process theory (p. 117)**
___ **36. Negative afterimage (p. 117)**
___ **37. Monocular cue (p. 118)**
___ **38. Binocular cue (p. 118)**
___ **39. Convergence (p. 118)**
___ **40. Stereoscopic vision (p. 118)**

A. *A theory that proposes that color vision is based on the operation of three different kinds of cells, each sensitive to a different range of wavelengths. The theory is correct for the processing of color vision by cones in the retina.*
B. *The situation in which an organism has two eyes with overlapping fields of vision so that the images received by each eye are slightly different and become more disparate as the object moves closer; an important cue for judging distance.*
C. *A type of feature detector discovered in the visual cortex of the cat. Responds best to a line, turned in a certain orientation and moving in a specific direction, presented in its receptive field.*
D. *The process used to verify the trichromatic theory of color vision in which a tiny beam of light is shone on a single cone and the amount of light reflected back is measured.*
E. *A binocular cue for depth perception involving signals from the muscles surrounding the eyes.*
F. *An illusion of seeing an image of one color, such as green, after staring at the same image in another color, such as red, apparently produced by the sudden change of firing in opponent process cells.*
G. *A cue for depth perception based on the cues available to one eye only.*
H. *A theory that proposes that color vision is based on the operation of cells, each of which responds to two different colors, such as green and red, or blue and yellow. The cells fire fast for one color and slow for the other.*
I. *A cue for depth perception requiring simultaneous messages from both eyes.*
J. *A type of feature detector discovered in the visual cortex of the cat. Responds best to a straight line or bar presented in its receptive field.*

___ **41. Audition (p. 120)**
___ **42. Sound (p. 120)**
___ **43. Compressions (p. 121)**
___ **44. Rarefaction (p. 121)**
___ **45. Frequency (of a sound wave) (p. 121)**
___ **46. Hertz (p. 121)**
___ **47. Pitch (p. 121)**
___ **48. Outer ear (p. 121)**
___ **49. Middle ear (p. 121)**
___ **50. Inner ear (p. 121)**

A. *The part of the ear that transduces sound into neural messages. Includes the cochlea, the basilar membrane, and the hair cells.*
B. *Cycles of a sound wave per second.*
C. *One part of a sound wave in which the molecules of air are spread out.*
D. *The sense of hearing.*
E. *The outer fleshy part of the ear, the auditory canal, and the eardrum.*
F. *The physical energy transformed into neural messages by the auditory system, produced by the vibration of things in a medium such as air or water.*
G. *Contains the tiny bones located in the ear (the malleus, incus, and stapes) that transmit vibratory motion from the eardrum to the inner ear.*
H. *One part of a sound wave in which the molecules of air are pushed closer together.*
I. *The number of waves passing through a point per unit of time, usually one second.*
J. *The experience by humans of a sound along a continuum from high to low.*

___ **51. Oval window (p. 122)**
___ **52. Cochlea (p. 122)**
___ **53. Basilar membrane (p. 122)**
___ **54. Hair cells (p. 122)**
___ **55. Vestibular system (p. 122)**
___ **56. Semicircular canals (p. 123)**
___ **57. Vestibule (p. 123)**
___ **58. Conduction deafness (p. 123)**
___ **59. Nerve deafness (p. 123)**
___ **60. Decibel (p. 126)**

A. *The long membrane inside the cochlea that follows its curvature and vibrates in response to sound.*
B. *A part of the vestibular system in the inner ear that functions in the detection of head orientation.*
C. *A sensory system that provides unconscious information needed to maintain posture and head orientation and to control eye movements; the sense organ is part of the inner ear.*
D. *A type of deafness caused by damage to the hair cells or to the auditory nerve.*
E. *The snail-shaped inner ear that contains the receptors for hearing.*
F. *Unit used for measuring noise intensity levels.*

G. *Part of the inner ear that functions in the vestibular sensory system, particularly to detect rotary motion.*

H. *The membrane of the inner ear that receives the vibrations coming from the stapes of the middle ear.*

I. *A type of deafness caused by a problem along the route from the eardrum to the cochlea.*

J. *The receptors for hearing, located along the basilar membrane.*

___ 61. **Epidermis (p. 127)**
___ 62. **Dermis (p. 127)**
___ 63. **Pacinian corpuscle (p. 128)**
___ 64. **Stress-induced analgesia (p. 129)**
___ 65. **Gate control theory (p. 129)**
___ 66. **Endorphins (p. 130)**
___ 67. **Placebo (p. 131)**
___ 68. **Olfaction (p. 132)**
___ 69. **Gustation (p. 132)**
___ 70. **Labeled lines (p. 133)**

A. *Proposes that a mechanism in the spinal cord controls whether information about painful stimulation will reach the brain. The mechanism's actions are determined by the proportion of painful stimulation to other kinds of stimulation and by efferent messages from the brain.*

B. *The phenomenon in which an organism's sensitivity to pain decreases during stressful situations.*

C. *An inert substance given to a patient who is told that the treatment is a drug with powerful healing properties; a "sugar pill."*

D. *The inner layer of skin, containing most of the receptors for the skin senses.*

E. *The sense of taste.*

F. *A group of chemicals produced by the brain that act like opiates and relieve pain.*

G. *A receptor in the skin that seems to transform mechanical pressure on the skin into neural information.*

H. *The sense of smell.*

I. *Sensory neurons with highly specific responses to particular stimuli.*

J. *The outer layer of skin.*

___ 71. **Pheromone (p. 133)**
___ 72. **Perceptual constancy (p. 136)**
___ 73. **Principle of similarity (p. 138)**
___ 74. **Principle of proximity (p. 138)**
___ 75. **Principle of closure (p. 138)**
___ 76. **Principle of good continuation (p. 138)**
___ 77. **Perceptual set (p. 139)**
___ 78. **Attention (p. 140)**
___ 79. **Shadowing (p. 140)**
___ 80. **Bottleneck model of attention (p. 140)**

A. *States that there is a biological limitation on the amount of information that can be processed at one time.*

B. *The expectancies or predispositions that affect the perceptions of an observer.*

C. *Selection and perception of certain components of the environment.*

D. *When a space is enclosed by lines, it tends to be perceived as a figure.*

E. *Similar objects are seen as members of the same group.*

F. *An experimental technique in which the subject listens to different messages in each ear and tries to repeat aloud one of the messages; used in studies of selective attention.*

G. *A biological odor that is used in communication between members of the same species.*

H. *The ability to perceive an object as constant, despite changes in size, color, or shape at the retina.*

I. *Objects that are closer to one another are seen as part of a group.*

J. *Images that appear to follow in the same direction are perceived as part of a group.*

___ 81. **Extrasensory perception (ESP) (p. 142)**
___ 82. **Telepathy (p. 142)**
___ 83. **Clairvoyance (p. 142)**
___ 84. **Precognition (p. 142)**
___ 85. **Psychokinesis (p. 142)**

A. *The ability to perceive future events.*

B. *The transference of one person's thoughts to another's.*

C. *Perception that does not require stimulation of a sense organ.*

D. *The ability to move objects without touching them.*

E. *The ability to perceive objects or events not present or affecting the person's senses.*

ANSWERS

81. C, 82. B, 83. E, 84. A, 85. D

65. A, 66. F, 67. C, 68. H, 69. E, 70. I, 71. G, 72. H, 73. E, 74. I, 75. D, 76. J, 77. B, 78. C, 79. F, 80. A.

50. A, 51. H, 52. E, 53. A, 54. J, 55. C, 56. G, 57. B, 58. I, 59. D, 60. F, 61. J, 62. D, 63. G, 64. B.

34. F, 35. H, 36. F, 37. G, 38. I, 39. E, 40. B, 41. D, 42. F, 43. H, 44. C, 45. I, 46. B, 47. J, 48. E, 49. G.

18. I, 19. A, 20. D, 21. E, 22. H, 23. C, 24. F, 25. B, 26. A, 27. D, 28. J, 29. I, 30. I, 31. J, 32. C, 33. A.

1. F, 2. D, 3. I, 4. A, 5. J, 6. E, 7. C, 8. H, 9. B, 10. G, 11. C, 12. E, 13. H, 14. F, 15. B, 16. J, 17. G.

SELF-TEST

1. Sensation involves
   (a) the interpretation of information about the environment by the brain.
   (b) the transmission of information about the environment to the brain.
   (c) events that take place in the sensory receptors and the pathways to the brain.
   (d) both b and c.
   (LO 1; p. 108)

2. A measure of the sensitivity of a sensory system is the
   (a) absolute threshold.
   (b) just noticeable difference.
   (c) measurement of individual difference in judgment about stimuli.
   (d) both a and b.
   (LO 2; p. 109)

3. In vision, the process of transduction occurs in
   (a) the rods and the cones.
   (b) the lens and the retina.
   (c) the vitreous humor.
   (d) the pupil.
   (LO 3; p. 114)

4. A receptive field of a cell
   (a) is a receptor cell such as an individual rod or cone.
   (b) can be a part of the focusing mechanism.
   (c) is an area in the environment in which the presentation of a stimulus will cause a change in the cell's firing rate.
   (d) is part of the nervous system.
   (LO 4; p. 115)

5. The trichromatic and opponent-process theories of color vision
   (a) appear to be useful ways to understand processes in the brain and the retina, respectively.
   (b) appear to be useful ways to understand the processing of color information in the retina and the brain, respectively.
   (c) have been replaced with a more recent and technologically sophisticated theory.
   (d) are part of an unresolved controversy.
   (LO 4; p. 117)

6. Stereoscopic vision
   (a) is produced by convergence.
   (b) results from the two eyes seeing the world from slightly different perspectives.
   (c) is the most importance monocular cue for distance and depth perception.
   (d) is not as important for distance perception as a sure knowledge of the actual distance from the object seen.
   (LO 4; p. 118)

7. The stimulus for hearing is
   (a) composed of alternating compressions and rarefactions in the air.
   (b) frequency.
   (c) amplitude.
   (d) loudness.
   (LO 5; p. 119)

8. The actual receptor cells for the sense of hearing are
   (a) located in the middle ear.
   (b) located in the inner ear along the basilar membrane.
   (c) located along the outside of the cochlea.
   (d) directly stimulated by the eardrum.
   (LO 5; p. 120)

9. Space motion sickness that involves nausea is most likely the result of some sort of stimulation of the
   (a) middle ear.
   (b) cochlea.
   (c) vestibular system.
   (d) stomach or intestines.
   (LO 5; p. 123)

10. The brain's interpretation of the sensory information coming from the ear's receptor cells
    (a) depends upon where in the cochlea the stimulated cells are located.
    (b) depends upon the frequency of the sound stimulus.
    (c) depends upon which of the three bones of the middle ear are stimulated.
    (d) both a and b.
    (LO 6; p. 123)

11. Nerve deafness
    (a) is presently irreversible.
    (b) can be caused by loud noises.
    (c) can be treated with a hearing aid or surgically repaired.
    (d) both a and b.
        (LO 7; p. 123)

12. Painful sensations
    (a) requires a stimulus that actually damages tissue.
    (b) are due to activation of the Pacinian corpuscle.
    (c) have been hypothesized to be partly under the control of a "gate" in the spinal cord.
    (d) are always the result of tissue damage.
        (LO 9; p. 129)

13. Endorphins are
    (a) opiatelike substances, found in the brain.
    (b) modern drugs, based upon the chemical model of the opiates, that have been developed to treat pain and that have fewer side effects than the more traditional morphine.
    (c) found in the skin.
    (d) found in the pain receptors.
        (LO 9; p. 130)

14. The basic taste categories are
    (a) sweet, sour, salty, and bitter.
    (b) sweet, sour, and salty.
    (c) mint, musk, sweet, and salt.
    (d) carbohydrates, proteins, and fats.
        (LO 10; p. 132)

15. Perceptual constancy
    (a) refers to an inability to adjust for difference in viewing conditions.
    (b) refers to the ability to perceive objects as unchanging despite changes in the characteristics of the retinal image.
    (c) is inborn.
    (d) holds for size and distance perception but not for color.
        (LO 11; p. 135)

16. Most people see the following display as four groups of five dots: ". . . . ." This is an example of the perceptual organizing principle called
    (a) closure.
    (b) proximity.
    (c) figure.
    (d) familiarity.
        (LO 11; p. 138)

17. One way in which experience influences the way in which the world is perceived is through the formation of
    (a) figure-ground relationships.
    (b) new brain cells.
    (c) perceptual sets.
    (d) culture.
        (LO 12; p. 139)

18. The selective focusing or filtering of perception is called
    (a) attention.
    (b) perceptual constancy.
    (c) habituation.
    (d) perceptual organization.
        (LO 13; p. 140)

19. Extrasensory perception is a phenomenon
    (a) that is alleged to take place via the stimulation of an as yet undiscovered sense organ.
    (b) that is disbelieved by a majority of people.
    (c) that has had several important and clear experimental confirmations.
    (d) whose existence is supported largely by anecdotal evidence.
        (LO 16; p. 142)

20. The experimental procedures and controls of studies demonstrating ESP are usually
    (a) found to be sound.
    (b) designed by sophisticated scientists.
    (c) found to be flawed if examined.
    (d) unfairly attacked as unsound.
        (LO 16; p. 143)

ANSWERS

1. d, 2. d, 3. a, 4. c, 5. b, 6. b, 7. a, 8. b, 9. c, 10. d, 11. d, 12. c, 13. a, 14. a, 15. b, 16. b, 17. c, 18. a, 19. d, 20. c

SUGGESTED READINGS

Hansel, C. E. M. *ESP and parapsychology: a critical re-evaluation.* Buffalo, NY: Prometheus Press, 1980. A volume that debunks many of the claims of parapsychology.

Hubel, D. H., and T. N. Wiesel. Brain mechanisms of vision. *Scientific American.* September 1979. A description of their research on the activity of cells in the visual cortex by the two Nobel prize winners.

Melzack, R. *The puzzle of pain.* New York: Basic Books, 1973. An introduction to the nature of pain, and a description of Melzack and Wall's gate control theory.

Mishlove, J. *Psi development systems.* Jefferson, NC: McFarland, 1983. An unusual book that critically examines the programs that attempt to develop abilities in extrasensory perception.

Schiffman, H. R. *Sensation and perception: an integrated approach 2d ed.* New York: Wiley, 1982. An introductory text on the senses and perception.

Weale, R. A. *Focus on vision.* Cambridge, MA: Harvard University Press, 1982. A closer look at some of the properties of the visual system, including chapters on developmental changes and visual perception.

Wilding, J. M. *Perception: from sense to object.* New York: St. Martin's Press, 1983. A well-written book that emphasizes the active nature of the perception of events.

c h a p t e r

5

Learning

LEARNING OBJECTIVES

After reading this chapter, the student should be able to

1. define the term *learning*. (**p. 154**)
2. explain some of the problems associated with distinguishing learning from behavioral changes due to other factors. (**p. 154**)
3. describe classical conditioning, and identify several factors that influence the rate of conditioning. (**p. 155**)
4. explain the terms *stimulus generalization, stimulus discrimination,* and *extinction.* (**p. 159**)
5. define second-order conditioning, and show how it might affect the reward value of previously neutral stimuli. (**p. 161**)
6. show how classical conditioning might affect a person's tolerance to drugs. (**p. 161**)
7. define operant conditioning, and describe some of its properties, such as shaping, superstition, and extinction. (**p. 163**)
8. describe the concept of reinforcement. (**p. 168**)
9. define biofeedback, and show why it is an example of instrumental conditioning. (**p. 171**)
10. define insight learning, and provide an example of its occurrence. (**p. 175**)
11. define a cognitive map, and describe a study demonstrating that such a map exists. (**p. 176**)
12. define observational learning, and explain some of the studies that suggest that children can acquire aggressive responses through this form of learning. (**p. 176**)
13. describe a study dealing with flavor aversions, and explain its implications for general principles of learning. (**p. 180**)

Ten years after the Vietnam War, a veteran who had seen much combat was sitting at his desk in a plush Chicago bank building. In the men's room next door, a maintenance worker was replacing the mirror and accidentally dropped it on the floor. The veteran heard the shattering glass and froze. Sweat poured down his chalky white face and his heart raced.

The vet's colleague, who was passing by the door, saw his face and rushed into his office. She quickly scanned the room for an attacker. There was no one else. She got a glass of water for the man, and slowly he began to loosen his grip from the desk. He muttered something about broken glass and grenades.

Both of these bank employees heard the sound of the breaking mirror in the bathroom, but only the veteran reacted so strangely. The two people behaved differently in the face of the same event because of learning. One had learned to associate the sound of breaking glass with an exploding grenade because he had been in a hotel in Saigon when a guerrilla tossed a grenade through a window. The other had certainly heard glass breaking before, but she had never associated it with anything so traumatic.

What Is Learning?

Like any complex psychological phenomenon, learning is difficult to define. A good starting point is to define it as the relatively permanent changes in behavior that occur because of prior experience. For example, a puppy learns to sit in response to a "sit" command, or a child learns the alphabet. Prior experience refers to virtually any event in the environment and even includes internal events like an upset stomach. After one experience of eating rotten strawberries, for example, one learns to avoid them in the future. In many cases, the effects of the prior experience never even reach the level of consciousness.

Figure 5.1 Hopi woman holding child on a cradle board

The definition of learning is a very useful one, but it has certain deficiencies. In particular, it does not clearly make distinctions between learning and other things that affect behavior, such as maturation, genetic influences, motivation, and injury.

Learning, Maturation, and Genetic Influences

The behavior of any organism changes from moment to moment, and not all of these changes are due to learning. For example, a human baby begins to walk at about the age of one. We usually refer to this as "learning to walk," but evidence supports the view that maturation of the nervous system and the muscles is more important than prior experiences. Babies who never receive any training or encouragement to walk still learn, and at about the same age. For example, infants of the Hopi tribe, a group of Pueblo Indians living in northeastern Arizona, spend most of their first year in cradleboards, so they get little chance to practice walking or learning any of the motions. (See fig. 5.1.) Nevertheless, Hopi babies begin walking at about the same age as other babies.

Even though walking occurs primarily because of the maturation of the nervous system and the muscles, it is still affected by learning. Depending on the culture, people learn to walk with toes inward, toes outward, or with toes straight.

Behavioral changes may also be more closely related to the messages contained in the genes than it is to learning. Song sparrows, for example, begin to sing their own songs even if they are raised by a canary (Marler and Hamilton, 1966). They do not need to learn the song from any model. A great many behavioral changes, however, contain elements of learning as well as elements of genetic control. Human smiling, for example, might appear to be primarily under genetic control since even congenitally blind and deaf babies perform the response. But smiling is obviously influenced by learning too. In most cases, it is usually too simple to say that a behavior is either "genetic" or "learned." Genes and environment often interact in complex ways to produce behavioral change, as we will discuss again later in this chapter when we examine biological limitations on learning.

Learning and Performance. We ordinarily cannot measure learning; it is an inferred phenomenon. All we usually do is measure behavioral changes as they are reflected in performance. But anyone who has "frozen" during a test knows that performance may not always be an accurate measure of learning.

Suppose you work very hard to learn the names of all the people who will attend an important business meeting. Then the meeting is called off, so you never use the information. You learned the names, but you never say them, so the learning has not changed your behavior. However, the learning has produced the potential for a change in behavior, one that might be transformed into an actual change at another time. For such reasons, many psychologists like to include the notion of potentiality in their definition of learning.

Your performance may not reflect what you have learned for other reasons as well: for example, motivation, fatigue, injury, and emotional state may affect how you perform. A cat might have learned to associate the sound of a bell with dinnertime, but it may pay no attention because it isn't hungry, it's busy playing, or it's too tired to eat. And anxiety-ridden test-takers have trouble showing what they learned because of emotional factors.

In practice, it is not always possible to distinguish between changes in behavior due to learning and those due to maturation, genetic influences, motivational shifts, fatigue, or other factors. Nevertheless, it is best to define **learning** as *the relatively permanent changes in behavior, or potential for those changes, that occur because of prior experience, excluding behavioral changes due to maturation, genetic factors, changes in motivation, fatigue, or injury.*

GUIDED REVIEW

Learning Objectives 1 and 2

1. _____ is defined as the relatively permanent changes in behavior, or the potential for such changes, that occur because of prior experience. Behavioral changes that are due to maturation, genetic influences, motivational shifts, injury, or fatigue, are excluded.

ANSWER
1. *Learning*

Classical Conditioning

The Vietnam veteran's experience was an example of **classical conditioning,** *in which two stimuli are presented to an organism in a specific sequence and the organism forms an association or connection between them. One of the stimuli must automatically elicit some response from the organism; the other can be a neutral stimulus, one that has no meaning prior to the conditioning experience.*

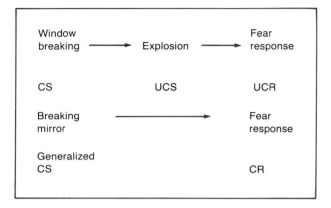

Figure 5.2   An example of classical conditioning

This simple form of learning is extremely common. It allows organisms to identify those events in the environment that are particularly relevant. The veteran had been conditioned to associate the sound of breaking glass with an explosion, for instance. Essentially, classical conditioning is a method used to predict events, although the "prediction" is not usually a conscious one. The vet certainly did not consciously predict a terrorist attack on the bank.

There are many stimuli in the world that will automatically elicit some response from an organism. A puff of air that touches your eye will cause you to blink, for example. Or a hot probe on the finger will make you withdraw your hand and feel pain. An explosion, or any sudden loud noise, will cause activation of the sympathetic nervous system. In classical conditioning, an **unconditioned stimulus** (UCS) *is an event that elicits an automatic response from an organism, one that is not learned.* The first component of classical conditioning is the presentation of a UCS which elicits the **unconditioned response** (UCR), *the automatic response to a UCS.* In the case of the veteran, the UCS was the explosion, and the UCR was the fear response (fig. 5.2).

The **conditioned stimulus** (CS) *is a neutral stimulus that precedes the UCS during classical conditioning;* it acts like a warning signal that the UCS is coming next. After many pairings, the organism begins to associate the CS with the UCS, and the CS, when presented by itself, will elicit a response. The **conditioned response** (CR) *refers to the organism's response to a previously neutral CS after it has been paired with a UCS.* For the veteran, the sound of shattering glass was the CS, and the fear response was the CR.

Pavlov's Dogs

The Russian physiologist Ivan Pavlov performed the first experiments on classical conditioning. As a young man Pavlov had incredible energy, and he directed almost all of it toward science. His indifference to earthly concerns was legendary. At one time he and his wife were living in poverty, unable to pay their bills. To help him out, his students took up a collection and asked him to give a lecture series. He gave the speeches but used the money to buy lab animals instead of necessities for the family.

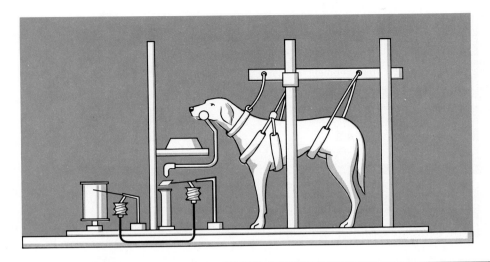

Figure 5.3 Pavlov's conditioning stand. Once a dog was strapped into a stand as shown, an experimenter could begin testing the effects of various stimuli on the salivary response. Saliva could be collected in a glass funnel.

When Pavlov began working with dogs, he was not studying behavior; he was investigating digestion. By putting meat powder in a dog's mouth, he could elicit salivation and collect the saliva in a tube (see fig. 5.3). Pavlov soon noticed, however, that the dog started to salivate before he offered it the meat powder, first when the dog saw the bowl, then when he heard Pavlov open the door. To learn more about this strange phenomenon, Pavlov began using a clicking metronome as a CS. Immediately following this sound, he placed food in the dog's mouth. After doing this several times, he noticed that the dog began to salivate as soon as it heard the metronome (fig. 5.4).

These observations led Pavlov to a turning point in his career. He did not know whether to continue his studies of digestion or to begin investigating how the dog's salivary gland "learns." Fortunately for psychology, Pavlov chose to study conditioning. He later won a Nobel prize for his work.

Properties of Classical Conditioning

The basic model of classical conditioning is deceptively simple. A UCS that elicits an automatic UCR is paired with a CS. Eventually, the CS itself can elicit a response from the organism, without the presentation of the UCS. This response is the CR. Pavlov, and many later researchers, investigated variations of this model to determine the properties of classical conditioning. Research on this topic is still very active; all of its properties are not yet entirely clear (Rescorla and Holland, 1982). Some of the questions about classical conditioning include the following:

1. How fast does conditioning occur?
2. What characteristics of the CS affect conditioning?
3. How does the pairing procedure affect conditioning?
4. How does an organism forget a conditioning experience?
5. Can a CS that elicits a response be used as a UCS and paired with a new CS?

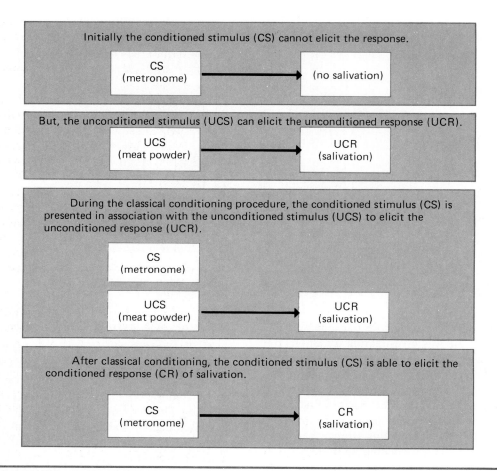

Figure 5.4 *A diagram of classical conditioning*

The Rate of Conditioning.   Pavlov found that the more times the metronome was paired with the food, the more quickly the dog would come to salivate to the sound of the metronome alone. This observation is very logical and suggests that the association became stronger each time the two stimuli were paired. However, the first few pairings are the most important in classical conditioning. After this, the CR usually does not get very much stronger. (See fig. 5.5.) Under some conditions, even a single pairing can be powerful enough to produce conditioning. This can happen if the UCS is particularly traumatic, as it was for the Vietnam veteran.

The usefulness of the CS as a predictor, and hence the rate of conditioning, are also affected by how consistently it is followed by the UCS. If the CS sometimes occurs alone, it will not be a completely reliable

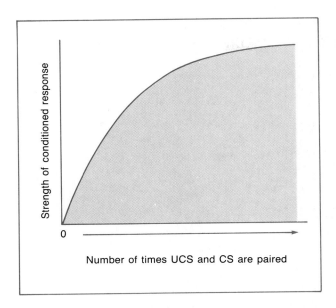

Figure 5.5 A graph showing the theoretical relationship between the number of times the UCS and CS are paired and the strength of the CR when the CS is presented alone. Actual data will depend on many factors, such as the delay between the UCS and the delay between the UCS and the CS and the emotional impact of the UCS.

predictor, and learning will be slower. The fastest learning takes place if the two events are consistently paired and neither one occurs by itself. This means that certain CS's will work better than others: novel, unusual, and intense CS's are usually more effective than familiar ones.

The Conditioned Stimulus—Stimulus Generalization. Once the organism has made an association between the UCS and the CS, it will begin to respond to the CS alone. It will continue to respond, even if you change the CS slightly. For example, the veteran originally learned to respond with fear to the sound of a grenade breaking a window. But a breaking mirror on a bathroom floor produced almost as much fear. And the dog that responded to the metronome by salivating will

probably also respond to a buzzer by salivating at least slightly. This phenomenon is called **stimulus generalization.** *The more similar a stimulus is to the original CS, the more likely it is that the organism will demonstrate a CR.*

Stimulus generalization often involves similarities in sound, sight, or other physical characteristics. In humans, though, a stimulus generalization can be much more abstract. In an early study, a researcher found that generalizations could even be based on similarities in meanings of words (Razran, 1939). He classically conditioned human subjects to salivate to the sight of certain words, such as style, urn, freeze, and surf. Then he presented some words that are similar in sound (stile, earn, frieze, serf), and others that are similar in meaning (fashion, vase, chill, wave). The subjects showed much more significant responses to the words similar in meaning.

The Conditioned Stimulus—Stimulus Discrimination. **Stimulus discrimination** *refers to the fact that an organism can learn to distinguish between a CS that reliably precedes a UCS and similar stimuli that are not paired with the UCS.* For example, dogs trained to salivate at the sound of a bell can learn to ignore a buzzer simply if the buzzer is presented alone several times. Pavlov found that dogs could make very subtle distinctions between sounds, and the technique is frequently used to assess the sensitivity of sensory systems in animals. In one of Pavlov's studies, dogs were able to discriminate between a metronome ticking at 98 beats per minute, and another at 100 beats per minute.

One of Pavlov's colleagues, N. R. Shenger-Krestovnikova, wondered what would happen if the dog's ability to discriminate were pushed to its limits. He conditioned the dog to salivate when it saw a circle but to ignore an ellipse. Then he slowly began to make the ellipse more like a circle and the circle more elliptical. Pavlov's description of the dog's behavior is fascinating.

The hitherto quiet dog began to squeal in its stand, wriggling about . . . and bit through the tubes connecting the animal's room with the observer. . . . In short, it presented all the symptoms of a condition of acute neurosis. (Pavlov, 1927, 291)

Pavlov called this behavior **experimental neurosis;** *it consists of severe agitation and aggressive behavior in an organism when a previously established learned response is disrupted in some way* (Allen, 1984). Pavlov hypothesized that some forms of mental illness might be due to similar disruptive conditioning experiences.

The Pairing Procedure. The manner in which the UCS is paired with the CS has turned out to be an interesting and controversial issue. First, conditioning does not seem to occur at all unless the neutral CS comes first. If it comes after the UCS, even very soon after, the organism never learns to make the CR to the CS alone. This kind of **backward conditioning,** *in which the UCS precedes the CS,* probably is ineffective because the CS cannot be used to predict the occurrence of the UCS. If the sound of breaking glass followed the explosion, the veteran would pay little attention to it and would certainly not become fearful each time he heard it. By the same token, **simultaneous conditioning,** *in which the CS and the UCS occur at the same time,* is also not very effective. Again, the sound of breaking glass cannot be used as a predictor if it occurs at the same time as the explosion.

Under most circumstances, the most successful conditioning occurs when the CS begins just a fraction of a second before the UCS is presented. For example, the dog would learn fastest if the bell was rung about one-half second before the food was put in its mouth. Shorter or longer intervals than this usually produce slower learning. (See fig. 5.6.) There are some exceptions to this general rule, however, as we shall see later in the chapter.

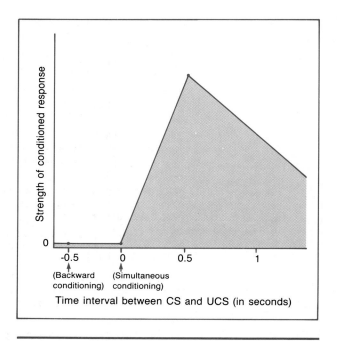

Figure 5.6 A graph showing the theoretical relationship of the CR and the time interval between the CS and the UCS. When the UCS comes either before the CS (backward conditioning) or at the same time as the CS (simultaneous conditioning), learning does not occur. In general, the best conditioning occurs when the time interval is about one-half second.

Extinction. **Extinction** *occurs when the CS is presented repeatedly without the UCS, causing the response to the CS to gradually diminish.* The dog's salivation response to the bell, for example, could be extinguished by ringing the bell over and over without following it with food.

Extinction may seem to be like forgetting, but the two are not quite the same. If a response has been extinguished, it is not forgotten in the sense that it will never happen again. If time is allowed to pass after the dog has stopped salivating to the sound of the bell, the dog will start again.

Extinguishing the veteran's response to breaking glass would take some time and patience. He would need to be exposed to the CS (the sound of breaking glass) repeatedly without pairing it with any UCS in order to extinguish the fear response.

Second-Order Conditioning. One of the most important features of classical conditioning is the way in which one conditioning experience can lay the groundwork for another. After many pairings of the CS and the UCS, the CS begins to elicit a response from the animal when it is presented alone. This CS can then be paired with another neutral stimulus; after many pairings, the organism will come to respond to the new stimulus. In effect, the CS can now act as a UCS. This phenomenon is called **second-order conditioning;** *it occurs when a previously established CS that reliably elicits a CR is used as a UCS in a new conditioning experience.*

In the example of the salivating dog, the dog first is conditioned to respond to the original CS, the bell, by salivating. In the next phase, a new stimulus, perhaps a light, is presented immediately before the bell, and the original UCS, the meat, is omitted. In the first few trials the dog responds to the bell by salivating. After several pairings of the light and the bell, the dog begins to salivate in response to the light presented alone.

If the circumstances are right, the light can then be paired with another new stimulus, which can then be paired with another one, and so on. But if the first CS, the bell, is repeatedly presented without pairing it with the original UCS (the meat), the bell will eventually lose its ability to elicit a response. The response will undergo extinction. For second- and higher-order conditioning to occur, the original CS must occasionally be paired with the original UCS to ensure that extinction does not occur.

Second- and higher-order conditioning are important because they help explain how certain stimuli can acquire the ability to elicit responses, even when they never seem to have been paired with any obvious UCS. A check in the mail, for example, might have been paired with money, which was paired with packages of food, which is paired with satisfaction of hunger.

Classical Conditioning and Preparation

An important function of classical conditioning is to provide the organism with a reliable warning signal that a significant event is about to occur. The conditioning will often result in a CR that very closely resembles the UCR. But in some cases, the CR is rather different. It appears to be more of a preparation for the upcoming UCS than an early response to the UCS.

For example, the appearance of a rival male in the territory of certain species of fish acts as a UCS that produces a typical UCR of aggressive behavior. If a warning signal, like a red light, reliably precedes the appearance of the rival, the fish will learn a conditioned response. It approaches the site of the signal and the place where the intruder will appear, all fins erect and ready for battle. In a sense, the fish is preparing for the contest. And this preparation helps it win, as well. Conditioned fish show considerably more aggression in these contests (Hollis, 1984).

Another example in which the CS may be helping the organism to prepare for the upcoming UCS is in the development of tolerance to psychoactive drugs, a phenomenon discussed in Chapter 3. The development of tolerance appears partly due to physiological changes in the body, especially in the brain and the liver. Tolerance also appears to be a function of conditioning (Siegel, 1975).

In one experiment, rats received fairly large doses of alcohol every other day for eighteen days in order to develop tolerance. The experimenters removed them from their home cages, took them into another room that had dim lights and a blaring radio, measured their rectal temperatures, and then injected the alcohol. The rats' temperatures were taken again after forty-five, sixty, and seventy-five minutes. (Le, Poulos, and Cappell, 1979).

Rats get drunk when they consume alcohol, just as humans do. One of the symptoms of their intoxication is a drop in body temperature, perhaps by two degrees Centigrade. But they show tolerance after they have received several injections, and their body temperatures might drop less than one degree. As expected, the same dose of alcohol produced a smaller effect on their bodies after they had used the drug for a while.

All of these tests were conducted in a strange noisy room with dim lights. But what would happen if the animals were tested in their home room, where they had never received any alcohol and where they were not expecting any? If tolerance is purely a physiological phenomenon, the results should be the same. The experimenters injected these same rats in their home rooms. They suddenly lost much of their tolerance to the drug. But when they were injected again the next day in the noisy room, their tolerance seemed to come right back.

This study shows that tolerance is not just a physiological phenomenon, it is also related to classical conditioning. The drug injection is the UCS, and the UCR is the drop in body temperature (and probably all the other effects of alcohol as well). The CS is the noisy room, which the rats had come to associate with the coming injection. The nervous systems of the rats produced a CR in response to the noisy room, and this CR was an *increase* in body temperature, which helped their bodies prepare and compensate for the imminent alcohol injection. Because of this preparation, the alcohol only produced a very slight drop in body temperature (less than one degree), rather than the large one observed previously. Since the rats had not formed any association between their own home rooms and the alcohol injection, they did not exhibit any CR in their home rooms.

We mentioned in Chapter 3 that a large proportion of deaths attributed to drug overdoses may not really be due to overdoses at all, especially since many of the victims did not seem to be injecting, sniffing, or swallowing particularly large quantities relative to their usual doses. The studies on classically conditioned responses to drugs leads to the conclusion that this simple form of learning plays an important role in a person's tolerance to a drug at any particular time. Tolerance is a physiological phenomenon that varies from moment to moment depending on psychological factors.

GUIDED REVIEW

Learning Objectives 3, 4, 5, and 6

1. During classical conditioning, an _____ (UCS) that automatically elicits an _____ (UCR) is paired with a _____ (CS). After many pairings, the animal learns the association between the UCS and the CS and begins to respond to the CS presented alone. This response to the CS is called the _____ (CR).

2. _____ performed the first studies of classical conditioning, using dogs. The UCS was meat in the dog's mouth, and the UCR was salivation. He taught the dogs to associate a sound (CS) with the meat, and after many pairings, the sound elicited a CR when it was presented alone.

3. The _____ depends on several factors, including how many times the UCS is paired with the CS and how novel the CS is to the animal.

4. The CS must precede the UCS for conditioning to occur; the most rapid conditioning takes place when the CS-UCS interval is about _____ .

5. After conditioning, the animal will generalize its learning to stimuli that are similar to the CS, a phenomenon called _____ . If similar stimuli are presented without the UCS, the animal will come to discriminate between the CS and other, similar stimuli in a phenomenon called _____ .

6. _____ may occur when a previously established learned response is disrupted, for example, by presenting two similar stimuli between which the organism cannot discriminate, and following only one stimulus with the UCS.

7. A CR can be inhibited through _____ . The CS is presented repeatedly without the UCS until the animal stops responding to the CS.

8. After conditioning, a CS can be used as a UCS in a new conditioning procedure with a new, neutral stimulus serving as the CS. This phenomenon is called _____ .

9. The development of _____ to drugs appears to be partly a physiological phenomenon, and partly due to classical conditioning experiences. Rats that were conditioned to associate a particular room with a drug injection began to make physiological preparations to compensate for the coming injection as a CR to the special room.

ANSWERS

9. *tolerance*
6. *Experimental neurosis* 7. *extinction* 8. *second-order conditioning*
4. *one-half second* 5. *stimulus generalization; stimulus discrimination*
stimulus; conditioned response 2. *Ivan Pavlov* 3. *rate of conditioning*
1. *unconditioned stimulus; unconditioned response; conditioned*

Operant Conditioning

In classical conditioning the organism is learning to associate two events in the environment because one of them can be used to predict the onset of the other. In **operant conditioning** *the organism is learning to associate its own behavior with events in the environment. It is learning the consequences of its actions.*

A woman whose children had just become old enough to enter school went on her first job interview in seven years. She was very nervous and anxious to please the personnel officer at the insurance company where she was applying for an assistant manager position. Instead of asking a series of questions, the interviewer made one simple request: "Tell me about yourself." The woman began talking about her home, family, volunteer activities, and education. Most of the time, the interviewer remained passive and looked down at her papers on the desk. But whenever the woman mentioned anything about organizational skills, the interviewer glanced up, looked her in the eye, and encouragingly said, "mmmm." By the end of the interview,

the applicant was only discussing her skills at organizing volunteer work. She didn't get the job, but at her next interview she skipped any discussion of home and family and concentrated on her volunteer work.

Learning by Consequences

Operant conditioning is the way organisms learn to modify their behavior by learning what the consequences of that behavior are. Although she may not have been aware of it, the applicant for the assistant manager position was learning which topics were followed by rewards and which were not. When she discussed her volunteer activities, the interviewer showed interest, clearly a rewarding event. As she continued talking, she began to speak more and more of her organizational skills rather than her home and family, topics that were not followed by any rewards. The general principle of operant conditioning is simple: if a behavior is rewarded, we repeat it.

There are three important components in operant conditioning: the stimulus, the response, and the reinforcer. In the preceding example, the general environment of the job interview is the stimulus, and the woman's verbal behavior is the response. The reinforcer is the interest of the interviewer as shown by her eye contact and verbal approval. *A* **reinforcer** *is anything that tends to strengthen the response that immediately preceded it.*

Thorndike's Cats and Skinner's Rats

At the same time Pavlov was unraveling the puzzles of classical conditioning, an American graduate student, Edward L. Thorndike, was studying animal intelligence. Unlike most of his contemporaries, Thorndike was convinced that most people were overimpressed with the intelligence of animals. Anecdotes of dogs or cats that traveled hundreds of miles in a successful search for their owners were common, but stories of

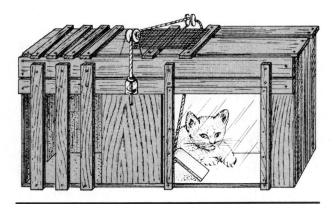

Figure 5.7 *A puzzle box for cats, developed by Thorndike*

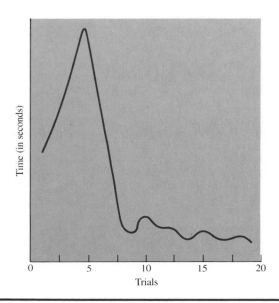

Figure 5.8 *A learning curve showing how the time a cat took to escape from the puzzle box decreased*

animals who got lost in their own neighborhoods were never reported in the news. In fact, he thought the topic of his research should be animal stupidity rather than animal intelligence.

Thorndike's most promising line of investigation dealt with the way cats solve problems. He put a hungry cat in a puzzle box (shown in fig. 5.7), and placed some food just out of its reach. A wire loop hanging from the inside top of the box would open the door if the cat pulled it. At first the cat tried to squeeze through the bars or reach its paw toward the food. Eventually, it accidentally pulled the wire, and the door opened. The next time it was placed in the box, the cat performed unsuccessful escape routines for a shorter period of time and then pulled the loop. After several experiences in the box, the cat went directly to the loop, pulled it, and got out of the box immediately. Thorndike timed the cat's escape performance on each trial, and it gradually decreased. (See fig. 5.8.)

Thorndike did not see much "animal intelligence" in the cat's behavior. Instead, he saw the cat performing a great deal of random behavior that eventually included the correct response. This response was followed by a reward (escape and food), and the cat then began performing it more frequently, whenever it was placed into the puzzle box. It was as if the cat tended to stop performing responses that were followed

by nothing and continue to perform those that were followed by a reward. (See fig. 5.9.) He called this phenomenon the **Law of Effect;** *it states that the probability of a response depends upon that response's effect on the environment. Responses that are followed by a reward tend to be repeated.*

Thorndike used the term "instrumental conditioning" rather than operant conditioning to refer to the process whereby an organism learns the association between behavior and its consequences. The term "operant conditioning" was introduced by B. F. Skinner, who began studying the phenomenon in the 1930s, developing techniques that eventually became standard for investigations of the phenomenon. Much of what we know about operant conditioning was learned in his laboratories and those of his students. He placed a rat into a **Skinner Box,** *a special cage, equipped with a lever and a food bin, used for investigating operant conditioning.* Each time the rat pressed the lever, a pellet of food was released into the bin. Some boxes were also equipped with lights and buzzers, and some

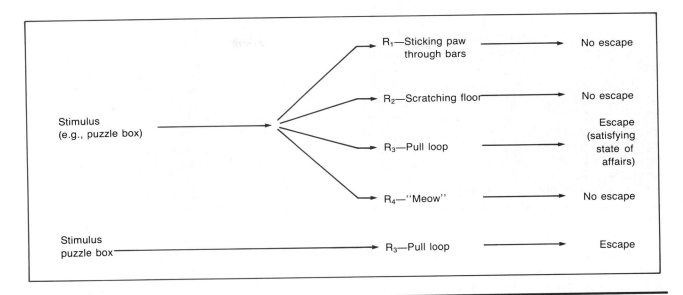

Figure 5.9   Thorndike's Law of Effect

Figure 5.10   A Skinner box

had grid floors for delivering shock. The lever was usually wired to a **cumulative recorder,** *which is an instrument with moving chart paper on which a pen moves a notch each time the organism makes a response, in this case, pressing a lever* (fig. 5.10). (The term "Skinner Box," by the way, was not invented by Skinner, and according to one author [Harris, 1971], he detests the nickname.)

Skinner's focus was on **operants,** *or responses such as lever pressing that occur in the absence of any particular stimuli, or at least any that are immediately obvious.* Before conditioning, the person or animal spontaneously emits these responses at some baseline rate. In his learning theories, Skinner used the term operant conditioning rather than instrumental conditioning to emphasize the way in which the conditioning procedure affects the frequency with which this response, or operant, is emitted. In his research he usually obtained a baseline rate of spontaneous responding, say of lever pressing, using the cumulative recorder. Since rats will rarely press the lever unless they receive training, the baseline for this response would be close to zero. Then he introduced an operant learning scheme, for example, a partial reinforcement schedule, and observed the change in the frequency of lever pressing.

Instead of the term "classical conditioning" Skinner prefers "respondent conditioning" to emphasize that the response in the situation is not freely emitted. The **respondent** *is equivalent to the UCR.*

Characteristics of Operant Conditioning

Some of the properties of operant conditioning and classical conditioning are quite similar, and others are very different or at least not applicable to the classical conditioning situation. For example, if the time between the behavior and the reinforcement is very short, about one-half second, learning proceeds very quickly. Giving a dog a bone for a trick it performed an hour ago is useless. The short time interval between the CS and the UCS was important in classical conditioning also. It seems as though organisms need predictors that predict something that is going to happen very soon, rather than minutes or hours later, although there are some exceptions.

Other characteristics of operant conditioning that bear some resemblance to classical conditioning are stimulus generalization and discrimination. For instance, the woman at the job interview would probably generalize what she had learned to other stimulus situations, such as other job interviews in banks, retail stores, or factories. Just as in classical conditioning, however, the amount of generalization decreases as the

stimulus becomes less and less similar to the one in which the learning occurred. She probably would not generalize what she had learned to an afternoon conversation with a neighbor. The process of stimulus discrimination in operant conditioning involves learning that a response produces a reward in one context but not in another.

Shaping. One of the characteristics of operant conditioning that is not present in classical conditioning is shaping. Suppose you are trying to train your dog to lie down, and you are using dog biscuits as rewards. The dog is too excited to lie down, so you never reward him. The solution to this problem is **shaping,** *a technique in which you reward successively closer approximations of the desired response;* in this case, until the dog finally performs the behavior. For example, you first reward the dog when he crouches slightly; then you only reward him when he crouches almost to the ground. Finally, you only reward him when he touches the ground with his belly and actually lies down. Professional dog trainers use shaping extensively. The technique is described in the Career Box: Dog Trainer.

A manager might use shaping techniques with a new employee. Suppose the employee's job is to write summaries of scientific articles and she does a very poor job in the beginning. The manager might wait a few days and finally give her a reward, perhaps a smile and a positive comment, for a summary that is at least grammatically correct. Before another reward is forthcoming, however, the summaries must be improved, at least in the manager's eyes.

The advantage of shaping is that it permits operant conditioning of responses that do not occur. If a parent has a son whose room is always a mess, it is difficult to reward him for cleaning up the room. But the parents can still use shaping by rewarding the boy for cleaning up a little corner or perhaps for putting up a poster. The parents would then raise the criterion for the next reward.

CAREER BOX

Dog Trainer

A rewarding career for dog lovers is that of a dog trainer, although few people rely on this occupation for their entire income. Talented trainers often run schools that specialize in teaching certain kinds of skills to dogs, such as obedience, hunting, tracking, police work, guide work for the blind, and even movie work. These schools sometimes double as kennels, and many trainers supplement their incomes by breeding dogs.

Regardless of which skills a trainer is trying to teach a dog, a good deal of knowledge about the characteristics of operant conditioning is required. Trainers are not necessarily familiar with the terms *discriminative stimulus* or *extinction schedule,* but they do know the principles of learning, particularly as they apply to the various breeds of dogs in different situations.

Trainers who teach dogs to track, for example, make ample use of the technique of shaping (Adam, 1983). First the trainer sets out a stake, scuffs the ground around it, and walks straight across an open field for about thirty yards, leaving his glove or sock on the ground. Then the pup is led to the stake, told to "Find it!," and then led to the sock. The trainer rewards the pup with praise and a treat as soon as it arrives at the sock. In later trials, the criterion for success (and reward) gradually gets more difficult. The distance between the stake and the sock is increased, and a few turns are added to the trainer's path. In advanced training, a few other people cross the trainer's path to add confusing scents.

Well-trained tracking dogs are valuable in police work, and especially in search and rescue operations. For example, in the spring of 1982, avalanches devastated a ski resort in California, trapping a 22-year-old employee in a locker room. The snow and debris poured in from all sides, forming a small triangular air space four feet long and two feet high. After five days of search operations, Bridget, a German shepherd tracking dog that is a member of a search-and-rescue (SAR) team called WOOF, located the woman's scent and led the rescuers to her. Bridget had previously assisted SAR workers in finding bodies, but this was the first time an SAR dog was able to help rescuers locate a living avalanche victim in North America (Bergstrom, 1982).

Superstition. The conditions under which operant conditioning occurs require that the response be followed by a reward. They do not necessarily require that the response must *cause* the reward. What would happen if a reward happened to follow a response accidentally?

Skinner (1948) answered this question by delivering food into the bin of a pigeon's Skinner box every fifteen seconds. Just before the food arrived, the pigeon was doing something, perhaps scratching the floor, turning in circles, or pecking the wall. Even though the reward arrived regardless of what the pigeon did or did not do, the particular behavior the pigeon was performing just before the reward increased in frequency. Skinner called this behavior **superstitious;** *it involves the formation of a false association between a response and a reinforcer when there is no cause-and-effect relationship between the two.*

Superstitious behavior is not restricted to pigeons; human beings show similar behavior. For example, a man gets in an elevator and presses the button for the floor to which he wants to go. The elevator is programmed to delay closing the door for several seconds after a button is pushed, but the man does not know this. Since the elevator does not move, he is not rewarded, so he presses the floor button again. Now the door closes and the elevator rises. The next time the man gets in the elevator he immediately presses the button *twice,* as if he must do this before the elevator will move. Since the elevator will always move after he presses a button twice, he will continue to receive rewards for his superstitious behavior.

Extinction.   The problem of getting rid of undesirable behavior can usually be solved by extinction. In classical conditioning, you may recall, extinction involves presentation of the CS alone, without pairing it with the UCS. In operant conditioning, extinction involves withholding the reward for a response. For example, if a rat has learned to press a lever for a pellet of food, withholding the reward will eventually result in the extinction of the lever-pressing response.

Let us consider a more practical problem. Suppose a one-year-old baby will not go to sleep at night unless her mother walks with her, sometimes for hours on end. The mother becomes exhausted and needs some means to solve the problem. She must first find out why the baby is crying. If she needs food, water, a change of diaper, or security, it is important that the mother provide her with these things. However, if she just wants to stay up as long as possible, the mother could put the baby on an extinction schedule, a somewhat drastic solution, but sometimes the only one. The mother would put the baby in bed at some reasonable hour, leave the room, and not go back. On the first night the baby might cry for over an hour. She may cry for only fifteen minutes on the second night. By the third night, as long as no one goes in to reward her crying, she may cry for only five minutes. And on the fourth night she probably wouldn't cry at all. In this situation the baby's sleepiness, the fact that it is nighttime, and all the elements associated with bedtime are the stimulus; the baby's crying is the response; and the mother's attention is the reinforcement. If the mother stops reinforcing the baby's crying in this context, the baby should stop crying and go to sleep.

Reinforcement

The concept of reinforcement is central in operant conditioning. Most psychologists maintain that during operant conditioning, the organism is learning an association between its own response and the reinforcer. It is called a "reinforcer" because it reinforces, or strengthens, the response that preceded it.

Positive Reinforcement, Negative Reinforcement, and Punishment.   Psychologists usually distinguish between positive and negative reinforcers. A **positive reinforcer** *is a reward for performing some response that tends to strengthen that response.* The food pellet in the Skinner box, for example, provides positive reinforcement for the pigeon pressing the lever. A **negative reinforcer** *is a stimulus, such as a loud noise or a shock, that is removed following the performance of some response, thereby strengthening that response.* For example, suppose you walk into a room with a dreadful buzz that seems to be coming from one of the fluorescent lights. You make several responses, such as pulling out one or two plugs, or flipping some unidentified switches on the wall. Finally, the buzzing stops. The response that immediately preceded the silence is the one that is rewarded with negative reinforcement.

Punishment *is not reinforcement at all because it does not strengthen a response. It is a stimulus that tends to decrease the probability of the response that immediately preceded it.* If a personnel officer made a gruff "hmph" each time a job applicant said something about her family during an interview, the applicant would quickly decrease that response because it was followed by a punishing stimulus.

Although punishment is an effective way of suppressing undesirable behavior, it has several problems. First, it teaches a person what behavior he should *not* do, but it does not teach what he *should* do. Using positive reinforcement for desirable behavior and punishment for undesirable behavior is much more effective than using punishment alone. Another problem with punishment is that it elicits an emotional reaction, such as fear or anger. The more severe the punishment, the more intense the reaction. This automatic reaction is very important in classical conditioning. The person doing the punishing is the CS, the punishment is the UCS, and the emotional reaction, perhaps fear, is the response. Eventually, the person being punished shows a classically conditioned fear reaction to the person who does the punishing. Parents might easily become a CS for a fear reaction if they use too much punishment on their children.

Schedules of Reinforcement. **Continuous reinforcement** *involves reinforcing a response every time it occurs.* This method of reinforcement is best during the first stages of conditioning, when the person or animal is just learning the response. It produces the fastest learning. Although it may seem that this method would be the most effective way to maintain some behavior, Skinner and his students found that **partial reinforcement,** *in which a response is rewarded intermittently,* is actually more effective.

A response maintained through partial reinforcement is very resistant to extinction. Under a continuous reinforcement schedule, the person or animal comes to expect a reward every time, so when the reward stops, the behavior extinguishes rather quickly. But under a partial reinforcement schedule, the organism does not expect a reward every time. If you try to extinguish the response by not rewarding it anymore, the organism will continue to respond for some time.

One of the major hazards in any extinction schedule is the chance that the response will receive a reward and the organism will be moved from a continuous reinforcement schedule to a partial schedule. For example, the parent who is trying to extinguish the baby's crying behavior at bedtime may feel so desperate by the second or third night that he or she goes in to comfort the baby. Now the baby learns that bedtime crying is not rewarded all the time, but at least some of the time, so the crying will be much more persistent. Maintaining the extinction schedule under these conditions takes nerves of steel, but it is the fastest way to a more peaceful bedtime for both baby and parents. The slowest way is to let the baby cry on some nights and to comfort her on other nights.

There are four different kinds of partial reinforcement schedules: fixed ratio, variable ratio, fixed interval, and variable interval. The **fixed ratio schedule** *reinforces a response after it occurs a certain number of times.* For example, a supervisor might reward an assembly-line worker on a piece rate arrangement, perhaps awarding $10 for every five completed toasters. In the laboratory, a rat that received a food pellet for every fifteen lever presses would be on a fixed ratio reinforcement schedule.

The **variable ratio schedule** *rewards a response after it occurs a certain number of times, on the average.* Sometimes, perhaps because a few toasters were sent back with defects, the worker might have to produce eight of them to get the reward. At other times, five would be enough. A slot machine also works on a variable ratio schedule.

The ratio schedules maintain a high rate of responding, which is one reason management has tended to adopt piece rate systems. Historically, however, trade unions have opposed the system. They argue that it encourages high production to the point of being inhumane.

In the interval schedules, a reinforcement is provided for the first response that occurs after an interval of time, usually measured from the last reinforcement. It does not make any difference how often the subject responds during the interval. No reinforcement will be forthcoming until the interval is over and the organism makes one more response.

A **fixed interval schedule** *provides a reward for any correct response that occurs after a specific time interval passes since the last reinforcement.* For example, a rat might have to wait exactly thirty seconds after each reinforcement before a lever press will result in another pellet of food. A **variable interval schedule** *provides a reward for any correct response that occurs after a variable time interval passes since the last reward.* For the rat, sometimes the interval might be twenty-two seconds; at other times it might be thirty-seven seconds. The average interval would be thirty seconds.

For another example of a fixed-interval schedule, consider a child who is fed after specific intervals, say every three hours, despite the fact that he says he is hungry between meals. Regardless of the child's crying, the parent only feeds the child when he cries after the specific interval is over.

An interesting behavior pattern appears in fixed-interval schedules of reinforcement. The animal or human begins to estimate the time interval rather well, showing a "scalloped" pattern of responding. For example, immediately after a reinforcement the organism shows very little response, but the rate of responding increases dramatically toward the end of the time period, until the next reinforcement is given. The child might cry very little immediately after a meal, but his crying would increase considerably when the three hours were nearly over.

The Nature of Reinforcement. Determining what will and what will not act as a reinforcer is a very difficult problem. The reinforcing nature of some things, such as food to a hungry animal, has a certain intuitive reasonableness. The term **primary reinforcers** *refers to events that aid biological survival.* Other examples would include water to a thirsty animal or warmth to a cold one.

The vast majority of reinforcing events, however, are not so obviously reinforcing. The slot machine delivers shiny circular pieces of metal to the person who is very persistent at pulling its lever. These pieces of metal have no intrinsically rewarding qualities. They do not quench thirst, satisfy hunger, warm cold hands, or provide gratification for sexual urges. Yet they act as a very potent reinforcer since they maintain "lever pressing" (or pulling) at an incredibly high rate. **Secondary reinforcers** *are those that tend to strengthen responses but do not aid biological survival directly.* Whether an event will have secondary reinforcing properties depends on the learning history of the organism rather than on biological survival needs. For instance, the first time a person walks into a candy store with a nickel to exchange for a piece of chocolate, he or she learns to associate money with primary reinforcements. Using classical conditioning, the money has become the CS and the candy the UCS. Second or higher order classical conditioning experiences would lay the foundation for other things that have been paired with money becoming potent reinforcers.

An important category of secondary reinforcers is called social reinforcers. A smile from the boss, a pat on the back, praise from a parent, are all very powerful reinforcers that can produce dramatic changes in the frequency of responses. They are so powerful and widespread that many scientists wonder whether they are indeed "secondary." Perhaps the need for social approval is almost as important for biological survival as food or water.

The Research Box: Human Verbal Learning discusses how a psychologist rewarded himself for memorizing boring lists; his secondary reward may have been acclaim from colleagues.

The definition of a reinforcer is that it is something that strengthens a response. But this only defines reinforcement after the fact. For example, you won't know whether marbles will act as reinforcers for little Johnny until you offer them as rewards for finishing homework assignments. The definition of a reinforcer is not entirely circular; if marbles work in one context, they are likely to work in another. Thus, once you know that something is a reinforcer for a person, you can use it to modify many different kinds of behavior (Meehl, 1950).

David Premack developed another approach to the definition and prediction of reinforcement (1959, 1965). He saw reinforcement as the opportunity to participate in some activity, such as eating, rather than as the thing itself, in this case food. The reward value of these different activities depends on how frequently the animal normally participates in it. The **Premack principle** *states that activities that are more common or probable in the animal's life will act as reinforcers for activities that are less probable.*

For example, lever pressing is a much less probable activity than eating, so eating will reinforce lever pressing. In instrumental conditioning, then, it is possible to use the eating response as a reinforcement for lever pressing, but it is not possible to use lever pressing as a reward for eating. If playing with marbles is a highly probable activity in Johnny's life, then the opportunity to do it will serve as a reinforcement for doing his homework, an activity that is less probable. On the other hand, if Johnny is working on a fascinating science project related to his beetle collection and has never played marbles in his life, the opportunity to play marbles will not reinforce doing his homework. Instead, the reverse would be true. Allowing him to work on his homework would serve as a reinforcement for playing with marbles. The Premack principle provides a theoretical basis with which to predict whether something will be reinforcing, without actually testing it.

Biofeedback

One example of how instrumental conditioning can be applied is **biofeedback.** *This is a technique in which a person learns to gain control over some physiological response by having access to information about the ongoing state of the response.* Until the late 1960s, most scientists thought it would be impossible to gain any voluntary control over internal physiological functions. But the development of biofeedback made everyone question this assumption. For example, a person can learn to reduce his heart rate simply by watching a monitor that provides feedback about tiny changes in heart rate. Each time it decreases, he is rewarded by his success and repeats the behavior that immediately preceded the slight drop. This causes the heart rate to decrease still further, providing another rewarding success. Eventually, responses that do not reduce heart rate extinguish, and responses that do become more frequent.

When you ask subjects what behavior they are performing in order to reduce their heart rates, they are usually quite vague. They might say, "Oh, I just try to relax," or "I think about a very calm day I had last week when I was in the mountains." They rarely say they are moving certain muscles or concentrating on their hearts. No one is quite sure *what* response is being rewarded in heart rate biofeedback, except that whatever it is, it results in the drop in heart rate. It most likely involves activation of the parasympathetic nervous system, a division of the autonomic nervous system discussed in Chapter 2. This system helps restore the body to normal after a stressful event. Activation of it would produce lowered blood pressure and slower respiration, as well as decreased heart rate.

Biofeedback has become a useful tool in some areas of medicine (Olton and Noonberg, 1980), particularly in treating tension and migraine headaches, ulcers, asthma, high blood pressure, and circulatory problems.

RESEARCH BOX

Human Verbal Learning

Whereas many of the early psychologists who were interested in learning were using rats in mazes or Skinner boxes for studying the details of reward and motivation, Herman Ebbinghaus was studying the way humans learn verbal material (Ebbinghaus, 1885). He acted as his own "rat," collecting data about his performance in learning and remembering lists of verbal stimuli.

Ebbinghaus chose to use consonant-vowel-consonant "nonsense syllables" like caj, cik, or gej. He reasoned that words or phrases would be too complex and that any investigations using them would not reveal very much about the elemental associations being formed during a learning experience. The words would have built-in associations that would complicate the learning process. Ebbinghaus argued that his 2300 nonsense syllables represented a pool of minimal verbal units that were free of previous associations. (Later experiments demonstrated that these so-called nonsense syllables are not always nonsensical to people and often have strong associations. For example, a syllable such as "bal" has a much higher association value than one like "cij." The higher the association value of the syllable, the easier it is for subjects to learn and remember it.)

A typical experiment for Ebbinghaus involved serial learning. He made up a list of syllables and read through it at a rapid and uniform rate. Occasionally he would stop and test himself to see if he could remember the next syllable before seeing it. He continued this way until he could recite the entire list in the correct order without any errors. He usually scored his performance by noting either the amount of time or the number of trials required to learn the list perfectly. After an interval of time, Ebbinghaus would use the "savings method" to measure

A study conducted on patients with stomach ulcers demonstrates how biofeedback is used (Welgan, 1974). One of the symptoms of ulcers is excess stomach acid, so the five men who participated in the study used biofeedback to learn to control the acidity in their stomachs. Tubes were placed into their stomachs so samples of the contents could be obtained and information about its acidity relayed to each subject. After baseline acidity levels were obtained, the men received feedback about any changes in pH. At the end of the sessions, these patients' stomach acidity was reduced to about twenty percent of its original level.

The usefulness of biofeedback depends somewhat on whether the training carries over to the person's everyday life. Some studies have shown that it does. For example, patients who received biofeedback treatment to control tension headaches reported having fewer headaches for two months after training (McKenzie, Ehrisman, Montgomery, and Barnes, 1974).

Biofeedback, however, does not always produce such reliable results. In some studies, the changes that appeared to be due to biofeedback were actually due to other things. Treatments that attempt to alter brain-wave patterns are particularly controversial (Plotkin,

how much of the material he had retained. He relearned the list and compared his performance to his original learning performance. Generally, it took a much shorter period of time and fewer trials to relearn a list, and the difference was the amount "saved." The saving score is usually expressed as a percentage of the original learning score.

Using this technique, Ebbinghaus and his followers were able to demonstrate many things about the learning and retention of nonsense syllables. For example (and not surprisingly), longer lists take longer to learn. This is not only because there are more items on the list; the learner seems to devote more time to each item as well. Also, the more meaningful the nonsense syllables (in terms of association value), the easier they are to learn. Studies using nonsense syllables found the serial position effect, which means that the subject makes more errors on items in the middle of the list than on items in the beginning or end. Ebbinghaus's data contributed considerably to our understanding of retention. The amount of savings on a relearning task drops dramatically during the first hours after the learning task. Thereafter, the percent saved hardly drops at all.

Most psychologists no longer use Ebbinghaus's methods of studying human verbal learning, partly because the serial learning technique is fraught with complications. Also, many now prefer to use material rich in meaning in order to learn more about how humans process larger units of information. Nevertheless, Ebbinghaus's contributions to the field were enormous, and his influence lasted for many years.

1979). For example, biofeedback has been used to treat epilepsy by training patients to produce more brain waves in the six- to twelve-cycles-per-second range. Although many patients have fewer seizures after such training, some scientists wonder whether the simple relaxation training is the cause, rather than the brain-wave biofeedback (Kaplan, 1973).

Although biofeedback has not turned out to be the great breakthrough in medicine that many hoped for, at least with respect to the treatment of stress-related illnesses, it seems to offer some advantages in the treatment of severe muscular disorders. Patients with cerebral palsy or spinal cord injuries, for example, use computers and electrodes attached to muscle groups to obtain feedback about any tiny muscular changes. The electrodes detect muscular activity that is invisible to the naked eye, and the computer patiently provides rewards for increasing the intensity or duration of muscular activity. Children with cerebral palsy, for example, who showed no improvement in motor function over a five-year period, learned to use their hands well enough to drink from a glass or dress themselves. Although the techniques are experimental and need much refinement, they are promising.

GUIDED REVIEW

Learning Objectives 7, 8, and 9

1. Operant conditioning occurs when an organism learns the consequences of its actions in particular contexts. The three principal components are the _____ , _____ , and the _____ .

2. Thorndike developed his _____ by observing cats in puzzle boxes. Responses that were followed by reward (escape and food) were repeated the next time the cat was placed in the box. Responses that were not followed by reward became less frequent.

3. B. F. Skinner studied _____ conditioning in rats, using lever pressing in the _____ as the response, food for reward, and a _____ to chart the animal's behavior.

4. Operant conditioning proceeds most quickly if the time interval between the response and reinforcement is short. Other properties of operant conditioning include stimulus generalization and discrimination; _____ , in which the organism is rewarded for successively closer approximations of the desired behavior; and _____ , in which the organism learns an association between a response and its consequence by accident, since that response did not actually cause the consequence to occur.

5. A _____ reinforcement refers to a reward that increases the frequency of the behavior that preceded it. A _____ reinforcement also increases the frequency of the behavior that preceded it, but it is rewarding because it terminates an annoying state of affairs. A _____ decreases the frequency of the response that precedes it.

6. One major problem with the use of _____ as a means of behavioral control is that it produces an emotional reaction in the subject, and the punisher may elicit a classically conditioned fear reaction.

7. Schedules of reinforcement include _____ , _____ , and various kinds of partial reinforcement schedules such as _____ and _____ schedules.

8. Reinforcement increases the strength of the response that precedes it. _____ satisfy biological needs, whereas the reinforcement value of _____ comes from learning. _____ suggests that the more probable activities in an organism's life can reinforce less probable activities.

9. _____ is an application of the principles of operant conditioning. Patients learn to voluntarily control ongoing physiological processes, such as heart rate, by receiving feedback about the activity of those processes.

ANSWERS

1. stimulus, response, reinforcer 2. Law of Effect 3. operant; Skinner box; cumulative recorder 4. shaping; superstition 5. positive; negative; punishment 6. punishment 7. continuous, partial; ratio, interval 8. Primary reinforcers; secondary reinforcers; Premack's principle 9. Biofeedback

Learning and Cognition

The principles underlying operant and classical conditioning can explain a great deal of the learning accomplished by both animals and humans. By emphasizing the important role of the stimuli and rewards in the environment, conditioning theory can explain some very complicated behaviors. In fact, it almost seems possible to explain *all* behavior in terms of stimuli, responses, and rewards, without ever having to talk about cognition, or what is happening inside the head.

However, there are many instances of learning that cannot be fully understood by referring to the principles outlined in operant or classical conditioning. As psychologists began to study these instances more thoroughly, they learned that cognition plays an important role in learning, particularly in the higher primates and in human beings. The thoughts and mental activities that take place during the learning process are as important as the time delay between the CS and UCS, the strength of the reinforcement, or the schedule of rewards.

The contribution of cognitive psychology has been significant, and it certainly is not limited to the psychology of learning. We have already examined some of these contributions in the discussion of consciousness in Chapter 3. The cognitive approach to understanding human behavior has also provided important new insights to studies of perception and memory. In terms of learning, though, the cognitive approach has been of primary importance because it has offered more complete explanations of some instances of learning than have conditioning theories. For example, any explanation of more complicated learning processes, such as insight learning, cognitive maps, and observational learning, would be incomplete if it simply included references to stimuli, responses, and reinforcements. They can be better understood if we also describe the cognitive process.

Insight Learning

Unscramble the letters in "OTAPI." One way to do it is to write down the letters in slightly different sequences until you recognize a word. Another way is to simply look at "OTAPI" and try to visualize different sequences in your head until you come up with the answer. If you did it the second way, you probably pondered for a minute or so, and then "saw" the solution very suddenly. You had an insight. Now try to unscramble "OREEHCI."

The original studies on insight learning were not conducted with humans but with chimpanzees. Wolfgang Kohler, a psychologist working at the University of Berlin's primate colony in the Canary Islands during World War I, was studying their problem-solving abilities. Kohler maintained that learning is a cognitive phenomenon, particularly in apes and human beings. The animal studies the problem, trying out different solutions in its head, and finally "comes to see" the solution. When the insight finally comes, it is sudden, and it allows the animal to perform the solution without any errors.

Kohler invented all sorts of problems for the chimps to solve. In one experiment he placed a banana outside the cage of the smartest chimp, Sultan. Inside the cage were some boxes, and also two hollow sticks, one slightly thinner than the other. Both sticks were too short for Sultan to use to reach the fruit. But one could be placed inside the other to form a longer "double stick." After an hour of unsuccessful attempts to reach the fruit with his arm, one of the sticks, or even the box, Sultan seemed to have given up—but not quite:

> Sultan first of all squats indifferently on the box . . .
> then he gets up, picks up the two sticks, sits down again
> on the box and plays carelessly with them. While doing
> this, it happens that he finds himself holding one rod in
> either hand in such a way that they lie in a straight line;
> he pushes the thinner one a little way into the opening
> of the thicker, jumps up and is already on the run
> towards the railings, to which he has up to now turned
> his back, and begins to draw a banana towards him with
> the double stick. (Kohler, 1925)

The chimp's solution to the problem of reaching the banana is an example of insight learning. Although we can never know what was going through Sultan's mind, we can guess that *something* was happening. He acted as though he had solved the problem in his head, because as soon as he put the sticks together, he ran over and got the banana.

Based on studies like this, **insight learning** *can be defined as follows:*

1. The learning appears to be sudden and complete.
2. The first time the solution is performed, it is usually done so with no errors.
3. The solution is remembered very well.
4. The principle underlying the solution is easily applied to other situations.

The characteristics of insight learning cannot be fully explained using the principles of operant or classical conditioning. The animals don't show many successive approximations of the solution that can be rewarded. In insight learning, the animal seems to know the correct solution to the problem even though it has never been rewarded for it, or anything like it, before.

Cognitive Maps

The way an organism learns about its territory seems to involve more than simple stimulus-response connections. For example, you know a direct route from home to work, but even though you have never taken a longer route, you would probably be able to without making any mistakes because you have "in your head" a cognitive map of the area.

A **cognitive map** *is a hypothetical representation of a situation stored in memory, or a kind of mental picture of a situation or learning event.* Much of the research on cognitive maps deals with how people and animals acquire and use representations of space, but the term refers to mental pictures of any kind of learning situation. Humans and many animals seem to acquire these maps without ever having been rewarded for making a long series of stimulus-response connections.

An early study investigating this kind of learning involved rats running around in mazes and learning to use long detours to get to their food (Tolman and Honzik, 1930). The maze had three different paths of different lengths that the rats could use to get to the food. After a few trials, they began to prefer the shortest path, A. The next shortest path, B, was their second favorite, and the longest, path C, was third.

The experimenters blocked off path A to see whether the rats would go back and choose their second favorite path, B, or the longer one, C. Because of the location of the barrier, the rats could use only path C to reach their food. But unless the rats had acquired a cognitive map of the maze, they would have chosen their second favorite, path B. They chose the longer path, demonstrating that they did have a "map" of the area and were not simply performing well-established responses.

Rats will acquire a cognitive map of their environment even if they are not rewarded. In a related series of experiments, the rats were allowed to explore for ten days a maze without any food in it. On the eleventh day, they were given a food reward in the goal box. The next time they were placed in the maze, they ran directly to the goal box, making almost no mistakes, just as though they had been receiving a reward there for the past ten days. They did not have to slowly learn the correct path by trial and error, requiring a reward for each successive approximation of the correct solution. They had a cognitive map and could use it.

Animals that are more intelligent than rats are even better at learning the spatial layout of their environment. One experiment with chimpanzees showed that they acquire remarkable maps of their terrain (Menzel, 1973, 1978). The chimps were kept in a one-acre enclosure containing trees, fences, and other landmarks. An experimenter would take out the chimps, one at a time, and hide eighteen pieces of food in different places, allowing the chimp to watch. Then the chimp would be set free to find the food.

As soon as they were let loose, the chimps scrambled from one hiding place to another, finding and eating the food. However, consistent with the theory of cognitive maps, they did not retrace the experimenter's steps and get the food in the same order in which it was hidden. They used a much more efficient route, collecting all the food in one area before moving on to the next.

Observational Learning

Learning how to drive a car by yourself, without ever having watched someone else do it, would be perilous, to say the least. You might accidentally step on the accelerator and learn that that makes the car move. But what about stopping? There is precious little time to randomly try several different responses before you hit the brick wall. You would not have time to learn that

Figure 5.11   Children imitating an aggressive model in Bandura's studies of observational learning

turning on the lights, setting the clock, or pushing the automatic gearshift into D2 were all unrewarded responses.

Fortunately, humans and some of the other higher animals do not need to learn everything by direct experience with responses and rewards. They can learn through **observational learning,** *in which an organism acquires a response by imitating a model.*

A fascinating series of experiments by Albert Bandura and his colleagues investigated observational learning in children (Bandura, 1977). In a typical experiment, children sit and watch a model performing some action on TV, and then they are given an opportunity to imitate the model. (See fig. 5.11.) One study examined children's responses to an aggressive model (Bandura, 1965). The child actor on TV walked into a

room in which there was a large, inflatable Bobo doll and shouted "Clear the way!" When the Bobo doll didn't respond, the actor knocked it down, screaming "Pow, right in the nose, boom, boom." Then she struck the doll with a mallet, saying "Sockeroo, stay down." In one version of the TV program the model was rewarded for behaving so aggressively. An adult came in and gave the child candy and soft drinks. In another version, she was punished with a spanking and several verbal admonishments: "Hey there, you big bully, you quit picking on that clown." In a third version, the model was neither rewarded nor punished, but ignored.

After watching the program, each child was taken into a room with many toys, including a Bobo doll, and the experimenters observed whether the child imitated the aggressive model in any way. Some children were offered incentives for imitating the model, including juice treats and praise, while others were not.

Boys, especially, were very likely to imitate the actor, even if they saw the actor punished on television. They were even more likely to imitate the actor if they were offered some incentive for doing so. Girls, who showed less aggression toward the Bobo doll in most cases, were nearly as aggressive as the boys if they were offered some incentive. Clearly, both the boys and girls had learned something from observing the model on TV. The girls, though, were more likely to show what they had learned if they knew they would receive some reward.

Whether a person will imitate a model depends on many factors, including the model's status, the model's similarity to the person in age and sex, whether the model's behavior is rewarded or punished, and whether the model's behavior is unfamiliar to the observer. Why a person will imitate a model, in the absence of direct rewards and punishments, is still a matter of some controversy. Albert Bandura (1965) proposes that when observers pay attention to something going on around them, they form mental pictures, or cognitive representations, of what they observe. What they have learned, therefore, is not so much a response but a cognitive representation of a response.

Television Violence and Aggression.   Watching television is America's third most time-consuming activity, after sleeping and working. Children, for instance, spend more than three hours a day watching television. Many people have become very concerned about this, particularly because the amount of violence on TV is astounding. A survey of all the programs on television's three major networks revealed some sobering facts:

1. Violence occurred in eight of ten programs.
2. Violence occurred in 93.5% of all cartoons directed at children.
3. More than half the major characters were violent.
4. The "good guys" committed as much violence as the bad guys.

5. The programs rarely show any pain or suffering connected with violence.
6. Nearly half the killers received no punishment.
7. For every bystander who attempted to prevent violence, there was another who encouraged or assisted it. (Baker and Ball, 1969).

A more recent study conducted by the National Institute of Mental Health shows that TV violence has not decreased since the first survey. This report also cites very convincing evidence that television violence increases aggression in children.

For example, the Chicago Circle Study examined the viewing habits and aggressive behavior of more than five hundred children over a three-year period (Eron, 1982). The children were asked many questions about their television viewing habits, including what shows they watched and how much they felt they were like the main characters. The aggressive behavior of each child was also measured in several ways. In one method, the child was asked to rate his own aggressive behavior by responding to the question, "Steven often gets angry and punches other kids. Are you just like Steven, a little bit like Steven, or not at all like Steven?" In another method the child's classmates were asked to rate his or her aggressive behavior.

The experimenters found a strong correlation between the measures of aggressive behavior and the amount of violent TV a child watched. This study was correlational and, based on this study alone, we cannot absolutely conclude that TV violence is the cause of heightened aggression in heavy TV watchers. It is possible, for example, that children who are more aggressive will seek out TV programs that have more violent content. Nevertheless, combined with all the experimental investigations of observational learning of aggression, the studies lead to the almost inescapable conclusion that TV violence contributes to aggressive behavior in children.

GUIDED REVIEW

Learning Objectives 10, 11, and 12

1. Some more complicated instances of learning, particularly by higher primates, require an understanding of _____ during the learning process. These instances cannot be entirely explained by simple associations between stimuli, responses, and rewards.

2. _____ , which can sometimes be observed in higher animals, occurs when the organism seems to reason out a problem and then perform the solution. The principle features of the phenomenon include a learning curve that is sudden and complete (or "scalloped"), rather than slow and arduous; an error-free performance of the solution the first time it is attempted; a good memory of the solution; and the ability to transfer the principle learned to other, similar situations.

3. Learning about the layout of the environment involves the acquisition of _____ , rather than simple stimulus-response connections. Using these maps, animals and humans can reach goals despite complicated detours that require them to use paths and motor actions that they have never used and for which they have never been rewarded.

4. The ability of some animals, particularly human beings, to learn through observation also demonstrates the importance of cognition in some types of learning. Subjects will mimic the actions of a model even though the subjects have never been rewarded for performing the action. In general, the principles of _____ are very similar to those of operant conditioning, except that the subject is not being rewarded directly. For example, subjects imitate a model who is being rewarded for a particular action more than they imitate a model who is not being rewarded.

ANSWERS

1. cognition 2. Insight learning 3. cognitive maps 4. observational learning

The Limits of Learning

Two animal trainers, Keller and Marian Breland, were trying to teach a cow to perform a lively act on stage in a skit about a miner.

> It was a hilarious script . . . it required the cow to perpetrate various outrages on the poor old miner—kick over his bucket, chase him around the campfire, knock down his tent, and finally stage a wild bull fight with him. . . . we put a considerable amount of money into developing and selling this show before we had even trained the cows . . . however, when we started into production of the behavior, interesting but painful problems began to develop. Aside from the matter of kicking the bucket, which we could not condition with food reinforcement at all, we were able to condition all the required behavior in the cow . . . but all in lugubrious slow motion no matter how hungry she became. The whole slowed down performance looked quite ridiculous. (Breland and Breland, 1966)

Apparently, cows can only learn some things through operant conditioning and food rewards, and then only slowly. There are some things they have a great deal of trouble learning and some they may not be able to learn at all.

Animal trainers have known this for years, but it came as something of a surprise to psychologists. Traditional learning theory had always maintained that it made no difference what response was paired with what reward. The animal should learn to associate the two, as long as they occurred close together in time and as long as the beast was physically capable of the response. But as the Brelands discovered, they simply could not teach the cow to kick the bucket with its rear leg. Furthermore, they could not teach the cow to do anything quickly; she did all her tricks at her own bovine pace.

Why should it be so difficult to teach the cow to kick the bucket and so easy to teach it to chase the miner, although slowly? Studies on animals have shown that the principles of learning derived from conditioning studies are not quite as universal as we once believed. Organisms seem to have many built-in biological predispositions that make it easy for them to learn some associations but almost impossible to learn others, regardless of how much reward or punishment is used. These predispositions appear to have evolved, and they are connected with the animal's life-style and habitat. The Brelands think that it is extremely difficult to teach a cow to move quickly for a food reward because in the cow's environment there is no need to rush for food. Grass doesn't get up and run away. A dog might easily learn to perform some trick quickly for a food reward because it is a hunting species that must move fast to get its food.

Flavor Aversions

Some of the best studies on these predispositions deal with **flavor aversions,** *which involve the avoidance of specific tastes.* A team of researchers demonstrated that it is easier to teach a rat an association between the taste of food and an illness than between the taste of food and a shock (Garcia and Koelling, 1966). In part of this experiment, they offered one group of rats some flavored water and another group some "bright and noisy" water, made so by flashing lights and clicking sounds. Then half of each group was made sick by exposure to X rays, and the other half was given a shock.

According to traditional learning theory, the rats that had been punished for drinking flavored water should have avoided flavored water; those that were punished for drinking the bright noisy water should have avoided that kind of water. As it turned out, their avoidance behavior depended on what *kind* of punishment they received. If they became sick, they avoided only the flavored water. The rats that had drunk the bright and noisy water did not associate it with the sickness. Also, the rats that were shocked did not associate the shock with the flavored water—only with the bright and noisy water.

This study, and other more recent ones, shows that there are particular associations that are very easy to make and some that are very difficult. Which ones are easy to make depends on the species of animal. Birds, for example, do not easily associate the taste of food with illness, but they readily associate illness with the color of the food. Perhaps this is because visual rather than taste cues play a large role in the bird's normal food-getting behavior. In humans, tastes are paired with illness. A person who gets the flu after trying Szechuan stir-fry pork for lunch may form an association between the Chinese food and the sickness. He may never want to taste the food again, claiming that he hates the taste. This occurs even when the person knows that the onset of the flu had nothing to do with the novel food.

One important application of the flavor aversion phenomenon has been in the control of predation by coyotes. If these predators have one or two experiences in which the taste of sheep is followed by sickness, they seem to leave the sheep alone and find other prey (Garcia, Rusniak, and Brett, 1977). In a preliminary study in California, sheep carcasses laced with a mild poison were scattered across an open range. The wild coyotes took a few bites, became sick, and then began avoiding live sheep. The same technique is being used to alter the hunting habits of wild cougars and hawks that prey on sheep. The use of flavor aversions to control predation by crows is described in the Application Box.

Biological Predispositions and Learning

The flavor aversion studies made it clear that animals, and probably humans as well, have biological predispositions that make it easier to form some associations and more difficult to form others. They also challenged another assumption about learning: that the reward (or punishment) must immediately follow the response. Under some circumstances, animals can learn to avoid a particular food even if the sickness comes hours later.

APPLICATION BOX

Controlling Predation By Crows, Using Flavor Aversions

Farmers and ranchers are understandably troubled by predation on their livestock. Hawks, cougars, coyotes, and crows all take their toll on the domestic animals, often finding them easy prey. The most common means of controlling these wild species is to shoot them or poison them, but scientists are studying other means as well. The use of flavor aversions offers one possible solution.

When an animal eats a substance that makes it sick, it tends to avoid that substance in the future. Coyotes, for example, will avoid sheep meat if they previously ate some that was laced with a poison. Most mammals rely heavily on smell and taste to help them choose their food, and when they avoid a certain food, they usually avoid it because its smell has become associated with illness. Birds, however, rely more on visual cues in their feeding habits. So, instead of learning an association between taste, smell, and illness, the bird can learn an association between taste, visual cues, and illness.

In some applied research designed to find means to control predation by crows, the investigators placed chicken eggs in nests at ten different sites near Fargo, North Dakota (Nicklaus, et al., 1983). Some of the eggs were painted green, and at five of the sites these green eggs were injected with UC 27867, a poison that would make the crows sick but not kill them. At the other five sites, both the green eggs and the white eggs were harmless.

Every day the experimenters checked the sites for predation by the crows in the area. At first the crows ate equal numbers of green and white eggs at both the experimental sites (where the green eggs contained poison), and the control sites (where the green eggs were harmless). After a few days, however, the crows began to ignore the poisoned green eggs at the experimental sites, instead preying on the white ones. At the control sites, the crows continued to eat both white and green eggs in equal numbers. The birds had formed a long-lasting association between the taste of the egg, its green appearance, and the illness produced by the poison. Once this learning had taken place, the birds avoided the green eggs, even if they no longer contained any poison.

Research like this shows that flavor aversions are not just a peculiar phenomenon exhibited by tame white rats in psychological laboratories. They are a common form of learning in wild animals. With proper procedures, the phenomenon can be used to alter the feeding habits of many species, thereby protecting both the domestic animals and the wild ones that prey on them.

After much research on flavor aversions and other phenomena that show the limits of learning in various animals, most psychologists agree that we do not have to develop new laws of learning for each species. The principles of conditioning may need to be slightly modified, but they needn't be discarded (Rescorla and Holland, 1982). For example, although an animal does learn to avoid a taste even if the sickness comes hours later, the learning is stronger if the delay is short. Nevertheless, it is clear that a complete understanding of the phenomenon of learning will require some study of the life-style and evolutionary history of the animal doing the learning.

GUIDED REVIEW

Learning Objective 13

1. Animals and humans possess biological _____ that allow them to learn some associations very easily but make it very difficult to learn others.

2. _____ studies show how associations between taste and illness occur very easily in rats and other mammals.

ANSWERS

1. predispositions 2. Flavor aversion

SUMMARY

I. Learning represents changes in behavior as a result of experience.   (p. 154)

  A. It is very difficult to separate learning from changes in behavior due to maturation or genetic influences.   (p. 154)

  B. Learning cannot be observed directly; we merely observe performance. Despite the difficulty of separating learning from other variables, learning should be defined as the relatively permanent changes in behavior, or potential for those changes, that occur because of prior experience, excluding behavioral changes due to maturation, genetic factors, changes in motivation, fatigue, or injury. (p. 155)

II. Classical conditioning involves the formation of an association between two stimuli, one of which (UCS) automatically elicits a response (UCR), the other of which (CS) reliably precedes the UCS and after many pairings will produce a response (CR) when it is presented alone.   (p. 155)

  A. Ivan Pavlov first demonstrated the principles of classical conditioning using a dog's salivation response to meat powder.   (p. 156)

  B. Classical conditioning has a number of properties   (p. 157):

1. The rate of conditioning depends on factors such as how many times the UCS is paired with the CS and whether the CS is a novel or familiar stimulus.   (p. 158)

2. Organisms exhibit stimulus generalization, in which they will respond to stimuli that are similar to the CS.   (p. 159)

3. Organisms also exhibit stimulus discrimination after training. An organism trying to perform a very difficult discrimination may show experimental neurosis.   (p. 159)

4. The best pairing procedure involves presenting the CS about one-half second before the presentation of the UCS. (p. 160)

5. A CR can be inhibited by an extinction procedure.   (p. 160)

6. Second-order conditioning involves using a previously neutral CS that reliably elicits a CR as a UCS in a new conditioning experience.   (p. 161)

  C. The CR may or may not be similar to the UCR; in some cases, the CR is a preparation for the UCS. Tolerance to drugs may be affected by classical conditioning because of physiological preparation.   (p. 161)

III. Operant conditioning involves the formation of an association between a particular response and the consequences of that response.   (p. 163)

  A. The three important components of operant conditioning are the stimulus, the response, and the reinforcer.   (p. 163)

  B. Early researchers who investigated the properties of operant conditioning include Thorndike, who formulated the Law of Effect, and Skinner, whose theories of behaviorism are based on the fundamental properties of operant conditioning.   (p. 163)

  C. Some of the characteristics of operant conditioning are similar to those of classical conditioning. Others, such as the following, are somewhat different   (p. 166):

    1. Shaping is a technique in which successively closer approximations to the desired response are rewarded.   (p. 166)

    2. Superstition involves the formation of spurious associations between a response and a reinforcer.   (p. 167)

    3. Extinction in operant conditioning involves withholding the reward for a previously rewarded response.   (p. 168)

  D. A "reinforcement" strengthens the response that preceded it.   (p. 168)

    1. Both positive and negative reinforcement strengthen the preceding response. Punishment tends to decrease the probability that the preceding response will occur again. Punishment may produce a classically conditioned fear reaction.   (p. 168)

    2. Schedules of reinforcement include continuous, partial, and various kinds of partial reinforcement schedules including fixed ratio, variable ratio, fixed interval, and variable interval.   (p. 169)

    3. Primary reinforcers satisfy biological needs; secondary reinforcers acquire their rewarding properties through learning experiences.   (p. 170)

  E. Biofeedback is an example of operant conditioning in which a person learns to control a physiological response by having access to information about its activity.   (p. 171)

IV. Some examples of learning are not easily explained by the principles of conditioning. These examples involve cognition.   (p. 174)

  A. Insight learning appears in some problem-solving situations; the organism seems to learn the correct solution suddenly, performs the solution with no mistakes the first time, remembers the solution, and applies it in other situations.   (p. 175)

  B. Cognitive maps are hypothetical representations of a situation stored in memory.   (p. 176)

  C. Observational learning occurs when an organism acquires a response by imitating a model.   (p. 176)

    1. Observational learning appears to play an important role in the effects of TV violence on aggression in children.   (p. 178)

V. Learning is limited partly because of biological predispositions.   (p. 179)

  A. Flavor-aversion research demonstrates that for certain animals it is easier to form associations between taste and illness than between other stimuli, such as visual cues and illness.   (p. 180)

  B. Studies on flavor aversion suggest that biological predispositions exist for each species that make it easier to form certain associations and difficult or impossible to form others.   (p. 180)

ACTION GLOSSARY

Match the terms in the left column with the definitions in the right column.

____ 1. **Learning (p. 154)**
____ 2. **Classical conditioning (p. 155)**
____ 3. **Unconditioned stimulus (UCS)**
       (p. 156)
____ 4. **Unconditioned response (UCR)**
       (p. 156)
____ 5. **Conditioned stimulus (CS)**
       (p. 156)
____ 6. **Conditioned response (CR)**
       (p. 156)

A. *In classical conditioning, the stimulus that automatically elicits a response from an organism without prior learning.*
B. *A stimulus which, through classical conditioning, comes to elicit a conditioned response because it was paired with an unconditioned stimulus that automatically elicited an unconditioned response.*
C. *A response elicited by a conditioned stimulus after classical conditioning.*
D. *Relatively permanent changes in behavior that occur because of prior experience. Can be theoretically discriminated from changes in behavior that are primarily due to maturation, genetic influences, fatigue, injury, disease, or drugs.*
E. *The process by which an organism forms an association between two stimuli in the environment. One stimulus is neutral; it has no particular meaning prior to the conditioning process. The other automatically elicits some response from the organism. When the neutral stimulus reliably precedes the stimulus that automatically elicits a response, the previously neutral stimulus comes to elicit a conditioned response.*
F. *In classical conditioning, the response automatically elicited by the unconditioned stimulus.*

____ 7. **Stimulus generalization (p. 159)**
____ 8. **Stimulus discrimination (p. 159)**
____ 9. **Extinction (p. 160)**
____ 10. **Second-order conditioning**
       (p. 161)
____ 11. **Reinforcer (p. 163)**
____ 12. **Law of Effect (p. 164)**
____ 13. **Operant conditioning (p. 163)**

A. *In operant conditioning, a rewarding consequence to an action by an organism.*
B. *A type of classical conditioning in which the original conditioned stimulus is used as an unconditioned stimulus in a new conditioning procedure, with a new conditioned stimulus.*
C. *In classical conditioning, the process in which the organism learns that a particular stimulus is associated with an unconditioned stimulus whereas another stimulus is not. The organism learns to make a conditioned response to only one of the two stimuli. In instrumental conditioning, the organism learns that a response is followed by reinforcement under some circumstances but not under others.*
D. *The probability of a response depends upon that response's effect on the environment; responses followed by a reward tend to be repeated.*
E. *In classical conditioning, a procedure in which the conditioned stimulus is presented repeatedly without pairing it with the unconditioned stimulus. Diminishes the size of and gradually eliminates the conditioned response. In instrumental conditioning, it refers to the withholding of a reinforcement following a response.*
F. *In classical conditioning, once a conditioned response has been established to a particular stimulus, similar stimuli will also evoke the response. In instrumental conditioning, an organism tends to repeat a response in circumstances that are similar to the ones in which the response was originally learned.*
G. *The process by which an organism comes to associate a response with the consequences of that response.*

____ 14. **Skinner box (p. 164)**
____ 15. **Cumulative recorder (p. 165)**
____ 16. **Operant (p. 165)**
____ 17. **Respondent (p. 166)**
____ 18. **Shaping (p. 166)**
____ 19. **Superstition (p. 167)**

A. *An instrument with moving chart paper on which a pen moves up a notch each time an organism makes a particular response, such as a lever press by a rat. It is used to show changes in the rate of responding over time.*
B. *In operant conditioning, organisms come to repeat responses followed by rewards even though those responses did not cause the reward and their pairing was only coincidental.*
C. *The unconditioned response in classical conditioning. The term, used by B. F. Skinner, emphasizes the fact that the response is not freely emitted.*
D. *The process by which unusual or difficult responses are conditioned. Successive approximations that come closer and closer to the desired response are rewarded.*

E. *The experimental apparatus used to study operant conditioning in animals. Contains some means to provide rewards, such as a food cup, and some task for the animal to learn, such as pressing a lever or pecking a lighted disk.*

F. *A response that is spontaneously emitted; it occurs in the absence of any particular or obvious stimuli.*

____ 20. **Positive reinforcement (p. 168)**
____ 21. **Negative reinforcement (p. 168)**
____ 22. **Punishment (p. 169)**
____ 23. **Continuous reinforcement (p. 169)**
____ 24. **Fixed ratio schedule of reinforcement (p. 169)**
____ 25. **Variable ratio schedule of reinforcement (p. 169)**
____ 26. **Fixed interval schedule of reinforcement (p. 170)**

A. *A partial reinforcement schedule in which a response is rewarded after it occurs a fixed number of times.*

B. *Any rewarding stimulus that increases the probability of the response that immediately preceded it.*

C. *A method of reinforcement in which a reward is supplied after every response.*

D. *A partial reinforcement schedule in which the first response that occurs after a fixed time interval is rewarded, but all other responses are ignored.*

E. *A procedure used to decrease the probability that a response will occur by presenting an aversive stimulus whenever the response occurs.*

F. *A partial reinforcement schedule in which a response is rewarded after it occurs a certain number of times. The number of times varies from trial to trial.*

G. *Removal of a stimulus, such as a loud noise or shock, following the performance of some response, thereby strengthening that response.*

____ 27. **Variable interval schedule of reinforcement (p. 170)**
____ 28. **Secondary reinforcer (p. 170)**
____ 29. **Premack principle (p. 171)**
____ 30. **Biofeedback (p. 171)**
____ 31. **Insight learning (p. 175)**
____ 32. **Cognitive map (p. 176)**
____ 33. **Observational learning (p. 177)**

A. *A type of learning in which the learner acquires a response through observation of the consequences of the actions of a model.*

B. *An advanced form of learning seen in primates in which the organism seems to grasp the solution to a problem suddenly and perform the required responses completely and without error the first time.*

C. *A perceptual representation of an area that an organism develops through experience in the area, without necessarily being rewarded.*

D. *A partial reinforcement schedule in which the first response that occurs after an interval of time is rewarded, whereas all others are ignored. The interval of time varies from trial to trial.*

E. *Activities that are more common or probable function as reinforcers for activities that are less probable.*

F. *An application of operant conditioning in which an individual learns to gain control over some physiological response by receiving feedback about the ongoing state of the system.*

G. *A reinforcer that does not obviously aid biological survival, but which probably acquired its reinforcing value through classical conditioning.*

ANSWERS

1. D, 2. E, 3. A, 4. F, 5. B, 6. C, 7. F, 8. C, 9. E, 10. B, 11. A, 12. D, 13. G, 14. E, 15. A, 16. F, 17. C, 18. D, 19. B, 20. B, 21. G, 22. E, 23. C, 24. A, 25. F, 26. D, 27. D, 28. G, 29. E, 30. F, 31. B, 32. C, 33. A

SELF-TEST

1. Since learning itself cannot easily be measured, most researchers demonstrate that learning has occurred by measuring changes in
   (a) a potential to act.
   (b) the actual performance of some behavior.
   (c) the presentation of the conditions for learning.
   (d) both a and c.
     (LO 1; p. 155)

2. The procedure for classical conditioning involves pairing
   (a) two previously neutral stimuli, with the same one always coming second.
   (b) a neutral stimulus with an unconditioned stimulus, the neutral one coming second.

(c) a neutral stimulus with an unconditioned stimulus, but presenting only the unconditioned stimulus if the subject makes the response (e.g., salivation).

(d) a neutral stimulus with an unconditioned stimulus, with the neutral stimulus coming first. (LO 3; p. 156)

3. The unconditioned stimulus

(a) is neutral before the conditioning session.
(b) produces the conditioned response as a consequence of the training session.
(c) elicits an automatic and unlearned response from the subject before the training session.
(d) is a cue for learning. (LO 3; p. 156)

4. Stimulus generalization is

(a) the tendency for stimuli (CSs) similar to the original CS to elicit the CR.
(b) the ability to reliably distinguish between the original CS and similar stimuli.
(c) the tendency to make other similar (to the CR) responses to the original CS.
(d) a characteristic of operant conditioning but not classical conditioning. (LO 4; p. 159)

5. Stimulus discrimination

(a) involves the CR appearing after some stimuli but not others.
(b) involves the tendency to make a variety of conditioned responses to the original CS.
(c) is a characteristic of classical conditioning but not operant conditioning.
(d) involves the same stimulus eliciting different behaviors. (LO 4; p. 159)

6. Presenting the CS by itself, without the UCS, produces

(a) extinction.
(b) observational learning.
(c) generalization.
(d) discrimination. (LO 4; p. 160)

7. Second-order conditioning

(a) involves the same stimulus (CS) eliciting two responses (CRs).
(b) involves relearning after extinction.
(c) involves the distinction between classical conditioning and operant conditioning.
(d) is a classical conditioning procedure in which a CS becomes a UCS in a new learning session. (LO 5; p. 161)

8. The key element in operant conditioning is

(a) the type of stimulus used.
(b) the age of the subject.
(c) the consequence of the behavior.
(d) whether the response is elicited or emitted. (LO 7; p. 163)

9. A reinforcer is

(a) the same as motivation.
(b) a stimulus that strengthens the preceding response.
(c) the same as an unconditioned stimulus.
(d) learned, as opposed to an unconditioned response, which is not. (LO 8; p. 163)

10. A mouse is put into a box and observed. In the first five minutes the mouse grooms, sniffs, and walks around the box, picking up bits of dust. These behaviors are

(a) operants.   (c) reinforcers.
(b) respondents.   (d) artificial. (LO 7; p. 165)

11. The reinforcement of successive approximations of the desired terminal behavior is called

(a) classical conditioning.
(b) discrimination.
(c) generalization.
(d) shaping. (LO 7; p. 166)

12. If the relationship between emitted behavior and the reward is accidental and coincidental, the behaviors resulting are called

(a) generalized.   (c) superstitious.
(b) operants.   (d) random. (LO 7; p. 167)

13. The procedure called extinction is performed in operant conditioning

   (a) by not following the to-be-extinguished behavior with a reinforcer.
   (b) by presenting the CS without the UCS.
   (c) by following the to-be-extinguished behavior with an aversive stimulus.
   (d) by terminating conditioning trials and allowing the subject time to forget the behavior.
   (LO 7; p. 168)

14. The reinforcement of the first response that occurs after a set time interval

   (a) is called a fixed ratio schedule.
   (b) is called a fixed interval schedule.
   (c) is called continuous reinforcement.
   (d) is an application of classical procedures to operant conditioning.
   (LO 8; p. 170)

15. Biofeedback is a

   (a) technique in which brain stimulation and other physiological techniques are used with learning.
   (b) technique in which classical conditioning is used by physicians to control body responses.
   (c) technique in which an individual uses operant conditioning to learn to control body responses using only information for the reinforcer.
   (d) generally accepted technique in which a person learns control over body responses even to the point of reversing the effects of epilepsy and heart disease.
   (LO 9; p. 171)

16. A cognitive map is

   (a) an example of insight learning.
   (b) the result of classical conditioning.
   (c) characteristic of human learning but not of other animals.
   (d) a kind of a mental picture or diagram of a situation.
   (LO 11; p. 176)

17. Observational learning is

   (a) the result of classical conditioning that goes on unconsciously.
   (b) the result of operant conditioning that goes on unconsciously.
   (c) imitation of a model.
   (d) only possible in human subjects.
   (LO 12; p. 177)

18. Observing violent episodes, for example, on television,

   (a) results in increased aggression by subjects compared to controls.
   (b) results in decreased violence because the subjects "get it out of their systems" by watching.
   (c) has no effect on violent or aggressive behavior.
   (d) increases aggression in girls but decreases it in boys.
   (LO 12; p. 178)

19. An interesting and important observation about learning is that

   (a) any response can be trained in any subject if the reinforcer is chosen correctly.
   (b) there are biological limits on what responses can be learned effectively by which subjects.
   (c) classical conditioning is only possible with mammals.
   (d) operant conditioning will not work at all with animals more primitive than the mouse.
   (LO 13; p. 179)

20. The relationship between a particular taste and a subsequent illness

   (a) cannot be learned effectively.
   (b) is learned effectively by some animals but not by humans.
   (c) is innate.
   (d) is easier for the rat to learn than the relationship between a particular taste and a subsequent shock.
   (LO 13; p. 180)

SUGGESTED READINGS

Bandura, A. *Social learning theory*. Englewood Cliffs, NJ: Prentice-Hall, 1977. A description of Bandura's theories concerning social development and observational learning in children.

Glaser, R. Instructional psychology: past, present, and future. *American Psychologist,* 37 (1982): 292–305. An article discussing psychology applied to instruction.

Kohler, W. *The mentality of apes*. New York: Harcourt Brace, 1925. A classic in cognitive psychology that describes the experiments conducted with chimpanzees and insight learning.

Schwartz, B. *Psychology of learning and behavior*. 2d. ed. New York: Norton, 1984. An undergraduate text on learning that emphasizes the role of cognition and species-specific constraints on learning.

Skinner, B. F. *The behavior of organisms*. New York: Appleton Century Crofts, 1938. The classic work describing the principles of operant conditioning.

Woolfolk, A. E., and L. McCune-Nicolich. *Educational psychology for teachers*. 2d ed. Englewood Cliffs, NJ: Prentice-Hall, 1984. An introduction to the field of educational psychology, especially for students interested in a teaching career.

c h a p t e r

6

Remembering and Forgetting

LEARNING OBJECTIVES

After reading this chapter, the student should be able to

1. describe the nature of the sensory store. **(p. 193)**
2. describe short-term memory, and explain how information is maintained in STM, transferred to long-term memory, or lost from short-term memory. **(p. 194)**
3. describe long-term memory, and explain how information is stored in it and lost from it. **(p. 197)**
4. identify and describe two strategies for searching long-term memory. **(p. 202)**
5. explain some of the processes involved in memory reconstruction. **(p. 205)**
6. Compare "recall" and "recognition," showing how the two kinds of retrieval are different from one another. **(p. 208)**
7. explain some of the changes that occur in the brain during learning, relying on evidence from studies of animals. **(p. 210)**
8. define the "engram," and describe several studies that attempted to find its location and identify its properties. **(p. 212)**
9. describe several ways that memories can be modified. **(p. 213)**
10. list and describe several methods that can be used to improve the storage process. **(p. 215)**
11. explain how memory can be improved by improving retrieval. **(p. 218)**
12. describe the study strategy called SQ3R. **(p. 219)**

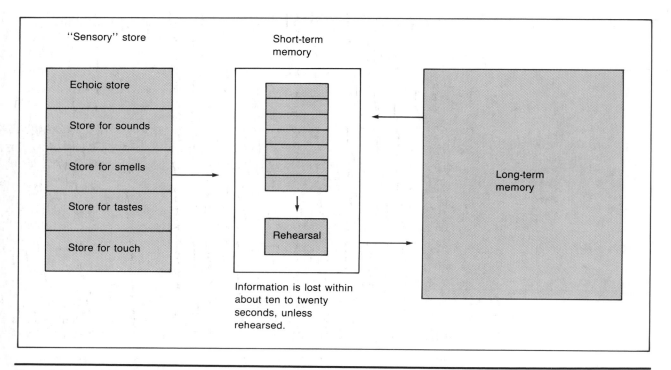

Figure 6.1   *A model for the three storage systems of memory*

How we remember—and forget—the events in our lives has always been an important topic to psychologists. In recent years, they have taken a very cognitive approach to memory research; much of the research we will describe involves human beings trying to remember rather complicated material. Whereas the last chapter concentrated on the simpler forms of learning, particularly those that have been investigated within a stimulus-response framework (such as classical conditioning), this chapter will focus more on the cognitive events involved in learning and memory. Much of the research in this field uses an information processing approach, in which the operations going on inside our heads are compared to the programs of a computer. Thus, we will be discussing how people store information and retrieve it later, and we will occasionally borrow some concepts and terms from computer science.

The Three Storage Systems

Human memory consists of three different but interacting storage systems: the *sensory store, short-term memory* (STM), and *long-term memory* (LTM). Each of these systems has its own functions, and information can be transferred from one to another (Atkinson and Shiffrin, 1968).

A simple model of how these three storage systems operate together will help you to better understand human memory. (See fig. 6.1.) Suppose your spouse writes the grocery list containing three items and puts it on the bulletin board. The information first is received by one of your sense organs, in this case your eyes. Then it is deposited into the sensory store for vision. This storage system holds everything that the eyes see, but it can only hold it for a very brief moment. If you are going to remember the grocery list long enough to buy the items at the supermarket, you must store the items in STM.

STM can only hold a limited number of items, and it can only hold them for about fifteen seconds (Brown, 1958; Peterson and Peterson, 1959). Unless you "rehearse" the grocery list, you will forget it by the time you get to the market; but if you keep rehearsing it to yourself, the information can remain in STM indefinitely. Unfortunately, if a dog runs out in front of your car while you are on your way to the store and your rehearsal is disrupted, you will probably forget the list.

When we say we want to remember something, to commit it to memory, or learn it "by heart," we mean that we want to store it in LTM. If you rehearse the grocery list, organize it, and integrate it with information already present in your LTM, at least some of it will be stored in LTM. Once there, it can be stored indefinitely. Furthermore, there appears to be no limit to the amount of information we can place into this remarkable storage compartment. With this brief overview, we can examine each of the storage systems in more detail.

Sensory Store

The **sensory store** *is the component of the memory system that receives information from the environment first. This storage system can maintain a very accurate and complete representation of the environment as it is received by each sensory system, but it can only maintain it for a fraction of a second.* Although there is probably a sensory store for each of the five senses, practically everything we know about the sensory store comes from studies using visual or auditory input. The **iconic store** *is the sensory store for visual information,* coming from the Greek word "eikon," which means "image." The **echoic store** *is the auditory sensory store.*

The existence of a sensory store for visual input was first demonstrated by some classic experiments by George Sperling (1960). He presented letters on a screen for 1/20 of a second and asked the subject to write them down. When there were only four or five letters on the screen, the subject could usually recall all of them, but when there were more than that, the subject usually could still recall only four or five items.

It would seem that the subject could see only four or five of the letters, even when there were twelve of them. But the subjects in the experiment said that was not so. They could see them all, but they began forgetting them after they had written only four or five items.

Sperling devised a very clever means of proving that what his subjects said was true. He presented the subjects with a slide containing twelve letters, arranged in three rows. Just after the slide was turned off, he sounded a high, medium, or low tone that was a signal for the subject to report the top, middle, or bottom row. Then the subjects were able to repeat any row, even though the screen was blank. This study made it clear that people can store a great deal more than just four or five items at a time, even if only for a brief moment.

Studies on the echoic store demonstrated a very similar phenomenon (Moray, Bates, and Barnett, 1965; Darwin, Turvey, and Crowder, 1972). The main difference between the iconic and echoic stores seems to be the length of time it takes information in them to decay. Information in the iconic store decays in less than a second; decay from the echoic store takes several seconds.

Some of the information held in sensory store is transferred to STM, where it can be remembered for longer than a few milliseconds. Attention is one important determinant of which information is transferred. Whenever you view a scene and place images into your iconic store, you can transfer some of those images to your STM simply by paying attention to them.

Another important element in the transfer process is the meaning of the images. Look at the Japanese kanji in figure 6.2 for a very brief moment, and then look away. In your mind's eye, or iconic store, you can see the image. However, if you wait a few more seconds

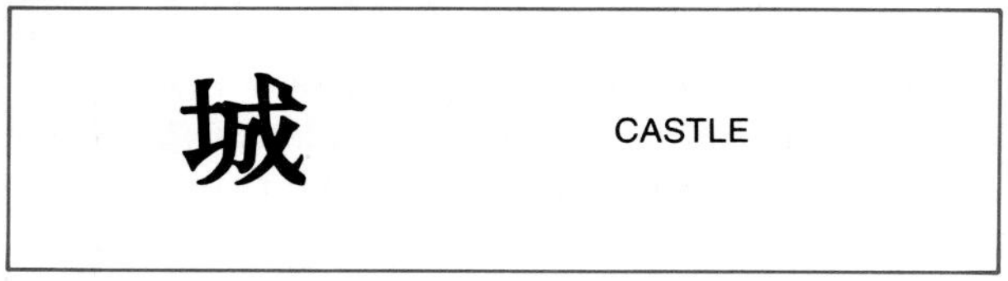

城   CASTLE

Figure 6.2 *Recognition and meaning are determinants in the transfer of information storage systems*

and then try to write the symbol, you will not be able to. Now look at the word next to the kanji for a brief moment; then look away. It is a very simple matter to wait a few seconds and then write the word down even though the word contains more lines. The English word has meaning to you; but unless you can read Japanese or Chinese characters, the kanji character for the word does not. You are able to recognize patterns in the English word, but the kanji seems to be little more than random lines. Transferring an item from iconic store to STM means that you must analyze the item for meaning and recognize the visual pattern that makes up the image. We will see that attaching meaning to patterns is also a critical factor in the transfer of information from STM to LTM.

Short-Term Memory

Anyone who has looked up a telephone number in a directory already knows a great deal about STM. You repeat the number to yourself until you dial, and then you forget it. If the number is busy, you may have to look it up again. **Short-term memory** *is the component of the memory system that holds information the individual is consciously thinking about at the moment. Its capacity appears to be limited to about seven items, and unless the information is rehearsed, it will be lost from STM in about fifteen seconds.*

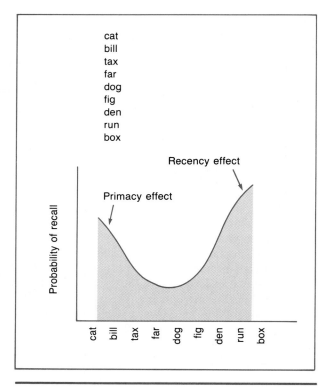

Figure 6.3 *The serial position effect*

Evidence for the existence of STM comes from studies of the **serial position effect,** *a phenomenon in which a person's ability to recall items from a list depends on the item's position in the list.* (See fig. 6.3.) The **primacy effect** *occurs when items in the beginning of the list are recalled well;* the **recency effect** *refers to occasions when the items toward the end of the list are recalled well.* Those words that come in the middle of the list are usually not recalled very well under most circumstances. The reason for these serial position effects is that words in the beginning of the list have been committed to long-term memory. But words near the end are still in STM, so the subject can recall them

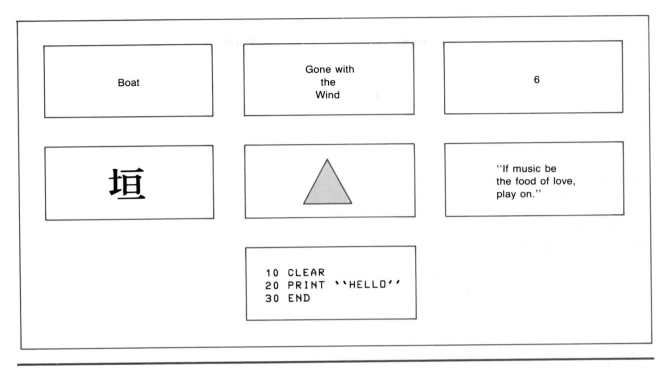

Figure 6.4 "Chunks"

from that storage compartment. If the subject is distracted, perhaps by doing some arithmetic problems after hearing the list, those items at the end of the list that had been in STM will be forgotten. Under these circumstances, there will be no recency effect at all. Studies like these make it clear that human beings do indeed have a short-term memory.

The Capacity of Short-Term Memory. The amount of information that can be held in STM is an intriguing question. Your own experience should tell you that STM's capacity is limited, perhaps to the amount of information in a seven-digit telephone number. Experiments that test a subject's ability to recall a series of items usually report similar results.

This finding created quite a puzzle for psychologists because it was difficult to define the abstract term "item." People could remember seven numbers, seven proper names, seven letters, seven faces, seven Shakespearean verses, or seven proverbs. Clearly, the amount of information in each of these "items" is very different. One psychologist addressed this problem in 1956 in a paper called "The Magical Number Seven, Plus or Minus Two" (Miller, 1956). He suggested that STM could hold about seven *chunks* of information. A **chunk** *refers to anything that is represented in long-term memory as a single unit.* Look at the boxes in figure 6.4. Most of them will be chunks to you. A few of them might only be chunks to a student of Shakespeare, a computer programmer, or a person who reads kanji.

A chunk can contain a great deal of information, but STM can only hold about seven chunks at a time. The capacity of STM cannot be increased by trying to remember more than seven or eight chunks, but it can be dramatically increased by reorganizing information into larger chunks. One student with an average memory, for example, tried to improve his ability to repeat back a sequence of digits that were read to him (Ericsson, Chase, and Faloon, 1980). At first he could only correctly repeat seven or eight digits, but after twenty months of practice, he was able to correctly repeat almost eighty digits.

The researchers found that the student's improved skill was entirely due to the reorganization of information into ever-larger chunks. For example, if the sequence 3492 appeared, it was recoded from four chunks into one, as "3 minutes and 49.2 seconds, near world-record time" (for the mile). Most of his larger chunks were running times for races, but he also recoded strings of numbers into dates or ages. His remarkable ability could only be demonstrated on number strings, however. When they read him a list of letters, his memory span dropped down to six. This shows conclusively that the capacity of his STM had not changed—only the size of his number chunks.

Besides a limited capacity, the STM also has a limited ability to hold items for any length of time. In one classic experiment, subjects tried to remember three letters of the alphabet. After eighteen seconds, they could not remember the letters (Peterson and Peterson, 1959). These people were not slow-witted; they were simply not allowed to rehearse because they were counting backward by threes during those eighteen seconds. Unless the chunks in STM are rehearsed, they are forgotten fairly rapidly.

Losing Information from Short-Term Memory. The relationship between the capacity of STM and the kind of chunks that exist in a person's LTM is a close one.

In fact, many psychologists see STM not so much as a storage system for information but as a group of seven or eight "slots" that can be filled with chunks from LTM. When you try to hold 591–4675 in your STM, you are filling each slot with a single digit. If you forget the digits, you have not lost them from your LTM. They have simply "slipped out" of the slot.

A long-running controversy exists over the way that information slips out of a slot in STM. The **decay theory of forgetting** *maintains that the chunk in the slot simply decays or fades over time, usually within fifteen seconds, unless it is constantly rehearsed.* The **interference theory of forgetting** *proposes that the slots in STM remain filled with the information until new information interferes with or replaces it.*

Attempts to confirm one of these theories and discard the other have been frequent, but not terribly successful. For example, the study described earlier (Peterson and Peterson, 1959), in which the subjects forgot three letters after just eighteen seconds because they were counting backward and could not rehearse, would suggest that the decay theory is correct. Since the subjects were not trying to add any new information to their STM during the eighteen-second interval, there should have been no interference, but they forgot the letters anyway.

Another study, however, found that subjects could recall three words quite easily after a fifteen-second delay if the task used to prevent rehearsal involved detection of an auditory stimulus rather than counting (Reitman, 1971). Perhaps the counting task provided at least some interference, but the auditory task provided none. It is likely that both the decay theory and the interference theory are partially correct. Forgetting from STM probably involves elements of each.

Transfer to Long-Term Memory. The manner in which information in STM is rehearsed is important to whether it will eventually be transferred to LTM. If you simply want to remember the information, say a

---

Watching a Peace March from the 40th Floor

The view was breathtaking. From the window one could see the crowd below. Everything looked extremely small from such a distance, but the colorful costumes could still be seen. Everyone seemed to be moving in one direction in an orderly fashion and there seemed to be little children as well as adults. The landing was gentle, and luckily the atmosphere was such that no special suits had to be worn. At first there was a great deal of activity. Later, when the speeches started, the crowd quieted down. The man with the television camera took many shots of the setting and the crowd. Everyone was very friendly and seemed glad when the music started.

Figure 6.5 *The importance of organizational framework in the transfer of information from STM to LTM*

---

phone number, for a short period of time, perhaps until you dial it, you will use **maintenance rehearsal;** *using this technique, a person maintains information in STM by repeating it over and over. When the person stops repeating, the information is lost.* **Elaborative rehearsal** *is the technique that facilitates the transfer of information from STM to LTM. This process involves organizing the information and integrating it with the knowledge that already exists in LTM* (Craik and Lockhart, 1972).

A fascinating study demonstrates how important the integration process is in the transfer of information from STM to LTM (Bransford and Johnson, 1973). A group of people read the story in figure 6.5 under the title "Watching a Peace March from the 40th Floor." Another group read the same story under the title "A Space Trip to an Inhabited Planet." Each person performed a distracting task for a short time afterward, and then each was asked to recall the story.

The researchers were very interested in how well each group was able to recall the underlined sentence about the gentle landing. This sentence did not fit in well with the "Peace March" story, but it was an important element if the story was about a space trip. Only eighteen percent of the group that read the "Peace March" story recalled anything about this sentence. But fifty-three percent of the people who read a story with a space trip title recalled something from this key sentence. This simple experiment demonstrates how important the organizational framework is when a person is trying to transfer information from STM to LTM.

Long-Term Memory

Long-term memory *is the relatively permanent memory storage system that holds information indefinitely.* In it we store last year's Superbowl score, the plot of the detective novel we read last month, and our memory of our first day at school.

LTM appears to include at least two kinds of memory systems: episodic and semantic, although the way they relate to one another is not entirely clear (McKoon, Ratliff, and Dell, 1985; Tulving, 1985). **Episodic memories** *record our life experiences* (Tulving, 1972), such as the first day at school. Retrieval of these usually involves associations with particular times or places. **Semantic memory** *stores information that has no association to times or places. It includes all the organized knowledge we have about words, other verbal symbols, their meanings, and how we manipulate them.*

How Is Information Stored in Long-Term Memory?
Information is stored in terms of its meaning in LTM, rather than in terms of its sound. For example, suppose you were shown a list of words: car, lamp, chair, plane. If you tried to recall them fifteen seconds later, you might confuse "car" with "char" or "lamp" with

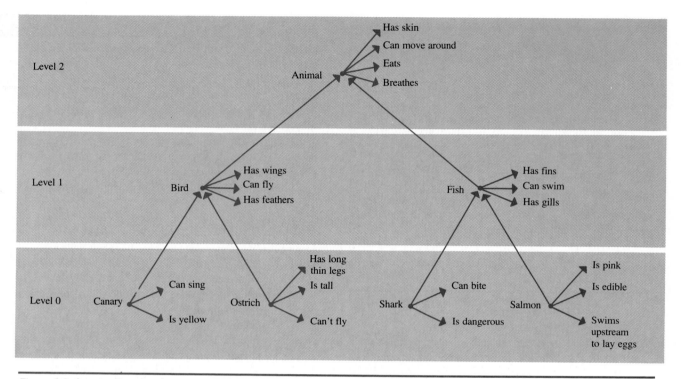

Figure 6.6 A semantic network

"lamb." But if you stored the words in LTM and tried to recall them twenty-four hours later, you would be more likely to confuse "car" with "auto." LTM seems to contain concepts, and it seems to be arranged in terms of the meanings and relationships of those concepts.

The way in which semantic information is stored and organized is a very active field of research in psychology. How, for example, do we answer the question, "Is a robin a bird?" We need a very elaborate categorization and organizational system in our memories, one that permits access to the properties of things, their relationships, examples of instances of the thing, and probably counterexamples as well (such as "bat is not bird").

One theory proposes that our knowledge is organized in **semantic networks,** *which are hypothetical hierarchical structures for semantic memories* (Collins and Quillian, 1969). Figure 6.6 shows how a semantic network might be arranged. Each **node,** *or concept in a semantic network, such as bird, animal, or canary,* is organized into a hierarchy in which one node is a subordinate of another. Characteristics of the general class of "animal" are stored with the node "animal" but not with subordinate nodes such as "bird."

One way to test this model is to ask subjects to answer questions such as, "Does a canary have wings?" and measure how long it takes them to respond (Collins and Quillian, 1969; Freedman and Loftus, 1970)

RESEARCH BOX

Infantile Amnesia

an you recall what happened on your first birthday? Your second? Can you remember anything at all about what happened the day you were born? A peculiar thing about human memory is that it suffers almost complete amnesia for events that occurred during the first few years of life. Even though the infant is learning a great deal about language, object permanence, smells, tastes, the behavior of mom and dad, and many other things, she will not be able to recall events that occurred during this time. Her episodic memory for the first few years of life is strangely deficient.

An early study of infantile amnesia investigated the childhood memories of college students (Waldfogel, 1948). The subjects recorded all their memories for events that occurred before their eighth birthdays. No one recalled anything that happened before the age of three and a half, and most of the events occurred much later. (See fig. 6A.) It appears that adults are much better at recalling events that happened after the age of four or five.

The amnesia is not simply due to the fact that more time has passed. For example, a person who is fifty years old can remember many events that occurred thirty years ago (when he was twenty years old), but someone who is thirty-two can remember nothing about events that occurred thirty years ago. The amnesia is also not simply due to the fact that language has not developed completely; even animals show the

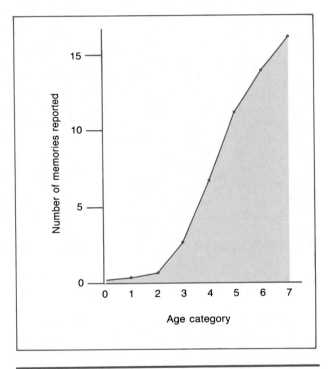

Figure 6.A *The average number of events during infancy and early childhood recalled by college students (Source: Waldfogel, 1948)*

phenomenon. They, too, show a puzzling inability to recall events that occurred during infancy (Spear, 1979). Researchers have proposed a variety of factors that might account for this phenomenon.

Freud suggested that the amnesia was due to repression of sexually unacceptable thoughts and desires. He suggested that the memories were not forgotten but rendered inaccessible to consciousness. Freud's theory postulates that the child's first few years are filled with erotic fantasies about the parents, and since they cannot be fulfilled and cause great anxiety, they are pushed out of consciousness and repressed.

Another hypothesis suggests that infantile amnesia is not so much due to guilt or anxiety as to our changing category systems. In order to remember a birthday cake, for example, you must have certain storage categories containing general information about cakes, birthdays, and candles, as well as associations between these categories. You must store the information about the cake in these categories. When you retrieve the memory later, you retrieve it based on the same category system. A candle, for example, will remind you of the cake at your tenth birthday party. An infant, however, must have quite different category systems from the adult, partly because he does not use language yet. As the child grows, the category system becomes more and more adultlike, and events are more easily recalled. The candle will probably not bring forth the retrieval of a memory about your first birthday cake, because when you stored the information about that cake, you had a very different category system.

Infantile amnesia may also be related to the drastic changes in the sensory world. The images associated with an event must seem very different to a one-year-old, and perhaps the same images seen by the twenty-year-old are simply incapable of acting as retrieval cues. To an adult, for example, a table looks like a flat surface about waist high; to an infant it looks like a massive overhead structure.

Many researchers think that some of the physiological changes in the developing brain play an important role in infantile amnesia. It is possible that the brain stores episodic memories only inefficiently during the first few years of life while brain structures are still maturing. Maturation of the hippocampus, a structure very much involved in memory, is not complete until the child is four or five years old. Perhaps the ability to retrieve memories about events coincides with the maturation of this important brain area.

None of these explanations for infantile amnesia is mutually exclusive. Physiological changes in the brain may be occurring at the same time the child's category system shifts. Or the child may be experiencing changing sensory experiences along with social pressures not to discuss certain embarrassing events. The phenomenon is an intriguing one that is likely to have multiple causes (White and Pillemer, 1979).

The model predicts that subjects would take longer to answer questions that contain nodes more distant from one another in the network. For example, it should take longer to answer the question "Does a canary have skin?" than "Does a canary sing?" The results of studies like this confirmed the hypothesis. It did indeed take longer to answer a question about a canary's skin.

This semantic network model represents just one way that information might be arranged in LTM; other models have been proposed (Smith, et al., 1974; Anderson, 1983). The study of how information in LTM is organized should be a fertile field for research for many years to come.

Forgetting from Long-Term Memory. Forgetting the name of your first-grade teacher, your spouse's birthday, or your social security number are common experiences. People forget things. Indeed, people forget just about everything that happened during their first few years of life. (See Research Box: Infantile Amnesia.) But whether we actually ever lose information from LTM is a controversial issue. There are two major theories on forgetting, one of which proposes that no information is ever lost—it just becomes extremely difficult to retrieve. This proposal views forgetting primarily as a failure in the retrieval process. The second theory proposes that information is forgotten through the process of interference. We mentioned this theory earlier in connection with the loss of information from STM.

The work of Wilder Penfield (1975), a brain surgeon who used electrical stimulation to learn more about the function of parts of the human cortex, led people to wonder whether memories might be permanent and forgetting was simply a failure in retrieval. (His main motivation was to perform needed brain surgery, and he was electrically stimulating the patient's brain to make sure the operation would not destroy critical brain tissue.) Sometimes he would stimulate the patient in the frontal or temporal lobe, and the current

would cause the patient to remember some event in vivid detail. During one operation, for example, the patient appeared to relive a long-forgotten childhood experience. During another, the patient heard Christmas songs in her church at home in Holland.

These studies suggest that memories are stored permanently. If we can't remember them, it is because we can't retrieve them efficiently. Using special techniques, such as electrical brain stimulation and others, some of these long-forgotten memories might be retrieved.

The interference theory states that forgetting occurs because something else that was learned prevents the event from being remembered. In other words, one event blocks another. *In* **retroactive interference,** *the learning of new material blocks the retrieval of old material.* A person who learns French, for example, and then years later studies Japanese might try to recall the French word for cat. Instead of *chat,* the Japanese word *neko* keeps coming to mind. Another form of interference, called **proactive interference,** *occurs when previously learned material interferes with the retrieval of new information.* The linguist, for example, might be speaking to a Japanese waiter in Tokyo and say "Sukiyaki, s'il vous plait." His old memory for the French *please* has interfered with his new memory for the Japanese phrase for please.

Experiments attempting to prove one theory and disprove the other have not been very successful, though there seems to be somewhat more support for the idea that forgetting involves primarily retrieval failure (Shiffrin, 1970). Probably, forgetting involves both processes, retrieval failure and interference.

Not all psychologists agree that memories are permanent, however. It may be that a memory for an event is really a very malleable thing and that subsequent events can cause it to change considerably (Loftus and Loftus, 1980). In the next section we will see how this might happen.

GUIDED REVIEW

Learning Objectives 1, 2, and 3

1. Human memory consists of three interacting storage compartments, called _____ , _____ (STM), and _____ (LTM).

2. Information is first processed through the sensory store, which receives a great deal of information from the external environment. There is probably a separate store for each sensory system, although research has focused on the _____ for vision and the _____ for audition.

3. The _____ , in which the recall of items from a list depends on the item's position in the list, demonstrates the existence of STM. The beginning items benefit from the _____ and have been stored in LTM. The last items on a list, however, benefit from the _____ and are held in STM until the subject has to recall them.

4. The capacity of STM is about seven _____ , a term which means anything that is represented in LTM as a single unit. Additional information can be held in STM only by increasing the size of the chunk, not by holding more of them.

5. STM is like a series of "slots" that are filled with information. STM contains the information we are thinking about at the moment. Information is lost from STM either through _____ , _____ from incoming information, or (probably) both.

6. Information in STM will be lost within about fifteen seconds unless it is rehearsed, using _____ . Transferring STM's information to LTM, however, requires _____ . This involves organizing the information and integrating it with knowledge already existing in LTM.

7. Information in LTM is stored in terms of its meaning, rather than its sound. It includes _____ and _____ memories. The _____ theory proposes that our knowledge is organized by concepts, or _____ , in a hierarchical fashion.

8. One theory to account for forgetting from LTM proposes that memories are permanent and that forgetting involves a failure to retrieve information. A second theory proposes that the memory that is forgotten has been blocked, or interfered with, by material that was learned either after (_____) or before (_____) the material that the subject is trying to recall.

ANSWERS

1. sensory store; short-term memory; long-term memory 2. iconic store; echoic store 3. serial position effect; primacy effect; recency effect 4. chunks 5. decay; interference 6. maintenance rehearsal; elaborative rehearsal 7. episodic, semantic; semantic network; nodes 8. retroactive interference; proactive interference

Retrieving Information

What is the capital of New York?

Where were you on September 3, 1980?

Who wrote *The Grapes of Wrath*?

To answer these questions, you must retrieve information from your LTM. This is no easy matter, considering that it contains millions of bits of information. However, much of the time we have no trouble at all. In this section, we will discuss how to go about searching

our LTM for information, how we recognize information that already exists in this unlimited storehouse, and finally, how we elaborate on and reconstruct a memory using bits and pieces of information that we are able to retrieve.

Search Strategies

One way to find a particular item of information in LTM is to use a **sequential search,** *which is a retrieval strategy that searches every piece of information, one at a time, until the desired item is found.* If you used a sequential search to find a book in a library's collection, beginning with the first book on the first shelf, it would be very time-consuming; the process is time-consuming for searching LTM as well.

A sequential search, however, is used to examine the contents of STM. In a series of very clever experiments, subjects looked over a list of a few numbers or letters until they felt they had stored the whole list in STM. Then various test items were presented, and the subjects simply identified whether each had been in the original set (Sternberg, 1966, 1967, 1969). The more items that were in the original set, the longer it took for the subjects to respond to each of the test items. This suggested that the subjects searched their STM's sequentially to decide whether the test item matched any of those in the original set. (Longer lists required longer sequential searches.) Strangely, the response times for "no" and "yes" answers was about the same. This meant that the sequential search was exhaustive; it continued through all the items contained in STM even though the subject might have found a match early in the search. An exhaustive sequential search of LTM would probably take centuries. But it is quite useful for STM.

Another kind of search, one that appears to be used for a search of LTM, depends on narrowing down the search set. Using **retrieval cues,** *which are pieces of information that are used to help locate other, related items of information in memory,* a much more efficient search of LTM can be conducted.

Retrieval Cues. Retrieval cues are absolutely essential in any search of LTM. In one experiment, subjects were given a list of categories, such as fruits, animals, or crimes, and then shown instances of each category (horse, plum, murder) and asked to memorize them (Tulving and Pearlstone, 1966). The next day, some subjects were given the category titles (fruit, for example), and then asked to recall the instances within that category. They could recall about thirty instances.

Other subjects tried to recall the instances without the category titles, and they could only recall about twenty instances. Later they were given the category titles, and they were able to recall about twenty-eight instances. Giving the subjects the category title as a retrieval cue was clearly very useful in helping them remember.

No one really knows exactly how long-term memory is searched, but figure 6.7 shows one plausible strategy that relies on semantic networks to recall the capital of New York. The retrieval cue "New York" causes the node labeled "New York" to be activated. The activation spreads out from there, moving from node to node until it reaches the one labeled "Albany," which has as one of its characteristics "state capital."

Trying to recall where you were on September 3, 1980, really taxes the retrieval system of your brain, and retrieval cues become even more important. One answer might go like this:

> I have no idea . . . wait, I must have been living in D.C., working for NASA. That fall I was going back and forth to Cocoa Beach, since the shuttle was about to go up. . . . Let's see . . . we had a bad hurricane that season. Was that around September? Yes, I remember I was trying to call my mother on her birthday, which is Sept. 4, from the motel in Florida, and the lines were down. I had to spend the whole weekend in that fleabag. . . .

State-Dependent Memory. Retrieval cues can be sights, sounds, smells, tastes, or anything that helps you find information. They can also include your state when you learned the material in the first place. A phenomenon called **state-dependent memory** *occurs when a person who learns material in a particular state, such as when he or she has been drinking alcohol, is able to recall it better when in the same state again.* The phenomenon applies to alcohol intoxication, other drugged states, and even mood (Overton, 1964; Swanson and Kinsbourne, 1976).

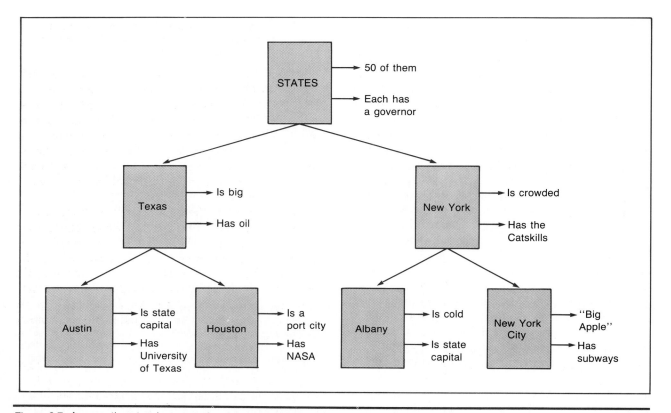

Figure 6.7 A semantic network strategy for searching long-term memory

In one experiment, subjects wrote down in a diary all their emotional experiences for a week. At the end of the week, each person was hypnotized and put into either a happy or a sad mood, using a simple hypnotic suggestion (Bower, 1981). While in the trance, the volunteers tried to recall the incidents they had written in their diaries. The ones in a sad mood tended to recall many more unhappy incidents, whereas those in a happy mood recalled the pleasant experiences. The mood the person was in during the recall test was an important retrieval cue that helped locate memories that were formed when the person was in a similar mood.

The phenomenon also occurs in the laboratory. Subjects in their normal moods were shown a list of sentences containing adjectives such as small, short, new, or full. Afterwards, half of them were placed into a depressed mood by special suggestions from the experimenter, and these people were able to recall fewer adjectives, compared to people whose moods were not altered (Ellis, Thomas, McFarland, and Lane, 1985).

There is some evidence that the right hemisphere plays an important mediating role in the effects of mood states on memory. In one experiment, people in either a happy or sad mood viewed photographs showing emotional facial expressions. The photos were presented to either the right or left visual fields so the information would first reach the right or left hemisphere, as we discussed in Chapter 2. Later, for part of the experiment, the subjects were placed in the opposite mood and shown the photos again. Although the different mood did not effect their ability to recall faces shown to the left hemisphere, they did very poorly when recalling the faces shown to the right. This suggests that the right hemisphere stores the information about mood during the encoding process, and its memory is particularly disrupted when the mood at retrieval time is different (Gage and Safer, 1985).

Memory Reconstruction

Once a memory has been located in LTM, it would seem to be a simple matter to "read it off," and recall it exactly as it happened. But recall is not so simple. Even memories that seem very vivid may be partly reconstructions. For example, people often make mistakes trying to date important world events. In one study, subjects were asked to recall the dates of events like the assassination attempt on Ronald Reagan by John Hinckley (March, 1981), or the shooting of Pope Paul II (May, 1981). Probably because the Reagan shooting was more accessible and they recalled more details about it, most people thought it occurred more recently. It may seem logical to assume that vividly recalled events are more recent, but it is not always correct (Brown, Rips, and Shevell, 1985).

People also seem to perform reconstructions based on an attempt to make an event more realistic or plausible. Sometimes the reconstruction is correct, but sometimes it turns into an almost incredible distortion.

The distortions that usually occur in the "rumor game" show how reconstructions occur. In one game, the first person in line heard the following story:

> Five men on a subway in New York held up a black man on his way to a business meeting. They all had knives, and none of the three other people on the train

offered any help. The victim handed over his wallet, saying, 'Shalom to all of you, brothers.' The muggers got off the train at the next stop.

Each person who heard the story was able to recall only one or two critical incidents and reconstructed the rest, and their reconstructions usually filled in the gaps imperfectly. One person mentioned that "the muggers held up some Jewish person." Someone later in line said "three guys held up a rabbi." The last person heard that "a black guy mugged a priest on a train." Each person filled in gaps, using information and assumptions that already existed in his LTM.

People are most likely to make reconstructive mistakes and distortions when they learned something after the event that contradicted what they originally saw. The new information seems to get incorporated into the original memory, and when we retrieve the original memory it has been subtly changed. American courts are very concerned about this kind of mistake, as we discuss in the Application Box: Judging the Accuracy of Eyewitness Testimony.

Eyewitness Testimony. Laboratory studies of eyewitness testimony confirm the view that our reconstructions can be distorted by new information. In one study, college students were shown a series of thirty color slides of the events at a staged traffic accident (Loftus, Miller, and Burns, 1978). Half the subjects saw a red Datsun traveling along a side street approaching a stop sign, and the other half saw the Datsun approaching a yield sign. In both cases, the Datsun then turned right and hit a pedestrian in a crosswalk.

After viewing the slides the subjects were asked many questions about the accident, including one very critical one: "Did another car pass the red Datsun while it was stopped at the stop sign?" In legal jargon, this is a leading question because it implies that a stop sign was there. Half the subjects from each group heard this question, while the other half heard an identical question except that the "stop" sign was called a "yield"

Figure 6.8 *Studies of memory show that even eyewitness testimony is subject to a great deal of error, partly because of the process of memory reconstruction.*

sign. Thus, half the observers were being given correct information about the version of the accident they witnessed. The other half were given false information.

Later on, the subjects saw a pair of slides—one showing the Datsun at a yield sign and the other showing a stop sign—and were asked to indicate the one they originally witnessed (fig. 6.8). Nearly all the subjects who were given correct information in the questionnaire chose the correct slide. On the other hand, more than eighty percent of those who received misleading information picked the wrong slide—the one they had never seen. They did this even though the one

they actually had seen was being shown at the same time. The leading question had apparently caused a change in the subjects' memories, or at least in the way they reconstructed their memories of the event.

New information can have powerful effects on memory of faces as well, a point that is extremely worrisome to legal professionals who must rely on eyewitness testimony for identification of suspects. In a series of three experiments, subjects saw a person's face in a photo, in a film, and live. Later they were exposed to a description of that person, ostensibly given by another witness. When the other witness's description included

APPLICATION BOX

Judging the Accuracy of Eyewitness Testimony

In the 1972 case of *Neil* v. *Biggers,* the U.S. Supreme Court made it clear that they are aware of the problems with eyewitness testimony. The annals of criminal justice include a number of case histories detailing the miscarriage of justice because of mistaken eyewitness identifications. In *Neil* v. *Biggers,* the Court was concerned with the factors that should be considered in determining whether an eyewitness's identification is accurate. The Court decided that the following five factors should be considered in judging the accuracy of an identification:

1. the opportunity of the witness to view the criminal at the time of the crime;
2. the witness's degree of attention;
3. the accuracy of the witness's prior description of the criminal;
4. the level of certainty demonstrated by the witness at the time of the confrontation; and
5. the length of time between the crime and the confrontation.

These criteria were established with very little input from psychologists, primarily because they had little to give at the time. The subject of eyewitness identification attracted very little research interest until the mid 1970s, when many investigators began studying the phenomenon. Now psychologists have some information about the usefulness of the Court's criteria and can make some suggestions for criteria that might be added (Wells and Murray, 1983).

For example, a witness's certainty about an identification is a very convincing element in trials, so it is not surprising that the Court included this criterion. When a witness says, "That's the woman. I'd know her anywhere!" judges and juries are very likely to believe him, often regardless of evidence to the contrary. However, study after study has found that there is little or no relationship between an eyewitness's certainty and his or her accuracy in making an identification.

an incorrect feature, such as a moustache that didn't exist, the subjects were much more likely to incorporate the mistaken feature into their own idea of what the person looked like. When they tried to pick out the correct person from a lineup of twelve people, seventy percent of the subjects identified someone who had the mistaken feature. Only thirteen percent of the control subjects, who had not heard the misleading "evidence" from another witness, picked a person with the wrong feature (Loftus and Greene, 1980).

Such studies demonstrate that memories are malleable and shifty things. When we try to remember some event, we retrieve some accurate bits of information

In one study, unsuspecting subjects witnessed a staged crime—an act of vandalism. Later they were asked to pick out the perpetrator from a live lineup and state how certain they were that their choices were correct. (Sometimes the perpetrator was in the lineup and sometimes he was not, a circumstance that is typical of actual lineups.) The correlation between the subjects' accuracy and their certainty was zero. Subjects were just as likely to be dead sure they were right when they were wrong as they were to be accurate but rather unsure of themselves. Most of the people who were certain but wrong had chosen someone out of the lineup in which the perpetrator did not appear. The ones who made no choice in the lineup without the perpetrator seemed much less sure of themselves. The researchers hypothesize that a person's certainty about an identification comes more from making a choice in the first place; if they make one, then they are sure (Malpass and Devine, 1981).

A criterion that probably should be added to the Court's list is *the conditions under which the witness makes the identification.* Some conditions, because of their suggestiveness, seem almost to provoke witnesses into making inaccurate judgments. In an experiment, for example, some of the subjects who were trying to pick out the vandal from the lineup were given the suggestion that the vandal was present, even though sometimes he was not. The error rate for these subjects was extremely high— 51.5%, compared to 25% for subjects who did not hear the suggestion.

If and when the U.S. Supreme Court reassesses the issue of the accuracy of eyewitness identification, psychologists will have learned a great deal more about the phenomenon and will be able to offer useful advice.

about it and fill in gaps to round out the story. The memory reconstructions are especially affected by new information, some of which may be wrong.

Recognition Memory

Recognizing something you have seen before is quite different from recalling it. The difference is obvious on college tests, for instance. Multiple-choice questions ask you only to recognize the correct answer when you see it; essay questions require that you recall the answer.

Students generally agree that essay questions are more difficult and that you must know the material better in order to do well. This is because the essay question gives you few retrieval cues to help you remember information; the multiple-choice test gives you the ultimate in retrieval cues—the answer itself.

Recognition memory is spectacularly good for visual information. In one experiment, subjects were given a chance to study 612 pictures of common scenes at their own pace, usually a few seconds per picture (Shepard, 1967). On the recognition test, they averaged ninety-seven percent.

"It's on the Tip of My Tongue." The **tip-of-the-tongue phenomenon** *refers to the failure to recall information when you are certain the information is contained in your LTM.* Suppose you are trying to think of the author of *The Grapes of Wrath.* You are fairly sure you know the answer—it is on the tip of your tongue—but you just can't recall it. You know that if you saw it, however, you would recognize it instantly. (If this description fits you, look at the bottom of the page and try to recognize the author's name.)

People are usually very accurate in their predictions about whether they can really recognize a correct answer. It seems that they know what is in their LTM, even though they cannot always retrieve it easily.

Some studies suggest that recognition memory may be different from recall memory, and not only because people perform one better than the other. For example, when subjects are asked to memorize a list of words and then later are asked to recall them, they tend to recall the more common words first (Shepard, 1967; Gorman, 1961). If the list contained names like Bob, David, Wentworth, Jim, and Humperdinck, they would tend to recall Bob, David, and Jim, more often than Wentworth or Humperdinck. If their memory is tested using recognition, however, perhaps by showing them a long list of names and asking them to pick out the ones they saw earlier, they tend to recognize the odd names better than the common ones.

Furthermore, the strategies people use to learn information that will later be tested by recall or by recognition appears to be different (Tversky, 1973). Subjects do much better on tests of learned material if they are correctly told which method of testing will be used. If they are misled about the testing method, they do not do as well. Students might be justifiably irate if they are told to expect an essay test and get multiple choice instead.

Recognizing Familiar Faces. Our ability to recognize the faces of familiar people seems to be separate from other memory skills. The main reason that many scientists hold this view is that there are some brain-damaged people who have a very peculiar defect: they cannot recognize their friends' faces (Benton, 1980). The case history of a 24-year-old woman who suffered from this defect illustrates the problem.

Three weeks after giving birth to her baby, a right-handed woman was admitted to the hospital because of severe headaches and occasional grand mal seizures. Her EEG was abnormal. After a few days in the hospital she began to improve, but it became clear that she was having trouble with her memory. She could speak and understand language normally, perform arithmetic problems, and repeat back sequences of digits. Her vision was normal, and she could remember most things quite well. She could even easily discriminate the faces of strangers. But when her husband or her mother came to visit, she didn't recognize them until they began to speak. When she looked at pictures of her children, she said, "They don't look like they should."

Ordinarily, when people suffer brain damage from disease or injury, they show a wide range of behavioral changes, some slight, some more severe. But occasionally a person shows a disability in a single function. The woman in the above example simply could not recognize familiar faces. Studies of patients like this one lead researchers to believe that the underlying brain mechanisms for facial recognition are different from those for other memory skills, or even for other visual abilities. Perhaps the ability to recognize familiar faces is so important to human beings that we have evolved special biological underpinnings for it. As the next section will show, psychologists have learned a great deal about the biological events that take place when a person learns and remembers, although many mysteries remain.

Learning Objectives 4, 5, and 6

1. Retrieving information from STM might be accomplished through an exhaustive _____ , in which you search items one by one, but this kind of search of LTM is very time-consuming. _____ narrow down the search set; they include anything that helps you find the correct location in LTM. They might also include your state of mind when you learned the material. Memories are _____ for states like intoxication or mood.

2. The retrieval process is partly an accurate "reading off" of information contained in LTM and partly _____ . The reconstruction process is vulnerable to distortion, particularly when you receive new information that contradicts what you had learned first.

3. _____ is easier than recall because a person simply has to identify that an item is in her LTM but not retrieve it. The _____ phenomenon refers to the failure to recall information when the person knows the information is contained in LTM.

4. Recognition of _____ seems to be based on different underlying biological mechanisms. People with brain damage in a particular area of the brain sometimes have trouble with this ability, but not with other memory skills.

ANSWERS

3. *Recognition; tip-of-the-tongue 4. familiar faces*
1. *sequential search; Retrieval cues; state dependent 2. reconstruction*

Biological Basis of Learning and Memory

The human brain, a four-and-a-half-pound mass of tissue, can hold all the memories you are able to store in it. It can process the information, decide which information to ignore and which to attend to, put some of it into short-term memory, and place some of that into long-term storage where it could last almost a century. Nevertheless, the way in which it learns and remembers is still very poorly understood.

A very old but still workable theory of how the brain accomplishes learning and memory was proposed by D. O. Hebb (1949). He suggested that information processing begins with changes in the firing patterns of particular neural networks in the brain. The transfer of information to permanent storage, however, probably involves physical changes in the brain, most likely in the synaptic connections between neurons.

Changes in the Brain During Learning

Tracing what happens in the brain during a learning experience is a formidable task, to say the least. The brain contains some ten to fifteen billion neurons, and changes in firing patterns might be limited to a very small network. Simply recording the activity of one or two neurons in the hope that they might show some changes during learning is like hunting for the proverbial needle in the haystack. However, there are several more efficient ways to approach the problem (Farley and Alkon, 1985). One way involves using an animal with very few neurons, and the other approach involves recording the activity in groups of neurons rather than in individual cells.

Learning in Aplysia. A snaillike creature that is rapidly becoming a favorite of some researchers who are studying learning and memory is *Aplysia* (Kandel, 1976). The attraction of this unassuming beast is its tiny nervous system. Unfortunately, a creature this simple cannot study nonsense syllables or press levers, but it does show some plasticity in its behavior. If someone squirts water on *Aplysia's* siphon, for instance, the animal will withdraw its gill. If its siphon is repeatedly stimulated, the gill withdrawal response habituates, growing weaker and weaker. Some psychologists argue whether **habituation,** *which refers to the gradual diminishing of a response after repeated* *presentations of the stimulus,* is really a form of learning. But most psychologists certainly consider it to be related to learning in the sense that the animal is making a behavioral change with experience.

All the neurons involved in the habituation of the gill withdrawal reflex have been mapped, and researchers have been able to follow the activity in each one while the animal "learns." By eliminating one neuron after another, they finally concluded that most of the change in the nervous system accompanying this kind of habituation occurs at the synapse between the sensory neuron and the motor neuron. The sensory neuron releases less and less neurotransmitter as habituation proceeds, and the motor neuron's response predictably becomes weaker and weaker (Kandel, 1976).

The patience required to perform a study like this one has paid off. Now it is clear that changes in the synapse can and do occur during habituation, at least in the gastropod. The change is not a permanent one, and the synapse returns to normal a short time after the experimenters stop stimulating the siphon. Most researchers had tacitly agreed that plastic changes in the nervous system must involve some kind of change at the synapse. But proving it in a live animal, even one as simple as *Aplysia,* was a very difficult challenge.

The Rabbit's Eyelid. Following the course of neuronal events during a learning experience in a mammal is a cyclopean task, but at least one group of workers has made the attempt (Thompson, Patterson, and Berger, 1978). They used a simple example of learning: classical conditioning of the rabbit's inner eyelid. A puff of air directed toward the rabbit's eye (UCS) automatically elicits a blinking response (UCR). If the rabbit always hears a tone (CS) just before the puff of air, it will eventually begin to blink in response to the tone by itself (CR).

Since the mammalian brain contains so many neurons, they chose to use larger electrodes and measure the activity of a group of neurons, rather than individual ones. One of the first areas they investigated was the hippocampus, a structure that has been implicated

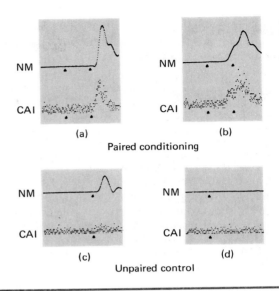

Paired conditioning

Unpaired control

Figure 6.9   Change in the activity of the rabbit's eyelid and in the activity in the hippocampus before conditioning (a), and after conditioning (b). The responses in (c) and (d) were taken from a rabbit that was not exposed to a paired CS and UCS.

in learning and memory for some time. People with damage in this area, for example, often have problems with memory. One man, H. M., whose hippocampus was damaged during surgery was never again able to transfer information from STM to LTM. We discussed his case in Chapter 2.

Figure 6.9 shows how the activity in the rabbit's hippocampal neurons changed. First, these neurons showed a significant increase in firing just after the puff of air (a), but before the eyelid response. After many conditioning trials, the hippocampal neurons increased their firing sooner; in fact, the change began after the tone, but before the puff of air. This means that the hippocampal neurons were anticipating the puff.

The precise role of the hippocampus in learning is still very unclear, but many scientists suspect that it is very much involved, particularly in STM and in the transfer of information from STM to LTM. Perhaps information stored in STM "slots" sets up special firing patterns in the hippocampus, patterns that eventually trigger changes in other parts of the brain as the information is stored in LTM.

Making a Memory

Although all the neurons you will ever have already exist by the time you are two years old, they do not remain the same throughout your life. They form new synapses, lose old ones, strengthen or weaken the ones they have, and grow new branches all the time. Scientists hypothesize that the formation of a memory requires just such changes in the brain. The **engram** *refers to the memory trace, or the hypothetical neuronal changes that occur when an organism learns something.*

Where Is the Engram?   Hunting for the location of a stored memory may seem rather simple. One approach is to teach an animal a task and then lesion part of its brain. If the animal cannot remember what it had learned, the part of the brain that was lesioned contained the memory.

Or did it? Karl Lashley (1959) performed experiments like this and obtained very confusing results. He found that despite some very extensive lesions, a rat would continue to perform a task it had learned. It would only forget the task, which involved learning the difference between a light and a dark alley in a maze, if the visual cortex were completely removed. Lashley wondered whether the rat "forgot" simply because it could no longer see. After many such experiments, he concluded that the engram for a particular event is very widespread, at least within the area of the brain that processes the kind of sensory information that was used in the task. A visual memory, for example, would be stored diffusely throughout the occipital lobes of the brain. (Lashley also concluded, incidentally, that the results of lesion studies are very difficult to interpret. When you damage part of the brain and the animal no longer performs, it is hard to tell whether you damaged the engram or some other function that is required for performance, such as vision, hearing, pattern discrimination, or motivation.)

Earlier we discussed brain-damaged people who were unable to recognize close friends by sight. This is a good example of how memories might be stored diffusely within a sensory area. The right occipital lobe is the brain area that is most often damaged in such people (Benton, 1980). Perhaps memories of familiar faces are stored in this general location. The patients can still recognize their friends' voices, however, suggesting that the auditory engrams are stored elsewhere, probably in the auditory cortex.

What Is the Engram?   Most scientists agree that the memory trace must involve changes in neuronal branching patterns and changes in synaptic connections. Nevertheless, in the billions of neurons in the brain and in the trillions of possible connections, the engram has been extremely evasive.

A typical study that might tell us something about the nature of the engram compares the brains of animals that have learned something to the brains of ones that have not. For example, one group of rats learned to avoid a shock by jumping onto a platform whenever a buzzer sounded (Rees, et al., 1974). A second group heard the buzzer but could not avoid the shock, and a third simply remained in its home cage. The animals were injected with radioactive tracers, and their brains were examined for any changes.

The most common finding in studies like this one is that an animal that learns something shows greater synthesis of both proteins and **RNA,** *a substance produced by DNA that directs the manufacture of proteins.* Furthermore, at least some of the time, the changes in synthesis activity are larger in certain parts of the brain, the hippocampus in particular. It is tempting to conclude that the formation of a memory trace requires the synthesis of proteins that might be acting as key enzymes or neurotransmitters. Perhaps these substances are involved in structural modification of existing synapses or even in the creation of new ones. However, the interpretation of these studies is somewhat cloudy (Dunn, 1980).

Modifying Memory

The attempt to describe the nature of the engram has been so difficult that many scientists have turned their attention to learning about those events that can modify memory. Most of these studies have used "memory disruptors;" however, a few have discovered means to improve the process of memory formation.

Memory Disruptors.   A variety of substances and events can disrupt memory. Drugs that inhibit protein synthesis are remarkably effective, again supporting the view that the formation of an engram requires protein synthesis. Another disruptor is **electroconvulsive shock (ECS),** *which refers to a treatment in which electric current is passed through the brain to the point at which convulsions occur.* It has been used as a treatment for various mental disorders, especially depression, since the 1930s. One reason that the use of ECS has decreased is that it produces **amnesia,** *or memory loss.* A patient might be unable to recall very much about the twenty-four hours preceding the treatment. This characteristic of ECS, however, interested memory researchers.

Whether ECS interferes with the consolidation of memories or their later retrieval is not certain. At first, the research suggested that memories take some time to form and that during the early stages they are very vulnerable to disruption by the drastic changes in neuronal firing patterns produced by ECS. If memories are "left alone" and allowed to consolidate for a period of time, they seem to become more and more resistant (Duncan, 1949; Gold, Macri, and McGaugh, 1973). Other work, however, suggests that ECS may affect retrieval more than memory consolidation. For example, memories whose consolidation was disrupted by ECS are sometimes retrievable through "reminders," such as electric shocks. Also, memories that should have been well-consolidated have been disrupted by ECS days after the event (Robbins and Meyer, 1970). Some scientists propose that memories are formed within moments after a learning experience and that ECS disrupts the hypothetical "cataloging" process by which a stored memory is retrieved (Miller and Springer, 1973).

Memory Improvement Drugs.   Although there is no magic pill that will suddenly make you a memory expert, there are some drugs that mildly improve memory. One such drug is **arecholine,** *a substance that increases activity at synapses in the brain that use the neurotransmitter acetylcholine* (Sitaram, Weingartner, and Gillin, 1978). Volunteers received injections of arecholine and then were shown a list of ten words. The subjects receiving the drug recalled slightly more words than did the controls, especially toward the end of the testing session. The drug hardly made the people into nightclub "memory experts," but it did produce a noticeable improvement in the subjects' ability to recall their list.

An important factor in senility appears to be a disruption in the network of neurons using acetylcholine (Bartus, Dean, Beer, and Lippa, 1982). Studies of aging animals have found changes in this network, and similar changes have been seen in the brains of people who were senile. Also, drugs like arecholine are sometimes effective in improving the memories of aged people. Again, these drugs do not work miracles, and they do have side effects, but this important clue is leading to a better understanding not only of aging and senility but of the biology of memory.

Stress and Memory.   Ted Kennedy had a very poor memory of the events of Chappaquiddick. On a summer weekend in 1969, he went to a party and slipped away early to catch the last ferry home. On the way, he made a wrong turn, and while crossing a narrow wooden bridge, his car flipped over into the water. Kennedy was able to get out of the car and swim to shore, but his companion, Mary Jo Kopechne, drowned.

Years later, especially when Kennedy was running for President, the press would ask him questions about the Chappaquiddick incident. His answers sounded very evasive: "I wish I could help you . . . I don't recall that . . . I have no recollection . . . That is the best I can give you . . . I have no memory. . . ." Some said he just didn't want to tell the whole story. Others guessed that his mind actively "forgot" the painful experience, pushing it into his subconscious, using the Freudian strategy called repression. Another hypothesis, though, is that the biochemical changes associated with acute stress actually can disrupt the formation of a memory.

In an experiment designed to explore the role of stress in memory formation, rats were given a footshock each time they tried to run into the dark side of a two-chambered box (Gold and van Buskirk, 1978). Immediately after this training, some of the rats received **epinephrine,** *one of the hormones released by the adrenal glands during stress.* Later, the animals given epinephrine seemed to forget what they had learned. They ran right into the dark compartment, hardly hesitating a moment. The footshock alone was fairly stressful, but when the experience was made even more stressful, at least biologically speaking, the formation of a memory was disrupted.

Stress, however, not only interferes with memory formation. Under some circumstances it improves the process. For example, in another study, six groups of rats were given a mild footshock each time they tried to enter the dark side of the box. The control group received an injection of saline after training, and each of the five experimental groups received a dose of epinephrine. The rats receiving a very small dose of this "stress hormone" did not remember the task very well. They ran right into the dark side the next time they were placed into the box, just like the control rats. Also, the animals that got a large dose of the drug performed poorly, but the ones receiving intermediate doses did very well. All three of those groups were very hesitant to enter the dark side; they clearly remembered what they had learned (Gold and van Buskirk, 1975).

These studies on epinephrine explain why stress can either be a boon to memory, or its nemesis. The formation of a memory is clearly affected by this important hormone. If the learning experience is too stressful, or not stressful enough, the memory of it will be weak. The formation of a memory appears to be most efficient when the stress level is somewhere in the middle. The studies relating stress to performance on a memory task offer an explanation for a widely known phenomenon called the Yerkes-Dodson Law (1908), which we discuss in more detail in Chapter 8. An individual who is extremely aroused, excited, and under a great deal of stress, rarely performs very well on any task, whether it involves learning and remembering, driving a car, or running a footrace. But very low levels of arousal also result in poor performance. The best performance is obtained when the individual is in a moderate level of arousal.

GUIDED REVIEW

Learning Objectives 7, 8, and 9

1. One hypothesis about the biology of learning and memory states that _____ involves changes in the firing patterns of neural networks in the brain and _____ requires physical changes in neurons.

2. Studies of *Aplysia* have identified the neural changes occurring during _____ , a phenomenon in which the response to a stimulus diminishes as the stimulus is repeatedly presented.

3. Brain activity during classical conditioning in the rabbit has been monitored. During the conditioning process, neurons in the _____ show increases in firing that might be related to learning.

4. Finding the location of the _____ , or memory trace, for a particular memory has been impossible, at least using lesion studies. Memories of an event appear to be stored diffusely, throughout the sensory area of the brain that was primarily involved in the learning experience.

5. The nature of the engram has been equally evasive. However, most studies show that the formation of a memory requires the synthesis of _____ .

6. Memory formation or retrieval can be disrupted by several procedures, including _____ , a treatment in which electric current is passed through the brain to the point at which convulsions occur.

7. Too much or too little _____ , one of the hormones released during stress, retards memory formation. However, injection of an intermediate amount of this hormone can improve memory formation.

ANSWERS

1. STM. LTM 2. habituation 3. hippocampus 4. engram 5. protein and RNA 6. electroconvulsive shock (ECS) 7. epinephrine

Improving Your Memory

Improving your memory is really not very difficult. In this section, we will explore a wide variety of methods you can use, depending on what you are trying to remember.

Improving the Storage Process

Storing information in LTM can be improved in several ways. First, you can pay more attention to what it is you want to store. Second, you can begin the storage process by actively rehearsing informaton you want to remember. Third, you can organize it better and integrate it into the information that already exists in your LTM. Finally, you can learn more efficiently by applying some of the principles of learning discussed in the last chapter.

Paying Attention.   You have probably had the experience of reading a paragraph and then not being able to recall a single idea or message even immediately after you are finished. Your mind wandered. You were thinking about the dog barking or the noisy air conditioner. You were daydreaming. In other words, you were not paying attention to the words in the paragraph. The only information in sensory store that is transferred to STM is that to which you are paying attention. It does not even have a chance to be stored in LTM unless you give it your attention.

> *John:* Hi there, Joe. I want you to meet Sara Armo.
> *Joe:* Glad to meet you. I'm Joe Downing.
> *Sara:* So you're a friend of John's. What did you say your name was again?

If you have ever been introduced to someone and almost immediately forgot his name, you are not alone. The reason people do this appears to be that they are not paying attention. The information never got out of sensory store, let alone transferred to LTM.

Rehearsal.   Holding Joe's name in STM for longer than a few seconds requires a rehearsal:

> *Joe:* It's Joe Downing.
> *Sara:* Well, I'm very happy to meet you, Joe.
> *Joe:* And I'm glad to meet you. John has told me a lot about you.
> *Sara:* Nothing bad, I hope. Do you also work for National Industries, Joe?

Rehearsal by itself, however, does not transfer information from STM into LTM. And if you really want to remember this person's name the next time you see him, you must store it in LTM. As we discussed earlier, you need to perform elaborative rehearsal, not just maintenance rehearsal. Organizing the material and integrating it into your present network of knowledge are the keys to elaborative rehearsal.

Organizational Strategies. Organizing and integrating a new piece of information can be accomplished in many ways. Two of the most effective are using a mnemonic device and chunking.

> *Joe:* Yes, I sure do.
> *Sara:* Downing, Downing . . . like 10 Downing Street. Are you British?
> *Joe:* That's right, mate!

Sara's technique for remembering Joe's name was first to rehearse it. Then she performed an elaborative rehearsal using a **mnemonic device,** *or a system that helps integrate new information with information already existing in LTM.* She associated the name with an image that already existed in her memory, and she made the connection between Joe, the name, and the image. The strategy of using old knowledge as a framework for storing new pieces of information, especially relying on mental imagery, is the mnemonic device.

A mnemonic device that is very effective in remembering grocery lists, speeches, or anything that must be recalled in a specific order, is the **method of loci.** *This memory improvement technique associates each item in a list with the parts of a well-known physical location, such as your house.* Imagine a tour of your house. First you enter the foyer, then the living room, the dining room, the kitchen, then the staircase, and so on. Then, make a mental association between the places on your tour and each item or idea you must remember. For example, with the grocery list, imagine the front door blocked with apples, the living room floor covered with butter, the dining room table stinking of vinegar, and so on.

Mnemonic devices are common tools in many professions, particularly those that require a great deal of memorization. Every musician knows about "*Every Good Boy Does Fine,*" for example.

While mnemonic devices are certainly useful for remembering grocery lists and musical notes, they also can help you remember more difficult material. Suppose you have to give a presentation on business computer systems to a group of potential customers, and you want to discuss several main computer applications, including inventory, accounting, and communications. You can use the loci system, imagining stacks of boxes blocking the entrance to your home, adding machines and calculators piled on your coffee table with their paper spilling onto the floor, and an old-fashioned telephone attached to the wall in your dining room. This method will insure that you don't leave out any major points. Mnemonic devices are also frequently used to make computer software more "user-friendly." (See Career Box: Software Developer.)

Another strategy to help you organize and integrate new information is the method of chunking. We saw how this method could be used to remember incredibly long strings of digits. You can use chunking to help you store more useful information as well. Suppose you are trying to remember the ten most important companies that do business with your law office: National Employment Bureau, Standard Coin Company, Delta Freight, Energy and Gas, Inc., Keller Cash Registers, Charley's Carburetors, Reliable Temporary Employment Counselors, New York Executive Search Company, New Jersey Money Markets, and BST Motorcycles. Trying to recall each item individually would tax your retrieval system, but you could chunk them into categories. One chunking system might group the companies according to their general purpose: transportation, money, and jobs. Then, all you have to do is recall the categories.

Transportation
Delta Freight
Energy and Gas, Inc.
Charley's Carburetors
BST Motorcycles
Money
Standard Coin Company
Keller Cash Registers
New Jersey Money Markets

CAREER BOX

Software Developer

An occupation that is in a growing industry is in software development. Computers are very useful gadgets, but in order for people to use them they must be accompanied by instructions. The software developer is involved in the production of programs (or instructions) for the computer to make the equipment perform certain functions. One program, for example, might ask the operator to type in all the data from a psychological experiment. The program would then take the data and compute statistics for it, make graphs, and even draw conclusions. Programs can be written in several different computer "languages," such as BASIC, FORTRAN, or PASCAL. They must be written very logically because the computer needs logical instructions in order to function properly.

Usually the software developer does not actually write the programs; that task is left to a computer programmer. The developer conceives the program and tries to make it meet the needs of the potential user by making it "user-friendly." Some programs are very difficult to learn to use, but others can be operated by almost anyone. A skillful software developer creates software that is easy to use. In order to do that, the developer must understand a great deal about psychology, particularly human memory.

One very popular program, called VisiCalc*, uses every kind of mnemonic device to help the user. The program is an "electronic spreadsheet" that permits rapid recalculation of figures all over a table. Some of the functions it can perform include deleting columns, blanking out entries, moving columns from one place to another, and clearing the entire table. One reason this program is so popular is that it is easy to remember all the commands. You press MC to move a column, MR to move a row, C to clear the table, B to blank out entries, DC to delete a column, and so on. Less user-friendly programs might ask you to press numbers for each function, and it takes many weeks to remember all the commands. The software developer for Visicalc obviously had a clear notion of how human memory works and thus was able to design a better computer program.

*VisiCalc is a registered trademark of Paladine.

Jobs
National Employment Bureau
Reliable Temporary Employment
Counselors
New York Executive Search Company

Efficient Learning. Although much of the material in the last chapter dealt with very simple forms of learning, it included some useful strategies that can aid the storage of more complicated information. In particular, you can make liberal use of rewards, and you can space your learning experiences.

Suppose you have a report to read and comprehend and must give a presentation on it the next morning. Tell yourself that as soon as you have learned the report to your satisfaction, you will reward yourself with a movie, a new shirt, a trip to the ice cream store, or perhaps a cold mug of beer. The reward will help you more if you get it very soon after the learning experience. Delaying the reinforcement too long will make learning less effective.

Studies of conditioning find that learning is much more efficient if the trials are spaced some time apart rather than one after another. If you want to learn a list of foreign words, for example, you could do so more easily by studying it a short time each day for several days rather than a long time on a single day. The effects of spaced trials on learning explain why students who "cram" the night before an exam usually do not perform very well. The same amount of study time can be used more effectively if it is broken into shorter segments.

Improving Retrieval

One way to improve retrieval is to use better retrieval cues. Finding your lost car keys is much easier if you focus on retrieval cues rather than hunt throughout your house. First, imagine when you had them last. What were you wearing? (Check pockets.) Did you have a purse or briefcase with you? Which room of the house did you enter first? Second? Did you open the trunk of the car? Using each of these retrieval cues in succession will help you remember where you put those elusive car keys.

In one experiment, subjects were asked to recall the names of their high school classmates years after they had graduated (Williams, 1976). The people explored one retrieval cue after another, and sometimes they recalled hundreds of names:

> Now, people I knew through my sister—hm—I didn't know them very well, they were just acquaintances, there's Leanne, and don't even remember his name . . . wow, OK, I just lo-located a storehouse of people. There was an afterschool thing where I used to go all the time, and there was lots of people there, and I have a whole building full of people, but I can't remember a lot of those names. There's Ruth Bower, Susan Younger, Sue

> Cairns—oh, wow, Jeff Andrews, Bill Jacobsen, I just located a whole another group of people, whew (laugh) wow-um.

When subjects tried to recall the names of high school classmates, they also included the names of people who were not in their class at all but whom they knew in different settings. Retrieval is a process of reconstruction, as we discussed earlier, and incorrect information will often be included in the retrieval.

An important retrieval cue can be your state when you learned the information. As we saw earlier, memories can be state-dependent and thus more easily remembered in the same state. For example, if you were drinking when you lost your address book, perhaps having a drink will help you remember where you put it. Or, if you were extremely happy when you lost it, getting into another happy mood may also help you find it.

Long-forgotten memories are sometimes successfully retrieved using special techniques, such as hypnosis. For instance, subjects recall the happenings at their fifth birthday party, the events at their mother's second wedding, a foreign language they haven't spoken for years, and even license-plate numbers on a van. (See Chapter 3.) However, hypnotized subjects can also fabricate information quite convincingly. In one experiment, subjects confidently recalled information not only from their past but from their future (Barber, 1965).

Other special retrieval techniques include brain stimulation and psychoanalysis. We don't recommend that you try the former, but the latter can have interesting results. Under certain circumstances, a person will forget a particularly traumatic experience because remembering it is just too painful. In psychoanalytic terms, this is "motivated forgetting," or repression. The memory may not be completely lost, however, and may make its presence known in dreams or in free associations. A person who saw her brother drown, for example, may seem to have forgotten the whole experience, but she may still have bad dreams about water.

SQ3R—A Study Strategy

As a student, you should have a very effective strategy for remembering the kind of information that appears in textbooks. This information is usually arranged in chapters, each perhaps about 30 to 50 pages long. The chapters are usually broken down into subheadings, and sometimes these are broken down still further. A single assignment might involve reading one or two of these chapters.

SQ3R is an excellent device for helping you store information that is arranged in a "textbook" format. SQ3R stands for:

1. Survey
2. Question
3. Read
4. Recite
5. Review

Many people just begin reading on page 1 of the chapter and continue until they finish, fall asleep, get bored, or have to do something else. However, this strategy does not help you form an organizational framework for your elaborative rehearsal. Instead, before you begin reading, you should survey the chapter to make sure you know what the author intends to cover. If there is an outline, read it; if there are subheadings, read them. Form a map in your mind of the contents of the chapter. Then, as you read, you will be filling in the gaps with details, rather than charting unknown terrain with each new paragraph. The chapter outlines in this book, for instance, help you establish this framework.

Although here we are mainly discussing the importance of the "survey" step in studying a single chapter, it is equally important in studying a whole book. Some readers skip the preface and the introductory chapter (if there is one), thinking that this material is not important. It is. It usually will give you a broad overview of the entire book, helping you construct that vital organizational framework for fitting in new information.

After you survey, you should question yourself to make sure you have a clear idea about the contents of the chapter, how they are arranged, and what the main points are going to be. You should be able to close the book and describe to yourself the main points of the chapter.

The third step is to begin reading. Don't try to read fifty pages at one time. It is better to stop and perform the other two "R's" after you have completed each major subheading. This is because of the effect of spaced rather than massed trials on learning. Fifty pages of technical, information-packed prose is too much for most people to absorb at one sitting.

Close the book and recite the main points of the section you have just finished reading. Don't rush yourself. If they don't come immediately, try to use retrieval cues. Seeing the image of a graph in the text might help, for example.

The final step is to review the new material. Check on the information you were not able to recall in the "recite" step. Summarize the material. In this book, we have provided guided reviews at the end of each section, rather than the end of each chapter, to help you with the "review" step. Read a single section of the chapter (perhaps about ten pages); then recite and review it. As long as you have performed the "survey" step well, you will be able to integrate the material into the overall theme of the chapter. Stopping after shorter segments will also encourage you to use spaced learning trials.

When you are studying a textbook or report with no outlines, few subheadings, no key words, no summaries, and vague chapter titles, the SQ3R method will be even more valuable. You can use it for studying manuals on fixing a Volkswagen, reports on nuclear power plant accidents, articles in *Psychological Review,* and just about anything else.

GUIDED REVIEW

Learning Objectives 10, 11, and 12

1. Improving your memory can be accomplished by first improving the storage process. Important elements of this process include paying attention, rehearsing, and an organizational strategy to integrate the information into your LTM. A _____ , for example, uses old information as an anchor for storing new data, particularly relying on mental imagery. The _____ links items or concepts to places on a tour of a well-known location, and it helps you remember those items in order. _____ organizes material into ever-larger units so they can be stored in LTM as single entities. Rewarding yourself and spacing your learning trials will also help you improve the storage process.

2. The retrieval process can be improved by using better _____ , including your state of mind when you originally stored the material. It might also be improved by special retrieval techniques, such as hypnosis or psychoanalysis.

3. A study strategy that is useful for learning information in most textbooks is called _____ . The strategy involves the following five steps: (1) _____ , (2) _____ , (3) _____ , (4) _____ , and (5) _____ .

ANSWERS

1. mnemonic device; method of loci; Chunking 2. retrieval cues 3. SQ3R; survey, question, read, recite, review

SUMMARY

I. The three storage systems of human memory are the sensory store, short-term memory (STM), and long-term memory (LTM).   (p. 192)

  A. The sensory store initially processes information from the environment and appears to hold virtually all the information impinging on the sensory systems.   (p. 193)

  B. Short-term memory holds information about which the individual is consciously thinking. (p. 194)

    1. The capacity of STM is about seven chunks of information.   (p. 195)

    2. Unless the information is rehearsed, it is lost from STM within about fifteen seconds through decay, interference, or both.   (p. 196)

    3. Information in STM can be transferred to LTM using elaborative rehearsal. (p. 196)

  C. LTM is the relatively permanent storage system with an unlimited capacity.   (p. 197)

    1. Information in LTM is stored in terms of its meaning, rather than in terms of its sound. The semantic network theory proposes that semantic memories are organized in nodes arranged in hierarchical structures.   (p. 197)

    2. Forgetting from LTM may be due to an inability to retrieve stored memories or due to the effects of interference.   (p. 201)

II. Retrieving information from LTM requires a search of its contents.   (p. 202)

  A. Search strategies include sequential search and the use of retrieval cues.   (p. 202)

    1. Rapid searches of LTM rely on retrieval cues, perhaps using semantic networks. (p. 203)

    2. State-dependent memory involves the facilitation of recall when the person is in the same biological state during learning and retrieval. The person's biological state acts as a retrieval cue.   (p. 203)

B. The retrieval of memories from LTM often involves some reconstruction and distortion, apparently in an attempt to make vaguely recalled memories more realistic and plausible. (p. 205)

    1. Studies of eyewitness testimony demonstrate some of the processes involved in memory reconstruction. (p. 205)

C. Recognition differs from recall partly because a person has more retrieval cues available during a recognition test. (p. 208)

    1. The tip-of-the-tongue phenomenon occurs when a person fails to recall information he knows is contained in LTM but is able to recognize the information. (p. 209)

    2. The ability to recognize familiar faces appears to be separate from other memory skills. (p. 209)

III. Learning and the formation of memories involve changes in neuronal activity and in synaptic connections in the brain. (p. 210)

A. Scientists have attempted to trace the changes that occur during learning by studying simple animals and systems. (p. 210)

    1. Studies of *Aplysia* show synaptic changes correlated with simple forms of learning. (p. 210)

    2. Studies of the activity of large populations of neurons in the rabbit brain show changes associated with classical conditioning. (p. 211)

B. Research on the engram, or memory trace, has not clearly demonstrated either its location or its nature. (p. 212)

    1. Memories for a particular event appear to be stored diffusely within the sensory area involved in the learning experience. (p. 212)

    2. The physiological changes that occur during learning include increases in protein and RNA synthesis. These events may be related to the changes that probably occur in synapses. (p. 212)

C. Researchers are examining the events that modify the formation of memories in an attempt to learn more about the process. (p. 213)

    1. The formation of a memory can be disrupted by electroconvulsive shock and by protein synthesis inhibitors. (p. 213)

    2. Certain drugs improve the formation of memories. (p. 213)

    3. Stress can either facilitate or inhibit the formation of a memory, probably through the action of epinephrine. (p. 213)

IV. Improving your memory can be accomplished in several ways. (p. 215)

A. The storage process can be improved by (p. 215)

    1. paying closer attention; (p. 215)

    2. rehearsing important information; (p. 215)

    3. using organizational strategies to improve elaborative rehearsal; (p. 216) and

    4. using more efficient learning strategies. (p. 217)

B. Retrieval can be improved by using better retrieval cues, including the state in which you learned the material initially. (p. 218)

C. SQ3R refers to a five-step study strategy: survey, question, read, recite, and review. (p. 219)

ACTION GLOSSARY

Match the terms in the left column with the definitions in the right column.

____ 1. **Sensory store** (p. 193)
____ 2. **Iconic store** (p. 193)
____ 3. **Echoic store** (p. 193)
____ 4. **Short-term memory (STM)** (p. 194)
____ 5. **Serial position effect** (p. 194)
____ 6. **Recency effect** (p. 194)
____ 7. **Chunk** (p. 195)
____ 8. **Decay theory of forgetting** (p. 196)
____ 9. **Interference theory of forgetting** (p. 196)
____ 10. **Maintenance rehearsal** (p. 197)

A. *Anything that is represented in LTM as a single unit, such as digit, a word, or a well-known quote.*
B. *The sensory store for auditory information.*
C. *A method by which information can be kept in STM by repeating it over and over.*
D. *A theory that attempts to explain the loss of information from STM by stating that the information gradually fades as time passes.*
E. *One of the three storage systems for memory. Information is received from the environment through the sense organs and maintained in this system for a very short time.*
F. *The storage system for memory that includes the information that an individual is consciously thinking about at the moment. Its capacity is limited to about seven items; unless the information is rehearsed, it is lost from this system in less than a minute.*
G. *A theory that attempts to explain forgetting from STM. It states that the information is lost when new information intrudes or replaces it.*
H. *The sensory store for visual information.*
I. *Items at the end of a list are recalled more accurately than are items in the middle of a list.*
J. *A phenomenon in which a person's ability to recall items from a list depends on the item's position in the list.*

____ 11. **Elaborative rehearsal** (p. 197)
____ 12. **Long-term memory (LTM)** (p. 197)
____ 13. **Episodic memory** (p. 197)
____ 14. **Semantic memory** (p. 197)
____ 15. **Semantic network** (p. 198)
____ 16. **Retroactive interference** (p. 201)
____ 17. **Proactive interference** (p. 201)
____ 18. **Sequential search** (p. 202)
____ 19. **Retrieval cue** (p. 203)
____ 20. **State-dependent memory** (p. 203)

A. *Information contained in LTM that has no association to a particular time or place. It includes the organized knowledge concerning words, other verbal symbols, their meanings, and how they are manipulated.*
B. *A piece of information that is used to help locate another related item of information in memory.*
C. *The relatively permanent memory storage system in which information can be stored for an indefinite period of time.*
D. *The phenomenon in which previously learned material blocks or interferes with the retrieval of material that was learned more recently.*
E. *The phenomenon in which the retrieval of information is facilitated when the person is in the same biological state as when the information was learned. The biological state acts as a retrieval cue.*
F. *The record of personal life experiences contained in LTM.*
G. *A retrieval strategy in which items of information in memory are examined one at a time in a search for a particular item of information.*
H. *A proposed type of hierarchical organization for semantic memory.*
I. *A method that permits transfer of information from STM to LTM. The information is integrated with knowledge already existing in LTM.*
J. *The learning of new material blocks the retrieval of old material.*

____ 21. **Tip-of-the-tongue phenomenon** (p. 209)
____ 22. **Habituation** (p. 210)
____ 23. **Engram** (p. 212)
____ 24. **Electroconvulsive shock (ECS)** (p. 213)
____ 25. **Amnesia** (p. 213)

A. *A hormone released by part of the adrenal glands during stress; a neurotransmitter.*
B. *The memory trace; the hypothesized neuronal changes that occur when an item of information is stored.*
C. *A system for improving memory in which the items of information are associated with the parts of a well-known physical location, such as your own house.*
D. *Failure to recall a piece of information when the person is certain the information is contained in his LTM.*

_____ 26. Arecholine (p. 213)
_____ 27. Epinephrine (p. 214)
_____ 28. Mnemonic device (p. 216)
_____ 29. Method of loci (p. 216)
_____ 30. Primacy effect (p. 194)

E. *The gradual diminishing of a response as a result of continuous exposure to the stimulus which evoked the response.*
F. *A system for improving memory that helps integrate new information with information already existing in LTM.*
G. *A technique sometimes used to treat depressed patients that involves delivering an electrical current to the brain that is intense enough to produce convulsions.*
H. *A drug that increases activity at acetylcholine synapses.*
I. *Memory loss for past experiences.*
J. *Items in the beginning of the list are recalled well.*

ANSWERS

18. G, 19. B, 20. E, 21. D, 22. E, 23. B, 24. G, 25. I, 26. H, 27. A, 28. F, 29. C, 30. J.
1. E, 2. H, 3. B, 4. F, 5. J, 6. I, 7. A, 8. D, 9. G, 10. C, 11. I, 12. C, 13. F, 14. A, 15. H, 16. J, 17. D.

SELF-TEST

1. Of which storage system is echoic memory a part?

    (a) sensory store
    (b) short-term memory
    (c) long-term memory
    (d) semantic memory
       (LO 1; p. 193)

2. The time limit on iconic store is approximately

    (a) less than one second.
    (b) several seconds.
    (c) fifteen seconds.
    (d) one minute.
       (LO 1; p. 193)

3. Rehearsal is a technique that maintains information in which storage system?

    (a) iconic store
    (b) echoic store
    (c) short-term memory
    (d) long-term memory
       (LO 2; p. 196)

4. The capacity limit on short-term memory is about _____ chunks of information.

    (a) three or four
    (b) seven or eight
    (c) twelve or thirteen
    (d) unlimited
       (LO 2; p. 195)

5. Remembering what you ate for dinner last night is an instance of

    (a) sensory store.
    (b) short-term memory.
    (c) semantic memory.
    (d) episodic memory.
       (LO 3; p. 197)

6. An exhaustive sequential search is a strategy used more often to retrieve information from _____ rather than from _____ .

    (a) sensory store; long-term memory
    (b) long-term memory; short-term memory
    (c) short-term memory; long-term memory
    (d) short-term memory; sensory store
       (LO 4; p. 203)

7. You learn a list of definitions for words after drinking two cups of coffee. Later you discover that you recall the definitions better after drinking two cups of coffee than after no coffee. Your learning illustrates which of the following?

    (a) episodic memory
    (b) semantic memory
    (c) the use of retrieval cues
    (d) state-dependent memory
       (LO 4; p. 203)

8. _____ refers to the fact that memory can be distorted when new information is learned after the event that contradicts what is originally seen.
   (a) recognition
   (b) reconstruction
   (c) chunking
   (d) habituation
       (LO 5; p. 205)

9. In retrieving information from memory, _____ tasks are easier than _____ tasks.
   (a) recall; recognition
   (b) reconstructive; recall
   (c) recognition; recall
   (d) reconstructive; recognition
       (LO 6; p. 208)

10. The ability to recognize _____ appears to be controlled by brain mechanisms different from those involved in other memory functions.
    (a) faces
    (b) words
    (c) numbers
    (d) places
        (LO 6; p. 209)

11. The kind of learning studied in the snaillike creature *Aplysia* is
    (a) classical conditioning.
    (b) operant conditioning.
    (c) habituation.
    (d) orientation.
        (LO 7; p. 210)

12. Training a rabbit to blink its eye to a tone, instead of to a puff of air (which originally accompanied the tone), involves
    (a) the sensory neuron releasing less neurotransmitter into the synapse.
    (b) hippocampal neurons increasing their firing after the tone, before the puff of air.
    (c) the frontal lobes increasing their firing after the tone, before the puff of air.
    (d) operant conditioning.
        (LO 7; p. 211)

13. Research by Karl Lashley, designed to determine the location of a stored memory, found that
    (a) a memory for a particular event is stored in the hippocampus.
    (b) a memory for a particular event is stored in the visual cortex.
    (c) a memory for a particular event is stored in the hypothalamus.
    (d) a memory is stored in a widespread area, not a particular location.
        (LO 8; p. 212)

14. Studies of rats have found that rats who have learned something show greater amounts of both _____ and _____ than do rats who have not learned.
    (a) RNA; proteins
    (b) RNA; DNA
    (c) DNA; proteins
    (d) neurotransmitters; RNA
        (LO 8; p. 212)

15. Which of the following enhances rather than reduces memory by affecting acetylcholine synapses?
    (a) electroconvulsive shock
    (b) stress
    (c) epinephrine
    (d) arecoline
        (LO 9; p. 213)

16. The first step in improving one's memory is
    (a) rehearsal.
    (b) attention.
    (c) organizing information.
    (d) elaborating information.
        (LO 10; p. 215)

17. Which of the following is most likely to transfer information from STM into LTM?
    (a) attention
    (b) maintenance rehearsal
    (c) organizing information
    (d) repetition
        (LO 10; p. 215)

18. Which of the following processes might produce an apparent, but not actual, increase in the size of STM?

    (a) attention
    (b) maintenance rehearsal
    (c) elaborative rehearsal
    (d) chunking
       (LO 10; p. 195)

19. Which of the following is not a technique that specifically improves retrieval?

    (a) maintenance rehearsal
    (b) retrieval cues
    (c) hypnosis
    (d) brain stimulation
       (LO 11; p. 218)

20. In the SQ3R method of studying, the second "R" stands for

    (a) review.
    (b) recite.
    (c) read.
    (d) remember.
       (LO 12; p. 219)

ANSWERS

13. d, 14. a, 15. d, 16. b, 17. c, 18. d, 19. a, 20. b
1. a, 2. a, 3. c, 4. b, 5. d, 6. c, 7. d, 8. b, 9. c, 10. a, 11. c, 12. b,

SUGGESTED READINGS

Ellis, H. C., and R. R. Hunt. *Fundamentals of human memory and cognition.* 3d ed. Dubuque, IA: Wm. C. Brown Company Publishers, 1983. A good introduction to the field of memory and cognition; emphasizes practical examples.

Kihlstrom, J. F., and F. J. Evans, eds. *Functional disorders of memory.* Hillsdale, NJ: Erlbaum Associates, 1979. A selection of articles on memory disorders, including one on infantile amnesia.

Lindsay, P. H., and D. A. Norman. *Human information processing.* 2d ed. New York: Academic Press, 1977. A text that emphasizes the cognitive approach in the study of memory and other cognitive processes.

Loftus, G. R., and E. F. Loftus. *Human memory: the processing of information.* Hillsdale, NJ: Lawrence Erlbaum Associates, Publishers, 1976. A well-written introduction to the experimental investigation of human memory. The book includes a good chapter on the practical applications of research on human memory.

Rosenzweig, M. R. Experience, memory, and the brain. *American Psychologist,* 1984, *39,* 365–376. An excellent article that reviews some of the research on the brain mechanisms underlying learning and memory.

Yarmy, A. D. *The psychology of eyewitness testimony.* New York: Free Press, 1979. A book that examines the problem of human memory as it relates to eyewitness identification in the American judicial system.

c h a p t e r

7

Communicating and Thinking

LEARNING OBJECTIVES

After reading this chapter, you should be able to

1. describe the nature of language, its structure, and the way people use language to communicate and comprehend meaning. **(p. 228)**

2. outline the steps children go through during the acquisition of language and the theories proposed to account for language learning. **(p. 231)**

3. explain the progress and the conclusions of the research that attempts to teach a language to apes. **(p. 235)**

4. discuss the relationship between language and thought. **(p. 240)**

5. explain the nature of concepts as they relate to the structure of thought. **(p. 241)**

6. explain how concepts are learned. **(p. 243)**

7. list the three steps involved in solving a problem. **(p. 245)**

8. explain several factors that influence how a problem is initially analyzed and whether the analysis will be successful. **(p. 245)**

9. explain and provide examples of the two general types of search strategies, called algorithms and heuristics, that are used by problem solvers. **(p. 248)**

10. discuss the nature of creative problem solving, and describe how incubation can facilitate the process. **(p. 251)**

11. describe the attempts scientists have made to measure intelligence, and describe the tests that are currently used. **(p. 253)**

12. discuss some of the practical and ethical issues involved in intelligence testing, including the issues of the reliability and validity of the tests. **(p. 256)**

13. describe two theories of the nature of intelligence. **(p. 260)**

14. discuss the studies that attempt to analyze the factors that influence intelligence. **(p. 261)**

When the child was found hiding in the woods, he was nearly eight years old. He had long straggly hair, was covered with dirt, bruises, and scars, and could not stand erect for more than a few minutes. Physical and psychological tests showed him to be basically healthy, though he could not speak, walk on two legs, or use eating utensils. Doctors concluded that he had been abandoned as an infant and raised by wolves.

Three years of intensive training enabled the "wild boy of Aveyron" to master some basic skills, such as eating with a knife and fork, walking erect, sleeping in a bed, and bathing and dressing himself. However, at the age of eleven he still behaved more like a two-year-old than a child nearing puberty. His speech consisted only of grunts and a few badly-formed words. Despite years of effort to teach him speech, he never fully learned the language, remaining at the level of a three- or four-year-old. He never seemed to acquire the ability to reason or solve problems, and he tended to rely heavily on the trial-and-error method of performing complex tasks.

The wild boy of Aveyron may have been mentally retarded, but the fact that he survived at all argues against this hypothesis. It is more likely that he had difficulty developing the cognitive abilities typical of any normal adult, like language or reasoning, because he was without the benefit of human contact during an important phase of development, one in which human children acquire language at an astounding pace. Although the boy was able to perform some of the basic cognitive processes, such as perceiving and remembering, he was tragically deficient in some of the cognitive abilities that are so critical to the human species. Because he never acquired much language, he was unable to think, reason, and solve problems like a normal adult.

Speaking, thinking, reasoning, and problem solving are all important cognitive processes and fall under the general heading of "cognition." They are of tremendous interest to psychologists because they are so characteristic of human beings and so uncharacteristic of

most animals. Although scientists certainly agree that animals are capable of solving problems, and some suggest that the higher primates may even be able to learn a human language, no one would deny that human beings have elevated these cognitive processes to a fine art. It is hardly surprising that human psychologists would spend a great deal of time studying behaviors that are characteristically human.

Language

Language *is the system of sounds and symbols by which we communicate meaning.* It is a universal trait of human beings; everyone speaks and understands a language, unless a physical or mental handicap prevents him or her from doing so. (In fact, tests of language abilities are used to diagnose neurological impairment. See the Application Box: Diagnoses of Speech Disorders.) The ability to use language is such an important trait that it even helps to define what we mean by "being human;" it enables us to think extremely complex thoughts and to imagine and represent ideas or objects that are not physically present in space or time. It also enables us to communicate our thoughts to one another, albeit imperfectly at times. And perhaps most important, it permits us to have a culture: a tradition of beliefs, rules, and artifacts that we can pass on to subsequent generations.

But what is a language? How do we manage to use it to express our thoughts? How can we possibly acquire such a complex vocabulary and system of rules long before we even start kindergarten? This section will consider these questions and also examine the various systems of communication used by other members of the animal kingdom.

The Nature of Language

There are approximately 2800 different languages in the world. Each one communicates meaning through its own vocabulary and phrasing, a fact that creates

APPLICATION BOX

Diagnoses of Speech Disorders

Knowing whether there is a problem with a person's language and speech is often crucial. The following two cases demonstrate that knowing when to intervene and when not to may have critical effects on people's lives.

Jimmy was an alert two-year-old who understood directions and conversations appropriately for his age but who was speechless. His mother was concerned, but not to the point of seeking help until a year later, when Jimmy passed his third birthday without emitting a single meaningful word. The family physician calmly acknowledged all the information offered by Jimmy's mother and then offered his professional opinion: "Jimmy will grow out of it." As the child approached his fourth birthday, he spoke his first words, his first phrase, and indeed his first sentence, all at the same time. "Mamma, kitty's got a robin!" came the shriek from the backyard. She knew at once that the voice was that of her son and that the doctor's advice was correct. By the time he was five, Jimmy's language was completely normal.

In contrast is the case of Vernon N., a 43-year-old former teamster and self-educated amateur archeologist, who was living in a nursing home. Following a stroke almost one year earlier, his relatives insisted upon admitting him, claiming that he was senile and incapable of handling his affairs. Like many aphasics (those without speech), Mr. N. did seem infantile. He lacked expressive language, except for some automatic speech, which he generally used inappropriately. He cried easily and appeared apathetic and withdrawn. He used the phrase "I can't think" over and over, and he too was convinced of his mental incapacity.

On testing, we found that he indeed could think; he scored at the ninetieth percentile on a test of recognition vocabulary and showed good auditory comprehension for short, simple messages. It took a great deal of supportive counseling and . . . therapy before he agreed to enter treatment; but once he did, Mr. N. made excellent progress. He later took a seasonal position as a receptionist in a local museum that featured an extensive collection of American Indian lore.

It is sobering to speculate how many untested and untreated aphasic individuals are languishing in nursing homes or occupying some dim corner in private residences on the mistaken premise that they are mentally defective. (Emerick and Hatten, 1974, p. 220)

great problems for diplomats. Yet despite their enormous differences, all human languages have three important characteristics in common. They all are creative, they all are governed by rules, and they all use arbitrary symbols that represent objects and events.

Languages are creative because the number of ways in which the words can be combined into sentences is theoretically infinite. Although you repeat certain sentences several times each day, for example, "How do you do?," most sentences are new. With a limited number of sounds and words, human beings are capable of creating novel sentences throughout their lifetimes.

A second important property of natural languages is that they are all governed by **grammar,** *a set of rules that governs the use of words, their functions, and their relations in a sentence.* The creation of a sentence must follow certain rules about using words as verbs, nouns, adjectives, and other parts of speech; the arrangement of the word order; and even the inflections. Utterances that do not follow these rules are difficult for others to understand and may even be unintelligible. Although some elementary schools and high schools stress the study of grammar through a variety of mechanical means, such as sentence diagramming, they are really reinforcing what most people learned when they were two or three years old. By the time a child is five, the vast majority of her sentences are easily understood by others because she follows the rules of grammar (for her language) quite well.

The Structure of Language. Although language involves both sounds and symbols, we will focus primarily on the spoken component. The basic unit of oral language is the **phoneme,** *a single sound element from which spoken words are formed.* In the English language, there are approximately forty-five phonemes. The phonemes /p/ and /b/, for example, help us distinguish between the words "pill" and "bill." Many of the phonemes in other languages are quite similar or identical to those in the English language; however, some may be quite different. For instance, English has two separate phonemes for /f/ and /h/, but Japanese has only one phoneme, somewhere between the two sounds. The Japanese language also has only one phoneme that falls somewhere between the English /r/ and /l/. This feature of the Japanese language helps explain why a Japanese speaker sounds to an American as if he is saying "herro" (for "hello"). Anyone who tries to imitate accents has to pay special attention to the phonemes in each language.

The **morpheme** *is the smallest unit of meaning in a spoken language.* Morphemes consist of one or more phonemes. Some morphemes are words, such as "run" and "walk," but any syllable or group of syllables that conveys meaning and indicates functions or relationships is a morpheme. The "ing" at the end of verbs and the "s" at the end of plural nouns are both morphemes. The English language contains about fifty thousand such morphemes.

One or more morphemes constitute a word, and words combine into phrases and finally sentences. The sentence is the normal unit of conversation, and a great deal of study and research has gone into how people produce and comprehend sentences.

Communicating through Language. Any sentence, even the simplest one, contains information at two different levels. One level is called the **surface structure** *and represents the organization of words in the sentence in the spoken form.* The second level is called the **underlying representation,** *and it is the meaning that the speaker is actually trying to convey.* In many cases, the surface structure and the underlying representation are the same: for example, "Mary loves John." But in some ambiguous sentences, the underlying representation may not be so obvious. Consider the following examples:

Nothing is better than Brand X.

He shot off his mouth.

The shooting of the hunters was terrible.

For each of the examples, the underlying representation is not entirely clear. The first sentence might mean that no other brand is better than Brand X, or it could mean that having nothing is better than having Brand X. Alternate representations for the second and third examples are too ghastly to describe.

A distinction between the surface structure and the underlying representation can also be seen in cases in which the surface structure can vary but in which underlying representation remains essentially the same.

Jake sold some shoes to Bob today.

Propositions:

1. Jake sold some shoes.

2. The shoes were sold to Bob.

3. The shoes were sold today.

Figure 7.1 A sentence contains one or more propositions, each of which expresses a unitary idea.

The sentences, "Psychology is an interesting subject," "I find psychology interesting," and "Among all the interesting subjects I know, psychology is number one," all have essentially the same underlying representations, although their surface structures are different.

Before speaking, we must establish the nature of the underlying representation and then choose a surface structure for a sentence that conforms to our language's grammatical rules. The mental operations that accompany this feat are obscure. Further, the method we use to interpret the surface structure of the utterances of others is also poorly understood.

The **semantic approach** *is one method that has been used to explain the relationship between surface structure and underlying representation, emphasizing the sentence's division into propositions* (Clark and Clark, 1977). The **proposition** *is a unit of meaning or an idea that consists of a verbal unit and one or more nouns.* A sentence consists of one or more propositions. For example, the sentence, "Jake sold some shoes to Bob today" contains a series of three propositions combined into one sentence (fig. 7.1).

In many ways, a proposition seems to correspond to a single thought. One study found that people took longer to read a sentence that contained more than one proposition, even when the number of words were the same (Kintsch and Keenan, 1973; Kintsch, 1977). As

people are reading or listening to language, they are attempting to extract propositions, or thoughts, from it. If there are more propositions, it takes longer to comprehend the material (Anderson and Bower, 1973).

Whereas the speaker has to transform her underlying representation into a surface structure, the listener has the opposite task. He must listen to the surface structure and somehow divine the underlying representation. Most psycholinguists believe that listeners automatically divide spoken speech into **constituents,** *which are phrases and subphrases.* In the sentence, "The furry mouse ran into the garage," there would be two major constituents: "The furry mouse," and "ran into the garage." Each of these could be divided into smaller units, but people seem to make a special effort to preserve the integrity of each constituent. For example, subjects who listened to sentences through one earphone were occasionally interrupted by a click in the other ear. They tended to recall that the click occurred very near or at the boundaries between the constituents of sentences, even though the click actually occurred right in the middle of some constituents (Fodor, Bever, and Garrett, 1974). The listener apparently analyzes the meaning of these constituents rather than the individual words contained in them one at a time.

The Acquisition of Language

Perhaps the most remarkable achievement of childhood is the development of the ability to understand and speak a language by the age of two. If you have tried to learn a second language as an adult, you probably recognize how extraordinary are the child's linguistic accomplishments. On their way to fluency, children pass through identifiable stages of language development.

The Course of Language Development. **Cooing** *refers to the vocalizations of the very young infant.* They are often vowellike sounds in which the phoneme /u/

appears frequently, although the phoneme may occasionally be preceded by a single consonant, resulting in sounds like "moo" or "coo." *The infant begins* **babbling** *around six or seven months of age; these vocalizations include strings of consonants and vowel phonemes.* During the babbling phase, the baby utters the phonemes from languages all over the globe but eventually comes to use those in his own language more and more frequently.

In addition to the sounds of the language, the baby is learning a great deal about communication and conversation in general during these early months (Rosenthal, 1973). The "conversations" that take place between the mother and the baby show particular temporal arrangements that seem to reflect precursors of later verbal communication. For example, some interactions show reciprocal turn-taking (Bruner, 1977).

One study investigated the interactions between newborns and their mothers in the hospital during breast-feeding. The researchers watched the mothers from the moment they took their babies out of the crib to breast-feed until they returned them, usually for about 15 minutes. Every five seconds the researcher recorded on a checklist the activities of the mother and baby. One of the things they observed was that there were large individual differences in the way the mothers and babies interacted. Some babies almost never gazed at their mothers, and some mothers spent almost the entire time vocalizing. The largest proportion of the babies' vocalizations occurred when the mother was already vocalizing. They tended to "join in" when the mother was speaking or cooing (Rosenthal, 1982).

By the end of the first year, the child is making **holophrases,** *or single-word utterances that carry a great deal of meaning, usually using only a few phonemes.* Children typically utter words like mama, dada, baby, milk, or kitty. Although they are only using holophrases and their vocabulary is quite small, they are able to communicate quite a range of meanings through inflections, pitch, and other devices. Imagine the differences in the word "Mama" when uttered by a child

who sees his mother come home from work and one who is demanding candy. Also, the child uses the same word to communicate different meanings in different contexts. For example, the word "bye-bye" might mean "good-bye," "he went bye-bye," or "I want to go bye-bye," (or "I wish you'd get lost").

Telegraphic speech *refers to the utterances of children who are beginning to use two-word sentences such as "Daddy come" or "cookie gone."* The tiny sentences are called **telegraphic** (Brown, 1973) because they omit the small words such as "the," "to," "for," and "be," thereby making the informational yield somewhat like that of a telegram. But even though the child is using only about two words per sentence, her speech is amazingly complex. Several researchers hypothesize that this stage is characterized by a system of rules for sentence construction (McNeill, 1970; Bowerman, 1973; Nelson, 1978).

When the child begins speaking four- and five-word sentences, another new development occurs. She begins to master certain inflections, like the plural "s" and the present-progressive verb form ending in "ing." According to some research on the topic (Brown, 1973), most children seem to acquire these morphemes in a specified order. The "ing" is learned first, followed by the prepositions "in" and "on," followed by the plurals, and so forth. The ones that are acquired earlier seem to be grammatically simpler.

Watching children master these rules is a fascinating experience. When they first acquire a rule, they are likely to apply it incorrectly. Although they had previously been saying "feet" as the plural of "foot," they may start saying "foots" when they acquire the rule for plural "s." As they learn more about how the "s" is used, they may say "footses" or "feetses" before finally returning to "feet." The application of the general rule of adding "s" to make a noun plural is *overgeneralized* by the child. Overgeneralization indicates that the child is constructing language by applying rules, even though in this case the rule may not be applicable. The manner in which the child learns these rules is a controversial subject in theories of language learning.

Theories of Language Learning. The way in which psychologists and psycholinguists have viewed the process of language development has changed rather dramatically over the last fifty years. John B. Watson, the father of American behaviorism, argued in 1924 that language is a complex behavior that is learned primarily through the laws of classical conditioning and stimulus-response associations. Later behaviorists stressed the importance of operant conditioning and imitation (Skinner, 1957; Staats, 1971; Bandura, 1971). An infant utters meaningless sounds, imitating some of the sounds around him, and is selectively rewarded for those sounds that duplicate or approximate the morphemes in the parents' language. When a babbling infant says "da da," her father picks her up, smiles, and says, "Yes, I'm dada." In this way, the child's verbal behavior is shaped and rewarded, and the child gradually comes to speak the language of his or her parents.

The effects of operant conditioning and imitation are apparent in the way that a child learns the particular phonemes associated with the language spoken in his home. Babies babble all kinds of sounds, but soon their babbling begins to "sound" more like the parents' speech in the sense that the phonemes are more recognizable and typical of the parents' language.

Nevertheless, the behavioristic view of language learning seems to fall short for a variety of reasons. For example, Noam Chomsky (1959), a psycholinguist, pointed out that a child's language acquisition is anything but slow and gradual. Instead, it is breathtakingly fast. And rather than merely duplicating sounds, words, and sentences that have been reinforced, children say many things that have not been reinforced and that they may not even have heard before. A two-year-old, for example, might begin saying, "I dooed it!" after he had already been using the correct form of the past tense verb. He is overgeneralizing the rule about using "ed" for the past tense.

Recent research on language acquisition stresses that the process is essentially one in which the child actively attempts to induce rule systems from the speech he hears every day. His progress suggests that he is actively generating hypotheses based on certain operating principles and that he is testing his hypotheses. For example, a child learning to use "ed" to change a verb to the past tense seems to be formulating a hypothesis about the nature of the language. She might then test that hypothesis by using "ed" on many verbs, such as "Baby cried" or "I walked." She might then, as we discussed earlier, extend her hypothesis to "I falled down" or "Daddy goed," by overgeneralizing.

In order to efficiently develop hypotheses like this one, some scientists have suggested that the child uses certain operating principles, such as paying attention to the ends of words, avoiding exceptions, looking for prefixes or suffixes that change the meaning of the word, and looking for systematic changes in the forms of words (Ferguson and Slobin, 1971; Slobin, 1979).

The question of how the child comes to induce these rule systems so well, and why he does it in the first place, seems to require the interplay of three main forces. First, all human beings appear to have a genetically endowed predisposition that enables them to acquire a language and discover the grammar that underlies the speech to which they are exposed. Second, children hear a steady barrage of speech, appropriate to their level of development, that further enables them to grasp the essentials of their own language and provides important feedback for their learning. And finally, children seem to have an incredibly strong motivation to learn language. All of these forces combine to enable the child to actively induce rule systems from the speech they hear every day and to become fluent in their native tongue even before they enter kindergarten.

That a genetic predisposition for language learning exists is supported by many arguments. For example, recall the studies on the specializations of the left and right hemispheres in human beings that we discussed in Chapter 2. For most people, language functions are lateralized on the left side of the brain. The brain contains important areas that are critical for language development, and if these are damaged in some way, language abilities are affected.

There appears to be a critical period for language development, a fact that adds further weight to the argument that such a genetic predisposition exists. The term **critical period** *refers to a period of development during which the organism is particularly vulnerable or susceptible to certain environmental influences.* During the first few years of life, children acquire language at an astounding rate. However, if they are not exposed to language during those years, as in the case of the wild boy of Aveyron, their ability to acquire language from then on is limited. It is as if there is a period of life during which the individual's brain is particularly sensitive to environmental factors that encourage language development. During other periods of life, the person can still learn a language, but the process is much more tortuous. A child who grows up in a bilingual home, for example, acquires both languages and usually becomes fluent in both rather easily. The person who tries to learn Russian in college may spend years on the task, but despite great effort, the person rarely becomes completely fluent and usually speaks the second language with an accent. It is very difficult for most people to correctly pronounce phonemes that are not typical of their own native language and that they had no opportunity to acquire during the first few years of life.

Although many psychologists agree that a critical period for language does exist, most would prefer to call it a "sensitive" period rather than a critical one. It is still possible for a person to acquire a second language after childhood, and there has been at least one case of a severely isolated and abused youngster who acquired her first language in her teens (Curtiss, 1977). Genie was reared in the attic of her parents' home, away from nearly all human contact, during the first thirteen years of her life. When she was discovered by the authorities, her behavior was about like that of a one-year-old. Despite her tragic isolation, she was able to learn language after several years of intensive therapy, although she is still not proficient.

Most psycholinguists agree that the environment is extremely important for language development, although not as all-important as the behaviorists had argued. Children would find it very difficult to induce the rule systems in language if they were exposed only to extremely complex sentences. And of course the task would be almost impossible if they heard only very few samples with which they might test their hypotheses. Parents and other adults provide a simple version of the language for children, one that has shorter sentences and simpler grammatical constructions and that is spoken more clearly and more slowly than normal speech (e.g., Cross, 1978). The parents' speech becomes more complex as the child's language development progresses. A conversation between one of the authors and her one-year-old child, for example, is shown in figure 7.2A. As the child grew, the complexity of the mother's sentences increased. The same conversation about an elephant, which took place when the child was two years old, is shown in figure 7.2B.

These exchanges provide the child with important feedback about the language and about the child's own progress. First, the parent prompts the child, encouraging her to talk. Second, the mother repeats what the child says, using correct pronunciation and grammar, often offering an expanded version of the primitive utterance of the child (Cazden, 1972).

Finally, the child seems quite strongly motivated to learn language. He is not by any means simply a passive recipient of either a genetically programmed predisposition or the environmental forces surrounding him. Some psycholinguists argue that the child's repeated attempts to induce rule systems, even in very difficult circumstances, is a part of the genetic inheritance associated with language. Others are not so sure. However, it is certain that children try very hard to learn to communicate even in the most inauspicious circumstances. Sometimes, for example, the normal, hearing parents of deaf children will choose not to teach them sign language based on the theory that it will be easier for the children to learn to speak and read lips.

A. Between the mother and the one-year-old.

Mom: (pointing to a picture of an elephant)
What's that?

Daughter: Doggie

Mom: I think it's an...elephant.

Daughter: Efant?

Mom: Yes! It's a big elephant!

B. Between the mother and the two-year-old.

Mom: What is this animal called?

Daughter: Elephant?

Mom: Yes! That's very good. It's a big gray
elephant with big ears.

Daughter: What's he doing?

Mom: What do you think he's doing?

Daughter: Taking a baf?

Mom: Yes, he's taking a bath in an
enooormous bathtub.

Figure 7.2 *Conversations with a growing child*

An investigation of some of these children found that they often began using a system of gestures that began to acquire some of the properties of language, even before they learned anything at all about English. The "language development" of these children was surprisingly similar in pattern to that of hearing children in the sense that it began with single signs and progressed to two- and three-sign sentences (Feldman, Goldin-Meadow, and Gleitman, 1978).

Animal Communication

It has often been said that language is the trait that clearly separates humans from other species (Descartes, 1637). In recent years, this distinction has been questioned, and psycholinguists now agree that many species of animals have extremely complex systems of communication, using visual cues, sounds, touch, and even odors and tastes. Although no species has been demonstrated to use language with the richness and variety that humans do, some researchers believe that a few species either possess a communication system that qualifies as a very primitive language or can be trained to use one.

Some of the communication systems based on sound in animals are truly remarkable (Thomas, 1974). Termites signal one another by drumming their heads against the floor, resonating corridors in their nests. To the human ear, the sound is like that of sand falling on paper, but an analysis of these drumming sounds reveals a high degree of organization and complexity. The beats occur in regular, rhythmic phrases, differing in duration and signaling important messages to members of the species. Lewis Thomas (1974) describes the termite's signal rather eloquently:

> From time to time, certain termites make a convulsive movement of their mandibles to produce a loud, high-pitched clicking sound, audible ten meters off. So much effort goes into this one note that it must have urgent meaning, at least to the sender. He cannot make it without such a wrench that he is flung one or two centimeters into the air by the recoil (p. 21).

Animals produce sounds by many different means. Prairie hens, rabbits, and mice tap their feet; woodpeckers bang with their heads, fish make sounds by clicking their teeth, blowing air, or drumming with special muscles against inflated air bladders. The proboscis of the death's-head hawk moth is used as a kind of reed instrument—the insect blows through it to produce high-pitched notes. Gorillas beat their chests. Turtles, alligators, crocodiles, snakes, and even earthworms make vocal sounds.

Figure 7.3 *The communication systems used by certain animals, such as the dolphin, can be extremely complex.*

Birds have a whole glossary of warning calls, mating signals, territorial pronouncements, calls for assistance, and demands for dispersal. The recorded songs of the humpback whale sound like music to many humans, but no one knows what the sounds mean to the whale. They may be simple statements about navigation, the location of food sources, or territorial signals; or perhaps they are music.

Does Animal Communication Qualify as Language?
There is no doubt that these various forms of signaling among animals constitute methods of communication,

but do they constitute language? To be considered language, a communication must meet the criteria listed earlier, including creativity, the use of a grammar, and the use of arbitrary symbols for objects or events. Animal communication systems often show one or more of these characteristics, at least to some degree.

One approach is to characterize the communication systems of animals along a continuum, with simple, primitive communication systems existing at one end and human language at the opposite end (fig. 7.3). Many species are able to respond only to dramatic changes in their environments; the chirping of the cricket, for example, is related to temperature. Birds and bees are able to communicate a much wider variety of messages from one member of the species to another. The communication systems of primates are quite complex, incorporating vocalizations, facial expressions, body gestures, and even odors. The communication system of humans reaches quite another level of sophistication, employing its enormously complex grammar, vocabulary, and symbolic written messages to convey information.

Teaching Primates a Language. Since the 1930s, psychologists have attempted to teach human language to chimpanzees, our closest animal relatives (Kellogg and Kellogg, 1933; Hayes and Hayes, 1951). They raised chimps in their homes and treated them as much like children as possible in an effort to encourage language development, but they were not successful. Although the chimps could understand a great many words, they were never able to speak more than a very few simple words, such as "cup" or "mama."

Recently, teams of psychologists reasoned that the chimps did not learn to speak because they lacked the proper vocal apparatus, not because they lacked the ability to acquire language (Gardner and Gardner, 1971; Premack, 1971; Premack and Premack, 1982). They decided to teach chimpanzees communication systems that did not include speaking. One group focused on American Sign Language (Ameslan); another used "Yerkish," an artificial language involving a large number of computer-generated symbols developed at Yerkes Primate Laboratory in Georgia; and a third team invented still another language, involving colored plastic symbols.

Sarah, a chimpanzee, was one of the pupils who learned to read and write with variously shaped and colored pieces of plastic (Premack, 1971; Premack and Premack, 1982). The teaching process with Sarah began with simple conditioning procedures: she was shown an object, such as a banana, and the symbol for banana, a pink plastic square. To obtain the banana she had to place the plastic square on a magnetic board. In the first phase of the project, Sarah was required to place only one word on the board, for instance, the name of the fruit she wanted. After she learned the symbols for some verbs, she had to place two words in the appropriate sequence to receive what she wanted, for example, "Give apple." When she had learned the name of her trainers, three-word sentences were required, such as "Give apple Gussie." Finally, Sarah had to use four-word sentences: "Gussie give banana Sarah." Sarah's language development differed considerably from that of normal, human children. Children are not usually required to say certain things in a certain way to get their food, and children do not usually show clear-cut three- or four-word sentence stages.

One of the essential features of language is **displacement;** that is, *the ability to talk about things that are not actually present.* When Sarah was given a piece of fruit and two plastic words, she was required to select the correct word for the fruit before being allowed to eat it. Often, however, she selected the wrong word. In many cases, these "errors" seemed to reflect her preferences in fruit rather than any mistake in selection. She tended to choose the symbol for the fruit that she liked best, even though the other fruit was present. This behavior suggested that Sarah could generate the meaning of the fruit names from the plastic symbols alone (Premack and Premack, 1982).

Sarah also learned to use conditional "if . . . then" sentences. For example, if she wished to receive a piece of chocolate, which was a favorite, she had to follow closely the meaning of a sentence like "Sarah take banana *if then* Mary no give chocolate Sarah."

Sarah's accomplishments were astounding. She eventually developed a vocabulary of over 125 words that she used with a reliability of over seventy-five percent. The achievements of the chimps in the other "language" programs were equally impressive. Washoe, the first chimp that learned American Sign Language, made up several words. For example, she combined the signs for "water" and "bird" to identify a duck.

Figure 7.4   Scientists are attempting to teach human languages, such as American Sign Language, to chimpanzees and many of the chimps have proven to be enthusiastic language learners.

Although the chimpanzee language training programs all broke new ground and the remarkable pupils continue to surprise their trainers, some scientists question whether the chimps have actually learned to use a human language. Detailed analyses of some videotapes taken of Nim Chimsky (a chimp named after Noam Chomsky), who acquired Ameslan, raise serious questions about whether the chimp was truly using a language the way human children do (Terrace, Pettito, Sanders, and Bever, 1979).

Herbert Terrace raised Nim like a human infant, with bottle feedings, diaperings, and much cuddling (fig. 7.4). When he was less than a year old, he became the first chimp to take classes at Columbia University. On at least one occasion, Nim's ability with sign language saved his life. Someone spotted him about to drink some cleaning fluid in the kitchen and frantically signed, "No! Stop! Don't eat!" Nim moved the jar away from his mouth and put it down (Glass, Holyoak, and Santa, 1979).

Despite Nim's remarkable progress, Terrace noted that nearly ninety percent of Nim's signs were responses to his teachers' signs and that about half of his signs repeated some or all of what the teacher had just signed. Nim was mainly reproducing language, rather than producing it. Based on the tapes, Terrace wondered whether very much two-way communication was taking place. Nim frequently interrupted the trainer while she was signing, for example.

Other scientists involved in the training programs have also begun to question the reliability of some of the highly original and spontaneous phrases that are sometimes used by the chimps. Researchers working with Lana, a chimp that learned "Yerkish," noted that she first called a cucumber "a banana which is green." They question, however, whether such a performance is reliable (Rumbaugh, Gill, and VonGlasersfeld, 1973). Although the achievements of the apes have been remarkable, the evidence that they use language in a creative way is not compelling.

Since language abilities are based partly on the existence of genetic predispositions, they are a product of evolution. Yet the evolution of those abilities may have occurred rather recently (Chomsky 1972, 1979; Lenneberg, 1967). Although apes may have evolved some of the abilities essential to the development of language, particularly the ability to apply arbitrary symbols to name objects, as the apes have clearly demonstrated (Terrace, 1985), they may not have evolved the ability to generate creative sentences the way humans do.

Scientists will undoubtedly continue to design language training programs for apes, however, partly to learn more about language in humans. Another motive, though, is to learn more about the thought processes of animals and how humans might communicate with some of the other species sharing our planet.

GUIDED REVIEW

Learning Objectives 1, 2, and 3

1. Language is the system by which we communicate meaning through sounds and symbols. All natural human languages have three important characteristics: they are all creative, they all use arbitrary symbols to represent objects and events, and they all are governed by rules, called _____ .

2. The basic unit of oral language is the _____ , which is a single sound such as /p/ or /b/. The smallest unit of meaning in a language is the _____ , which consists of one or more phonemes.

3. A sentence possesses a _____ , which consists of the words and their organization, and an _____ , which is the meaning the speaker is trying to convey.

4. The _____ suggests that the underlying representation of a sentence consists of one or more _____ , or unitary ideas.

5. The speaker must transform the underlying representation into a surface structure, and the listener must listen to the surface structure and grasp the underlying representation. The listener divides speech into _____ , or phrases, to aid in this task.

6. Children go through stages during language acquisition, including _____ and _____ , single-word utterances called _____ , and two-word sentences. The two-word sentences are called _____ because they omit the small articles, verbs, and prepositions.

7. The most widely accepted theory of how children learn language argues that language is only partly acquired through _____ and _____ . Other factors include a _____ that lays the groundwork for language learning during the early childhood years, and a strong motivation to acquire language. Some call these years a _____ for language acquisition, but they are best thought of as sensitive years since it is still possible to acquire language outside of this age range.

8. Although animals have very complex communication systems, there is much controversy over whether any of them meet the criteria of a _____ . Several attempts have been made to teach language to primates, using American Sign Language, plastic symbols, or a computer-operated keyboard containing symbols. Most of the subjects in these experiments performed extremely well, acquiring hundreds of symbols and learning complex relationships and word orderings. Despite their accomplishments, however, the apes do not seem to be able to use language _____ in the same way in which humans are able.

ANSWERS

1. *grammar* 2. *phoneme; morpheme* 3. *surface structure; underlying representation* 4. *semantic approach; propositions* 5. *constituents* 6. *cooing, babbling; holophrases; telegraphic* 7. *imitation, reinforcement; genetic predisposition; critical period* 8. *language; creatively*

Thinking

The study of human thought is one of the most difficult tasks in all of psychology. Although everyone thinks during practically every waking minute, the thought processes are not at all easy to examine in an objective, scientific way. They are very private, and verbal explanations of our thought processes often are inadequate.

During the early part of this century, psychologists explored the nature of human thought with the technique called introspection, discussed in Chapter 3. The method required trained observers to analyze their own thought processes as objectively as possible. The technique had many drawbacks, not the least of which was its reliance on second-hand information rather than direct observations of the thinking process, and many psychologists lost interest in it. The behaviorists of the early twentieth century emphasized the use of strictly observable and measurable behavior, and the introspection method fell out of favor. As a result, scientists did not attempt to systematically study thinking or consciousness until recently.

The growth of cognitive psychology in the sixties and seventies signaled renewed interest in the study of human thought, despite the difficulties of studying such private phenomena. Psychologists have developed remarkably inventive tools to study thought processes, and some even use modified versions of introspection. A psychologist might ask a subject to work on a geometry problem, for example, and to "think out loud," tracing the steps she goes through to reach the solution. Studies using reaction-time measures are especially popular. Subjects are asked to process some information, usually presented visually; computerized displays and digital timing devices enable researchers to examine the most minute differences in processing time for various tasks.

Thinking is a very broad subject, encompassing many topics that we have already covered or will cover in other chapters. It includes consciousness, memory, perception, attention, problem solving, decision making, planning, meditating, daydreaming, and imagination. Also, it relies heavily on language, and we will first consider the relationship between thought and language. Second, we will explore some of the fundamentals of the thinking process, including the structure of thought and the nature of concepts.

Language and Thought

As adults we do most of our thinking with language, and it is difficult to imagine how, as young children, we were ever able to think without it. (Recall the stroke victim who had almost no language abilities—he kept repeating, "I can't think!" over and over.) To early behaviorists, thought itself was seen as a form of speech, although it was speech that was inaudible, internal, and subvocal. But psychologists generally agree that speech is not necessary for thought. Mathematicians and musicians certainly seem able to think about their subjects without using language. Very young children and animals demonstrate some remarkable problem-solving abilities without the aid of language.

One view of the relationship between language and thought, proposed by some early cognitive psychologists such as Jean Piaget, argues that language and thought have separate origins. This theory suggests that language develops from interaction and communication with other people. Thinking develops from interaction with objects in the environment. As the child grows to adulthood, the systems underlying language and thought become interdependent, and language comes to function as the servant of thought.

Another view of the connection between language and thought states that thinking is determined to a considerable extent by language. The **linguistic relativity hypothesis,** *first proposed by Benjamin Lee Whorf (1956), states that an individual's perceptions, thinking, and view of the world depend on the particular language he or she speaks.*

Language, according to this hypothesis, sets limits on what we can experience and think (Fishman, 1982). If we do not have a term or phrase to describe a concept, the linguistic relativity position would argue that we would have great difficulty thinking about the concept and may not even be capable of doing so. An example might be the word for "give." In English, the word is used when one gives something to friends, strangers, children, bosses, or the President. The Japanese, however, have several words for "give," and the use of each one depends on the status of the giver, relative to the receiver. One verb is appropriate when the speaker is higher in status than the receiver, another when she is lower. Whether or not the receiver is a member of the speaker's family or circle of friends is also significant in choosing the correct verb. According

to the linguistic relativity hypothesis, these fine distinctions in the Japanese language would enable people to perceive subtle differences in status and group membership. In contrast, the nature of the English language would make it much more difficult for native speakers to perceive such distinctions.

Critics of this hypothesis point out, among other things, that people can use long strings of words to describe and communicate concepts in any language (Au, 1983, 1984). Even though English speakers do not have a range of words for "give" that are appropriate in different contexts, English speakers can add words that make the phrasing distinctive in each case: "I'm giving you this book" (to an equal); "I would very much like to give you this book as a token of my great appreciation" (to royalty). A modified view of the relationship between thought and language is that language makes it easier to experience events for which we have an adequate vocabulary (Cole and Scribner, 1974; Slobin, 1971). It is easier to recognize and recall objects or events that can be linguistically coded.

The Structure of Thought

Randy: A penny for your thoughts.
Tim: Oh . . . I was just wondering whether that collie intends to run across the street.

In order for a person to have thoughts about "collies," "running," and "streets," he must have concepts. **Concepts** *are the mental constructs that enable us to make classifications; they are categories that represent classes of things with shared characteristics, rather than any particular member of a class.* The world consists of an enormous number of objects, actions, and abstractions, and human beings must somehow order and classify these into some meaningful arrangement to make sense of the world. As we discussed in Chapter 6, concepts are hierarchically arranged (Collins and Quillian, 1969). A collie is an instance of a dog, running is an instance of movement, and street is an instance of roadway.

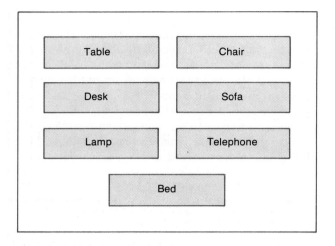

Table	Chair
Desk	Sofa
Lamp	Telephone
Bed	

Figure 7.5   Which are the best examples of the concept "furniture"? What attributes do they share?

The Nature of Concepts.   A concept is defined by one or more **attributes,** or *features of an object or event that are used to identify it as a member of a particular class.* For example, "the possession of wings" constitutes one of the attributes for the concept "bird." Members of a class will of course have many attributes, but only some of them will be relevant to the concept itself. Somebody's pet bird might be yellow, for example, but this attribute is irrelevant to the concept "bird." The concept "voter" might have the following relevant attributes: age 18 or older, United States citizen, registered to vote. Attributes such as sex, race, religion, and occupation are irrelevant to the concept "voter." They may be quite relevant to other concepts, however.

The assignment of attributes to a concept is not always clear-cut. For example, it is quite difficult to come up with appropriate attributes for the concept "furniture," even though everyone knows an example of a piece of furniture when he or she sees one (fig. 7.5). Sometimes, attributes are connected by some kind of rule, such as "either-or." An attribute of "furniture"

might be that it is either "something to sit on" or "something to put objects on." Judging from the examples in figure 7.5, however, the attributes of furniture are more complex than this.

One approach to the nature of concepts divides the attributes of a concept into defining features and characteristic features. The **defining features of a concept** *are those attributes that are essential for category membership.* A bird, for example, must have wings and feathers (at least according to taxonomists). **Characteristic features of a concept** *are those attributes that many members of a class possess, but not all.* The ability to fly would be a characteristic feature of the concept "bird" because there are many birds, such as penguins and ostriches, that do not fly (Smith, Shoben, and Rips, 1974). An instance of a category with all the defining features and all the characteristic features of the concept would thus be a "better" instance than one that had only a few of the characteristic features. A robin, for example, is probably a better example of a bird than a penguin is, because the robin has more characteristic features, such as the ability to fly. When speaking about penguins, a person might use a kind of verbal hedge before placing it into a specific category (Lakoff, 1972). He might say *"Technically speaking, a penguin is a bird."* This tells the listener that the instance is lacking many of the characteristic features of the category.

Another approach to understanding concepts involves the notion of the **prototype,** *a term that refers to the best example of an object or event within a particular category* (Rosch, 1973; 1975). This approach suggests that the boundaries of a concept are not clearly delineated and that some members of a class are "better" than others because they are closer to the prototype. For example, a table might be considered an excellent example of "furniture," but a telephone or lamp might be further away from the prototype.

The concepts we hold for colors seem to fit well into the notion of prototypes. People seem to organize their understanding and perception of colors into a limited number of **focal,** or *basic* colors (Berlin and Kay, 1969).

The English names for these focal colors are black, white, red, green, yellow, blue, pink, orange, brown, and purple. Although people from various cultures may place different boundaries between two focal colors, they tend to agree on the color that best represents red or blue, for example. Some scientists argue that the focal colors, or prototypes, for these colors are physiologically based.

Eleanor Rosch (1973) investigated the nature of color concepts in a group of people living in New Guinea, called the Dani. Their language has only two color terms: *mili,* which means dark, and *mola,* which means light. She selected eight sets of three colors each. Each set contained one focal color, such as green, and two colors that were slightly above or below it on the color spectrum (slightly yellowish green and slightly bluish green). Rosch asked the Dani subjects to learn eight different names; each name applied to one focal color and its two surrounding colors. In a second series, she asked them to learn names for another eight sets of colors; however, this time each set contained a focal color and two colors that were both on the same side of the spectrum. The green set, for example, might contain the focal color green, a slightly yellowish-green, and a very yellowish-green.

Rosch found that the Dani learned the names for the focal colors faster than the names for nonfocal colors, even when the focal color was not at the center of the set in terms of the color spectrum. However, the Dani learned the name of the focal color fastest in the first experiment, when it was in the center. It seems that a focal color represents a prototype for a color category and that the category is most easily learned when the instances of it are organized around the prototype.

Learning Concepts. A Luddite visitor to a modern office might approach an IBM PC and hear that it is a microcomputer. Having never seen or touched any computers, the visitor might begin to form a concept for the term "microcomputer," including tentative attributes like "many labeled keys," and "a greyish color." On another desk, the visitor might see an Apple II⁺,

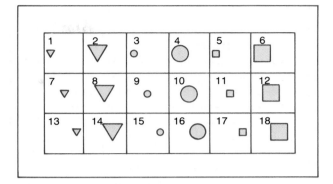

Figure 7.6 An array of cards presented to a subject in a hypothetical concept-learning experiment.

notice the keys and the color, and guess that it, too, is a microcomputer. On the next desk, however, is an old manual typewriter. The visitor, using his tentative attributes, might incorrectly guess that the typewriter is a microcomputer and hear that it is not. Now the visitor must search more critically for common features of the Apple and the IBM PC, and also features that those two machines do not share with the typewriter. In this way, the visitor uses both positive and negative examples of a concept to identify the concept's relevant attributes.

Two of the major tasks in learning a new concept are to separate relevant from irrelevant attributes and to determine which ones might be defining and which ones are only characteristic. Early research on this topic has led to the conclusion that many people use trial and error to grasp the nature of new concepts, although many use more efficient and sophisticated hypothesis-testing strategies (Bruner, Goodnow, and Austin, 1956).

For example, one method that researchers use to study concept learning strategies involves a series of cards with a single geometric shape on each: the kind of shape, the size of the shape, and the position of the figure differ on each card (fig. 7.6). The concept to be acquired is chosen by the experimenter, and it might be "large figure," "squares," or something else. The subject's job is to determine the attributes of the concept, just as he might have tried to learn the attributes of microcomputers from examples.

In the experiment, the subject picks one card after another, and the experimenter simply says whether the card is a positive or negative instance of the concept. If the concept for figure 7.6 were "large figure," all the odd-numbered cards represent positive instances.

One kind of strategy a subject might use to acquire a concept in a problem like this is the **conservative focusing strategy.** *A learner using this approach uses one positive instance of the concept as the focus and then tests individual hypotheses, one at a time, to ascertain the nature of the concept.* For example, the subject might choose #1 in figure 7.6, hear "positive" from the experimenter, and then use this as the focus card. He would then choose #3, which differs in shape but not size or position. The experimenter would also say this is a positive instance, and the subject would conclude that shape was irrelevant to the concept. He might then choose #2 to test whether size is relevant to the concept.

Concepts, and the language underlying them, are the building blocks of knowledge and thought. From very early childhood, adding one block at a time, each of us constructs an enormous edifice of interlocked ideas, and no two of them are exactly alike. What you believe to be the defining and characteristic features of a concept like "collie" may be very similar to those of another person who is familiar with dogs. But what about the concept "husband?" Some parts of our knowledge structure may be relatively stable; others, particularly those that were acquired recently, may be volatile. Researchers are only beginning to study the structure of human thought and the processes by which the structure develops.

GUIDED REVIEW

Learning Objectives 4, 5, and 6

1. Language and thought are closely related. The _____ proposes that an individual's perceptions, thinking, and view of the world depend heavily on the particular language he or she speaks. Less radical views suggest that it is easier to experience events for which we have an adequate vocabulary.

2. The structure of thought appears to be arranged as a _____ of concepts, or mental classifications of objects and events. A _____ has one or more attributes that are used to place members of a class.

3. The attributes of a concept can either be _____ , which are essential for category membership, or _____ , which are typical features but not essential ones.

4. Some scientists suggest that each concept has a _____ , which is a good example of the category, and that other members of the category match the prototype to a greater or lesser extent. Studies in which naive subjects are taught the names for colors suggest that certain prototype colors exist and that it is easier to learn the names for these.

5. People acquire concepts either through trial and error or through more efficient strategies, such as the _____ .

ANSWERS

1. linguistic relativity hypothesis 2. hierarchy; concept 3. defining features; characteristic features 4. prototype 5. conservative-focusing approach

1. Is the following analogy true or false?

2. Connect the nine dots below with four straight lines, without lifting your pencil from the paper.

3. Arrange six matchsticks to make four triangles. The triangles must be the same size, with each side equal to the length of one match.

4. Given an arrangement of matchsticks like the one below, in which the pattern forms five squares, move three sticks to form four squares.

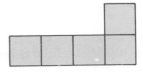

Figure 7.7 These problems require some creative solutions. The answers to these and other problems presented in the text are at the end of this chapter.

Problem Solving

One of the most fascinating aspects of thinking is that it includes the ability to solve problems like the ones in figure 7.7. We are capable of thinking abstractly, of mentally testing hypotheses, and of trying out various solutions in almost unlimited ways. By using concepts and the relationships between them, we are able to solve problems in geometry, semantics, algebra, business, politics, and even art. Some people are able to solve problems in astonishingly creative ways. Some have used their problem-solving ability to "crack" enemy codes (see Career Box: Cryptographer).

Any problem contains three main parts: a **given state,** *which is the state one is currently in,* a **goal state,** *which is the place where one wants to be,* and a **path,** *which is the route from the given state to the goal state.* The job of the solver is to find a path through the **problem space,** *which is composed of all the possible knowledge and operations that can apply to the problem.*

Steps of Problem Solving

Regardless of what kind of problem a person is trying to solve, there is usually a series of steps involved, including (1) analyzing the problem, (2) searching for a solution, and (3) deciding that a solution has been discovered.

Analyzing the Problem. Analyzing the problem is essentially the job of gaining an understanding of and encoding the "givens." In some problems the givens are all provided to the solver, but in most the solver is expected to provide some givens from his or her own experience and knowledge. For example, a question that might appear on a college entrance exam might ask you to apply principles of geometry.

CAREER BOX

Cryptographer

Cryptographers, many of whom work in government or military intelligence agencies, are master problem solvers. They invent codes, called ciphers, and they use a variety of strategies to break codes that are used in communications. The word "cryptographer" comes from the Greek words "kryptos," meaning "hidden," and "graphein," meaning "to write."

Many codes involve the substitution of each of the letters of the alphabet with different letters of the alphabet, or with altogether different symbols. The cipher shown below is a very early one of this kind that was developed by a Benedictine abbot named Trithemius. Each word or short phrase, such as "incessantly," stands for a particular letter. The abbot added small conjunctions and prepositions between the phrases to make the message read more fluidly and thus not arouse suspicions in anyone who chanced upon the text.

In his reign in perpetuity and in paradise in one infinity. Incessantly for perpetuity and in glory and in divinity. Irreversibly in the light and of the light in perpetuity in one infinity and irreversibly in heavens in His Kingdom in perpetuity in glory to the throne.

The bar graph in figure 7.A shows the frequency distribution of letters in a sample of ordinary English language text, 200 characters long. "E" is easily the most common letter, followed by "t," "a," and "o." A cryptographer would first prepare a frequency distribution of

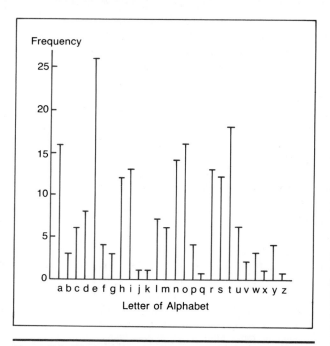

Figure 7.A *The frequency distribution for 200 letters of ordinary English language text*

the symbols in the code sample and then make the assumption that the most frequent symbol represented an "e." From there, the cryptographer might employ other heuristics, such as assuming that a three-letter word ending in "e" was "the." As with any heuristic, these do not guarantee a solution to the problem. They merely provide plausible hypotheses to test.

Not surprisingly, familiarity with the elements of the problem, as well as the information that might be needed to fill in the gaps of the givens, is very useful to a solver. Recent research suggests that people do their best problem solving when the problem is concrete rather than abstract, apparently because people are more familiar with the ideas in the problem and can form a kind of mental model to manipulate (Johnson-Laird, 1983). For example, suppose four cards, showing the symbols E, K, 4, and 7, are presented to you. Which of these cards should you turn over to verify the following statement: "If a card has a vowel on one side, then it has an even number on the other side"?

Most people realize they must turn over the E, but few recognize the need to overturn the 7. People tend to solve the problem more easily, however, if it is presented in concrete terms with which they are more familiar. The four cards might read "Manchester," "Sheffield," "Train," and "Car." The hypothesis to test would be "Every time I go to Manchester, I travel by train."

Although familiarity is useful most of the time, it can sometimes be a hindrance to problem solving in this early stage. The person may prematurely define the problem space too narrowly and close his mind to information that might be useful. The example of the nine dots shown in Problem #2 (fig. 7.7) shows how this can happen. If you defined the problem space by thinking that you should not move your pencil outside the imaginary square delineated by the outer dots, you will never reach a solution. Your previous experience with squares and with playing "connect the dots," may have led you to define the problem space too narrowly.

The term **set** *refers to the tendency to cling to a certain interpretation of the requirements of a problem, an interpretation that is familiar to you and that led to correct solutions on previous occasions.* You may have been influenced by a set on Problem #3 (fig. 7.7).

A classic demonstration of the effects of a set on problem solving was demonstrated in early research on the "water-jar problem" (Luchins, 1942). Subjects

GIVEN JARS OF THE FOLLOWING SIZES			OBTAIN THE AMOUNT
A	B	C	
21	127	3	100
14	163	25	99
18	43	10	5
9	42	6	21
20	59	4	31
14	36	8	6

Figure 7.8 Luchin's water-jar problem

were shown pictures of three water jars with different volume capacities and were told they had an unlimited supply of water. In the first problem, Jar A could hold 21 quarts; Jar B, 127 quarts; and Jar C, 3 quarts. The task was to use the jars to obtain 100 quarts of water.

A simple solution is to fill Jar B, pour out enough water to fill Jar A, leaving 106 quarts in Jar B. Then Jar C could be filled twice from Jar B, thereby leaving 100 quarts in Jar B. The mathematical solution is $B - A - 2C$.

A group of subjects were given one problem after another, like those in figure 7.8, all of which could be solved using $B - A - 2C$. The last problem, however, could be solved simply by filling up Jar C (8 quarts) from Jar A (14 quarts) to arrive at 6 quarts. But most of the subjects who had done the earlier problems relied on the more complex, but tried and true, $B - A - 2C$ formula. They had developed a set.

Sets can exist because an experimenter induces them, as in the water-jar problem. They can also exist because of previous experiences and expectations. In another classic experiment, subjects were given the objects

Figure 7.9 *The candle problem. The figure contains a candle, matches, and a box full of tacks. Your task is to think of a way to get the candle on the wall so that it would burn properly. You may use only the objects illustrated in the figure. From Bourne/ Ekstrand/Dominowski,* The Psychology of Thinking, *© 1971, p. 52. Reprinted by permission of Prentice-Hall, Englewood Cliffs, New Jersey.*

in figure 7.9 and told to mount the candle on the wall in such a way that it would burn without dripping wax on the floor. The solution (fig. 7.10) is to use the box as a ledge for the candle and tack it to the wall. Most subjects, however, were unable to discover this solution because of **functional fixity,** *which is the tendency for people to have difficulty imagining new uses for familiar objects.* They saw the box as a container rather than a ledge. When people were given the boxes separately, without the tacks in them, their functional fixity was reduced, and they were better able to solve the problem.

The initial analysis of the problem often has an important impact on how easily and quickly a solution is reached. Some research suggests that people who take longer to analyze and encode the information solve the problem more quickly than people who breeze through this step. Consider Problem # 1 in figure 7.7. This is an analogy problem requiring **inductive reasoning,** *which is the ability to take specific experiences and form general rules, ideas, or concepts,* and it is similar to the concept learning discussed earlier. People who do well at this kind of task are quick to make inferences and

Figure 7.10 *The solution to Duncker's candle problem. From Bourne/Ekstrand/Dominowski,* The Psychology of Thinking, *© 1971, p. 52. Reprinted by permission of Prentice-Hall, Englewood Cliffs, New Jersey.*

apply them, but they often take longer to analyze and encode the initial information. In this problem, the superior reasoner might carefully encode the nature of the relationship between the figures on the left of the colon before going on to analyze the set of figures on the right. She might verbalize the relationship mentally, perhaps by describing it as "the outer figure is rotated about 45 degrees to the right, and the inner figure is enlarged."

Search Strategies.
> I forgot the combination for my bike lock. Fortunately, the lock only has three numbers, and I remember that all three of them were 7 or higher.

Once a problem has been understood, the solver must next attempt to find a solution. One way might be to use trial and error, though this method is rather inefficient. The bicyclist might, for example, simply try 789, then 998, then 777, and so on, hoping to come upon the solution by chance. For most problems, however, some kind of strategy would be much more efficient. Psychologists have identified quite a number of strategies typically used by problem solvers, including algorithms and heuristics.

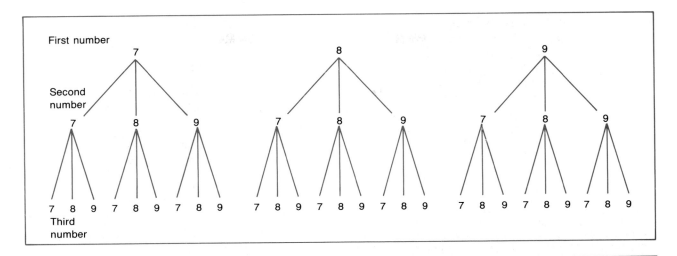

Figure 7.11 An exhaustive search for a three-digit combination in which all digits are seven or higher

An **algorithm** *is a general procedure that guarantees a solution to a problem.* For example, if you were asked to find the length of the hypotenuse of a right triangle whose legs were two inches and five inches long, you could use the algorithm $a^2 + b^2 = c^2$. For most problems, there are no mathematical algorithms available, and the only method of guaranteed solution is an exhaustive search of all possibilities. The person who forgot her lock combination might try a "tree" like the one in figure 7.11.

One of the disadvantages of algorithms is that the number of possible choices is often extremely large. In the eight letter anagram TERALBAY, for example, there are 40,320 possible letter combinations. Using the algorithm approach to checkers would involve the consideration of 10^{40} possible moves. Even at three choices per millisecond, a move would take 10^{21} centuries to consider (Samuel, 1959). A more commonly used technique in problem solving is the employment of a **heuristic,** or *rule of thumb.* The heuristic is a general principle that can be used to solve the problem, although its use does not necessarily guarantee a solution. The heuristic is actually a selective search through the possible solutions. When the number of possible solutions is very large, the heuristic reduces the cost of the search at the risk of not solving the problem.

One commonly used heuristic is called **means-end analysis.** *This approach to problem solving examines the difference between the present state of affairs and the final goal state, and it tries to reduce that difference by setting up subproblems.* Consider a simplified version of the problem of the hobbits and the orcs:

> Two hobbits and two orcs are sitting on the west bank of a river. They have access to a boat that will hold no more than two creatures at a time, and they all want to get across. Orcs are nasty creatures, however, and if at any time they outnumber the hobbits on either side of the river, the hobbits will be eaten. How can you get them all across to the other side of the river?

Using means-end analysis, we would first examine the difference between the given state, with all the creatures on one side, and the goal state, in which all the creatures were on the other side. We would begin moving creatures two at a time, perhaps one hobbit and one orc, to the other side of the bank. Then we would have to bring the boat back, so we would have to decide whether to let the orc or the hobbit take it. If we let the orc take it, the hobbit on the west bank would be eaten. So we send the hobbit. Solving each subproblem brings us closer to the final goal.

People generally rely on heuristics that worked for them in the past. An anagram solver may have had some luck solving anagrams with a T and H in them by first placing those two consonants together in the beginning of the word. The anagram RTIEH would be quickly solved with this heuristic. The anagram GHIETH would not. It is not uncommon for people to develop a set about certain heuristics and to continue to rely on them when they clearly no longer work or when much simpler solutions are possible. The people trying to solve the water-jar problem were victims of such a set.

The focusing strategy we discussed earlier in connection with concept learning is another kind of heuristic. It is a very useful one to use in the game Mastermind, in which a codebreaker has to try to guess the codemaker's color scheme in a row of four pegs. There are six possible colors, so there are a total of 1296 possible codes (6^4). The codebreaker makes a guess on the first trial, and the codemaker tells him how many pegs of the right colors were in the right positions and how many correct colors were in the wrong positions (fig. 7.12).

A study of strategies used in a simpler version of the game, containing four pegs and only three colors, found that the most successful players used a focusing strategy (Laughlin, Lange, and Adamopoulos, 1982). Thirty-six percent of the players began with a guess that contained only one color, such as red, red, red, and red. This focusing strategy would tell the player how many red pegs were in the answer. The second guess might be blue, blue, blue, and blue, thereby telling the player how many blue pegs were in the final answer. The number of yellow pegs could be deduced by subtraction. Thereafter, the player would choose only sequences that contained the correctly colored pegs, thus reducing the size of the problem space considerably.

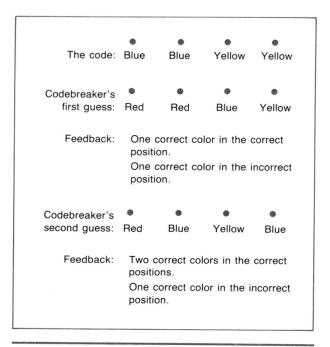

Figure 7.12 A simplified version of Mastermind

A theoretically even more efficient strategy, which might be called "tactical," was used by thirty-one percent of the players. This approach requires that the player collect hypotheses into two approximately equal subsets so that the feedback will allow him to reject one set of hypotheses on each guess (Johnson, 1971, 1978). It requires rather deep insight into the game and a great deal of memory and information processing, probably much more than most people have. A tactical first guess of blue, blue, red, yellow, for example, would divide the hypotheses into two sets that are more nearly equal than a first guess of red, red, red, red, which only provides feedback about how many red pegs are present. But the information from the feedback would overload most people and place too many demands on their short-term memories. In practice, the people who used the focusing strategy solved the problem in an average of 5.27 guesses, compared to 5.98 for those who used the theoretically more efficient tactical strategy.

Deciding When to Stop. A **well-defined problem** *provides the necessary information, either directly or indirectly, for a single possible correct solution.* Deciding when to stop is an easy matter when solving these problems. A person solving an anagram, for example, knows when to stop when she has made a word out of a string of letters. In contrast, an **ill-defined problem** *is one in which all the needed information is not given and for which there may be more than one correct solution, although some may be better than others.* Most problems in life fall into this category. Deciding when to stop trying to solve ill-defined problems is much more difficult. It may involve weighing the benefits of an optimal solution against the drawbacks of the amount of time and the increased cost that a better solution might require. For example, say a chemist who is developing a new insecticide is faced with deadlines and budget constraints. His or her decision about whether the problem is solved may be based more on these factors than on an evaluation of the new poison as the best solution to the problem.

Creative Problem Solving

Many of the problems discussed earlier can only be solved by what most people would call a "creative" approach. The subject of creativity is one that has interested psychologists for many years, and there is much controversy over what it is, who has it, and how it can be encouraged.

The type of problem like that of the lost bicycle combination is best solved by using **convergent thinking,** *a type of thinking in which a person applies his knowledge and the rules of logic* (Guilford and Hoephner, 1971). Many problems, however, such as the ones involving the arrangement of matchsticks (fig. 7.7, problems 2 and 3), are best approached with **divergent thinking.** *This mode of thought involves stretching the imagination to conceive of new possibilities.* It is divergent thinking that appears to be the most important ingredient in the creativity required for certain kinds of problems. Creative people are able to free themselves from the limitations of sets and other obstacles to problem solving, and they can examine potential solutions and possibilities that are unusual and often unique.

More creative approaches to problems generally can be fostered by two techniques. First, the solver should not attempt to define the problem too quickly. She should look for new relations between the elements of the problem, new ways to conceive the problem, or new "givens" that are implied by the stated facts but not directly supplied. If the solver is first relying on a means-end analysis, she might try to work backward from the goal state to obtain a fresh look at the problem. The solution to the following problem is facilitated by this approach:

> A man had four chains, each with three links. He wanted to join the four chains into a single closed chain. Having a link opened cost two cents, and having a link closed cost three cents. The man had his four chains joined into a closed chain for 15 cents. How did he do it?

For most problems that apply to everyday life, a broad knowledge of many subjects is invaluable. A person who has a grasp of a wide range of topics will be better able to bring fresh insights to a problem, and those insights are more likely to be relevant and realistic.

Another technique that appears to aid the problem-solving process is **incubation,** *in which the person sets a problem aside for a while after a series of unsuccessful attempts at a solution.* The solver should engage in other pursuits, although his mind may still be devoting a limited amount of processing capacity to the problem, perhaps unconsciously. When he returns to the problem, his approach may be freed of previously acquired mental sets.

An experiment involving the above problem about the chains demonstrated that incubation can really help people find solutions to problems (Silveira, 1971). A control group of subjects worked continuously on the problem for about half an hour, and about half of them found the correct solution. Several experimental groups spent a limited amount of time in their initial attempts and then took a break for a while, during which they were involved in other activities. The experimental groups, especially those taking the longest break (four hours) were more successful in solving the chain problem compared to the control group, even though the amount of total time spent on the problem was the same. The incubation period appeared to facilitate the problem-solving process.

Sometimes the incubation period ends with an "insight" like the kind we described in Chapter 5, on learning. The story of how Archimedes helped determine whether his King's crown contained the correct amount of gold illustrates this process. The King of Syracuse had given a goldsmith a certain amount of gold to use in the crown. When the crown was constructed, the King suspected that the gold in it was not pure. Perhaps the goldsmith had mixed the gold with another metal and stolen the leftover gold. He asked the famous mathematician, Archimedes, to find out if the crown contained the right amount of gold without damaging the crown.

Archimedes studied the problem and examined all the ways he knew to analyze the metal, including melting it or cutting it. He could not think of any method of analyzing the metal without damaging it, so he set the problem aside, allowing it to incubate. One day he stepped into his bath and noticed the water displacement, and the solution came to him. He ran (naked) through the streets shouting "Eureka! Eureka!" He knew that different metals displaced differing amounts of water. All he had to do was compare the displacement of the crown to an amount of pure gold equal to what the King had given the goldsmith.

GUIDED REVIEW

Learning Objectives 7, 8, 9, and 10

1. Any problem consists of a _____ , a _____ , a _____ from the given state to the goal state, and a _____ .

2. The three steps in problem solving are (1) _____ , (2) _____ , and (3) deciding that a solution has been discovered.

3. The analysis of a problem involves acquiring an understanding of the _____ . Familiarity with the elements of the problem can facilitate problem solving since people do better with concrete, familiar problems than with abstract problems. Familiarity can hinder problem solving when the person develops a set or functional fixity.

4. Two common search strategies in problem solving are the use of an _____ and the use of a _____ . One example of a heuristic, or rule of thumb, is _____ .

5. Deciding when a solution has been discovered is simple when the problem is well defined. For _____ problems, this decision is often based more on factors other than whether the solution is optimal.

6. Creative problem solving requires _____ thinking rather than convergent thinking. Creativity can be encouraged by incubation.

ANSWERS

1. given state, goal state; path; problem space 2. analyzing the problem; searching for solutions 3. given state 4. algorithm; heuristic; means-end analysis 5. ill-defined 6. divergent

Intelligence

It probably will surprise no one that people differ in the degree to which they are able to learn, solve problems, think logically, use language eloquently and precisely, understand and acquire concepts, deal with abstractions, integrate ideas, attain goals, and perform many other cognitive tasks. Most people believe that these skills, as well as other cognitive abilities, make up a person's intelligence (Sternberg, 1985). Yet the concept of intelligence is very abstract, and there is a tremendous amount of controversy over what it is, how it should be measured, and even whether anyone should be trying to measure it at all.

Entire texts have been devoted to the nature of intelligence, so it is not easy to define in a sentence or two. A working definition of **intelligence** is *a combination of abilities that enable a person to learn from experience, to think abstractly, and to adapt successfully to the environment.* However, our notions about the concept of intelligence have been very closely linked to our attempts to measure it in different people, and many lay people believe that the word intelligence is synonymous with the scores people achieve on various tests of mental ability. In order to fully understand the nature of intelligence, it is first necessary to understand how scientists and educators have tried to measure the phenomenon.

Measuring Intelligence

Early philosophers and scientists did not allude to intelligence as a separate trait, and they did not appear to try to measure it in any way. Instead, intellectual activity was seen as a part of sensation and perception, of soul, and of consciousness. It was not until modern times, particularly during the late nineteenth and early twentieth centuries, that scientists became interested in intelligence as a separate entity and wondered how one might measure it.

Figure 7.13 Alfred Binet

Sir Francis Galton, the naturalist and mathematician who was related to Charles Darwin, developed the first set of tests designed to measure intelligence. Galton was convinced that intelligence ran in families, based especially on his observations of the titled families of England, and that the trait probably had some biological underpinning. With these ideas in mind, he decided to measure a number of anthropometric and sensory-motor traits (such as head size, strength of hand grip, breathing capacity, and reaction time), and sort out those that were capable of distinguishing the eminent British scientists from the people he considered less intelligent. He examined thousands of people, but none of the traits he measured correlated with his concept of intelligence. He did, however, invent and use the correlation coefficient.

The Concept of Mental Age.   In the early twentieth century, Alfred Binet made a breakthrough in the attempt to measure intelligence (fig. 7.13). The French government commissioned Binet to develop techniques for identifying those schoolchildren who would be too slow to benefit from the regular elementary school program. He had done extensive research on the subject of cognitive abilities and had especially studied the growth in intelligence of his own two daughters. His earlier work had led him to the conclusion that intelligence was a global process that perceives external stimuli, organizes, chooses, directs, and adapts such stimuli, and that individuals differed widely in this global capacity.

In his initial research, Binet and his colleague Theodore Simon collected a series of short tasks that would be related to everyday problems, for example, placing weights in ascending order. Trained examiners administered the tests to individual students. Binet hoped that by using a wide range of test items, he would tap enough different abilities to be able to assess each child's general potential. The items sampled quite a wide range of functions, including judgment, comprehension, and reasoning, which Binet felt were the most important factors in intelligence (Matarazzo, 1972).

After several years of refining the scale, Binet and Simon suggested the notion of **mental age,** *which reflects a child's score on a test compared to the scores of a large, representative group of children of the same age.* A child who scored the same as the average of a group of six-year-olds, for example, would have a mental age of 6, regardless of the test taker's actual age in years.

A few years later, the German psychologist William Stern argued that the child's mental age should be divided by his chronological age to yield an **intelligence quotient,** or **IQ.** *The IQ was expressed as*

$$IQ = \frac{MA}{CA} \times 100,$$

where MA = mental age as determined by the standardized tests of intelligence and CA = chronological age. If a ten-year-old child successfully completes the tasks that a majority of twelve-year-olds are able to complete, the child's IQ is:

$$\frac{12}{10} \times 100 = 120.$$

Although IQ has become commonly used to express levels of intelligence, it is not what Binet believed intelligence to be. He thought intelligence was too complex to be expressed by a single number and that it could not be measured as linear surfaces are measured.

The Development of the Stanford-Binet Test. **The Stanford-Binet test of intelligence** *is a widely used modification of Binet's original test; in this revision, there are several test items for each age group, and each item successfully completed earns the child a "score" of two months of mental age.* Table 7.1 shows some examples of the test items. The Stanford-Binet test takes into account the fact that some children will fail one or more items at one age level but then pass several for an older age level.

An important modification in the contemporary version of the Stanford-Binet is the use of tables to ascertain the IQ, rather than the formula of MA/CA. In this method, the average score for all people of a particular age is assigned the value of 100, with a standard deviation of 16. A person's score on the test is compared to the scores of other people of his or her own age. For example, a score of 116 on the test would mean that the person was one standard deviation above the mean of his or her age group. This score would be approximately at the eighty-fourth percentile rank.

The Wechsler Adult Intelligence Scale. David Wechsler (1939) pointed out that the Binet tests of intelligence were primarily designed for children and that there were no useful tests to measure intelligence in adults. Although more difficult items could be included on the Binet tests, the items were not really relevant to the lives of adults. They were designed to determine the abilities and interests of the schoolchild; thus, adults found them boring. Another problem with the Binet tests was that they emphasized speed and the routine manipulation of words, factors that might handicap the older person. Furthermore, the tables for ascertaining scores were based on scores from young people.

Table 7.1 Examples of items from the Stanford-Binet Intelligence Test	
Age	**Task**
2	**Naming parts of the body.** Child is shown a large paper doll and asked to point to various parts of the body.
3	**Visual-motor skills.** Child is shown a bridge built of three blocks and asked to build one like it. Can copy a drawing of a circle.
4	**Opposite analogies.** Fills in the missing word when asked: "Brother is a boy; sister is a _____." "In daytime it is light, at night it is _____." **Reasoning.** Answers correctly when asked: "Why do we have houses?" "Why do we have books?"
5	**Vocabulary.** Defines words such as *ball*, *hat*, and *stove*. **Visual-motor skills.** Can copy a drawing of a square.
6	**Number concepts.** Is able to give the examiner nine blocks when asked to do so.
8	**Memory for stories.** Listens to a story and answers questions about it.
9	**Rhymes.** Answers correctly when asked: "Tell me the name of a color that rhymes with Fred." "Tell me a number that rhymes with free."
12	**Verbal absurdities.** Tells what is foolish about statements such as, "Bill Jones's feet are so big that he has to put his trousers on over his head."
14	**Inference.** Examiner folds a piece of paper a number of times, notching a corner with scissors each time. Subject is asked the rule for determining how many holes there will be when the paper is unfolded.
Adult (15 years and older)	**Differences.** Can describe the difference between "misery and poverty," "character and reputation." **Memory for reversed digits.** Can repeat six digits backwards (that is, in reverse order) after they are read aloud by the examiner.

Adapted with permission of The Riverside Publishing Company.

Wechsler devised the **Wechsler Adult Intelligence Scale,** or **WAIS,** *to measure the mental abilities of adults, rather than children, for whom the Binet Test and the Stanford-Binet were primarily designed.* An important feature of the WAIS was that it was divided into eleven subtests that were grouped into a verbal scale and a performance scale. Each subtest was designed to measure specific components of intelligence, and the scales were created to permit an overall assessment of verbal and performance abilities.

Refining the Intelligence Test with Computer Technology. The breakthroughs that have been made in cognitive psychology have led to proposals for improving the tests used to measure mental abilities in ways that would enable us to better understand the meaning of the test scores. With the aid of computer technology, for example, it would be possible to record not only whether an answer was correct, but how long the test taker took to respond. By constructing tests that include problems that vary in specific dimensions, it is possible to obtain a great deal more than just an overall performance score; the computer could record and compute the test taker's encoding speed, inference speed and accuracy, as well as other measures.

For example, the two analogy problems shown in figure 7.14 each require only one transformation. In the first, the number of figures is doubled; in the second, the outer figure is enlarged. They differ in the number of elements the test taker has to encode: in the first problem there is only one, but in the second there are two. If we can assume that the amount of time to perform a single transformation remains the same for both

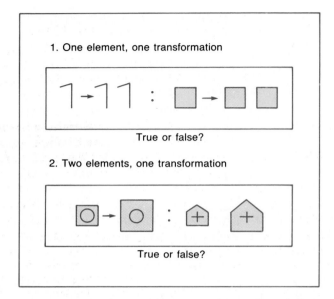

1. One element, one transformation

True or false?

2. Two elements, one transformation

True or false?

Figure 7.14 Two analogy problems that differ in the number of elements that must be encoded

problems, then subtracting the time the person takes to solve the second problem from the time to solve the first results in an estimate of the time it takes the person to encode a single element.

Measures like these might lead to a better understanding of a person's strengths and weaknesses with respect to how he is reasoning and solving problems, not just whether he is solving them.

Practical Issues Involved in Testing

The use of intelligence tests is a very controversial subject for both practical and ethical reasons. The two main practical issues involve the reliability of the tests and the validity of the tests.

Reliability.   In psychological testing, the term **reliability** *refers to the consistency of scores obtained by the same subjects when they are reexamined on the same test on different occasions.* It does not refer to whether the test is accurate or a useful measure of a particular trait; it refers only to whether people tend to get the same scores the second time they take the test. This concept is important because it provides some information about the error of measurement. If the test has a great deal of error in it because of factors that are irrelevant to the test's purpose, then the test would not be reliable. Your IQ score on one day might be very low because of irrelevant factors such as fatigue, depression, or perhaps because the examiner failed to explain the instructions adequately. On another day, your IQ score might be much higher because these factors all combined in some favorable way. If your score on the test is affected by these factors to any great degree, the test would not be reliable.

The most common means of providing information about the reliability of any test is the correlation coefficient. The reliability of a test can be determined in several ways, including the test-retest method and the alternate-form method. In the **test-retest method,** *a group of people are given a test twice, on two different occasions usually separated by a time interval of less than six months, and the correlation between their two scores is calculated to obtain an estimate of reliability.* In the **alternate-form method,** *a group of people take one form of the test on one occasion and another, comparable form on another occasion; their scores are correlated to obtain an estimate of reliability.* This latter method is more appropriate when the scores of the people taking the test might be changed simply by the practice they gained during the first administration.

Studies of the reliability of the Stanford-Binet show that it is quite high; most of the correlations between scores on one form and scores on another are around .9 (McNemar, 1942). When the scores of a group of seven-year-olds who took two different forms of the test are compared, the children generally tended to receive approximately the same score on both tests. It is interesting that the reliability of the test was not as high in the upper IQ ranges, a common finding on studies of the reliability of IQ tests (Anastasi, 1982).

Validity. The **validity** *of a test reflects whether or not the test actually measures what it is supposed to measure.* The validity gives some indication of what can be inferred from test scores and what conclusions might be drawn. Although the names of most IQ tests suggest that they are measuring "intelligence," or "abilities," the actual traits that are being measured are probably much narrower.

Validity is ordinarily determined by analyzing the relationship between performance on the test and performance on some independent indication of the trait. For example, one validity measure of the IQ test might relate the scores of a group of subjects to their grades in school. Or, the test scores might be correlated to teachers' ratings of students' abilities. Correlations of this kind for the Stanford-Binet are usually in the range of .4 to .75 (Anastasi, 1982). These measures of validity would not necessarily indicate that the test is a valid measure of intelligence, because that question would have to depend on how intelligence is defined. They only suggest that it is reasonable to use the test as a valid predictor of performance in school.

Ethical and Legal Issues Surrounding IQ Testing

In the last decade, the use of intelligence or ability tests has become an extremely controversial issue. A person's score on these tests can influence many events in his life, including admission to college, advanced placement in high school, assignment to special education programs, acceptance in particular career fields, and assignment to special training programs. The usefulness of these tests and the wisdom of using them as predictors have become the subjects of increasing concern, not just to psychologists, but to the public and the courts as well (Linn, 1982; Kaplan, 1982; Messick, 1980; London and Bray, 1980; Glaser, 1981).

For example, in the California case of *Larry P.* v. *Wilson Riles,* the plaintiff argued that minority children were overrepresented in classes for the mentally retarded, primarily because the decision to place children in these classes was based on the results of IQ tests. According to the plaintiff, these tests do not fairly assess the abilities of black children and should not be used as assessment instruments. The state supreme court agreed and imposed a moratorium on the use of intelligence tests in the placement of students in special education programs for the mildly mentally retarded (Lambert, 1981). Although evidence was presented in favor of the validity of these tests for this purpose, particularly when they are used in conjunction with other assessment tools, the judge decided that being placed in a special program might stigmatize children for life. The court concluded:

> . . . to remedy the harm to black children who have been misidentified as EMR (educably mentally retarded) pupils and to prevent these discriminatory practices from recurring . . . the defendants shall direct each school district to reevaluate every black child . . . without including in the psychological evaluation a standardized intelligence or ability test that has not been approved by the court. . . . (*Larry P.* v. *Wilson Riles,* 1979)

A report by a committee of the National Academy of Science addressed the controversy over intelligence and ability tests (Holden, 1982). The committee reviewed all the literature and court cases on the subject and decided that on the whole, these tests are valid and useful in predicting an individual's academic performance, for minority groups as well as whites. The tests are biased in that the items in them depend heavily on experience in mainstream American culture, but according to the committee, there is no way to produce a test that is not culture-dependent.

The committee cautioned that the tests are of limited use and should not be the sole criterion for making any decision. They also argued that testing should be conducted in an ethical manner and that the testing program and any classifications of children must have "instructional validity"—it must be useful for the child. For example, a test designed to assess ability in young

RESEARCH BOX

Measuring Creativity

Researchers have as much difficulty defining and measuring creativity as they have with intelligence. The term is a very rich one that suggests a wide range of abilities, interests, and accomplishments. Definitions of the term vary widely. Some definitions emphasize the production of socially valued products, such as inventions or works of art. Others describe creativity more as an ability than as a set of extraordinary accomplishments, and some subjects might be called "highly creative" even though they have never produced anything. Almost all scientists who study creativity agree that it is not the same as intelligence, although the two overlap slightly (Getzels, 1975; Richards, 1976; Barron and Harrington, 1981; Sternberg, 1985).

The most widely used measures of creativity are tests of divergent thinking, based on the work of J. P. Guilford (1967). These tests include items, such as those shown, that assess the subject's ability to provide many answers to a single question. They differ from the items on most intelligence tests that measure convergent thinking, because those items usually have only one correct solution.

Guilford believed that the major components of creative thinking included fluency, flexibility, elaboration, and originality. Fluency, for example, might be measured by asking the subject to think of as many words as possible that contain the letter "z." The subject's originality might be assessed by asking him to name a variety of unusual uses for a familiar object, such as a brick.

Another widely used test of creativity that also emphasizes divergent thinking is the *Torrance Tests of Creative Thinking,* devised by Paul Torrance. The test is appropriate for school-age children. In the "Just Suppose" component of the test, for example, the child is shown a strange picture, such as clouds linked to the ground with strings. The child is asked to think of things that might have caused this situation.

The question of how valid these tests are is a very controversial one. Do scores on these tests of creative ability actually relate to the number or quality of an individual's creative accomplishments? A survey of the many studies that attempted to correlate scores on creativity tests to assessments of a person's creative accomplishments suggests that the tests are valid, at least to some degree (Barron and Harrington, 1981); however, the correlations are usually low.

Newer tests of creativity are attempting to assess the kinds of creativity required by different fields and to relate scores on the more specific tests to accomplishments within the field. It seems reasonable to assume, for example, that the kind of creativity required of an architect is not quite the same as that required of a composer. Perhaps more specific tests, for example, ones that assess creativity in the musical domain, may be able to assess creative ability in different fields (Torrance, 1969; Frederiksen and Ward, 1972; Lunneborg and Lunneborg, 1969).

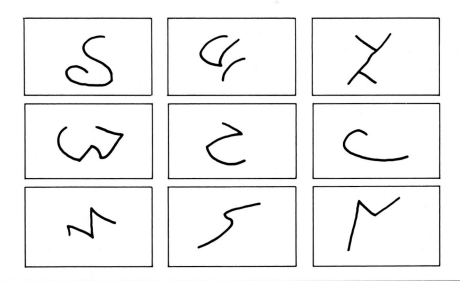

Figure 7.B *Sample items from creativity tests*

Sample Items from Creativity Tests

1. Name as many objects as you can that weigh less than one pound.
2. Write as many sentences as you can that have four words, each word starting with these letters: t,a,s,a. (One sentence might be Tomorrow a salesman arrives.)
3. Write as many meanings as you can for the following words:
   a. duck
   b. sack
   c. pitch
   d. fair
4. Name as many uses as you can think of for:
   a. a toothpick.
   b. a brick.
   c. a paper clip.
5. The child is shown pictures like those in figure 7.B and is asked to make meaningful drawings and to label them.

children should lead to opportunities to improve weak areas. If the test finds that a particular child has very poor reading skills, the information should be used to provide the child with required instruction rather than to label the child as a nonreader.

The report emphasized that a procedure that used tests to select people for various programs is more equitable than a procedure that did not use such tests. Abolishing tests would not alter the fact that test scores of blacks and Hispanics are usually lower than those of whites or the fact that minority children are more likely to be included in special education programs. As long as some groups have more members with less education and fewer advantages than other groups, the disadvantaged groups are likely to be overrepresented in remedial programs.

The Nature of Intelligence

The nature of intelligence can easily become lost amid all the controversies and debates about the measurement of intelligence and the use of IQ test scores. The term "intelligence" is commonly used to refer to a combination of abilities that enable an individual to survive and adapt to the environment. These abilities vary depending on the nature of the culture, the historical period, and the kind of career a person chooses. For example, the skills and abilities that lead to successful adaptation in rural Indonesia are different from those in contemporary urban America. Most people use the word "intelligence" to refer to the kinds of skills required for their own contemporary culture.

Although the word "intelligence" is used very broadly, the IQ tests only measure a limited number of abilities. They very heavily stress verbal reasoning and the ability to deal with numerical and abstract symbols, but they ignore other abilities that might reasonably be included in any definition of intelligence. Mechanical skills, motor skills, musical abilities, artistic talents, and creativity (see Research Box: Measuring Creativity) in general are all examples.

Furthermore, IQ tests do not measure "practical knowledge," which is not taught in schools but is more closely related to a person's success in business or other professions than is his score on an IQ test (Wagner and Sternberg, 1985). Neither are motivation and attitudinal variables assessed. Thus, the IQ tests sample only a few of the abilities required for successful adaptation to contemporary American culture.

Based solely on the results of studies using the IQ tests, and therefore limited to the kinds of behaviors sampled by these tests, two main hypotheses have emerged about the nature of intelligence. The **two-factor theory of intelligence,** *proposed by the English psychologist Charles Spearman, suggests that intelligence is made up of two principal components: (1) the* **g-factor,** *which is the general component of intelligence and the major determinant of performance on cognitive tests; and* **s-factors,** *which are special factors that contribute to an individual's performance in specific cognitive areas, such as verbal reasoning or spatial relations.*

Both Binet and Wechsler assumed that intelligence was a general and fundamental trait. Even though their tests sampled many different abilities, there were few children who performed extremely well on some and very poorly on others. For the most part, children with high scores in one area tended to have high scores in most of the others as well.

A second theory of intelligence, proposed by L. L. Thurstone (1938), argued that intelligence consists of seven separate and independent abilities, not a single undifferentiated g-factor, as Spearman suggested. Thurstone referred to the concept of **primary mental abilities,** *which are independent abilities including verbal comprehension, word fluency, number, memory, space, perceptual speed, and reasoning.* According to this theory, individuals differ in each of these mental abilities, some showing greater capacity in one area and others in another area. This theory has only received limited support, partly because the determination of the "primary abilities" depends on which items are included in the test. Some researchers have argued that there are twenty different factors, and others suggest that there may be more than a hundred (Ekstrom, et al., 1976). Also, test scores on each primary ability are correlated, indicating that children who do well in one area tend to do well in others. This provides more support for the g-factor theory.

Factors Influencing Intelligence. Because efforts to determine what factors influence intelligence have relied on IQ tests as measures of intelligence, this section might more appropriately be titled, "Factors Influencing Performance on IQ Tests." The research on this topic has been extraordinarily controversial, and in fact, has caused some of the most heated debates in the entire field of psychology. The debate centers around the relative contributions of environmental influences and genetic factors.

The general approach is to collect IQ scores from people who are genetically related in varying degrees, especially from **monozygotic twins,** *who are identical and have 100% of their genes in common,* and **dizygotic twins,** *who are fraternal and as genetically related as regular siblings.* Studies like these generally find that people who are closely related tend to perform similarly on tests of IQ, a fact that is not very surprising considering that they share many common genes and many of the same environmental influences. For example, a large number of studies on monozygotic twins have found high correlations between their IQ test scores, ranging around .86 (table 7.2) (Bouchard and McGue, 1981).

What is somewhat surprising is that the correlations between the test scores of related people tend to follow a pattern. The closer the genetic relationship, the higher the correlation. Of particular interest is the comparison between the correlations for monozygotic twins reared together and dizygotic twins reared together. Although both kinds of twins are reared in the same home at the same time by the same parents, the similarity in IQ scores is much higher for the monozygotic twins. One possible reason for this is that genetic factors play a very important role in performance on IQ

Table 7.2 Correlations of scores on IQ tests between people who are related genetically in varying degrees, and who also vary in the degree to which their environments are similar

Relationship	Correlation on IQ test scores*
Monozygotic twins reared together	.86
Monozygotic twins reared apart	.72
Average of parents correlated with child reared in parents' home	.50
Dizygotic twins reared together	.60
Siblings reared together	.47
Siblings reared apart	.24
Cousins	.15
Adopting parent and adopted child	.19

*Correlations represent a weighted average of the values obtained in several studies. From Bouchard, T. J., and M. McGue, "Familial Studies of Intelligence: A Review," in Science, Vol. 212, pp. 1055–1058, Fig. 1, May 1981. Copyright © 1981 by the American Association for the Advancement of Science.

tests. Thus, the monozygotic twins are more similar to one another primarily because they share all of their genes, and dizygotic twins only share about half of theirs.

Perhaps even more surprising is that individuals who are closely related genetically, but who are reared apart in different homes, still perform similarly on IQ tests, although not as similarly as if they had been reared together. The correlation between the IQ test scores of monozygotic twins reared apart, for example, is around .72, not very much lower than the .86 found for monozygotic twins reared together.

Data like these are enormously difficult to interpret, for many reasons. For instance, monozygotic twins look identical, so the parents may treat them more similarly than do the parents of dizygotic twins. Thus, the difference in the correlations between monozygotic and dizygotic twins may not be entirely due to genetic factors. Also, monozygotic twins separated at an early age are not necessarily placed randomly by adoption agencies; many agencies would try to find a home that is similar to the one from which the twin came. Therefore, just because members of a twin pair are reared apart does not necessarily mean they do not share common environmental influences.

As we will discuss in more detail in Chapter 9, the behavior of any organism is the result of the interactions between its genes and its environment. Performance on IQ tests, and probably intelligence itself, is made up of behaviors that are influenced by both genes and environmental factors. Genetic factors appear to determine a range within which the environment can then modify behavior. For example, one person might inherit genes that would enable him to have an average to superior intelligence, provided he received at least some physical and emotional care. Whether his ultimate IQ is average, above average, or superior would depend on the environment to which he is subsequently exposed. The kinds of environmental influences that might affect his ultimate performance would include his prenatal and postnatal nutrition, the stimulation he receives in infancy, the encouragement and rewards he receives from his parents and teachers, the quality of the academic training he receives, and the attitudes of his peers toward intellectual pursuits.

Fortunately, the debate over the relative contributions of genes and environment to performance on IQ scores has cooled somewhat, and many scientists have become more concerned with the steps we need to take to raise intelligence-test scores and encourage the development of intelligence in general. There is no doubt that a person's performance on an IQ test can change dramatically. In one study of California schoolchildren, fifty-nine percent of the children showed changes of fifteen points or more between the ages of six and eighteen. Another thirty-seven percent showed changes of twenty or more IQ points, and nine percent changed by more than thirty points (Honzik, Macfarlane, and Allen, 1948). Some of the approaches that are being used to encourage the cognitive development of children will be explained in the discussion of infancy and childhood in Chapter 9.

GUIDED REVIEW

Learning Objectives 11, 12, 13, and 14

1. _____ is a combination of abilities that enables a person to learn from experience, think abstractly, and adapt to the environment. It often includes a span of cognitive abilities, such as problem solving, language comprehension, concept formation, and many others, but different theorists have emphasized different cognitive abilities.

2. _____ designed one of the first instruments to measure intelligence. The test consisted of a series of items related to everyday problems, and Binet determined the items that could be passed by a majority of children at each age level. The child's IQ score was his _____ divided by his chronological age, multiplied by 100.

3. One of the most widely used IQ tests today is the _____ , a modified version of Binet's test. Another widely used test is the _____ , which includes items more appropriate for adults.

4. Techniques used in cognitive psychology, especially _____ , offer ways to obtain information about how a person solves problems on IQ tests, measures that may be more useful than overall performance scores.

5. The _____ of an intelligence test refers to the consistency of scores obtained by the same subjects when they are reexamined on the same test on different occasions. Two methods used to assess reliability are the _____ and the _____ .

6. _____ of an IQ test reflects whether the test measures what it is designed to measure, and what conclusions can be drawn from the scores.

7. Since intelligence refers to the ability to adapt to the environment, any measure of intelligence will depend on the _____ to which the individual is adapting. IQ tests developed in the United States measure a narrow range of abilities that might be included in intelligence, and they are specifically biased toward adaptation to contemporary American culture.

8. There are two hypotheses concerning the nature of intelligence, both based on the abilities assessed in typical IQ tests. One is called the _____ , which proposes that intelligence consists of a general _____ and a number of special _____ , each of which contributes to a specific cognitive area. The second theory suggests that intelligence consists of separate and independent _____ .

9. Studies of the correlations between the IQ test scores of individuals who are genetically related in varying degrees suggest that genetic factors contribute to performance on IQ tests. However, these studies are difficult to interpret. The safest conclusions are that both genes and environment _____ in their effects on behavior, and that genetic factors determine a range of intelligence within which the environment is able to modify the behavior.

ANSWERS

1. Intelligence 2. Alfred Binet; mental age 3. Stanford-Binet; Wechsler Adult Intelligence Scale 4. computer-assisted testing 5. reliability; test-retest method, alternate form method 6. Validity 7. culture 8. two-factor theory of intelligence; g-factor; s-factors; primary mental abilities 9. interact

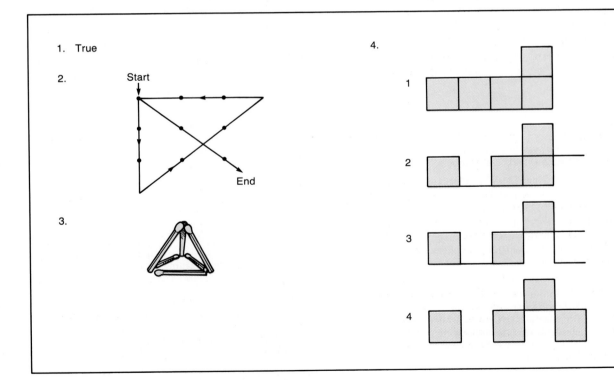

1. True

2.

3.

4.

Figure 7.15 Solutions to problems from figure 7.7. Answers continue on p. 264.

5. The Hobbits and the Orcs   (page 249)

Send over one hobbit and one orc. Have the hobbit bring the boat back, pick up another hobbit, and take him to the other bank. Have the hobbit bring the boat back again and pick up the orc.

Anagrams: (page 250)

RTIEH = THEIR

GHIETH = HEIGHT

The Chain Links Problem   (page 251)

Take one of the four chains, and open all the links (3 X 2 cents = 6 cents). Connect two of the four chains with one link (3 cents), use another to link the third three-link chain to the chain that now contains seven links (3 cents), and use the third opened link to connect one end of the chain that now contains eleven links to the other end (3 cents). The total cost is 15 cents.

Analogy Problems   (p. 256)

1. True
2. True

Cipher (from Career Box: Cryptographer) [page 246]

SEND HELP IMMEDIATELY

Figure 7.15, Part 2   Solutions to problems from figure 7.7, continued

SUMMARY

I. Language is the system by which we communicate meaning through sounds and symbols.   (p. 228)

   A. All natural languages share three characteristics: creativity, the use of arbitrary symbols to represent objects and events, and governance by a grammar.   (p. 228)

      1. The structure of oral language includes a number of elements: the phoneme, the morpheme, the word, the phrase, and the sentence.   (p. 230)

      2. To communicate, a speaker transforms the underlying representation of a sentence into a surface structure. To understand, the listener grasps the underlying representation from the surface structure by dividing the speech into constituents. (p. 230)

   B. Language acquisition is one of the most remarkable achievements of the child. (p. 231)

      1. The course of language development involves several stages, including cooing, babbling, holophrases, and telegraphic speech.   (p. 231)

      2. The most widely accepted theory of language learning proposes that several factors are important, including imitation and reinforcement, genetic predisposition for language learning, and the child's strong motivation to acquire language by inducing the rule systems underlying the language.   (p. 233)

   C. Many animals have very complex communication systems.   (p. 235)

      1. Animal communication systems do not meet the criteria for human language. (p. 236)

2. Attempts to teach language to apes have met with much success, although the apes do not appear to use the language creatively as humans do.   (p. 237)

II. Cognitive psychology includes the study of human thought.   (p. 240)

  A. Language and thought are closely related in humans. The linguistic relativity hypothesis proposed a very close relationship between the two.   (p. 240)

  B. The structure of thought is arranged as a hierarchy of concepts.   (p. 241)

   1. Each concept has one or more attributes that are used to place objects or events into the class.   (p. 242)

   2. People acquire concepts through trial and error or through more efficient strategies, such as the conservative-focusing approach.   (p. 243)

III. Any problem consists of a given state, a goal state, a path from the given state to the goal state, and a problem space.   (p. 245)

  A. There are three major steps in problem solving.   (p. 245)

   1. The analysis of the problem involves acquiring and understanding of the givens. Familiarity with the elements of the problem can either facilitate this step or hinder it if the solver forms a set.   (p. 245)

   2. The search for a solution might involve one of several strategies, including use of an algorithm or the use of a heuristic.   (p. 248)

   3. The decision that a solution has been reached is simple for well-defined problems but much more difficult for ill-defined ones.   (p. 251)

  B. Creative problem solving requires divergent, rather than convergent thinking. Creativity can be encouraged by incubation.   (p. 251)

IV. Intelligence is a combination of abilities that enable a person to learn from experience, think abstractly, and adapt successfully to the environment.   (p. 253)

  A. Alfred Binet designed the first intelligence test for children.   (p. 253)

   1. Stern used the formula of mental age/chronological age to obtain an intelligence quotient.   (p. 253)

   2. The Stanford-Binet test of intelligence is a modification of Binet's test.   (p. 254)

   3. The Wechsler Adult Intelligence Scale (WAIS) is a test designed to measure mental abilities in adults.   (p. 254)

   4. Further refinements in the intelligence test may involve the use of the computer to assess the speed of responses.   (p. 255)

  B. There are several practical issues involved in intelligence testing.   (p. 256)

   1. Reliability of a test refers to the consistency of scores obtained by the same subjects when they are reexamined on the same test on different occasions.   (p. 256)

   2. The validity of a test reflects whether the test is measuring what it is supposed to measure.   (p. 257)

  C. IQ testing has raised many ethical and legal issues, particularly because some children of minority groups tend to score poorly and their test scores are used to place them in special education programs.   (p. 257)

  D. Theories have been proposed to explain the nature of intelligence, including the two-factor theory. Another theory proposes that intelligence consists of several independent and separate mental abilities, called primary mental abilities.   (p. 260)

   1. Factors that influence intelligence test scores include both genes and the nature of the environment.   (p. 261)

ACTION GLOSSARY

Match the terms in the left column with the definitions in the right column.

_____ 1. **Language** (p. 228)
_____ 2. **Grammar** (p. 230)
_____ 3. **Phoneme** (p. 230)
_____ 4. **Morpheme** (p. 230)
_____ 5. **Surface structure** (p. 230)
_____ 6. **Underlying representation** (p. 230)
_____ 7. **Semantic approach** (p. 231)

A. *A single sound element from which spoken words are formed; the basic unit of oral language.*
B. *The organization of words in a spoken sentence.*
C. *The system of sounds and symbols by which we communicate meaning.*
D. *The smallest unit of meaning in a spoken language. Can be either a single word, such as "run," or any syllable that conveys meaning, such as "ing" at the end of a verb.*
E. *A method of explaining a sentence's underlying representation; emphasizes a sentence's division into propositions.*
F. *A set of rules that governs the use of words, their functions, and their relations in a sentence.*
G. *The meaning that the speaker is trying to convey in a sentence.*

_____ 8. **Proposition** (p. 231)
_____ 9. **Constituents** (p. 231)
_____ 10. **Cooing** (p. 231)
_____ 11. **Babbling** (p. 232)
_____ 12. **Holophrase** (p. 232)
_____ 13. **Telegraphic speech** (p. 232)
_____ 14. **Critical period** (p. 234)

A. *A period of development during which the organism is particularly vulnerable or susceptible to certain environmental influences, such as exposure to language.*
B. *Vowellike sounds or sounds beginning with a single consonant; characterizes the vocal behavior of the very young infant.*
C. *The speech patterns characteristic of children who are beginning to use two-word sentences.*
D. *The phrases or subphrases of a sentence.*
E. *A unit of meaning or an idea that consists of a verbal unit and one or more nouns.*
F. *Single-word utterances, which often carry a great deal of meaning, produced by a child who is just learning to talk.*
G. *The vocal behavior of infants at age six months or older; includes strings of consonants and vowel phonemes.*

_____ 15. **Displacement** (p. 237)
_____ 16. **Linguistic relativity hypothesis** (p. 241)
_____ 17. **Concepts** (p. 241)
_____ 18. **Attribute** (p. 242)
_____ 19. **Defining feature** (p. 242)
_____ 20. **Characteristic feature** (p. 242)
_____ 21. **Prototype** (p. 242)
_____ 22. **Focal** (p. 242)

A. *An attribute that is present in all members of a particular class or concept and is necessary for categorization into that concept.*
B. *That which is the best example of an object or event within a particular category and which is matched to a greater or lesser degree by other examples of the category.*
C. *A feature of an object or event that is used to identify it as a member of a particular class or concept.*
D. *The ability to talk about things that are not actually present.*
E. *An attribute that is present in many, but not all members of a particular class or concept.*
F. *One of several basic colors that are perceived by human beings.*
G. *Suggests that an individual's perceptions, thought patterns, and view of the world are dependent upon the particular language he or she speaks.*
H. *The mental constructs that enable us to make classifications based on shared characteristics.*

_____ 23. **Conservative focusing strategy** (p. 244)
_____ 24. **Given state** (p. 245)
_____ 25. **Goal state** (p. 245)
_____ 26. **Path** (p. 245)
_____ 27. **Set** (p. 247)
_____ 28. **Functional fixity** (p. 248)
_____ 29. **Inductive reasoning** (p. 248)

A. *The ability to take specific experiences and form general rules, ideas, or concepts.*
B. *A method of learning concepts in which the learner uses one positive instance of the concept as the focus and then tests individual hypotheses, one at a time, to determine the nature of the concept.*
C. *The strategy one uses to move from the given state to the goal state in problem solving.*
D. *The tendency for people to have difficulty imagining new and unusual uses for familiar objects.*

E. *The solution to the problem or the place where one would like to be.*

F. *The state one is currently in.*

G. *The tendency to cling to certain interpretations of the requirements of a problem, especially ones that have been successful in finding a solution to a similar problem.*

____ 30. **Algorithm** (p. 249)
____ 31. **Heuristic** (p. 249)
____ 32. **Means-end analysis** (p. 249)
____ 33. **Well-defined problems** (p. 251)
____ 34. **Ill-defined problems** (p. 251)
____ 35. **Convergent thinking** (p. 251)
____ 36. **Divergent thinking** (p. 251)

A. *A person who is solving a problem applies the rules of logic to arrive at a single correct solution.*

B. *Problems that provide the necessary information for a solution and for which there is only one correct solution.*

C. *A rule of thumb, or general principle, that involves a selective search through the possible solutions to a problem.*

D. *Problems for which all the needed information is not given and for which there may be more than one correct solution.*

E. *A general procedure or operation that guarantees a solution to the problem.*

F. *An approach to solving problems in which the solver tries to reduce the difference between the given state and the goal state by setting up and solving subproblems.*

G. *A person who is solving a problem stretches his imagination to conceive of a variety of possible solutions to a particular problem.*

____ 37. **Incubation** (p. 251)
____ 38. **Intelligence** (p. 253)
____ 39. **Mental age** (p. 254)
____ 40. **Intelligence quotient (IQ)** (p. 254)
____ 41. **Stanford-Binet** (p. 254)
____ 42. **Wechsler Adult Intelligence Scale (WAIS)** (p. 255)
____ 43. **Reliability** (p. 256)

A. *The abilities that enable a person to learn from experiences, to think abstractly, and to adapt successfully to the environment.*

B. *A term used in psychological testing that refers to the consistency of scores obtained by the same subjects when they are reexamined on different occasions.*

C. *The most widely used revision of the early Binet test of intelligence.*

D. *A measure that expresses a person's mental attainment in terms of his/her test scores relative to the scores of a large representative group of people of the same age.*

E. *A test that measures the mental abilities of adults.*

F. *A technique used to aid the problem-solving process; a difficult problem is set aside after a series of initial unsuccessful attempts at solving the problem.*

G. *A number used to express a person's intelligence; determined by dividing mental age (as measured by Binet's early intelligence test) by chronological age and multiplying by 100.*

____ 44. **Test-retest method** (p. 256)
____ 45. **Alternate form method** (p. 256)
____ 46. **Validity** (p. 257)
____ 47. **Two-factor theory of intelligence** (p. 260)
____ 48. **Primary mental abilities** (p. 260)
____ 49. **Monozygotic twins** (p. 261)
____ 50. **Dizygotic twins** (p. 261)

A. *The concept that intelligence consists of seven separate and independent abilities, including verbal comprehension, memory, and reasoning.*

B. *A method of assessing reliability in which subjects are given different forms of the same test on two different occasions, and their scores are correlated.*

C. *Fraternal twins.*

D. *Identical twins.*

E. *Suggests that intelligence consists of a general g-factor, which affects performance on all kinds of cognitive ability tests, and several specific s-factors, which affect performance in specific cognitive areas.*

F. *Reflects whether a test actually measures what it is supposed to measure and gives some indication about what conclusions can be drawn from test scores.*

G. *A method of assessing reliability. Subjects are given the same test on two different occasions, and the scores are correlated.*

ANSWERS

48. A, 49. D, 50. C

33. B, 34. D, 35. A, 36. G, 37. F, 38. A, 39. D, 40. G, 41. C, 42. E, 43. B, 44. G, 45. B, 46. F, 47. E.

18. C, 19. A, 20. E, 21. B, 22. F, 23. B, 24. F, 25. E, 26. C, 27. G, 28. D, 29. A, 30. E, 31. C, 32. F.

1. C, 2. F, 3. A, 4. D, 5. B, 6. G, 7. E, 8. E, 9. D, 10. B, 11. G, 12. F, 13. C, 14. A, 15. D, 16. G, 17. H.

1. Which of the following characteristics is *not* a universal characteristic of all languages?

    (a) creativity
    (b) rule governed
    (c) standard tenses for verbs
    (d) use of arbitrary symbols to represent objects and events
    (LO 1; p. 229)

2. The unit that is a sound element from which spoken words are formed is called a

    (a) phoneme.   (c) word.
    (b) morpheme.   (d) semantic approach.
    (LO 1; p. 230)

3. The sentence "They are eating apples" has two

    (a) surface structures.
    (b) underlying representations.
    (c) morphemes.
    (d) inflections.
    (LO 1; p. 230)

4. The stage of single-word utterances appears at about the age of

    (a) two to three months.   (c) twelve months.
    (b) two and one-half years.   (d) eighteen months.
    (LO 2; p. 232)

5. The behavioral view of language learning argues that infants and children learn language

    (a) through the creative generalization of rules.
    (b) through a biological predisposition for learning language.
    (c) by actively attempting to test hypotheses about language.
    (d) through reinforcement and imitation.
    (LO 2; p. 233)

6. The linguistic relativity hypothesis claims that

    (a) language determines thought.
    (b) thought determines language.
    (c) thought and language are completely independent.
    (d) thought and language are initially independent, but language eventually comes into the service of thought.
    (LO 4; p. 241)

7. The defining feature of a concept is one that is true for

    (a) some but not all members.
    (b) most but not all members.
    (c) few members.
    (d) all members.
    (LO 5; p. 242)

8. The "best" example of a category is called a

    (a) focal color.   (c) defining feature.
    (b) prototype.   (d) characteristic feature.
    (LO 5; p. 242)

9. As a result of her research with the Dani, Rosch reported that they learned the names for color categories best when

    (a) focal colors were the center of the category.
    (b) focal colors were not the center of the category.
    (c) a focal color was not in the category.
    (d) They were unable to learn color names under any circumstances.
    (LO 5; p. 243)

10. Learning new concepts requires

    (a) identifying relevant attributes.
    (b) determining which attributes are defining and which characteristic.
    (c) developing a conservative focusing strategy.
    (d) both a and b.
    (LO 6; p. 243)

11. The three steps in problem solving in order are

    (a) searching for a solution, analyzing the problem, and deciding that a solution has been discovered.
    (b) analyzing the problem, searching for a solution, and deciding that a solution has been discovered.
    (c) analyzing the problem, deciding that a solution has been discovered, and searching for a solution.
    (d) searching for a solution, deciding that a solution has been discovered, and analyzing the problem
    (LO 7; p. 245)

12. A person who solves a problem in a more complicated way than necessary because of prior experience in solving more difficult but similar problems may be demonstrating
    (a) functional fixity.
    (b) inattention to the problem.
    (c) a set.
    (d) lack of familiarity with the material.
       (LO 8; p. 247)

13. A person who cannot solve a problem because he or she cannot imagine new uses for a familiar object is demonstrating
    (a) functional fixity.
    (b) inattention to the problem.
    (c) a response set.
    (d) lack of familiarity with the material.
       (LO 8; p. 248)

14. A general procedure that guarantees a solution to a problem is called a(n)
    (a) heuristic.   (c) algorithm.
    (b) response set.   (d) means-end analysis.
                                (LO 9; p. 249)

15. Creative problem solving is best approached with _____ rather than with _____ .
    (a) convergent thinking; incubation
    (b) incubation; divergent thinking
    (c) convergent thinking; divergent thinking
    (d) divergent thinking; convergent thinking
       (LO 10; p. 251)

16. The intelligence test developed by Binet was designed to
    (a) support his theory of intelligence.
    (b) examine racial differences in intelligence.
    (c) identify children who would not benefit from the regular elementary school program.
    (d) compare mental age with chronological age.
       (LO 11; p. 253)

17. Elizabeth is seven years old and has a mental age of nine. Elizabeth's IQ, according to the Stern's formula for calculating IQ, is
    (a) 135.   (c) 78.
    (b) 129.   (d) 108.
                                (LO 11; p. 254)

18. The extent to which a test measures what it is supposed to measure refers to the concept of
    (a) validity.   (c) legality.
    (b) reliability.   (d) culture dependence.
                                (LO 12; p. 257)

19. Spearman argued that intelligence is made up of
    (a) primary mental abilities.
    (b) a general factor.
    (c) both a general factor and specific factors.
    (d) independent abilities, such as divergent and convergent thinking.
       (LO 13; p. 260)

20. Correlations of scores on IQ tests are highest for which of the following?
    (a) siblings reared together
    (b) parents and their children
    (c) dizygotic twins reared together
    (d) monozygotic twins reared together
       (LO 14; p. 261)

ANSWERS

1. c, 2. a, 3. b, 4. c, 5. d, 6. a, 7. d, 8. b, 9. a, 10. d, 11. b, 12. c,
13. a, 14. c, 15. d, 16. c, 17. b, 18. a, 19. c, 20. d

SUGGESTED READINGS

Chomsky, N. *Knowledge of language: its nature, origin, and use.* New York: Praeger, 1985. A brief discussion of the nature of language by one of the important scientists in the field of psycholinguistics.

Curtiss, S. *Genie: a psycholinguistic study of a modern-day "wild child."* New York: Academic Press, 1977. An account of a child who was reared in isolation.

Fancher, R. E. *The intelligence men: makers of the IQ controversy.* New York: Norton, 1985. An unusual discussion of the nature-nurture controversy and its relevance to intelligence, which revolves around the biographies of several of the scientists who participated in it.

Gardner, H. *The mind's new science: a history of the cognitive revolution.* New York: Basic Books, 1985. A readable book for a general audience that covers the history and emergence of cognitive science from its interdisciplinary origins.

Johnson-Laird, P. N. *Mental models: towards a cognitive science of language, inference, and consciousness.* Cambridge, MA: Harvard University Press, 1983. An advanced text that proposes new ideas about reasoning and understanding language.

Matlin, M. *Cognition.* New York: Holt, Rinehart and Winston, 1983. A comprehensive introductory text on cognition that includes chapters on language, concept learning, and problem solving.

Miller, G. A. *Language and speech.* San Francisco: W. H. Freeman, 1981. An introductory text on the topic of language.

Wickelgren, W. A. *How to solve problems.* San Francisco: Freeman, 1974. Contains tips on improving problem-solving abilities.

c h a p t e r

8

Motivation
and Emotion

LEARNING OBJECTIVES

After reading this chapter, you should be able to

1. define the term motivation, and describe four theories that have attempted to exlain it. **(p. 272)**

2. describe one system that attempts to classify motives. **(p. 276)**

3. discuss the brain mechanisms underlying motivation. **(p. 277)**

4. describe some of the biological and psychological factors underlying hunger. **(p. 279)**

5. describe some of the biological and psychological factors that affect the human sex drive and human sexual behavior. **(p. 284)**

6. define the term *sensation-seeking,* and discuss the theories that attempt to explain the existence of this motive. **(p. 286)**

7. define the motive called *need for achievement,* explain how it is measured, and discuss the characteristics of people who score high or low on this motive. **(p. 289)**

8. define the term *emotion,* and explain how researchers have attempted to categorize the many different emotions. **(p. 292)**

9. discuss how human beings express emotions. **(p. 293)**

10. discuss some of the physiological factors associated with emotion, including activity in the autonomic nervous system and in the brain. **(p. 294)**

11. identify and describe several different theories of emotion. **(p. 298)**

The study of motivation explores why people do what they do—from why they work hard, to why they eat, to why they seek thrills in skydiving. One reason that the concept of motivation is an intriguing one is that people display such an enormous range of motives. Several theories have been proposed that attempt unifying explanations for the concept.

Probably the most important motive of all is emotion. Anger can make people fight, kick garbage cans, or abuse children; happiness can make us give money to charity or smile at our neighbors; and sadness can lead some people to commit suicide. Emotions are not simply motives, however; they are much more complicated. They can also be the goal for other motives. For example, we might read a novel because we know it has a happy ending and will make us feel good.

In the decades of the sixties and seventies, there was a revival of interest in mental activities, or cognition. No longer did researchers depend exclusively on observable behavior as they studied the human being, as they did during the dominance of behaviorism. Perhaps the eighties and nineties will see a revival of interest in motivation and, especially, emotion. Human beings cannot be entirely explained by their observable behavior, but neither can they be explained entirely by their conscious thoughts and cognitions. They are complicated creatures with behavior, thoughts, and feelings.

Motivation—A Description

The term *motivation* comes from the Latin word meaning "to move." A **motive** *is something that moves an organism to act.* It is *why* we do things, rather than what we do or how we do them. **Motivation** *refers to internal states of an organism that lead to the instigation, persistence, energy, or direction of behavior* (Ferguson, 1984). *It is a process that effects changes in the environment consistent with a person's plans.* (Often those plans are of a person's own designs, but the advertising business has become very sophisticated in subtly influencing human motivation, as we discuss in the Career Box: Copywriter.)

Theories of Motivation

Explanations for the "why" of human behavior are plentiful. They range from "the devil made me do it" to sophisticated mathematical models of relationships between habits, drives, rewards, and other variables. Several theories have been proposed to explain motivation: drive reduction theory, optimum level of arousal theory, expectancy theory, and the theory of opponent processes. Attempts have also been made to explain motivation on the neurophysiological level.

Drive Reduction Theory. One of the earlier theories of motivation, called the **drive reduction theory,** *proposed that organisms experience the arousal of a drive when an important need is not satisfied, and they engage in behavior to reduce the arousal and satisfy the need.* **Primary drives** *are those that motivate the organism to fulfill some basic need that is necessary for its survival (or the survival of the species), such as hunger, thirst, or sex.* One of the early proponents of the theory was Clark Hull (1943, 1952).

An important component of the drive reduction theory is **homeostasis.** *This term refers to a state of balance that is necessary in many physiological systems.* For example, temperature control requires a balance between hot and cold stimulation, and the control of body weight requires a balance between food intake and energy expenditure. Organisms are motivated to maintain homeostasis in their physiological systems, and their drives help them accomplish this.

The primary drives are the biological ones necessary for personal and species survival. There are also **acquired drives** *which develop through learning.* For example, a child learns that she never gets to eat unless she washes her hands first. She will probably develop an acquired drive to keep clean, based on this learning experience. Or a teenager who learns that possessing money attracts more members of the opposite sex may thus develop an acquired drive for money.

The drive is the force that motivates an organism to action. Which action the organism finally performs depends on the strength of the organism's **habit.** *A habit*

CAREER BOX

Copywriter

Careers in advertising are usually fast-paced, high pressure, and competitive, and the job of a copywriter is no exception. The copywriter is a member of a large team of people who produce advertising for products and services. He or she develops the headlines and text to be used in the ads, working in cooperation with the artists and layout designers. Usually a college education is required, though many advertising agencies do not necessarily want their new copywriters to major in advertising, or even business. Many employers prefer liberal arts graduates because they feel that a broad background in English, psychology, journalism, history, or other fields helps develop the copywriter's imagination.

In addition to having a creative flair for writing, the copywriter must have an understanding of human motivation, particularly what motivates people to buy. Most advertisements appeal to the various needs of the buying public. They may appeal to emotional needs, such as the need for social approval or the need for achievement. For example, one Chivas Regal ad reads, "Your friends won't think less of you if you don't serve Chivas Regal . . . But they certainly will think more of you if you do." Ads may also help satisfy more rational needs, such as the need for information. An ad for a Texas Instruments Professional Computer includes a chart that compares its features to those of major competitors. The headline reads, "The Texas Instruments Professional Computer gives you more for the money. Tear and compare."

Some ads may even be designed with very subtle appeals to various human needs. Little gimmicks sometimes appear in an advertisement, and consumers are supposed to perceive them unconsciously, or subliminally (Key, 1973). Whether consumer behavior can be influenced by subliminal appeals is a matter of some controversy, but it is clear that copywriters must have substantial knowledge of how to tap human motivations. Judging from the effects of successful advertising on product sales, many copywriters are indeed very knowledgeable.

---

is a response to some stimulus, and the strength of the habit depends on the connection between the stimulus and the response that influences what kind of behavior the drive will energize. For example, a drive will motivate a rat to move through a maze to find food. Whether the rat turns right or left at a certain point is determined by the animal's habit strength. If it has often turned right and found food, it will probably turn right again.

The drive reduction theory is simple and straightforward, but there are some human behaviors that it cannot explain. For instance, the theory assumes that human beings, and other animals as well, are always driven to reduce their arousal levels (by seeking food, water, shelter, etc.). It would seem logical to conclude, then, that we are happiest when we are stuffed with food and drink, sexually satiated, and lazing around doing nothing. However, for human beings especially, this state would rapidly lead to boredom. Humans are curious creatures who seek arousal; they are not always motivated to reduce it. If they were, why would they climb mountains, skydive, or even just go to a movie? Also, human beings do not always behave in accordance with their own biological self-interest. They diet

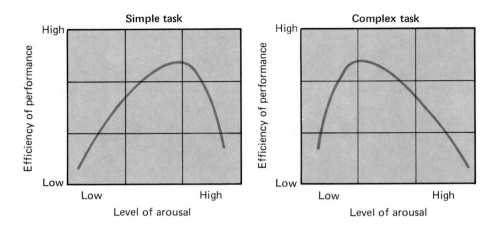

Figure 8.1 The Yerkes-Dodson Law shows the relationship between the level of arousal, the complexity of the task, and the efficiency of performance.

until they are extremely thin, sit in unbearably hot sauna baths, and occasionally even sacrifice their own lives for an important cause.

Optimum Level of Arousal Theory.   The drive reduction theory was eventually revised to take into account these criticisms. The new version, called the **optimum level of arousal theory,** *stated that drives did not necessarily motivate the organism to seek the lowest level of arousal. Instead, they provided motivation to seek an optimum level of arousal. What the optimum level is depends partly on the circumstances and partly on the person.* For example, a person who has been deprived of stimulation for most of the day might seek a high level of arousal that evening by going to an exciting football game. Another person, home from a hard day of selling encyclopedias to reluctant parents, might seek a lower arousal level by sitting in an easy chair and watching a TV show. This theory better explained why people sought out excitement and stimulation.

As early as 1908, a pair of comparative psychologists named Robert Yerkes and J. D. Dodson were emphasizing the effects that different arousal levels had on learning (Yerkes and Dodson, 1908). They varied arousal levels in mice by changing the intensity of electric shocks and observing how well the animals performed in simple and more complex mazes. The mice performed best in difficult mazes when the shock level was intermediate. This finding can be presented in a graph as an inverted, U-shaped function (fig. 8.1). The **Yerkes-Dodson Law** *states that performance on a learning task is related to arousal; the best performance results from intermediate levels of arousal.* Performance is also related to the difficulty of the task. Yerkes and Dodson found that the mice performed simple tasks better when the stimulation was more intense. For complex tasks, low to intermediate arousal was best. The Yerkes-Dodson Law shows how the optimum level of arousal theory can be applied to a specific kind of behavior: performance on a task.

A rather unnerving demonstration of the Yerkes-Dodson Law in humans involved arousal levels in simulated combat (Berkun, et al., 1962; Berkun, 1964). Inexperienced recruits and experienced combat-ready soldiers were each placed at a post during field operations and told that their radios required repair in order for them to regain communications with the command post. The repair involved reading and following instructions on a connection wire diagram. Some recruits and some experienced soldiers were in the "high stress" group, although they didn't know it. During the operation, artillery shells were set off to simulate an emergency, and many of them appeared to hit quite close to the subject. No simulated emergencies occurred for the control, or "low stress" subjects.

In rating the performance of these people in terms of how well and how quickly they were able to repair the radio, the experienced troops under simulated artillery fire did better than the experienced controls. For the recruits, though, the artillery fire caused them to perform poorly.

The Yerkes-Dodson Law can help explain these findings. For the experienced troops, the non-emergency setting was probably rather boring. Adding some excitement in the form of artillery fire increased their arousal to an optimum, intermediate level at which they would perform their best on the repair task. For the recruits with no field experience, the low stress condition was arousing enough, and optimum for them. When the simulated emergency was added, their arousal level was pushed too high, and their performance went down. Some recruits never even finished the task. They deserted their posts as soon as the firing began.

Studies on the effects of epinephrine on learning and memory may provide clues to the biological underpinnings of the Yerkes-Dodson Law. As we discussed in Chapter 6, rats were trained to avoid entering the dark side of a two-sided compartment by being given a mild footshock each time they entered. Moderate doses of the hormone administered just after training seemed to make it easier for the rats to remember what they had learned. But rats that received either small or large doses of the substance did not perform as well on the retention test (Gold and vanBuskirk, 1975, 1978). Perhaps moderate levels of epinephrine, released by the organism's own body during a moderate arousal level, facilitate learning in some way. However, too much epinephrine released during high levels of arousal may interfere when the task is difficult.

The Yerkes-Dodson Law appears to apply to many kinds of activities, such as learning, running, radio repair, multiplication, and public speaking. If the task is a challenging one for the person, high levels of arousal impede performance, and low levels also seem to produce poorer performance. If a person is seeking to perform well on a task, the optimum level of arousal would depend on the difficulty of the task.

Expectancy Theory. The drive theory and the optimum level of arousal theory emphasize an internal state that "pushes" the organism into action to satisfy some need. **Expectancy theory** (or theories, since there are many versions) *emphasizes the importance of rewards or goals, as well as how a person's expectations of consequences can influence his behavior.* This theory stresses "pull" rather than "push."

According to expectancy theory, the hunger drive is only part of the reason a hungry rat is motivated to find its way through a maze. It is also motivated because of previous learning experiences in which it had come to expect a bit of food at the end. Its motivation is composed of two major features: the **valence,** or *attractiveness of the goal,* and the **expectancy,** *or the likelihood that its behavior will lead to the goal.* A simple way of explaining the expectancy theory is to say that motivation = valence $\times$ expectancy.

The actions that a hungry person takes to satisfy her hunger depend very much on valence and expectancy. Let's say there is a deli on the corner of the person's block that sells foot-long hot dogs. This person loves to eat these dogs, so the valence is high. But what about expectancy? How does the person evaluate whether her actions will lead to the desired reward? If she has no money, she will probably not go to the deli even though she is hungry and the valence of the hot dogs is high. Her motivation to walk down to the deli is tempered by (1) the valence of the hot dogs, and (2) the expectancy that walking down there will lead to eating one.

First stimulation

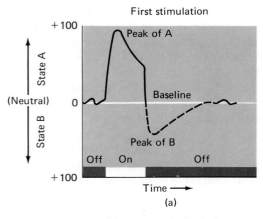

(a)

After repeated stimulations

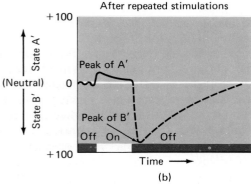

(b)

Figure 8.2 *Response to a UCS (a) the first few times it occurs and (b) after many stimulations*

Opponent Process Theory. The **opponent process theory** *proposes an explanation for the way in which acquired drives are acquired* (Solomon and Corbit, 1974; Solomon, 1980). *It suggests that a stimulus is first followed by a particular response and that this initial response is followed by an opposite reaction. After repeated stimulus presentations, the first response diminishes, but the opposite reaction that occurs after it grows in strength.* The **a-process** *is the initial reaction to the stimulus,* and the **b-process** *refers to the opposite reaction that occurs after the initial reaction.* (See fig. 8.2.)

For example, when a person is injected with heroin, the initial response is euphoria. This lasts for a few hours and is followed by discomfort, until eventually the person returns to the resting state. After repeated injections, the a-process, which in this case is euphoria, diminishes and is replaced by a weaker kind of contentment. The b-process, or discomfort, grows into the agony of withdrawal. Thus, the user continues to inject the drug even though it only produces contentment at first, primarily to avoid the painful b-process that would follow.

Another example concerns how a sauna bather comes to seek the seemingly painful heat of the sauna. The first time the person enters the sauna the experience is probably a painful and burning sensation. Afterwards, relief is experienced, followed by a slow return to normal. After several exposures to the sauna, the pain (a-process) diminishes and the relief (b-process) grows into long-lasting exhilaration. The opponent process theory is a useful one because it helps explain why something that would seem to be painful, like sauna bathing, can come to be a powerful acquired motivation.

Classification of Motives

The list of motives is almost as long as the list of different kinds of human behavior. In early theories of motivation, psychologists equated motives with instincts, and they began making lists that included the obvious ones, such as hunger, thirst, and sex, as well as more exotic ones, such as pugnacity and curiosity. By the 1920s, psychologists had added so many instincts that the list totalled nearly 6000! (One rather curious one was "the instinct to avoid eating apples in one's own orchard.")

H. A. Murray (1938) developed a more useful (and shorter) list of motives. His list focuses on social motives and includes achievement, aggression, and sex.

The **needs heirarchy system,** *devised by Abraham Maslow* (1954), *is a commonly used scheme for classifying human motives. It involves five categories of*

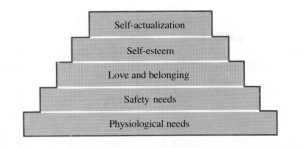

Figure 8.3 Maslow's hierarchy of needs

motives arranged in a pyramid; lower-level needs on the bottom of the pyramid must be satisfied first, before the ones higher in the pyramid come into play (fig. 8.3). For example, Maslow predicts that people who are hungry will not show a strong need for love. Or people who have enough food, water, clothing, housing, safety, companionship, and love, will probably begin showing a strong interest in obtaining personal recognition for their accomplishments. The motive that will be most prominent in an individual's behavior is the one that is the lowest, still-unsatisfied motive in the hierarchy.

This theory has been particularly popular in management circles because it seems to help explain what motivates people at different socio-economic levels and on different rungs of the corporate ladder. Some cross-sectional research has tended to support the theory. One investigation (Porter, 1961) studied people in lower and middle management, trying to determine the importance of various needs for these two groups. The researcher concluded that the higher levels of the organization offered more opportunities for fulfilling higher-level needs, such as self-esteem and self-actualization. The lower levels of the organization provided the opportunity for fulfilling only the more basic needs, such as safety.

Longitudinal studies, however, do not support Maslow's need hierarchy theory (Wahba and Bridwell, 1976; Hall and Nougaim, 1968; Lawler and Suttle, 1972). For example, Maslow's theory predicts that as a person achieves satisfaction for needs in a particular category, the importance of those needs should go down, and the importance of needs in the next highest category should go up. A person might emphasize safety needs at one time, but as his house is paid off and his job becomes secure, for example, safety should become less important and social needs should receive more attention. When people are studied over time, however, they do not necessarily show patterns like this.

Critics of Maslow's theory point out that the term *need* is poorly defined. Also, there is no particular reason to suppose that human needs are arranged in a fixed heirarchy that does not vary between people. Despite the criticisms, Maslow's theory is well known and has important historical value.

Motivation and the Brain

Research on the biological basis of motivation began when James Olds and his colleagues made some startling discoveries about the rewarding properties of electrical stimulation of the brain (ESB) (Olds, 1958). As we discussed in Chapter 2, tiny electrical shocks to certain parts of the brain, the areas around the hypothalamus in particular, can be very rewarding. Rats will press levers thousands of times per hour to receive these shocks and will sometimes ignore food (Routtenberg and Lindy, 1965). In some cases, rats will even neglect their own newborn pups (Sonderegger, 1970). The studies on ESB suggested that the brain contains some integrated "reward system" that is not specifically tied to a particular motive, such as hunger, but that is involved in all kinds of motivated behavior.

Since Olds's original discovery, the studies on ESB have uncovered many interesting things about the phenomenon (Olds and Fobes, 1981). For one thing, stimulation of the hypothalamus is very rewarding, but this is not the only rewarding site. Rewarding sites have been found in many brain regions, including the cortex, the hippocampus, the thalamus, and even the olfactory bulbs. The reward system seems to be widespread, a finding that is not so surprising considering how important it is to our behavior and our survival.

One very widespread pathway that seems to be quite involved uses the neurotransmitter norepinephrine. Electrical stimulation along this pathway is usually rewarding, and drugs that affect the neurotransmitter usually affect motivation as well. However, the brain uses many neurotransmitters, and it is unlikely that only one is involved in anything as important as reward. For example, **dopamine,** *a close chemical relative of norepinephrine,* has been implicated in the brain's reward system. The pathways in the brain that seem to be most rewarding for electrical stimulation are rich in neurons that use norepinephrine as well as dopamine (Olds and Fobes, 1981).

The way in which the brain's reward system works is still very mysterious. In some instances, its activation reduces drive; in others it increases it. In human beings, electrical stimulation of rewarding brain areas evokes quite a variety of sensations. One patient reported, "I have a glowing feeling . . . I feel good" (Heath, 1964). Another kept pressing a button to stimulate his own brain because each shot of ESB produced a vague memory. He wanted to know more about the memory and bring it into clearer focus, as he kept pressing the button. There is still much to learn about this important brain system, particularly the way it might operate in human beings.

GUIDED REVIEW

Learning Objectives 1, 2, and 3

1. The study of motivation explores the _____ of behavior, rather than the "how" or the "what."

2. The _____ of motivation proposes that organisms have certain needs, such as the need for food or water. When the organism is hungry, it enters a _____ in which it is motivated to action that will reduce the hunger drive. Motivation is the striving to maintain _____ , or balance, in the organism, by reducing drives. The behavior that the organism finally performs depends on the organism's _____ strengths, developed through learning.

3. The _____ theory of motivation takes into account the fact that people do not always seek to reduce their drives to the lowest possible level. They sometimes seek to _____ drive rather than reduce it.

4. The _____ points out the relationship between performance and arousal, and also the difficulty of the task. For a _____ task, a moderate level of arousal produces the best performance; high and low levels of arousal hinder performance. For easier tasks, _____ levels of arousal facilitate performance.

5. The _____ theory of motivation emphasizes the "pull" of goals in the motivation process, rather than the "push" of drives. Motivation is a function of both the attractiveness, or _____ , of the reward, and the _____ , or the likelihood that some behavior on the part of the organism will lead to the reward.

6. The _____ theory of motivation explains how motives are acquired. A stimulus triggers an _____ that diminishes with repeated presentations and a delayed and opposite _____ that strengthens over time.

7. The variety of human motives have been named and classified in many ways. A common scheme is Maslow's _____ , which lists five categories arranged in a pyramid.

8. The brain contains a _____ that functions in all kinds of motivated behaviors. Electrical brain stimulation of sites along the system is rewarding. The _____ norepinephrine and dopamine seem to be involved.

ANSWERS

1. "why." 2. drive reduction theory; drive state; homeostasis; habit 3. optimum level of arousal; increase 4. Yerkes-Dodson Law; difficult; higher 5. expectancy; valence; expectancy 6. opponent process; a-process; b-process 7. need heirarchy 8. reward system; neurotransmitters

Human Motives: Four Examples

The number of human motives is almost equal to the number of humans. As we saw in the last section, psychologists have attempted to classify these motives, using one scheme or another, into groups. Most scientists distinguish between primary and acquired motives, a distinction that separates motives based on biological needs from those based on learned needs. However, this separation is not always very clear and in some cases is quite arbitrary. The motive to quench thirst, for example, would seem to fall into the category of primary drive, and the body contains several controls to ensure that the drive for fluids is activated when supplies are low (see Research Box: Thirst). But learning plays a very large role in everyone's drinking behavior. Passing a cola vending machine or a soda shop might easily arouse one's drive for fluids well before any physiological regulatory mechanisms were activated.

Trying to categorize all motives as acquired or primary would involve us in a lengthy discussion of the relative contributions of heredity and environment in human behavior, a discussion we will take up in other chapters. For the moment, it is safe to say that some motives are mostly primary, others are mostly acquired, and many fall somewhere between the two extremes. In choosing the examples of motives for this section, we tried to select ones that covered this range. Our four examples are hunger, sex, sensation seeking, and the need for achievement.

Hunger

If you were to fast for a day, it is likely that your mind would be obsessed with thoughts of food by dinnertime. It might be difficult to concentrate on reading the newspaper because you keep noticing the ads for a new Greek restaurant, a cake sale at the local church, and the twelve-cents-off coupon for steak. You would experience how compelling the motive to eat can be.

Human beings have a failsafe mechanism for survival—if they do not get enough to eat, they begin to focus all their attention on food until their hunger is satisfied. The way this mechanism works, how it arouses the hunger drive, how it usually prevents overeating, and how it occasionally fails, have been the subject of a great deal of research. Scientists have been hunting for this mechanism, especially to find out why it fails and why so many people become overweight. They have actually been successful in finding not one mechanism, but many; and they keep finding more. Some of them are in the stomach, the intestines, the liver and other organs, and some are in the brain, mouth, and tongue.

Peripheral Controls. If you asked a person why he knew he was hungry, he would probably say that his stomach was growling. If you asked him why he stopped eating, he might say that it is because his stomach felt full. The stomach and its contractions certainly provide signals that tell you to start and stop eating, but they do not provide the only signals. For example, people whose stomachs have been removed continue to consume food and say they feel hungry, so messages about the need for food must come from other places as well.

Another signal seems to come from the intestinal tract. **CCK,** *which is a hormone released from the intestinal tract when the contents of the stomach pass into the small intestine, appears to provide one of the signals that says you have had enough to eat.* When animals are injected with CCK, they stop eating (Smith and Gibbs, 1976). Researchers became very interested in this substance because it might have been used as an effective diet aid; however, doses of CCK only inhibit eating for a short time. If the animal continues to receive injections, it goes back to eating normally after a few days (Mineka and Snowden, 1978). Apparently you can only fool the hunger system for a while. Since there are multiple controls over hunger and satiety, another one probably steps in and overrides the CCK signal.

RESEARCH BOX

Thirst

Without water, a human being will begin to die within a few days. The motivation to drink will be so compelling that the individual will be able to think of little else. The body contains elaborate regulatory mechanisms to control fluid balance and to ensure that the organism takes some action if the balance is disrupted (Fitzsimons, 1972).

The human body is made of more than half water, and this water is distributed into separate "compartments." About two-thirds of it is inside the cells of the body; another one-fourth is in the extracellular fluid, and the rest is in the blood plasma. The regulation of fluid balance not only involves making sure the body contains enough water; it also requires that the fluid is properly distributed among these compartments. For example, if the amount of fluid in the blood plasma drops too far, blood pressure may fall to a dangerously low level.

Experiments that artificially reduce the amount of water in one of these compartments, without affecting any of the others, have shown that the body has several different mechanisms to regulate fluid balance. For instance, it is possible to reduce the amount of fluid in the extracellular fluid of rats by injecting a colloid, or gluelike substance, into their abdominal cavities. The colloid absorbs water from the extracellular fluid without actually affecting intracellular water or the total amount of water in the animal's body. Within a short time these rats become thirsty and begin drinking to replace the water taken from the extracellular fluid (Fitzsimons, 1961).

Another way to produce thirst is to draw water out of the cells rather than the extracellular fluid. This can be done experimentally by an injection of water with a high quantity of salt. The sodium cannot get into the cells, so water is drawn out of the cells to dilute the salty extracellular fluid. This also causes the animal to drink, even though again, its total quantity of water did not change.

The body contains several kinds of detectors involved in fluid balance—some detect changes in blood pressure, and others detect substances that the kidneys release during a period of water imbalance. Still others appear to detect a deficiency of sodium, the substance that is so critically involved in the maintenance of water balance in the body (Stricker, 1980). The control of fluid balance is extremely complicated and not well understood, but it is clear that the body contains many redundant mechanisms to cope with and prevent dehydration. In fact, most animals, and people as well, never get particularly thirsty. They anticipate their future water needs and drink *before* their bodies become dehydrated.

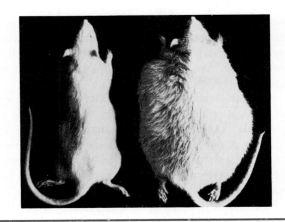

Figure 8.4 *A normal rat and a rat that has been made obese by lesions in the ventromedial hypothalamus*

The liver also plays an important role in hunger by monitoring and filtering the blood so that it always contains the correct amount of nutrients, including glucose and proteins. To accomplish this vital task, the liver has **glucoreceptors,** *that monitor glucose levels in the blood.* If the blood contains too much, perhaps because you have just finished a meal and the circulatory system has absorbed many nutrients, the liver stores the excess. These fascinating glucoreceptors were first discovered in experiments on dogs. An injection of glucose directly into the vein that carries blood from the intestines to the liver caused the hungry dog to stop eating for quite a while (Russek, 1975). The liver's main role then, is to monitor the body's fuel supply, particularly to signal satiety.

The Brain's Role in Hunger.   Figure 8.4 shows an obese rat. In slightly more than one month, this rat nearly doubled its body weight, going from a slim 200 grams to almost 400. In human terms, this would be equivalent to a normal-sized person gaining 150 pounds in four weeks. What happened to make this rat so fat?

The rat became a voracious eater about one week after its **ventromedial hypothalamus (VMH)** had been destroyed. *A lesion in this tiny part of the brain results in a dramatic increase in food consumption.* Scientists speculated that the neural activity in the VMH might be involved in satiety. Without this brain area, rats simply could not stop eating (Brobeck, et al., 1943).

If the VMH might be involved in satiety, then the **lateral hypothalamus (LH)** might be involved in hunger. *Lesions in this brain area, which is right next to the VMH, cause an animal to hardly eat at all.* In fact, it must be forcefed to survive. Perhaps brain activity in the LH triggers hunger, and without the LH the animal simply never feels hungry.

Further support for the complementary roles of the LH and VMH came from electrical stimulation studies. Stimulation of the LH led to feeding in rats, whereas stimulation of the VMH caused animals to stop eating.

The discovery of the effects of lesions in the VMH and LH was an important breakthrough in psychology. As is usually the case, however, the more we learned about these two syndromes, the more confused the story became. For example, animals with VMH lesions overeat if food is easily available, but under many testing conditions they will not work very hard for their food. In fact, they will lose weight if they have to do anything too strenuous to obtain their huge portions. Normal rats, on the other hand, will work quite hard to obtain a reasonable number of calories for the day. VMH lesioned rats are also very finicky about the taste of their food. They readily eat chocolate cookies but refuse any food that tastes a little bitter. Thus, they were not simply very hungry. A hungry rat works very hard to get food and will eat even foul-tasting rat food to maintain its body weight. These findings were puzzling and suggested that the whole story was not yet told.

In addition to the hypothesis that lesions in the VMH produce obesity by destroying the "satiety" center, others have been proposed. One suggests that the lesions damaged parts of the animal's reward system, the brain mechanism that underlies all different kinds of motivation discussed earlier (Powley, 1977). The damage might enhance the rewarding value of food, causing the animal to overeat. This explanation might also help us understand why the animal with a lesion in the LH refuses food. Another proposal suggests that the lesions alter metabolism so that fat tissue continues to absorb nutrients, and the animal has to overeat to maintain its energy balance (Friedman and Stricker, 1976). Perhaps both explanations are at least partly correct.

Obesity. According to the *Guinness Book of World Records,* Robert Earl Hughes weighed 1041 pounds when he died at the early age of 32. Clearly, whatever signals the brain or the body uses to stop eating were not working in his case. Despite our progress in understanding these signals, we know very little about how to control obesity. If we did, Americans would not be spending billions of dollars each year on diet books, low-calorie foods, weight-loss programs, and diet drugs.

Attempts to find a single cause of obesity have met with failure. Obesity is not a single disorder, and it is not likely to have a single cause. The chubby baby, the woman who fails to return to normal weight after pregnancy, the overweight executive, and the sumo wrestler all have overweight in common, but the causes are probably quite different.

Some of the factors that explain why people get fat include genetic predisposition, hormonal imbalance, too many fat cells in the body, improper eating habits, boredom, and even viral infections (Lyons, et al., 1982). One recent theory, called the **emotional arousal theory (EAT)**, *proposes that overeating is an instrumentally conditioned behavior that serves to reduce anxiety in the obese* (Leon and Roth, 1977). Some studies of obese people under stress have supported this hypothesis (e.g.,

Pine, 1985; McKenna, 1972). Animals, too, seem to react to stress by overeating. For example, rats that were stressed every day by mild pinches on the tail increased their food intake considerably (Rowland and Antelman, 1976).

Another popular theory maintains that people who become obese are those who rely too heavily on external cues, such as the taste of food or the time of day, to decide when it is time to eat. In contrast, people who can maintain a normal weight rely more on internal cues, such as stomach pangs, to decide when and how much to eat.

In one study, overweight and normal-weight subjects were brought into the laboratory near the dinner hour, ostensibly to participate in an experiment on personality. While they were filling out some bogus questionnaires, they were offered crackers. For half the obese and half the normal subjects, there was a clock in the testing room that was deliberately set to run fast. For these subjects, the dinner hour approached more quickly than normal. When it was actually around 5:30, the subjects' clock read 6:00. For the other half of each group, the clock was set to run very slowly, so 6:00 came and went while the clock was still reading around 5:30. The experiment was really designed to find out how many crackers each group of subjects would consume (Schacter and Gross, 1968; Schachter, 1971). The obese subjects ate more crackers when they thought it was the dinner hour, even though it was not. The subjects of normal weight, however, ate more crackers when it actually was the dinner hour, even though they thought it was not. The obese subjects seemed to be relying on the clock to trigger eating, while those of normal weight were probably relying on internal cues.

The reliance on external cues seems to be a cause of overeating, rather than an effect. At the beginning of a summer camp, a group of normal-weight girls were tested to see how responsive they were to external and internal cues (Rodin and Slochower, 1976). Candy, cakes, and other good-tasting treats were easily available at the camp. At the end of eight weeks, the girls were weighed. Those girls who were most responsive to external cues at the beginning of the summer were the ones who gained the most weight.

Unfortunately, no one knows why some of these children were more responsive to external cues. Perhaps there is some genetic predisposition involved, or perhaps they learned it at an early age. A baby who is fed on a rigid four-hour schedule might learn to ignore hunger cues that come at other times and instead rely more on the external cues, such as the sight of the bottle, to trigger hunger and feeding. A baby fed on demand might learn to rely more on internal cues.

Obesity is not a simple problem, however, and studies trying to find differences between overweight and normal-weight subjects in their responses to external cues have not always been successful (Rodin, 1981). There are some obese people who rely very much on internal cues, and there are some thin people who rely completely on the taste of food or the time of day to trigger eating. Clearly, obesity has many causes, and an overreliance on external eating cues may be just one of them.

Although it is not always clear why a person becomes fat, it is a little clearer why he stays fat. First, the larger a fat cell becomes, the more easily it can store more and more fat. Thus the fat person, who already has more fat cells, can put on weight more easily than the thin person. Second, obese people usually have higher levels of a hormone from the pancreas, called insulin, that is needed to allow glucose to enter cells. This means that the storage of fat is more efficient in the fat person. Higher insulin levels also produce a higher level of hunger, so the fat person feels hungrier most of the time.

A third reason fat people stay fat is that whenever they try to diet, they are fighting their own **setpoint,** *which is the weight that a person can maintain effortlessly, without dieting* (Bennett and Gurin, 1982). The body automatically feels hungry when weight drops below this setpoint. When weight surpasses the setpoint, the person feels less hungry and eats less, and his

or her weight drops back. Unfortunately, a person's setpoint may not equal ideal weight, and it rarely equals that of a fashion model.

Going on a diet is really an attempt to get below the setpoint, and the body responds as though it were in a state of starvation. Metabolism drops to conserve energy, hunger increases, and physical exercise is avoided. The person may lose weight rapidly during the first few days of a diet, but as soon as these mechanisms to counteract starvation are activated, it becomes more and more difficult to lose each pound. Even though the person may consume only a few hundred calories a day, the weight loss may be very small. The feeling of hunger will persist, not only as long as the diet lasts, but until the person's weight goes back up to its setpoint. This may explain why so many people lose weight but so few keep it off. The most effective way to lose weight permanently is probably to change the setpoint. Unfortunately, no one knows how to do that.

This may be gloomy news for people who want to be thinner. But the picture may not be entirely dark. Frequent physical exercise seems to be a promising way to change the body's setpoint. Also, recent studies have found specific receptors in the brain that are related to appetite and are clearly affected by amphetamine, a drug that depresses appetite (Paul, Hulihan-Giblin, and Skolnick, 1982). There is strong hope that scientists can now produce drugs that block these receptors in the way amphetamines do but that do not have the same hazardous side effects, especially the production of tolerance.

A person's attitude also seems to be a key ingredient in whether or not he will lose weight. In one study, people's answers to a question about the likelihood that they would lose weight over the next six weeks turned out to be the best predictor of their success (Schifter and Ajzen, 1985).

Psychologists may have an overpessimistic view of weight-loss programs, according to one scientist (Schacter, 1982). Clinicians tend to see only those obese people who seek treatment, not the ones who succeeded on their own. Also, clinical psychologists often only see the patient make a single attempt. Interviews with a wide range of people revealed that around sixty percent of those who had been obese at one time in their lives were now at a normal weight, thanks to their own persistent attempts at weight loss.

Sex

The human sex drive is one of the most complicated motives we have. It is influenced by biological, psychological, sociological, and cultural factors. As we mentioned earlier, it is usually called a primary drive because the species would die out if it did not exist. As far as we know, however, an individual suffers no physical problems from abstention.

Biological Influences. In the lower animals, hormones are the most important factor regulating sexual behavior. **Estrogen** and **progesterone** *are the sex hormones released by the female's ovaries,* and **androgens** *are the sex hormones released by the male's testes.* The mating behavior of animals like the rat or the mouse, for example, is very closely tied to the levels of these hormones circulating in the blood. If the male rat's testes are removed so that no androgens are released, the animal will stop mating, usually within a few weeks, although a few continue to show sexual behavior for several months (Davidson, 1966). If the animal is later given injections of **testosterone,** *one of the important androgens,* its sexual behavior will return.

The sex behavior of some animals with normal levels of circulating androgen can be increased by adding hormones. Normal male rats given testosterone show more intense sex behavior than is normal by some measures. For example, they tend to ejaculate more quickly after the mating sequence is begun (Beach, 1942; Cheng and Casida, 1949).

In female animals, the role of hormones is equally important. Unlike humans, female rats are sexually receptive only at the time at which mating would most likely result in pregnancy. The fluctuation in the female's receptivity is controlled by the changing levels of estrogen and progesterone in the female's bloodstream. Removal of the source of these hormones eventually causes the animal to lose interest in sex behavior. Also, replacement of the hormones through an appropriate sequence of injections will result in the reappearance of typical mating responses.

In human males, the relationship between hormones, sex behavior, and sex drive is similar but less direct. When men lose their testes for one reason or another, perhaps through accident or disease, some lose their potency almost immediately, and others show a gradual decline over a period of years. Once they begin hormone replacement therapy, their sex drive and sex behavior return (Money and Ehrhardt, 1972). Thus, the presence or absence of the hormone is related to the presence or absence of sex drive and sex behavior in men.

Whether smaller fluctuations in testosterone level have any influence on the sex behavior of a man from day to day is a very difficult question to answer. Testosterone levels do vary from one day to the next, often in response to stressful situations. For example, the stress of war seems to lower testosterone levels in troops (Rose, Bourne, Poe, Mougey, Collins, and Mason, 1969). Also, testosterone levels appear to be affected by the anticipation of sex. Men who know they are about to leave an isolated Arctic military base sometimes report that their beards start growing faster, a sign of increased testosterone production. In monkeys, testosterone levels appear to be related to dominance level in the group. One study found that the monkeys that became dominant in a newly formed group showed remarkable increases—as much as 238 percent—in their testosterone levels (Rose, et al., 1975). The testosterone levels decreased in the monkeys that became subordinate.

Despite these fluctuations in hormone levels, investigators have not been able to find any clear relationship between the amount of hormone circulating in a human male's bloodstream and the intensity of his sex drive or amount of his sex behavior. It seems that men require a minimum amount of male sex hormone for normal sex behavior; once the man has this amount, fluctuations in his sex drive or behavior are due more to psychological factors than to biological ones.

The role of hormones in the sex behavior of women is much less direct than it is in men. Women show sex drive and sexual behavior throughout their entire menstrual cycle, demonstrating that the link between the levels of circulating estrogen and progesterone and sex behavior is very weak or nonexistent. Nevertheless, some scientists have reported survey data showing that women report more frequent sex behavior around the middle of their cycles—about the time when they would be ovulating (Hart, 1960; Udry and Morris, 1968). Others, however, have found evidence that there is a peak of sexual behavior around the time of menstruation rather than at midcycle (James, 1971; Spitz, Gold, and Adams, 1975). The controversy surrounding this topic is due to disagreements about the way survey data are interpreted and to the variability in the length of women's cycles.

When a woman loses her ovaries through surgery, she ordinarily experiences little or no change in sex drive. Although the loss of estrogen and progesterone probably will cause vaginal dryness and other physiological changes that may indirectly affect sexual behavior, she usually reports that her sex drive is just as strong as it was before the surgery. The loss of ovarian function after menopause also seems to have little or no effect on sex drive in women (Kinsey, et al., 1953). This adds further weight to the hypothesis that the relationship between sex drive and ovarian hormones is either very weak or nonexistent, and quite different from the relationship between sex drive and testicular hormones in men.

Some research suggests that sex drive in women is related to the presence of low levels of androgen, probably released by the adrenal glands. For example, injections of testosterone increase sexual interest in some women (Salmon and Geist, 1943; Bancroft and Skakkebaek, 1978). This treatment, however, has to be conducted very cautiously because of its masculinizing side effects.

Psychological Influences on Sex Behavior and Sex Roles. Individuals are treated differently from the day they are born, depending on whether they are male or female. They learn their **sex roles,** *or the attitudes and behaviors believed by their culture to be appropriate for each sex.* Even children as young as eighteen months begin to show a great deal of interest in play usually considered appropriate for their own sex. Researchers observing toddlers in their homes note that girls are more likely to play with soft toys, dolls, and dress-up clothes, whereas boys play more often with blocks, trucks and cars, and toys that require some form of manipulation (Fagot, 1974).

By the time people reach adulthood they have developed clear pictures of what it means to be a man or a woman as defined by their society, and these images have important effects on their sex behavior. Our culture's definition of a man usually includes traits like "aggressive, ambitious, willing to take risks." Adjectives like "emotional, passive, dependent, and affectionate" are usually applied more frequently to women. These expectations about the behavior of men and women can have effects on sex behavior and attitudes toward sexuality.

Attitudes toward premarital sex, for example, are quite different among adolescent girls and boys. According to one survey (Sorensen, 1973), girls attached less importance to their first experience of intercourse than the boys did. However, the girls were more likely to experience negative reactions such as fear, guilt, sorrow, and disappointment. The boys tended to feel a sense of maturity and excitement.

Since the beginning of the twentieth century, attitudes toward sex have changed considerably. The changes have been reflected in the way people respond to the many surveys conducted about sexual attitudes and practices (Sorensen, 1973; Hunt, 1974; Glen and Weaver, 1979; Kinsey, et al., 1953). What is most clear from these surveys is that people's attitudes toward sex change more quickly than their actual sexual behavior. For example, the question, "Do you think it is all right for either or both parties to a marriage to have had previous sexual intercourse?" was asked of people in the 1930s, the 1950s, and in the 1970s. For the surveys conducted in the thirties and fifties, about twenty-two percent of the respondents said that premarital sex was acceptable for both men and women. In the seventies, well over two-thirds of the respondents said it was acceptable. It is interesting that the double standard for men and for women present in the thirties' and fifties' survey was still in evidence in the seventies. In general, more people approve of premarital sex for men than for women.

Although attitudes about sex may have changed considerably over the past decades, sexual behavior has changed more gradually. According to the surveys, the age at the time of first intercourse has been declining. In the 1940s and 1950s, about seventy percent of the men reported having had premarital sex, compared to thirty-three percent of the women. In the seventies, these percentages increased to ninety-seven percent and sixty-seven percent. But this increase really doesn't indicate a dramatic departure from the sexual standards of the past (Perlman and Cozby, 1983). Most of the women who engage in premarital sex, for example, have only one partner, whom they eventually marry. Men have an average of six partners (Hunt, 1974).

Cultural Influences on Sexual Behavior.   There are cultures in which nearly every form of what Americans would consider sexual excess or deviance is accepted, and may even be expected. Among the Gusii of southwestern Kenya, for example, hostility and humiliation are normal features of sexual activity. A Gusii man believes that he must overcome the woman's natural resistance and cause her some form of physical pain and humiliation (Davenport, 1977).

In other cultures, sex is clearly associated with pleasure. In Mangaia, one of the Cook Islands of Polynesia, premarital intercourse is strongly encouraged for both sexes. Men are expected to express their virility by experiencing many successive orgasms. Even though sexuality is assumed to be stronger in men than in women, women are expected to be eager and active sex partners. Romantic love is not seen as a necessary part of a youthful heterosexual relationship. Affection is thought to develop out of satisfactory sexual relations; love is expected to grow much later as sexual appetite declines.

One of the major generalizations that emerges from studies of sex behavior in different cultures is that all societies regulate sexuality in some way. The nature of the regulations vary from culture to culture, but apparently sex is so important to the survival of the species that all societies have developed regulatory mechanisms. In a classic survey of sexual attitudes and practices in different cultures, Clellan Ford and Frank Beach (1951) concluded that the American culture was one of the more restrictive ones. However, the changes that have taken place during the years since they conducted their survey probably have made the United States one of the more permissive societies, in terms of sexual attitudes and practices.

Sensation Seeking

Climbing mountains, taking drugs, and trying new sexual experiences are all characteristic of people who are seeking sensations. This motive is a fascinating one that is part curiosity, part thrill-seeking, and part adventure. **Sensation seeking** *refers to the need for varied, novel, and intense forms of stimulation and experience.* Studies on this motive are trying to explain why human beings do so many "crazy" things that sometimes conflict with the motive for personal survival.

Low and High Sensation Seekers.   Not everyone finds rappelling off a mountain an exhilarating experience. People differ considerably in the extent to which the sensation-seeking motive drives their behavior. Marvin Zuckerman and his colleagues (Zuckerman, 1979) devised the **Sensation Seeking Scale,** *which measures how*

Table 8.1 A portion of the sensation seeking scale

Sensation seeking scale—form I

Interest and preference test form I

Directions: Each of the items below contains two choices, A and B. Please indicate *on your answer sheet* which of the choices most describes *your likes* or the way *you feel.* In some cases you may find items in which both choices describe your likes or the way you feel. Please choose the one which better describes your likes or feelings. In some cases you may find items in which you do not like either choice. In these cases mark the choice you dislike *least.*

It is important you respond to *all items* with only *one choice,* A or B. We are interested only in *your likes or feelings,* not in how others feel about these things or how one is supposed to feel. There are no right or wrong answers as in other kinds of tests. Be frank and give your honest appraisal of yourself.

1. A. I like the tumult of sounds in a busy city.
   B. I prefer the peace and quiet of the country.
2. A. I prefer my meals at regular times.
   B. I like to eat when the mood strikes me.
3. A. I dislike the sensations one gets when flying.
   B. I enjoy many of the rides in amusement parks.
4. A. I would like a job which would require a lot of traveling.
   B. I would prefer a job in one location.
5. A. I do not find gambling worth the risk.
   B. I like to gamble for money.
6. A. I am invigorated by a brisk, cold day.
   B. I can't wait to get into the indoors on a cold day.
7. A. I like a lively party with a lot of people and noise.
   B. I prefer a quiet party where I can relax and converse with a few friends.
8. A. I find a certain pleasure in routine kinds of work.
   B. Although it is sometimes necessary, I usually dislike routine kinds of work.
9. A. I often wish I could be a mountain climber.
   B. I can't understand people who risk their necks climbing mountains.
10. A. I dislike all body odors.
    B. I like some of the earthy body smells.
11. A. I get bored seeing the same old faces.
    B. I like the comfortable familiarity of everyday friends.
12. A. Society should maximize the individual's freedom and opportunity for the "pursuit of happiness."
    B. Society should protect mankind from all extremes of hunger, fear and insecurity.

From Zuckerman, M., Sensation Seeking: Beyond the Optimal Level of Arousal. *Copyright © 1979 by Lawrence Erlbaum Associates, Inc. Reprinted by permission.*

important sensation seeking is in a person's life. Some of the items on the scale are shown in table 8.1. The test measures four different aspects of the sensation-seeking motive: thrill and adventure seeking, experience seeking, disinhibition, and susceptibility to boredom. Questions in the first two categories try to determine how much the person needs risky adventures or novel experiences. Questions relating to disinhibition refer to an individual's motive to behave in an uninhibited way and to seek experiences that break or bend social rules. One item, for example, states, "I often like to get high (drinking liquor or smoking marijuana)." The last group of questions tries to determine how easily the person is bored and how upset the person gets by boredom.

People who score high on this scale are quite different from those who score low. High scorers are more likely to be male, and they are also more likely to be in their late teens. As people get older, the motive to seek sensations becomes less compelling. Not surprisingly, high sensation seekers differ from low sensation seekers in their behavior as well; high sensation seekers tend to engage in riskier sports like parachuting and scuba diving, and they like the idea of traveling to exotic places. They are drawn to gambling, prefer higher odds, and make bigger bets. They are also more likely to volunteer for psychology experiments, particularly those that promise a little excitement. For example, they volunteer more readily for experiments involving hypnosis, sensory deprivation, and drug taking, but not for experiments that require subjects to learn lists of nonsense syllables. This finding is particularly unnerving to psychologists who seek volunteers for their research because it may mean that they are testing a biased sample.

Why Seek Sensation?   It is not too difficult to see why curiosity in an animal could be necessary for its survival. Acquiring information about the environment in which one lives is not an idle and worthless pastime; it is one that might easily be considered a primary motive. An animal's curiosity can help it to find out about hiding places, food sources, shelter, and the location of prey. Such information may become vital in the animal's future. Sensation seeking goes beyond mere curiosity, however; it is a search for novel, varied, and exciting experiences. The sensation-seeking motive is so strong in some humans that it sometimes conflicts with the motive to stay alive.

One way to understand the motive of sensation seeking is to use the opponent process theory of acquired motivation described earlier. For example, how can we explain why a person seeks out skydiving? During the first free-fall, parachutists may experience terror: their eyes may bulge, their lips may retract, and they may even experience involuntary urination. After landing, the jumpers may look stunned and dazed for a few minutes, but then they may begin lively chatter with the other jumpers. After several jumps, the a-process of terror diminishes while the b-process of relief grows. Now the parachutists experience thrill during the jump and extreme exhilaration afterwards. Some parachutists claim this "high" lasts as long as eight hours (Epstein, 1967; Solomon, 1980). The increase in strength of the opponent b-process is the key to the acquired motivation. It offers a good explanation for why a person might come to exhibit some rather dangerous acquired motives.

Another approach that may help us understand the sensation-seeking motive is to look at it in terms of the optimal level of arousal theory. As we discussed earlier, this theory predicts that a person will not necessarily strive to reduce arousal by satisfying drives but will seek the optimum level of arousal. For high sensation seekers, that level might be quite high.

A test of this hypothesis examined people's physiological responses to a novel stimulus (Neary and Zuckerman, 1976). Both high and low sensation seekers wore earphones while a tone was presented over and over, for ten trials. On the eleventh trial a different sound was presented to test the subjects' reactions to a novel auditory stimulus. During all the trials, the experimenters recorded the subjects' **galvanic skin response (GSR),** *which is a measure of activity in the autonomic nervous system. When the sympathetic division of the autonomic nervous system is activated by some stressor, one of the responses is increased sweating in the hands and feet. The GSR is a measure of this increased sweat-gland secretion.*

The high sensation seekers tended to show a large GSR response the first time they heard the tone and also when they heard the novel tone in the eleventh trial. They reacted more strongly to novelty than did the low sensation seekers; however, after hearing the first tone once, their autonomic arousal dropped down to about the same level as that of the low sensation seekers. This study shows that the high sensation seekers are more easily aroused by novelty, but they do not necessarily have a higher baseline level of arousal.

This finding presents a problem with respect to the optimum level of arousal theory. Perhaps the term "arousal" is just too general, and the sensation seekers are not seeking an overall higher level. They seem instead to be seeking new sensations that are pleasurable, not annoying or irritating. Zuckerman's (1979) new theory takes this into account. He proposes that high sensation seekers have a more active and more efficient general reward system in their brains, made so partly by greater activity at those norepinephrine synapses we mentioned earlier. As a result of the greater activity in the reward pathways, the person is peculiarly responsive to novel stimulation and also especially alert to it. Zuckerman supposes that whether a person is high or low on the sensation-seeking motive depends to a considerable extent on such biological factors, some of which may have a genetic component.

The Need for Achievement

When John Opel began doing well in business, he did very well. In 1981 he became the chief executive officer of IBM. When a hometown reporter asked Opel's father what he thought of John's success, he replied, "I always knew Johnny was a good boy" (Stacks, 1983).

The **need for achievement** or **n Ach** *involves the desire to independently master objects, ideas, and other people, and to increase one's self-esteem through the exercise of one's talent.* Opel's father equated John's remarkable achievements in the business world with being "good." A father whose child chooses a less achievement-oriented path might supply a less desirable label, such as "bum."

Research on the need for achievement has focused on many different aspects of the motive. Early research investigated individual differences in both the strength and the characteristics of the motive as well as the measurement of those differences.

Measuring n Ach.   The **Thematic Apperception Test,** or **TAT,** *is one of the more common tests used to measure motivation, including the need for achievement* (Murray, 1938). The theory behind this test is that an individual's fantasies and dreams can reveal a great deal about a person's motives. An experimenter shows a subject a picture containing ambiguous figures, and the subject makes up an imaginative story about what is happening. Below is a story about a picture showing a boy with a vague operation scene in the background. The story was scored high in n Ach. Notice that it contains imagery relating to achievement, and especially long-term involvements.

> The boy is thinking about a career as a doctor. He sees himself as a great surgeon performing an operation. He has been doing minor first aid work on his injured dog, and discovers he is suited for this profession and sets it as an ultimate goal in life at this moment. He has not weighed the pros and cons of his own ability and has let his goal blind him of his own inability. An adjustment which will injure him will have to be made. (McClelland, et al., 1953)

In contrast, following is a story that was scored low in n Ach because it contains little achievement-oriented imagery:

> Young fellow is showing anxiety toward impending operation.
> Some malady has been diagnosed.
> The doctor has prescribed an operation to remove the source of illness and the boy wonders about the advisability of such a plan.
> The operation will be performed and successfully. (McClelland, et al., 1953)

The TAT is also used extensively as a tool to assess personality. We discuss the TAT and other measures in Chapter 11.

High and Low n Ach. People who score high in n Ach on the TAT and other tests tend to behave much differently than do those who score low. For example, high n Ach scorers are more likely to become entrepreneurs or to do well in business. The choice of tasks in an experimental situation is also related to a person's n Ach score. In a well-known experimental game, subjects are asked to toss rings at a vertical post for money (Atkinson and Litwin, 1960). They can choose how far they wish to stand from the post, and their choice affects the monetary payoffs for each successful toss. If they stand very close to the post, their chance for success is of course very high, but the payoff is low. If they stand far away, the chance for success is very low but the reward is much greater. High n Ach people tend to choose an intermediate spot; those people lower in n Ach tend to choose locations either close to the post or very far away. In one study (Hamilton, 1974), the high n Ach subjects chose distances that made their likelihood for success about 0.4. Low and moderate n Ach subjects chose distances that resulted in success probabilities that were either very high or very low.

Studies like the ones using the ring-toss game suggest that people high in n Ach are not gamblers. They focus their attention on tasks that are challenging but that allow a fair chance of success based on the subject's own abilities. They seem to be driven more by a motive to seek success rather than one to avoid failure. They are also more persistent on difficult tasks (e.g., Feather, 1962).

As research on achievement motivation progressed, it became clear that the motive was a very dynamic one. People high in n Ach behave differently in different situations, and low n Ach people sometimes show remarkable needs for achievement. The interaction between the situation and the personality of the person in determining how much achievement motivation might be demonstrated has received a great deal of attention. According to earlier theorists (McClelland, et al., 1953; Atkinson and Feather, 1966) the expression of the achievement motive in any particular situation depends on several factors, including (1) the person's expectation of success in the situation, (2) the value the individual places on the reward being offered, and (3) the individual's perception of how instrumental his or her own behavior will be in bringing about success. (You may notice that there is a certain similarity between these three factors and the concepts of valence and expectancy, which were discussed earlier in this chapter.)

The theory is not without its critics. In particular, many scientists question the reliability of the TAT testing method. The tests may be good at assessing n Ach in white American middle-class males, but they seem to be much less useful for other groups, such as women and blacks. One study, for example, found that women whose stories about pictures of men were scored high in n Ach, but whose stories about pictures of women were scored low in n Ach, tended to be underachievers (Lesser, et al., 1963). Also, critics argue that achievement-motivation theory has focused too heavily on personality and not enough on the situation (Maehr and Nicholls, 1980).

Studies of achievement motivation are now taking new directions. Scientists are questioning the influence of culture on achievement motivation. The traditional approach to achievement motivation emphasized challenges, goal setting, risk taking, delay of gratification, and other variables that seem to reveal a bias toward the Protestant work ethic and American notions of "good." People in other cultures may be motivated to achieve in ways very different from ours. Another new direction involves the study of changes in achievement motivation through the life span. Studies have found that older men have lower n Ach scores than younger men (Veroff, Atkinson, Feld, and Gurin, 1960). But is this finding another artifact of the bias of the test? Perhaps older people seek different ways of achieving, ones that stress internal rewards rather than prestige and success (Maehr, 1974; Maehr and Kleiber, 1981).

GUIDED REVIEW

Learning Objectives 4, 5, 6, and 7

1. The motivation to eat is controlled by multiple biological and psychological factors. Signals from the stomach signal both hunger and satiety, and a hormone from the digestive tract, called _____ , also signals satiety. The liver contains _____ , which monitor glucose levels.

2. Lesions of the _____ produce overeating and obesity; lesions in the nearby _____ cause an animal to stop eating altogether. These brain areas are involved in hunger and satiety, but they cannot be called "feeding" or "satiety centers." Damage to these brain areas may interfere with food intake by damaging the brain's reward system.

3. Obesity has multiple causes, one of which may be stress. Another may be an overreliance on _____ to trigger eating, such as the time of day, rather than internal cues such as stomach contractions. Once a person becomes obese, it is very difficult to lose weight because the body's weight _____ is set at a higher level.

4. The human _____ is influenced by a combination of biological, psychological, and cultural factors. In lower animals, biological factors are most important, especially the ovarian hormones _____ and _____ in females and the testicular hormones called _____ in the male.

5. A minimum amount of male sex hormone is required for normal sexual behavior in men. Loss of the _____ will result in the loss of sex drive and behavior. However, day-to-day fluctuations in the level of circulating _____ are not related to changes in sex drive or behavior.

6. In women, changes in the level of _____ hormones do not appreciably affect sex drive or behavior. However, sex drive in women is affected by _____ , probably from the woman's adrenal gland.

7. One of the main psychological influences on sex behavior involves the acquisition of _____ , the expectations and behaviors believed to be appropriate for each sex by the individual's culture.

8. Although _____ about sex behavior have become increasingly permissive over the last fifty years, actual sexual practices have changed more slowly.

9. _____ vary widely in their attitudes toward sexual behavior, but all cultures regulate it in some way.

10. Another human motive is _____ , which means that a person seeks novel, varied, and intense forms of stimulation and experience. Low and high sensation seekers score very differently on the _____ , which is designed to measure this motive.

11. Attempts to explain the sensation-seeking motive include the _____ theory of motivation and the _____ theory. Another hypothesis suggests that the motive may be related to the activity of the _____ in the brain.

12. The need to achieve is sometimes measured by the _____ . High n Ach people are persistent and tend to seek challenges of intermediate difficulty in which their chance of success is fair and in which their own behavior is instrumental in obtaining the reward. Critics of the conclusions drawn from achievement motivation research argue that the TAT is biased and unreliable and that the effects of environmental factors, such as culture, have not received enough attention.

ANSWERS

1. CCK; glucoreceptors 2. ventromedial hypothalamus; lateral hypothalamus 3. external cues; setpoint 4. sex drive; estrogen; progesterone; androgens 5. testes; testosterone 6. ovarian; androgens 7. sex roles 8. attitudes 9. Cultures 10. sensation seeking; Sensation Seeking Scale 11. opponent process; optimum level of arousal; reward system 12. Thematic Apperception Test

Emotions

Emotions may be the most potent motivators of all. We can get into fights because we are angry, risk our lives for love, stop eating because of grief, and jump (as the old cliché tells us) for sheer joy. Emotions can also be the goal of motivated behavior. We might carefully plan a vacation to experience happiness and relaxation or go to a horror movie seeking to experience fear. Avoiding emotions, particularly very severe and unpleasant ones, might also be a goal. According to the Food and Drug Administration, Americans take about five billion tranquilizers every year in an attempt to avoid anxiety, depression, or pain. And the United States military took special steps during the Korean and Vietnam Wars to help people avoid the severe emotional reaction called battle fatigue, described in the Application Box: Battle Fatigue.

Finally, emotions may just accompany motivated behavior. Pleasure for example, is not just a goal of sexual arousal. It also accompanies it. The relationship between motivation and emotion is a very complex one and still is not well understood. Nevertheless, no one would deny that emotions are extremely important to human beings.

Describing Emotions

The definition of the term *emotion* varies, depending on who is defining it, as we see when we discuss the various theories of emotion. As a starting point, however, we can say that an **emotion** *is a complex reaction with two main components. One component involves a series of physiological changes; the other is a subjective experience or "feeling."*

The dictionary lists literally thousands of words that have some emotional content (see fig. 8.5). But are there thousands of different emotions? Many psychologists argue that there are only a few *primary emotions,* perhaps six to twelve. Silvan Tomkins (1981), for example, maintains that there are nine: interest,

abase	affectation
abash	affection
abhor	affinity
abysmal	afflict
acclaim	affright
accursed	affront
acerbity	afficionado
acquisitive	afoul
acrid	afraid
admire	agape
admonish	aggravate
adorable	aggress
adulate	aggrieve
adulterate	aghast
adventurer	agitate
adversary	agreeable
adversity	alack
aesthetic	alacrity
afeared	alarm
affect	alert

Figure 8.5   A partial list of words in the dictionary with emotional overtones

enjoyment, surprise, fear, anger, distress, shame, contempt, and disgust. Each of these primary emotions has its own underlying biological accompaniments in the form of facial expression, voice patterns, muscular changes, and brain activity.

Other psychologists see human emotions not as independent categories but as states that are more or less related to one another. Figure 8.6 shows a "circle of emotions" that suggests how different emotions are related. States opposite from one another on the wheel are also opposite emotions. Happy, for example, is the opposite of miserable, but is very closely related to delighted, pleased, and glad (Russell, 1980). This circle was designed by asking subjects to sort twenty-eight emotion-laden words into groups of four, seven, ten, and thirteen, based on similarity.

The two most important dimensions on which emotions seem to be categorized are the pleasantness of the emotion and the intensity of the arousal. These two di-

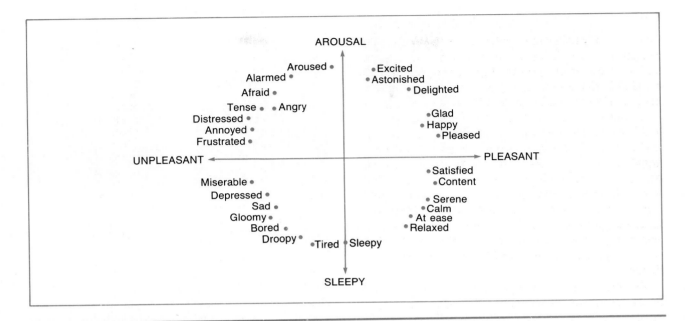

Figure 8.6   A circle of emotions

mensions are represented by the axes in figure 8.6. Alarmed and bored, for instance, have about the same degree of moderate unpleasantness, but they are very different in arousal. Serene and miserable are about equal in their arousal but are very different along the pleasantness dimension. Pleasantness and arousal seem to be the two critical factors that account for the way people categorize their emotions.

Expressing Emotions

Emotions are expressed in many ways: by what we say and how we say it, by our gestures and postures, and especially by our facial expressions. The facial expression of many emotions is remarkably similar in people from different cultures (fig. 8.7). All people smile when they are happy and frown when they are sad. People from widely different cultures usually have no trouble identifying the emotions expressed in photographs. Even people from remote tribes in New Guinea are able

to identify the emotional expressions in photographs of westerners (Ekman and Friesen, 1975). People appear to be able to make distinctions between facial expressions quite early, at least by five months of age (Schwartz, Izard, and Ansul, 1985), and adults do quite well at identifying the emotional expressions of infants, especially for expressions of joy, interest, distress, and surprise (Emde, et al., 1985). All this evidence supports the view that many facial expressions of emotion are universal in human beings and that they begin quite early in life, adding weight to the hypothesis that only a few primary emotions exist and that these have at least some biological basis.

Despite the overall universality in the facial expressions of emotions, cultural factors do appear to play a role. Sticking out your tongue, for example, usually means disgust to an American; to a Chinese it means surprise (Klineberg, 1938).

Figure 8.7 The facial expressions of many emotions are very similar and easily identified in different people.

Emotions are also communicated especially well through the nonverbal aspects of speech. Arousal is associated with increases in pitch, loudness, and rate of speech, whereas anger appears to be communicated by an even speech with occasional sharp increases in pitch and loudness. These cues are recognizable and used by people of different cultures, again suggesting a certain universality in emotional expression (Trick, 1985).

Measuring Emotions

Although it is fairly simple to tell what emotion a person is experiencing by looking at her face, it is not as simple to identify an emotional state by recording other physiological changes, such as heart rate or blood pressure. Many physiological changes are quite similar because intense emotion activates the sympathetic nervous system. Records of heart rate changes, blood pressure rises, sweat gland responses, or pupil dilations are not likely to reveal very much about which emotion the person is feeling. They will only tell you that the person is feeling some intense emotion.

The anatomical arrangement of the sympathetic nervous system explains why the physiological changes during an emotion are so global. A single signal from the brain sends out messages to all the organs and glands that are innervated by the sympathetic division. The signal is designed to prepare the body for an emergency. It does not single out individual organs or glands, speeding up their activity during some emotions and slowing them down during others.

Although many kinds of measurements do not reveal differences between the emotions, most scientists hypothesize that physiological differences do exist. It is most likely that these differences would be in places not so affected by the sympathetic nervous system, such as the brain or the facial muscles.

Emotions and the Brain.   Most of what we know about the relationship between emotional states and brain chemistry comes from studies of patients who are diagnosed as having either bipolar or unipolar affective disorders, formerly called manic-depression and depression. These disorders represent abnormal emotional states, not the normal ones most of us experience. Yet many scientists hypothesize that the brain mechanisms underlying them all share many characteristics.

The symptoms of unipolar affective disorder, discussed in more detail in Chapter 14, include depression, loss of appetite, loss of zest for living, sleeping

APPLICATION BOX

Battle Fatigue

A very extreme form of emotional reaction sometimes occurs in individuals involved in combat, usually after they have just completed a difficult mission. The military calls this reaction "battle fatigue." Initial symptoms include increased emotionality, irritability, sleep disturbances, and exaggerated startle responses. In some cases, soldiers may show severe tremors, muteness, hallucinations, hysterical blindness, stupor, or uncontrollable panic (Chermol, 1983).

The causes of battle fatigue are not very well understood, although most agree that it is the inevitable result of continual combat, rather than isolated cases of "nerves" in a few soldiers with previous personality problems. Statistics on the incidence of the problem show some interesting trends that indicate potential causes. For example, during World War II, armored divisions had the highest incidence of battle fatigue, and air crews had the lowest. The air crews, however, sustained higher battle casualty rates. Soldiers in armored divisions were probably more vulnerable to battle fatigue for a number of rea-

sons, including their long confinements inside tanks, their almost continual mobility, and particularly, their inability to take any personal action against threats in hazardous situations. Soldiers in armored divisions may develop greater feelings of helplessness than do air crews, thus increasing the risk of battle fatigue.

The air crews may have had fewer cases of battle fatigue for other reasons as well. They had more regular sleeping schedules, better nutrition, and more opportunities for recreation and rest between missions. Even though their casualty rates were higher, they felt themselves to be members of an elite group and had high morale and esprit de corps. The importance of morale is also demonstrated by the fact that volunteer infantry units, such as the paratroopers, had lower battle fatigue rates than nonvolunteer units, even though the former may have had higher casualty rates.

The treatment for battle fatigue varies, though the military generally tries to return the victim to his unit as quickly as possible. Infantrymen who

problems, irritability, and sometimes suicidal thoughts. All of us feel "blue" at one time or another, but unipolar affective disorder is much more serious. Although it might be triggered by a tragedy, it is much deeper and more severe than normal, and it lasts much longer. Also, it sometimes begins for no obvious reason at all. People with bipolar affective disorder have moods that swing back and forth between extremes. For some months they will show severe depression, and then,

within a period of a few days, switch to the other emotional extreme. During their manic phase, they will be excitable, energetic, talkative, and often in a very high mood.

One hypothesis that attempts to explain these moods suggests that they are related to levels of a group of related chemicals in the brain, one of which is norepinephrine (Schildkraut, 1974, 1978; Maas, 1978).

suffer battle fatigue, for example, might be treated right at the brigade clearing station. In severe cases, the victim might be returned to the division rear and treated by mental health officers or trained NCOs. About eighty or ninety percent of these people can be returned to their units within a few days. Those who do not recover may be evacuated to corps-level medical facilities, but this option is not a very desirable one. At least some of these patients exhibit long-term psychological problems partly *because* their symptoms caused them to be removed from combat. They apparently feel overwhelming guilt at having deserted their unit, and they try to justify their removal by unconsciously perpetuating their symptoms. Studies of motivation in combat usually point strongly to the importance of this kind of group loyalty in combat. It is not unusual for soldiers wounded in battle to return to their unit before they have recovered so they won't "let their buddies down."

Preventing battle fatigue is an issue of great concern to the military. Some of the recommended countermeasures include the following (Chermol, 1983):

1. Ensure that individuals involved in combat operations get adequate sleep.
2. Train soldiers to function in an NBC (nuclear, biological, chemical) warfare environment. Lack of knowledge about and confidence in safety equipment can be a major contributor to stress during combat.
3. Provide rigorous physical training programs during peacetime, since physically fit soldiers can tolerate stress better.
4. Provide accurate and timely information to troops; rumors and dishonesty will create more stress, particularly during a nuclear attack.
5. Establish the "buddy system" to help build cohesion; squad members can observe one another for signs of battle fatigue.

This is the same neurotransmitter that seems to be so important in the brain's reward system. It seems very logical that the pathways mediating reward and those mediating the emotions should overlap. High levels of norepinephrine in certain brain pathways lead to manic moods, and abnormally low levels lead to depressed moods.

Some evidence for this hypothesis comes from studies that measure the amounts of norepinephrine byproducts excreted in the urine. Patients with bipolar affective disorder usually show larger amounts of these byproducts when they are in their manic phase and less-than-normal amounts when they are in their depressed phase. This is less clear in unipolar patients; however, at least some of those patients have low levels of **MHPG**, *one of the important byproducts of norepinephrine.*

Drugs that affect norepinephrine also affect mood, adding further support to the hypothesis. Those that increase activity at norepinephrine synapses are often useful in treating unipolar affective disorder. They are especially useful in those patients who show low levels of norepinephrine byproducts in their urine. This finding suggests that there are many categories of patients who, on the surface, appear to have similar symptoms. Some have a decrease in activity in their norepinephrine pathways, and they will respond well to drugs that increase norepinephrine activity. Others, however, are depressed for unknown reasons, and these patients are less likely to respond to drug treatment.

Polygraphy. Although simple recording equipment that measures heart rate, blood pressure changes, and other changes related to sympathetic activity cannot easily distinguish between fear, rage, sadness, joy, or any other emotion, it can tell the difference between relaxation and intense emotion. The technique of **polygraphy** *attempts to use physiological measures of heart rate, blood pressure, GSR, and respiration to detect deception.* The basic premise of polygraphy is that under the right conditions, a person's sympathetic nervous system will be activated when that person is telling a lie.

One kind of polygraph session begins with a lengthy interview (Reid and Inbau, 1977). The polygrapher asks many questions, trying to learn something about the subject's background, attitudes, and personality. Then the examiner reviews the questions that will be asked during the actual test. Most examiners use three types of questions: irrelevant questions that have nothing to do with the crime, relevant questions that pertain directly to the crime, and **control questions,** *which are designed to stimulate the innocent person to tell a lie.* The examiner might ask, "Other than what you have told me, have you ever stolen anything?" This polygraph technique relies on the assumption that most people will not be able to recall everything they have ever stolen, or at least will not have told the examiner about every single theft. There are many small thefts that people might forget about—taking money from our mother's purse, "borrowing" pens from the office, or keeping silent when a cashier hands back too much change.

During the test, the examiner will observe the responses, especially to the relevant and the control questions. Presumably, innocent subjects will show greater responses to control questions; deceptive subjects will respond more to the relevant questions.

Many psychologists have strongly criticized the polygraph technique. The reasons are that its accuracy has not been demonstrated and that it is often more like a game of cat and mouse between the examiner and the subject, using subtle psychological techniques and crude physiological measures (Kleinmuntz and Szucko, 1984b). The technique relies on very shaky assumptions, one of which suggests that an innocent person will be more nervous while telling a small white lie than while telling an extremely consequential truth. Another is that lying is a simple response that results in a certain pattern of physiological changes.

Although the polygraph is widely used in settings ranging from employment interviews to national security investigations, its validity is quite questionable. In both laboratory and field settings, trained polygraph examiners declare many innocent people guilty, based on their physiological responses, and many guilty people are declared innocent. In one study using charts obtained from actual criminal investigations, examiners found thirty-seven percent of the innocent subjects guilty (Kleinmuntz and Szucko, 1984a). The test is also rather unreliable because trained polygraph examiners reading the same charts do not always draw the same conclusions.

The human consequences of the fallibility of the polygraph examination can be very serious. One innocent man, for example, was convicted of a murder charge and sentenced to life on the basis of the results of a polygraph test. In prison, he studied the technique, learned how to beat it, and taught other inmates the same skill. He was released after the real murderer was apprehended (Cimmerman, 1981).

Theories of Emotion

Why do we feel happy, sad, afraid, or disgusted? Popular wisdom says that emotions are mostly reactions to external events. We grieve because a dog died, feel happy because another person entered our lives, or become depressed because of a lost promotion. But one of the first theories of emotion claimed that feelings were the result of internal, not external, events. This theory was proposed in 1890 by William James, the pioneering American psychologist mentioned in Chapter 1, and also by Carl Lange, a Danish physiologist, at about the same time.

The James-Lange Theory.   This theory proposes that the emotional state we feel is the result, rather than the cause, of the physiological changes occurring in the viscera and muscles. For instance, a person feels afraid because her heart is racing; her heart does not race because she is afraid. Thus, the **James-Lange theory** *suggests that the physiological changes in the body come before the subjective experience of emotion; feedback from the viscera and muscles then result in the emotion.*

Studies of patients with spinal-cord damage have generally supported the James-Lange theory (Hohmann, 1962, cited in Schachter, 1971). These patients have no feedback from their muscles or viscera below the injury, and many of them say that their feelings of emotion changed considerably after the injury. They say that their emotions have become rather "cold" and "mental."

> Seems I get thinking mad, not shaking mad, and that's a lot different.
> I say I am afraid, like when I'm going into a real stiff exam at school, but I don't really feel afraid, not all tense and shaky, with that hollow feeling in my stomach, like I used to.

More recently, some scientists have proposed the **facial feedback hypothesis,** *which suggests that feedback from the facial muscles contributes to the experience of emotion,* in addition to feedback from the viscera. In his book *The Expression of Emotion in Man and Animals,* Darwin first pointed out how important facial expressions are. He suggested that outwardly expressing emotion in the face intensifies the emotion. The appeal of this hypothesis is that facial expressions of emotion, unlike visceral changes, are very rapid, and they are clearly different for each emotional experience.

In one study designed to test the role of facial feedback, subjects watched six videotaped scenes: two pleasant comedy skits, two unpleasant scenes of traffic accidents and a ritual suicide, and two neutral sequences about the use of computers in the apple harvest. Some subjects were told to pose the appropriate facial expression for each scene, so that judges observing their faces could tell what scene they were watching. Other subjects were told to suppress their facial expressions so that judges would not be able to tell which scene they were watching. A third group was given no instructions (Zuckerman, Klorman, Larrance, and Spiegel, 1981). During the scenes, the experimenters recorded heart rate, GSR, and blood pressure. Afterwards, the subjects filled out questionnaires asking about their actual emotions during the scenes.

The subjects who exaggerated their facial expressions showed the largest changes in autonomic activity, whereas those who suppressed their facial expressions showed the smallest autonomic reactions. Although the results appear to provide evidence for the role of facial feedback in emotion, they are controversial (Tomkins, 1981; Buck, 1984, Tourangeau and Ellsworth, 1979). In particular, critics wonder whether subjects who voluntarily control their facial expressions, in accordance with the experimenter's directions, can really provide valid evidence about whether feedback from natural expressions can affect the experience of emotion. Another problem with the hypothesis is the rather odd finding that naturally expressive people tend to have smaller autonomic reactions to emotional stimuli than do people whose faces show less emotion (Buck, 1980). More research is needed to determine exactly what role feedback from the face might play in emotional experiences.

Cannon's Theory of Emotion. Walter B. Cannon objected to the James-Lange theory for several reasons. For example, Cannon argued that people whose viscera were surgically separated from their central nervous system still reported some kind of emotional experience. He also pointed to the fact many physiological changes are very similar in most intense emotions, a point we made earlier. **Cannon's theory of emotions** *suggested that emotion originates in the activity in lower brain areas rather than in the viscera; these circuits then activate both the cortex and the viscera.* As we discussed earlier, activity in the brain is critically important for certain emotions, thereby supporting Cannon's viewpoint. The research thus far particularly implicates specific brain networks in depression.

Emotion and Cognition. Neither the James-Lange theory nor Cannon's theory give much attention to cognition. Another theory of emotions proposed in the 1960s, sometimes called the **cognitive-physiological theory of emotions,** *emphasized the role of the person's thoughts and their interaction with physiological arousal* (Schacter and Singer, 1962; Lazarus, 1984). *This theory suggested that whenever we are emotionally aroused, we decide which emotion we are feeling by cognitively evaluating and appraising situational cues.*

Suppose you are walking down a dark alley and a mugger appears from the shadows, brandishing a handgun. Your sympathetic nervous system will, most definitely, be activated. You will cognitively appraise the situation, noting the gun, the dark alley, the mugger's snarl, and feel fear, rather than joy, sadness, or disgust.

In an early experiment, some subjects were given injections of epinephrine, a drug that mimics sympathetic activation. Some of these subjects were told about the drug's effects; others were either misinformed or given no information. Then all subjects were placed into one of two different situations: an anger-producing one and a euphoria-producing one. In the "anger" situation, the subject was supposed to fill out a very insulting questionnaire. One item, for example, asked "With how many men (other than your father) has your mother had extramarital relationships? 4 and under——; 5–9——; 10 and over——." The situation that was supposed to encourage euphoria included a confederate who laughed a lot, flew paper airplanes, and sometimes asked the subject to join in the fun.

The subjects who were either misinformed or not informed about epinephrine's effects were more likely to join in if they were placed in the "euphoria" situation or to feel angry if they were filling out the "questionable questionnaire." These people did not expect to feel emotionally aroused, and when they did, they appraised their emotion in terms of the situation in which they were placed. In contrast, those who knew about the side effects of epinephrine already had a cognitive "excuse" for their bodies' reactions. They did not need to attribute their sympathetic activation to the situation.

Although this study was criticized on many grounds, and some labs have failed to replicate it, it did call attention to the relationship between emotions and cognitions. For example, college students were divided into two groups and given harmless placebos. One group was told to expect that the pill would make them yawn and make their eyes tired; the other was told the pill would produce heart rate increases, flushed face, and other symptoms of sympathetic activation. Then all the subjects were tempted to cheat on a test. The subjects who thought the pill was causing their high arousal levels were more likely to cheat than were those who were expecting only tired eyes. The people all felt sympathetic arousal; one group had a "logical" explanation for it (the pill) and therefore did not interpret the feeling as guilt. Perhaps it was easier for them to cheat because they interpreted their arousal as a drug side effect, rather than as guilt. The other group cognitively appraised their arousal as guilt and were thus inhibited from cheating (Dienstbier and Munter, 1971). Cognitions and emotions seem to be related, though their relationship is probably not as simple as the early experiment suggested.

A Network Model of Emotions. A more recent view of the relationship between emotions and cognitions, which grew out of the information-processing approach, is the **network model** (Bower, 1981; Levanthal, 1980; Berkowitz, 1983). *This theory expands on the semantic network notion discussed in Chapter 6 (e.g., Collins and Quillian, 1969), and it suggests that nodes for various emotions and their autonomic manifestations are linked in the brain to memories for the experiences in which those emotions were aroused.*

The model proposes that an event is represented in memory by concepts, or nodes, and the associations between them. Suppose an event happens to John: "Mary kisses me." This would produce linkages between the concepts of "Mary," "kissing," and "me." Linkages would also be formed between these nodes and the nodes that represent the place and the time of the event. Most important, a link would be formed between these nodes and the specific node in memory that represents "joy." Linked to this emotion node are nodes representing the appropriate autonomic reactions, the standard roles expected during the emotion, the expressive behaviors associated with it, and probably a number of events that typically lead to the emotion. Nodes for "heart racing," "grin," "clap hands," and "big pay increase" might be linked to "joy."

According to the theory, a particular node can be activated, or brought into the contents of consciousness, by two different means. First, the stimulus, such as "Mary," can be presented in some way. John might hear her name mentioned, see her photograph, or happen to meet her at the airport. Nodes can also be activated through the activation of an associated thought, or linked node, provided the linkage is strong enough. When any node is activated, the activation spreads out first to all those most closely linked. When John meets Mary at the airport, the "Mary" node will be activated, followed by "kissing," "me," "joy," and other associated nodes. John will recall and feel the emotion again. The network model would suggest that John might think of Mary if he feels joy for another reason, say because he won the state lottery.

The network model suggests that particular memories, thoughts, and actions become associated, or linked, with emotions. A cognition can activate a particular emotion, and an emotion can activate cognitions. If one is sad, the linked nodes that receive the most activation probably represent other, previous sad happenings. Thus, you are more likely to think your life has been filled with disaster, a proposition that will make you even sadder. If a woman is having an argument with her spouse because he came home late from an office party, the nodes "husband" and "anger" are activated. As the activation spreads out from these two nodes, she might easily recall other occasions on which she felt angry toward him.

Emotions and Evolution. The brain areas important in emotions, particularly the hypothalmus and other subcortical structures, do not exist only in human beings. They are very primitive structures. They were the first parts of the brain to evolve and can be found in creatures as far removed from humans as alligators, birds, fish, and frogs. Whether these animals feel emotions the same way we do is a fascinating question that is not easy to answer. These animals certainly behave emotionally. A frightened bird shows rapid heart beat, increased blood pressure, heightened activity, squawking, and many of the same signs of fear that human beings show. This kind of emotional behavior appears to be important in the bird's survival. A bird that faces a large predator with no emotional behavior would be quick to become the main course for dinner, and would probably not leave very many offspring. Thus, the importance of emotions in helping organisms survive may explain why they evolved and, indeed, why they exist now.

It is easy to see how the emotion of fear is important for survival. Without fear and all the physiological changes accompanying it, an animal might not move quickly enough to escape from a predator. Other emotions might also have an evolutionary basis. Disgust, for example, might be the emotional reaction that helps prevent organisms from eating poisonous foods. When you put something in your mouth that has a foul taste, you show disgust and spit it out. The reason a particular food tastes bad to us is that it is poisonous, so we have evolved taste buds that react to the substance, signalling an unpleasant taste. But the emotion of disgust that accompanies the taste adds a certain urgency to the situation. The food doesn't just drop out of your mouth. You actively and urgently spit it out, thus avoiding a bellyache, at the very least, and a premature demise at the most.

The importance of emotions in our survival, and also their existence in animals with little or no cortex, suggests that although cognition may affect emotions, cognitive activity may not be necessary for an emotion to occur (Zajonc, 1984). One theorist maintains that emotions are a primary and independent system that combines with other systems (such as cognition or perception), adding an element of urgency to them (Tomkins, 1981). Whereas the cognitive theory of emotions emphasized the importance of cognitive appraisal of arousal, an evolutionary approach deemphasizes the role of cognition. For example, human infants begin to cry and smile long before they acquire the verbal skills necessary for cognitive appraisals (Zajonc, 1980).

An experiment that supports this point of view shows that a person can feel an emotion about something without really ever analyzing it cognitively at all. Many different polygons were presented one at a time to a group of subjects for a very brief moment, 1/1000 second. Later, the subjects were shown more polygons, some of which they had already seen. They rated each one for "liking," and they also reported whether or not they recognized the polygon from the first series. Their chances of being able to identify which polygons they had seen before were no better than simply guessing. However, when they rated the shapes for liking, they tended to like those they had seen before better than those they had not. Cognitively, the subjects could not tell the old shapes from the new, but emotionally they could. This suggests that a person can form an emotional attachment very quickly, with little or no cognitive appraisal (Kunst-Wilson and Zajonc, 1980). Studies like this suggest that it is possible for emotion to precede cognitive appraisal.

The evolutionary approach to emotions does not altogether exclude any role for cognitions, although it does deemphasize them. The approach is not incompatible with the network model, for example. An evolutionary viewpoint looks at emotions from a different level of analysis and highlights some important features of the phenomenon. It helps explain why there seem to be so few emotions and why the expression of these is for the most part universal. It also shows why human beings sometimes make decisions emotionally and then later try to justify them rationally. One psychologist, for example, was trying to decide whether to accept a new job at another university. She made up a very rational balance sheet listing the pros and cons of each decision, but then she said, "Oh hell, it's not coming out right! Have to find a way to get some plusses over on the other side!" (Zajonc, 1980, note 6, p. 155).

GUIDED REVIEW

Learning Objectives 8, 9, 10, and 11

1. Emotions are complex reactions involving two components: a _____ component and a _____ . There appear to be a limited number of _____ . Emotions can be discriminated along two dimensions: pleasantness and arousal level.

2. Emotions are expressed by facial expressions, the verbal and nonverbal aspects of speech, gestures, and body movements. Facial expressions of _____ appear to be universal in human beings.

3. Activity in the _____ is similar for intense emotions. However, facial expression can distinguish one emotion from another, and brain activity and chemistry may also be able to. The emotional disorders of depression and manic-depression are related to the activity of certain brain chemicals, including _____ .

4. _____ attempts to use physiological measures of autonomic activity to detect deception. The validity and reliability of the technique are controversial.

5. The _____ theory of emotions suggests that emotions are the result, rather than the cause, of visceral and muscular changes. A newer hypothesis includes feedback from the _____ as being important in the experience of emotions.

6. _____ states that activity in the lower brain areas is critical in emotions, rather than visceral activity.

7. A _____ of emotion suggests that the bodily changes are interpreted as a particular emotional experience after a cognitive appraisal of the situation.

8. The _____ of emotions, couched in information-processing terms, proposes that events are represented by linkages between nodes in memory, and that emotions have their own nodes and associated linkages. Activation of an emotion will facilitate recall of events associated with that emotion. Also, activation of events will activate linked nodes for emotions.

9. An _____ approach to emotion suggests that emotions have evolved because they help organisms to survive. This approach suggests that organisms can feel emotions without requiring any cognitive appraisal.

ANSWERS

1. physiological; subjective experience; primary emotions 2. primary emotions 3. autonomic nervous system; norepinephrine 4. Polygraphy 5. James-Lange; facial muscles 6. Cannon's theory 7. cognitive-physiological theory 8. network model 9. evolutionary

I. The study of motivation attempts to explain the "why" of behavior.   (p. 272)

   A. Several theories of motivation have been proposed.   (p. 272)

      1. The drive reduction theory proposes that organisms experience the arousal of a drive when an important need is not satisfied, and they engage in behavior to reduce the arousal.   (p. 272)

      2. The optimum level of arousal theory of motivation suggests that organisms do not always seek the lowest level of arousal; they seek an optimum level, which depends on the circumstances and the organism.   (p. 274)

      3. Expectancy theory emphasizes the role of rewards in motivation.   (p. 275)

      4. The opponent process theory attempts to explain how drives are acquired.   (p. 276)

   B. One scheme used to classify motives is Maslow's need hierarchy system.   (p. 276)

   C. Brain mechanisms underlying motivation appear to involve a pathway in the lower brain areas that mediate reward for all kinds of motivation.   (p. 277)

II. Four examples of human motives are hunger, sex, sensation seeking, and the need for achievement.   (p. 279)

   A. The mechanisms that control eating behavior include both biological and psychological ones.   (p. 279)

      1. Peripheral controls include signals from the intestines and the liver.   (p. 279)

      2. The brain, especially the hypothalamus, plays an important role in hunger.   (p. 281)

      3. Obesity appears to have multiple causes, including psychological ones.   (p. 282)

   B. Sex behavior is affected by biological, psychological, and cultural factors.   (p. 284)

      1. The major biological influences on sex behavior involve sex hormones.   (p. 284)

      2. Psychological factors affect the development of sex roles in human beings.   (p. 285)

      3. Cultures differ considerably in their regulations and traditions regarding appropriate sexual behavior.   (p. 286)

   C. Sensation seeking refers to the need for varied, novel, or intense forms of stimulation or experience.   (p. 286)

      1. People who score high on the Sensation Seeking Scale behave differently from those who score low.   (p. 288)

      2. Various theories of motivation have been used to explain sensation seeking, including the optimum level of arousal theory and the opponent process theory.   (p. 288)

D. The need for achievement (n Ach) involves the desire to independently master objects, ideas, and other people, and to increase one's self-esteem through the exercise of one's talent. (p. 289)

1. N Ach is often measured with the Thematic Apperception Test. (p. 289)

2. People who score low or high on tests that measure N Ach behave differently in several ways. (p. 290)

III. Emotion consists of two components: a physiological component and a subjective experience. (p. 292)

A. There appears to be a limited number of primary emotions; these appear to differ along the dimensions of pleasantness and arousal. (p. 292)

B. Emotions are expressed by facial expression, the verbal and nonverbal aspects of speech, gestures, and body movements. Facial expressions of primary emotions appear to be universal in humans. (p. 293)

C. Emotions are accompanied by activity in the autonomic nervous system, although different emotions produce very similar patterns of response. (p. 294)

1. Activity in various brain regions and changes in brain chemistry are associated with different emotions. (p. 294)

2. Polygraphy is a controversial technique that attempts to use physiological measures of autonomic activity to detect deception. (p. 297)

D. Various theories of emotion have been proposed: (p. 298)

1. The James-Lange theory suggested that emotions are the result of visceral and muscular changes. (p. 298)

2. Cannon's theory of emotion emphasized the importance of brain activity in emotions. (p. 299)

3. The cognitive-physiological theory suggests that bodily changes are interpreted as a particular emotion after a cognitive appraisal of the situation. (p. 299)

4. A network model of emotions suggests that emotions, like memories, are represented by their own nodes and linkages in memory. (p. 300)

5. An evolutionary approach to emotion suggests that emotions have evolved because they help organisms to survive. (p. 300)

ACTION GLOSSARY

Match the terms in the left column with the definitions in the right column.

____ 1. Motive (p. 272)
____ 2. Drive reduction theory (p. 272)
____ 3. Primary drive (p. 272)
____ 4. Acquired drive (p. 272)
____ 5. Habit (p. 272)
____ 6. Optimum level of arousal theory (p. 274)
____ 7. Yerkes-Dodson Law (p. 274)
____ 8. Expectancy theory (p. 275)

A. A revision of the drive reduction theory that takes into account the fact that people do not always seek a lower level of arousal.
B. That which motivates an organism to satisfy some basic biological need, such as hunger or thirst.
C. Organisms are driven to reduce their state of arousal and achieve homeostasis.
D. A drive that develops through learning.
E. Performance on a difficult learning task is related to arousal; the best performance results from intermediate levels of arousal.
F. Something that moves an organism to act.
G. Stresses the importance of rewards and goals, and how a person's expectations of consequences can influence his behavior.
H. A connection between a stimulus and response.

____ 9. Valence (p. 275)
____ 10. Expectancy (p. 275)
____ 11. Opponent process theory of motivation (p. 275)

A. In the opponent process theory of motivation, the reaction that follows the initial response to a stimulus, and is opposite to it.
B. The attractiveness of the goal.
C. A neurotransmitter that is chemically related to norepinephrine.

_____ 12. a-process (p. 276)
_____ 13. b-process (p. 276)
_____ 14. Needs hierarchy (276)
_____ 15. Dopamine (p. 278)
_____ 16. CCK (p. 279)

D. *Attempts to explain how acquired drives are acquired. Proposes that a stimulus is followed by a particular response and that the response is followed by an opposite reaction. After repeated stimulus presentations, the first response diminishes in strength and the reaction increases.*
E. *A hormone released from the intestinal tract that acts as a signal for satiation of hunger.*
F. *A system of classifying motives devised by Maslow. Lists physiological needs at the bottom and self-actualization needs at the top.*
G. *The likelihood that an individual's behavior will lead to a particular goal.*
H. *In the opponent process theory of motivation, the response that occurs immediately after the presentation of a stimulus.*

_____ 17. Glucoreceptors (p. 281)
_____ 18. Ventromedial hypothalamus (p. 281)
_____ 19. Lateral hypothalamus (p. 281)
_____ 20. Emotional arousal theory (EAT) (p. 282)
_____ 21. Setpoint (p. 283)
_____ 22. Estrogen and progesterone (p. 284)
_____ 23. Testosterone (p. 284)

A. *Proposes that overeating is instrumentally conditioned behavior that serves to reduce anxiety in the obese.*
B. *Lesions of this area of the brain produce overeating and obesity in experimental animals.*
C. *The particular weight that an individual can maintain effortlessly, without dieting.*
D. *One of the androgens released by the testes.*
E. *Monitor the levels of glucose, a form of sugar, in the bloodstream or other body compartment.*
F. *Sex hormones released by the ovaries.*
G. *Lesions in this area of the brain inhibit eating in experimental animals.*

_____ 24. Sex roles (p. 285)
_____ 25. Sensation seeking (p. 286)
_____ 26. Sensation Seeking Scale (p. 286)
_____ 27. Galvanic skin response (GSR) (p. 288)
_____ 28. Need for achievement (n Ach) (p. 289)
_____ 29. Thematic Apperception Test (p. 289)
_____ 30. Emotion (p. 292)
_____ 31. MHPG (p. 296)

A. *A metabolic byproduct of norepinephrine.*
B. *A measure of activity in the autonomic nervous system; used as an indicator of emotional arousal.*
C. *Used to measure motivation, including the need for achievement; based on the theory that fantasies and dreams can reveal a great deal about a person's motives.*
D. *The attitudes and behaviors believed by a society to be appropriate for males and females.*
E. *The need for varied, novel, and intense forms of stimulation and experience.*
F. *A psychological test designed to measure individual differences in sensation seeking.*
G. *A complex reaction involving two components: a series of physiological changes and a subjective experience or "feeling."*
H. *The motive to achieve success, to independently master objects, events, and other persons, and to increase self-esteem through the development of talent.*

_____ 32. Polygraphy (p. 297)
_____ 33. Control question (p. 297)
_____ 34. James-Lange theory (p. 298)
_____ 35. Cannon's theory of emotions (p. 299)
_____ 36. Network model of emotions (p. 300)
_____ 37. Facial feedback hypothesis (p. 298)

A. *The technique of recording physiological responses while the subject answers a standard series of questions, usually related to a criminal act, for the purpose of detecting deception.*
B. *Suggests that facial expressions contribute to the experience of emotion.*
C. *Based on the semantic network concept; suggests that nodes for various emotions and their autonomic manifestations are linked to memories for the experiences in which those emotions were aroused.*
D. *Used on a standard polygraph examination; designed to stimulate an innocent person to tell a lie.*
E. *Proposed that the physiological changes occurring in the viscera and muscles were the cause, rather than the result, of the emotion.*
F. *Suggests that emotions originate in the activity in lower brain areas rather than to activity in the viscera.*

ANSWERS

SELF-TEST

1. The theory of motivation that proposes that the purpose of behavior is to reduce arousal is called
   (a) drive reduction theory.
   (b) optimum level of arousal theory.
   (c) expectancy theory.
   (d) opponent process theory.
   (LO 1; p. 272)

2. The motivation of a housewife who is home alone all day and who wants to go out to dinner and to a movie in the evening could best be explained by which of the following theories?
   (a) drive reduction theory
   (b) optimum level of arousal theory
   (c) expectancy theory
   (d) opponent process theory
   (LO 1; p. 274)

3. In expectancy theory, the attractiveness of the goal is termed
   (a) homeostasis.
   (b) acquired drive.
   (c) expectancy.
   (d) valence.
   (LO 1; p. 275)

4. In opponent process theory, the first response _____ over time, and the second response _____ .
   (a) is stable; increases
   (b) increases; decreases
   (c) decreases; increases
   (d) decreases; is stable
   (LO 1; p. 276)

5. Longitudinal research on Maslow's need hierarchy has found that
   (a) his formulation was accurate.
   (b) two of his needs should be in the opposite order.
   (c) people do not necessarily show the predicted pattern.
   (d) there was nothing accurate about his formulation.
   (LO 2; p. 277)

6. Which of the following brain areas appears to have pathways that are most intimately involved in reward?
   (a) hypothalamus
   (b) medulla
   (c) cerebellum
   (d) temporal lobe
   (LO 3; p. 277)

7. Which of the following substances, when injected into the liver of a dog during feeding, will cause the hungry dog to stop eating?
   (a) CCK
   (b) insulin
   (c) glucose
   (d) caffeine
   (LO 4; p. 281)

8. A lesion in what part of the brain will prevent a rat from ceasing to eat when it is full and eventually will lead to obesity?
   (a) lateral hypothalamus
   (b) ventromedial hypothalamus
   (c) hippocampus
   (d) lateral thalamus
   (LO 4; p. 281)

9. If a male rat has its testes removed, what hormone will cause its sexual behavior to return?
   (a) testosterone
   (b) ACTH
   (c) estradiol
   (d) progesterone
   (LO 5; p. 284)

10. Sex roles refer to
    (a) a person's sexual behavior.
    (b) the attitudes and behaviors believed by a person's culture to be appropriate for each sex.
    (c) the sexual attitudes a person adopts during adolescence.
    (d) alternate life-styles.
    (LO 5; p. 285)

11. Which theory of motivation seems best able to explain high sensation-seeking behavior?
    (a) drive reduction theory
    (b) classical conditioning
    (c) expectancy theory
    (d) opponent process theory
    (LO 6; p. 288)

12. People who are high sensation seekers show _____ galvanic skin response to a novel stimulus than do people who are low sensation seekers.
    (a) much weaker
    (b) slightly weaker
    (c) similar
    (d) stronger
    (LO 6; p. 289)

13. In a ring-tossing game, people with high n Ach scores tended to stand _____ to/from the post while people with low n Ach scores tended to stand _____ to/from the post.
    (a) close/far
    (b) far/close
    (c) at an intermediate distance/close or far
    (d) close or far/at an intermediate distance
    (LO 7; p. 290)

14. In the "circle of emotions," the two dimensions for describing emotions are
    (a) pleasantness and arousal level.
    (b) pleasantness and physiological.
    (c) intensity and physiological.
    (d) physiological and expressive.
    (LO 8; p. 293)

15. The facial expression of emotions has been found to be
    (a) completely culturally specific.
    (b) universal for some basic emotions.
    (c) universal for all emotions.
    (d) difficult to interpret across cultures.
    (LO 9; p. 293)

16. For people with bipolar affective disorders, different levels of the neurotransmitter _____ appear to be associated with the manic and depressive parts of the cycle.
    (a) dopamine   (c) acetylcholine
    (b) norepinephrine   (d) CCK
    (LO 10; p. 295)

17. In the James-Lange theory of emotion, what is the sequence of events in emotional response?
    (a) physical arousal followed by subjective feelings of emotion
    (b) emotion followed by physical arousal
    (c) only physical arousal
    (d) cognitive appraisal followed by emotion, and physical arousal
    (LO 11; p. 298)

18. According to Cannon, emotion originated in the _____ rather than in the viscera, as suggested by the James-Lange theory.
    (a) heart   (c) lower brain stem
    (b) cortex   (d) hypothalamus
    (LO 11; p. 299)

19. In an experiment by Schacter and Singer, subjects were given injections of epinephrine and were then put in different situations. Who were most likely to show anger in this situation?
    (a) People who were misinformed about the effects of the injection.
    (b) People who were correctly informed about the effects of the drug.
    (c) People who were given an insulting test to fill out.
    (d) People who were misinformed and were given an insulting test to fill out.
    (LO 11; p. 299)

20. The evolutionary perspective on emotion suggests that although _____ may affect emotions, it may not be necessary for emotions to occur.
    (a) physiological arousal
    (b) feeling
    (c) expression
    (d) cognitive activity
    (LO 11; p. 300)

ANSWERS

13. c, 14. a, 15. b, 16. b, 17. a, 18. b, 19. c, 20. d

1. a, 2. b, 3. d, 4. c, 5. c, 6. a, 7. c, 8. b, 9. a, 10. b, 11. d, 12. d.

SUGGESTED READINGS

Deci, E. L., and R. M. Ryan. *Intrinsic motivation and self-determination in human behavior.* New York: Plenum, 1985. An advanced text covering research on human motivation, especially as it relates to human performance.

Ekman, P. *Emotion in the human face* (2d ed.). New York: Cambridge University Press, 1982. An interesting book on facial expressions that display emotions in various cultures.

Franken, R. E. *Human motivation.* Monterey, CA: Brooks, Cole, 1982. An introductory textbook on the topic of motivation.

McClelland, D. C. *Human motivation.* Glenview, IL: Scott, Foresman and Co., 1984. An introductory text on motivation, by the researcher who spent years studying achievement motivation.

Plutchik, R. *Emotion: a psychoevolutionary synthesis.* New York: Harper and Row, 1980. A presentation of the theory that emphasizes the role of evolution in emotion.

Strongman, K. T. *The psychology of emotion* (2d ed.). New York: Wiley, 1978. An introductory treatment of emotions.

p a r t

III

DEVELOPMENT

c h a p t e r

9

Life-Span Development: Infancy and Childhood

LEARNING OBJECTIVES

After reading this chapter, you should be able to

1. describe the two major types of studies conducted to explore human development. **(p. 310)**
2. describe three major perspectives used to approach the study of human development. **(p. 311)**
3. explain how genes can affect behavior, and describe the kind of study scientists use to learn more about the role of genetics in behavior. **(p. 314)**
4. provide examples of how the nature of the prenatal environment can affect later behavior. **(p. 316)**
5. discuss the nature-nurture issue. **(p. 317)**
6. explain some of the recent trends in childbirth in the United States. **(p. 320)**
7. describe the sensory-motor abilities of the newborn. **(p. 321)**
8. explain what is meant by the term "attachment," and provide examples of studies that show the effects of the nature of attachment on the behavior of the young child. **(p. 324)**
9. describe Piaget's theory concerning the nature of cognitive development. **(p. 327)**
10. explain the roles of the family and of a child's peers in social and emotional development. **(p. 330)**
11. discuss Piaget's and Kohlberg's theories of moral development. **(p. 333)**
12. define the term "gifted," and explain two methods that are used to educate the gifted. **(p. 335)**

The process of development begins with conception. From the time an egg and sperm are joined, a human being begins to develop, first into a fetus and then a tiny infant. The infant develops into a child, the child into an adolescent, and the adolescent into an adult. The process does not stop here, however. The adult continues to go through important developmental stages, especially involving marriage, career, and parenting. Finally, the adult begins to age and faces the prospect of death. Development ends only when the individual dies. In this chapter we explore the early stages of human life: infancy and childhood. Chapter 10 continues the discussion of development in the adolescent and the adult.

The Study of Human Development

The discussion of development in this chapter is different from all the other chapters. Rather than focusing on a particular aspect of human behavior, such as personality, sensation and perception, or learning, it focuses on chronological periods of human life. Instead of examining how people learn, socialize, or alter their states of consciousness, the chapters on development examine how these behaviors *change* across the life span. In this context, **development** *refers to patterns of forward movement or change, beginning at conception and continuing through the entire life span*. Obviously changes do not just occur in one area of a person's life; they occur in cognition, social behavior, physical attributes, and just about every aspect of human beings.

Cross-Sectional and Longitudinal Studies

Because developmental psychologists are interested in changes over time, sometimes very long periods of time, their approach to their subject is slightly different from that of other psychologists. They follow all the usual rules of science that we discussed in the first chapter, and they take advantage of experimental and correlational methods. They also, however, must consider the aspect of change across time, and there are two basic ways to do this. One is called the **cross-sectional study,** and the other is the **longitudinal study.**

The **cross-sectional study** *compares the characteristics of groups of individuals of different ages on some behavior*. For example, ultrasound examinations of women at different stages of pregnancy have found that fetuses show different kinds of eye movements related to age. Rapid eye movements seem to begin around twenty-three weeks (Birnholz, 1981).

The **longitudinal study** *follows the same group (or groups) of people through time, observing whatever changes in behavior occur at different ages*. Another study on eye-movement patterns monitored rapid eye movements in a group of infants during the first month of life, then again at three months, six months, and one year of age. The year-old infants were given a test of mental development, and their scores were compared to their previous rapid eye movement patterns. Babies who had frequent rapid eye movement storms at six months of age were more likely to have lower mental development scores (Becker and Thoman, 1981).

Both the cross-sectional and longitudinal methods have advantages and disadvantages. In the cross-sectional method, for instance, the age groups might be different because of factors other than just age, including age of the parents, quality of schools, and historical factors. People in their sixties probably have a vivid memory of the Depression and might behave differently from fifty-year-olds because of that memory, not because of age differences. A disadvantage of the longitudinal study is that it can be very time consuming and expensive. Another potential problem is that subjects may move to new towns and lose track of the experimenter. A more recent approach is a combined cross-sectional and longitudinal study. In the first testing session, groups of different ages are compared. Then each group is followed up at later ages.

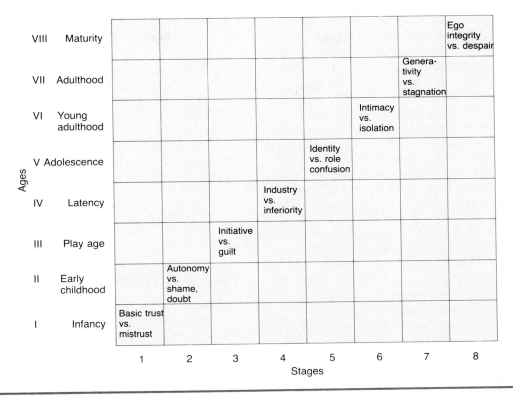

Figure 9.1 Erikson's eight stages of development

Perspectives in Human Development

Just as psychologists approach the subject of human behavior in different ways and on different levels of analysis, they have different approaches to the subject of changes in human behavior. Three perspectives in the study of development are the psychoanalytic approach, the cognitive-structural approach, and the behaviorist approach.

Psychoanalytic thinkers have contributed much to our understanding of human development; for example, Sigmund Freud, whose theories are elaborated in more detail in a later chapter, emphasized the notion that events and outcomes early in development would have important influences on the individual's later behavior. Erik Erikson is a contemporary psychologist

with a psychoanalytic approach. He proposed that human beings face major conflicts involving both psychological and social dimensions at several stages in life (see fig. 9.1). During each of these eight stages, the individual must resolve a particular conflict; the person's success at each stage will have a significant impact on personality development. For example, **autonomy vs. shame and doubt** *is one of the psychosocial crises proposed by Erikson that must be resolved by the child. The child who successfully masters control over bladder and bowels gains a healthy attitude of autonomous control and self-efficacy. However, the child who experiences discouragement and failure in self-control and bodily regulation may experience shame and doubt.* We discuss other Eriksonian psychosocial crises throughout our exploration of development.

Another important perspective in human development, the **cognitive-structural approach,** *focuses primarily on stages of intellectual development and the way the child's thinking is organized at each stage.* Jean Piaget, a Swiss psychologist who carefully observed the behavior and thinking processes of his own children, is the towering figure in this area. The notion that development includes qualitatively different stages through which people move in invariant sequence is central to the cognitive-structural approach. It has been an important feature in the theorizing of other developmental psychologists as well, such as Lawrence Kohlberg, who conducts research on moral development.

Behavioristic thinking has also affected theories of human development and constitutes a third significant perspective in the field. The important role that reinforcement plays in learning is a key issue in this approach. In particular, this approach stresses the fact that the process of development involves the accumulation of more and more learning experiences and that each individual's learning history is likely to be unique.

These and other perspectives have guided much of the research on human development in psychology. On some issues the perspectives have conflicting viewpoints, whereas on others they disagree mainly in emphasis. Often, the theories differ on the topics they choose to investigate; psychoanalytic adherents usually focus on personality development, and advocates of the cognitive-structuralist stage theory are more interested in cognitive development.

GUIDED REVIEW

Learning Objectives 1 and 2

1. Studies of development involve all the experimental and correlational approaches discussed in earlier chapters. They also involve _____ designs, in which groups of people of different ages are compared, and _____ designs, in which the same people are observed as they develop over time.

2. Three major perspectives in human development include the psychoanalytic, the cognitive-structural, and the behaviorist. The _____ approach stresses the effects of early developmental experiences on later behavior, particularly personality development. _____ , for example, proposed eight stages of development, each of which involves the resolution of a psychosocial conflict. The _____ approach focuses on stages through which individuals move during development. The cognitive developmental theory of _____ is a good example. The _____ approach features the importance of reinforcement in development and the unique learning history of each individual.

ANSWERS

1. cross-sectional; longitudinal 2. psychoanalytic; Erik Erikson; cognitive-structural; Jean Piaget; behaviorist

The Forces That Shape Development

The two major forces that shape development are genes and environment. These two forces never act independently, however. They always work together in their effects on the developing organism. Even at the very first, when a sperm cell and an egg join, the organism is more than just the genetic information contained in those two cells. The egg cell, in particular, contains an enormous quantity of nutrients and thus is already providing an environment that will interact with the genetic instructions.

Genetic Forces

Jim Springer and Jim Lewis are identical twin brothers who were adopted into separate families at four weeks of age. They had no contact until they were thirty-nine years old. Nevertheless, the similarities between the twins were uncanny. Both were named Jim, and both had first married a woman named Linda, were divorced, and then remarried a Betty. They each had a dog named Toy and a son called James Allen or James Alan. They both liked math in school but hated spelling. In adulthood, they each enjoy mechanical drawing and carpentry. They smoke and drink about the same

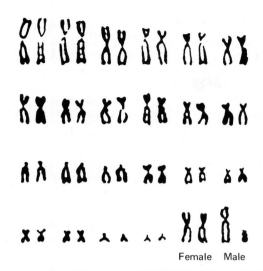

Female   Male

Figure 9.2 Human chromosomes

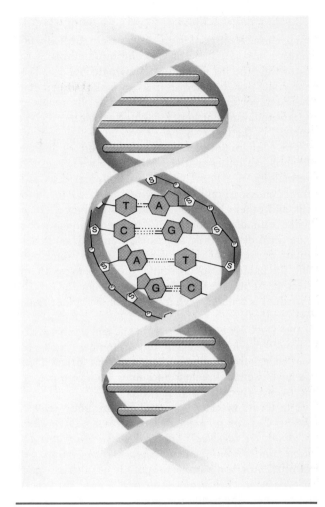

Figure 9.3 A schematic diagram of the double-helix structure of DNA. T = thymine, A = adenine, C = cytosine, and G = guanine

amount, and they both bite their fingernails. They have the same pulse, blood pressure, sleep patterns, hemorrhoid and headache problems, and they both gained ten pounds at about the same time of life. Many of these similarities are simply remarkable coincidences. But investigators who study twins reared apart notice that such coincidences are usually frequent in their subjects, and some of them must surely be due to the effects of genes on behavior (Bouchard, cited by Holden, 1980). The role that genes play in the development of the human being is not limited to eye color or bone structure. The effects of the genes go far beyond physical characteristics.

The Gene. Almost every cell of the human body has forty-six **chromosomes,** *which are long chains of genetic material located in the nucleus of the cell* (fig. 9.2). Each chain consists of **DNA,** *the remarkable substance that contains the genetic information.* DNA molecules are made up of three elements, arranged more or less like a ladder: sugar, phosphates, and bases. Figure 9.3 shows an example of a very small segment of the DNA making up a chromosome. **Adenine, thy-**mine, guanine,** and **cytosine** *are the four bases that make up DNA, and it is the sequence of these bases arranged along the chromosome that is the genetic code.*

A **gene** *is a very short length of DNA, consisting of perhaps only a few hundred bases; the gene is the basic unit of heredity.* Some genes give instructions to other genes. Other genes actually code for specific proteins that are used in physiological processes in the body. For example, a single gene on one chromosome codes for one of the proteins that breaks down alcohol. Another gene codes for an enzyme used to make norepinephrine, an important neurotransmitter. The chromosomes contain thousands of genes, each of which has its own function in the body.

The complex interactions of these proteins and the metabolic activities that they direct are what goes into the making of a human being. In different cells, different genes are active; this is why some become kidney cells and others become neurons, for instance. Genes do not begin coding for proteins at conception and continue until death; they function on and off, and some remain dormant for years. Whatever genes are responsible for baldness, for example, do not express themselves until middle adulthood, and then only if the individual is a male, perhaps because of the hormonal environment.

The forty-six chromosomes in the cell are arranged in pairs. You inherited one chromosome in each pair from your mother and the other from your father. Thus, you have twenty-three chromosomes from your mother and twenty-three from your father.

The terms **heterozygous** and **homozygous** *refer to whether the complementary genes on a pair of chromosomes are identical; "hetero" means they are different, and "homo" means they are the same.* For example, a person who has type AB blood has a gene for type A on one chromosome and a gene for type B on the other. She is heterozygous for this trait because the two genes are different. A person who is type O has a gene for type O on both chromosomes and is called homozygous for this trait.

The blood groups can illustrate the phenomena of dominance and recessiveness as well. A **dominant gene** *is one that will be expressed regardless of which gene is on the paired chromosome.* A **recessive gene** *is one that is expressed only if it is paired with another recessive gene.* For example, a person with type A blood

has at least one gene for type A—a dominant gene—on one of his chromosomes. But the other chromosome might have either another gene for type A or perhaps a gene for type O blood, which is recessive. The only people who have type O blood are those with the genes for type O on *both* chromosomes. Both the gene for A and the gene for B are dominant over the gene for O. But A and B are **co-dominant** with one another, *meaning both genes are expressed.* This is why a person with a gene for A and one for B has type AB blood, rather than type A or type B. Recessive genes are not rare. In the United States, more people have type O blood than any other.

There are many genes that affect proteins in the blood that can now be detected. Tests are sometimes used to determine whether it is possible that a man is the father of a child in a paternity suit. For example, a type O man who believes that a type A baby of a type O mother is his child is mistaken. The father would have to be either type A or type AB. Examples of other genes that act as dominant or recessive in humans are listed in table 9.1.

Genes and Behavior. Genes cannot directly affect behavior; they can only code for specific proteins or direct the activities of other genes. But to the extent that these different proteins can affect behavior differently, genes can affect behavior. Suppose, for example, a person whose genes code for a very efficient enzyme that breaks down alcohol consumes an average of two drinks per night for fifteen years. Since this person had the physiological ability to break down the alcohol rapidly, she would probably never get drunk. Another person, however, who had genes coding for a less efficient version of the same enzyme, might feel woozy for a couple of hours each evening after having two drinks. This person may, because of her genes, be more predisposed to become alcoholic, given a similar pattern of social drinking and environmental stresses.

Scientists have not been able to find specific genes that are involved in complex behaviors like alcoholism, intelligence, psychosis, or personality. Our example,

Table 9.1 Examples of dominant and recessive genes in humans

Dominant	Recessive
Ability to roll the tongue	Inability to roll the tongue
Freckles	No freckles
Free earlobes	Attached earlobes
Inability to fold tongue	Ability to fold tongue
Huntington's Chorea	Tay-Sachs Disease
Achondroplastic dwarfism	Hemophilia (located on the X chromosome)
Nail-patella syndrome	Color blindness (located on the X chromosome)
	Sickle-cell anemia
	Albinism
	Phenylketonuria (PKU)

relating a single "inefficient" gene to drinking, is only hypothetical. If there are genes that can predispose some people to alcoholism, it is much more likely that there are many "alcoholism" genes, rather than just one. A person who inherited several of these would thus be more likely to develop the disorder.

Even though no one has yet been able to determine any specific connection between genes and behavior, it is possible to determine how large a role genes play in complex behaviors using the **adoption study** (Plomin, Loehlin, and DeFries, 1985). *In this method, the similarity between an adopted child and the adoptive parents is compared to the similarity between the child and the biological parents.* In theory, the biological parents contribute only genes to the child, but the prenatal environment, and perhaps the postnatal environment as well, also come from the biological parents. For some traits, such as eye color, one would expect the adopted child to closely resemble the biological parents rather than the adoptive parents. For other traits, the child would resemble the adoptive parents much more than the biological ones. The language the child learns is a good example: a Japanese child reared from birth by English-speaking American parents is not likely to speak Japanese.

Most behavioral traits, however, seem to fall somewhere between these two extremes. Children of alcoholic parents, for example, are more likely to become alcoholic even if they are reared by nonalcoholic adoptive parents (Goodwin, 1979). Sons of alcoholics are particularly vulnerable. One study found that they were four times more likely to become alcoholic than were sons of nonalcoholic parents, even if they were reared in normal homes. The adopted children of the alcoholic parents were not more likely to develop other behavioral disorders—they were only more likely to become alcoholic. This study suggests that the children inherited genes from one or both of their parents that predisposed them to alcoholism later in life, perhaps by affecting the way their bodies metabolized alcohol.

There are many common misconceptions about the role of genes in behavior. One is that genes predetermine a particular behavior, rather than predispose an individual toward the behavior. Thus, people with an alcoholic parent might mistakenly assume, after reading about the relationship between genes and behavior, that they are destined to become alcoholics. This is clearly not true. It only means that they may be more vulnerable. Genes do not predestine; they only predispose.

Another myth about genes is that if something is "genetic," meaning that genes are involved, then it must be universal. People often claim that human aggression cannot have any genetic basis, since some cultures are not aggressive at all. Unfortunately, this line of reasoning is not valid, even though the conclusions might be. The most important characteristic about genes is that they are different for every individual. If a genetic predisposition exists for a particular trait, that trait will be expressed differently for different people, even if they are reared in the same environments, simply because their genes differ.

A third misconception is that if some behavior is "genetic," then it can't be changed; it is inevitable. As we just pointed out, any predispositions produced by genetic factors can often be mitigated or changed completely by environmental influences. A good example of this involves **phenylketonuria (PKU)**, *a disease transmitted through two recessive genes that causes a lack in the enzyme needed for metabolizing one of the amino acids, phenylalanine. Toxic byproducts build up in the individual's body, resulting in severe retardation and light skin and hair.* If the trait is detected early, however, the baby can be placed on a diet low in phenylalanine. Fewer toxic byproducts accumulate, and the child is much less affected. Babies are generally tested for this hereditary problem soon after birth.

There are many other misunderstandings about the role of genes in behavior. Most of them seem to have arisen because people see genes and environment as acting independently, rather than together. As we shall see later in this section, genes and environment operate together.

Environmental Forces

The effects of the environment on human development begin at the moment of conception. The "environment," as we discuss it in psychology, includes a great deal more than the child's room and family life. It includes the prenatal, hormonal, and nutritional environments. In fact, it includes every component of the environment, both inside and outside the womb, and inside and outside the person, that is not in the DNA. Environmental effects can range from the drugs the mother took during pregnancy, to a death in the family when the person is in middle age, and even to the unpredictable effects of chance happenings (Bandura, 1982). In this section, we will discuss a few examples of how the environment affects development.

The Prenatal Environment.   While the genes are directing some cells to specialize, the environment in which they are acting is having important effects. The hormones present are particularly critical. If the fetus is a male, it begins to release a male sex hormone that causes the fetus to develop male sex organs. If the fetus is a female, no male sex hormone is released; the fetus develops female sex organs. These prenatal hormones affect the brain as well. Many scientists are convinced that the sexual behavior of the adult is partly dependent on the presence of these hormones in prenatal life.

Another important component of the prenatal environment is the drugs the mother is taking. During the 1960s, some pregnant women were prescribed a minor tranquilizer, called *thalidomyde,* to help relieve morning sickness. The babies of many of the women who took the drug during the first few weeks of pregnancy were born with tragic limb deformities.

Thalidomyde, however, is certainly not the only drug that can affect development in the human fetus. As more research is conducted on the problem, it is becoming clear that many otherwise safe drugs are not safe at all for pregnant women. Alcohol, for example, can produce the *fetal alcohol syndrome* in babies (Chapter 3). Babies born to mothers who drink a great deal during pregnancy can have a variety of problems, including weak sucking abilities, hyperactivity, delayed development, and mental retardation (Streissguth, 1980). Tests on animals are revealing more and more that commonly used drugs are harmful to the fetus. For example, **cimetidine,** *a drug used to treat ulcers,* produces strange effects on the sexual behavior of male rats whose mothers received the substance during pregnancy. The sex organs of the males were smaller, and their sex drive and performance were lowered (Anand and Van Thiel, 1982).

Drugs are not the only things that can affect prenatal development. Even the mother's emotions can affect the growing fetus. Severe stress results in the release of hormones in the mother that can cross the placental barrier and increase activity levels in the fetus, an effect that may extend until after birth (Yang, Zweig, Douthitt, and Federman, 1976).

The prenatal environment seems to be a very vulnerable one. The DNA does not unfold in a vacuum, and the characteristics of the environment modify development considerably. Whether or not we understand the effects of all the thousands of drugs on the market, a prudent person would be wary of taking *any* drug during this important phase in her child's development.

Nutrition.   Food is the source of energy for all the cells in our body, so it is hardly surprising that the nature of that food can affect how our cells work. What is surprising is how little we know about the role of nutrition in development. We know enough, however, to realize that nutrition can play a very large role, especially in the development of the brain.

Eating too little, or eating too little protein, is particularly harmful if it occurs during the early part of life when the brain cells are still dividing (Winick and Rosso, 1975). The effects of malnutrition on the brain usually are reversible if they occur later. If they occur while the brain cells are still dividing, however, the individual will be left with fewer brain cells and will probably suffer some mental impairment. In animals, early malnutrition can have devastating effects, including reduced brain weight, loss of myelin, delayed brain development, delayed physical and motor development, and increased aggression. In humans, early malnutrition may have similar effects. Some human brain cells continue to divide until well after birth, probably until the age of two.

The role of nutrition in development can sometimes be quite subtle. Some scientists believe, for example, that synthetic food colorings can result in hyperactivity in certain responsive children (Weiss, 1981). Others maintain that aggressive behavior in children is sometimes part of a "junk-food syndrome" (Bland, 1982). Eating too many empty calories deficient in key vitamins and minerals may alter biochemical activity in the brain, resulting in aggression, bad dreams, fatigue, and stomach pains. Eating too many calories, even if they are nutritionally sound and don't result in obesity, may hasten the aging process.

The Interaction between Genes and Environment in Development

A very old debate in psychology deals with the **nature-nurture issue.** *This issue revolves around the question of the relative importance of genetic factors (nature) and environmental factors (nurture) in shaping the characteristics of the developing human.* The argument has surfaced in many forms over the years. The behaviorists, for example, were closely aligned with "nurture" because of their emphasis on the environment. Scientists interested in evolution, and with more biological training, usually emphasize the important role of the genes in development and behavior.

The current attitude is that neither extreme point of view is correct. Since genes and environment cannot operate independently, they both must contribute to development and behavior by interacting. Some behaviors seem to have more genetic predisposition than others, and deciding just how much each one has is another topic for debate.

One very good example of the way in which genes and environment interact is the concept of critical periods discussed in Chapter 7. We have mentioned that some environmental influences, such as malnutrition, are particularly devastating if they occur within a certain age range. Although the environment can usually have a good deal of impact outside of this age range, the critical period is particularly sensitive and vulnerable. Malnutrition, for example, will affect the organism outside the critical period, but its effects may not be so great. The genes dictate when that critical period will be, and the characteristics of the environment, combined with the timing of the genes, determine how development will proceed.

Critical periods exist for many environmental effects. We mentioned earlier that thalidomyde had negative effects only on children whose mothers took the drug during the first few weeks of pregnancy. There also appear to be critical periods for attachment to the mother and probably for language learning as well (see Chapter 7). Nevertheless, human beings are remarkably adaptive. It would be much too rigid to suggest that a baby who did not develop a close relationship with a caregiver would forever be deficient in intimacy.

The nature-nurture debate continues, and it is not a trivial issue. The outcome of the debate has implications for the way that we choose to intervene in social problems. For example, if you support the theory that alcoholism has a strong genetic predisposition, you might support programs that attempt to prevent alcoholism in the siblings of known alcoholics. If you believe that environmental factors are the dominant influence in the disorder, you would perhaps attempt to remove alcoholics from their environmental stressors. Because genes and environment interact, however, it is quite possible that *both* strategies might help alleviate the problem of alcoholism.

GUIDED REVIEW

Learning Objectives 3, 4, and 5

1. _____ and _____ are the two major forces that shape development.

2. Most body cells contain forty-six _____ , or long chains of _____ , the material that contains the genetic code. The code is the sequence of bases _____ , _____ , _____ , and _____ along the DNA. A _____ is a short sequence of bases, and each chromosome contains thousands of genes.

3. Genes can affect behavior indirectly by altering body chemistry and physiological functions. The _____ is one method used to determine whether genetic factors influence the development of complex behavioral traits.

4. Environmental factors begin affecting development from the moment of _____ . The prenatal environment, for example, is critical in development. Drugs such as thalidomyde can have tragic consequences, and others, such as alcohol and cimetidine, are also harmful to the developing fetus.

5. Nutrition is an important environmental variable that affects development throughout life. Malnutrition is particularly harmful to the developing brain if it occurs when brain cells are still _____ .

6. The _____ issue argues about the relative importance of genes and environment in human development. Most scientists agree that genes and environment must always _____ in their effects on development.

ANSWERS

1. Genes; environment 2. chromosomes; DNA; adenine; thymine; guanine; cytosine; gene 3. adoption study 4. conception 5. dividing 6. nature-nurture; interact

Birth and Infancy

The most rapid developmental changes in a person's life, particularly biological ones, occur during the nine months preceding birth and the year after birth. From the microscopic fertilized egg, the developing human being's weight is multiplied about 11 million times by the time of birth (fig. 9.4). Fortunately, during the baby's first year, weight gain slows down considerably, but it still usually triples by the first birthday. Never again in the life of a human being will biological changes proceed at such a rapid pace.

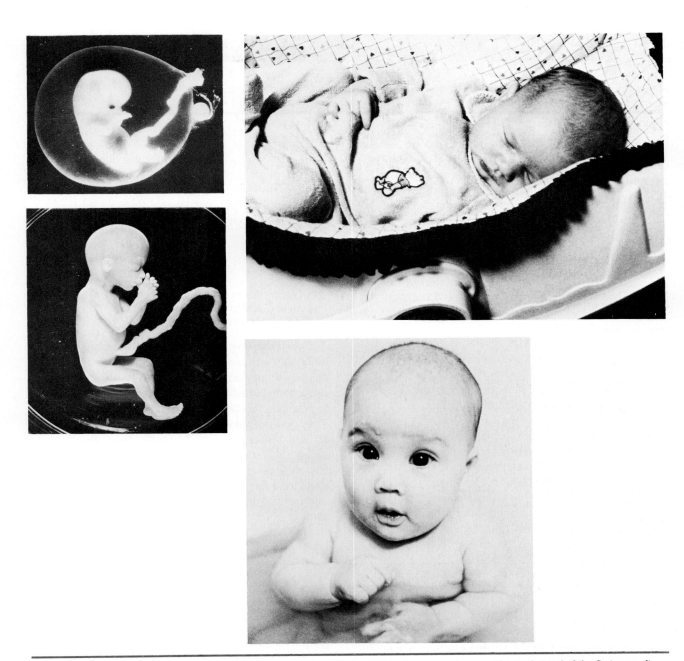

Figure 9.4 *Tremendous changes occur in the developing human being from the moment of conception to the end of the first year after birth.*

CAREER BOX

Nurse-Midwife

A growing profession both in Europe and the United States is the nurse-midwife, an individual who has received specialized training in obstetrics, particularly labor and delivery. Most nurse-midwives began as registered nurses, perhaps obstetrical nurses, and then pursued further education in a nurse-midwife program. Depending on the laws of the state in which he or she is practicing, the nurse-midwife can participate in at least part of the maternity care of a patient and can sometimes do everything necessary, including help the mother deliver the baby.

One reason the profession is growing is that many women and their husbands desire more natural surroundings for their child's birth and more flexible and individual care than may be typical of most hospital births attended by physicians. Some women want to use the Leboyer method, for example, which emphasizes the importance of a gentler and softer environment for the newborn. The delivery room lights are dimmed, and the baby is immediately placed directly into a warm bath after delivery. The nurse-midwife usually is able to offer more options to the couple and allow them to make many of the choices concerning the birth of their baby.

Some people enter the nurse-midwife field because they feel frustrated by the constraints of the typical obstetrics ward. Evelyn Francis, a nurse-midwife trained at the State University of New York's College of Health Related Professions in Brooklyn, emphasizes this point:

> I worked six years in obstetrics after I got my RN. It was fun, but I felt frustrated. I only saw the mothers for a couple of days while they were hospitalized. When they left, I'd lose touch. Now, as a certified nurse-midwife, I can follow them for almost a year. It's much more satisfying for both of us (Zimmerman and Smith, 1978).

The nurse-midwife has a more personal relationship with each patient, partly because he or she can spend more time with her. Midwives pay special attention to developing the psychological bond between the mother and her baby. They generally like to give the baby to the mother as soon after birth as possible, thus encouraging the attachment process. In many ways, the profession of nurse-midwife offers people a chance to express the motivation that led them into nursing in the first place: a sincere desire to help people.

The process of childbirth is truly magnificent and often ranks among the most important experiences of a woman's life. The experience is very different in different cultures. Even in the United States, ideas about childbirth have changed many times. During the twentieth century, advances in medical science have been able to reduce the rate of birth injuries and infant mortality during the birth process. The result, however, has been to take childbirth out of the home and into the sterile environment of the hospital. Giving birth came to be seen as a condition of sickness, requiring medication and medical intervention, rather than a normal developmental process. At the peak of this trend, mothers were receiving many kinds of drugs—to relieve the pain of childbirth, to speed up labor, and even to make them forget the entire experience.

Recently, however, the trend seems to be moving in the direction of viewing childbirth as a very normal process, one that requires little or no medication, and one that can even take place at home. An important part of this trend is the **Lamaze method** *of childbirth. In this method, both the father and the mother attend classes, prior to the birth of their child, that cover prenatal development, labor, and delivery. Principles of relaxation, neuromuscular control, and breathing techniques are taught during the classes to aid the mother during labor and delivery.* The method is partly based on the sound psychological principle of conditioning. The mother is conditioned to begin breathing exercises with each contraction and to relax between contractions, thereby learning to control her pain and reduce her fear. The Lamaze method also emphasizes the father's role in childbirth; he acts like a "coach" for the mother, helping her through all the stages of labor, timing her contractions, pacing her breathing, and giving moral support and encouragement. He is present in the delivery room and usually holds the newborn baby immediately after birth.

Other new trends in childbirth include **rooming-in,** *in which the baby stays in a bassinet in the mother's hospital room rather than in the nursery with all the other babies,* and **birthing rooms** *in the hospital, where the furnishings are more homelike.* The number of mothers breast-feeding their infants is also increasing rapidly.

These trends are beneficial for the baby as well as the mother. For example, babies born to mothers who receive heavy medication during labor often are sluggish for at least three days after birth. Reducing the amount of medication, therefore, helps the baby adjust to the outside world more quickly. Also, allowing mothers and infants to be together sooner after birth, and allowing the baby to stay in the room with the mother, has advantages as well. In addition to reducing

the number of infections that spread rapidly in the crowded nursery, rooming-in encourages the growth of love and attachment between the two. Later in this section we will further discuss why the attachment process is an important component of development in infants.

The Abilities of the Newborn

To the untrained eye, the newborn may seem more like a mass of leaky protoplasm than a human being. The newborn's main motivation seems to be the avoidance of hunger, coldness, and other discomforts, and his sole means of communication seems to be crying. Some might say that if the baby is not sleeping, he is crying or sucking. But by carefully observing newborns, using some very creative techniques, we get a much different picture. Researchers have learned to record subtle changes in babies' heartbeats, sucking patterns, and eye movements, and have found that the baby is an astonishingly capable individual.

Motor Behavior. The infant is born with a group of reflexes, some of which are critical to survival. Sucking is an example. The **rooting reflex** is *another reflex present at birth; when infants are stroked near the mouth, they will open their mouths and turn their heads in the direction of the stimulation.* Other reflexes are less obviously connected with important biological functions. The **Babinski reflex,** for example, *results in bending of the toes when the sole of the foot is stroked; normal infants curl their toes upward; older children and adults curl them downward.*

The motor areas of the cortex are not well myelinated at birth, so the infant's voluntary motor coordination is not yet developed. However, as the months go by, the infant gains more and more control over the large muscle groups (see table 9.2). Control first appears in the head and extends downward as the baby grows older. For example, at two months the baby can hold her head and chin up; at three months she can raise her chest as well.

Table 9.2 Milestones of motor development in three areas

Age in Months	Control of		
	Head	Trunk and arms	Legs
Birth			
1	Side-to-side movement		Limited-support stepping reflex
2	Hold head and chin up		
3		Hold chest up in face-down position	
4		Reach for objects in sight (without success)	
5	Head erect in sitting position		
6		Sit up with some support	
7		Roll over in prone position	
8			Walk with assistance
9			
10			Support self alone
11			Pull self up in standing position
12			
13			Walk alone
14			

The Sensory World. The newborn can sort out the sensory environment very early. In one study, three-day-old babies listened to tape recordings of either their mothers or female strangers reading a story. During the readings, the babies sucked on a pacifier containing electronic equipment that controlled the tape recorder. The baby could control which voice came on by changing the sucking pattern. To everyone's surprise, these tiny infants changed their sucking patterns in order to hear more of their mothers' voices. Not only could they discriminate between the two voices, they clearly preferred their mothers' voices and would work to hear them (DeCasper and Fifer, 1980).

The world of sound is obviously not a big confusing jumble to newborns. Besides being able to discriminate their mothers' voices, they can discriminate their own voices too. Calm babies begin to cry when they hear the tape-recorded crying of other babies, but they cry very little if they hear a recording of their own crying. Listening to their own crying on tape often stops babies from crying, even when they are only eighteen hours old (Martin and Clark, 1982; Simner, 1971; Sagi and Hoffman, 1976). Some psychologists maintain that this represents the earliest glimmerings of empathy, a clear sign of social behavior. Empathy in this sense is only a very primitive ability to detect the emotional state of another being and to respond in kind.

During the 1960s, experts in child care believed that babies could see little more than light or dark patterns during the first weeks of life. Today psychologists know that newborns see shapes very well, although their color vision takes longer to develop. Classic studies of infant perception have been conducted by Robert Fantz and his coworkers (Fantz, 1961; Fantz, et al., 1975a, b).

ONE-MONTH-OLD

TWO-MONTH-OLD

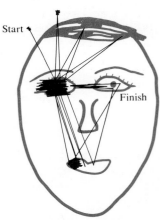

Figure 9.5 *How one- and two-month-old infants scan human faces*

These researchers presented two images to infants and observed how long they looked at each. Using this technique, they found that babies prefer facelike figures to bull's eyes and prefer bull's eyes to solid circles. They also found that babies spend more time looking at curved lines rather than straight ones and at images with many large elements in them.

Newborns are even able to imitate facial expressions, suggesting rather advanced development of both sensory abilities and motor control of the facial muscles. Babies who were only thirty-six hours old watched models make happy, sad, and surprised facial expressions, while observers watched the babies and rated their facial movements. The observers, who were unable to see the model, could guess which facial expression the model was posing just by watching the baby's face. These babies, less than two days old, were actually imitating the poses (Field, Woodson, Greenberg, and Cohen, 1982).

Studying the perceptual abilities of human infants has been very challenging; researchers must be quite inventive to design testing methods. For example, one group of studies tried to determine what features of the environment draw the attention of infants (Salapatek, 1975; Banks and Salapatek, 1981; Maurer and Salapatek, 1976). Infants are shown pictures or drawings, and their eye movements are recorded photographically. The photographs can then be correlated to the images, showing how the infant scans visual scenes in her environment.

Figure 9.5 shows how one- and two-month-old infants scan the faces of people (not drawings or photographs) through a mirror arrangement. The scanning patterns of the two-month-old babies were somewhat different from those of the younger babies. The older infants scanned more of the faces, focusing their attention on the eyes and mouth. The one-month-old baby paid more attention to certain areas on the head and the chin.

Another spark of creativity was shown by Richard Walk and Eleanor Gibson (1961), the scientists who developed the visual cliff apparatus to study depth perception (fig. 9.6). The "cliff" is actually a solid glass tabletop suspended over a checkerboard-covered

Figure 9.6   The visual cliff. The side with the pattern several feet below the glass looks ominously like a sharp cliff to the infant.

"shallow" side and "deep" side. Infants refuse to crawl across the deep side despite coaxing by the parents and the conflicting message they are receiving from their hands, demonstrating that they have excellent depth perception. Even before they can crawl, infants show an increase in heart rate when they are placed face down on the deep side, suggesting that depth perception appears very early.

The Newborn's "Speech."   The rudiments of speech communication seem to be present in the infant as well. They engage in various kinds of "vocal dialogues" with their mothers. In one experiment, researchers recorded the vocalizations of three-day-old infants and their mothers during breast-feeding (Rosenthal, 1982). The infants were more likely to start vocalizing when the mother was vocalizing than when she was silent; the

baby seemed to "join in." In other experiments, older babies developed patterns of vocalization in which they alternated with their mothers, much like the normal pattern of conversation.

Attachment

One of the most important events that occurs during the first year of life is the development of an attachment between the child and the caregiver, whether it is the mother, the father, both, or some other person. Attachment is not simply a matter of finding a person who will take care of a baby's physical needs. It is an important part of emotional and social growth, and it is vital to the development of a healthy personality. (Sroufe, 1985).

Mother Love in Monkeys.   Studies of monkeys reared without their mothers show very clearly how important the attachment process is (Harlow, 1962). Infant monkeys were taken away from their mothers soon after birth and kept in cages with two surrogate, or artificial substitute, mothers. Both were wire models with heads, and one had a terrycloth covering. The infant monkeys became quite attached to the cloth-covered "monkey," running to it in times of stress and spending a great deal of time holding on to it. The monkeys preferred this cloth surrogate even when the wire surrogate was the one that always provided the food (fig. 9.7).

Formerly, many psychologists believed that infants became attached to their mothers through classical conditioning—the mother became associated with food. But the attachment of these monkeys to the cloth surrogate was not based on food rewards; it was based on other factors, one of which seemed to be the softness of body contact from the terrycloth. Later studies showed that infant monkeys prefer cloth surrogates that move gently, rather than those that are stationary. No one would conclude that the essence of mother love is soft skin or a swaying motion, but body contact and the normal motion accompanying carrying a baby around seem to contribute to the phenomenon.

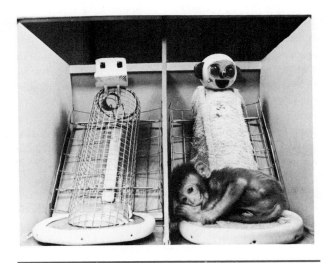

Figure 9.7 A "wire surrogate mother" (left) and a "cloth surrogate mother" for an infant monkey (Courtesy Harlow Primate Lab, University of Wisconsin)

The monkeys reared with the lifeless surrogate mothers, even cloth surrogates, did not develop normally. They became very fearful and aggressive, and the females lacked mothering skills. Monkeys, it seems, need "mother love" to develop normally. Although similar studies have never been conducted on human beings, of course, there is good reason to believe that the attachment process is at least as important to humans as it is to monkeys. Infants reared in institutional settings, where they get adequate physical care but are unable to develop an attachment with one individual, develop abnormally. They become socially apathetic and usually have poor cognitive development as well.

Attachment and Personality Development. Many psychologists see the attachment process as being particularly important in personality development. Erik Erikson's theory (1972), mentioned earlier (table 9.1), suggests that **trust vs. mistrust** *is the first psychosocial task the human faces in life. This conflict revolves around whether the baby can successfully form a trusting attachment with his caregiver.* If he can, he develops a sense of trust and learns that it is possible to depend on adults in his world to give him reliable and loving care. If he fails to develop this sense of trust, his personality development will be affected.

A British study illustrates what can happen to children who do not develop an attachment during the early part of life (Tizard, 1979). The subjects were babies who were reared in residential nurseries run by British voluntary societies. Although they had wonderful physical care, and in fact received a fair amount of attention from adults, they could not form lasting attachments to specific people. Turnover among the staff was high because the institutions were used to train student nurses. As the children grew up, they were much more clinging and dependent on the nurses than were children reared in normal families. They cried and whined more, they were less willing to share their belongings with other children, and many were unusually aggressive. Their mental development was slightly retarded, and they generally became toilet trained at a later age than children reared in their own homes. Whether these personality disturbances continued into later childhood depended on whether the child was adopted, restored to its natural mother, or left in the institution. The adopted children fared quite well; the adopting parents were carefully screened, very loving people who probably provided an environment in which the child could form a normal attachment. The children restored to their own mothers, however, often continued to show personality disturbances. Several natural mothers had ambivalent feelings toward the youngsters, and some did not want the child home.

In the extreme case of institutional rearing, a baby might not form an attachment to one particular person, but even in normal families babies can form different kinds of attachments. Mary Ainsworth and her colleagues developed the **Strange Situations Test,** *which is designed to assess the nature of the attachment between an infant and mother or other caregiver.* It consists of a sequence of episodes in which the mother and a stranger leave the room and return while researchers carefully observe the child's behavior. (The Research Box: Measuring Attachment describes this test in more detail.)

Some babies show **secure attachments** *to their care-givers; they show a healthy balance between depen-dence and exploration, using the mother as a secure base for exploration of a new environment but de-creasing their explorations when she leaves the room.* They actively greet the mother when she returns. Other babies show **insecure attachments,** *which are charac-terized by several different reactions to the mother's departure and return, including avoidance, resistance, or ambivalent emotional responses* (Ainsworth, Blehar, Waters, and Wall, 1978).

The effects of these attachments on later behavior is the subject of recent research. For example, re-searchers observed the behavior of preschool children whose attachment behavior had been measured in in-fancy. The children who had developed secure attach-ments during infancy, especially the girls, tended to be more socially adept and competent with their peers, participate more, and generally attain higher social status, compared to those with insecure attachments in infancy (La Freniere and Sroufe, 1985).

The nature of the attachment an infant forms early in life may have wide-ranging effects during the child's later development, and more research is needed to un-derstand these effects (Sroufe, 1985).

GUIDED REVIEW

Learning Objectives 6, 7, and 8

1. _____ is an important developmental transition, for both infant and mother. New trends in the United States include the use of the _____ method of prepared childbirth, rooming-in, and birthing rooms. The trends make childbirth less a medical event and more a personal one that involves less medication and more opportunity for _____ between mother and baby.

2. Motor abilities of the newborn primarily consist of reflexes, such as sucking, _____ , and the _____ . The infant's motor skills develop from the head downward. Tests of sensory abilities show that the baby can discriminate sounds and visual stimuli at a very early age.

3. The attachment process is important for the baby's normal development. Studies of motherless monkeys demonstrated that infant monkeys need mothers not just for food but for body contact and security. In humans, the first year is important for the development of trust, a process that requires attachment. Different kinds of attachment in infants have been demonstrated by the _____ , including _____ and various kinds of insecure attachments.

ANSWERS

3. Strange Situations Test; secure attachments
1. Childbirth; Lamaze; attachment 2. rooting; Babinsky reflex

Childhood

The years between the ages of one and about twelve, when puberty is beginning, are exciting for both the child and the parents. Biologically, the child is growing much more slowly than during prenatal life or even during the first year. Still, the changes are remarkable, and they occur in every area of development. The child develops physically: adding weight, gaining control over

major and minor muscle groups, learning to walk, run, hop, and play ball. Socially, the child's world expands from just the mother to the family group, and even-tually to children and adults at school. The child begins to develop morally as well. First the concepts of good and bad are associated with whatever is approved or disapproved by the parents. Later "good" and "bad" are linked to rewards and punishment. And still later, toward the end of childhood, children acquire a sense of justice and fair play.

RESEARCH BOX

Measuring Attachment

The way that a child becomes attached to the primary caregiver has been a topic of considerable interest to psychologists and parents alike. However, studying attachment behavior, and measuring it in real-life situations, has been extremely difficult. A great deal of information has been accumulated through interviews with the parents, but this technique has many drawbacks. Parents' memories are notoriously selective when they are discussing their children and the way they interact with them. Many parents tend to report that they used whichever child-rearing practices were endorsed by the experts of the era.

Researchers in child development are now depending more heavily on actual observations of interactions between the caregiver and the child to obtain data on attachment behavior. Videotape recordings are especially useful here because researchers can play the tapes over and over to different people, making sure that their judgments of the events are reliable.

One very popular strategy for assessing attachment behavior is the Ainsworth Strange Situation Test (Ainsworth and Bell, 1970). It consists of a sequence of episodes designed to determine how the child behaves in a series of introductions, separations, and reunions with the child's mother and a stranger. Some of the episodes are described below:

Episode 1: Mother, accompanied by an observer, carried the baby into the room. Then the Observer left.

Episode 2: Mother put the baby down in the specified place, then sat quietly in her chair, participating only if the baby sought her attention. (Duration: 3 minutes.)

Cognitive Development

Jean Piaget proposed the most influential theory of cognitive development, based mainly on observations of his own children. He presented them with problems and noted not so much whether they could solve them, but how much they understood about their own solution. Piaget noticed that at different ages children's ideas about objects and events changed considerably. Even though children of different ages might be able to solve a particular problem, their cognitions about the objects and events were dramatically different. Consider the game of tiddlywinks, played on a carpet:

Experimenter: Try and get one of the pawns (her word) into the box. (She puts the small counter on the large one and then presses down on the former, with all her attention on the movement of her hand and none on the target.) Where did it go?
Flo (age 4): Onto the table.
E: How did you do it?
F: I pressed very hard.
E: Can you do it on the table?
F: (She tries.) No, because it slides.
E: Why?
F: Because the table isn't soft.

Episode 3: A strange entered, sat quietly for one minute, conversed with the mother for one minute, and then gradually approached the baby, showing him a toy. At the end of the third minute the mother quietly left the room.

Episode 4: If the baby was happily engaged in play, the stranger was nonparticipant. If the baby was inactive, the stranger tried to interest him in the toys. If the baby was distressed, the stranger tried to distract or comfort him. If he could not be comforted, the episode was curtailed; otherwise it lasted 3 minutes.

Episode 5: The mother entered and paused in the doorway to give the baby an opportunity to respond spontaneously to her. The stranger then left unobtrusively. What the mother did next was not specified, except that she was told that after the baby was again settled in play with the toys she was to leave again, after pausing to say "bye-bye." (Duration of episode undetermined.)

Although the Strange Situation Test provides much richer and more meaningful information about attachment than do interviews, it has been criticized. In particular, the sequences are very fluid, and experimental controls are lacking. For example, if the baby begins to cry in the middle of episode 4, can we assume it is because the mother is gone? Or should we attribute the baby's distress to an inability to relax in the presence of a stranger? Despite these difficulties in interpretation, most researchers agree that direct observation of this kind is very informative.

Flo was able to get the tiddlywink into the target box, but she did not understand why. She thought that the main action was simply pressing, rather than pressing the edge of the small counter on the edge of the larger one. She also could not fully grasp why the game worked on the carpet and not on the table. Older children would describe the events quite differently since they perceive the role the small counter plays (Piaget, 1976).

Based on his observations, Piaget concluded that a child's thought goes through a series of fundamental changes, such that the later ways of thinking are dependent upon, yet quite distinct from, earlier ones. Each stage is progressively more logical than the last. He proposed four stages of cognitive development: sensorimotor stage, preoperational stage, concrete operational stage, and formal operational stage. (See table 9.3.)

Sensorimotor Stage.   The **sensorimotor stage** *is the earliest of Piaget's stages of cognitive development. It extends from birth to about age two. During this period, the infant gradually develops the capability to coordinate his sensations and perceptions with his physical actions.*

One ability acquired during this stage is called **object permanence,** *which refers to the understanding that an object exists independent of the self and continues to exist even when it cannot be immediately perceived.*

Table 9.3 Piaget's stages of cognitive development

Stage	General descriptions	Age level
Sensorimotor period	The child progresses from instinctual reflexive action at birth to symbolic activities to the ability to separate self from object in the environment. He develops limited capabilities for anticipating the consequences of actions.	0 ½ 1 1½ 2
Preoperational period	The child's ability to think becomes refined during this period. First, he develops what Piaget calls preconceptual thinking, in which he deals with each thing individually but is not able to group objects. The child is able to use symbols, such as words, to deal with problems. During the latter half of this period, the child develops better reasoning abilities but is still bound to the here-and-now.	2½ 3 3½ 4 4½ 5 5½ 6 6½ 7
Concrete operations	At this stage, the child develops the ability to perform intellectual operations—such as reversibility, conservation, ordering of things by number, size, or class, etc. His ability to relate time and space is also matured during this period.	7½ 8 8½ 9 9½ 10 10½
Period of formal operations	This is the period in which the person learns hypothetical reasoning. He is able to function purely on a symbolic, abstract level. His conceptualization capacities are matured.	11 11½ 12 12½ 13 13½ 14 14½ 15

From Belkin, Gary S., and Jerry L. Gray, *Educational Psychology: An Introduction.* © 1977 Wm. C. Brown Publishers, Dubuque, Iowa. All Rights Reserved. Reprinted by permission.

For example, when you show a toy to a five-month-old, he tracks it visually and may reach for it. If you hide the toy under a scarf, the baby acts as though the toy no longer exists. By the age of ten months, however, the baby will actively search for the hidden toy, demonstrating his acquisition of object permanence.

The way babies of different ages respond to the unexpected appearance of a toy shows how object permanence develops. Babies of five, nine, and sixteen months were seated in an infant seat in front of a screen. A toy on a circular track moved in front of the screen, behind it out of sight, and then around in front again.

After several rounds, the experimenters replaced the familiar toy with a new one, behind the screen. When the new toy came into the babies' view, the experimenters rated their facial expressions for raised brows, dropped jaws, or other signs of surprise. None of the five-month-old babies showed any surprise when the unexpected toy appeared. But all the sixteen-month-olds, and some of the nine-month-olds, did (Gratch, 1982). The youngest infants had no sense that the first toy was permanent and continued to exist after it went behind the screen, so they were not surprised when a new toy appeared.

Preoperational Stage.   The **preoperational stage,** *extending from about two to seven years of age, is characterized by the acquisition of language, the growth in the use of symbols, and a limited kind of logical thinking.* Even though the child is beginning to talk like an adult, he is not yet thinking like an adult. His cognitive processes are different in several ways.

One such difference involves **egocentrism,** *which refers to the failure to appreciate that another person's perceptions may differ from one's own.* The preoperational child's world is dominated by her own visual impressions, and she thinks that everyone sees what she sees. She might, for example, cover her eyes and claim that you can't see her. Another example of the limitations of preoperational thought involves **conservation,** *a term which refers to the fact that the basic properties of objects often remain unchanged despite superficial changes in appearance.* If you show a six-year-old child two equal-sized lumps of clay and ask whether they were about equal, he would say "yes." If you then rolled one into a snake before his eyes and asked the same question, the child would probably say that the snake had more clay. Because visual impressions are so important to the preoperational child, he cannot grasp that a change in shape did not affect the amount of clay present in the lump.

Concrete Operational Stage.   The **concrete operational stage** *lasts from about age seven to age eleven and is characterized by the need to anchor thought in concrete events.* Many of the limitations of logical thought characteristic of the preoperational stage are gone. For example, children in this stage are able to grasp the concept of conservation, and they lose the egocentric perspective typical of the younger child. Children in this stage can think logically in many ways; they can draw a diagram of a neighborhood and trace the route to a friend's house, organize objects by increasing size, and classify objects according to dimensions such as color or shape.

Formal Operational Stage.   The **formal operational stage** *usually begins around puberty. It is characterized by the ability to think about both concrete and abstract events, as well as the ability to formulate and test hypotheses to solve problems.* An adolescent can solve algebra problems, for example, using only abstract symbols. For Piaget, this stage was the most advanced, though other theorists argue that many advances in cognitive development come during adulthood.

Piaget's theories have been remarkably durable, as far as psychological theories are concerned. Further research on the cognitive stages suggests that there may be more than four stages, that they may be more flexible than Piaget thought, and that children sometimes exhibit elements of more than one stage at the same time. Some research suggests that the sequences are not entirely invariant since children sometimes move back and forth between stages during a transition phase (Fischer and Silvern, 1985). Nevertheless, Piaget's formulation of how cognition develops seems to represent quite well how children actually think.

Social and Emotional Development

Human beings begin their social and emotional development from the first day of life. As we previously discussed, the attachment process is important for babies; the kind of attachment a baby develops for its primary caregiver has effects that last for at least one or two years, and perhaps much longer (Matas, Arend, and Sroufe, 1978). In the years after infancy, the child's family is the most important variable in the socialization process. As the child grows older, especially after school begins, friendships play key roles in social and emotional development.

With respect to Erikson's theory, psychosocial tasks during early and middle childhood reflect how the child interacts first with parents and then with siblings and friends (see table 9.1). After the trust vs. mistrust conflict, children are faced with the task of resolving autonomy vs. shame and doubt, discussed earlier in this chapter. During this stage the child should be developing independent and autonomous actions. The child next faces **initiative vs. guilt,** *an Eriksonian psychosocial task of early childhood, which concerns whether the child learns to initiate actions or to feel guilty if he initiates ones that are disapproved.* **Industry vs. inferiority** *is the psychosocial task faced during the period of middle childhood; using neighborhood and school friends as a yardstick to measure her own competence, the child will be inclined more toward industriousness if she finds herself basically competent. If she feels incompetent and inferior, an unhealthy negative attitude may color her ability to attack challenging problems.*

The Family. The styles of interaction in different families are very diverse. Some parents insist on maintaining strict control over their children while others adopt a more lenient attitude. One researcher (Baumrind, 1971) found three styles of parenting that were particularly associated with social and emotional development: authoritarian, authoritative, and permissive.

The **authoritarian parent** *is restrictive and emphasizes punishment in the control of behavior.* The **authoritative parent,** *typically very warm and nurturing, encourages independence in the child but still places limits and controls on his actions.* The **permissive parent** *is nonpunitive, places low demands, and allows considerable freedom.* Research has found these parenting styles associated with different patterns of social and emotional development. Children of authoritarian parents tend to be anxious about social comparisons and generally ineffective in social interactions. Permissive parenting is associated with immaturity and regressive behavior in children, as well as an inability to assume leadership. The most positive qualities appear to be related to the authoritative style. Children of such parents demonstrate social competency and self-reliance.

When you think of the word "family," images of a mother and father probably come to mind, and perhaps images of one or two brothers or sisters. This is the nuclear family in which the majority of American youngsters grew up in previous eras. The mother usually did not work outside the home, and the father was typically the main breadwinner. No longer are most children exposed to this kind of family situation. They develop in a much broader range of environments, including homes in which both parents have outside employment and homes with a single parent, usually the mother. The increase in single-parent homes has been staggering. About twenty-five percent of children born between 1910 and 1960 lived in a single-parent home for at least some period of their development. In the 1970s the figure rose to between forty and fifty percent (Bane, 1978). Another rising statistic is the number of children living in "blended" families, containing stepparents, unmarried cohabiting adults, stepchildren, or half-siblings.

The effects of these changing family environments on the development of children are not entirely clear. Studies of children whose mothers work outside the home have found both positive and negative effects. For example, one study found that boys whose mothers stayed at home were more competent intellectually but were more fearful, inhibited and conforming as adolescents. The day-care boys (but not the girls) were also more likely to disagree with their mothers and ignore punishments (Moore, 1975). Many studies find very little difference between children with full-time mothers and children of employed mothers (Etaugh, 1980). Even very young children appear to suffer few ill effects from having substitute caregivers part of the time. For example, studies of the attachment behavior of toddlers using the Strange Situations Test find highly similar patterns of attachment in the two groups (Barahal, 1978).

APPLICATION BOX
Nurturing Fathers

With the entrance of so many women with young children into the labor force, the job of child rearing is increasingly a shared one, shouldered by both mother and father. The children in such families see less of their mothers but more of their fathers, as the dads take on more nurturing roles. Husbands whose wives are employed outside the home share in diapering, feeding, cuddling and comforting, as well as household chores.

More traditional people view these trends with surprise, although not necessarily alarm. Gail Kaufman, a working wife with a daughter now in her teens and a husband who shares child-rearing responsibilities, was out of town on a business trip when Jennifer, then two years old, got bronchitis. The pediatrician asked Barry, her husband, if he knew how to take the child's temperature. Barry not only knew, he was quite familiar with all the other aspects of child care as well (Peterson, 1983).

Psychologists who study the children from such homes find that it benefits them in important ways. Diane Ehrensaft, a psychologist from Berkeley, California, believes they are more confident and creative than other children, and also more comfortable with their own sexuality. The boys are masculine but not frantic about being macho, and the girls appear competent and feminine. Gail Kaufman believes some of the benefits lie in the fact that Jennifer always has two adults she can count on. The daughter is comfortable with both parents and trusts both men and women.

An important variable in any conclusion about the effects of substitute caregivers is the quality of the care. While high quality day-care appears to produce no obvious ill effects, poor quality care could well be very detrimental.

The Influence of Peers. Most children have one or more siblings who contribute to their social and emotional development. In observations of forty-seven families with two or three children, the children teased, whined, yelled, talked, touched, laughed, and performed many behaviors one might expect of children. But most of the negative interactions were with one another, whereas most of the positive ones were with the parents (Baskett, 1974). Although siblings can be serious rivals, particularly with respect to parental attention, they can also have very positive effects on one another. Older siblings seem to understand many of the problems of younger children and can communicate with them about friendships, teachers, physical appearance, and sex.

The impact of peer groups becomes almost overwhelming in the adolescent years; but even in early and middle childhood the peer group plays a critical role in social and emotional development. Peers provide the developing child with a source of information about the world and give her a chance to compare her abilities and accomplishments with others her own age. Infant monkeys who grow up without normal mothers show very abnormal behavior, as we discussed earlier. But if they have opportunities to interact with other young monkeys, their abnormalities are very much reduced (Suomi and Harlow, 1972). The evidence that human children can be very effective "therapists" for one another is growing stronger. Some schools are even developing structured programs in which this kind of activity can take place, and children can assist one another in such areas as trust, cooperation, and leadership.

The development of friendships begins quite early. Infants as young as six months interact by smiling, touching, and vocalizing. During the second year, children's friendships revolve primarily around toys, using the object as a focus for the interaction. When the toddlers begin to use language more fluently, interactions increase in complexity.

An interesting observational study of two- to four-year-old children revealed some of the facets of the development of friendships in a nursery school (Corsaro, 1981). The children's behavior suggested they shared two concerns: to gain entry to ongoing interactions, and to protect those interactions once they started by resisting the efforts of other children to join in. In the following sequence involving three-year-olds, Linda is trying to join Nancy, Barbara, and the researcher:

> Barbara to Linda: You can't play!
> Linda to Barbara: Yes I can. I can have some animals too.
> Barbara to Linda: No, you can't. We don't like you today.
> Nancy to Linda: You're not our friend.
> Linda to Barbara and Nancy: I can play here too.
> Barbara to Nancy: No, her can't—her can't play, right Nancy?
> Nancy to Barbara: Right.
> Linda to Researcher: Can I have some animals, Bill?
> Researcher to Linda: You can have some of these. . . .

Linda's persistence in trying to join the group, and Barbara and Nancy's equal persistence in refusing her entry, demonstrates how important children consider peer interactions. They seem to be aware of the fragility of peer interactions and try hard to enter them and then protect them against intrusion. Children also seem to be aware of the power of friendship in social control.

What constitutes a "friend" to a child changes dramatically, and some researchers have suggested a series of stages (Selman, 1981). At first, children consider a friend to be anyone with whom they play and who lives nearby, a condition that might better be called "playmateship." In the next stage, friendships are "one way." A person is a friend if he does what the child wants. In later stages, the child develops two-way friendships, in which the child appreciates cooperation and the reciprocal nature of a two-way interaction.

Moral Development

The way a child comes to know right from wrong, to feel guilty, to empathize with other people, and to help them when they are in distress are all components of moral development. It is a complicated process that is integrally related to both cognitive development and socialization.

Piaget proposed that children pass through stages of moral development just as they do during their cognitive development. **Moral realism** *is the first stage of moral development proposed by Piaget; in this stage, right and wrong are judged by the consequences of the action rather than by the intention of the actor.* For example, a child who accidentally knocked everything off a table would be judged more harshly than one who deliberately knocked over a glass of juice. **Moral autonomy** *is the second stage of moral development, according to Piaget; in this stage, children can take into account both the intentions of the actor and the consequences of the action.*

Another theorist, Lawrence Kohlberg, elaborated on Piaget's two stages (Kohlberg, 1976; Levine, Kohlberg, and Hewer, 1985). He poses a moral dilemma to his young subjects and asks them what they would do. The most famous dilemma involves a man who cannot afford to pay the exhorbitant price demanded by a druggist for a drug needed by his dying wife. Should he steal the drug or not? Kohlberg assesses a person's stage of moral development not so much by whether the person says yes or no, but by a standard scoring scheme that probes the person's moral reasoning

Table 9.4 Kohlberg's stages of moral development		
Stage	**Brief description**	**Reasons for doing right**
Level I: 1	Preconventional Desire to avoid punishment	Avoidance of punishment and the superior power of authority; obedience for its own sake.
2	Desire to obtain rewards	Serves ones own needs and recognizes that other people have their interests, too; conforms to obtain rewards.
Level II: 3	Conventional "Good boy/Good girl"	Values the approval of others and tries to maintain mutual relationships involving trust, loyalty, respect, and gratitude; believes in the Golden Rule.
Level III: 4	Conventional Respect for authority	Values society's laws and tries to uphold them; tries to keep the institution going.
5	Respect for the social contract	Believes in upholding the social contract because it provides the "greatest good for the greatest number;" recognizes that a social contract is an agreement between people that benefits the public welfare.
6	Universal ethical principles	Personally committed to a set of self-chosen ethical principles, most of which may be compatible with the laws of society. When laws conflict with ethical principles, the person acts in accordance with his or her principles.

Source: Based on Kohlberg, L., "Stage and Sequence: The Cognitive-Developmental Approach to Socialization," in D. A. Goslin (ed.), Handbook of Socialization Theory and Research. *Chicago: Rand McNally, 1969; and Kohlberg, L., "Moral Stages and Moralization," in T. Lickons (ed.),* Moral Development and Behavior. *New York: Holt, Rinehart and Winston, 1976.*

(Colby, Kohlberg, Gibbs, Candee, et al., 1983). For example, if the subject answers "Yes, because the drug isn't really worth that much anyway," he would be in a very low stage of moral development. If he answered, "Yes, because he should act according to his principle of preserving and respecting life," he would be in a rather advanced stage. Table 9.4 details Kohlberg's six stages.

The notion that children pass through stages during their moral development has received some support (Kohlberg, 1984; Snarey, 1985). Their advancement appears to be particularly dependent on their cognitive development and their ability to reason about non-moral situations. Nevertheless, the stage theories, particularly Kohlberg's, have been criticized on many grounds. The subjects' answers to the stories are very difficult to score, and many scientists believe that the stories themselves are culturally biased and ethnocentric. Morality in one culture may be quite different from morality in another, and even some of Kohlberg's work supports this hypothesis. In one longitudinal study of adolescents living on a kibbutz in Israel, the girls and boys tended to pass progressively through the stages of moral development as expected, but these children did show a greater orientation toward the welfare of the group than did American children (Snarey, Reimer, and Kohlberg, 1985).

Critics have also argued with Kohlberg's emphasis on fair-minded rationality in morality and objected to the lack of attention paid to the role of emotions (Gibbs and Schnell, 1985). Emotions are an important motivator for moral learning and empathy, and they may be one of the important aspects of moral behavior.

The Gifted Child

Educational trends in the United States have, in general, been very favorable toward the education of the handicapped, the culturally disadvantaged, women, the retarded, and many other groups. In the last fifty years, laws have been designed to allow many of these children access to educational opportunities denied them in the past. For example, most schools now have provisions for children in wheelchairs, making it possible for them to attend class with normal children. And funds have been provided for girls' sports programs, giving them the chance to learn the teamwork skills typical on the playing field.

A group of children whose educational needs have somehow been ignored, however, is the gifted. The **gifted** *child is usually identified by a very high score on an IQ test, perhaps 130 or above. Recently, the gifted are also identified by their extraordinary talents in one or more areas, such as mathematics, verbal abilities, creativity, ability in the performing arts, or leadership.* Some gifted children show talent in all these areas; others tend to have gifted abilities in only one.

What is the Gifted Child Like? Some psychologists maintain that the gifted child is different by definition. They are more curious, very active (and sometimes labeled hyperactive), obnoxious, unruly, rebellious, and generally a pain in the neck. Because they are so different from their peers and family, they may feel lonely and depressed and may be ostracized by their parents and friends (Webb, cited by Holden, 1980).

Some of the research on these children, however, suggests that they are surprisingly healthy, both socially and emotionally. Tests of mathematically precocious youths, for example, found that their personalities were mostly quite normal, although they were emotionally and socially advanced (Stanley, 1976; George, Cohn, and Stanley, 1979). A classic longitudinal study of 1500 gifted children, which began in the 1920s, found that many of them had made remarkable accomplishments by adulthood (Terman, 1925). When contacted in their sixties, these people generally felt they were leading satisfying lives in both their work and family life (Sears, 1977).

Educating the Gifted. How to educate the gifted child is an important issue, not simply because these children have the same rights that other minority groups have. The gifted children, if they are properly nurtured, could perhaps make significant contributions to our civilization when they mature. The two primary methods of educating the gifted include enrichment and acceleration.

There are many types of enrichment programs that might be devised for gifted children. One style would provide all gifted children with similar, expanding experiences, ignoring the particular "gift" of each child. For example, an enrichment program might allow children to go on field trips, do extra school projects, and become involved in more creative endeavors. Another enrichment program might concentrate more heavily in the area in which the child shows exceptional talent. A musically inclined youngster, for example, would receive special training in music but would remain with her grade level in the other subjects. Other enrichment approaches include the opening of special schools and the establishment of special, fast-paced classes in particular subjects.

Proponents of acceleration maintain that enrichment programs are useful but that they do nothing to relieve the child's boredom in school. They think a better strategy is to allow the child to skip one or more grades. A program at Johns Hopkins University, called the Study of Mathematically Precocious Youth (SMPY), has been encouraging its gifted children to skip grades. Sean, for example, skipped ninth and tenth grades and entered eleventh grade at the age of thirteen. He took calculus, won a letter on the wrestling team, and was the "whiz" of the school's TV quiz team.

He also took advanced math courses, played golf, took some college courses, and managed a fourteen-year-old friend's campaign for the president of the student council. He entered Johns Hopkins as a sophomore at the age of fourteen.

The students in the SMPY project showed few personality and adjustment problems, despite their rapid acceleration through school. People who recommend acceleration rather than (or in addition to) enrichment wonder whether their mental health would be as good if they had been kept with their age mates. They also point out that few schools have qualified people to provide enrichment programs for the gifted because there are so few gifted children. Instead of worthwhile activities that keep the interest and stimulate the talents of these exceptional children, many "enrichment" programs become nothing more than extra busy work. One boy who eventually entered the SMPY project, for example, was required by his teacher to work every problem in his algebra text, rather than just the odd-numbered ones. The boy could have finished the whole course in a few hours, but the teacher wanted to hold him for 180 fifty-minute periods (Stanley, 1956).

The apparent lack of interest in the gifted may be due to the American distaste of elitism and our emphasis on egalitarianism. However, the gifted are gaining more visibility. The federal government has established an Office of Gifted and Talented within the Department of Education and is funding research on this special group of children.

GUIDED REVIEW

Learning Objectives 9, 10, 11, and 12

1. Piaget's theory of cognitive development states that children go through four stages: _____ , _____ , _____ , and _____ .

2. In Erikson's theory, children face a series of psychosocial tasks affecting their social and emotional development during early and middle childhood. These include _____ , _____ , _____ , and _____ .

3. The child's family is an important influence in his social, emotional, and moral development. Three parenting styles are _____ , a rigid, rule-oriented style; _____ , a warm nurturing style that provides limits and rules; and _____ , a laissez faire parenting style. The authoritative style appears to promote the most desirable characteristics in children.

4. Friends play key roles in socialization and emotional development. Even very young children interact with one another, and the concept of _____ becomes more sophisticated as the child matures.

5. Cognitive approaches to moral development emphasize stages of moral reasoning that advance with cognitive development. Piaget proposed two stages: _____ and _____ .

6. Kohlberg proposed a theory of _____ development that included six stages, each of which required greater cognitive abilities. The sixth stage involves adherence to universal ethical principles.

7. The _____ child has superior abilities in one or more areas. Although some gifted children have emotional problems because they are different, many are psychologically quite healthy.

8. The two main strategies for educating the gifted are _____ and _____ .

ANSWERS

1. sensorimotor stage; preoperational stage; concrete operational stage; formal operational stage 2. trust vs. mistrust; autonomy vs. shame and doubt; initiative vs. guilt; industry vs. inferiority 3. authoritarian; authoritative; permissive 4. friendship 5. moral realism, moral autonomy 6. moral 7. gifted 8. enrichment, acceleration

SUMMARY

I. Development refers to the patterns of forward movement or change, beginning at conception and continuing through the entire life span. (p. 310)

 A. Two methods of studying development are the cross-sectional study and the longitudinal study. (p. 310)

 B. Various perspectives have been used to approach the study of development, including the psychoanalytic approach, the cognitive-structural approach, and the behaviorist approach. (p. 311)

II. The two major forces that shape development are genes and the environment. (p. 312)

 A. Genetic forces begin their effects from the day of conception and continue throughout the life span. (p. 312)

 1. The gene is a very short length of DNA that is the basic unit of heredity; individual genes either direct the formation of specific proteins or control the activity of other genes. (p. 313)

 2. Genes can only indirectly affect behavior; the effects of genes on behavior is often investigated by use of the adoption study. (p. 314)

 B. Environmental factors influence development from conception. (p. 316)

 1. Aspects of the prenatal environment that can influence the development of the fetus include the presence or absence of hormones and the presence of drugs or alcohol. (p. 316)

 2. Inadequate nutrition is an environmental factor that is especially harmful to the growing organism if it occurs while the brain cells are still dividing. (p. 317)

 C. The interaction between genes and environment in development, and their relative importance in shaping the characteristics of the developing human, is often debated as part of the nature-nurture issue. The concept of critical periods demonstrates how genes and environment interact. (p. 317)

III. The first year of a baby's life is the time of the most rapid development after birth. (p. 318)

 A. Childbirth practices are undergoing many changes in the United States, including childbirth preparation classes, rooming-in, and birthing rooms. (p. 320)

 B. Careful observations of newborns show that they have many abilities from the moment of birth. (p. 321)

 1. The infant is born with several motor reflexes, such as the rooting reflex, sucking, and the Babinski reflex. Motor development proceeds from the head downward. (p. 321)

 2. Studies of the sensory abilities of infants show they can perceive sounds and visual images well very early in life, and show preferences for the sound of their mothers' voices and for visual stimuli that resemble faces. They can also perceive depth very early. (p. 322)

 3. Newborns show identifiable patterns in their vocalizations and participate in vocal "dialogues" with their mothers. (p. 324)

 C. Attachment to the primary caregiver is one of the most important processes during the first year of life. (p. 324)

 1. Studies of monkeys reared without their mothers show that they have various abnormal behavioral patterns in adulthood, even though they received proper nutrition. (p. 324)

 2. The nature of the infant's early attachment appears to influence personality development. (p. 325)

IV. Childhood includes the years between the ages of one and about twelve, when puberty is beginning. (p. 326)

 A. The most widely known theory of cognitive development was proposed by Jean Piaget. This theory suggests that children pass through four main stages. (p. 327)

1. The sensorimotor stage is characterized by the development of the capability to coordinate sensations and perceptions with physical actions.   (p. 328)

2. The preoperational stage is characterized by the acquisition of language, the growth in the use of symbols, and a limited kind of logical thinking.   (p. 330)

3. The concrete operational stage is characterized by the need to anchor thought in concrete events.   (p. 330)

4. The formal operational stage is characterized by the ability to think about both concrete and abstract events and to formulate hypotheses.   (p. 330)

B. Social and emotional development, according to Erikson, is affected by a child's ability to resolve several psychosocial conflicts. (p. 330)

1. The family is the focus of emotional and social development during early childhood. Styles of parenting that appear to affect social and emotional development include authoritarian, authoritative, and permissive.   (p. 331)

2. During later childhood, the influence of peers on social and emotional development grows.   (p. 332)

3. Moral development appears to be characterized by stages through which children pass in sequential order with increasing cognitive abilities. Kohlberg proposed six stages, using results from a test that presents the child with a moral dilemma.   (p. 333)

C. The gifted child has extraordinary abilities in a single area, or in several areas, such as academic aptitude, creativity, ability in the performing arts, and leadership.   (p. 335)

1. Gifted children tend to be socially and emotionally, as well as academically, more advanced than their age-mates.   (p. 335)

2. The two approaches generally used to educate the gifted include enrichment programs and acceleration programs. (p. 335)

ACTION GLOSSARY

Match the terms in the left column with the definitions in the right column.

____ **1. Development** (p. 310)
____ **2. Cross-sectional study** (p. 310)
____ **3. Longitudinal study** (p. 310)
____ **4. Autonomy vs. shame and doubt** (p. 311)
____ **5. Cognitive-structural approach** (p. 312)
____ **6. Chromosome** (p. 313)
____ **7. Adenine** (p. 313)

A. *A psychosocial task faced by toddlers, according to Erik Erikson, that involves the successful development of autonomous control over one's bodily functions. Failure to establish such control leads to shame and doubt.*
B. *Patterns of forward movement or change, beginning at conception and continuing through the entire life span.*
C. *A procedure for observing changes in the same group of people over time.*
D. *Long chains containing DNA, the genetic information, found in the nucleus of cells.*
E. *A procedure for comparing the characteristics of groups of people of different ages.*
F. *One of the four bases that make up DNA.*
G. *A perspective in human development that focuses on stages of intellectual development.*

____ **8. DNA** (p. 313)
____ **9. Cytosine** (p. 313)
____ **10. Gene** (p. 313)
____ **11. Homozygous** (p. 314)

A. *One of the four bases that make up DNA.*
B. *A gene that will be expressed regardless of which gene is on the paired chromosome.*
C. *Refers to the condition in which the two genes located on paired chromosomes and coding for the same function are identical.*

____ 12. **Dominant gene** (p. 314)
____ 13. **Recessive gene** (p. 314)
____ 14. **Co-dominance** (p. 314)

D. *A gene expessed only if it is paired with a recessive gene.*
E. *Characterizes the relationship between two genes that are both expressed on paired chromosomes in the same organism.*
F. *The basic unit of heredity. Consists of a short sequence of DNA arranged along a chromosome.*
G. *Deoxyribonucleic acid, the substance found in chromosomes that carries the genetic information.*

____ 15. **Adoption study** (p. 315)
____ 16. **Thymine** (p. 313)
____ 17. **Phenylketonuria (PKU)** (p. 316)
____ 18. **Cimetidine** (p. 316)
____ 19. **Nature-nurture issue** (p. 317)
____ 20. **Lamaze method** (p. 321)
____ 21. **Rooting reflex** (p. 321)

A. *A debate involving the relative importance of genetic factors and environmental factors in human behavior and development.*
B. *The infant's response to a touch on the cheek or corner of the mouth. The infant reflexively turns her head in the direction of the stimulation.*
C. *A procedure in which the similarity of an adopted child and the adoptive parents is compared to the similarity between the child and the biological parents.*
D. *A drug used to treat ulcers.*
E. *A method of childbirth that uses relaxation training, neuromuscular control, and specific breathing techniques in an attempt to reduce the sense of pain during labor and delivery.*
F. *One of the four bases that make up DNA.*
G. *A disease transmitted by two recessive genes that causes a lack in the enzyme required to metabolize a particular amino acid.*

____ 22. **Guanine** (p. 313)
____ 23. **Babinski reflex** (p. 321)
____ 24. **Trust vs. mistrust** (p. 325)
____ 25. **Strange Situation Test** (p. 325)
____ 26. **Secure attachment** (p. 326)
____ 27. **Insecure attachments** (p. 326)
____ 28. **Sensorimotor stage** (p. 328)

A. *The earliest stage of cognitive development, according to the theory of Jean Piaget. The infant develops the capability to coordinate his sensations and perceptions with his physical actions.*
B. *A pattern of behavior in which the infant shows a healthy balance between dependency and exploration, using the mother as a secure base from which to explore a novel environment.*
C. *A response in which the infant automatically curls his toes upward when the sole of his foot is stroked.*
D. *One of the four bases that makes up DNA.*
E. *A standardized procedure for measuring attachment between an infant and mother or other caregiver. The test involves a series of separations and reunions under controlled laboratory conditions.*
F. *A pattern of behavior in which the infant's behavior, in response to the mother's departure and return, includes avoidance, resistance, or ambivalent responses.*
G. *A psychosocial task faced by infants, according to Erik Erikson's theory of development. Successful resolution occurs when the baby's needs are met and she develops trust in the environment and her caregivers.*

____ 29. **Object permanence** (p. 328)
____ 30. **Preoperational stage** (p. 330)
____ 31. **Egocentrism** (p. 330)
____ 32. **Conservation** (p. 330)
____ 33. **Concrete operational stage** (p. 330)
____ 34. **Formal operational thought** (p. 330)
____ 35. **Initiative vs. guilt** (p. 331)

A. *An inability to appreciate that another person's perceptions of a situation may differ from one's own.*
B. *Refers to the fact that the basic properties of objects remain unchanged despite superficial changes in appearance.*
C. *The understanding that an object exists independently of the self and continues to exist even when it cannot immediately be perceived.*
D. *The psychosocial task of early childhood, according to Erik Erikson's theory of personality development. The child is learning to initiate actions or to feel guilty about initiating ones that are disapproved.*
E. *The third stage of cognitive development, according to Jean Piaget's theory. The stage is characterized by the need to anchor logical thought in concrete events.*
F. *The second stage in the theory of cognitive development proposed by Jean Piaget, characterized by acquisition of language, growth in the use of symbols, and a limited kind of logical thinking.*
G. *The fourth stage of cognitive development, according to Jean Piaget's theory. The stage is characterized by the ability to think about both concrete and abstract events as well as the ability to formulate and test hypotheses to solve problems.*

____ 36. **Industry vs. inferiority** (p. 331)
____ 37. **Authoritative parenting style** (p. 331)
____ 38. **Permissive parenting style** (p. 331)
____ 39. **Authoritarian parenting style** (p. 331)
____ 40. **Moral realism** (p. 333)
____ 41. **Moral autonomy** (p. 333)
____ 42. **Gifted** (p. 335)

A. *Children who show extraordinary talent or ability in one or more areas, such as mathematics, verbal skills, creativity, leadership, or the performing arts.*

B. *The psychosocial task of middle childhood, according to Erik Erikson's theory. The task involves the child's comparison of her own abilities with those of her friends and schoolmates.*

C. *The first stage of moral development in Piaget's thoery, in which children judge right and wrong by the consequences of an action rather than by the intention of the actor.*

D. *The second stage of moral development in Piaget's theory, in which the child can take into account the intentions of the actor and the consequences of the action.*

E. *A warm and nurturing style of parenting that encourages independence in the child but still places limits and controls on his actions.*

F. *A nonpunitive style of parenting that places low demands on the child and allows considerable freedom.*

G. *A restrictive style of parenting that emphasizes punishment in the control of behavior.*

ANSWERS

1. B, 2. E, 3. C, 4. A, 5. G, 6. D, 7. F, 8. G, 9. A, 10. F, 11. C, 12. B, 13. D, 14. E, 15. C, 16. F, 17. G,
18. D, 19. A, 20. E, 21. B, 22. D, 23. C, 24. G, 25. E, 26. B, 27. F, 28. A, 29. C, 30. F, 31. A, 32. B,
33. E, 34. G, 35. D, 36. B, 37. E, 38. F, 39. G, 40. C, 41. D, 42. A

SELF-TEST

1. The study that tests a single group of the same people repeatedly at different ages is termed a _____ study.
   (a) cross-sectional   (c) combined
   (b) longitudinal   (d) Both a and c.
   (LO 1; p. 310)

2. The developmental perspective that focuses on personality development and emphasizes the role of the outcome of early psychosocial conflicts on later behavior patterns is the _____ perspective.
   (a) psychoanalytic   (c) cognitive-structural
   (b) behavioral   (d) biological
   (LO 2; p. 311)

3. The developmental perspective that explains the development of behavior by stressing the role of reinforcement is the _____ perspective.
   (a) psychoanalytic   (c) cognitive-structural
   (b) behavioral   (d) biological
   (LO 2; p. 312)

4. An individual human inherits how many chromosomes from the mother?
   (a) 46 pairs of chromosomes
   (b) 46 chromosomes
   (c) 23 pairs of chromosomes
   (d) 23 chromosomes
   (LO 3; p. 314)

5. A gene that is expressed only when it is paired with another identical gene is termed
   (a) dominant.   (c) recessive.
   (b) sex-linked.   (d) codominant.
   (LO 3; p. 314)

6. Which of the following substances will, if ingested during early pregnancy, cause limb deformities in the developing offspring?
   (a) thalidomide   (c) caffeine
   (b) alcohol   (d) cimetidine
   (LO 4; p. 316)

7. Which perspective on development is most closely aligned with the nurture side of the nature-nurture issue?
   (a) psychoanalytic   (c) cognitive-structural
   (b) behavioral   (d) biological
   (LO 5; p. 317)

8. In the United States, there has been a recent trend from viewing childbirth as _____ to viewing it as _____ .
   (a) a normal developmental process; a painful process
   (b) a painful process; a condition of sickness
   (c) a condition of sickness; a normal developmental process
   (d) a condition of sickness; a painful process
   (LO 6; p. 321)

9. Which reflex in the newborn is characterized by turning the head and opening the mouth when the cheek is stroked?
   (a) sucking   (c) rooting
   (b) stepping   (d) Babinski
   (LO 7; p. 321)

10. An experiment in which newborn infants used a sucking response to control a tape recorder showed that an infant
    (a) prefers to listen to its mother's voice rather than a stranger's.
    (b) prefers to listen to a novel voice rather than its mother's.
    (c) prefers to listen to its father's voice rather than its mother's.
    (d) cannot discriminate between its mother's voice and a stranger's.
    (LO 7; p. 322)

11. Research with infant monkeys who were raised with a cloth and a wire mother found that they
    (a) showed no preference.
    (b) showed a preference for the surrogate mother who fed them.
    (c) showed a preference for the wire mother when it provided the food.
    (d) showed a preference for the cloth mother whether or not it provided the food.
    (LO 8; p. 324)

12. Erikson argues that the first psychosocial task in life revolves around attachment and is termed
    (a) industry versus inferiority.
    (b) autonomy versus shame and doubt.
    (c) initiative versus guilt.
    (d) trust versus mistrust.
    (LO 8; p. 325)

13. A critical ability that develops during Piaget's sensorimotor period is
    (a) conservation.
    (b) abstract thought and reasoning.
    (c) formal operations.
    (d) object permanence.
    (LO 9; p. 328)

14. During Piaget's concrete operational period, children become able to
    (a) appreciate the concept of conservation.
    (b) reason abstractly.
    (c) use language.
    (d) form hypotheses to solve problems.
    (LO 9; p. 330)

15. A parent who places limits on a child but is also warm and loving is termed
    (a) authoritarian.
    (b) permissive-indulgent.
    (c) authoritative.
    (d) permissive-neglectful.
    (LO 10; p. 331)

16. For both monkeys and children who show abnormal behavior, other young of the same species (monkeys for monkeys, other children for humans) can act as _____ in helping to reduce the abnormal behavior.
    (a) peers   (c) rivals
    (b) friends   (d) therapists
    (LO 10; p. 332)

17. According to Piaget, the first stage of moral development is called
    (a) moral autonomy.   (c) preconventional.
    (b) moral realism.   (d) conventional.
    (LO 11; p. 333)

18. Which of the following is *not* a criticism of Kohlberg's theory of moral development?
    (a) Subjects' responses to the stories are difficult to score.
    (b) Moral reasoning has nothing to do with moral development.
    (c) The stories are culturally biased.
    (d) The role of emotion is ignored.
    (LO 11; p. 334)

19. Research generally shows that the gifted child is
    (a) severely depressed.
    (b) handicapped.
    (c) emotionally well-adjusted.
    (d) never gifted in more than one area.
    (LO 12; p. 335)

20. Methods that are currently used to address the needs of the gifted child are
    (a) programmed instruction and reinforcement.
    (b) acceleration and enrichment.
    (c) alternate use of punishment and reward.
    (d) isolation from agemates.
    (LO 11; p. 335)

ANSWERS

13. d, 14. a, 15. c, 16. c, 17. b, 18. b, 19. c, 20. b
1. b, 2. a, 3. b, 4. d, 5. c, 6. a, 7. b, 8. c, 9. c, 10. a, 11. d, 12. d,

SUGGESTED READINGS

Brenner, A. *Helping children cope with stress.* Lexington, MA: Lexington Books, 1984. A brief volume designed for human service workers that explores the nature and treatment of childhood stressors, such as parental death, divorce, and child abuse.

Freeman, J., ed. *The psychology of gifted children: perspectives on development and education.* New York: Wiley, 1985. An advanced text that provides an overview of the theories and practices relating to gifted children.

George, W. C., S. J. Cohn, and J. C. Stanley, eds. *Educating the gifted.* Baltimore: Johns Hopkins University Press, 1979. A series of articles on approaches to the education of the gifted child.

Hale, J. E. *Black children: their roots, culture, and learning styles.* Provo, UT: Brigham Young University Press, 1982. A comprehensive treatment of the cognitive development of black children in America. Suggests ways of designing educational programs for disadvantaged youth.

Harris, J. R., and R. M. Liebert. *The child: development from birth through adolescence.* Englewood Cliffs, NJ: 1984. An introductory text for undergraduates covering the process of development from conception through adolescence.

Phillips, J. L., Jr. *Piaget's theory: a primer.* San Francisco: Freeman, 1981. A brief introduction to Piaget's theory of cognitive development.

Rosenblith, J. F., and J. E. Sims-Knight. *In the beginning: development in the first two years of life.* Monterey, CA: Brooks/Cole, 1985. An introduction to research on infancy.

Russell, G. *The changing role of fathers?* St. Lucia, Australia: University of Queensland Press, 1983. A descriptive and fascinating account of an interview study of fathers in Australia.

Woolfolk, A. E., and L. McCune-Nicolich. *Educational psychology for teachers.* 2d ed. Englewood Cliffs, NJ: Prentice-Hall, 1984. An introduction to the field of educational psychology, especially for students interested in a teaching career.

Yussen, S. R., and J. W. Santrock. *Child development: an introduction* (2d ed.). Dubuque, IA: Wm. C. Brown Publishers, 1982. A thorough, topically organized text on the psychology of infancy and childhood, with an especially good section on cognitive development.

c   h   a   p   t   e   r

10

Life-Span Development: Adolescence and Adulthood

LEARNING OBJECTIVES

After reading this chapter, you should be able to

1. describe the biological factors underlying sexual development and puberty. **(p. 346)**
2. identify some of the patterns of sexual behavior in adolescence. **(p. 349)**
3. describe the process by which the adolescent seeks to establish an identity separate from his or her parents. **(p. 350)**
4. explain how the adolescent's social development moves from a focus on parents to a focus on peer groups. **(p. 352)**
5. describe some of the major developmental tasks and life events facing a person during the early years of adulthood. **(p. 354)**
6. describe the mid-life transition and explain how it affects the individual during middle adulthood. **(p. 362)**
7. discuss the changes in cognitive abilities that occur during the adult years. **(p. 363)**
8. describe the aging process. **(p. 365)**
9. identify several of the adjustments that are often necessary during later adulthood. **(p. 366)**
10. describe the role of creativity and productivity in adjustment to later adulthood. **(p. 368)**
11. discuss the behavioral patterns people may experience when they learn they are going to die. **(p. 369)**

The years from the onset of puberty until death constitute adolescence and adulthood. This period can last the better part of a century, so it is not surprising that a person would go through a number of changes and would face many important life events during this time. Choosing a career is just one. Others include establishing an identity, getting married, having children, facing middle age, and eventually old age and death. In this chapter we explore the events and tasks of the longest portions of a person's life.

Adolescence

The word *adolescence* comes from the Latin "adolescere," to grow up. The boy turns into a man and the girl into a woman. The change is a profound one, involving much biological, social, moral, cognitive, and emotional growth. It is not an easy period of life; it is full of conflicts, confusions, and crises. In this section we will focus on the biological changes that take place during adolescence—sexual development, the adolescent's search for identity, and social development.

Biological Changes

Puberty *marks the end of childhood and the beginning of adolescence; it is the time of sexual maturation.* The age at which this event occurs varies between boys and girls, and among people of different countries as well. This age has been slowly declining in America as well as most of the other industrialized countries, partly because of improved nutrition (fig. 10.1).

Although the onset of menstruation is an obvious starting point for adolescence in girls, pubertal changes actually begin much earlier. The young girl begins a growth spurt around age ten; breast development and pubic hair appear soon thereafter. The onset of menstruation, somewhere around thirteen years of age, does not necessarily mean that the girl is now reproductively mature and can become pregnant. Although some girls

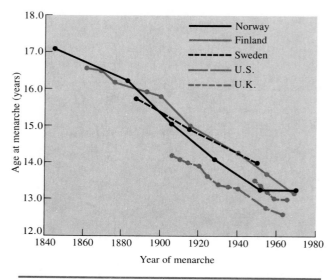

Figure 10.1 The lowering age of first menses in selected northern European countries and the United States from 1845 to 1969

are fertile at that age, most require several more months before their reproductive organs are able to function properly.

The growth spurt in boys begins about two years later than in girls and peaks about the age of fourteen. Most boys begin to show live spermatazoa in their urine by the age of twelve, and this is usually considered the onset of puberty. More obvious signals include the growth of the testes, penis, and scrotum (around age twelve), the appearance of pubic and facial hair, and the lengthening of the vocal cords, resulting in a deepening of the voice.

The hormones released during puberty result in the development of **primary** and **secondary sexual characteristics.** The **primary sexual characteristics** *include those that are directly related to reproduction, such as the penis, the testes, the ovaries, and the fallopian tubes.* The **secondary sexual characteristics** *include many of the features that appear during puberty but that are not directly related to reproductive functions.*

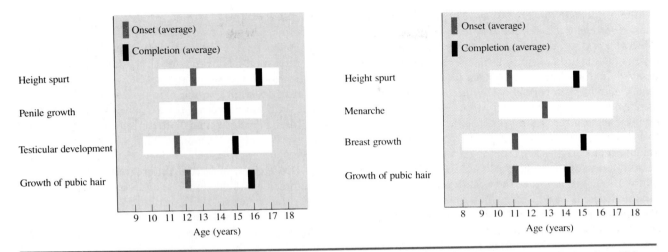

Figure 10.2 The sequence of events for puberty for boys and girls. (From "Growing Up," by J. M. Tanner, in Scientific American, Vol. 229. Copyright © 1973 by Scientific American, Inc. All Rights Reserved. Reprinted by permission.)

Examples include the change in the male voice, the growth of pubic hair and axillary hair, and muscular development in men.

The age at which developmental changes occur varies widely among individuals (fig. 10.2). In the adolescent years, these differences can become points of social comparison, affecting the socialization process. Early-maturing boys, for example, seem to have more positive self-concepts and more successful relationships with friends, compared to late-maturing boys (Mussen and Jones, 1957). Also, adults seem to respond more positively to boys whose physical maturation occurs early. One study found that the psychological characteristics associated with early maturation in boys, such as dominance and independence, were still prominent even when the individuals reached their thirties (Jones and Mussen, 1958). Early maturation, however, may have some negative effects on socialization and emotional development as well. Early maturers tended to be rigid and inhibitory, perhaps because they were being pushed into decisions about their identity too early (Peskin, 1967).

Sexual Development

The biological changes that occur during puberty are the result of forces that begin at the moment of conception. As we discussed in the previous chapter, all human beings have a total of forty-six chromosomes arranged in twenty-three pairs. The **sex chromosomes** *are one of these pairs of chromosomes; they determine the gender of the fetus. An X chromosome is present as one of the sex chromosomes in all normal people. Women have two X chromsomes, but men have only one. The Y chromosome is the other, smaller, sex chromsome that is present only in men.* Because a woman has two X chromsomes, all of her egg cells contain an X. The sperm that fertilizes the egg, however, can contain either an X or a Y chromsome from the father. If the sperm contains an X, the fetus will be a girl; if it contains a Y, the fetus will be a boy.

Sexual Differentiation. The sex of the fetus is determined at conception, but the unfolding of those genetic directions takes considerable time. **Sexual**

differentiation *is the process by which the physiological differences between males and females develop. The process has two primary components: one that involves the reproductive system of the developing organism, and another that involves the organism's brain and behavior.* **Androgens,** *which are sex hormones released by the fetal testes,* play a critical role in the process of sexual differentiation.

During the first two months of prenatal life, male and female embryos are indistinguishable except by an examination of their chromosomes. If the embryo contains a Y chromosome, the undifferentiated gonadal tissue develops into testes, which then begin to secrete male hormones that affect the further development of the reproductive system. Under the influence of these hormones, the cells that might have become female reproductive organs regréss, and those that are to become male reproductive organs develop normally. The tissue that might have become the ovaries, uterus, vagina, or fallopian tubes regresses, and the fetus develops a penis, prostrate gland, ejaculatory duct, and other male organs. If the embryo contains no Y chromosome, no testes develop, and no male hormones are released. In the absence of these male hormones the female reproductive organs develop normally (Wilson, George, and Griffin, 1981).

A very unusual phenomenon that demonstrates what can happen when this hormonal sequence is disrupted involves a small group of Dominican children who appeared to be girls at birth and were reared as girls. Isabel, for example, spent her early years as a girl but then began to feel very different in late childhood. At puberty she began adding muscle and speaking with a lower voice. What everyone thought was a clitoris became a penis. Finally, at age twelve, she put on men's clothes and became the muscular, masculine "Chi Chi." (Imperato-McGinley, et al., 1974).

Isabel, and a few others like her, inherited a genetic problem that interferes with the ability to produce **dihydrotestosterone,** *the hormone released during prenatal life that is responsible for the development of the male genitals.* Although they possessed a Y chromosome and were genetically male, their testicular tissue was unable to produce dihydrotestosterone during the first months of prenatal life. In the absence of this hormone, the genitalia of these children looked more like that of a girl, so the parents reared them as girls. They did have internal testes, however, and when the children reached puberty, these internal organs began producing male hormones. The hormone caused the development of male secondary sexual characteristics.

The process of sexual differentiation also involves the brain and behavior. The androgens released in the male during prenatal life, and the absence of those hormones in the female, have important effects on the developing brain. Some of the effects of these hormones are delayed; they are not apparent until the organism reaches puberty.

When females reach puberty, they begin their menstrual cycle because of the cyclic release of hormones from the pituitary gland. The brains of males, however, cause those pituitary hormones to be released in fairly steady amounts from puberty onward. This difference in the way the pituitary glands of males and females direct hormonal secretion is due to differences in the neurons of the brain that control the pituitary gland, mainly in the hypothalamus (MacLusky and Naftolin, 1981). Even though the difference between the brains of males and females is not apparent until puberty, it first appeared in prenatal life. The trigger for the development of differences in the brains of males and females is the hormones circulating in the embryonic male. If they are present, as they should be for a fetus with a Y chromosome, the brain is organized so that it will later direct the pituitary to release its hormones at a constant level, in the malelike fashion. If they are absent, the brain is organized so that the hormones are released cyclically after puberty, as they should be for females.

There are several differences in the brains of male and female animals, and at least some of them appear to be due to the presence or absence of early androgens. For example, in young monkeys the dendritic structure of the part of the brain involved in sex behavior shows a sex difference (Ayoub, Greenough, and Juraska, 1983). Since the monkeys had not yet reached puberty, it is likely that the sex difference in the brain is due to the presence or absence of prenatal androgens.

Whether structural differences in the brain produced by exposure to prenatal hormones have any behavioral significance is a very difficult question to answer (Deaux, 1985; Moore, 1985). One investigation studied girls who had been exposed to androgens during prenatal life for one reason or another, perhaps because the mother was given certain types of androgenlike drugs (Ehrhardt and Meyer-Bahlburg, 1981). Based on studies of the behavior of these girls, some scientists hypothesize that the early androgens make the child somewhat more active and inclined to expend more energy. However, the early hormones do not seem to play a very large role in the process of **gender identity,** *in which the child learns to feel like a girl or a boy and identify with the appropriate sex.* This process seems to be much more affected by the way a child is reared than by the hormones present during prenatal life. In the majority of cases, children seem to accept the gender assigned to them at birth and acquire that gender identity, even though biologically they may have been exposed prenatally to the hormonal environment of the opposite sex. In most cases, a girl like Isabel would have a great deal of trouble coping with her new lower voice and her masculine appearance. And in many instances, particularly in the United States, she might request surgery so that she can remain a female.

The Adolescent's Emerging Sexuality. Around the time of puberty, when the adolescent's body undergoes so many biological changes associated with the release of pubertal hormones, there is a large increase in interest in sex. The heightened attention to sexuality is probably caused by many factors, including the biological changes and the individual's awareness of them, the hormonal changes, and the emphasis placed on sexuality by peers, parents, and the entire culture.

Table 10.1 Adolescent sex information sources*			
Source	Male N–392 (%)	Female N–566 (%)	Total N–958 (%)
Peers	45.7	32.4	38.7
Literature	16.7	23.8	20.9
School	18.3	20.4	19.5
Mother	5.6	18.7	13.4
Father	4.1	.7	2.1
Experiences	8.0	2.8	5.0
Minister	1.0	.6	.7
Physician	.6	.6	.6
	100.0	100.0	100.0

From H. D. Thornburg, Contemporary Adolescence: Readings, 2nd ed. Copyright © 1975 by Wadsworth Publishing Company, Inc. Reprinted by permission of H. D. Thornburg.

Not surprisingly, the adolescent usually experiences considerable inner turmoil about sexuality. Accurate information about topics such as masturbation, homosexuality, venereal disease, pregnancy, contraception, or impotence is difficult to obtain. These subjects are taboo in many American homes, and most adolescents do not obtain very much information about sex from parents. (See table 10.1.) One woman enrolled in a class on human sexuality at a northeastern college reported her problems of communication:

I would like to write about my mother and the way she explained to me the facts of life. Actually, she didn't. My poor mom. Everytime I asked her anything about how babies were born, she answered so hesitantly that I almost felt sorry for her. . . . (G. L. Thornton, personal communication)

Although some adolescents are able to discuss sexual matters openly with one another, there are many topics that are not discussed. One study of sexually active adolescents, for example, found that although most had discussed birth control on at least one occasion, they had not discussed these matters prior to the first intercourse. One-fourth felt that contraception had not been adequately discussed. (Polit-O'Hara and Kahn, 1985).

Studies of sexual behavior in adolescents show a dramatic increase in all kinds of sexuality around the time of puberty. One such survey (Sorensen, 1973) obtained information from 393 adolescents, aged thirteen to nineteen, who filled out a questionnaire with the consent of their parents. A researcher was present to answer any questions about the items. This survey explored such topics as frequency of masturbation, attitudes toward premarital sex, homosexual behavior, and motives for having intercourse.

This study found that a common pattern among adolescents is serial monogamy without marriage. These adolescents establish a relationship with a partner, intending to be faithful, but they are never sure how long the relationship will last. For example, of those in the sample who had had premarital sex, about forty percent could be described as serial monogamists. Other surveys have found that adolescents usually do not engage in premarital sex randomly or in any way that might be described as promiscuous (Hunt, 1974; Kantner and Zelnick, 1972). A large number of women have only one partner, whom they eventually marry, for example. Although standards regarding premarital sex have changed considerably over the years, they have not been disregarded completely. Generally, adolescents appear to regard premarital sex as acceptable provided the two people love one another and are emotionally committed.

Seeking an Identity

How does a person decide who he is? How does he decide whether to vote Republican or Democratic or whether to apply to Princeton, West Point, or air-conditioning school? How does she decide whether to go to church or whether she believes in God? Why does one person become a tax accountant, eager to make money, another person devote her life to the world hunger problem, and another person run for mayor?

The answer to all of these questions involves the concept of identity, or the sense of self. Your identity is who you are, what your values, commitments, and beliefs are; it provides continuity to an individual life.

The primary task of the adolescent is to establish an identity separate from his or her parents. For some, this is a painful and time-consuming task—people can take years to complete it, and a few never do. For others the task is accomplished smoothly, and the change from adolescence to adulthood is not very difficult at all. The adolescent must establish a sexual identity, a vocational identity, and a social identity on his or her road to a stable sense of self. Adolescents must become individual people with their own principles, beliefs, friends, thoughts, and ideas, while they are still hanging onto childhood. They are at a crossroad, yearning for independence but still afraid of it and still showing a great deal of dependence on their parents.

Identity vs. identity diffusion *is the major psychosocial developmental task of adolescence, according to Erik Erikson (1972). This task concerns the young person's search for a role that fits, particularly with respect to social behavior and occupational choice.* Typical of this stage are rapid fluctuations between self-confidence and insecurity. One day the adolescent may yearn for more responsibility and complain of being "treated like a baby." The next day he may seek comfort in dependence on his parents. He is in a stage in which he must acquire a sense of wholeness, a feeling of continuity between the child he was and the adult he is becoming.

Researchers have found that adolescents, and indeed, adults as well, fall into one of several different categories with respect to their identity status. **Identity achievement** *is one category of identity status; it characterizes people who have gone through a period of crisis and have developed relatively firm commitments.* **Foreclosure** *is another category of identity status, characteristic of people who have never gone through any identity crisis but have nevertheless become committed to certain goals or values.* Most often, their commitments reflect an unexamined acceptance of those of their parents, teachers, or peers.

Moratorium *is another type of identity status and describes a person who is currently in an identity crisis.* Finally, **identity diffusion** *is a type of identity status in which one has never had a crisis, is not in one now, and has not formed any particular commitments or established any goals* (Marcia, 1976).

Children are only peripherally interested in questions of identity, but for adolescents the search for identity is a consuming task. Most people move from one status to another during their adolescent years, and many enter adulthood with a stable sense of self, in the identity achievement status. Though the process of forming an identity begins early in adolescence, changes in identity status are especially common during late adolescence, particularly in college. Adolescents begin college in the foreclosure status, or perhaps in the identity diffusion status, but many finish somewhere else. Seniors often have a much stronger sense of personal identity than freshmen do. They hold stronger commitments to and have clearer ideas about their vocational choices, their political beliefs, their feelings about sex, and their own self-worth. With respect to religious commitments, researchers have found that college experiences seem to undermine traditional religious beliefs without helping the students establish any alternative (Waterman and Goldman, 1976; Waterman, 1982). Some interviews with adolescents show how people in these different statuses feel:

Interviewer: Tell me how you feel about the election coming up in November.
Jan: I'm not much into politics—my parents are both staunch Republicans, really conservative, you know? But I never thought about it much. It doesn't matter whether I vote or care anyway . . . . (identity diffusion)

Interviewer: How do you feel about people who have sex before marriage?
Bill: Umm . . . that's a tough one. My best friend is going to bed with his girl, I know. Sometimes I want to, and I think [my girlfriend] does too, though we don't talk about it much. I think it's not a good idea because of pregnancy, and well, you know, morals, but I'm just not sure. I'd like to know what my father did, but I'd never ask. It's confusing, but at least I think you should be in love first and not just hop in the sack with any girl. (moratorium)

Interviewer: What are your plans for a career?
Darien: I've got it all set to join my father's law firm . . . of course I have to finish school, but it's a good life. My parents travel a lot, and somehow, it seems like that's what I should do. (foreclosure)

Interviewer: Have you made any decisions about what to do after college?
Sean: Boy, I really sweated last year about that one. I got really scared, wondering how I was going to get a _____ job in this economy. It's such a mess. First I took some welding classes, can you believe, in case I couldn't find a teaching job—there are so few of them, you know. But now I think I feel better about it. I did some subbing this year and loved it—teaching is what I want to do. So maybe I'll have to be a busboy on the side for awhile. Beats counting beans for Uncle Sam . . . . (identity achievement)

One of the variables related to which identity status an adolescent is in is the relationship with the family. Adolescents who have very close relationships with their parents are more likely to be in a foreclosure status. They view their parents as supportive and are very willing to involve family members in their life decisions. Those with very distant family relationships are more likely to be in a state of identity diffusion. Children from these families see their parents as rejecting, indifferent, detached, and lacking understanding. Adolescents in the moratorium and identity achievement statuses are more likely to be critical of their parents and to have conflict in their homes. No one knows yet whether the attitudes or behaviors of the parents are the cause of the adolescent's identity status; it could easily be the other way around. An apathetic youngster in a state of identity diffusion, showing no interest in jobs or school and having no commitments in life, is not likely to elicit enthusiastic encouragement from his parents.

It is clear that the college years are important ones for the development of identity in adolescents. The eighteen-year-old leaves home for the first time and is exposed to an enormous array of experiences for the first time. These conditions seem to push the adolescent into questioning her own beliefs and entering an identity crisis. But what happens to adolescents who do not go to college? And what happens to adults who fail to achieve a stable sense of identity during college? Later in this chapter we will see that many people have questions about identity during adulthood.

Social Development

During infancy, the baby's social world consists almost entirely of the mother and father. Neighborhood and school friends become more important during childhood, but the parents still are very significant in the child's world. For instance, what mother and father consider "good" and what they say about politics or world affairs are critical influences on the child's behavior and attitudes. During adolescence, however, the person's social world shifts. No longer are the parents so important; people of the same age assume a much more influential role.

The decision to smoke or not smoke cigarettes is a good example of social development during adolescence. Two groups of children, aged eleven and fourteen, filled out questionnaires about their smoking habits and also about the smoking habits and attitudes of their parents and friends. For the eleven-year-old preadolescents, smoking habits were related both to their parent's attitudes and smoking habits and to the smoking habits of their friends. Children who did not smoke were more likely to have parents with negative atttitudes toward smoking, whereas those who did smoke were more likely to have parents whose attitudes were more prosmoking. The influences on the fourteen-year-old adolescents, however, were slightly different. These children were more influenced by peers. The ones who smoked were more likely to have friends who also smoked; their parents' attitudes and smoking habits were less important in their own smoking behavior (Krosnick and Judd, 1982).

During adolescence, more than any other period of life, the person is concerned with the social group and with what they think (fig. 10.3). This change is due partly to the search for identity—the adolescent needs

Figure 10.3 *During adolescence, the importance of the peer group for social rewards and social comparisons grows dramatically.*

to establish himself as an individual, separate from his parents. The dependence on his peer group, however, seems to be a way to help him solve the identity crisis. If he uniformly adheres to the values and customs of a peer group, he is, at least temporarily, solving his identity crisis. He is adopting the identity of the group. In this way he can avoid some of the conflicts associated with the development of a separate identity, at least for a while. By wearing the same kind of jeans, buying the same makeup, using the same slang, listening to the same music, and inventing all kinds of fads that set the adolescent group apart from other groups but make up a kind of uniform for the group's members, the adolescent can postpone the painful search for individual identity.

GUIDED REVIEW

Learning Objectives 1, 2, 3, and 4

1. Adolescence begins with the onset of _____ , the time of sexual maturation.

2. Early maturing boys have more positive _____ and are viewed more positively by parents and teachers. However, early maturation may have negative effects as well.

3. The process of sexual development begins at conception. The newly conceived fetus either has two _____ and becomes a girl or has one X and one _____ and becomes a boy. The chromosomes then direct the process of _____ , whereby the physiological differences that exist between males and females develop.

4. If the fetus is a male, it begins to release _____ , which masculinize the reproductive system and the brain. If the fetus is female, no fetal hormones are released, the female reproductive system develops, and the brain will produce a cyclic release of hormones at puberty.

5. Whether the release of prenatal sex hormones influences behavior is not clear, although some scientists suggest that early androgens influence activity levels in childhood. The child's _____ , however, is mainly influenced by the gender assigned at birth rather than the prenatal hormone environment.

6. All kinds of sexual behavior increase markedly after puberty. Although sexual attitudes and practices have become more permissive during the last few decades, most adolescents do not show promiscuous sexual behavior. A common behavior pattern is _____ .

7. The developmental task of _____ is important in adolescence. The individual must establish an identity separate from parents and "tries on" many identities to see how they "fit." Identity status can fall into one of four categories: _____ , _____ , _____ , or _____ . The college years are particularly important for changes in identity status.

8. Social development in adolescence is very rapid. Individuals move from primary reliance on their _____ for social approval and support to primary reliance on their _____ . The social group is an important source of comparison during the adolescent years.

ANSWERS

1. puberty 2. self-concepts 3. X chromosomes; Y chromosome; sexual differentiation 4. androgens 5. gender identity 6. serial monogamy without marriage 7. identity vs. identity diffusion; identity achievement, foreclosure, moratorium, identity diffusion 8. parents; peers

Early and Middle Adulthood

Ten years ago this chapter would have ended with the discussion of adolescence. The field of developmental psychology was almost exclusively interested in the changes that occur between conception and the end of adolescence. Those that occur during adulthood were little understood and rarely studied. Now, however, psychologists recognize that important developmental changes may take place in many areas after adolescence.

The question of whether substantial personality changes occur during the course of adult development, for example, is an intriguing one for psychologists. Some theorists maintain that personality is formed during childhood and adolescence and remains stable after

that. Others argue that personality develops and changes throughout the life span. Much of the research, however, indicates a balance between these positions: some facets of personality tend to change during adulthood, particularly in conjunction with major life events and developmental tasks, whereas others remain stable. One longitudinal study spanning twenty years found that personality traits such as deference, need for order, succorance, and endurance tended to remain stable over time. Traits such as the need for achievement, autonomy, and dominance tended to increase in many people as they grew older (Stevens and Truss, 1985).

Another issue in adult development concerns whether there are identifiable patterns. In babies, children, and adolescents, there are several rather uniform life events, such as learning to walk, acquiring language, entering school, and reaching puberty. These events tend to occur at about the same age in all people. In adulthood, though, the course of life becomes much more variable. By the age of twenty-seven, for example, some people have found their career niches, are married, and have two or three children. Others might still be clinging to adolescence, trying out one role after another in their search for a sense of identity. Still others might be getting divorced.

Although the study of developmental changes in early and middle adulthood is still relatively new, it seems that familiar patterns do appear in people who, on the surface, seem to be leading quite different lives. One study of men, for example, found that biologists, novelists, factory workers, and business executives all showed some similar trends in their adult development (Levinson, 1978). This pattern, diagrammed in figure 10.4, found different developmental tasks facing people in their early adult years (their twenties, thirties, and early forties), and in middle adulthood (the forties through sixties).

The Early Adult Years

During the early years of adulthood, people face important developmental tasks. The first of these is simply to end adolescence. This means, on the practical side, establishing financial independence and usually a separate residence from the parents. Psychologically, the end of adolescence can be very wrenching, and a few people avoid this task for years. Our society expects that a person in the early twenties should have a clear idea of both personal and career goals. The adolescent years have been considerably extended in American culture, giving people a good deal of time to solve problems of identity and to adopt goals.

Choosing a Career.   Even though some people switch careers during their adult lives, most people, men in particular, become established in a career during their

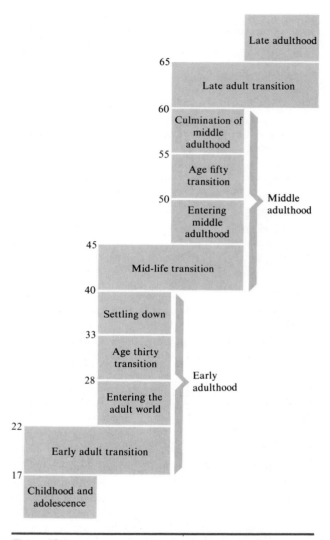

Figure 10.4 Developmental periods in adulthood

twenties. (Levinson, 1978; Super, 1980; 1985) The task of choosing a career, which occurs even earlier, is truly an overwhelming one because there are so many different occupations, and the patterns of employment are shifting so dramatically. In the late 1960s and early 1970s, many people with an interest in education chose to major in this subject in college. At the time, it seemed

Table 10.2 Projected distribution of employment by occupation in 1990

Clerical workers	22.5 million
Professional and technical workers	16.3 million
Service workers (except private household)	16.1 million
Craft workers	14.5 million
Operatives, except transport	12.8 million
Managers and administrators	12.5 million
Sales workers	7.5 million
Nonfarm laborers	5.0 million
Transport equipment operatives	3.8 million
Farm workers	2.4 million
Private household workers	0.7 million

Source: Bureau of Labor Statistics, U.S. Department of Labor

a wise decision because teachers were desperately needed by the public school systems. However, as the baby boom subsided and the number of pupils entering schools declined, teachers became less employable. By the late seventies, individuals graduating with teaching certificates in hand found it very difficult to obtain a job. For most people, the choice of a career is only partly dictated by interests and abilities. The growth and decline of industries also affect the decision because, not surprisingly, people want to know they will be able to find a job. (See table 10.2.) For instance, although the United States needs computer scientists now, there may be a glut in ten years. How do people make this difficult choice?

Most people in their late teens and early twenties have very little accurate information about occupations. What little information they have comes from their parents, the parents' friends, the media, and perhaps some limited career education in high school. One study of twelfth-grade boys tried to determine how much they understood about the requirements for particular jobs, in terms of both temperament and education. The occupations included civil engineer, physicist, psychiatrist, accountant, medical technologist, playground supervisor, credit investigator, insurance salesman, and window decorator (Nuckols and

Banducci, 1974). Some of these jobs (physicist, for example), require an investigative interest and a great deal of education. Others (such as accountant), would be more appropriate for someone with a more conservative or conventional personality. Sadly, the boys had very little idea about either the temperamental or educational requirements for these jobs. They were particularly ignorant of the requirements for the higher-level jobs.

Most people seem to learn about the requirements for the career they have chosen after they are well along in that career path. Students who enroll in nursing school are a good example:

Without exception our student nurses said that their main reason for choosing nursing as a career had been the wish to be of service to suffering people. When their freshman year began, they were disappointed upon finding that the entire first semester was devoted to academic classroom work; they had expected to learn things that were immediately useful in helping the sick. When basic nursing training began . . ., the students wanted to develop nurturant relationships with patients. They found that the faculty . . . [emphasized] specialized skills as well as proficiency in following routines and procedures. . . . During the two semesters of basic nursing, the gradual shift of interest from a humanistic concern with patients as individuals to a concern with mastery of technical repertoires was evident. . . . (Simpson, 1967)

Career counseling described in the Career Box, is becoming more available to help remedy this situation. It is usually offered in high schools and colleges, and some cities offer it in the form of noncredit workshops, not just to help people choose a career in early adulthood but to help them change careers later in life. Ideally, a person should consider his or her own abilities and interests in choosing a career, as well as predicted trends in the labor market.

Choosing a career is a somewhat different developmental task for men and women. Traditionally, men have been expected to enter a career or take a job and stay with it until they retire. Women have either been expected to get married and become homemakers after completing their education or to work for a few years first and then become homemakers. Psychologists have

CAREER BOX

Career Counselor

The career counselor does a great deal more than help a person find a job. As the field has evolved over recent years, the career counselor has come to be responsible for assisting people to develop and accept integrated and adequate pictures of themselves and of their roles in the world of work. We used to think of this process as occurring primarily during the teen years, when an individual was supposed to be choosing and preparing for his or her lifetime career. But now career counseling has become more developmental. As more people move in and out of careers during their lifetimes, the functions of the career counselor have become broader. Training to become a career counselor usually involves college, often with a major in psychology or a related field. The career counselor needs to know a good deal about the job market, and the outlook for various occupations and industries, as well as psychology.

Most career counselors use one of three approaches in helping clients. The "trait-and-factor" approach is historically the oldest; it emphasizes the notion that each person has particular abilities and interests, and each occupation has special psychological requirements. The job of the career counselor, then, is to match up the two. The approach is a cognitive one, relying on rational decision making by the client. Clients typically take a battery of tests that reveal their interests and abilities, and the counselor interprets their results and explains them to the client. One popular test is the Strong-Campbell Vocational Interest Inventory,

a test that assesses an individual's interest in the activities associated with different occupations. The person's interests are profiled both in terms of their general occupational themes and in terms of their similarity to people who are already in various occupations.

Two other approaches commonly used by career counselors are the "client-centered approach" and the "psychodynamic approach." The client-centered approach developed out of the general system of psychotherapy proposed by Carl Rogers, a system in which the counselor plays a much more reactive, reflective, and nondirective role than in the trait-and-factor approach. This method attempts to place the responsibility for career decision making squarely on the client, rather than on the counselor. The psychodynamic approach uses elements of both trait-and-factor and client-centered counseling. The approach focuses on the relationship between the person's motives, personality, and career choices, and often makes use of psychlogical tests designed to measure motivation.

Career counseling is a profession that requires substantial psychological background, often a bachelor's degree with a major in psychology or a master's degree in counseling. A great deal of a person's self-esteem is derived from career choices and advancement, and it is not surprising that people are beginning to rely on professionals to help them with these important decisions.

found that until recently, choosing a career was not a major developmental task for women in their early adult years, though it was a very salient one for men.

These differences between men and women are rapidly decreasing, however. More and more women are entering the work force, especially married women with children, because of desires to have both a family and a career and because of economic needs. Recent studies of occupational motivation among persons in late adolescence and early adulthood show fewer differences between the sexes (Grotevant and Thorbecke, 1982). Nevertheless, differences in attitudes toward the relationship between work and gender still exist, and these differences may affect each gender's career choices. In a recent survey of students in grades seven to twelve, for example, the majority listed household chores such as laundry, cooking, and childcare as women's work; yardwork and car repair were thought to be men's work (Hansen and Darling, 1985). Also, female adolescents tend to participate more in household chores (Sanik and Stafford, 1985).

Marriage and Family. Other important developmental tasks facing young adults include adjusting to married life and raising a family. Although some people are choosing not to marry and others are choosing alternative life-styles such as cohabitation, the vast majority of American men and women marry.

Intimacy vs. isolation *is the major psychosocial developmental task faced by young adults, according to Erik Erikson* (1972). *The focus of this task is to successfully establish relationships with other young adults and to establish an intimate relationship with one person.* The failure to achieve this intimacy results in isolation.

The adjustments that young adults have to make when entering a marriage are profound. If they have not lived together before marriage (and most couples have not), they must learn how to cope with each other's idiosyncrasies. One might prefer to watch TV in the evening, and the other may want to invite friends over. They both may find the financial burdens of marriage very difficult to cope with, and they are likely to feel acutely the loss of their personal freedom. Power is usually a source of controversy, particularly when both partners are working outside the home. The power equation was very much tilted toward the husband when it was the norm for the wife to stay home, but now the balance is a more equal one in many families. When both partners work and contribute to the marriage financially, who will make final decisions about what car to buy, how much to spend for a new stereo, or whether to spend the vacation in New York or Florida?

In addition to getting married, most people have children in the early adult years. Although there is a recent trend to postpone having children until the late twenties or early thirties, over ninety percent of American women eventually have at least one child. The care of the children has traditionally been almost the exclusive responsibility of the mother, but this too is changing. As traditional stereotypes about sex roles break down, fathers are becoming more and more involved in childcare; many now attend Lamaze classes and play a key role in the development of their children. Scientists are discovering that the attention of fathers is important, even for infants. They tend to provide their babies with more unpredictable physical kinds of play, whereas the mother is more likely to do the comforting and caretaking (Lamb, 1981). Although the effects of the father's early involvement on infant development are not clear, his involvement is very important for his own feelings of inclusion in the family (Palkovitz, 1985).

The coming of children represents an enormous stressor in the lives of young adults. Children bring heavy financial and emotional responsibilities, even when they are planned. Because of improvements in birth control, parents can now choose when to have children and how many to have, a choice which, according to some scientists, may influence the intellectual development of the children. (See the Research Box: The Confluence Controversy.) These influences may add yet another level of responsibility to the decisions young people must make during the early adult years.

RESEARCH BOX

The Confluence Controversy

One of the more controversial hypotheses in the field of human development is called the *confluence model* (Zajonc and Markus, 1975). The model deals with the influence of family factors in intellectual development through adolescence. In particular, the model emphasizes the importance of three family influences: (1) the number of children in the family, (2) the spacing between those children, and (3) whether the individual was an only or a last child.

The model proposes that an individual's intellectual development is related to the average intellectual environment to which he or she is exposed during early life. A child born to a family with six children, for example, would be exposed to a lower average intellectual environment than a child born to a family with only one other child. Also, a child in a family in which the only other sibling is ten years older would be exposed to a higher average intellectual environment than would a child with a sibling who is two years older. An illustration follows:

> Consider the absolute intellectual levels of the parents to be thirty arbitrary units each, and of the newborn child to be zero. Thus, the intellectual environment at the birth of the first child has an average value of 20. Suppose the second child is born when the intellectual level of the firstborn reaches four. The second born then enters into an environment of $(30 + 30 + 4 + 0)/4 = 16$. (Zajonc, 1976)

Studies of the intellectual performance of Dutch, American, French, and Scottish children suggested a relationship to family size and birth-order position. For example, intellectual performance declined steadily with increasing family size, and older siblings tended to perform better than younger ones, particularly for children whose siblings were closely spaced.

More recently, the confluence model has been criticized on many grounds. For example, one scientist has questioned some of the statistical procedures used in the original research (Galbraith, 1982), arguing that they may have led to false conclusions. In particular, the way that child spacing in families was measured may have been open to errors. The original research depended partly on national birth rate, reasoning that when it went up, the space between births went down. But critics argue that this deduction may be unfounded.

Attempts to confirm some of the hypotheses that can be derived from the confluence model have not proven very successful. One investi-

The birth of the first child represents an important event in the lives of young adults. One study of new parents found certain personality changes during those first few weeks of parenthood. Compared to childless control women, the new mothers tended to increase their feelings of confidence about their ability to care for a child. The new fathers tended to gain confidence about life in general. The new parents that perceived their babies as "easy," in the sense that they were more cheerful, more adaptable to schedules, and less active,

gation gave batteries of intellectual tests to more than fifty thousand children at age four and then again at age seven (Brackbill and Nichols, 1982). The children's intellectual performance at these ages seemed to bear little relationship to the family configuration factors emphasized by the confluence model. For example, the confluence model would predict that children from homes in which the father is absent should score lower than children whose fathers are present in the home, because the average intellectual environment would be boosted by the presence of both parents. In this sample, the father-absent children did indeed score lower, but they also tended to come from families of lower socioeconomic status. When the researchers compared the scores of father-absent and father-present children in the same socioeconomic status, there were no differences. This suggests that the lower scores of father-absent children are primarily due to their low socioeconomic status rather than to the lowered average intellectual environment produced by the absence of the father.

Zajonc and his coworker John Bargh (1980) later tried to determine whether the variables associated with family configuration have been part of the reason for the dramatic decline in Scholastic Apptitude Test scores over the past decades. Between 1965 and 1977 the average SAT scores dropped 34.5 points. They compared three groups who took the SATs in the 1970–71, 1973–74, and 1976–77 school years and found, not unexpectedly, that the SAT scores declined over time. The average birth order of these groups declined as well, because the size of families was progressively increasing during the years these people were born. Nevertheless, the increase in family size was very small compared to the enormous drop in the SAT scores. Zajonc and Bargh concluded that birth order could not possibly account for more than a tiny fraction of the alarming drop in the SAT scores.

Although birth order, family size, the presence of the father may all have influences on the intellectual development of children, the confluence model has not explained those influences very efficiently (McCall, 1985). It is a tempting theory because of its simplicity, but intellectual development is a very complicated process, and many variables are likely to play important roles.

tended to experience more positive personality changes than did the new parents with the "difficult" babies (Sirigano and Lackman, 1985).

Young people, and especially young men, do not seem to be very well-versed in child behavior. One survey of college students found a widespread lack of knowledge about child-development patterns, particularly with regard to the age at which children are able to recognize their own wrongdoing (Shaner, Peterson, and Roscoe, 1985). This is a troubling finding because it

APPLICATION BOX

Children of Divorce

By 1990, about thirty-three percent of the children in the United States will have experienced their parent's divorce before they reach the age of eighteen (Glick, 1979). The way that these millions of children adjust to this experience is becoming an issue of intense national concern. The success of their adjustment depends on a great many factors, including the age and sex of the child, the amount of conflict between the divorcing parents, the custody arrangements, the availability of support services, and the socioeconomic changes that accompany the divorce.

When a husband and wife are contemplating divorce, the atmosphere in the home is often not very conducive to successful childrearing. The adults are concerned with their own problems, and they may create conflicts and stress in the child by competing for the child's loyalty. Certainly in some cases the children of parents who are constantly fighting may be better off if their parents divorce and they live in a single-parent home. But even when the parents had a great deal of conflict, the year following the divorce is usually a very difficult one for the child.

If the mother is awarded custody, she may experience a sudden drop in standard of living, particularly since only about one-third of ex-husbands contribute to child support. She may be poorly trained for employment and capable of making only a meager living. If the parents are still in conflict, visits by the noncustodial parent may be traumatic for the child. Typically, the mother's style of childrearing becomes more restrictive and controlling, whereas the noncustodial father becomes more permissive but less available (Hetherington, Cox, and Cox, 1978). Both parents are often not very consistent.

Divorce may have more long-lasting effects on the behavior of children. A study of adolescent girls living with widowed mothers, divorced mothers, and with both parents revealed several differences, particularly with respect to the girls' attitudes about boys and sex. The daughters of the widowed mothers tended to be more withdrawn, passive, and inhibited, while the daughters of the divorced mothers were more aggressive and flirtatious. For example, when the girls were interviewed for the study by a man, the daughters of the widowed mothers tended to sit in the chair farthest away. In contrast, the daughters of the divorced mothers tended to sit in the closest chair (Hetherington, 1972). Follow-up studies of these daughters

may suggest that younger people expect children to be able to control themselves and discriminate right from wrong much sooner than they actually are.

Since the teenage years are generally ones in which the individual goes through so many changes, it is not surprising that their parental behavior changes as well.

In an observational study of mothers ranging from ages sixteen to twenty-two, researchers found that the different age groups interacted differently with their infants. The younger mothers showed more efforts to control the behavior of the infants and more nonverbal

continue to reveal differences. The daughters of the widows tend to marry men with more puritanical attitudes, and the divorcees' daughters were more likely to marry men with drug problems or job difficulties. The daughters of both widowed and divorced mothers tended to have more sexual adjustment problems, compared to daughters who grew up with both parents in the home (Hetherington, 1972; 1977).

Until the 1900s, children of divorcing parents were almost invariably placed into the custody of the father, since it was the father who possessed the means to support the family. The notion that both the children and the wife were the man's property also contributed to this practice. The twentieth century brought a greater concern for the welfare of the children, partly because of the influence of Freudian thinking, and mothers began gaining custody of young children. Today, courts no longer automatically award custody to the mother. Judges try to consider the welfare of the children and the home situations of each parent before they make their decisions. Preliminary psychological research suggests that children seem to adjust better after divorce if they live with the same-sex parent.

The age of the child is another important consideration. Preschool children are not very accurate in assessing the cause of the divorce, and many blame themselves. Children at this age are probably the most vulnerable of all, in terms of the likelihood of adjustment problems. Although adolescents experience a great deal of conflict and stress, they are better able to assign responsibility (Wallerstein and Kelly, 1980). Neverthless, surveys of adolescents whose parents have divorced show that they develop more negative attitudes toward their parents, and themselves, after the divorce (Parish and Wigle, 1985).

The divorce of a child's parents is a stressful event in almost all cases, but many of these stresses can be minimized. Adjustment problems seem to be fewer if the child is older, if the child's home environment remains economically stable, if the parents keep the conflict and hostility before and after the divorce low, if both parents agree about childrearing practices and discipline, if the noncustodial parent continues to show love and interest, and if the child has the opportunity to discuss divorce-related concerns (Kurdek, 1981).

behavior. The older mothers tended to engage in more stimulating, reciprocal interactions with their babies (Fry, 1985).

Possibly one of the most significant trends in the United States is the increase in the number of single-parent homes, testifying to the difficulty of adjusting to marriage and family life. The United States has the highest divorce rate in the world—about forty percent of all American marriages end in divorce. Families with young children have not been immune to this statistic: young couples with one or two children are at least as likely to end their marriage in divorce as are childless couples. The effects of divorce on the children are not clearly understood, but research suggests that the child living in a single-parent household is at some disadvantage. For example, data from a national sample demonstrate that adolescent children in single-parent homes show significantly more deviant behavior than do children living in two-parent homes (Dornbusch, et al., 1985). The effects of divorce on children are described further in the Application Box: The Children of Divorce.

The Middle Adult Years

Daniel J. Levinson and his colleagues (Levinson, et al., 1978) performed a study of men through their adulthood years that led to the conclusion that between the ages of forty and forty-five, men face awesome developmental tasks. They are at the peak of their careers, and most have made it just about as far as they are going to go in their jobs. They are reaching the midpoint of their lives. From age forty on, they begin to think in terms of "the number of years remaining" rather than "the number of years since birth." They begin to see signs of physical deterioration. Gray hairs, flab, failing eyesight, slower reaction times, imagined or real, become more troubling. Even though the aging process is a slow one and physical deterioration has been occurring in many systems almost since puberty, men in their forties are at a stage when these signs can create difficult adjustment problems.

At this stage of life, people begin to think about their own mortality. Although adolescents and young adults know intellectually that they are going to die, the person in midlife begins to grasp this much more fully. His parents may have recently died, or they may be entering old age and relying on him for care. As he sees his own body age, he is confronted with his own mortality. Although there is no easily identifiable "marker" for the midlife transition, as there is with the onset of

adolescence, Levinson and others believe that it is an important developmental period that repeats itself in most men at about the same age.

The Midlife Transition.   The **midlife transition** *is the period in middle adulthood when an individual changes perspectives, begins to confront his own mortality, and reevaluates many of the goals and values he held during early adulthood.* The way men handle this period varies considerably. Some adapt and adjust very well, and others seek to regain their lost youth by divorcing their wives, buying fast cars, and entering a series of casual sexual relationships. Some become more nurturant with their own families, finding time for things their career ambitions and eighteen-hour workdays had denied them in earlier years. Still others urgently seek a purpose to which they can devote the remaining years of their lives, disillusioned with the dreams they had when they were young adults. One of the men whom Levinson interviewed, a biologist, made this point:

> The thing that's distressing to me at the moment is the absence of a goal that I consider worthwhile. I have to couch it in the framework of science, because that's the only thing I'm really trained to do. But I think the problem is perfectly general. I don't in all honesty see a goal that's worth having at the moment. . . . This is what really shakes me up . . . (Levinson, 1978, p. 274–275).

Midlife Changes in Women.   Although most of the research on middle adulthood, particularly midlife transitions, has focused on men, some women may experience a similar kind of reevaluation period (Neugarten, 1970). Those who did not work outside the home during the years of childrearing are in the stage when the children are beginning to leave home. While most women feel positive about their new freedom, some may find the adjustment to the "empty nest" more difficult. They are faced with an enormous amount of free time that they must fill up with a new career or other activities. While these changes may be challenging, they also can create adjustment problems that are quite different from those experienced by men who have had steady employment over the years.

Whereas men gradually begin to notice the signs of aging, women experience an identifiable "marker"— menopause. Usually during the late forties, menses becomes irregular and eventually ceases altogether. The ovaries degenerate, and the secretion of female hormones, particularly estrogen, declines. This signals the end of the reproductive years, and even if the woman had decided long ago to have no more children, the experience of menopause can have important psychological effects. A study of the attitudes of women toward menopause revealed that the phenomenon is poorly understood (Neugaraten, 1968). Many dreaded it because they believed it would affect their appearance, their ability to have sexual intercourse, or their emotional stability. About fifty-eight percent found menopause to be unpleasant, but seventy-five percent reported they were happier and calmer after menopause than before. The majority also reported having better relationships with their husbands.

The physiological signs of aging may also have greater impact in American women because of the value our culture places on youth and beauty in women. Television anchorwomen, for example, may worry that their graying hair is not attractive and will cause the network executives to move them to less prominent jobs. Gray hair in anchormen, on the contrary, may make them seem distinguished and more credible.

Since the 1950s, the number of women who have continued to work outside the home during the child-rearing years has increased dramatically, as we discussed in the last chapter. The adjustment problems of these women as they approach middle age is likely to be similar to those facing men.

Beyond the Midlife Transition. The outcome of the midlife transition varies considerably in different men and women. Some establish closer relationships with their families based on much-improved lines of communication. After reexamining the dreams of youth, they are able to accept themselves and their limitations more readily and find a happier and more fulfilling life. No longer tyrannized by the passions of youth and the drive to succeed, they can do some of their most creative work. Relieved of the responsibility of childcare,

both men and women can find time to engage in other pursuits. A study of the productivity of people at various ages found that inventors show marked gain in creative output in their fifties (Dennis, 1966).

Some people emerge from their midlife transition with deep scars. They find their lives lacking in meaning and excitement and their family lives in turmoil. They may have been divorced and unable to establish a new intimate relationship. In their work, they may begin marking time until retirement, resenting what has become an oppressive and meaningless chore.

Erikson (1972) sees **generativity vs. self-absorption** *as the major psychosocial crisis of middle adulthood. The way an individual is able to cope with the adjustments required during the forties and fifties will in part determine whether middle adulthood is a period of creative life effort with deeper intimacies with others and deeper commitments to worthwhile goals, or one of self-absorption, self pity, and apathy toward the outside world.* The patterns the individual established during middle adulthood also affect how the person copes with the later years of life.

Cognitive Development in Adulthood

According to Piaget's theory of cognitive development, adolescents enter the stage of formal operations around the age of eleven. They are able to engage in abstract thought and reasoning, and in their approach to problem solving they can use deductive hypothesis testing.

Piaget proposed that there were few changes in cognitive abilities after adolescence and that adulthood was characterized by a continuation of formal operational ways of thinking. Not all psychologists agree with this point of view. Many believe that after childhood the process of cognitive development becomes more variable; some people may never reach the stage of formal operations, and others may develop a good deal further.

For example, during the college years and even later there seem to be some improvements in logical reasoning, particularly in individuals who pursue specialized and abstract subjects such as physics, law, or philosophy (Neimark, 1975). Some theorists maintain that there is another stage of cognitive development after formal operations, although not everyone reaches it. In this stage, the person would be capable of analyzing formal operational thought itself.

Early studies of intellectual ability through the adulthood years and beyond strongly suggested a progressive decline. Edward L. Thorndike (1928) tested people of different ages and found that the twenty-two-year-olds had the best learning abilities. His data suggested a decline of about one percent for each subsequent year until about age fifty.

One problem with the early studies on cognitive change is that they relied on the cross-sectional method, the interpretation of which can be difficult and troublesome. In the twentieth century, the levels of educational achievement by each generation climb steadily. In general, older people tend to be less educated than younger people. Researchers who used longitudinal studies to investigate cognitive changes across the life span reached quite different conclusions.

In one study combining the virtues of the cross-sectional and longitudinal methods, five hundred subjects ranging in age from twenty-one to seventy were given intelligence tests. After seven years, 301 of the subjects were tested again (Baltes and Schaie, 1977; Schaie, 1979). These tests yield scores on four different kinds of cognitive functioning: (1) **crystallized intelligence,** or *the ability to engage in formal reasoning and abstract thinking,* (2) **cognitive flexibility,** *the ease with which the individual can shift from one way of thinking to another,* (3) **visuo-motor flexibility,** *the ability to shift from familiar to unfamiliar patterns in visuo-motor tasks,* and (4) **visualization,** *the ability to organize and process visual information.* When the researchers examined their data from a cross-sectional perspective, comparing different people in different age groups, they found a decline in all the categories of intellectual function. When they analyzed it longitudinally, however, and noted how people changed after seven years, they found a decline only in visuo-motor flexibility.

From this and other carefully designed investigations, it has become clear that cognitive abilities do not necessarily decline with age. There may be declines in some abilities, but there may be no change or even increases in others, particularly abilities relating to crystallized intelligence. These aspects of cognitive development hold true not just for early and middle adulthood but for later adulthood as well. Many of the deficiencies seen in very old people may be due more to lack of education or, especially, poor health. Furthermore, when testing conditions are optimal, many very old people show cognitive abilities that are in the same range as young adults.

GUIDED REVIEW

Learning Objectives 5, 6, and 7

1. The study of _____ is a young branch of developmental psychology. The adulthood years can be divided into early (twenties, thirties, and early forties), middle (forties, fifties, and early sixties), and later adulthood (middle sixties and older).

2. Tasks of _____ adulthood include choosing a career, establishing intimate relationships, and raising a family. Choosing a career is often a very haphazard process. Adolescents know little about occupations, yet they are expected to choose a lifetime career soon after they leave high school.

3. In Erikson's view, the main developmental task of early adulthood is _____ . The main task of middle adulthood is _____ .

4. Middle adulthood is often characterized by a _____ , in which the individual begins to confront mortality and re-examines previous goals. The period may be a difficult time of adjustment. Midlife transitions appear to be common in men, and recent studies suggest that women may experience similar "gear shifting" in midlife.

5. Piaget's theory of cognitive development suggests that the _____ , reached in adolescence, continues through adulthood. Other theorists propose that some adults never reach formal operational thinking at all and that some bypass it to even more advanced modes of thinking.

6. Longitudinal studies of changes in cognitive abilities throughout the life-span reveal that some abilities decline, others stay the same, and some increase. _____ seems to suffer some decline, and _____ may increase somewhat.

ANSWERS

1. adulthood 2. early 3. intimacy vs. isolation; generativity vs. self-absorption 4. midlife transition 5. formal operations stage 6. Visuo-motor flexibility; crystallized intelligence

Figure 10.5 Dwight Eisenhower as a young man, at middle age, and late in life

Later Adulthood

The stereotypes many Americans have of older adults are not very flattering. Some see the old person as forgetful, cranky, dependent, senile, or lonely. Few people look forward to their later adult years, fearing the aging process and especially death.

In some cultures, however, signs of aging are valued highly. Older adults in China are considered wise, and younger members of the society seek their counsel. It is extremely unusual for anyone in China to be named to a powerful political post before reaching the age of seventy.

Our stereotypes about old age can make this a difficult period of adjustment. Even though our negative images are filled with misconceptions, people react to the old as though they were true. But the aging process is not nearly as bad as many people suspect. Though there are a variety of physiological changes and no one can expect to be as spry as they were during their twenties, most can and do lead very independent, creative, and fulfilling lives in the older adult years.

The Aging Process

The physical changes that were taking place during middle adulthood continue past age sixty-five. Although the changes may not be obvious from day to day, or even from year to year, the cumulative effects of the process are unmistakable (fig. 10.5). The hair turns gray or white and becomes sparse, the skin loses its natural elasticity and moisture and becomes wrinkled. The eyelids thicken, the spine begins to bow, and the person becomes shorter.

Why do people age and eventually die? Do their bodies just begin wearing out? Do the stresses and strains of life begin to take their toll? Do the poisons and pollutants in the food and environment finally catch up with us?

One proposal, called the **genetic theory of aging,** *asserts that the aging process is part of the genetic code.* The program in the code carries us through the maturational changes of infancy, childhood, adolescence, the reproductive years, and middle adulthood, but then finally begins to expire during later adulthood. In some animals, like flies, the code runs out of program after only a few days; in dogs the program lasts more than a decade. In humans the program lasts many decades. Other theories point out the importance of stress in the aging process, the degradation of the immune system, or the buildup of toxic substances or mutations.

No one lives forever, but some people age much more slowly than others. Three groups, in particular, are famed for their incredibly long life span: the Vilacambamba in Ecuador, the Hunza in Kashmir, and the Abkhaziain in the Soviet Republic of Georgia. These people often live past the age of 100, and they share many characteristics. Their diets consist mostly of vegetables, and they eat very little fat. They also stay quite thin and eat less than Americans.

Studies in mice have found that dietary restriction, down to almost half their usual caloric intake, resulted in longer life spans and lower incidence of cancer. The thin but apparently healthy mice received vitamin supplements and lived ten to twenty percent longer than control animals that were allowed to maintain their normal body weight (Weidruch and Walford, 1982). There may be something about undernutrition that decelerates the aging process, as long as it does not include malnutrition.

Although the diets of the Vilacambamba, the Hunza, and the Abkhaziain may be boring by American standards, their lives are not. They maintain active sex lives, smoke or drink occasionally, stay married, and have no equivalent of our retirement. They also *expect* to live a long time. Perhaps we can learn something from the habits and attitudes of these long-lived people.

Life Adjustments in Later Adulthood

Just as each developmental period brings with it its own characteristic tasks, pleasures, challenges, sources of stress, and conflicts, later adulthood has its own as well. **Integrity vs. despair** *is the major psychosocial developmental task of later adulthood, according to Erikson. During this time, the individual who has successfully worked through earlier tasks and is now able to accept the inevitability of death will experience integrity. The existence of previously unresolved conflicts and an inability to accept impending death will lead to despair.*

This developmental period is often characterized by many changes that can have profound effects on the adjustment process. The changes might include retirement, alterations in family relationships, widowhood, illness, or death in the family.

Retirement.   For those who are employed outside the home, an important adjustment during later adulthood will probably be retirement. The success with which the individual adapts to this change in life-style can be an important factor in how satisfying the later adult years will be. The change does not simply involve moving from the status of worker to nonworker. It has implications for the person's social life, personal adjustment, and self-esteem.

When a person retires, his or her income usually drops, sometimes dramatically. Through combined income sources, including Social Security, private pension plans, part-time work, or perhaps family contributions, many retirees live on no more than half of their pre-retirement income, and often live on much less.

Retirement also brings a change in friendships. Many retirees no longer try to maintain close relationships with their former colleagues and instead seek friendships with other retirees who can share their interests. The individual also must make changes in perceptions of self-worth. We live in a very work-oriented society that often judges people by their ability to make money, climb the ladder of success, and contribute to society. The retiree is not a part of this order any longer and must find new ways by which to measure self-worth.

Studies of retired men have found that most adapt to retirement very well. For example, the National Institute of Mental Health conducted a survey of retired people and found that fifty-seven percent felt positively toward retirement. Other studies have focused on individuals' adaptation styles. The largest category of retired men were well-adjusted, mature individuals who adapted very well, finding new interests and activities. Another group, called "rocking-chair men," relaxed more and enjoyed the freedom of retirement. The group called "armored men" were also well adjusted, but they developed highly organized and regimented life-styles as a defense against feeling old. The individuals who did not adjust well to retirement were unable to face aging and blamed others for their own inability to achieve their life goals. Many of these individuals became very depressed and bitter. These were the ones who were unable to successfully resolve the psychosocial conflict of integrity vs. despair.

Two important factors in whether a person's retirement is successful and well adjusted appear to be whether it is voluntary or involuntary and whether the individual plans for it. The age of sixty-five was first established as the age for mandatory retirement in nineteenth-century Germany by Otto von Bismarck, the "Iron Chancellor." He instituted the first comprehensive social insurance program and chose sixty-five as the age when "old age" began. (Some claim he chose this age because the life expectancy was then around forty-five and he wanted to save the government money.) Other Western countries followed his lead, making sixty-five the mandatory retirement age.

The arbitrary designation of sixty-five has been criticized severely, sometimes by individuals who are actively working well into their eighties and nineties. Congress finally enacted legislation to change the age of mandatory retirement to seventy and also passed laws prohibiting age discriminatory employment practices for people between the ages of forty and seventy. It appears our society is appreciating that people are quite capable of working long past age sixty-five and should be allowed to if they wish.

Family Changes. The later adult years are frequently characterized by changes in the structure of the family. Children are probably well into their own careers and families, and are also probably independent. The older adult may have to depend on children, especially financially, rather than the other way around. For some individuals this represents an enormous blow to self-esteem and triggers feelings of depression and hopelessness. An especially devastating change may be the death or serious illness of a spouse. After what might have been decades of married life, the individual loses her or his partner and must face this loss and learn to cope with widowhood.

One aspect of life that need not change much is sexual activity. It is one of the more destructive myths of aging that older adults lose interest in sex or lose their ability to have sexual relationships. Studies of sexual activity in older adults clearly show that these notions are false. For example, one survey found that seventy percent of married couples over sixty years old were sexually active (Meyners and Wooster, 1979). A continuation of sexual activity also seems to be one of the components of a successful and fulfilling older adulthood.

Aging and Health. Reasonably good health is one of the key criteria in most of the successful coping patterns of old age. A good sex life, a fulfilling social life, and an industrious and active retirement all depend to a large extent on good health. Although most older adults describe their health as reasonably good, health problems are more common in this period of life because of the aging process. The problems may also be partly due to the major life changes that people over sixty-five are likely to encounter.

Aging is not necessarily the only factor that aggravates health problems in later adulthood. These years are sometimes characterized by wrenching life changes, and it appears that severe change can trigger stress reactions in the body that make an individual more vulnerable to illness. For example, stressors are related to circulatory disorders and to reductions in immune responses. The **Life Events Questionnaire** (Holmes and Rahe, 1957; Holmes and Masuda, 1974) *is a short test that lists major life events, both positive and negative, such as marriage, divorce, pregnancy, retirement, and so forth, and asks people to check those they have recently experienced.* Various studies have found that people who rate high on this checklist are often the ones most likely to suffer physical symptoms and illnesses. Some of the most important life events are more likely to occur during later adulthood. An example is the death of one's spouse, which is considered the most stressful event of all. When this happens, the person must work through a lengthy period of grief to readjust to life without the loved one.

The grief process is not well understood. According to some research, it consists of eleven identifiable stages: (1) shock, (2) sobbing, (3) craziness, (4) relief, (5) physical symptoms of unresolved grief, (6) panic, (7) guilt, (8) anger, (9) limbo, (10) emerging hope, and (11) reaffirmation of reality (Tanner, 1976). These are not necessarily distinct stages; people seem to blend two or more at once and skip others. Some research, however, suggests that grief can lead to physical symptoms of illness. In a study of widowers aged fifty-five or older, 213 died during the first six months after their wives had died, a death rate that is much higher than expected for married men. Most of these men had died from cardiovascular disorders, which are particularly aggravated by stress.

Creativity and Productivity

Michelangelo became the chief architect of St. Peter's Church in Rome at the age of seventy-two. The president of a roofing supplies business says his highest sales are achieved by those over sixty; they belong to the "Sizzling Sixty Club." Colonel Harlan Sanders, founder of Kentucky Fried Chicken, made his first million at the age of seventy-three. At age ninety-seven, Joel Hildebrand was an active chemistry professor at the University of California, continuing to publish papers and start new projects. Justice Oliver Wendell Holmes

Intellectual Self-management in Old Age

Professor B.F. Skinner's suggestions for dealing with the "normal abnormalities" of the aging process include the following:

If you cannot read, listen to book recordings. If you do not hear well, turn up the volume on your phonograph (and wear headphones to protect your neighbors). Foods can be flavored for aging palates. Paul Tillich, the theologian, defended pornography on the ground that it extended sexuality into old age (Skinner, 1983, p. 240).

A particular problem for the aged, of course, is forgetting. Skinner has some practical advice here too. If you want to remember to take an umbrella with you when you go out because rain is in the weather forecast, hang the umbrella on the door handle so you won't forget to take it. If you think of things you must do sometime later but are afraid you will forget them, keep a notebook or a pocket tape recorder handy. If you forget the names of acquaintances you want to introduce to someone else, work out a plan with that person:

My wife and I use the following strategy: If there is any conceivable chance that she could have met the person, I simply say to her, "Of course, you remember...?" and she grasps the outstretched hand and says, "Yes, of course. How are you?" The acquaintance may not remember meeting my wife, but is not sure of his or her memory, either (Skinner, 1983, p. 240).

Figure 10.6 Intellectual management in old age

stayed on the Supreme Court into his nineties; his credo was "to live is to work." Creativity and productivity are not limited to the early or middle adult years. Especially if the older adult remains reasonably healthy, he or she has much potential for creative work. See figure 10.6 for a description of the way a famous psychologist handles the aging process.

Creativity and productivity seem to be important factors in adjustment to later adulthood. In one of the best studies of this adjustment process, Bernice Neugarten (1971) found several patterns in the 2000 men and women in their seventies who participated. The integrated older adults were those who were well-adjusted, open to new experiences, intact with regard to cognitive abilities, and generally high in life satisfaction. Other people in the sample showed more striving, achievement-oriented behavior and preferred to keep busy with regimented schedules. Some of the less well-adjusted individuals required considerable emotional support from family and friends, and a few showed very poor adjustment by withdrawing and engaging in almost no outside activities.

This study is important because it demonstrates that the patterns of development occurring during later adulthood are quite variable. Most people adjust to the many life changes extremely well, finding new activities, interests, and seeking new ways to be creative and productive. Many very well adjusted older adults adopt new values and motivations as well. For example, the famous psychologist D. O. Hebb noticed interesting changes as he grew older (1978). At the age of seventy-four, he said that he would rather devote his energies to putting a ten-acre farm in shape than to solving complex psychological problems. A highly achievement-oriented individual with financial obligations might not understand this motivation, but Hebb devoted as much energy and dedication to the farm as to his work in psychology.

Death and Dying

Despite the statistics, most adolescents and younger adults believe that they will die suddenly, by accident or perhaps by an unexpected heart attack. Most people, however, do not die suddenly. We become ill, often from cardiovascular disorders or cancer, before we die. Many have ample opportunity to face their own deaths, and some have described their attitudes and fears to psychologists. A group of cancer patients, for example, reported concern over pain, disfigurement, the future, loss of work role, dependency, being a burden on others, and alienation from others (Hinton, 1973).

Facing Death. Some research has found that terminally ill patients who are anticipating their own deaths move through a series of behavioral patterns on their way to accepting the inevitable. Elizabeth Kübler-Ross (1969) interviewed more than 200 such patients and found five different stages: denial, anger, bargaining, depression, and acceptance. Some patients move through all of these stages in sequence; others showed elements of more than one attitude at the same time.

In the denial stage, the person is stunned and refuses to believe what the doctors say, even if he or she has suspected the worst. Some seek exotic treatments from faith healers or untested drugs. These feelings are eventually replaced by anger, rage, envy of healthy people, and resentment. The person asks, "Why me?" In the bargaining stage, patients seem to accept their own death but seek to postpone it by repenting, taking their medicine regularly, going to church, or other means.

Depression is the fourth stage in the death process, a step Kübler-Ross viewed as a necessary step in accepting death. This depression represents a kind of anticipatory grief as the individual grieves for his or her own death before the fact. If they have enough time, the dying patients may arrive at the final stage of acceptance, in which they can openly discuss their own deaths and use their last days to arrange their affairs and say good-bye. Many express wistfulness rather than severe depression or anger at the prospect of the end of life.

The Choices of the Dying.   Dying people often do not have too many choices about how they will die, how much pain medication they will get, whether to talk about dying with other people, and even whether they will be told they are dying.

Patients sometimes cannot discuss their attitudes and feelings about death with those around them because many people are reluctant to do so. The attendants at a geriatric hospital used one of only a few stereotyped responses every time the patient wanted to talk about death. One was reassurance: "Don't think like that—you're doing very well. . . ." Another was denial: "You don't mean that! You're going to live to 100!" The least likely response was honest and genuine discussion about death (Kastenbaum, 1967).

Our society is gradually recognizing that people want to have control over some aspects of their own deaths. Some states have legalized "living wills" in which people can state whether they want to die natural deaths or be maintained by life-sustaining equipment for as long as possible. Surveys of older people show convincingly that most want to die a natural death and do not want to be kept alive by artificial means. Without a living will, however, or in states where such documents are not recognized, the removal of a patient from life-sustaining equipment constitutes euthanasia.

Death is the last developmental phase of life. We know almost nothing about the experience of death; however, many people have been close enough to give us some glimpses, though their reports cannot be taken as hard evidence of what actually happens. Such reports are often surprisingly similar. People report leaving their bodies and watching the resuscitation attempts from a distance. They also report having a sense of traveling through space very rapidly, a tunnel, a passage of some kind, and the awareness of a comforting presence. Not very many feel fear, and those that do are often the healthy ones faced with sudden death, by drowning, for example. Although the methods of science can reveal fascinating information about most developmental phases, this last one is likely to retain its mysteries.

GUIDED REVIEW

Learning Objectives 9, 10, and 11

1. The _____ process involves graying of hair, wrinkling of skin, and other physiological changes. The _____ proposes that aging and death are programmed in our genes.

2. According to Erikson, the major developmental task of later adulthood is _____ .

3. Major life adjustments in _____ adulthood include retirement, changes in family and social relationships, and changes in health. Retirement can be particularly difficult if it is accompanied by a large reduction in standard of living and if it is not voluntary. Most people adapt to retirement very well.

4. Health problems are more common during later adulthood because of the aging process and because of the increase in significant life changes. There is some evidence that grief can make people more vulnerable to _____ .

5. Later adulthood is often characterized by _____ and _____ . Integrated persons indicate high satisfaction in life and are open to new experiences.

6. Most people die from illness rather than accidents, so most can face the prospect of their own imminent deaths. Terminally ill patients may show a sequence of behavior patterns including _____ , _____ , _____ , _____ , and _____ .

7. Many states recognize _____ , which are documents that describe how the individual wishes to die, particularly whether they wish to die a natural death or be placed on life-sustaining equipment.

SUMMARY

I. The term *adolescence* comes from a Latin word meaning "to grow up." Adolescence begins at puberty. (p. 346)

   A. Biological changes occurring at puberty include the development of the primary and secondary sexual characteristics as a result of the release of sex hormones. (p. 346)

   B. A persons' gender depends on his or her sex chromosomes. Women have two X chromosomes, and men have one X and one Y chromosome. (p. 347)

     1. Sexual differentiation, which occurs during prenatal life, is the process by which the physiological differences between males and females develop. The presence or absence of androgens affects the body, the brain, and behavior. (p. 348)

     2. Interest in sexuality increases greatly during adolescence. Although sexual attitudes have changed markedly in recent decades, sexual behavior is much slower to change. (p. 349)

   C. An important developmental task of adolescence is the search for an identity separate from the parents, something Erikson referred to as identity vs. identity diffusion. Categories of identity status include identity achievement, foreclosure, moratorium, and identity diffusion. (p. 350)

   D. During adolescence, social development shifts from a focus on the parents to a focus on peer groups as a source of approval and comparison. (p. 352)

II. Early and middle adulthood span the years from the end of adolescence to the early sixties, although no clear demarcations can be used to identify these periods. (p. 354)

   A. The early adult years involve a great many developmental tasks. (p. 354)

     1. Choosing a career is an important task of early adulthood. (p. 354)

     2. Most people get married and start families during early adulthood, and these are also important life events. (p. 357)

   B. Middle adulthood appears on the surface to be very different for different people, but some researchers have found identifiable patterns of development. (p. 362)

     1. An important stage during middle adulthood is the midlife transition, in which the person changes perspectives, begins to confront mortality, and reevaluates earlier goals and values. (p. 362)

     2. Studies of women have shown important developmental transitions during the middle adulthood period, often associated with menopause or the "empty nest syndrome." (p. 362)

     3. Erikson sees generativity vs. self-absorption as the major psychosocial task of middle adulthood. (p. 363)

   C. Piaget proposed that there were few changes in cognitive ability after adolescence, but recent research suggests that there are improvements in logical reasoning. In middle and later adulthood, longitudinal studies have shown that some cognitive abilities improve, some decline, and many remain stable. (p. 363)

III. Our stereotypes of later adulthood are mostly negative, but research shows that this can be a very satisfying period for well-adjusted people. (p. 365)

   A. The aging process includes a number of cumulative changes that occur gradually. Although the reason why people age and die is not clear, the genetic theory of aging proposes that the process is genetically coded. (p. 366)

   B. Later adulthood involves a number of life adjustments that can be very difficult. Integrity vs. despair is the major psychosocial task associated with later adulthood, according to Erikson. (p. 366)

     1. Retirement involves many changes, including loss of income, change in friendships, and change in schedules. (p. 366)

     2. Later adulthood is associated with more health problems, which may be due not only to the aging process but to the stresses associated with life changes. (p. 367)

C. Creativity and productivity are characteristic of many people during later adulthood, and studies have found that the majority of older adults are very satisfied with their lives. (p. 368)

D. The process of confronting death is an important feature of later adulthood. (p. 369)

    1. Some research on terminally ill patients suggest that this process involves several behavioral patterns that often occur in sequence, including denial, anger, bargaining, depression, and acceptance. (p. 369)

    2. The choices of the dying patient are limited, partly because friends, family, and those in the medical profession are reluctant to share information and discuss the issue. (p. 370)

ACTION GLOSSARY

Match the terms in the left column with the definitions in the right column.

____ **1. Puberty** (p. 346)
____ **2. Primary sexual characteristics** (p. 346)
____ **3. Secondary sexual characteristic** (p. 346)
____ **4. Sex chromosomes** (p. 347)
____ **5. Sexual differentiation** (p. 347)
____ **6. Androgens** (p. 348)
____ **7. Dihydrotestosterone** (p. 348)

A. *A trait or organ directly concerned with reproductive function, such as the ovaries and uterus in the female, and the testes in the male.*
B. *The process by which the physiological differences between males and females develop.*
C. *A hormone released during prenatal life that is responsible for the development of the male genitals.*
D. *A trait typical of one sex, but not directly concerned with reproductive function, such as distribution of body fat or growth of facial hair.*
E. *The time of sexual maturation.*
F. *Sex hormones released by the fetal testes.*
G. *Chromosomes, called the X and the Y, that determine the gender of the fetus; a female has two X chromosomes, and a male has one X and one Y.*

____ **8. Gender identity** (p. 349)
____ **9. Identity vs. identity diffusion** (p. 350)
____ **10. Identity achievement** (p. 350)
____ **11. Foreclosure identity** (p. 350)
____ **12. Moratorium identity** (p. 351)
____ **13. Identity diffusion** (p. 351)
____ **14. Intimacy vs. isolation** (p. 357)
____ **15. Midlife transition** (p. 362)

A. *A category of identity status in which the person is actively involved in choosing an identity and seeking alternatives.*
B. *A period in middle adulthood when an individual changes perspectives, begins to confront mortality, and reevaluates many of the goals and values he or she held during early adulthood.*
C. *A category of identity status in which the individual has gone through a period of crisis and developed fairly firm commitments.*
D. *The process in which the child learns to identify with the appropriate sex; the feelings of a person about whether he or she is male or female.*
E. *A category of identity status in which a person has never had an identity crisis and has not formed any particular commitments or established any goals.*
F. *The major psychosocial task of adolescence, according to Erik Erikson.*
G. *According to Erik Erikson, the major psychosocial task faced by young adults.*
H. *A category of identity status in which the individual has never gone through any identity crisis but has become committed to goals and values, usually those of the parents.*

___ **16. Generativity vs. self-absorption** (p. 363)
___ **17. Crystallized intelligence** (p. 364)
___ **18. Cognitive flexibility** (p. 364)
___ **19. Visuo-motor flexibility** (p. 364)
___ **20. Visualization** (p. 364)
___ **21. Genetic theory of aging** (p. 366)
___ **22. Integrity vs. despair** (p. 366)
___ **23. Life Events Questionnaire** (p. 368)

A. *A short test that asks about the number and characteristics of changes and important events in a person's life, in an attempt to relate these to health and illness.*
B. *The ability to engage in formal reasoning and abstract thinking.*
C. *The ability to shift from familiar to unfamiliar patterns in visuo-motor tasks.*
D. *The ability to organize and process visual information.*
E. *The major psychosocial task of later adulthood, according to Erik Erikson.*
F. *According to the personality theory of Erik Erikson, the major psychosocial task of middle adulthood.*
G. *The ease and flexibility with which one can shift from one mode of thinking to another.*
H. *Asserts that the aging process is programmed into the genetic code of each species.*

ANSWERS

1. E, 2. A, 3. D, 4. G, 5. B, 6. F, 7. C, 8. D, 9. F, 10. C, 11. H, 12. A, 13. E, 14. G, 15. B, 16. F, 17. B, 18. G, 19. C, 20. D, 21. H, 22. E, 23. A

SELF-TEST

1. For girls, the approximate age at which the growth spurt begins is
   (a) ten years.
   (b) twelve years.
   (c) thirteen years.
   (d) fourteen years.
   (LO 1; p. 346)

2. The hormone(s) released during prenatal development and responsible for the development of the male genitals is (are)
   (a) estrogen.
   (b) progesterone.
   (c) dihydrotestosterone.
   (d) pituitary hormones.
   (LO 1; p. 348)

3. According to research on sexual behavior, a common pattern demonstrated by adolescents can be described as
   (a) promiscuity.
   (b) serial monogamy without marriage.
   (c) celibacy.
   (d) life-long monogamy.
   (LO 2; p. 350)

4. The identity status of an adolescent who accepts an identity based on parental expectations would be _____ , according to Marcia.
   (a) identity achieved
   (b) identity diffused
   (c) moratorium
   (d) foreclosure
   (LO 3; p. 350)

5. Adolescents who are in the identity achievement status are likely to
   (a) have supportive parents.
   (b) be critical of their parents and have conflict in their homes.
   (c) experience very distant family relationships.
   (d) have parents who are rejecting and indifferent and lack understanding.
   (LO 3; p. 351)

6. A close association with a peer group during adolescence is one way for an individual to
   (a) become an autonomous functioning individual.
   (b) hide feelings of dependence on the parents.
   (c) foreclose on an identity acceptable to the parents.
   (d) establish an identity separate from the parents.
   (LO 4; p. 352)

7. According to research, most people learn about the requirements for the career they choose
   (a) after being well along that career path.
   (b) by talking with people who are involved in that career, prior to the choice.
   (c) by reading about it prior to making any decisions.
   (d) All of the above.
   (LO 5; p. 355)

8. According to Erikson, the developmental task of early adulthood is

(a) industry versus inferiority.
(b) identity versus identity diffusion.
(c) intimacy versus isolation.
(d) generativity versus stagnation.
(LO 5; p. 357)

9. According to recent research, what personality change occurs in new fathers?

(a) They are more angry and are resentful of their infants.
(b) They are less confident about their abilities.
(c) They are more passive and withdrawn.
(d) They are more confident about life in general.
(LO 5; p. 358)

10. The period in life when one begins to confront his or her own mortality and reevaluates many of the goals and values held during early adulthood is called

(a) generativity versus stagnation.
(b) the midlife transition.
(c) menopause.
(d) old age.
(LO 6; p. 362)

11. According to Erikson, the psychosocial task of middle adulthood is

(a) integrity versus despair.
(b) identity versus identity diffusion.
(c) intimacy versus isolation.
(d) generativity versus self-absorption.
(LO 6; p. 363)

12. In longitudinal research in intelligence, an intellectual decline was observed in which of the following areas?

(a) crystallized intelligence
(b) cognitive flexibility
(c) visuo-motor flexibility
(d) visualization
(LO 7; p. 364)

13. Cross-sectional studies of cognitive change across the life-span have been criticized because

(a) older people generally have less education than younger people.
(b) older people do not understand the directions as well as younger people.
(c) older people are discriminated against because their reaction time is slower than that of younger people.
(d) more older people drop out than do younger people and therefore cannot be retested.
(LO 7; p. 364)

14. The three groups of people who often live past the age of 100 share all of the following *except*

(a) diets that include mostly vegetables and little fat.
(b) abstinence from alcohol and tobacco.
(c) an expectation that they will live a long time.
(d) active sex lives.
(LO 8; p. 366)

15. According to research with mice, _____ appears to be associated with longer life spans and lower incidence of cancer.

(a) undernutrition
(b) exercise
(c) moderate alcohol consumption
(d) hormone treatment
(LO 8; p. 366)

16. Which of the following situations is not usually a change associated with old age?

(a) retirement   (c) marriage
(b) widowhood   (d) illness
(LO 9; p. 366)

17. According to a report by the National Institute of Mental Health, what percent of retired people feel positively about retirement?

(a) 95%   (c) 57%
(b) 10%   (d) 34%
(LO 9; p. 367)

18. Which of the following is one of the key criteria in most of the successful coping patterns of old age?

(a) good health
(b) a good sex life
(c) an active retirement
(d) a fulfilling social life
(LO 9; p. 367)

19. Neugarten's study of adjustment to later adulthood found
    (a) that most elderly adults were withdrawn from activities.
    (b) that most elderly adults required a great deal of emotional support from family and friends.
    (c) that most elderly adults were housebound and infirm.
    (d) a great deal of variability in adjustment.
    (LO 10; p. 369)

20. According to research by Kübler-Ross, which stage is characterized by individuals asking, "Why me?"
    (a) denial
    (b) anger
    (c) depression
    (d) bargaining
    (LO 11; p. 369)

ANSWERS

1. a, 2. c, 3. b, 4. d, 5. b, 6. d, 7. a, 8. c, 9. d, 10. b, 11. d, 12. c, 13. a, 14. b, 15. a, 16. c, 17. c, 18. a, 19. d, 20. b

SUGGESTED READINGS

Baruch, G., and J. Brooks-Gunn, *Women in midlife*. New York: Plenum, 1984. A collection of articles dealing with the experiences of women during their middle years.

Doyle, J. *The male experience*. Dubuque, IA: Wm. C. Brown Publishers, 1983. An interdisciplinary and readable text on the male role in society.

Levinson, D. J., C. N. Darrow, E. B. Klein, M. H. Levinson, and B. McKee. *The seasons of a man's life*. New York: Alfred A. Knopf, 1978. An account of men's developmental changes during their middle years.

Little, M. *Family breakup: understanding marital problems and the mediating of child custody decisions*. San Francisco: Jossey-Bass, 1982. A summary of an interview study that examined the reactions of people to their own divorces.

Perlmutter, M., and E. Hall. *Adult development and aging*. New York: Wiley, 1985. An excellent undergraduate text on the topic of adult development.

Poon, L. W., ed. *Aging in the 1980s: psychological issues*. Washington, D.C.: American Psychological Association, 1980. A collection of articles dealing with the problems of older adults, ranging from neuropsychological issues to interpersonal relations.

Santrock, J. W. *Life-span development*. Dubuque, IA: Wm. C. Brown Publishers, 1983. An introductory text that covers development throughout life, organized by age groups.

Schneider, J. *Stress, loss, and grief: understanding their origins and growth potential*. Rockville, MD: Aspen Systems, 1984. A detailed look at the process of grieving after a loss, and especially how to help people who are experiencing grief.

Stevens-Long, J., and N. J. Cobb. *Adolescence and early adulthood*. Palo Alto, CA: Mayfield, 1983. An introductory text with good treatment of issues such as the differences between early and late developers and the importance of identity formation.

c h a p t e r

11

Personality and Assessment

LEARNING OBJECTIVES

After reading this chapter, you should be able to

1. define personality, and discuss different conceptions of personality. **(p. 380)**
2. draw the fundamental distinction between personality theories that define personality largely as a product of environmental factors and those that see it as the result of enduring forces within the individual. **(p. 380)**
3. identify the two basic concepts of Freud's psychoanalytic theory: the principle of psychic determinism and the principle of the unconscious. **(pp. 381–82)**
4. identify and describe the three components of the psychic apparatus: the ego, id, and superego. **(pp. 382–83)**
5. list and detail the five stages of psychosexual development: the oral, anal, phallic, latency, and genital stages. **(pp. 383–85)**
6. describe how fixation or regression, two key mechanisms for defending the ego against attack, may come into play when difficulties are encountered at any psychosexual stage. **(p. 385)**

7. discuss the ways in which the theories of the neo-Freudians differed from Freud's original psychoanalytic theory. **(pp. 387–89)**
8. explain how the theoretical and experimental roots of the social learning theory of personality lie in classical and operant conditioning and in observational learning. **(pp. 390–93)**
9. discuss the similarities and the differences between social learning and psychodynamic theories of personality. **(pp. 393–94)**
10. indicate how the existential/humanistic theories of personality emphasize the unique and singular worth of the individual. **(pp. 394–97)**
11. detail the ways in which unstructured, semistructured, and structured observational methods and projective and objective tests of personality are designed to reflect personality in its manifold forms. **(pp. 397–402)**

What Is Personality?

Personality psychologists have found it difficult to agree on a single definition of personality. This difficulty reflects the differences in theoretical position and research methods that divide psychologists who are interested in the study of personality. Most personality psychologists do agree, however, that personality is expressed through behavior and that the goal of personality theory and research is understanding and prediction of behavior. This emphasis on behavior as the key to understanding personality, combined with our conviction that no single approach to the study of personality does full justice to the complexity of personality, leads us to suggest the following definition of personality: **personality** *is composed of the traits, values, attitudes, physical and intellectual attributes, and social skills and interpersonal experiences that distinguish one person from another, help predict his or her behavior in new settings, and give some continuity to behavior that would otherwise seem to be subject only to the whims of fate and fortune.*

One of the most enduring controversies among personality theorists is how personality and behavior develop. Walter Mischel (1979) and other advocates of the social learning position believe that personality is the product of the environment in which the individual lives. To these theorists, personality and behavior cannot be viewed independently of the external, environmental forces that affect them. Seymour Epstein (1979) and other predominantly psychoanalytic theorists take another position. They see personality as the result of enduring forces within the individual that are acquired early in life. This position discounts the impact of the environment in favor of factors internal to the individual.

An important element of the "environmentalist" position is its understandable emphasis on the importance of environmental **states**, *immediate environmental influences,* in understanding behavior. Theorists taking this position believe that behavior and personality can be understood best by examining their environmental context. To these theorists, an unreasonable employer, a nagging spouse, or a demanding profession, along with the events of the day, explain most of what we need to know about the causes of behavior. The social learning theory of personality is a state theory.

In contrast, psychoanalytic personality theorists, along with others who see the roots of behavior in "enduring forces," explain behavior by emphasizing **traits,** *the enduring personal attributes like social skillfulness or ineptness, driving ambition or laziness, and loyalty or disloyalty.* Such enduring forces are thought to predict behavior and explain personality better than less enduring events in the environment, so far as these theorists are concerned. The psychoanalytic theory of personality is a trait theory.

Trait theorists or state theorists do not agree among themselves on all issues, however. Freud, the first modern trait theorist, believed that sexual and aggressive impulses (central components of the Freudian theory of personality) play unparalleled roles, from life's earliest years, in determining behavior and personality. Later "neo-Freudian" theorists, however, chose to emphasize social rather than biological mechanisms as key factors in personality development. They also saw these factors as less fixed and more changeable than Freud saw sex and aggression to be.

Likewise, whereas some social learning theorists like Joseph Wolpe believe that a single learning mechanism (classical conditioning) is responsible for most normal and abnormal behavior, others (like Albert Bandura and Terence Wilson) believe that operant conditioning, modeling, and cognitive mediating factors also influence behavior in important ways.

Because we believe that neither state nor trait theories by themselves do full justice to the complexity of human behavior, we think a theory of personality ought to call upon *both* states and traits to explain the development of personality and the expression of behavior.

GUIDED REVIEW

Learning Objectives 1 and 2

1. Most personality theorists agree that personality is expressed through _____ and that the ultimate goal of personality theory and research is the _____ and _____ of behavior.

2. _____ theories of personality explain behavior and personality as the product of immediate environmental influences; _____ theories stress the role of enduring traits of personality on behavior.

ANSWERS

1. behavior; understanding; prediction 2. State; trait

Freud's Psychoanalytic Theory of Personality

Psychoanalytic theory remains the most comprehensive, influential, and well-articulated theory of personality. Developed by Sigmund Freud (fig. 11.1) in successive stages through his years of clinical practice during the early part of the twentieth century, this theory has had an enormous impact on personality theory and research.

Basic Concepts

Central to the psychoanalytic theory are its two most basic concepts, the principle of psychic determinism and the principle of the unconscious. Both aroused much controversy when they were first proposed because they took a position so different from the prevailing ideas about the causes of behavior. Disagreement between psychoanalytic and social learning theorists on the same issues continues today.

The principle of **psychic determinism** *states that no behavior occurs by chance.* In other words, every human behavior—physical or psychological—occurs because of what has preceded it. Even such seemingly random events as dreaming, slips of the tongue, and forgetfulness stem from preexisting causes of which the individual is probably unaware. The source of these

Figure 11.1 Sigmund Freud (1856–1939)

behaviors, which appear to be products of chance but are not, is the unconscious. According to Freud, the **unconscious** *is that part of the individual's mental world that cannot be brought into consciousness by effort of will,* in that way distinguishing it from conscious processes of thinking.

The unconscious, according to psychoanalytic theory, is composed of the person's most primitive and least mature wishes, impulses, and desires. They remain unconscious (though they are quite capable of influencing behavior) because their conscious experience would be powerfully disruptive of normal functioning.

The behavior of small children is sometimes pointed to by psychoanalytic theorists as a model of how the unconscious can affect behavior. This behavior, straight from the child's uncensored unconscious, is sometimes referred to as **primary process** because it *conveys a primitiveness, an immaturity, an unsocialized impact that is not yet modified by society's rules and not yet altered by the child's wish to conform.*

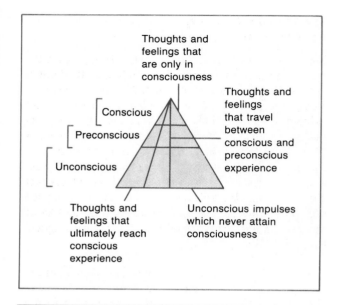

Figure 11.2 Freud's topography of the personality

Unconscious material can also seek expression in the behavior of adults: in "unconscious (Freudian) slips of the tongue," in dreams, or, during psychotherapy, by a gradual process that permits the unconscious to come to consciousness (fig. 11.2).

Psychic Apparatus

According to classical psychoanalytic theory (Freud, 1932), much of the content of the unconscious is derived from what Freud called the id, the first part of the psychic apparatus to make itself felt. The **id** *is a reservoir of primitive drives and desires untouched and unaffected by contact with the real world and its "civilizing" influence.* It is the first element of the psychic apparatus to emerge, and it does so during earliest childhood. Dominant in these early months of life, the id is guided by one aim, **the pleasure principle.** *The aim of the pleasure principle is to maximize pleasure.* (Dry diapers and a full stomach give the infant pleasure.)

According to psychoanalytic theory, the **ego** *comes into existence as a way to adjust the id to external reality by modifying id impulses so that they conform to society's moral and ethical standards and rules.* In essence, the ego is supposed to enable the organism to adapt and, when necessary, to compromise. The ego, in contrast to the id, is guided by **the reality principle,** *which means that reality, rather than pleasure, guides ego functioning.*

Sometimes known as the "executive" of the personality, the ego "manages" the functioning of the person the way an executive manages the functioning of an organization. The ego also mediates and arbitrates between the demands of the real world and those of the id, in that way permitting the individual to do many things: to learn complex motor skills like driving a car; to learn to write; to sense, perceive, and then reflect on environmental stimuli; to remember, compare, and think; and to test reality. It's not hard to see why some psychoanalytic psychologists believe the ego to be responsible for our most distinctly human social and intellectual capabilities.

As the child grows, the ego comes to have another job. That job is to deal with and sometimes moderate the superego. The last of the elements of the psychic apparatus to develop, the **superego** *is presumed to emerge gradually, when the child must begin to learn the rules by which society and interpersonal behavior are governed. Because parents are most responsible for teaching their children these rules, the superego comes to represent internalized parents.* In other words, the superego is at the root of conscience, a function parents typically serve until the child has evolved a conscience of his or her own.

Freud believed that the id is the reservoir of two basic drives, **the life instinct,** whose sources are *the sexual impulses and drives that reside in the id,* and **the death instinct,** powered by *the aggressive drives and impulses that are also a part of the id.* He also believed that the thoughts, feelings, wishes, and desires motivated by these drives are present at birth in every infant, hidden, safely or not, in his or her unconscious. It was this belief, particularly his conviction that infants and children have sexual feelings, that aroused so much hostility toward Freud when he first proposed the theory of infantile psychosexuality. Before he concluded, based upon years of clinical observation, that very young children have some of the same sexual and aggressive urges that adults have, children were assumed to be free from such thoughts and feelings. Freud wrote during the Victorian era, when sexuality was subject to strong repressive efforts, so his views were that much more suspect.

The ego must find socially acceptable ways, if at all possible, for id impulses to find conscious expression. Psychoanalytic theory teaches, for example, that the artist and the sculptor may be expressing their sexual feelings in the process of artistic creation, whereas the businessperson might well be competing in order to express (in disguised form) aggressive impulses.

The ego must also handle superego demands if and when they become too harsh and condemning of behavior. This can happen if an extremely critical, judgmental, punitive conscience has developed, one which prevents enjoyment from quite normal and usual pursuits. Such a situation can occur during early adolescence, when sexual drives are intense and the adolescent has not had sufficient experience to handle them adequately.

Freud assumed the existence of these three components of the psychic apparatus because he recognized that every healthy human being is capable of three distinct kinds of behavior: sexual and aggressive drives and wishes; the capacity to utilize reasoning in order to adjust to life's varying demands; and the capacity to govern oneself according to society's rules (Jones, 1963). By describing psychological behavior in this three-part fashion, Freud could attribute the many varieties of mental disorder to problems in early life that had an impact on one or more of the components of the psychic apparatus.

Psychosexual Stages of Personality Development

Freud's theory of personality (Freud, 1905) separated personality development during childhood into distinct phases. During these psychosexual stages of development, specific parts of the body become invested with psychic energy, or **libido,** defined as *the psychological energy that comes from instincts and energizes parts of the body involved in the successive stages of psychosexual development.* Believing that personality development involves passage through a set of distinct phases, Freud also believed that the "fit" between the child's behavior during a psychosexual stage and his or her environment determined the child's psychological health later on.

The Oral Stage. The first stage of psychosexual development, the **oral stage,** *lasts from birth to about eighteen months. Much of the child's behavior during this time is devoted to obtaining food.* As a result, the taste and touch receptors in and around the child's mouth, lips, and tongue become especially sensitive so that they provide stimulation and pleasure that Freud considered to be similar in important ways to sexual pleasure. A firm believer in evolutionary theory, Freud saw evolutionary significance in the fact that psychological energy (he called it libido) invested itself in that function of the body, food intake, that was most essential to healthy development at this time.

Freud also recognized that psychological as well as physical development occurred during this earliest psychosexual stage. Central to the psychological developments that take place during the oral stage was the child's realization that she or he could not be fed or comforted instantly. Instead, during the oral stage, *the child must learn that there are important aspects of the world over which he or she cannot have control.* To

Freud, this intrusion of the realistic demands of the environment was most important to the developing ego and to the development of personality during this first stage of psychosexual development.

The Anal Stage.   During the **anal stage** of psychosexual development, *which Freud believed lasts from about the ages of eighteen months to two and a half years, the young child's major focus of learning and experiencing is on controlling the elimination of waste products from the body.* Accordingly, the sensory receptors involved in elimination become especially sensitive during this time, ensuring that pleasurable sensations will be involved in elimination and that they will motivate the child to learn to eliminate urine and feces.

Further, Freud believed that children must also learn a psychological lesson during the anal stage: how to control other important aspects of their environment. They must learn, for example, that they can exert surprising control over their parents, pleasing or displeasing them profoundly simply by giving or withholding certain behaviors (for example, love, physical affection, even feces and urine). The importance of this lesson to the child's developing sense of self-esteem and competence is immense: the parent who refuses to let the child be his or her own person and who exerts control over some of his behavior prevents the child from developing the self-respect he or she needs for the rigors of what is to come in life.

The Phallic Stage.   Between the ages of three and six, according to psychoanalytic theory, the child's genital area is the major source of sensory focus and pleasure. In other words, Freud believed the child's genitals are a primary focus of potential pleasure during what he called the phallic stage of psychosexual development. Freud was severely criticized for taking this position,

as have been psychoanalysts ever since. The idea of considering a five- or six-year-old capable of deriving sexual pleasure from his or her genitals still astounds many nonpsychoanalysts.

It is during the phallic stage of development, Freud wrote, that the boy must deal with the "Oedipal conflict" and the girl with the "Electra conflict." The way in which these situations are resolved determines both sexual identity (the adult sexual role the person considers most appropriate for him- or herself), and later mental health or illness. The **phallic stage** *centers on concerns about the size and function of the genitals (which, at this age, are not yet capable of mature sexual functioning).* This focus leads the child into direct conflict with the same-sex parent and, at the same time, a closer relationship, one with sexual overtones, with the opposite-sex parent.

This shift in parent-child relationships culminates in a family conflict situation named for the central figures in two tragic Greek myths. In one of the myths, Oedipus, son of a royal Greek family, is fated to carry out a tragic prediction: that he will kill his father, the king, and marry his mother, the queen. And, true to the prediction, Oedipus ultimately does so despite heroic efforts to avoid his fate. In the other myth, Electra, daughter of a royal couple, incites her brother to kill both her mother and her mother's lover.

Observing themes in the fantasies of five-year-old boys and girls that seemed to him to resemble these myths, Freud speculated that these phenomena were universal ones, occurring across different cultures and different eras. He observed the frequent development of unconscious fantasies and wishes to assume the same-sex parent's place in the mind, heart, and bed of the opposite-sex parent. Freud saw little boys, then, as wishing (unconsciously, of course) to destroy their fathers and become their mothers' lovers; for little girls it was just the reverse. The successful resolution of this conflict, Freud felt, was essential to healthy adult functioning later on.

The Oedipal and Electra conflicts as Freud portrayed them are only by analogy and in fantasy. That is, the fantasies the child entertains are both unconscious and poorly formed. Few children are aware of the aims of these fantasies; of those few who may be, all are terribly ambivalent about wanting to displace an otherwise beloved parent.

The Latency Period. Following the stormy phallic period (to resolve the Oedipal conflict, the child must accept the reality that his/her ultimate sexual partner *will not be* a parent), the child enters an extended period of psychosexual quietude, the **latency period.** What takes place during this time is *the consolidation of the psychological and social lessons learned and behaviors acquired during the three earlier stages of psychosexual development.*

The Genital Stage. With the onset of puberty, the **genital stage** of psychosexual development begins. *It is during this time that the adolescent learns the perils and pleasures of adult sexuality.* How much pleasure and how much peril the adolescent experiences during this period depends very much on how well or poorly he or she has progressed through the earlier stages of psychosexual development. That is, central to Freud's theory is the conviction that the events of the oral, anal, and phallic stages largely determine both the personality and the ultimate psychological health of the adult.

Defense Mechanisms

To protect itself against excessively strong id or superego demands, even healthy strong egos must adopt **defense mechanisms,** *which prevent the insistent, powerful forces of the id or superego from ultimately overwhelming the "civilized" ego and seeking expression in behavior that might otherwise destroy or seriously harm the personality.* Many of these defense mechanisms are unconscious and involuntary; others are conscious or at least open to conscious recognition.

Though healthy egos resort to defensive maneuvers from time to time, excessive dependence upon certain of the less adaptive defenses signals a weak or otherwise inadequate ego. This dependence results in ineffective, maladaptive, or abnormal behavior, according to psychoanalytic theory (Freud, 1914, 1924).

The role of defense mechanisms in both adequate and inadequate adjustment is discussed in detail in Chapter 12. Two key defense mechanisms are discussed here, though, in order to clarify the means by which troublesome environmental events, those capable of causing psychological trauma, interact with the stages of psychosexual development to affect later personality functioning. The two defense mechanisms are fixation and regression.

Fixation *refers to the defense mechanism that causes a person to remain in a particular psychosexual stage because his or her development is interfered with.* The person is unable to progress toward a more advanced stage and greater psychological maturity. For example, the child whose every desire is gratified by his mother during the oral stage may grow to adulthood believing that "the world owes me a living." Or, if the child is neglected during the same stage, she may come to believe that the world will never satisfy her needs and that people are not to be trusted or relied upon.

Regression *describes the return to an earlier, less mature stage of development from a later, more mature one* in the face of severe environmental stress. Though all of us regress briefly, at times, when faced with acute stressors (crying is one of the most common of such regressions), psychologically mature persons recover quickly from ordinary stress and adapt to it satisfactorily. However, persons who have not built a firm personality on the foundation of successful passage through the stresses of childhood may be overwhelmed by later reverses. They may find it impossible to avoid returning to earlier, less adaptive levels of adjustment on a more or less permanent basis.

An Overall View of Psychoanalytic Theory

Freud believed that personality develops largely from crucial events, taking place during the first five or six years of life, that help determine the success or failure of the child's passage through the stages of psychosexual development. In doing so, they affect the relative balance and strength of the ego, superego, and id—and, in turn, personality functioning.

The events that are most constructive and most helpful psychologically are those that foster development of a strong healthy ego and those in which supportive loving parents challenge the child to function more and more independently and to confront age-appropriate stresses that lead to enhanced feelings of competence and self-esteem. Least constructive are circumstances that weaken the ego and strengthen the id and superego, relative to the ego.

Situations that prevent the child from acquiring basic trust in the world or developing the capacity to view his or her environment realistically can weaken ego function. Punishing or seductive parents, whose behavior fosters development of a harsh punitive superego or strong and uncontrollable id impulses, can unduly strengthen id or superego functions. In both of the latter instances maladaptive behavior may develop, either during childhood, as the result of fixation, or at some point later, following regression. In contrast, psychological health flourishes when the ego is successful in mediating the demands of the sexual and aggressive impulses (the id), conscience (the superego), and the environment (as conveyed by the ego).

Through the years since Freud and Josef Breuer, an early collaborator, launched the psychoanalytic movement with the publication of *Studies in Hysteria* in 1895, efforts have been made to subject psychoanalytic theory to empirical study and confirmation. Two factors have interfered with these efforts.

First, Freud and those who worked with and came after him were clinicians, not researchers. Accordingly, the theory they devised was a clinical theory that was not designed even in part for ease of empirical validation. Second, much of psychoanalytic theory is so complex and so abstract that it defies experimental investigation. As a result, psychoanalytic theory has come to be viewed as inaccessible to controlled study. One either accepts it on faith or chooses another theory of personality. Although efforts to validate the theory empirically do continue (see, for example, Lambert and Bergin, 1983, and Imber, Pilkonis, and Glanz, 1983), the basic problems associated with the scientific investigation of psychoanalytic theory remain.

GUIDED REVIEW

Learning Objectives 3, 4, 5, and 6

1. Psychoanalytic theory's two basic tenets are the principle of _____ and the principle of the _____ .

2. The psychic apparatus includes the _____ , the earliest part of the psychic apparatus to develop and the reservoir of primitive drives and impulses; the _____ , the means by which the id is forced to adjust to external reality; and the _____ , which functions as a conscience, or internalized set of parents.

3. During the _____ , _____ , _____ , _____ , and _____ stages of psychosexual development, successive parts of the body are invested with _____ , and important psychological and interpersonal lessons associated with those bodily parts are learned.

4. Even strong egos must adopt strategies to defend themselves against excessively strong id or superego demands. Two of the most common are _____ and _____ .

ANSWERS

1. *psychic determinism; unconcious 2. id; ego; superego 3. oral, anal, phallic, latency, genital; libido 4. fixation, regression*

Neo-Freudian Personality Theories

Three separate groups of psychoanalytic theorists have developed influential psychoanalytically based theories of personality that deviate from Freud's original theory.

Freud's "Inner Circle": Jung, Adler, and Rank

The earliest group of neo-Freudians was composed of those members of Freud's original inner circle who were unable to accept all aspects of his original theory. Carl Jung, for instance, a very religious man, would not accept Freud's conclusion that infantile psychosexuality plays an important role in the development of many of the emotional disorders of adulthood. The idea that very young children have sexual feelings strong enough to lead them to wish to replace a parent in the arms of the other parent was unacceptable to Jung. Instead, Jung traced the development of many emotional disorders to problems the patient's parents might be having.

Jung also differentiated between extraverted and introverted personality types. **Extraverts** *are most interested in the world around them and in other people.* On the other hand, **introverts** *tend to be preoccupied with their own thoughts and feelings, and as a consequence they are less involved in the world around them.* This fundamental personality type distinction has had a continuing impact on later personality theorists' conceptions of personality. Chances are that these terms are a part of your vocabulary as well!

Alfred Adler, another member of Freud's inner circle, concluded that many emotional disorders derived from the feelings of **inferiority** all children experience *in relation to bigger, wiser, more powerful parents as they are growing up,* not from specifically sexual conflicts, as Freud would have said. Otto Rank, also a member of Freud's original group, traced many emotional disorders to the **trauma of birth,** *or the infant's shock at being delivered from the security and warmth of the womb to the chaos and confusion of the outside world.*

To these fundamental changes in theory, each theorist subsequently added modifications to Freud's original therapeutic method. The resultant therapeutic approaches were named after their sponsors: for example, Adlerian psychoanalysis and Jungian psychoanalysis.

Horney, Fromm, and Erikson: The Impact of Culture and Society

A second group of "revisionist" psychoanalysts worked later, in the decade of the 1930s, when most of the world struggled with serious economic depression. Accordingly, these men and women modified psychoanalytic theory to emphasize the effects of culture and society on the development of personality. Such theorists as Karen Horney, Erich Fromm, and Erik Erikson emphasized the dual impact that stressful current life events (poverty, hunger, and hopelessness, for example) *and* the ease or difficulty with which the person had progressed through the stages of infantile psychosexuality, have on development of mental disorder.

Karen Horney (fig. 11.3) believed that anxiety and depression result from basic conflicts arising from contradictory trends common to human beings. She summed up these trends as (1) "moving toward people," (2) "moving against people," and (3) "moving away from people." Horney labelled the concrete behavioral expression of these trends as the "Ten Neurotic Needs":

1. *The neurotic need for affection and approval.* (Examples: automatic living up to the expectations of others; dread of self-assertion.)
2. *The neurotic need for a partner who will take over one's life.* (Examples: dread of desertion and dread of being alone.)
3. *The neurotic need to restrict one's life within narrow borders.* (Examples: urge to save rather than to spend; dread of making any demands.)
4. *The neurotic need for power.* (Examples: domination over others craved for its own sake; dread of uncontrollable situations.)

Figure 11.3 Karen Horney (1885–1952)

5. *The neurotic need to exploit others and by hook or crook get the better of them.* (Examples: pride in exploitative skill; dread of being exploited and thus of being 'stupid.')
6. *The neurotic need for social recognition or prestige.* (Examples: self-evaluation entirely dependent on nature of public acceptance; all things evaluated only according to their prestige value.)
7. *The neurotic need for personal admiration.* (Examples: inflated image of self; dread of losing admiration.)
8. *The neurotic ambition for personal achievement.* (Examples: need to surpass others not through what one presents or is but through one's activities; dread of failure.)
9. *The neurotic need for self-sufficiency and independence.* (Examples: distance and separateness the only source of security; dread of needing others, of ties, of closeness, of love.)

10. *The neurotic need for perfection and unassailability.* (Examples: relentless drive for perfection; feelings of superiority over others because of being perfect.) (Horney, 1942, 54–63)

Written in 1942, these descriptions of causes for anxiety and depression have as much relevance to the human condition today as they did more than forty years ago. How many of the ten can you see in yourself?

Erich Fromm's classic work, *Escape from Freedom,* was published in 1941, at the height of the threat to the world from Nazi Germany. The book's thesis was that in their search for maximum freedom and self-determination, modern men and women might find themselves disorganized by boundless opportunity for choice in life-style and individual freedom. So great would be their discomfort at their freedom of choice that they would choose to "escape from freedom" by agreeing to a totalitarian dictatorship (like that of the Nazis, for example). The parallel that Fromm drew between what was then happening in Hitler's Germany in the late 1930s and the fundamental thesis of his book was obvious to all who read the book:

> We have been compelled to recognize that millions in Germany were as eager to surrender their freedom as their fathers were to fight for it; that instead of wanting freedom, they sought for ways of escape from it; that other millions were indifferent and did not believe the defense of freedom to be worth fighting and dying for. (Fromm, 1941, 5)

One of the most influential of the neo-Freudians today is Erik Erikson. Erikson's emphasis on the social and cultural factors that influence personality, as described in Chapters 9 and 10, and his belief that personality continues to grow and develop through the lifespan have struck a responsive chord in our society. (For example, Levinson, 1978, Sheehy, 1976, and Vaillant, 1977, authors of popular books on the developmental crises of adulthood, all acknowledge important debts to Erikson.) Other signs of Erikson's impact on our society are the words for key Eriksonian concepts that are now a part of our everyday vocabulary: Identity crisis, life cycle, psychohistory, and role confusion are examples.

The Ego Psychologists: Hartman, Spitz, and Mahler

A third neo-Freudian movement in psychoanalytic theory and practice has come to prominence even more recently through the work of psychologists like Heinz Hartman, Rene Spitz, and Margaret Mahler. These theorists are called **ego psychologists** because they *stress the ever-changing, ever-reacting nature of the ego and its defenses.* Inspired by Freud's daughter Anna and her influential 1936 book, *The Ego and the Mechanisms of Defense,* these theorists give credit to the ego and to the mature adult for having the ability, under the right circumstances, to respond and adapt to a changing environment. Earlier psychoanalytic theorists, including Sigmund Freud, did not believe that the ego could develop this ability to be flexible and adaptive.

Stressing the concept of ego strength as a prime determiner of the ability to deal with stress in both childhood and adulthood, the ego psychologists emphasize that the first three years of life are most important for mature psychological health. The reason is that during these years the ultimate strength of the ego, its capacity to withstand the stresses of life and life's changing circumstances, either is or is not established. Understandably, the psychotherapy developed by these theorists emphasizes procedures designed to strengthen the ego in its dealings with a stressful environment and more traditionally, with the challenges posed by the id and the superego.

These theorists deviate from Freud and those in his inner circle in stressing the role of the ego (rather than, for example, sex and aggression [Freud], feelings of inferiority [Adler], or the trauma of birth [Rank]) in determining mental health and mental disorder. Also,

whereas Horney, Erikson, and Fromm believed in the power of culture and society to bend ego functions, the ego psychologists emphasize the ego's power to alter environmental stresses.

The Neo-Freudians: An Overview

At this point, you might ask how it is that a single personality theory, in this case Freud's psychoanalytic theory, has been subjected to so many attempts at modification and change despite its profound continuing impact. Does this mean that the original theory was seriously deficient? Does it mean that new information has come to light invalidating the original theory? Or does it mean that different personality theorists, like everyone else, are apt to see the same thing in different ways? We think that all these explanations are valid. Perfection in theory-building is unattainable, and men and women continue to strive to improve existing theories of personality, even influential theories like Freud's, whose primary value may ultimately be measured in terms of the theories to which it gives birth rather than the questions it can answer itself.

GUIDED REVIEW

Learning Objective 7

1. Three separate groups of psychoanalytic theorists have deviated from _____ classical psychoanalytic theory.

2. The first group were members of Freud's inner circle who rejected the emphasis he placed on _____ .

3. The second group of neo-Freudians emphasized the effects of _____ and _____ on personality development.

4. The third group, called _____ , stressed the adaptive role of the ego in effecting adjustment to the environment.

ANSWERS

1. Freud's 2. infantile psychosexuality 3. culture, society 4. ego psychologists

Social Learning Theory of Personality

The social learning theory of personality assumes that most human behavior, normal and abnormal, is learned (see Chapter 5).

This view of personality arose from several influences. One of the first and most important was the identification, during this century, of the basic learning modes: Ivan Pavlov's and John B. Watson's elucidation of the principles of classical conditioning during the first two decades of the century; Edward Thorndike's and B. F. Skinner's subsequent development of the operant conditioning model; and Albert Bandura's more recent discovery of the impact of modeling and vicarious reinforcement on human behavior.

However, identification of these models of learning, while necessary before learning-based theories of personality could develop, was not sufficient for this purpose. The reaction against Freud's psychoanalytic theory was also needed. This reaction was in response to psychoanalytic theory's complexity, inaccessibility to experimental confirmation, overemphasis on the role of sexuality in behavior development, and belief in human behavior as a continuous struggle against inborn forces leading to emotional disorder. Had there been no reaction against psychoanalytic theory, there would have been no great need for an alternative.

Classical Conditioning and Personality

Though Pavlov's discoveries (see Chapter 5) were derived from laboratory research with animals, an enormous amount of later research has established the importance of the classical conditioning learning model so far as human beings are concerned. Scientists and clinicians have concluded that much of the autonomic learning that human beings do (learning that involves our emotional reactions to people and places) obeys the principles of classical conditioning.

How are emotional responses acquired by classical conditioning? In a now-famous demonstration, John B. Watson, whom many consider the parent of behaviorism in this country, successfully conditioned fear of a white rat in an 18-month-old child ("Little Albert") who was previously unafraid of the animal (Watson and Rayner, 1920). They did so by first exposing the child to a white rat, to which the child responded with interest and no fear. Then they paired the sight of the animal with a loud, frightening noise, to which the child responded with tears and a startle response. After Watson and Rayner had repeatedly paired the frightening noise with the rat, the child began to cry as soon as he saw the rat: a conditioned aversion to the rat, based upon fear, had been established.

Following Watson's demonstration of the conditionality of fear, other researchers began to study the many other emotions that can be conditioned to environmental stimuli. Their conclusions were that most of our emotional responses to the environment come about as the result of this kind of learning (e.g., Bandura, 1977; Lazarus, 1981; Wilson, 1982).

Social learning theorists believe that maladaptive emotional responses are also acquired by means of classical conditioning. The South African psychiatrist Joseph Wolpe, one of the leading spokespersons for this position, believes that learning mechanisms that are strikingly similar to those responsible for Little Albert's fear of the white rat are also responsible for adult fears and anxieties. By these mechanisms, human beings acquire inappropriate, dysfunctional fear and anxiety about people, places, and things. The practical significance of Wolpe's views on the causes of these conditions is that they are learned by means of classical conditioning. It was this conclusion that led Wolpe to develop a learning-based treatment program designed to "counter-condition" neurotic anxiety and fear and, hence, to alleviate fear and anxiety (see Chapter 14).

Operant Conditioning and Personality

Most social learning theorists believe that much of the behavior that defines our personalities is powerfully influenced by operant conditioning mechanisms. Unlike classical conditioning, operant learning does not establish new relationships between already existing behaviors (for example, between the frightening loud noise and the white rat to which Little Albert was exposed). Instead, operant conditioning exerts its influence on preexisting behaviors, whose frequency is increased or decreased as a function of their consequences. As one example, let us consider the central role that operant conditioning plays in the process by which we develop social skills.

Social skills are important components of our personalities. Friendliness, charm, cooperativeness, and empathy are all social skills, and all are important determinants of how successfully we interact with the world. Approval (smiles, grins, applause, verbal praise) for a particular social behavior leads to a strengthening of behavior and an increase in the likelihood that it will be repeated. Disapproval (frowns, shakes of the head, tears, verbal criticism) leads us just as quickly to reduce the frequency of the social behaviors that elicit such responses. And that is how, according to the operant conditioners, we become "social animals."

Operant conditioning also plays an important role in the development and maintenance of maladaptive behavior. Behavioral clinicians now believe that the operant model helps explain many severe and disabling conditions, including depression and the alcohol and drug dependencies.

Observational Learning and Personality

Observational learning, also called vicarious learning or modeling (see Chapter 5), is the most recently developed social learning-based perspective from which to view personality development. Explored in detail first by psychologist Albert Bandura and his colleagues in the early 1960s, this learning model explains the part of our behavior that we acquire by watching others. Models typically include parents, teachers, and friends; movie stars, characters in cartoons, or sports heroes can also serve us in this way. In his research on this basic learning mode, Bandura has concluded that such behaviors as aggressiveness, the capacity to delay gratification, certain patterns of emotional responsiveness, and many forms of verbal and social interactions are acquired as a function of modeling. Others (see Research Box: From Whom Do We Learn Morality?) have concluded that even such complex behaviors as morality are acquired, at least in part, by modeling the behaviors of parents and friends.

In his Presidential Address to the American Psychological Association (1974), Bandura reminded his readers that "theories that explain human behavior as the product of external rewards and punishments present a truncated image of man because people partly regulate their actions by self-produced consequences." This excerpt emphasizes Bandura's belief that operant and classical conditioning (both of which depend on external rewards and punishments) do not account for all human learning.

Bandura's statement also makes the equally important point that observational learning may well take place because the observer *chooses* to model certain behaviors. Those choices, of course, involve cognitions, or thinking, which prominent social learning theorists have only recently begun to credit in the learning process (Kendall and Kriss, 1983; Meichenbaum and Cameron, 1982; Rosenthal, 1982). Admitting that people act on the basis of thoughts as well as learned patterns may seem a small step forward to those of you who know that people think as well as act. However, many behavioral psychologists, especially those in the

---

RESEARCH BOX

From Whom Do We Learn Morality?

Watch school-aged children on the playground as Janet Lever did (1976). A group of girls are playing and a dispute arises; they settle the issue by changing the rule or going on to a new game. Then turn and watch a group of boys at play. They too have just had a difference of opinion about the rule of a game. A prolonged debate erupts with considerable discussion of the alternative interpretations of the rule. Finally, it is resolved and the game resumes. These young people have just exemplified a difference in how boys and girls, men and women, make moral decisions. Females tend to focus more than males upon the interpersonal context in which decisions are made. They value the continuation of the friendship more than winning the game, and so they are more likely than males to avoid escalation of conflict and insistence upon winning.

Children learn rules of morality from parents and peers. Apparently, the rules that are acquired hinge to some extent upon whether one is male or female. Interestingly, the assumption over the years has been that the male perspective is somehow superior, and not just different from the female one. Theorists including Freud, Piaget, and Erikson have written essentially male theories of moral development and assumed that because females deviate from this picture, their development is inherently inferior. Carol Gilligan (1982), a Harvard professor of education, points out that when we say men and women are different, we are typically also saying that different is worse. "Thus, when women do not conform to the standards of psychological expectation, the conclusion has generally been that something is wrong with the women." (Gilligan, 1982, 14)

Recent social changes make it more possible for us than ever before to reevaluate our assumptions about what constitutes "right" behavior. Why have we assumed that it is better to be competitive and independent in our approach to life rather than cooperative and interdependent? Is it inherently better to follow rules that dictate moral decisions independent of interpersonal considerations? Or could we all learn to consider the effect of our decisions upon other people in their relationships to us?

Both men and women may have been burdened in past generations by the assumption that male rules of moral decision making are inherently better than female rules. How many men have made life decisions based on what they "ought" to do rather than listening carefully to themselves and acting in ways that made good sense in their relationships with others? As Gilligan states, "Sensitivity to the needs of others and the assumption of responsibility for taking care lead women to attend to voices other than their own and to include in their judgment other points of view." (p. 16) A new generation of men and women may learn to listen to these voices in themselves and others and draw what is best from the moral development of both men and women.

classical and operant traditions, have never given cognitions a central place in their theories of personality and behavior, largely because thinking cannot be measured reliably and objectively.

The role of modeling in the development of maladaptive behavior has only recently begun to be explored. However, there is considerable clinical evidence that patients who complain of intense fear of new situations or of meeting new people have modeled the behavior, as children, from a similarly timid, shy, and socially isolated parent. Behavioral theorists have also hypothesized that modeling may play a role in more serious psychiatric symptomatology. When one family member is seriously disturbed, for example, there is an increased incidence of serious psychiatric disturbance in other family members (Ullmann and Krasner, 1976).

GUIDED REVIEW

Learning Objective 8

1. Social learning theories assume that most of human behavior and personality is _____ .

2. Social learning theorists believe that most of the emotional learning that humans do is accounted for by _____ mechanisms.

3. _____ conditioning mechanisms are responsible for much of our social and interpersonal behavior. Central to this view is the fundamental assumption that behavior that is _____ will increase in frequency whereas behavior that is _____ or _____ will decrease.

4. _____ includes those aspects of our behavior that we have acquired by watching others engage in the same behaviors.

ANSWERS

1. learned 2. classical conditioning 3. Operant; reinforced; punished; ignored 4. Observational learning

Psychoanalytic and Social Learning Theory: Similarities and Differences

Personality theorists have identified similarities as well as important differences between psychoanalytic and social learning theories of personality.

The two theories are similar in their intents to place behavior and personality within a consistent framework, to explain both normal and abnormal behavior, and to see continuity as well as change in the lives of men and women.

The two theories differ primarily in their images of personality development. Psychoanalytic theory (a trait theory) views personality development as a function of crucial early life experiences interacting with the stages of psychosexuality, themselves the result of inborn genetic mechanisms; later life experiences are of much less importance in determining behavior and personality. In contrast, social learning theory (a state theory) emphasizes two other explanatory mechanisms: learning, which continues through life, and the immediate stimulus characteristics of the environment, which powerfully affect the behavior taking place within that environment.

The two theories also differ in their complexity, accessibility to empirical validation, focus, and breadth of explanation. Social learning theory, a much newer theory based largely on laboratory findings, is much less complex and hence "explains" less behavior than can psychoanalytic theory. At the same time, its roots in the laboratory and the college classroom (from which subjects for many of its experiments have been drawn) mean that its explanations fit normal behavior better than they do abnormal behavior.

Psychoanalytic theory, for all its breadth, depth, and history, cannot point to the experimental support that social learning theory can claim. The validation problem remains a central one for psychoanalytic theory. In addition, because it derived from Freud's clinical observations, many people believe that psychoanalytic theory explains abnormal behavior a good deal better than it does normal behavior.

Existential/Humanistic Theories of Personality

Existential/humanistic theories of personality have only recently begun to exert a major impact on our perceptions of personality growth and development. Both **humanistic and existential theories** *emphasize the significance of the individual, his or her uniqueness and singularity.* Both have led to the development of behavior change techniques that aim to help people feel better about their own individuality and uniqueness and more willing to value their behavior, opinions, and self-worth.

Existential and humanistic theories differ in their origins. Existential theory arose in the consulting room; like psychoanalysis, it is based on psychotherapeutic efforts with emotionally troubled individuals. Humanistic theory, like social learning theory, derived from the study of normal individuals. The two theories also differ in central focus: existential theory focuses on the anxiety people experience toward existence and death, and humanistic theory focuses on the fundamental worth of the individual human being.

Rogers's Client-Centered Theory— A Humanistic Theory

The psychologist Carl Rogers (fig. 11.4) developed his theory from his observations of troubled but essentially normal clients. His **client-centered theory of personality** *states that personality derives from the individual's perceptions and interpretations of his or her world* rather than from inherited potentialities (as in psychoanalytic theory) or acquired, more or less involuntary

Figure 11.4 Carl Rogers (1902–   )

behavior patterns (as in social learning theory). Because Rogers also takes a very optimistic view of men and women (remember, his theory came from his experiences with healthy persons facing "normal" adjustment problems), his theory emphasizes their potential power to effect changes in themselves and their environments to a much greater extent than most other personality theories (Rogers, 1942, 1961).

Because Rogers's views of what contributes to healthy personality growth and development are based on his extensive experiences as a counselor to normal (albeit troubled) persons, they are relevant to psychologically healthy people—including most of the readers of this book! Those views are summarized in the Application Box: Carl Rogers on the Healthy Personality.

Maslow's Concept of Self-Actualization

Humanistic theorist Abraham Maslow, like Carl Rogers and the other humanists, based his theories on one fundamental assumption: men and women are basically good; they can achieve their potential, or actualize themselves, if they can overcome the frustrations and anxieties that are also a normal part of modern life.

APPLICATION BOX

Carl Rogers on the Healthy Personality

The following statements, comprising the essence of Rogers's theory of personality, bear little resemblance to either the social learning theory or the psychoanalytic theory. Thus, many theorists have concluded that Rogers's writings do not comprise a theory of personality but are instead simply the poetically rendered observations of a bright and very sensitive human being.

However, these fundamental beliefs do encompass both a way of life and an approach to behavioral explanation. Moreover, they have had considerable impact on the views of personality and its development (though their impact has not been nearly as great as that of either social learning or psychoanalytic theory). Therefore, they belong here as another example of the diverse range of influential theories of personality.

1. In my relationships with persons I have found that it does not help, in the long run, to act as though I were something I am not.
2. I find I am more effective when I can listen acceptantly to myself, and can be myself.
3. I have found it of enormous value when I can permit myself to understand another person.
4. I have found it enriching to open channels whereby others can communicate their feelings, their private perceptual worlds, to me.
5. I have found it highly rewarding when I can accept another person.
6. The more open I am to the realities in me and in the other person, the less do I find myself wishing to rush to "fix things."
7. I can trust my experiences.
8. Evaluation by others is not a guide for me . . . only one person can know whether what I am doing is honest, thorough, open, and sound, or false and defensive and unsound, and I am that person.
9. Experience is, for me, the highest authority . . . It is to experience that I must return again and again, to discover a closer approximation to truth as it is in the process of becoming in me.
10. I enjoy the discovering of order in experience.
11. The facts are friendly . . . painful reorganizations are what is known as learning.
12. What is most personal and unique in each one of us is probably the very element which would, if it were shared or expressed, speak most deeply to others.
13. I have come to feel that the more fully the individual is understood and accepted, the more he tends to drop the false fronts with which he has been meeting life, and the more he tends to move in a direction which is forward.
14. Life, at its best, is a flowing, changing process in which nothing is fixed. (From C. R. Rogers, *On Becoming a Person*, pp. 16–27. Copyright © 1961 by Houghton-Mifflin. Reprinted by permission of Houghton-Mifflin, and by permission of Constable and Company, Ltd., London.)

Maslow talked of what he called a **hierarchy of needs.** *At the bottom of this hierarchy are the basic physiological needs (like food, water, and sex) that are necessary for survival of the individual and the species. Farther up the hierarchy are the basic social and interpersonal needs, like companionship and friendship; toward the top of the hierarchy are complex yet supremely important needs such as love, the esteem of oneself and others, and self-actualization.*

According to Maslow, normal individuals move slowly but surely through the hierarchy of needs as long as they live in supportive and facilitative family environments. It is such environments that permit us to **self-actualize,** to achieve our greatest potential, to reach the top of our hierarchy of needs. The self-actualized person, Maslow believed, was the person who could love and be loved, enjoy self-esteem as well as the esteem of others, and work at a job with the kind of constructive enthusiasm that leads to accomplishment—to doing the work of the world, whether it is studying, painting pictures, writing novels, laying bricks, or driving a taxi.

Maslow's theory is optimistic; he believes that we can be whatever we aspire to be if we find support in our environment. This is a refreshing contrast to the theories that see living as a continuous struggle against forces that are trying to hold us down or confront us with our darker sides.

Existential Theory

Though all theories of personality are ultimately concerned with the individual, **existential theory** *emphasizes the importance, legitimacy, and value of differences among people as well as their potential for enhancement of maximum human potential.* Whereas psychoanalytic theory assumes that all of us share important experiences (those of the Oedipal period, for example), and social learning theory teaches that classical and operant conditioning mechanisms are constant, existential theory recognizes each person's individuality—and values that difference.

Psychologist Lawrence Pervin, an existential theorist, has this to say about existential theory:

Existentialists emphasize the significance of the individual . . . Freedom is basic to the individual, as seen in man's ability to determine himself, to be reflective and see himself, to have consciousness, and to question his existence while seeking meaning in it. The existentialist assumes that each person has a world-design or reference point from which he interprets everything that exists. The goal is existential understanding; that is, an understanding of the existence of a particular person at a particular moment in his life. (Pervin, 1970, p. 61)

In other words the existential personality theorist is concerned with *being* and with the importance of finding a reason for being. Accordingly, existential theory is particularly relevant to the concerns of many of the readers of this book, who are likely to be preparing for adulthood and adult responsibilities and would like to believe that these responsibilities make some difference and have some meaning.

Central to existential theories of personality is the fact that human beings, unlike other animals, learn at an early age that there will be a time when they will die. Knowledge of this fundamental fact of existence confronts human beings with a range of choices. Should they value every moment of every day, live life to its fullest, seek constantly to make the very most of their strengths, and find fullest possible meaning in life? Or should they dwell on the certainty of life's end, with the result that they live with the ultimate finality of life in mind rather than with the desire to maximize the living of every hour? Not surprisingly, the therapy derived from existential theory focuses on psychotherapeutic solutions for the problems of those who have chosen the latter unhappy course.

Learning Objective 10

1. Rogers's _____ theory of personality, a humanistic theory, assumes that personality derives from the individual's own _____ and _____ of the world rather than from inherited potentialities or acquired behavior patterns.

2. Maslow's _____ determines the path the individual must take to achieve self-actualization.

3. Existential/humanistic theories of personality emphasize _____ between people, the importance, legitimacy, and value of those differences, and their _____ for enhancement of maximum human potential.

ANSWERS

3. differences; potential

1. client-centered; perceptions, interpretations 2. hierarchy of needs

How Personality Is Assessed

For almost as long as people have recorded their histories, they have also recorded their speculations about the behavior of fellow human beings. Until very recently most of these efforts at describing behavior and trying to capture the essence of individuality were more or less unsystematic, and they were more poetic than precise.

Real progress in assessing normal personality functioning and diagnosing abnormal behavior did not begin until the end of the nineteenth century, following the scientific revolution. At this time German psychiatrists, including Emil Kraepelin and Eugen Bleuler, put forth the first comprehensive system for categorizing psychiatric patients. It included a physical examination, diagnostic interview, and systematic behavioral observation. These contributions are described in greater detail in Chapters 12 and 13.

At the same time Sir Francis Galton (see Chapter 7) began to develop procedures for assessing intelligence and other components of normal personality functioning. Galton's contribution to psychological assessment was a respect for psychological tests, which permitted more objective examination of personality functioning. As we discussed, Galton influenced Alfred Binet, a French psychologist responsible for the development of the first reliable measure of intelligence.

Because of these early assessment efforts, psychologists now have at their disposal a vast array of personality tests and measures. With them clinicians can reach consensus on a diagnostic label, a treatment plan, or an expected therapeutic outcome. Personality researchers can compare personality functioning across groups or individuals. School psychologists can identify learning disability in school children. Industrial psychologists can assess the qualities of potential employees and predict their contribution to the organization. And psychologists in military settings can decide which draftee or enlistee ought to be sent to Officers' Candidate School, to an electronics training program, or to service in the infantry.

This list of the uses for psychological tests and other psychological assessment methods may surprise you, especially if you thought these assessment techniques were used only to diagnose or assess troubled behavior. In fact, psychological tests are at least as widely used for classification and assignment purposes in business, industry, education, and the military as they are with emotionally disturbed individuals. (See Career Box: Personality and Nuclear Energy.)

Two of the personality assessment methods described below involve forms of behavioral observation, and the other two involve the use of tests. All of them differ in the extent to which they provide both examiner and examinee with a structure for the examinee's response. In general, the more structured the assessment method, the more predictable the results of the assessment and the more easily the results can be analyzed by statistical means. However, highly structured methods sharply reduce the likelihood of observing spontaneous or unexpected behavior, which is especially helpful for an understanding of personality.

CAREER BOX

Personality and Nuclear Energy

P sychologists are not alone in employing personality assessment methods and measures for predictive purposes. Persons who are responsible for hiring men and women for sensitive, emotionally demanding, exceptionally stressful jobs frequently use personality assessment measures to help them predict how a given job candidate will perform in the taxing job for which he or she is being considered.

Among the jobs for which information on personality is commonly sought are those at nuclear power sites. Virtually everyone working in a nuclear power plant must be constantly aware of the necessity to completely obey all safety

and operational instructions and to respect the power of the nuclear reactor. Persons whose personalities lead them to defy authority, for instance, do not make good employees of nuclear power plants. Similarly, individuals whose personality structure leads them to take excessive risks, with themselves as well as others, are probably not well suited to operate a nuclear reactor. Since it is difficult to detect these basic personality features from an employment interview or reference letters, the use of personality measures aimed specifically at risk-taking potential and attitudes towards authority is a common part of the process of evaluating prospective employees of nuclear power plants.

Unstructured and Semistructured Observation

Many psychologists and psychiatrists depend almost entirely on unstructured behavioral observation and on interviews (in which patients relate their thoughts, feelings, and recollections) to assess personality or diagnose a psychiatric disorder. Unstructured interviews provide a lot of information about a wide range of behavior in a relatively short time.

Interviewers may also choose to provide some structure to the interview, however, if they have some idea what to look for in an interviewee's behavior or history. This being so, interviewers may ask specific questions designed to elicit information on some aspect of the individual's personality or behavior (for example, the way

the person handles anger; his reaction to frustration; or his history of emotional disturbance). The interviewee then responds at whatever length and in whatever way he chooses.

Structured Observation

The most useful structured observational techniques are behavior- or symptom-rating scales. The developers of these instruments base them on their own observations of behavior. Clinicians can then use the instruments to compare the behaviors of the people whom they are observing to the predetermined criteria. The advantage of structured observational methods is that they have greater **reliability** than unstructured methods, meaning

---

Table 11.1 A portion of a structured interview on drug abuse

Cardinal question

   1. Have you ever used pot, speed, heroin, or any other drugs to make yourself feel good?

Social significance questions

   2. Have drugs ever caused you problems in your life?

   3. Have drugs ever interfered with your school, your work, or your job?

   4. Have drugs ever caused you problems with your family or caused your family to worry about you?

 5–8. (Related social significance questions)

Auxiliary questions

Did you use any of the following drugs fairly regularly for at least six months at a time:

 9–15. ("Uppers," "downers," pot, narcotics, pain killers, hallucinogens, and tranquillizers are enquired about.)

  16. Have you ever used two or more different street drugs fairly regularly to get high?

  17. Have there been times when you stayed high or "stoned" on drugs throughout most of the day?

  18. Have you ever really wanted to cut down or completely stop taking a drug but found that you couldn't?

19–24. (Additional questions about physical and psychological consequences of heavy drug use.)

Time profile questions

  25. How old were you when drugs first caused you any problems?

  26. How old were you when drugs last caused you any problems?

  27. Have you experienced any problems because of drugs in the past month?

  28. Have you experienced any problems because of drugs in the last 2 years?

---

that *clinicians using the same behavior- or symptom-rating scales are more apt to agree with each other on diagnosis and personality assessment.*

Table 11.1 lists some of the questions asked in a structured diagnostic interview that is widely used to elicit information about possible drug abuse.

Projective Tests of Personality

Projective tests of personality, the most unstructured of all psychological test instruments (but more structured than observational and interview methods) were developed by psychoanalytic clinicians as a means of uncovering unconscious determinants of behavior that could not be explored by other means.

The **Rorschach Inkblot Test,** *the most widely-used projective test, consists of a series of ten cards, each of which contain a design made from inkblots.* The test was developed in 1921 by the Swiss psychiatrist Hermann Rorschach. Each card is presented to the subject, one at a time; the subject is asked to respond by telling what he thinks the blot resembles (fig. 11.5).

The Thematic Apperception Test, invented by Harvard psychologists Henry Murray and Christina Morgan in 1935, is another widely used projective test (fig. 11.6). As discussed in Chapter 8, the **Thematic Apperception Test (TAT)** *requires the subject to tell stories about a variety of pictures of people, places, and things, each pictured on a separate card.*

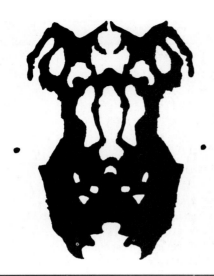

Figure 11.5 *The Rorschach ink blot test*

Figure 11.6 *Thematic apperception test example. (Reprinted by permission of the publishers from Henry A. Murray,* Thematic Apperception Test, *Cambridge, Mass.: Harvard University Press, Copyright © 1943 by the President and Fellows of Harvard College, © 1971 by Henry A. Murray.)*

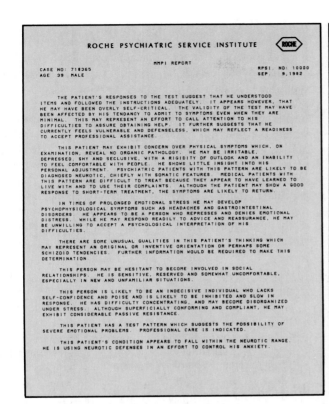

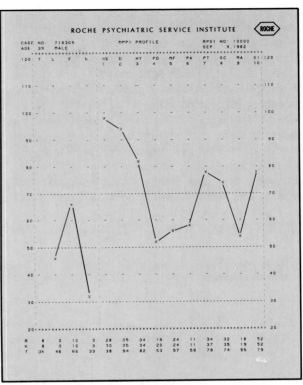

Figure 11.7   Sample MMPI report

Both the Rorschach and the TAT, along with other less commonly used projective devices, lend themselves to an unlimited range of differing interpretations. As a consequence, these measures permit the subject to *project* his or her thoughts, fantasies, feelings, and beliefs onto the intentionally ambiguous test stimulus. Thus, according to those who use these tests, the subject provides the examiner with insight into unconscious or forgotten dynamics of personality available in no other way than by lengthy psychoanalysis. Unfortunately, both the reliability and validity of the projective measures remain a problem.

Objective Tests of Personality

Objective tests were designed to confront the troubling problems of the unreliability of observational and projective measures of personality. The administration, scoring, and interpretation of these tests are usually more reliable. This is because detailed instructions accompany the test; the assumption is made that clinicians who use them will follow the instructions very carefully.

Figure 11.7, the Minnesota Multiphasic Personality Inventory (MMPI), an objective test of personality developed in 1940 by psychologists Starke R. Hathaway and John C. McKinley, is probably the most widely used personality measure. The test is employed both by personality theorists, who use it to provide information on the relative weightings persons give to different aspects of their behavioral repertoires, and by clinical psychologists, who employ it to help make diagnostic judgments about psychiatric patients.

The **MMPI** *requires direct self-reports of beliefs, feelings, attitudes, and self-perceptions for information on past, present, and future behavior.* The person being tested completes a booklet containing 550 statements; she is the judge whether or not each statement applies to her. The pattern of an individual's MMPI responses is compared directly to response norms gathered from groups of both psychiatric patients and normal controls. The ten clinical scales of the MMPI, so-called because they tap possible psychiatric symptoms, provide data on the extent to which a subject's behavior in ten different areas conforms to test patterns shown by the normal and psychiatric groups on which the test was validated. Research on the reliability, validity, and utility of the MMPI has been intense and productive. Nonetheless, the precise nature of relationships between patterns of responding and psychiatric diagnoses remains uncertain, even though the instrument's reliability appears to be comparatively high (Anastasi, 1983; Dahlstrom and Dahlstrom, 1979).

GUIDED REVIEW

Learning Objective 11

1. Personality assessment procedures include un-, semi-, and _____ observational techniques, _____ tests, and _____ tests.

2. The more structured the test, in general, the more _____ it is, although the _____ of all assessment devices remains somewhat uncertain.

ANSWERS
1. structured; projective, objective 2. reliable; validity

SUMMARY

I. Personality is expressed through behavior. The ultimate goal of personality theory and research is the understanding and prediction of behavior. (p. 380)

   A. State theories of personality explain behavior and personality as being the result of environmental influences.   (p. 380)

   B. Trait theories of personality stress the influence of enduring traits of personality on behavior. (p. 381)

II. There are two basic tenets of psychoanalytic theory. (p. 381)

   A. The principle of psychic determinism states that in the human mind nothing occurs by chance.   (p. 381)

   B. The principle of the unconscious states that there are causes of behavior of which the individual is likely unaware.   (p. 381)

C. The psychic apparatus includes three components.　(pp. 382–83)

　　1. The *id,* the earliest part of the psychic apparatus to develop, is the reservoir of primitive drives and impulses.　(p. 382)

　　2. The *ego,* which develops later, is the part of the psychic apparatus that interprets external reality to the id and forces it to adjust to external reality.　(p. 382)

　　3. The *superego,* which develops last, functions as a conscience, or internalized set of parents who convey society's rules to the growing child.　(p. 383)

D. During the *oral, anal, phallic, latency,* and *genital* stages of psychosexual development, successive parts of the body are invested with libido. In the process, important psychological and interpersonal lessons associated with those bodily parts are learned.　(pp. 383–85)

E. Even strong egos have to adopt strategies to defend themselves against excessive id or superego demands. Two of the most common are *fixation* and *regression.*　(p. 385)

III. Three separate groups of *neo-Freudian theorists* have deviated from Freud's classical psychoanalytic theory.　(pp. 387–89)

A. The first group, including Jung, Rank, and Adler, were the members of Freud's inner circle who rejected the emphasis he placed on infantile psychosexuality.　(p. 387)

B. The second group of neo-Freudian theorists, including Horney, Fromm, and Erikson, emphasized the effects of culture and society on personality development.　(pp. 387–89)

C. The third group of neo-Freudians, called *ego psychologists* and including Hartman, Spitz, and Mahler, stressed the adaptive role of the ego in helping the person adjust to the environment.　(p. 389)

IV. *Social learning theories* assume that most of human behavior and personality is learned.　(p. 390)

A. *Classical conditioning mechanisms* are thought by social learning theorists to account for most of the emotional learning humans do.　(p. 390)

B. *Operant conditioning mechanisms* are responsible for much of our social and interpersonal behavior, according to social learning theory.　(p. 391)

C. *Observational learning* refers to how we acquire behavior by watching others engage in the same behaviors, so far as social learning theory is concerned.　(pp. 391–93)

V. *Existential/Humanistic theories of personality* emphasize the significance of the individual, his/her uniqueness and singularity.　(p. 394)

A. *Rogers's client-centered theory of personality* assumes that personality derives from the individual's own perceptions and interpretations of the world.　(p. 394)

B. *Maslow's hierarchy of needs* shows the path the individual must take to achieve self-actualization.　(pp. 394–96)

VI. *Personality assessment procedures* include unstructured, semi-structured, and structured observational techniques, projective tests (including the Rorschach and the TAT), and objective tests (including the MMPI). In general, the more structured the test is, the more reliable it is.　(pp. 397–402)

ACTION GLOSSARY

Match the terms in the left column with the definitions in the right column.

____ 1. **Personality** (p. 380)
____ 2. **States** (p. 380)
____ 3. **Traits** (p. 381)
____ 4. **Psychic determinism** (p. 381)
____ 5. **Unconscious** (p. 381)
____ 6. **Primary process** (p. 381)
____ 7. **Id** (p. 382)
____ 8. **Pleasure principle** (p. 382)
____ 9. **Reality principle** (p. 382)

A. *A reservoir of primitive drives and desires untouched and unaffected by contact with the real world and its civilizing effects.*
B. *The principle that no behavior occurs by chance, that every psychological event is determined by events preceding it.*
C. *Immediate environmental influences.*
D. *A primitive, immature way of thinking that is not yet modified by society's rules or altered by the child's wish to conform.*
E. *The traits, values, attitudes, physical and intellectual attributes, and social skills and interpersonal experiences that distinguish one person from another, help predict his or her behavior in new settings, and give some continuity to behavior.*
F. *The aim that guides the id to derive as much pleasure as possible from its actions.*
G. *Enduring personal attributes like social skillfulness or ineptness, driving ambition or laziness, and loyalty or disloyalty.*
H. *The part of the individual's mental world that cannot be brought into conciousness by effort of will.*
I. *The aim that guides ego functioning.*

____ 10. **Ego** (p. 382)
____ 11. **Superego** (p. 382)
____ 12. **Life instinct** (p. 382)
____ 13. **Death instinct** (p. 382)
____ 14. **Libido** (p. 383)
____ 15. **Oral stage** (pp. 383–84)
____ 16. **Anal stage** (p. 384)
____ 17. **Phallic stage** (p. 384)

A. *The psychological energy that comes from instincts and energizes parts of the body involved in the successive stages of psychosexual development.*
B. *The third stage of psychosexual development. Centers on concerns about the size and function of the genitals.*
C. *That part of the psychic apparatus that helps the id to adjust to external reality by modifying its impulses so they conform to society's moral and ethical rules.*
D. *The first stage of psychosexual development. Gratification is focused on activity surrounding the lips, tongue, and mouth.*
E. *The second stage of psychosexual development. Gratification is focused on controlling the elimination of waste products from the body.*
F. *That part of the psychic apparatus that reflects parental and societal rules and expectations.*
G. *The aggressive drives and impulses that are a part of the id.*
H. *The sexual impulses and drives that reside in the id.*

____ 18. **Latency period** (p. 385)
____ 19. **Genital stage** (p. 385)
____ 20. **Defense mechanisms** (p. 385)
____ 21. **Fixation** (p. 385)
____ 22. **Regression** (p. 385)
____ 23. **Extravert** (p. 387)
____ 24. **Introvert** (p. 387)
____ 25. **Inferiority** (p. 387)

A. *A defense mechanism by which the individual remains in a particular psychosexual stage because his/her development is interfered with.*
B. *A person who is preoccupied with his or her own thoughts and is therefore less interested in the world.*
C. *A defense mechanism by which the individual returns to an earlier, less mature stage of development.*
D. *The stage of psychosexual development during which the adolescent learns about adult sexuality.*
E. *A person who is interested in the world and in other people.*
F. *Strategies that the ego uses to prevent the forces of the id and superego from seeking expression in harmful behaviors.*
G. *Feelings that all children experience, while growing up, in relation to bigger, wiser, more powerful parents.*
H. *A stage of psychosexual development during which there is a consolidation of the psychological and social lessons learned and behaviors acquired during earlier stages.*

_____ 26. **Trauma of birth** (p. 387)
_____ 27. **Ego psychologists** (p. 389)
_____ 28. **Humanistic theory** (p. 394)
_____ 29. **Hierarchy of needs** (p. 396)
_____ 30. **Self-actualize** (p. 396)
_____ 31. **Existential theory** (p. 396)
_____ 32. **Rorschach ink blot test** (p. 399)
_____ 33. **Minnesota Multiphasic Personality Inventory (MMPI)** (p. 401)

A. *A projective test of personality consisting of ten ambiguous designs made from inkblots. The subject is asked to respond, when shown the designs, by telling what he/ she thinks the designs resemble.*

B. *Emphasizes the significance of the individual, his or her uniqueness and singularity.*

C. *To achieve our greatest potential; to reach the top of our hierarchy of needs.*

D. *Emphasizes the importance, legitimacy, and value of differences among people and their potential for enhancement of maximum human potential.*

E. *An objective test of personality functioning that requires self-reports of beliefs, feelings, attitudes, and self-perceptions.*

F. *The neo-Freudian psychologists who stress the ever-changing nature of the ego and its defenses.*

G. *The infant's shock at being delivered from the security of the womb to the chaos of the outside world.*

H. *According to Maslow, the path an individual must follow in order to become self-actualized.*

ANSWERS

1. E, 2. C, 3. G, 4. B, 5. H, 6. D, 7. A, 8. F, 9. I, 10. C, 11. F, 12. H, 13. G, 14. A, 15. D, 16. E, 17. B, 18. H, 19. D, 20. F, 21. A, 22. C, 23. E, 24. B, 25. G, 26. G, 27. F, 28. B, 29. H, 30. C, 31. D, 32. A, 33. E

SELF-TEST

1. Personality is expressed through

   (a) thoughts.
   (b) feelings.
   (c) behavior.
   (d) test scores.
   (LO 1; p. 380)

2. The goal of personality theory and research is

   (a) understanding and prediction of behavior.
   (b) control of behavior.
   (c) modification of behavior.
   (d) description of behavior.
   (LO 1; p. 380)

3. Personality theories that define personality largely as a product of environmental factors are called

   (a) trait theories.
   (b) state theories.
   (c) environmental theories.
   (d) sociocultural theories.
   (LO 2; p. 380)

4. Trait theories of personality explain behavior as a function of

   (a) the environment.
   (b) drives and impulses within the individual.
   (c) enduring forces within the individual.
   (d) societal rules and regulations.
   (LO 2; p. 381)

5. The two basic concepts of Freud's psychoanalytic theory are the principles of

   (a) psychic determinism and ego development.
   (b) psychosexual development and the unconscious.
   (c) fixation and regression.
   (d) psychic determinism and the unconscious.
   (LO 3; p. 381)

6. The three components of the psychic apparatus include the

   (a) oral, anal, and phallic stages.
   (b) ego, id, and superego.
   (c) oral, anal, and genital stages.
   (d) ego, superego, and libido.
   (LO 4; pp. 382–83)

7. Which of the following is *not* one of the five stages of psychosexual development?

   (a) anal
   (b) phallic
   (c) latency
   (d) Oedipal
   (LO 5; pp. 383–85)

8. Fixation and regression are
   - (a) syndromes of mental disorder.
   - (b) signs of weak ego functioning.
   - (c) derived from the superego.
   - (d) ego defense mechanisms.
      (LO 6; p. 385)

9. The first neo-Freudians included
   - (a) Rorschach and Murray.
   - (b) Spitz, Hartman, and Fromm.
   - (c) Jung, Adler, and Rank.
   - (d) Rogers and Maslow.
      (LO 9; p. 387)

10. The first neo-Freudians objected to Freud's emphasis on
    - (a) childhood aggression.
    - (b) infantile psychosexuality.
    - (c) the unconscious.
    - (d) fixation and regression.
       (LO 7; p. 387)

11. Horney, Fromm, and Erikson emphasized the effects of
    - (a) culture and society on personality development.
    - (b) sex and aggression on personality development.
    - (c) infantile psychological trauma on personality development.
    - (d) World War II on behavior.
       (LO 7; pp. 387–89)

12. The ego psychologist stressed
    - (a) the vulnerability of the ego.
    - (b) the strength of the ego.
    - (c) the importance of ego defenses.
    - (d) all of the above.
       (LO 7; p. 389)

13. The social learning theorists assume that most human behavior is
    - (a) ultimately forgotten.
    - (b) learned by operant and classical mechanisms.
    - (c) acquired by observational learning.
    - (d) learned.
       (LO 8; p. 390)

14. The social learning theorists account for emotional learning by the mechanism of
    - (a) classical conditioning.
    - (b) operant conditioning.
    - (c) observational learning.
    - (d) vicarious reinforcement.
       (LO 8; p. 390)

15. According to the social learning theorists, operant conditioning mechanisms are responsible for
    - (a) emotional learning.
    - (b) social and interpersonal behavior.
    - (c) behavior we watch others perform.
    - (d) drives and impulses.
       (LO 8; p. 391)

16. The existential/humanistic theories of personality emphasize
    - (a) our inhumanity to others.
    - (b) our similarity to others.
    - (c) our essential uniqueness.
    - (d) our need to learn.
       (LO 10; p. 394)

17. Carl Rogers's theory of personality is called the
    - (a) other focused theory of personality.
    - (b) humanistic theory of personality.
    - (c) individualized theory of personality.
    - (d) client-centered theory of personality.
       (LO 10; p. 394)

18. At the bottom of Abraham Maslow's hierarchy of needs are needs for
    - (a) self-actualization.
    - (b) food and water.
    - (c) warmth and human understanding.
    - (d) sex and aggression.
       (LO 10; pp. 394–96)

19. The Rorschach and TAT are
    - (a) semistructured tests of personality.
    - (b) structured tests of personality.
    - (c) projective tests of personality.
    - (d) an objective test of personality rarely used nowadays.
       (LO 11; p. 399)

20. A reliable test
    - (a) accurately predicts behavior.
    - (b) is not useful for research purposes.
    - (c) is likely to be unstructured.
    - (d) is likely to be structured.
       (LO 11; pp. 398–99)

ANSWERS

1. c, 2. a, 3. b, 4. c, 5. d, 6. b, 7. d, 8. d, 9. c, 10. b, 11. a, 12. d,
13. d, 14. a, 15. b, 16. c, 17. d, 18. b, 19. c, 20. d

SUGGESTED READINGS

Freud, S. *A general introduction to psychoanalysis.* Chapters 1 (Introduction) and 21 (Development of the Libido and Sexual Organization). New York: Permabooks, 1953. In these two chapters, Freud places psychoanalytic theory in its historical and scientific context, then sets out the basic outlines of his theory of infantile psychosexuality.

Fromm, Erich. *Escape from freedom.* New York: Rinehart & Co., 1941. In this classic study of the effects on behavior of the multitude of choices urban society presents modern men and women, Fromm makes a convincing case for one of its effects: the ready acceptance of the totalitarian system of government, which removes the necessity for decision making from its citizenry.

Pervin, L. A. "The Case of Mrs. Oak." In *Personality: Theory, assessment and research.* New York: Wiley, 1970. This excerpt from Pervin's personality textbook illustrates Carl Rogers's theory of personality. Pervin quotes extensively from a counseling relationship Rogers had previously reported on, then evaluates these materials from the vantage point of a sympathetic critic of Rogers's theory.

Skinner, B. F. The steep and thorny way to a science of behavior. *American Psychologist,* 30 (1975): 42–49. This lecture, originally given at Oxford University, permits Skinner, Dean of living American behavioral psychologists, to respond to critics of his book, *Beyond Freedom and Dignity* (1971), and to add some additional comment on his view of the relative impact of hereditary and environmental factors on behavior.

c h a p t e r

12

Adjustment and Abnormality

LEARNING OBJECTIVES

After reading this chapter, you should be able to

1. differentiate among approach-approach, avoidance-avoidance, approach-avoidance, and double approach-avoidance conflicts. **(pp. 410–12)**
2. detail the ego's mechanisms of defense, and give examples of their use—appropriate or inappropriate—in everyday life. **(pp. 415–17)**

3. discuss the behavioral consequences of conflict and frustration, including alcohol and drug use and misuse, and anxiety and depression. **(pp. 417–19)**
4. discuss the bodily consequences of conflict and frustration, which include the psychosomatic disorders and Type A behavior. **(pp. 419–21)**
5. touch on the high points of the history of society's efforts to diagnose, treat, and prevent abnormal behavior from early times to our own. **(pp. 424–26)**
6. identify the most important similarities and differences between DSM-III and its predecessors. **(pp. 426–27)**
7. distinguish between acute and chronic organic mental disorders, and identify some of the causes of these central nervous system dysfunctions. **(pp. 427–28)**
8. categorize the behavioral and psychological effects of drug and alcohol abuse and dependence. **(pp. 428–29)**
9. list and describe the serious defects in cognitive, perceptual, and affective functioning of patients given schizophrenic or bipolar affective disorder diagnoses. **(pp. 429–31)**
10. discuss the relationship between depression and suicide, and put the facts about suicide in perspective. **(p. 431)**
11. detail the diverse nonpsychotic disorders formerly called the neuroses. **(pp. 432–33)**
12. describe and discuss the psychosexual disorders, which include transsexualism, the paraphilias, the sexual dysfunctions, and ego-dystonic homosexuality. **(pp. 433–34)**
13. discuss the deeply ingrained patterns of behavior that are termed the personality disorders. **(pp. 434–35)**

Conflict: Resolution and Adjustment

We are continuously confronted with the need to make decisions. Most of them are insignificant; few are monumental. Choosing between soft-boiled eggs or cereal for breakfast, the 8:10 or 8:20 bus to school, or wearing a sweater or a windbreaker to class are basically unimportant decisions, the kind each of us must make many times a day. However, decisions that affect our future or the futures of those we love (like whether to work after college or attend graduate school, to marry one person or another, or to take a job in another city) are much more important and much more difficult.

Conflicts *are the unavoidable obstacles in life that thwart our decisions and our choices.* Failure to resolve some of the minor conflicts we all face is normal and probably healthy. It leaves us the emotional energy to solve serious problems. But failure to resolve major conflicts is another matter. It may lead us in the direction of psychopathology, toward anxiety, depression, or another consequence of unresolved conflict. In contrast, resolving our conflicts (which includes adjusting to them) leads us toward personal maturity and enhanced self-esteem. **Adjustment** *describes a healthy and desirable process by which we resolve or learn to live with major conflicts in our lives.*

Psychologists have divided conflict situations into four categories, which differ in degree of conflict experienced. They also differ in the ease or difficulty of resolution of, or adjustment to, the conflict. An understanding of the challenges posed by each kind of conflict situation gives us the opportunity to deal objectively and, we hope, effectively with conflict in our own lives.

Approach-Approach Conflict

One of the most common conflicts, known as an **approach-approach conflict,** requires *a choice between two attractive alternatives that are mutually incompatible.* The best way to resolve such a difficult decision is generally to make the decision "up close," with as many of the facts at hand as possible. However, this is sometimes easier said than done, especially when the conflicts are between equally attractive alternatives. The trick is to learn enough about the alternatives to appreciate small but important differences among them.

After making a difficult decision among attractive alternatives, we often find ourselves justifying it again and again, to ourselves and others, to convince ourselves we made the right choice. Have you ever continued to convince yourself that you chose the right college major or selected the right summer vacation, long after finally committing yourself to them?

Why do we act this way? Theorists believe we are trying to reduce the **cognitive dissonance,** or *discomfort that results from the simultaneous presence of two or more ideas, attitudes, or beliefs that are in conflict.* Put another way, entertaining ideas that are incompatible with one another makes our lives unworkable. This state of cognitive dissonance, so named by psychologist Leon Festinger (Festinger, Riecken, and Schachter, 1956), is most troublesome when the decision has to be made between two or more alternatives that differ in very small ways. As a result, we must magnify these differences to make the option chosen more attractive than the alternative not chosen. Sometimes the process is difficult, sometimes it is easy, but in either case, it is a familiar feature of the need to make decisions, and then to adjust to them once they are made.

Avoidance-Avoidance Conflict

Avoidance-avoidance conflicts *require choices between equally disliked alternatives.* A common problem with avoidance-avoidance conflicts is that moving away from one disliked alternative automatically moves one closer to an equally disliked alternative, unless one chooses to avoid resolution of the conflict altogether—if that is possible.

College life is full of avoidance-avoidance conflict situations. Consider the student who hates studying but fears his parents' displeasure over low grades even more,

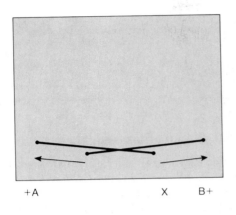

+A   X   B+

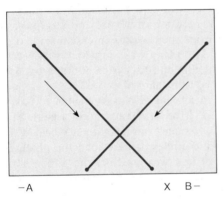

−A   X   B−

Figure 12.1 Diagram of (a) approach-approach conflict and (b) avoidance-avoidance conflict

or the senior who plans on attending graduate school, even though she abhors the thought of its rigors, because the world of work appears even more unpromising. In both cases, the choices are between unappealing alternatives.

Successful resolution of avoidance-avoidance conflict is not easy. Getting as close as possible to an alternative may simply lead to greater aversion to it and thus perpetuate the conflict without resolving it. Avoiding a choice altogether by refusing to choose either alternative is also possible, but only when a choice can appropriately be avoided, which is not always the case. So, this approach to resolution of avoidance-avoidance conflict is also ultimately unsatisfactory. It is also possible to postpone making a decision, which helps if one or another of the aversive alternatives disappears but hurts if the postponement of decision-making does nothing more than intensify the conflict. One of the most adaptive ways to confront avoidance-avoidance conflicts is to scrutinize each alternative as carefully and objectively as possible to try to identify positive features in one or the other.

Approach-Avoidance Conflict

Approach-avoidance conflicts *force us to choose to approach or avoid a single stimulus having both positive and negative features.* Few of us go through the day without being confronted with such conflicts: to eat a candy bar and gain weight; to go out with friends and be tired for the exam tomorrow; to sleep late but have to cut that eight o'clock chemistry lecture; all are common decisions having both attractive and aversive consequences.

Persons who cannot resolve approach-avoidance conflicts may choose instead simply to avoid a decision altogether and move on to other matters. This strategy takes them away from the conflictual object, but it also deprives them of its important positive features. Or a person may make a decision, either to approach or to avoid the object with positive and negative features, but then remain obsessed by his or her decision long after it has been made. Or the person may postpone a decision until it is too late to make it. Or, as most persons who resolve approach-avoidance conflicts successfully do, the person may decide that the stimulus object's positive features outweigh its negative ones, or vice versa.

Once a person makes an approach-avoidance decision, adjustment to it is usually most successful when he or she concludes that nothing more can be done about the decision and, accordingly, that it is no longer worth worrying about.

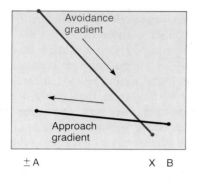

Figure 12.2 Diagram of approach-avoidance conflict

Double Approach-Avoidance Conflict

The **double approach-avoidance conflict,** a particularly demanding one, *necessitates a choice between two or more stimuli, each of which possesses both positive and negative features.* At college, for instance, students are faced with the choice of applying themselves diligently to achieve excellent grades or working only as hard as is necessary to graduate. The former commitment requires giving up some of the unique joys of college life, but it may also enable students to go on to graduate or professional school or simply to feel good about their academic accomplishments. Working only hard enough to get by permits students the time to enjoy a full range of social and extracurricular activities, but it may also mean running the risk of flunking out, earning parents' ire, or having fewer options on graduation.

GUIDED REVIEW

Learning Objective 1

1. The most common conflict, _____ conflict, requires a choice between two attractive alternatives that are mutually incompatible.

2. _____ conflicts require choices between equally disliked alternatives.

3. _____ conflicts require the individual to choose to approach or avoid a stimulus with both _____ and _____ features.

4. _____ conflicts demand a choice between two or more alternatives, each of which possesses both _____ and _____ features.

ANSWERS

1. approach-approach 2. Avoidance-avoidance 3. Approach-avoidance; positive, negative 4. Double approach-avoidance; positive, negative

Conflict, Frustration, and Their Responses

Conflict is a principal source of **frustration,** *the temporary or permanent failure to achieve a desired goal.* Frustration is important because it plays a central role in the development of both normal and abnormal behavior. According to psychoanalytic theory, for example, frustration of sexual and aggressive impulses that prevents their overt expression leads to emotional turmoil. The many ways in which this process occurs are detailed in our discussion of defense mechanisms a bit later in this chapter.

Frustration has also been known to motivate individuals to strive harder to obtain a goal. "The impossible takes longer" was a common World War II phrase in scientific circles; it described the process of development of new weapons like the A-bomb after many said it couldn't be done. Although it is uncertain precisely how conflict and frustration yield positive consequences, it is clear that they do so at times. Psychoanalytic theory entertains the same possibility. Certain of the defense mechanisms detailed below represent relatively effective and productive ways of converting conflict-induced frustration into socially desirable behavior.

When many such frustrations occur over a very short period of time, we may respond with more than frustration and irritation. We may begin to attribute responsibility for these frustrations to ourselves and our own inadequacies—or to an external source, to someone or something "out to get us." The student who fails a chemistry exam may blame the poor teaching of the professor; the jilted lover may blame the loss on the bad judgment or immaturity of his or her beloved; the fishing zealot may blame a poor catch on the bait or

CAREER BOX

Divorce Mediation—
A Career in Conflict Resolution

More and more attorneys, mental health professionals, and other human service workers have recently become involved in one of the newest of the helping professions: divorce mediation.

With the enormous increase in divorce rates in this country in recent years, the need for a better mechanism to resolve the conflicts between parting spouses (over child custody and visitation, finances, housing, and other community property) has come to be recognized. Divorce exacts a terrible toll on the divorcing couple, but an equal toll is often taken on their children, their parents, and their friends. The longer and more disharmonious the process of resolution of outstanding conflicts between divorcing spouses, the greater the psychological toll on all of those affected by the divorce.

Traditionally trained divorce attorneys have seen their job to be to arrange the best settlement for the spouse they represent. As a consequence, their efforts rarely facilitate a rapid, harmonious settlement because their position is an adversarial one. Divorce mediators, by contrast, see as their task the resolution of outstanding conflicts between divorcing spouses so as to shorten the settlement process and make it easier and less stressful. These persons consider themselves to be mediators between the divorcing couple, rather than adversaries of one or the other. If not attorneys themselves, they may bring them in to deal with the legal issues surrounding the various financial settlement options. Their major role, however, is to bring angry spouses together to work out a settlement that both consider fair to themselves and appropriate to the needs of their children.

Divorce mediators employ many of the principles of conflict resolution outlined in this section. Further, mediators quickly learn (if they are not trained as mental health professionals) the role that defense mechanisms (outlined in the next section of this chapter) play in retarding readiness or reducing ability to resolve conflicts. Above all, the divorce mediator must recognize that what may initially appear to be a conflict between two people may actually be the unresolved conflict of one person—a conflict that has profoundly influenced the troubled interaction between the two.

Although data are not yet available on whether divorce mediation is superior to traditional legal mechanisms for dissolving marriages and resolving financial and child custody conflicts, many divorcing couples have been quite vocal in proclaiming their satisfaction with what may be both a more humane and a more effective means of enabling two people to dissolve a marriage.

the weather; the discharged worker may blame the job loss on a hostile or envious boss. *In virtually all such cases the person is dealing inaccurately* (if understandably) with the causes of the frustration.

Confronted by conflict that cannot be resolved and thus leads to frustration, we adopt one or more of the well-defined responses to frustration that are described below. Some are effective; they permit us either to resolve the conflict or to get on with our lives without resolving it. Others are less effective, especially when they simply prolong the unresolved conflict or, even worse, involve us in a return to less mature, less adaptive behaviors in a vain effort to deal with the conflict.

Withdrawal and Aggression: Unsuccessful Responses

Withdrawal.   Perhaps the most common initial response to conflict or frustration is to **withdraw,** *think of running away from or ignoring it.* Unfortunately, escape and withdrawal are rarely realistic means for resolving conflicts (fig. 12.3). They simply postpone the time for the decision, often making the conflict more difficult to resolve when the passage of time has intensified it. The procrastination that bedevils many college students is a common, ineffective response to difficult conflict situations: putting off studying for an exam never delays the examination; it only increases the odds of doing badly on it.

Withdrawal and escape from interpersonal conflict are just as ineffective. The individual who deals with a tumultuous love relationship by withdrawing tends to find herself in similarly tempestuous relationships wherever she goes next. Generally speaking, there is no such thing as a "geographical" cure for conflict—or for the consequences of poorly handled conflict.

Aggression.   **Aggression** *represents a direct attack on whatever blocks attainment of a goal.* It is almost always a maladaptive response to frustration. From research with animals begun in the 1930s, pioneering behavioral psychologist B. F. Skinner observed that the

Figure 12.3   Withdrawal is a common though unrealistic response to conflict or frustration.

removal of an expected reward almost invariably elicited aggression from the animal whose behavior was suddenly no longer reinforced (Skinner, 1938).

Extending Skinner's findings to human beings isn't difficult. The frustration of losing a job, being jilted, getting a bad grade, or having a flat tire on the highway can result in aggressive feelings and, at times, violent responses. Who hasn't wanted to kick the telephone coin box or soda-pop machine that swallowed a coin but failed to deliver?

More recently, behavioral psychologist Albert Bandura (1973) has shown that aggression isn't an inevitable consequence of frustration and that the ways in which we respond to frustration also depend on who is doing the frustrating, what kind of frustration we are faced with, and where the frustration takes place. Undertaken as part of Bandura's research on observational learning (research described more fully in Chapter 11), this research program reveals that when children see other children and adults responding without marked anger to frustrating situations, they too respond without anger to like frustration. Children who witness models responding angrily to frustration, however, behave every bit as aggressively as do the models. Bandura's conclusion was that aggression is an acquired response to frustration that can be modified by appropriate environmental rearrangements. Another view of the relationship between aggression and frustration is described in Chapter 15.

The Defense Mechanisms: Successful and Unsuccessful Responses

Central to the psychoanalytic theory of personality, discussed in Chapter 11, is the belief that the ego employs defense mechanisms in the face of conflict and frustration to protect the integrity of the personality and permit optimal psychological functioning. Although Freud described some of these defense mechanisms, theorists who came after him, beginning with his daughter Anna (A. Freud, 1936), played a more important role in the current widespread interest in the ego's defense mechanisms. According to these "ego psychologists," some of the defense mechanisms are unconscious and, hence, beyond voluntary control; others are conscious and can be voluntarily controlled. Though everyone relies on defensive maneuvers from time to time, excessive reliance on the ego's mechanisms of defense can be problematic.

Repression and Suppression. Repression and suppression are the two most basic and most common defense mechanisms. **Repression** *describes the involuntary burying in the unconscious of unwanted, unacceptable, and threatening thoughts, feelings, or impulses.* Occasionally we have a vague memory of an early event that has the capacity to disquiet us; this partial memory, according to psychoanalytic theory, is likely the "tip of the iceberg" of a repressed, painful memory that would be too disturbing for us to deal with were we to fully remember it. Concentrating on the memory usually fails to provide any additional information about the earlier scene, though additional clues may appear in dreams, slips of the tongue, or during the process of psychoanalysis. Such traumatic early events as the loss of a parent, an incestuous relationship, or a serious accident, for example, are the types of experiences that we are likely to repress, since remembering them and their emotional accompaniments in detail would be very painful both to an older child and the adult he or she becomes.

Though we are not always aware of repression, we are perhaps much more familiar with **suppression,** *the deliberate decision to keep material from surfacing into consciousness.* We employ suppression when the memory of an event involving rejection, embarrassment, shame, or guilt, for instance, is especially painful, even in recall. Most people have probably purposely kept from consciousness such things as the memories and emotions associated with the end of a love relationship that shouldn't have ended, the automobile accident that shouldn't have happened, or the surprisingly bad grade that shouldn't have been received.

Reaction Formation. Freud believed that *we replace a particularly unpleasant feeling about someone or something with the opposite feeling by means of* what he called **reaction formation.** Hate is replaced by love, cruelty by gentleness and concern, or stubbornness by compliance. Psychoanalysts conclude, for example, that doting, overprotecting, "smothering" mothers may actually be defending against very ambivalent feelings toward their children by being overzealous mothers.

Reaction formation takes place unconsciously: we cannot choose to make it happen. If we discover the existence of a reaction formation (in the process of psychotherapy, for example) it may be a surprise to us. The constructive role played by reaction formation is obvious; maintaining negative feelings about people, places, or things is rarely helpful.

Sublimation. According to psychoanalytic theory, **sublimation** is an especially adaptive defense mechanism that *permits the psychological energy associated with unconscious desires and impulses to be translated into socially accepted, often creative, activities like painting, composing, writing, or plain hard work.* The empirical data of this hypothesized process are even less substantial than that supporting other aspects of psychoanalytic theory (Fine, 1979). Nonetheless, there can be no denying the positive value that many persons derive from active, enthusiastic immersion in creative activities, especially during times of stress and conflict. The great German composer Beethoven, for example, a man whose sexual and aggressive impulses were always very near conscious experience during an era in which such behavior was considered especially objectionable, has been singled out as a person who dealt with these strong, unacceptable impulses (unacceptable, that is, to the society in which he lived) by sublimating them in the process of creativity.

Rationalization. A basically harmless defense mechanism, if not used to excess, **rationalization** *permits us to give a behavior whose motivation may be obscure, unknown, irrational, or embarrassing a rational, logical, or intellectual explanation and purpose.* Justifying the decision to attend a pornographic movie "as an educational experience" or to leave school for a year and travel through Europe "to become a Renaissance man" are examples of rationalization.

Regression. This very common defense mechanism, introduced in Chapter 11, occupies a position somewhere between the defenses just described, which are fundamentally mature and adaptive, and the defenses shortly to be described, which are significantly less effective as responses to environmental stress and frustration.

Regression *involves either a brief and temporary or prolonged and permanent return to behaviors more characteristic of children.* When the regression is temporary, it may be constructive and adaptive because it relieves the individual of intense stress. Crying, sleeping more than usual, and seeking out close friends "to lean on" contribute to recovery from stress; all are regressive behaviors that give the individual "breathing space" in which to mobilize more adaptive responses. However, when regressive defensive maneuvers last too long, or when they interfere with efforts to adapt to the demands of the environment, they no longer serve a useful purpose. The man who forfeits all responsibility for his family by gambling or drinking away his resources, or the woman who stops seeing her friends and spends most of her time sitting in front of the television set watching soap operas because the world has gotten too complicated for her, have regressed to less complicated, less mature forms of existence in order to maintain some control over their own destinies, however diminished those destinies might be.

Displacement. *The experience of a feeling, usually unwanted, about a person to whom it does not really belong* is called **displacement.** Becoming angry at a friend when the anger actually stems from conflict with a roommate, or criticizing the behavior of one's children when one is actually critical of the behavior of a spouse, are common examples of displacement. Generally a harmless defense, displacement can become troublesome, especially when it influences our behavior toward whole classes or groups of people. The man who expects all women to belittle him because his mother did so, and avoids women for that reason, or the woman who believes that all men harbor sexual designs on her because of early experiences with her father, and refuses to relate to men because of that belief, are both distorting their worlds in unfortunate and troublesome ways.

The social learning theorist calls the same behavior overgeneralization; it derives, according to social learning theory, from a failure to discriminate important differences between one environmental stimulus (for example, a father, mother, sibling, or friend) and another (the stimulus classes "women," "men," "blue-collar workers," "blacks," "Jews," "Italians" and so on).

Denial. The defense mechanism of **denial** *represents a failure to feel the impact of a painful thought or feeling by denying, psychologically, that it exists.* In so doing, one avoids the pain that would result from directly confronting the thought or feeling. The student who fails to study for an important exam is denying that preparation for the course is necessary for adequate performance in it. In this way he or she can enjoy his or her activities the week before the exam and avoid worrying about the consequences of doing little or no work for the test. The "costs" of this behavior, though, may be considerable.

GUIDED REVIEW

Learning Objective 2

1. While most people resolve most conflict situations satisfactorily most of the time, they sometimes do not. When they don't, _____ may be a consequence.

2. When frustration is not dealt with successfully, one result may be _____ or _____ , neither of which constitutes a satisfactory response to frustration.

3. According to psychoanalytic theory, the _____ confronts conflict and frustration in a variety of other ways, some mature and effective, others less mature and less effective.

4. Some of the ego's mechanisms of defense are _____ while others are _____ .

5. The _____ include repression and suppression; reaction formation; isolation; sublimation; rationalization; regression; projection; displacement; and denial.

ANSWERS

1. *frustration* 2. *withdrawal, aggression* 3. *ego* 4. *conscious; unconscious* 5. *defense mechanisms*

Behavioral and Bodily Consequences of Conflict and Frustration

Fortunately, most of us handle conflict and frustration reasonably effectively most of the time. When we do not, we may experience behavioral or bodily consequences of conflict and frustration that range from the common behavioral and stress reactions detailed in this section of the chapter (conditions which may be troublesome but are rarely permanently disruptive), to the severe and disabling behavioral disorders detailed later in the chapter. While the bodily reactions to conflict and frustration can be life-threatening, more often they are temporary and self-limiting; they too are discussed in this chapter.

The Behavioral Consequences of Conflict and Frustration

The use of alcohol and drugs is a common behavioral reaction to conflict and frustration. The drugs used vary from the nicotine in cigarettes and the caffeine in coffee to more potent and dangerous drugs like alcohol and the drugs of abuse. Other reactions to conflict and frustration include anger, aggression, anxiety, and depression.

The line between normal and abnormal use of alcohol and other drugs, and the experience of anger, aggression, anxiety, and depression is a difficult one to draw. This chapter focuses on normal (though not always healthy) behavioral and bodily responses to conflict and frustration. We consider normal responses to conflict and frustration to be those which are generally within our control, which most of us can do something about if we feel they are beginning to be problems for us.

Alcohol and Drugs.   A problem once recognized only in the back alleys and flophouses of Skid Row, alcohol misuse is now acknowledged as a major social problem in the United States, affecting millions of people in all walks of life. But alcoholism is only the extreme on the continuum of alcohol misuse. Also included on the continuum is the occasional social drinker who has "one too many" one night and plows into an oncoming automobile, killing or maiming all the occupants of the other car; the heavy social drinker who invariably "loses his cool" at parties, insults hosts, embarrasses friends, and isolates himself in the process; and the problem drinker, whose drinking on the job threatens to cost her both the job and her remaining self-esteem. Included as victims, too, are the family and friends of those who drink too much. They suffer directly, when their loved one hurts her- or himself or others, as well as indirectly, when they conclude that something they have or haven't done has caused their loved one to drink abusively.

A recent study by Canadian psychologist Martha Sanchez-Craig (1983) suggests that teaching early problem drinkers (whose drinking has not yet progressed to alcoholism or been associated with serious physical or behavioral consequences) how to drink in a controlled, moderate fashion may yield marked decreases in overall consumption as well as in problems associated with drinking. Sanchez-Craig's data suggest that it may be possible to halt the common progression from heavy social drinker to problem drinker to alcoholic by providing early problem drinkers the skills of moderation that drinkers who never develop alcohol problems seem to possess naturally.

Research by two social psychologists exploring drug use in a medium-sized Colorado community (Jessor and Jessor, 1976) yielded surprising data on the widespread use of marijuana: over half of their large sample of high school students had tried marijuana during their four high school years, and fully one-third of this group were regular users of the drug by the time they graduated. Although some observers believe that "hard drug" use (e.g., heroin) is now lower, others believe that it has simply gone underground. Most observers agree that hallucinogen use is definitely on the wane. Marijuana appears to continue to be a drug of choice among high school and college-age youth (Fawzy, Coombs, and Gerber, 1983; Smart and Blair, 1978).

Peer pressure, novelty-seeking, and modeling of parental drug use are clearly involved in many adolescents' decision to try drugs. (See Research Box: Do You Smoke and Drink?)

Anxiety and Depression.   All of us experience the feelings of aggression, anger, anxiety, and depression that accompany frustration and conflict. Most of the time, however, these feelings dissipate quickly, leaving us to anticipate more successful confrontations with our environment. All of us, in the face of frustrating, conflictual situations, have learned to resolve them when we can and, when we cannot, to employ adjustment maneuvers, including the defense mechanisms, to minimize their impact on us. One of the most frequent consequences of unresolved conflict and frustration is anxiety. The word describes a feeling familiar to everyone, yet sufficiently different from person to person that agreement on the word's precise meaning is almost impossible to achieve. We choose here to define **anxiety** as *a sense of foreboding, a feeling of apprehension, an ill-defined fear that is independent of specific objects or situations.*

The subjective experience of anxiety, which varies from individual to individual, nonetheless typically includes bodily sensations ("butterflies in the stomach," dizziness, sweating, etc.), along with worry, preoccupation with real or imagined problems, and a vague, overriding sense of unease. Sometimes, anxiety is intense enough that we must take steps to do something about it. Some of us turn to relaxation exercises and other self-administered behavior-change methods to deal with undue stress (Walker, et al., 1981). Others of us structure our lives to avoid it as much as possible.

Depression is another very common consequence of stress and conflict. All of us experience depression from time to time, when the world appears gray and our usual optimism turns to pessimism. Death of parents or other relatives, loss of friends, and rejection by a lover all have the obvious potential to induce marked depression. But lesser stressors and conflicts—disappointments in school, at home, or on the job, the stresses of a new job, new course, new relationship, or new career option, conflicts over living arrangements or life-styles—also have the potential to induce depression. The typical signs of **depression** are *feelings of dejection and downheartedness, a sense of decreased self-worth and self-esteem, reduced interest in the future and in planning for it, difficulty concentrating, problems in getting to sleep or staying asleep, and a pervasive feeling of fatigue and ennui.*

Fortunately, the normal feelings of depression we all experience rarely last long enough to interfere with our ability to confront life's normal stresses and strains. When we do experience depression, and all of us do from time to time, it helps to remember that time, friends, and some perspective on the normal ups and downs of life have been sufficient to get us through before and will be sufficient again.

The Bodily Consequences of Conflict and Frustration

The emotional and behavioral reactions to conflict and frustration have another set of effects. They may well be linked, in a cause-and-effect manner, with physical diseases like stomach ulcers, high blood pressure, skin diseases, and asthma. These are the so-called psychosomatic disorders, and conflict and frustration can largely explain them. Conflict and stress are also assumed to contribute to unhealthy life-styles. Persons whose lives are in turmoil may speak of their tendency to overeat, smoke more heavily than usual, and forego exercise, for example. (See Application Box: The Secrets of Successful Dieters, for hints on how to avoid being overweight.)

Theories of Psychosomatic Disorder. Most theories of the psychosomatic disorders stress the interaction of psychological *and* physical causes. The most influential psychoanalytic explanation of these disorders was put forth by psychoanalyst Franz Alexander (1935, 1948, 1962). It stresses the impact of specific traumatic events, occurring during childhood, on the development of specific physical disorders in adulthood. According to this view, frustration of dependency needs in childhood, for example, at the hands of an unloving mother, a distant father, or punitive parents, is associated with the development of stomach ulcers in adulthood. Other kinds of trauma in childhood lead to other psychosomatic problems in adulthood.

A more recent behavioral explanation of the psychosomatic disorders has been offered by Roy Lachman (1963, 1972). He believes we develop these disorders following prolonged exposure to current stressful situations. These situations, in turn, cause chronic maladaptive alterations in physiological functioning, in heart rate, blood pressure, muscle tension, and gastric secretion. It is these alterations in physiological functioning, associated with prolonged stress, that are responsible for development of psychosomatic disorder.

General Adaptation Syndrome. One of the most influential theories of psychosomatic disorder is based on the empirical research of Canadian physician Hans Selye. His research has established that *whenever stress is imposed on a person, regardless of its precise causes, the person's body progresses through a series of reactions* Selye terms the **General Adaptation Syndrome (GAS).**

RESEARCH BOX

Do You Smoke and Drink?
Chances Are Your Parents Do Too

When 256 California adolescents, ages thirteen through seventeen, and their parents were interviewed about their drug use recently, a striking relationship between adolescent drug use and drug use by their parents was found (Fawzy, Coombs, and Gerber, 1983). Though this finding doesn't prove that heavy drug use by parents always leads to heavy drug use by their children or, for that matter, that parents who don't smoke or drink will always have children who don't use drugs, the strong parent-child drug use relationship Fawzy and his colleagues identified does cast some light on two factors that may lead to youthful drug use and abuse.

The study's findings included the following:

1. Coffee consumption by parents was strongly associated with youthful substance use (defined as the use of alcohol or illegal drugs, or prescription drugs obtained illegally): eighty-two percent of heavy coffee-drinking parents, but only 37% of parents who don't drink coffee, have substance-using offspring.

2. Smoking by parents is also strongly associated with substance use by children: eighty-five percent of mothers and 64% of fathers who smoke heavily have substance-using children; parents who smoke less or not at all are much less likely to have children who use drugs.

3. Seventy-two percent of fathers and 77% of mothers who drink wine or beer daily, and 76% of parents who drink hard li-

quor frequently have offspring who use drugs; parents who do not drink alcoholic beverages are 50% less likely to have substance-using children.

4. Eighty-one percent of fathers and 78% of mothers who use marijuana or hashish have substance-using children; parents who do not use these drugs are much less likely to have substance-using children.

One interpretation of these findings by the study's authors calls on social learning theory to emphasize the role of youthful modeling of parental drug-use behavior in the development of their own drug-use behavior. That is, children whose parents use alcohol, drugs, or cigarettes will likely model that behavior themselves—though they may "go their parents one better" by using hard drugs as well as the alcohol, coffee, and cigarettes their parents use.

The authors put forth a "deviancy/pathology" view of their findings by hypothesizing that parents who are heavy users of drugs and alcohol are more apt to be socially deviant—rejecting of society's behavioral norms. Their deviance, in turn, is likely to be conveyed to their children, who will then be more likely to use illegal drugs.

While studies of this kind do not prove that parental and adolescent drug use are invariably related, they do provide important information on factors—probably important factors—that influence adolescent substance use and abuse.

The first of these bodily stages of response to stress is the **alarm reaction,** during which *the body produces a variety of endocrine gland hormones (ACTH, adrenalin, noradrenalin, corticoids) designed to deal with the stressor.* During the next GAS stage, the stage of **resistance,** *the body system best able to cope with the stress becomes most strongly activated.* If this mechanism fails to reduce the stress, the stage of **exhaustion** sets in. During this stage, *the body is either able to reduce the stress and eliminate the stressor or the organism expires.*

Taking note of the fact that different persons experience different physical symptoms in the face of the same set of stressors, Selye has acknowledged that, "In some people the heart, in others the nervous system or the gastrointestinal tract, may represent the weakest link. That is why people develop different types of disease under the influence of the same kind of stressors" (Selye, 1977).

Type A Behavior. A recent and very controversial theory of psychosomatic disorder focuses on cardiovascular disease, the nation's leading cause of death, and its relationship to a specific personality pattern, the so-called Type A personality. The **Type A pattern,** supposedly found more often in persons with cardiovascular problems, *describes hard-driving, competitive individuals intensely interested in achievement and easily angered.* These are the persons who rush to work, rush home, and rush to appointments, even though there may be plenty of time available. In contrast, the Type B pattern involves greater relaxation, less time- or competition-urgency, much less hostility—and less risk of cardiovascular disease (Rosenman and Friedman, 1974).

How can something as nonspecific as a personality pattern cause blockage of coronary arteries? Although no one understands this disease process completely, it is clear that emotions and stress interact with other risk factors for coronary artery disease to heighten the chances of having the disease (Steptoe, 1981). These risk factors include age (older persons are at greater risk), sex (males are at greater risk), cholesterol levels in the blood (high levels increase risk), blood pressure

Table 12.1 Type A behavior
Time urgency
Impatience
Excessive drive
Ambition
Competitiveness
Hostility
Achievement-oriented behavior
A tendency to be ordered and well planned
Self-control
Self-confidence
A preference for working alone when challenged
Concentration on task performance even in the face of distracting events
Outgoingness
Hyperalertness
A tendency to be fast-paced, tense, and unrelaxed
Deep involvement in one's vocation
An inability to relax away from work
Denial of failure
Suppression of symptoms and fatigue

(From Rosenman, R. H., and M. A. Chesney, "The Relationship of Type A Behavior Pattern to Coronary Heart Disease," in Activitas Nervosa Superior, *1980, 22, 1–45. Copyright © 1980 by Avicenum, Czechoslavak Medical Press. Reprinted by permission.)*

(high levels increase risk), smoking (which increases risk), diabetes (which increases risk), genetics (a family history of cardiovascular disease places one in a high-risk category), weight (obesity increases risk), and physical activity level (inactivity increases risk). Specifically, it seems that the general activation of the sympathetic nervous system during times of emotional stress is a key factor in cardiovascular disease (Friedman, Rosenman, and Carroll, 1958). The Type A person shows more intense emotions in many situations, particularly negative emotions like hostility, and this may lead to increases in cholesterol levels, blood pressure, smoking, or eating (see Table 12.1).

Positive life-style change programs, discussed below, may be having some success dealing with some of the bodily consequences of Type A behavior (Nathan, 1984).

APPLICATION BOX

The Secrets of Successful Dieters

Along with anxiety, depression, substance abuse, aggression, and the psychosomatic diseases, overeating that results in obesity is also believed by many to be a result of unresolved conflict and frustration. (There are also several other reasons for obesity that have little or nothing to do with unresolved conflict and frustration.)

A notoriously difficult condition to treat, obesity has long resisted a variety of heroic efforts to induce weight loss that will be maintained over more than a very short time. A recent study of highly successful dieters—men and women who have lost significant weight and been successful at maintaining the loss—has identified some of the weight loss methods and personal characteristics of people who have been successful in maintaining weight loss. (Colvin and Olson, 1983).

The subjects of the study were forty-one women and thirteen men who had lost at least 20% of their body weight and been able to maintain the loss for at least two years. Over half the men reported that they began to lose weight following a "critical incident"—which generally involved having a physician tell them to lose weight "or else." Most women could not identify such a critical incident for their decision to begin to lose weight.

Though factors that appeared to be crucial to maintaining weight loss in men could not be reliably identified, four factors crucial to maintaining weight loss in women were found. They included the following:

1. These women had lost enough weight to feel that they had attained the loss they originally felt was appropriate for them— they had reached their weight loss goal.
2. They had become much more aware of what they eat; they had developed diets that worked for them: they eat less sugar and fats, more fish, fowl, fruits, and green vegetables, and they no longer like feeling "full."
3. Most of the women no longer spend the day at home; whereas most were full-time housewives and mothers before, more than 60% are now business and professional women.
4. The women are now much more concerned about their appearance and physical condition than before; they exercise on a regular basis, and they weigh themselves daily.

Successful maintenance of weight loss takes continued effort and vigilence. But it is possible to lose weight and to maintain weight loss, contrary to popular opinion.

Stress, Coping, and Healthy Life-styles

Psychologists and others have recently become interested in helping induce positive life-style change in healthy persons whose life-styles nonetheless have the potential to cause health problems later in life. Healthy persons who smoke heavily, fail to exercise, overeat, or fail to follow good nutritional practices can all be helped to change these poor health practices and, in so doing, enhance the quality of their life now and their health later on. One of the authors of this text (Nathan, 1984) was involved for several years in the implementation of the Live for Life program, a positive life-style change program designed to change unhealthy life-styles among the 60,000 employees of one of the country's largest companies. A substantial number of employees were persuaded to stop smoking, start exercising, and reduce excessive food intake by attending weekly "action groups" aimed at smoking cessation, weight control, exercise, and better nutritional practices, a variety of educational activities, on-site exercise facilities, and other inducements. Similar smoking cessation and weight-control programs are likely to be offered on your campus several times a year.

Another feature of the Live for Life program, and a frequent component of such programs elsewhere, was a stress management program, extending over eight weeks, that was designed to teach highly stressed, hard-driving business people to cope with the stressors that were an inevitable part of their jobs. Relaxation training, cognitive restructuring ("You don't have to be letter-perfect every time"; "Even successful managers make a mistake once in a while."), and more flexible time management skills were all elements of a program designed to reduce the effects on mind and body of the stressful lives these successful business-people were living.

GUIDED REVIEW

Learning Objectives 3 and 4

1. _____ afflicts more than nine million Americans. With problem drinking and heavy social drinking, which may also exact a high price, _____ is one of the most destructive of the behavioral consequences of conflict and frustration.

2. Hard-core _____ and recreational _____ are also consequences of conflict and frustration; their impact on vocational, familial, and interpersonal effectiveness is every bit as disastrous as is that of alcohol abuse, though the numbers of drug abusers in this country are significantly _____ than the numbers of alcohol abusers.

3. Among the most frequent behavioral consequences of unresolved conflict and frustration are _____ and _____ , which can both interfere markedly with functioning. One of the most unfortunate complications of depression, in turn, is _____ ; each year in this country, 200,000 people attempt it and 25,000 are unlucky enough to succeed.

4. Conflict and frustration also have bodily consequences. Many people believe that the _____ come about as a part of the body's natural response to stress.

5. One of the most influential models of the psychosomatic disorder disease process is called the _____ ; it was first described by _____ .

ANSWERS

1. Alcoholism; alcoholism 2. drug abuse; drug use; fewer 3. anxiety, depression; suicide 4. psychosomatic disorders 5. General Adaptation Syndrome (GAS); Hans Selye

A Brief History of Abnormal Behavior

Natural Forces and Supernatural Forces

Through much of human history, two conflicting views on the causes of abnormal behavior have struggled for supremacy. One position saw abnormal behavior as a product of natural forces; the other viewed it as the responsibility of supernatural forces.

As early as the seventh century B.C., Chinese physicians concluded that abnormal behavior was a natural phenomenon. An imbalance of the two essential human forces, yin and yang, resulted in physical or mental illness; yin and yang in balance assured health.

Hippocrates, the Greek "father of medicine," writing in the fourth century B.C., took a similar view. He considered mental disorder to be the result of brain disease. Specifically, he believed it to be the product of an imbalance of the four essential fluids or humors—blood, phlegm, yellow bile, and black bile. Depending on the nature of the imbalance, **mania** (extreme excitement), **melancholia** (*depression*), or **phrenitis** (a condition we call *schizophrenia* today) was the result.

Although the belief that mental disorder is caused by supernatural forces (by demons, devils, and evil spirits) has always been an influential one (even today, as we discuss below), this belief reached its unfortunate heights in the sixteenth and seventeenth centuries A.D. in Europe and America. This belief was powerfully influenced by *The Witches' Hammer,* a book written by two Dominican brothers and published in 1487. The book "proved" that sin and mental disorder are invariably linked.

Believing that all those who suffered from mental disorder had sinned and hence "deserved" their affliction and its consequences justified widespread efforts by the Church of the Middle Ages to curb mental disorder by exorcizing or otherwise destroying the evil spirits that caused it. This "treatment" sometimes involved burning "witches" at the stake. The abuses of

the "witch hunters" were equalled in many parts of the world by those who treated the mentally disordered like criminals. Some unfortunates eked out a living as beggars; others were imprisoned as petty criminals.

Pinel's Reforms

The French and American revolutions of the last quarter of the eighteenth century coincided with a new sense of human dignity and social responsibility throughout the Western world. This wave of humanity led, in turn, to the establishment of mental hospitals designed to offer both refuge and humane treatment for those for whom there had previously been no safe place. In 1793, a French physician, Philippe Pinel, was made physician-in-chief at the Bicetre, a Paris hospital for psychotics. Believing that his charges deserved treatment for their disorder rather than punishment for their sins, he ordered removal of the chains with which most of the patients had been bound (fig. 12.4). Later, Pinel expanded his reform efforts, generally considered the first in the Western world, by requiring attendants to provide humane treatment to their charges and providing his patients a regular routine designed to be therapeutic. Pinel's reforms in Paris gradually spread through Europe and America. Influenced by Pinel, Dorothea Dix humanized psychiatric hospitals in the United States in the 1840s and led a movement that ultimately prohibited imprisonment of the insane in this country.

The Rise of the Disease Model of Mental Illness

As more patients were admitted to more humane psychiatric hospitals following Pinel's reforms, better records of these patients began to be kept, again following Pinel's lead. As a consequence, systematic efforts to classify and categorize mental disorder began. The work of German physicians in the latter half of the nineteenth century, about sixty years after Pinel's reforms,

Figure 12.4   Philippe Pinel freeing the insane from their chains

led this effort. Notably, three different German physicians described serious **psychoses,** or *disorders typically involving hallucinations, delusions, and bizarre behaviors.* Two decades later, another German physician, Emil Kraepelin, concluded that these observers were all describing variations of a disorder he labelled dementia praecox. That serious disorder was renamed schizophrenia by the Swiss psychiatrist Eugen Bleuler shortly thereafter. Its description as a single disorder with several subtypes (caused by damage to the central nervous system, according to Kraepelin) constituted an extremely important diagnostic advance. Kraepelin was also centrally involved in the classification of **organic brain disorders,** *disorders of the central nervous system that have behavioral consequences,* and in what are now called the **bipolar affective disorders,** *extreme and uncontrollable mood swings.*

The Psychoanalytic Revolution

Shortly before the turn of the century, a very important advance of a very different sort gave rise to modern psychiatry. This advance was marked, in 1895, by the publication of *Studies in Hysteria,* written by Austrian psychiatrists Josef Breuer and Sigmund Freud. This book, now seen as the beginning of the psychoanalytic movement, set forth the then-radical views that psychological rather than physical factors could affect behavior in very powerful ways; that a "talking" treatment might be more effective for disordered behavior than the harsh physical treatments then in use; that behavior might be influenced by thought patterns, impulses, wishes, and desires of which the individual might be quite unaware; and that nonpsychotic behavioral disorders were nonetheless worthy of attention and treatment by psychiatrists.

GUIDED REVIEW

Learning Objective 5

1. Abnormal behavior has been recognized, categorized, and treated for _____ .

2. Two conflicting views on the causes of mental disorder have been widely held. One saw mental disorder as the product of _____ ; the other believed it to be caused by _____ .

3. _____ , published in 1487, marked the high point of the demonological, _____ view of the causes of mental disorder.

4. _____ , shortly after the French and American revolutions, humanized French psychiatric hospitals.

5. Following Pinel's reforms, the newly humane mental hospitals brought together enough patients for the first time to permit systematic efforts to _____ and _____ the mental disorders represented among the patients in them.

6. German physicians working in the latter half of the nineteenth century, by systematizing the diagnosis of _____ , setting this disorder off from what is now termed _____ , and determining the physical etiology of several central nervous system (_____) disorders having behavioral consequences, established the medical model of mental illness.

7. The publication in 1895 of Breuer and Freud's _____ marked the formal beginning of the _____ movement, which then proceeded to revolutionize theory and research on etiology and treatment of the mental disorders.

ANSWERS

1. many centuries 2. supernatural forces, natural agents 3. The Witches' Hammer; supernatural 4. Philippe Pinel 5. classify, categorize 6. schizophrenia; bipolar affective disorder; organic 7. Studies in Hysteria; psychoanalytic

The Third Edition of the *Diagnostic and Statistical Manual of Mental Disorders*

DSM-III, the third edition of the *Diagnostic and Statistical Manual,* was published in 1980 by the American Psychiatric Association. It represents this country's most widely accepted system for categorizing the mental disorders. The major diagnostic categories included in DSM-III are shown in table 12.2.

DSM-III is a marked revision of its predecessors, DSM-I and DSM-II, published in 1952 and 1968, respectively. In turn, they had evolved gradually over a period of about seventy-five years, with roots extending back to Kraepelin, Bleuler, and other German diagnosticians working in the latter part of the nineteenth century. Because of this heritage, DSM-III takes a decidedly "disease-model" approach to mental disorder, categorizing syndromes according to signs and symptoms and implying the existence of a disease process for most of its entries.

Table 12.2 Categories of abnormal behavior in DSM-III

Disorders of infancy, childhood, or adolescence (45 diagnoses)
Organic mental disorders (58 diagnoses)
Substance use disorders (19 diagnoses)
Schizophrenic disorders (5 diagnoses)
Paranoid disorders (4 diagnoses)
Psychotic disorders not elsewhere classified (4 diagnoses)
Affective disorders (9 diagnoses)
Anxiety disorders (10 diagnoses)
Somatoform disorders (5 diagnoses)
Dissociative disorders (5 diagnoses)
Psychosexual disorders (22 diagnoses)
Factitious disorders (3 diagnoses)
Disorders of impulse control (6 diagnoses)
Adjustment disorders (8 diagnoses)
Psychological factors affecting physical condition (1 diagnosis)
Personal disorders (12 diagnoses)

DSM-III is both larger and more comprehensive than its predecessors, encompassing half again as many separate diagnostic descriptions as did DSM-II and more than double the number in DSM-I. Much of DSM-III's increase in diagnostic breadth reflects the decision of its authors to include all conditions that might be the object of attention by mental health professionals. That is, no arbitrary set of standards setting off what are "mental disorders" from what are not "mental disorders" influenced the contents of DSM-III. If a set of behaviors, or syndrome, regularly comes to the attention of mental health professionals, it has been included in DSM-III.

Other "new departures" that characterize DSM-III were designed to increase the usefulness of diagnosis to the person who must plan treatment for a newly diagnosed patient, to increase the level of agreement among clinicians who may be called upon to diagnose the same individual, and to make the diagnostic process as specified in DSM-III conform more closely to actual clinical diagnostic practice.

GUIDED REVIEW

Learning Objective 6

1. The _____ , the "official" nomenclature, published in 1980, is markedly different from its predecessors. It has been strongly influenced by the disease model of mental disorder.

ANSWER
1. *Diagnostic and Statistical Manual of Mental Disorders*

The Categories of Abnormal Behavior

Abnormal behavior, as we observed at the beginning of this chapter, is behavior that differs markedly from what is expected of us in the society in which we live. In this section, we describe categories of behavior (they are listed in table 12.2) that occur sufficiently often among persons in our society that they require special attention, understanding, and help from specially trained persons.

We categorize abnormal behavior because the process of systematic categorization, or diagnosis, allows us to convey a great deal of information about a person's behavior in a very few words. The categories "schizophrenia" or "bipolar affective disorder," for example, convey a great deal of information to the mental health professional called upon to work with someone who carries one of these diagnoses.

Organic Mental Disorders

The organic mental disorders are either **acute** *(temporary and reversible)* or **chronic** *(permanent and irreversible)* dysfunctions of brain tissue. They may afflict either children or adults. Signs and symptoms of these disorders include an impairment in memory and orientation: in severe cases, the individual may not be able to remember where he lives, what she had for breakfast, or where the bathroom is located in the home or hospital; or the person may not know where she is, what his name is, or what day and year it is. Another sign of organic mental disorder is impaired intellectual functioning and judgment: the person may no longer be able to think and reason as well as before and may take risks or make decisions that are both unwise and at variance with earlier behavior. Finally, persons with this diagnosis often show impaired affect: they may respond with a smile to another's pain or with tears to events that please others.

Infections of the brain constitute one organic factor responsible for organic mental disorders. For example, untreated syphilis may infect the brain and cause a devastating chronic brain disorder called general paralysis. Before the discovery of penicillin, more psychiatric patients were hospitalized because of general paralysis than any other disorder, including schizophrenia. High fevers associated with other infections, including pneumonia, typhoid fever, malaria, and acute rheumatic fever, can also induce acute, temporary delirium, a form of organic mental disorder. Fortunately, the delirium disappears when the patient recovers from the physical disorder.

Alcohol and drug intoxication and prolonged usage can also cause both acute and chronic organic mental disorders. Simple alcohol intoxication and delirium tremens, a severe alcohol withdrawal reaction, are temporary organic disorders; Korsakov's psychosis, characterized by a profound, permanent memory loss, is a consequence of severe, chronic alcoholism.

Organic mental disorders are also caused by brain tumors, epilepsy, and diseases associated with aging. The latter include senile dementia, Alzheimer's disease, cerebral arteriosclerosis, and Parkinson's disease. All involve injury or death to portions of the brain because of reduced blood circulation or changed brain metabolism, both of which are a consequence for some of the aging process.

One of the most common consequences of brain function changes resulting from aging are the memory problems that so many older people experience. Harvard psychologist B. F. Skinner, a distinguished behavioral researcher and theorist now in his eighties, continues to be a perceptive observer of behavior. He engagingly describes techniques he has adopted to counter some of the troublesome problems of aging, which even a famous psychologist cannot entirely avoid, in the Applications Box: Intellectual Self-Managment in Old Age.

Substance Use Disorders

Eleven million Americans are said to drink enough to be called alcoholic. The estimated cost of alcoholism in the country is more than $50 billion annually (NIAAA, 1984). One out of three arrests is for drunken behavior. Drunken driving accounts for more than 35,000 deaths a year on the highways. One-fourth of the serious crimes that come to public attention are linked to alcoholism, and it is now the third major cause of death in the United States. Furthermore, alcoholism appears to be on the rise, with perhaps 200,000 new cases diagnosed each year. It is distressing that many of these new cases involve young people; alcoholism among adolescents is estimated to be increasing at several times the rate among older persons (Nathan, 1983).

Firm data on the prevalence and costs of drug addiction are only now beginning to be reported, despite the fact that drugs other than alcohol have been used throughout human history. While still only an "informed guess," it is estimated that there are fewer than 250,000 heroin addicts in the United States, a surprisingly small number given the public attention this addiction has received (Zinberg and Harding, 1982). Though comparable data on numbers of men and women who abuse prescription drugs like the barbiturates, the amphetamines, and minor tranquilizers like Librium and Valium are not available (Hunt, 1982), it is likely that these "legal" addictions ("legal" because the drugs were initially prescribed legally for a medical or psychiatric condition) constitute an even larger number. The private nature of this kind of drug use makes it difficult to determine firm figures.

The Distinction between Abuse and Dependence. DSM-III draws the useful distinction between persons who abuse alcohol (problem drinkers) and those who are dependent upon it (alcoholics). The **alcohol abuser** has:

1. *abused alcohol for more than a month,*
2. *adopted a "pathological pattern of use"* (that is, needs to drink daily for adequate functioning, is unable to cut down or stop drinking, or has consumed a fifth of spirits [vodka, gin, scotch, or bourbon] or its equivalent in wine or beer in a single day), and
3. *experienced "impairment in social or occupational functioning due to alcohol use"* (by becoming violent while intoxicated, losing time from work, or being arrested for driving while intoxicated).

Alcohol dependence *is signalled by these three criteria and the presence of signs of physical withdrawal when heavy drinking ceases* (including nausea, vomiting, "the shakes," and other physical symptoms) or tolerance (needing more and more alcohol to achieve the desired effect or experiencing a decreased effect at the same consumption level). Equivalent distinctions are made between the abuse and dependence of the other drugs of abuse besides alcohol.

Drugs of Abuse. Whereas DSM-III's predecessors only listed alcoholism and drug dependence as possible diagnoses, DSM-III lists a wide range of drugs of abuse, in large part because of the apparent surge of drug abuse in this country since 1968, when DSM-II appeared, and 1980, the year DSM-III was published. The substances listed in DSM-III include alcohol, sedatives (including Valium and Librium), the opioids (including heroin and morphine), cocaine, the amphetamines, PCP, the hallucinogens, cannabis (including marijuana and hashish), tobacco, and caffeine. Although it might seem strange to talk of an addiction to tobacco or caffeine, both are capable of inducing dependence and, accordingly, are categorized in this section of DSM-III.

Genetic factors have been implicated in the development of alcoholism (Goodwin, 1983), but social and environmental factors also appear relevant to the substance use disorders. Drug abuse and, to a lesser extent, alcoholism are particular problems for the poor, undereducated, and underemployed in our society. Some believe that the excessive use of alcohol and drugs serves to temporarily "blind" those at the bottom of our society to the emptiness and despair in their lives.

Schizophrenic Disorders

The word "schizophrenia" comes from two Latin roots meaning the splitting of the mind. The word, coined by Eugen Bleuler (referred to earlier in this chapter), recognizes the fact that the mood and affect, intellectual capacities, and behavior of the schizophrenic are not coordinated, as they are in nonschizophrenic persons. Schizophrenics suffer from a psychotic disorder, which means that on occasion they lose touch with reality.

Table 12.3 Schizophrenic associations

Eugen Bleuler includes the following excerpt from a letter written by one of his schizophrenic patients to his mother. It illustrates very well the symptom of schizophrenia called "loose associations":

Dear Mother: I am writing on paper. The pen which I am using is from a factory called 'Perry & Co.' This factory is in England. I assume this. Behind the name of Perry Co. the city of London is inscribed; but not the city. The city of London is in England. I know this from my schooldays. Then, I always liked geography. My last teacher in that subject was Professor August A. He was a man with black eyes. I also like black eyes. There are also blue and gray eyes and other sorts, too. I have heard it said that snakes have green eyes. All people have eyes. There are some, too, who are blind. These blind people are led about by a boy. It must be very terrible not to be able to see. There are people who can't see and, in addition, can't hear. I know some who hear too much. . . . (Bleuler, 1950 (1911), 17)

Accordingly, schizophrenic patients may act, at times, on the basis of imagined or fantasized reality rather than on what is real in their environments.

The way schizophrenic persons think and use language, their cognitive ability, is among the first and most obvious signs of this psychotic disorder. As table 12.3 illustrates, language has lost much of its communication value for the schizophrenic. As the figure indicates, the continuity (chain of associations) in a schizophrenic's thought is disrupted: the pattern by which he or she links words and thoughts together is different from the plan used by nonschizophrenic persons.

Another hallmark of psychosis, and a very common accompaniment of schizophrenia, is delusions. **Delusions** *are false beliefs that are rarely altered, even in the face of facts or common-sense explanations.* Schizophrenic patients are most likely to experience paranoid delusions, which serve to justify or explain a pervading sense of persecution. Patients can also experience grandiose delusions (delusions of self-importance), sexual delusions, religious delusions, hypochondriacal delusions (in which they imagine themselves physically ill) and self-destructive delusions.

Schizophrenics and other psychotic patients also frequently experience **hallucinations,** which are *false perceptions by which patients see, hear, smell, taste, or feel environmental stimuli that do not in fact exist.* The hallucinations are often in line with delusions being experienced. The most common hallucinations of the schizophrenic are auditory (Al-Issa, 1977). The patient typically hears voices talking to or about him or her. The voices may be those of God, Jesus, Satan, a long-dead parent, or a long-absent friend.

Another hallmark of the schizophrenic process is **affective disorder,** *the failure in emotional responsivity that typically accompanies schizophrenia.* Schizophrenics often fail to respond to both usual and unusual events in their lives with the appropriate range of emotions. Instead, they may appear withdrawn and emotionally indifferent in situations to which the nonschizophrenic person will respond with pleasure or pain. Schizophrenics may also show inappropriate affect by taking pleasure in the pain of someone else or experiencing obvious displeasure on news that would generate pleasure in nonschizophrenics.

Subtypes of Schizophrenia. One of Emil Kraepelin's great contributions, made about ninety years ago (Kraepelin, 1896), was to recognize that the syndromes several colleagues described and labelled separately as catatonia, hebephrenia, and vesania typica (a condition characterized by paranoid delusions and hallucinations) were really subcategories of a single psychotic disorder Kraepelin called dementia praecox. Eventually, at the urging of Bleuler, who renamed the disorder schizophrenia (Kraepelin's term inaccurately presumed that the disease is always progressive and first observed in late adolescence), a fourth subtype, simple schizophrenia, was identified (Bleuler, 1911).

Despite an enormous amount of research on the disorder since Kraepelin's time, our diagnostic conceptions of the disorder are very much in line with his. DSM-III identifies the following subtypes of schizophrenia:

Disorganized: Patients with disorganized schizophrenia, labelled hebephrenic by Kraepelin, demonstrate severely disordered thinking processes and grossly inappropriate affect. Giggling, silliness, childlike behavior, poor judgment, and few social skills characterized their behavior. The symptoms of schizophrenia appear early in patients with this diagnosis. They are least likely of all schizophrenic patients to recover from the disorder.

Catatonic: Excitement and withdrawal are two conflicting aspects of the subtype of catatonic schizophrenia. The excited catatonic demonstrates excessive, sometimes violent, motor behavior, and the withdrawn catatonic may be negativistic, mute (without speech), and stuporous (barely conscious, often motionless, and speaking or moving little or not at all). This subtype is very rare today because the major tranquilizing drugs used to treat schizophrenia tend to prevent catatonic behavior from occurring.

Paranoid: Kraepelin's "vesania typica," this subtype of paranoid schizophrenia is the most common of the subtypes of schizophrenia (Romano, 1977). It is characterized most often by paranoid, persecutory delusions and hallucinations. As a result, paranoid patients are often suspicious, hostile, and violent physically and verbally.

Undifferentiated: Formerly accorded Kraepelin's simple schizophrenic label, undifferentiated schizophrenic patients do not show a clear-cut syndrome pattern. Since their symptoms are drawn from more than one subtype of schizophrenia, they are given this diagnosis.

Residual: The diagnostic label of residual schizophrenia is given patients who were previously diagnosed psychotic and schizophrenic but are not now psychotic. Mild or moderate symptoms of the disorder, like a moderate thought disorder or mild affective disturbance, may remain as residuals of the schizophrenic process.

Affective Disorders

Among the signs and symptoms of depression are those familiar to everyone—sadness, melancholy, despondency, despair, pessimism, tearfulness, and sorrow. Experienced clinicians also look for the inability to get to sleep, early morning awakening, anxiety, a loss of appetite, lowered energy level, and trouble concentrating as additional cues to depression. In psychotic depressions, the individual may suffer from delusions of sinfulness and guilt, auditory hallucinations of a persecutory nature, and disordered and confused thinking.

Mania or hypomania (a less extreme state of mania) typically involve *an exalted, grandiose view of oneself, an increase in amount of food eaten and a decrease in amount of sleep required, "racing thoughts" and difficulties in concentration, and the need to be constantly "on the move."*

Bipolar Affective Disorder. The **bipolar affective disorder** patient typically *alternates among periods of mania, depression, and relative or complete psychological health.* The normal periods often last longer than those of either mania or depression. The severity and chronicity of manic depressive disorders have been reduced markedly since lithium carbonate came into widespread use to treat mania and reduce the likelihood of depression.

Major Depressive Disorder. Major depressive disorder involves one or more episodes of depression. Mania is not a feature of the disorder. The depressive episode, which may last for weeks or months, is self-limiting (unless antidepressant medication succeeds in terminating the depression earlier). It is often associated with severe dysfunction. The depressed patient is often unable to function normally and may spend most of his or her time at home, sitting in a chair or lying in bed, unable to think or act clearly and effectively enough to work.

Dysthymic Disorder. One of the most common DSM-III diagnoses, **dysthymic disorder** refers to *mild to moderate depression that interferes with daily functioning but is not as disabling as the major affective disorders* reviewed above. Patients with the dysthymic disorder diagnosis are not psychotic. They generally feel sad, pessimistic, and inadequate, may have sleeping and eating problems, and may consider suicide. They are not, however, so impaired that they cannot work, study, or take care of children, though their effectiveness in these activities may well be significantly affected. Psychotherapy and antidepressant medication are often effective treatments for this disorder.

Depression and Suicide. No discussion of serious depression is complete without some consideration of suicide, one of the ten leading causes of death overall and third among young people in the United States. Each year some 200,000 people attempt suicide, and of these about 25,000 are unlucky enough to succeed. Suicide affects people in all stations of life, apparent successes as well as failures, rogues and heroes, the famous and the infamous, urban blacks as well as suburban whites. The list includes actresses Marilyn Monroe and Judy Garland, socialite Amy Vanderbilt, news columnist Dorothy Kilgallen, and author Ernest Hemingway. Nazi leader Hermann Goering committed suicide before he could be executed for his war crimes; ironically, so did the United States psychiatrist, Douglass M. Kelley, who had treated Goering at Nuremberg.

Given the incidence of suicide in our society and, hence, the likelihood that it has touched many of this book's readers, it would be comforting to believe that only those suffering from serious mental disorders choose to end their lives at their own hands. Yet everything we know about suicide convinces us that many of the people who commit suicide are not victims of serious mental illness (Farberow, 1980).

The reasons for suicide are as diverse as the people who attempt it and the ways they do so. Some commit suicide for altruistic reasons. The Buddhists who burned themselves to death to protest the war in Vietnam and the young Japanese kamikazee pilots of World War II are striking examples. Other suicides are romantics. Goethe's morbid novel *The Sorrows of Young Werther* (1774) led a generation of lovers to consider suicide in the belief that once they had attained their lady loves, there was nothing else to live for.

Still others take their lives under severe stress or when feelings of failure and unworthiness overwhelm them. For instance college students may impetuously try to end it all after getting a "C" in an important course or at the end of a relationship that had once seemed to be permanent. Still other young people kill themselves by mistake, after a suicidal "gesture" that is not intended to end their lives but, rather, to call attention to their unhappiness and their emotional need.

Finally, there are those who kill themselves when meaning and hope have disappeared from their lives, usually when they are afflicted by a chronic physical or psychiatric illness. Psychologist Norman Farberow, a leading suicide researcher, reports that suicide can even occur, incredibly enough, when a terminally ill patient has only a few hours to live (1980).

Anxiety Disorders

Persons who suffer from a **phobic disorder** are subject to *intense periods of fear of objects, situations, or events that they recognize are not really harmful or dangerous.* As long as the person avoids the feared object, no anxiety is experienced. However, when the object or event must be faced (when the person must leave his or her home, for example), anxiety intense enough to cause the person to become dysfunctional may result.

The recurrent experience of panic attacks, when *terrifying anxiety suddenly and unexpectedly overwhelms the individual,* is at the core of **panic disorder.** The person experiencing a panic attack may fear he or she is going crazy or is about to die. A racing heart, chest pain, nausea, dizziness, a feeling of unreality, sweating or hot and cold flashes, and faintness can all accompany the intense anxiety. Lasting from a few moments to several hours, these episodes are especially frightening because it is rare that the person can identify the events responsible for them.

Insistent, unwanted thoughts, urges, and behaviors characterize the **obsessive-compulsive disorders. Obsessions** involve *the unavoidable, irresistible preoccupation with certain thoughts or ideas.* **Compulsions** are *behaviors that the individual feels compelled to perform, sometimes over and over again;* the penalty for failing to repeat a compulsive ritual is intense anxiety. Although some persons are preoccupied primarily with obsessions and others are most troubled by compulsions, the two occur together in the same individual often enough to be considered two facets of the same disorder. From four to twenty percent of all neurotic patients carry this diagnosis (Coleman, 1972; Goodwin, Guze, and Robins, 1969).

Chronic and persistent anxiety that has lasted at least six months merits the **generalized anxiety disorder** diagnosis. These patients live in a state of continuous anxiety, which varies from mild to intense. Also, they experience chronic autonomic symptoms, which may include motor tension, sweating, racing heart, feelings of dread and apprehension, impatience, and the sense that one must be constantly on one's guard. The anxiety is not focused on any specific object or event. Hence, these patients are said to suffer from "free-floating anxiety." Along with dysthymic disorder, this disorder is the most common of the so-called neurotic conditions.

Somatoform Disorders

Conversion Disorder. One of the most striking of the somatoform disorders is **conversion disorder,** which describes *the experience of dramatic physical symptoms that have no organic or physical cause.* The patient may come to the attention of a mental health professional because, on awakening one morning, he/she has lost sensation in a hand or an arm, or cannot see from one or both eyes, or has lost control over all the voluntary muscles on one side of the body, all in the absence of physical findings to justify the condition. Another patient with the same diagnosis may suffer from frequent, intense headaches or frightening heart palpitations, both without any sign of physical illness. It is interesting that this dramatic condition has become increasingly rare since Freud described the syndrome in several of his patients. Perhaps its increasing rarity reflects our greater sophistication with respect to both physical and psychological health and disorder. Most of us now know that most of the physical symptoms of conversion disorder make little anatomical sense.

Hypochondriasis. In **hypochondriasis,** *the person is preoccupied with his or her body and health, to the exclusion of any other interests in life.* (Though all of us have concerns about our health, these concerns do not preoccupy us and prevent us from thinking about other things.) Although not delusional, these people simply cannot believe that they are not seriously ill. They usually know the symptoms of an astounding array of illnesses, from cancer and heart disease to leprosy and Courvoisier's gallbladder, and are constantly anticipating the appearance of symptoms of these disorders in themselves. A slight headache may signal a stroke, and mild muscle pain may mean terminal cancer to the hypochondriac. Such persons are prime targets for quack physicians and makers of "miracle drugs," who encourage them to believe that their complaints have an actual physical basis—which they do not.

Psychosexual Disorders

Gender Identity Disorder. Persons suffering from **transsexualism** are convinced that *they are in the body of a person of the wrong gender*—that they are a male in a female's body or a female in a male's body. The separation of this syndrome from the sexual deviations (called the **paraphilias** in DSM-III) recognizes the widespread clinical belief that this condition is not really a sexual deviation since the sexual choice of the transsexual is a person whose sex is opposite to the transsexual's experienced gender.

The Paraphilias. The **paraphilias** represent *"gross impairment in the capacity for affectionate sexual activity between adult human partners."* The paraphiliac's choice of sexual object or manner of achieving sexual gratification with that object deviates significantly from the normal. Although most paraphiliacs are men, nobody knows for sure why that is so. Similarly, though there are many theories of causation, there are essentially no definitive data on why some persons develop this disorder whereas most of us do not.

The **fetishist** *achieves sexual gratification from inanimate objects;* the **transvestite** *by wearing clothes of the opposite sex.* The **zoophiliac,** whose diagnosis is quite rare, *prefers sex with animals;* the **pedophile** *with children.* The **exhibitionist** can be *gratified sexually by displaying his genitals to women and children;* the **voyeur** *by watching others who are engaged in sexual activity.* The **sexual masochist** *gets sexual pleasure when pain is inflicted on him by a sexual partner;* the **sexual sadist** *does so when he can inflict pain on a sexual partner,* who may or may not be willing.

Psychosexual Dysfunction. The **psychosexual dysfunctions** represent *problems in sexual functioning and sexual desire.* Contrary to earlier belief, they are quite widespread and therefore very troubling, since sexual proficiency is so often considered a mark of the whole man or the complete woman in our society. These conditions are known to many clinicians as the "Masters and Johnson" disorders. Pioneering sex therapists William Masters and Virginia Johnson described the conditions and the details of their successful treatment in books and journal articles that enjoyed great popularity among clinicians and the public in the 1970s.

These conditions include inhibited (inadequate or deficient) sexual desire or sexual excitement (sexual desire or excitement that is less than the person or his or her partner wishes); inhibited orgasm (orgasm that is delayed longer than the person desires); premature ejaculation (orgasm by the male that occurs more quickly than he or his partner wishes); functional dyspareunia (painful menstruation), and vaginismus (painful intercourse). All these disorders represent problems that prevent normal sexual functioning.

Because Masters and Johnson (1976), Helen Singer Kaplan (1974, 1979), and other influential sex therapists have concluded that psychological factors play an important role in these disorders, they are included as a subcategory of the psychosexual disorders in DSM-III.

Ego-Dystonic Homosexuality.   Ego-dystonic homosexuality is included as a fourth subcategory of psychosexual disorders. It is not a paraphilia because it was not considered a sexual deviation by the drafters of this section of DSM-III. It is included as a psychosexual disorder, however, when the behavior is unwanted and a source of distress. When it is desired and a source of pleasure, it is not considered appropriate for inclusion in the nomenclature.

Contrary to popular belief, homosexuality takes as many forms as heterosexuality. Some people become homosexual only by necessity (when they are in prison, for example), and others remain homosexual throughout their lives. Some homosexual relationships last no more than a single evening, and others last a lifetime. Some homosexuals prefer a passive role, in

lovemaking and in daily living, and others choose to be the active partner. Some homosexuals are quite open about their sexual preference; others choose to keep their sexuality to themselves.

Further, some homosexuals are unhappy with the "hassles" of homosexuality and would prefer being "straight," whereas others are totally satisfied with the homosexual way of life. And though some homosexuals suffer from anxiety, depression, alcoholism, and other psychological and behavioral disorders, others are as healthy psychologically as it is possible to be (fig. 12.5). In other words, like heterosexuals and heterosexuality, few generalizations about homosexuals and homosexuality are apt to be valid for all.

The Personality Disorders

Personality disorders are *deeply ingrained habits and patterns of behavior recognized early in life that are considered a distinguishing feature of the person's behavior,* both by him- or herself and by others. They are disorders and are listed in DSM-III because they disturb or concern friends and family or otherwise affect the person's interaction with the world. Because the personality disorders are the most vaguely defined and diverse of the DSM-III categories, appropriate use of this diagnostic category is difficult. The line between these disorders and the anxiety disorders, for example, is a very hard one to draw at times.

Among these disorders are the schizoid personality (persons who are typically withdrawn and seclusive, tend to avoid close interpersonal relationships, and find it difficult to make emotional investments in people); the compulsive personality (who seem driven by the need to attain perfection and orderliness in everything they do, sometimes at the expense of feelings of affection and caring for others [because these feelings are not orderly]); the passive-aggressive personality (persons who combine passivity with aggressiveness and

Figure 12.5 *Many homosexuals are satisfied with their way of life and their behavior is not considered a disorder.*

hostility; unable to express aggression directly, these people do so indirectly, for example, by being obstructive, stubborn, or slow and, in those ways, impeding the goals of others); the dependent personality (persons who seem for all the world to be spending their lives looking for people who will assume life's responsibilities for them, people to whom they can subordinate their wishes, desires, and aspirations in return for being taken care of); and the antisocial personality (persons who come into conflict with society, sometimes serious conflict, by refusing to conform to its established rules of conduct).

GUIDED REVIEW

Learning Objectives 7, 8, 9, 10, 11, 12, and 13

1. The _____ are either acute or chronic dysfunctions in brain tissue with behavioral consequences.

2. The substance use disorders categorize the behavioral and psychological effects of _____ and _____ and _____ .

3. The _____ are signalled by serious defects in cognitive ability, delusions, hallucinations, and affective functioning.

4. The affective disorders include the _____ (formerly manic-depressive psychosis), major _____ disorder, and _____ disorder.

5. The anxiety and somatoform disorders categorize some of the diverse nonpsychotic disorders formerly called the _____ .

6. The psychosexual disorders include _____ , the _____ (formerly the sexual deviations), the sexual _____ (the "Masters and Johnson disorders"), and _____ (when the gay man or lesbian woman experiences distress because of it).

7. The _____ are deeply ingrained patterns of behavior that are troublesome either to the person who receives the diagnosis or to those around him or her.

ANSWERS

1. organic mental disorders 2. drug; alcohol abuse; dependence 3. schizophrenic disorders 4. bipolar affective disorders; depressive; dysthymic 5. neuroses 6. transsexualism; paraphilias; dysfunctions; homosexuality 7. personality disorders

SUMMARY

I. Adjustment involves a healthy and desirable process by which we resolve or learn to deal with conflict. Most conflicts are described according to one of the four following models: (p. 410)

  A. Approach-approach conflicts require a choice between attractive alternatives that are mutually incompatible.   (p. 410)

  B. Avoidance-avoidance conflicts require choices between equally disliked alternatives. (pp. 410–11)

  C. Approach-avoidance conflicts force a choice to approach or avoid a single stimulus that possesses both positive and negative features. (p. 411)

  D. Double approach-avoidance conflicts necessitate a choice between two or more stimuli, each of which possesses both positive and negative features.   (p. 412)

II. Conflict is a principal source of frustration, defined as temporary or permanent failure to achieve a desired goal.   (p. 412)

  A. Unsuccessful responses to frustration include withdrawal and aggression.   (pp. 412, 414)

  B. The ego's mechanisms of defense, which represent efforts (sometimes successful, sometimes unsuccessful) to deal with environmental and personal stress and frustration, include the following: (pp. 415–17)

    1. Repression describes the involuntary burying in the unconscious of unwanted, unacceptable, and threatening thoughts, feelings, or impulses.   (p. 415)

    2. Suppression involves the deliberate decision to keep potentially painful material from surfacing into consciousness. (p. 415)

    3. In reaction formation, we replace a particularly unpleasant feeling about someone or something with the opposite feeling.   (pp. 415–16)

    4. Sublimation permits the psychological energy associated with unconscious desires and impulses to be translated into socially acceptable, often positive, activities. (p. 416)

    5. Rationalization gives a behavior whose motivation may be obscure, unknown, irrational, or embarrassing a rational, logical, or intellectual explanation. (p. 416)

    6. Regression involves either a brief and temporary or a prolonged and permanent return to behaviors more characteristic of children.   (p. 416)

    7. Displacement involves the experience of a feeling, usually unwanted, about a person to whom it does not really belong. (pp. 416–17)

    8. Denial represents a failure to feel the impact of a painful thought or feeling by denying, psychologically, that it exists. (p. 417)

III. Conflict and frustration have both behavioral and bodily consequences.   (p. 417)

  A. The behavioral consequences of conflict and frustration include the use and, sometimes, abuse of alcohol and drugs, along with the universal experience of anxiety and depression. (pp. 417–19)

  B. The bodily consequences of conflict and frustration can include experience of the General Adaptation Syndrome in the face of profound stress, as well as development, over the longer term, of the Type A behavior pattern.   (pp. 419–22)

  C. One approach to prevention of the behavioral and bodily consequences of conflict and frustration has been the development, by industry, of positive life-style change programs. (p. 423)

IV. History of abnormal behavior.   (pp. 424–25)

  A. Through much of human history, two conflicting views on the causes of abnormal behavior struggled for supremacy.   (p. 424)

    1. One position saw abnormal behavior as the product of natural forces.   (p. 424)

    2. The other position viewed abnormal behavior as the responsibility of supernatural forces.   (p. 424)

B. A turning point in the history of attitudes toward the mentally ill were Pinel's reforms of the mental hospital system in France. (p. 424)

C. Another landmark in the history of our views on abnormal behavior came with the rise of the disease model of mental illness, which coincided with Kraepelin's efforts to classify what he called dementia praecox. (pp. 424–25)

D. The psychoanalytic revolution constitutes another key advance in conceptions of mental disorder. (p. 425)

V. A current legacy of Kraepelin is the 1980 edition of the Diagnostic and Statistical Manual of Mental Disorders, Third Edition. (pp. 426–27)

VI. The categories of abnormal behavior include the following: (pp. 427–35)

A. The organic mental disorders are either acute or chronic dysfunctions of brain tissue. They usually involve significant impairment of behavior. (pp. 427–28)

B. The substance use disorders include both alcoholism and drug dependence. (pp. 428–29)

C. The schizophrenic disorders are serious psychotic conditions that typically involve disturbances in cognitive, perceptual, and affective functioning. The subtypes of schizophrenia include disorganized, catatonic, paranoid, undifferentiated, and residual schizophrenia. (pp. 429–31)

D. The affective disorders include bipolar affective disorder (a psychotic condition), major depressive disorder, and dysthymic disorder. Depression is often associated with suicide, a leading cause of death among young people. (pp. 431–32)

E. The anxiety and somatoform disorders include many of the conditions previously termed neuroses. (pp. 432–33)

F. The psychosexual disorders include transsexualism, the paraphilias, the psychosexual dysfunctions, and ego-dystonic homosexuality. (pp. 433–34)

G. The personality disorders are deeply ingrained habits and patterns of behavior recognized early in life that are considered a distinguishing feature of a person's behavior. (pp. 434–35)

ACTION GLOSSARY

Match the terms in the left column with the definitions in the right column.

____ 1. Conflict (p. 410)
____ 2. Adjustment (p. 410)
____ 3. Approach-approach conflict (p. 410)
____ 4. Cognitive dissonance (p. 410)
____ 5. Avoidance-avoidance conflict (pp. 410–11)
____ 6. Approach-avoidance conflict (p. 411)
____ 7. Double approach-avoidance conflict (p. 412)
____ 8. Frustration (p. 412)
____ 9. Withdrawal (p. 414)

A. *Running away from or ignoring conflict or frustration.*
B. *Requires a choice between equally disliked alternatives.*
C. *The temporary or permanent failure to achieve a desired goal.*
D. *Requires a choice between two attractive alternatives that are mutually incompatible.*
E. *The unavoidable obstacles in life that thwart our decisions and our choices.*
F. *Requires the decision to approach or avoid a single stimulus that possesses both positive and negative features.*
G. *Requires a choice between two or more stimuli, each of which possesses both positive and negative features.*
H. *A healthy and desirable process by which we resolve or learn to live with major conflicts in our lives.*
I. *The psychological discomfort that results from the simultaneous presence of two or more beliefs, ideas, or attitudes that are in conflict.*

____ **10. Repression** (p. 415)
____ **11. Suppression** (p. 415)
____ **12. Reaction formation** (p. 415)
____ **13. Sublimation** (p. 416)
____ **14. Rationalization** (p. 416)
____ **15. Regression** (p. 416)
____ **16. Displacement** (p. 416)
____ **17. Denial** (p. 417)
____ **18. Anxiety** (p. 418)
____ **19. General Adaptation Syndrome** (p. 419)

A. *A defense mechanism by which the psychological energy associated with unacceptable unconscious desires and impulses is translated into socially acceptable, often creative, activities.*

B. *A defense mechanism that involves the experience of an unwanted feeling about a person to whom it does not really belong.*

C. *A sense of foreboding, a feeling of apprehension, an ill-defined fear that is independent of specific objects or situations.*

D. *A defense mechanism that involves the involuntary burying in the unconscious of unwanted, unacceptable, and threatening thoughts, feelings, or impulses.*

E. *A defense mechanism that permits us to give a behavior whose motivation may be obscure, unknown, irrational, or embarrassing a rational, logical, or intellectual explanation and purpose.*

F. *A defense mechanism involving a brief and temporary or prolonged and permanent return to behaviors more characteristic of children.*

G. *The series of bodily reactions through which Hans Selye said the body progresses whenever stress is imposed on a person.*

H. *A defense mechanism that involves a failure to feel the impact of a painful thought or feeling by denying, psychologically, that it exists.*

I. *A defense mechanism by which a particularly unpleasant feeling about someone or something is replaced by the opposite feeling.*

J. *A defense mechanism that involves the deliberate decision to keep painful memories from surfacing into consciousness.*

____ **20. Alarm reaction** (p. 421)
____ **21. Resistance** (p. 421)
____ **22. Exhaustion** (p. 421)
____ **23. Type A pattern** (p. 421)
____ **24. Melancholia** (p. 424)
____ **25. Phrenitis** (p. 424)
____ **26. Psychosis** (p. 425)
____ **27. Organic brain disorder** (p. 427)
____ **28. Acute** (p. 427)
____ **29. Chronic** (p. 427)

A. *A condition in which the body is either able to reduce the stress and eliminate the stressors or the organism expires.*

B. *The temporary and reversible dysfunction of brain tissue.*

C. *The ancient Greek term for what is today called depression.*

D. *A response to stress in which the body produces a variety of endocrine gland hormones designed to deal with a stressor.*

E. *A mental disorder that typically involves hallucinations, delusions, and bizarre behaviors.*

F. *The permanent and irreversible dysfunction of brain tissue.*

G. *A response to stress in which the body system best able to cope with the stress becomes most strongly activated.*

H. *The ancient Greek term for what is today called schizophrenia.*

I. *Disorders of the central nervous system that have behavioral consequences.*

J. *Behavior found typically in hard-driving, competitive individuals intensely interested in achievement and easily angered.*

____ **30. Alcohol abuse** (p. 428)
____ **31. Alcohol dependence** (p. 428)
____ **32. Delusions** (p. 429)
____ **33. Hallucinations** (p. 430)
____ **34. Affective disorder** (p. 430)
____ **35. Depression** (p. 431)
____ **36. Mania** (p. 431)
____ **37. Bipolar affective disorder** (p. 431)
____ **38. Dysthymic disorder** (p. 431)
____ **39. Phobic disorder** (p. 432)

A. *Intense periods of fear of objects, situations, or events that are not really harmful or dangerous.*

B. *Behavior that typically includes an exalted, grandiose view of oneself, an increase in eating and a decrease in sleeping, "racing thoughts," psychomotor hyperactivity, and difficulty in concentration.*

C. *Marked by both the symptoms of alcohol abuse and either withdrawal symptoms, tolerance, or both.*

D. *Behavior characterized by feelings of dejection and downheartedness, a sense of decreased self-worth and self-esteem, reduced interest in the future, difficulty concentrating, problems getting to sleep or staying asleep, and a pervasive feeling of fatigue and ennui.*

E. *Marked by a month or more of heavy drinking, a pathological pattern of alcohol use, and impairment in social or occupational functioning due to the alcohol use.*
F. *The failure in emotional responsivity that typically accompanies schizophrenia.*
G. *A condition characterized by alternation among periods of mania, severe depression, and relative or complete psychological health.*
H. *False beliefs that are rarely altered, even in the face of facts or common-sense explanations.*
I. *False perceptions in which a person sees, hears, smells, tastes, or feels environmental stimuli that do not in fact exist.*
J. *Mild to moderate depression that interferes with daily functioning but is not as disabling as a major depressive disorder.*

___ 40. **Panic disorder (p. 432)**
___ 41. **Obsessive-compulsive disorder (p. 432)**
___ 42. **Obsession (p. 432)**
___ 43. **Compulsion (p. 432)**
___ 44. **Generalized anxiety disorder (p. 432)**
___ 45. **Conversion disorder (p. 433)**
___ 46. **Hypochondriasis (p. 433)**
___ 47. **Transsexualism (p. 433)**
___ 48. **Paraphilias (p. 433)**
___ 49. **Fetishist (p. 433)**

A. *The unavoidable, irresistible preoccupation with certain thoughts or ideas.*
B. *Preoccupation with one's body and health, to the exclusion of any other interests.*
C. *A person who achieves sexual gratification from inanimate objects.*
D. *A disorder in which the person is convinced he or she is in the body of a person of the wrong gender.*
E. *Characterized by insistent, unwanted thoughts, urges, and behaviors.*
F. *Sudden and unexpected anxiety sufficient to overwhelm the person.*
G. *The experience of dramatic physical symptoms that have no organic or physical cause.*
H. *Represent gross impairment in the capacity for affectionate sexual activity between adult human partners.*
I. *A behavior that the individual feels compelled to perform, sometimes over and over again.*
J. *Chronic, persistent anxiety that lasts at least six months.*

___ 50. **Transvestite (p. 433)**
___ 51. **Zoophile (p. 433)**
___ 52. **Pedophile (p. 433)**
___ 53. **Exhibitionist (p. 433)**
___ 54. **Voyeur (p. 433)**
___ 55. **Sexual masochist (p. 433)**
___ 56. **Sexual sadist (p. 433)**
___ 57. **Psychosexual dysfunctions (p. 433)**
___ 58. **Personality disorders (p. 434)**

A. *Problems in sexual functioning and sexual desire.*
B. *Deeply ingrained habits and patterns of behavior that disturb or concern friends or family or otherwise affect the person's interaction with the world.*
C. *A person who achieves sexual gratification with animals.*
D. *A person who gets sexual pleasure when he or she inflicts pain on a sexual partner.*
E. *A person who gets sexual pleasure when pain is inflicted on him or her by a sexual partner.*
F. *A person who achieves sexual gratification with children.*
G. *A person who achieves sexual gratification by wearing the clothing of the opposite sex.*
H. *A person who derives sexual gratification from displaying his genitals to women and children.*
I. *A person who achieves sexual gratification by watching others who are engaged in sexual activity.*

ANSWERS

1. Approach-approach conflicts
   (a) are easily resolvable.
   (b) require a choice between mutually incompatible alternatives.
   (c) require a choice between two alternatives.
   (d) necessitate closest inspection of possible alternatives.
   (LO 1; p. 410)

2. Approach-avoidance conflicts
   (a) are easily resolvable.
   (b) are notoriously difficult to resolve.
   (c) require choices between disliked alternatives.
   (d) force a choice to approach or avoid a single stimulus with both positive and negative features.
   (LO 1; p. 411)

3. The ego's mechanisms of defense were first described in detail by
   (a) Anna Freud.   (c) Erik Erikson.
   (b) Sigmund Freud.   (c) Erich Fromm.
   (LO 2; p. 415)

4. The defense mechanism defined as the deliberate decision to keep potentially painful material from surfacing into consciousness is termed
   (a) repression.   (c) denial.
   (b) suppression.   (d) displacement.
   (LO 2; p. 415)

5. The defense mechanism defined as the experience of a feeling, usually unwanted, about a person to whom it does not really belong is termed
   (a) repression.   (c) denial.
   (b) suppression.   (d) displacement.
   (LO 2; p. 416)

6. Depression is
   (a) a behavioral consequence of conflict and frustration.
   (b) associated with suicide.
   (c) a universal affect.
   (d) all of the above.
   (LO 3; p. 417)

7. Suicide is
   (a) an inevitable consequence of serious depression.
   (b) the leading cause of death among the aged.
   (c) the third leading cause of death among young people.
   (d) a relatively uncommon event among the middle-aged.
   (LO 3; p. 431)

8. The General Adaptation Syndrome was first described by
   (a) Anna Freud.   (c) Selye.
   (b) Rosenman.   (d) Friedman.
   (LO 4; p. 419)

9. The Type A behavior pattern is associated with
   (a) cancer.   (c) hives.
   (b) emphysema.   (d) heart disease.
   (LO 4; p. 421)

10. The two conflicting views on the causes of abnormal behavior that have struggled for supremacy through history include
    (a) the genetic and the environmental.
    (b) the natural and the unnatural.
    (c) the learning and the dynamic.
    (d) the natural and the supernatural.
    (LO 5; p. 424)

11. The man who reformed French mental hospitals in the eighteenth century was
    (a) Pinel.   (c) Lafayette.
    (b) Napoleon.   (d) DeGaulle.
    (LO 5; p. 424)

12. Kraepelin coined the term
    (a) schizophrenia.   (c) general paresis.
    (b) catatonia.   (d) dementia praecox.
    (LO 5; p. 425)

13. DSM-III was published in
    (a) 1980.   (c) 1885.
    (b) 1905.   (d) 1968.
    (LO 6; p. 426)

14. Organic mental disorders
    (a) can be caused by psychological variables alone.
    (b) are inevitably severely disabling.
    (c) can be acute or chronic.
    (d) all of the above.
        (LO 7; p. 427)

15. The substance use disorders
    (a) have been diminishing in this country during the past decade.
    (b) are most prevalent in the U.S.
    (c) include alcoholism and drug dependence.
    (d) categorize the central nervous system effects of alcohol and drug abuse.
        (LO 8; p. 428)

16. The subtypes of schizophrenia include
    (a) catatonic, paranoid, and disorganized.
    (b) acute, chronic, and residual.
    (c) endogeneous and exogeneous.
    (d) process and reactive.
        (LO 9; p. 430)

17. Bipolar affective disorder was formerly termed
    (a) major depressive disorder.
    (b) dysthymic disorder.
    (c) manic-depressive psychosis.
    (d) none of the above.
        (LO 9; p. 431)

18. The anxiety and somatoform disorders were formerly termed the
    (a) functional disorders.
    (b) neuroses.
    (c) nonpsychoses.
    (d) dissociative disorders.
        (LO 11; p. 432)

19. Masters and Johnson concerned themselves with
    (a) the psychosexual dysfunctions.
    (b) transsexualism.
    (c) ego-dystonic homosexuality.
    (d) the paraphilias.
        (LO 12; p. 434)

20. The personality disorders are
    (a) responses to environmental stress.
    (b) products of impaired brain function.
    (c) deeply ingrained habits and patterns of behavior.
    (d) never disabling.
        (LO 13; p. 434)

ANSWERS

1. b, 2. d, 3. a, 4. b, 5. d, 6. d, 7. c, 8. c, 9. d, 10. d, 11. a, 12. d, 13. a, 14. c, 15. c, 16. a, 17. c, 18. b, 19. a, 20. c

SUGGESTED READINGS

American Psychiatric Association. *Diagnostic and Statistical Manual of Mental Disorders.* 3d ed. Washington, D.C.: American Psychiatric Association. The new nomenclature, complete with careful comparisons with preceding versions of the *DSM.*

Bleuler, E. *Dementia praecox or the group of schizophrenias.* New York: International Universities Press, 1950. Originally published more than seventy years ago, this classic text still provides some of the best descriptions of the signs and symptoms of schizophrenia.

Breuer, J., and S. Freud. "Fraulein Anna O." In *Studies in hysteria.* New York: Basic Books, 1957. The case of Anna O. describes a most interesting patient who suffered from an incredible array of hysterical symptoms. The treatment she received and the theories her case and its treatment led to were very important to the development of psychoanalysis.

Davidson, P. O., and S. M. Davidson, eds. *Behavioral medicine: Changing life-styles.* New York: Brunner/Mazel, 1980. One of the first books to bring together discussions of such different behavioral health problems as smoking, obesity, sedentary lifestyle, and alcoholism. The book also presents data on how life-style changes can be put into effect to counter these negative life-style factors.

Farberow, N. L., ed. *The many faces of suicide: Indirect self-destructive behavior.* New York: McGraw-Hill, 1980. One of the world's authorities on suicide has edited a book bringing together informed discussions of a whole host of behaviors that have not before been considered suicidal. High-risk sports, cigarette smoking and alcoholism, and failure to cooperate with medical regimens, with many other behaviors, are discussed as self-destructive behaviors.

Kraepelin, E. *Psychiatry: A textbook.* Leipzig: Barth, 1913. Kraepelin's most complete presentation of the varieties of psychosis, which was essentially a first in the history of psychiatry.

Ray, O. *Drugs, society, and human behavior.* St. Louis: Mosby, 1983. Written by one of the nation's leading authorities on alcohol and drugs and their effects on the body, this book is designed specifically for college students who want to learn as much as possible about alcohol and drugs, their role in society, and their potential for abuse. The book effectively "deromanticizes" and "demythologizes" alcohol and drug abuse.

c h a p t e r

13

Therapies

LEARNING OBJECTIVES

After reading this chapter, you should be able to

1. identify and describe the most important psychoanalytic techniques. **(pp. 444–45)**

2. discuss the two crucial phenomena characterizing and defining the psychoanalytic relationship. Explain how one of these phenomena interferes with the therapeutic relationship whereas the other facilitates it. **(p. 445)**

3. distinguish between psychoanalysis and psychoanalytic psychotherapy in terms of goals and methods. **(p. 446)**

4. describe systematic desensitization, and identify those conditions for which it is appropriate. **(p. 447)**

5. describe the therapeutic roles that classical and operant conditioning methods and observational learning can play. **(pp. 447–49)**

6. discuss the role of behavior modification and token economies in the management of institutionalized psychotic patients. **(pp. 450–52)**

7. summarize the assumptions and the elements comprising client-centered therapy. **(p. 453)**

8. discuss the goals, methods, and applications of group therapy procedures. **(pp. 454–55)**

9. describe the somatic treatment procedures, and delimit their applications. **(pp. 456–58)**

10. distinguish among primary, secondary, and tertiary prevention. **(pp. 460–61)**

Treatment of Abnormal Behavior

Treatment of abnormal behavior aims to restore the individual to normal interpersonal and psychological functioning. Psychotherapy, behavior therapy, group and family therapy, and somatic therapy all have specific applications and utilize different methods. However, all have essentially the same ultimate goal. And though the training of psychotherapists proceeds along different pathways (see Career Box: The Training of Psychotherapists), the products of these diverse training experiences share the same basic goal of treatment: restoration of the individual to effective interpersonal and psychological functioning.

Freud's Psychoanalytic Method

Classical or Freudian psychoanalysis remains attractive to many people, though its greatest popularity may have peaked a decade or more ago. The psychoanalyst, in accord with the psychoanalytic theory of personality, believes that the deep-seated causes of disturbed psychological functioning stem from repressed feelings and memories from childhood. **Psychoanalysis,** then, *attempts to uncover these repressed feelings so they can be faced and dealt with by the conscious mind of the more mature adult.*

Many alternatives to psychoanalysis have arisen in recent years, including briefer, more direct therapies like psychoanalytic psychotherapy and behavior therapy. Nonetheless, psychoanalysis is still a widely accepted form of intervention that many believe is the best method for exploring the complex mechanisms of the mind.

Basic Psychoanalytic Techniques

Although there are many "schools" of psychoanalysis besides the Freudian (Adlerian, Rankian, Jungian, and Sullivanian, to name but a few), basic techniques are similar (Weiner and Bordin, 1983).

CAREER BOX

The Training of Psychotherapists

Who practices psychotherapy in our society? Many persons, some with formal training to do so, some without it. Beyond the core mental health professions—clinical psychology, psychiatry, social work, and psychiatric nursing—all of which require some psychotherapy training, a variety of other professionals, including the clergy, counselors of one kind or another, and guidance workers, often benefit from some formal training in the skills necessary to effective therapy.

Clinical psychologists and psychiatrists receive the most extensive formal training in psychotherapy in the course of their medical or graduate school educations. This is because they have a greater period of time for psychotherapy practice and supervision: the psychologist has five years of graduate training, and the psychiatrist has four years of medical school and three years of residency. The social worker and the psychiatric nurse, on the other hand, generally have two years of graduate training. Nevertheless, members of all four core disciplines who are especially interested in psychotherapy can add to graduate training in psychotherapy in a variety of formal and informal ways to sharpen their therapeutic skills.

The most important psychoanalytic technique, and one of Freud's most important discoveries, is **free association,** in which *the stream of one's thoughts are unburdened or "talked out."* Freud did not discover free association all at once. In line with the practice of the day, Freud had been hypnotizing his patients— many of whom were middle-class Viennese women prone to fainting spells, migraine headaches, inexplicable paralytic conditions, and other signs of what we call somatoform disorder today. His object was to deliver them of the repressed memories, many of them sexual, which he believed were responsible for these disorders.

Freud was not a good hypnotist, and he was not always successful in uncovering the memories of his patients. So he gradually developed the method of free association to replace hypnosis, ineffective in his hands for this purpose. To make the effort easier Freud started having his patients lie relaxed on a couch (ever since, the symbol of the psychoanalyst), speak freely, and wander, without control or censorship, through the forest of thoughts and memories available to all of us.

Another technique important to psychoanalysis is dream interpretation. Although generations of soothsayers, shamans, fortune-tellers, and temple priests had relied on dreams to foretell the future and explain the past and present, Freud was the first to propose specific rules for uncovering the meaning of dreams and to clarify the extent of their behavioral influence. Above all, Freud believed that **dreams** *were symbolic representations of unconscious conflicts rearoused by the previous day's activities and events.*

The path of psychoanalytic treatment is neither smooth nor predictable, but certain stages are recognizable. In the course of treatment and especially during the process of free association, *patients find areas in which they feel blocked; they cannot talk anymore; they find it difficult to recollect crucial events from the past; they start forgetting appointments.* These behaviors constitute phases or episodes known as **resistance.** Essentially the same phenomena also appear during virtually every other kind of psychological counseling and therapy because they reduce the pain of exploring areas of functioning that gave pain in the past and promise to do so again in the future.

Another central component of the psychoanalytic process is transference. Rarely are the patient's thoughts and feelings about the relationship with the therapist based upon a realistic assessment of the therapist's behavior during treatment. Indeed, the therapist makes every effort to convey as little of himself or herself as possible in order to highlight the distortions the patient inevitably brings to his or her feelings about the analyst. *These distortions of the analyst by the patient constitute* **transference;** *they reflect a natural tendency to see in the therapist behaviors that actually belonged to other important persons in the patient's life,* most often the mother and father.

As a consequence of these distortions, the patient responds emotionally to the analyst in many of the same ways he or she responded to parents. It is the responsibility of the analyst to help the patient experience growth-inducing insights so that the patient will see more clearly the nature of these distortions and their potential for trouble. Implicit in all of this is the conviction that distortions revealed during analysis reflect similar distortions occurring outside analysis, which are presumably responsible for the patient's troubled and troubling behavior.

Interpretation is *the means by which transference phenomena and other resistances are brought to the patient's attention when he or she has not observed them spontaneously.* (Transference is a resistance and an impediment to therapeutic progress even though it is also a means by which progress is achieved.) The therapist's interpretive statements are designed to confront the patient in the most nonthreatening way possible with both the significance and the sources of defensive, resistant behavior.

Who Benefits Most from Psychoanalysis?

Contrary to common belief, psychoanalysis seems to work best with individuals who are in relatively good psychological health. According to many practicing psychoanalysts, patients who benefit most from psychoanalysis are in good contact with reality (that is, they are not psychotic), function adequately in both cognitive (thinking) and affective (feeling) spheres, and have a history of adequate functioning. Furthermore, patients must be highly motivated for treatment and not drop out when they begin recognizing some of the disquieting negatives about themselves that are an inevitable component of virtually every therapy. Despite these indications for successful psychoanalysis, some therapists have written convincingly of their success in treating schizophrenia with psychoanalysis.

Psychoanalytic patients must also be willing and able to "think psychologically"—to search the inner recesses of their minds, reflect intensively about their feelings toward happenings in early life, and connect them to similar feelings occurring in the therapeutic relationship. Finally, these patients must be able to afford the high fees charged for three or more analytic sessions a week, often extending for three or more years.

GUIDED REVIEW

Learning Objectives 1 and 2

1. The most important psychoanalytic technique is _____ ; it permits patients to dredge up the unconscious determinants of their behavior.

2. _____ is another way of reaching the unconscious.

3. _____ is an inevitable accompaniment of analysis and psychotherapy; it mobilizes diverse _____ designed to protect the patient from troubling memories.

4. _____ , by which patients distort the psychoanalyst's thoughts, feelings, and behavior to reflect those of parents and other important figures in their lives, is central to the _____ process.

ANSWERS

1. free association 2. Dream interpretation 3. Resistance; defense mechanisms 4. Transference; analytic

Psychoanalytic Psychotherapy

Psychoanalytic psychotherapy calls on many of the assumptions and techniques of psychoanalysis, but it is less intense and less demanding of patients. Furthermore, whereas psychoanalysis aims at nothing less than total self-understanding and complete personality reorganization, **psychoanalytic psychotherapy,** having more limited goals, *seeks to help patients come to terms with their environments and face their specific life problems.*

Psychotherapists are more active and more direct than psychoanalysts. They are less concerned with uncovering unconscious motivation and, since they reveal more of themselves in the process of therapy, are less apt to depend heavily on transference as a vehicle for behavior change. Whereas psychoanalytic sessions are typically held three to five days a week, psychoanalytic therapy generally takes place once a week. It is less intense, demanding, all-consuming, and involving than psychoanalysis; it is also a much more realistic treatment option for people who must continue to work full-time. One of the newest forms of psychoanalytic psychotherapy is time-limited psychotherapy, which is designed to achieve significant behavior change in a matter of six months with techniques that hasten transference and the mobilization of interpretable resistances (Malan, 1976; Mann, 1973).

GUIDED REVIEW

Learning Objective 3

1. _____ involves many of the same elements as _____ . It seeks to help patients come to terms with their _____ , though, rather than to bring about the total self-understanding that is the goal of psychoanalysis.

ANSWERS

1. Psychoanalytic psychotherapy; psychoanalysis; environments

Behavior Therapy

Behavior therapy is *a term that encompasses a number of methods designed to change maladaptive behavior directly* instead of searching for its deep-seated causes as the route to behavior change. Following are brief descriptions of some of these methods and procedures.

The Roots of Behavior Therapy

The potential of behavior therapy was completely unknown when, in the first decade of this century, the Russian physiologist Ivan Pavlov revolutionized the world of experimental psychology by showing that a dog will learn to salivate at the sound of a bell if that sound is first paired with food, a substance to which the dog naturally salivates (Pavlov, 1906). This form of learning—now known as classical conditioning—was augmented by the discovery of an American, Robert Thorndike, another one of psychology's early behavior theorists, that an animal can also learn if the consequences of its own learning are reinforcing; this form of learning is operant conditioning (Thorndike, 1931).

Both kinds of conditioning were eventually shown to be fundamental to learning by human beings, but it wasn't until midcentury that their capacity to modify maladaptive behavior was demonstrated. Today, behavior therapy is used in the United States not only in mental hospitals but also in schools, juvenile institutions, rehabilitation wards, prisons, day-care centers, community health centers and, some cynics contend, in movie theaters and every family's television room.

Systematic Desensitization, Relaxation Training, and Assertive Training

Systematic desensitization, *a behavior therapy procedure for dealing with distressing levels of anxiety,* derives from behavior therapist Joseph Wolpe's clinical observations (1952, 1958) that the anxiety disorders are learned patterns of responding that can also be unlearned. Wolpe's inspiration stemmed from the famous experiment by the early behavioral psychologist J. B. Watson and his associates (1920), reviewed earlier in this book.

Today, the behavior therapist who chooses to use systematic desensitization generally begins the process by teaching the patient deep muscle relaxation through **progressive relaxation training.** The therapist teaches the patient first to contract, then to relax, successively selected muscle groups. By the fourth or fifth session patients typically report that they can achieve states of relaxation accompanied by warmth, a sense of increased inner peace, and pleasant feelings of comfort and lassitude.

sertive training, *in which the patient and therapist role play situations that require assertive responses on the patient's part, responses that many people have trouble making, like disagreeing effectively with a boss or teacher or making a date.* Besides being an effective way to interact with the world, assertive behavior helps inhibit anxiety. It is difficult to be appropriately assertive and terribly anxious at the same time.

Refer to the Application Box: Do You Have an Assertiveness Problem? How many of the scenes typically elicit an assertive response from you? How many elicit either ineffective anger or resigned silence?

Desensitization begins after patient and therapist draw up a list of anxiety-producing situations arranged in order of their stress-inducing potential. The situations often include parents, spouses, friends, or employers, since these kinds of relationships are most often anxiety-producing. Once the list is drawn up, patients are asked to concentrate on the least threatening scene in the hierarchy and to describe it in as much detail as possible. If the relaxed patient can imagine the scene in detail for several seconds without experiencing the anxiety she experiences in real life, the therapist asks the patient to proceed to the next scene. When the patient does experience anxiety about a scene, she returns to the next lowest step.

Do You Have an Assertiveness Problem?

Do you have an assertiveness problem? When behavioral innovator Joseph Wolpe sets out to assess the assertiveness of a potential candidate for assertiveness training, he asks them to respond to the five imaginary situations given below. In how many of them would you be able to be properly assertive?

1. What do you do if after having bought an article in a shop you walk out and find that your change is a dollar short?
2. Suppose that, arriving home after buying an article you find it slightly damaged. What will you do?
3. What do you do if somebody pushes in front of you in line (e.g., at the theatre)?
4. At a shop, while you wait for the clerk to finish with the customer ahead of you, another customer arrives and also waits. What do you do if the clerk subsequently directs his attention to that customer instead of you?
5. You order a steak rare and it arrives well done. How do you handle the situation?

In all these situations, the individual ought to be able to stand up for himself, and is likely to feel upset when he does not. Insofar as he does not, assertive training is indicated. (Reprinted by permission from J. Wolpe, *The Practice of Behavior Theory,* 3rd Edition, p. 122. Copyright © 1982, Pergamon Press.)

It is common practice for behavior therapists to ask desensitization patients to "try out" less anxiety-arousing situations in the real world. When they can do so to situations that arouse only modest amounts of anxiety, they may be asked to move on to more anxiety-provoking real-world situations.

Positive Reinforcement and Extinction

Positive reinforcement and extinction, which typically *involve rewarding desirable behavior and failing to reward—or punishing—undesirable behavior,* respectively, are commonly used to confront psychotic behavior. Similar methods have been used to treat the anxiety disorders. Several years ago, for instance, researchers (Leitenberg, et al., 1968, 1976) at the Universities of Vermont and Mississippi focused successfully on **anorexia nervosa,** *an increasingly common eating disorder characterized by rapid, life-threatening weight loss associated with uncontrollable vomiting that has no apparent physical cause.* The therapists found that positive reinforcement for greater and greater food intake, combined with selective non-reinforcement of other symptoms of the disorder (like vomiting and other sympathy-inducing behaviors) increased food intake dramatically and eventually extinguished the vomiting.

The same group of behavior therapists also used positive reinforcement and extinction to treat **agoraphobia** (*fear of open spaces*) and **claustrophobia** (*fear of closed spaces*). Agoraphobic patients were asked to travel down a certain path from the medical center to downtown (Agras, et al., 1968). Each time a patient covered a bit more of the distance, he or she received graded positive reinforcement until the patient could maneuver the entire route. During intervals when either time or distance were reinforced, the agoraphobic patient walked farther and spent more time away from the hospital than when one or both were not reinforced.

The therapists also provided claustrophobic patients with the same kind of reinforcement, reporting that this treatment enabled these patients to spend more and more time alone in a small room that at first had made them scream in agony (Leitenberg, et al., 1968).

Observational Learning

One of the three basic modes of learning (see Chapter 5), observational learning has also been tried out clinically. In one of the most influential early efforts to use observational learning for therapeutic purposes, Bandura and his coworkers (Ross, et al., 1971) used modeling, along with what they called "guided participation," to modify a six-year-old boy's social withdrawal. The boy's social withdrawal had grown so severe that it had induced what was then called school phobia. During the early sessions of a seven-week treatment program, the child developed such a warm relationship with the therapist that he began to imitate the therapist's behavior. Patient and therapist then went to the boy's school, where the patient watched the therapist interacting with his classmates. Privately, the therapist used a technique called **role-playing,** in which *the therapist and the patient act out potentially more effective behaviors.* In this case, the therapist and the boy *acted out some of the social situations into which the boy might be drawn at school.* The therapist then began to include his patient in play situations with other six-year-olds at the school so that by the end of the seventh week, patient and therapist fully shared these interactions with the child's classmates. Two months later, a check revealed that the patient had continued to maintain improved social functioning and no fear with his peers.

It is now routine to use modeling procedures to teach more appropriate self-care and social skills to both isolated and withdrawn children (Conger and Keane, 1981) and mentally retarded children (Matson, Kazdin, and Esveldt-Dawson, 1980). An intriguing new behavior-shaping method that also calls on modeling is the use of peer models to demonstrate appropriate social and verbal behavior to severely disturbed autistic children. In a recent study in which four autistic children were being taught color and shape discriminations to encourage interest in their environment, using three normal children and a high-functioning autistic child as models for correct discrimination led to rapid increases in correct discrimination responding (Egel, Richman, and Koegel, 1981). These increases were much greater than those that followed modeling by adult teachers, who were the children's usual models.

Cognitive Behavior Therapy

Cognitive behavior therapy is a new development in behavior therapy. It recognizes the very important impact that thoughts, beliefs, expectations, and attitudes have on behavior. Through **cognitive behavior therapy,** *therapists change attitudes and expectations in order to change the behavior these cognitions influence.*

One of the most influential cognitive behavior therapy procedures was first developed by psychologist Donald Meichenbaum (1977). Called **self-instructional training,** *it aims to teach the use of self-instruction as an aid to more adequate behavior.*

Let us assume that your fear of elevators prevents you from using them to get to your Wednesday morning class, which is on the seventh floor of an academic building. If you were to present this problem to Donald Meichenbaum, he might well train you to say, first out loud, then to yourself, some or all of the following:

> I know that elevators are safe and that there is nothing to fear from using them. I must take this elevator to get to the seventh floor of this building, to attend class. I know how to relax and so do not have to become overwhelmed by anxiety during the ride. And, besides, a little nervous tension simply energizes me before I have to sit in class. The trick is to relax, think of the instructor I am going to listen to, then I'm there.

Although grossly oversimplified and condensed here, self-instructions of this kind are designed to interfere with the patient's self-defeating, destructive verbalizations and, in that way, to alter behavior that is maladaptive.

Behavioral Treatment of Psychotics

In 1959, psychologists Teodoro Ayllon and Jack Michael developed a series of simple behavior modification strategies to alter several typical psychotic behaviors by patients at a psychiatric hospital in Canada. Their efforts represented the first substantial use of behavioral techniques for therapeutic purposes with psychotic patients.

The basic behavioral approach was deceptively simple and surprisingly powerful: punishment of unwanted psychotic behaviors (two of the most powerful behavior-change techniques were withdrawal of food reinforcement and systematic withdrawal of attention) and reinforcement of nonpsychotic behavior (by providing edible "goodies" for and systematic increase in attention to the desired nonpsychotic behavior). Bizarre psychotic verbalizations and unnecessary, attention-getting, repetitive visits to the nursing station, for instance, decreased dramatically when no attention was given to them; assaultive behavior was eliminated by reinforcing behavior incompatible with it, like quiet conversation with nurses. As figures 13.1 and 13.2 show, food stealing (and the excessive weight gain that accompanied it) was eliminated when it led to immediate removal from the dining room.

It might seem incredible that psychotic behaviors could be controlled so readily by such simple manipulations, but behavior therapists quickly learned that many kinds of human behavior can be modified almost immediately by systematic and consistent manipulation of such powerful consequences of human behavior as verbal praise and punishment ("good," "bad"), nonverbal signs of approval or disapproval (a smile, a frown), or, as with Ayllon and Michael, selective inattention to unwanted behavior.

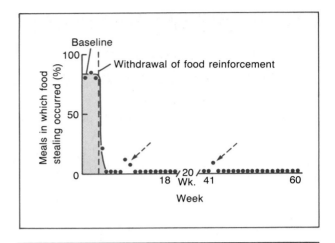

Figure 13.1   A response, food stealing, is eliminated when it results in the withdrawal of food reinforcement. The dotted arrows indicate the rare occasions when food stealing occurred. For purposes of presentation a segment comprising twenty weeks during which no stealing occurred is not included.

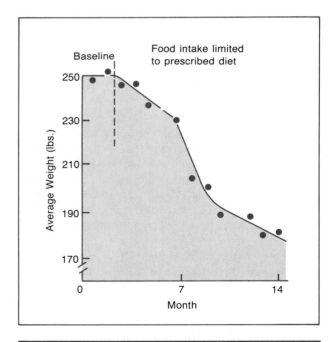

Figure 13.2   The effective control of food stealing results in a notable reduction in body weight. As the patient's food intake is limited to the prescribed diet, her weight decreases gradually.

A Comparison of Two Inpatient Treatments for Psychosis

In 1977 Gordon Paul and R. L. Lentz published their report on a six-year effort to develop behavioral assessment instruments for continuously recording the behavior of patients and staff on two inpatient units in a large Illinois state hospital. This represented a landmark in the effort to develop methods to compare the effectiveness of different treatment programs for inpatient psychotics.

The report documented the superiority of a social learning ward-based treatment program (based on the pioneering work of researchers like Teodoro Ayllon, Nathan Azrin, and Leonard Krasner) over traditional standard hospital and milieu (ward community) programs. All three programs were as comprehensive and well-run as possible, and all three program staffs were as thoroughly trained and as highly motivated as possible. Yet,

> . . . the overall comparative results on the relative effectiveness of the programs in the current project could not be clearer. The social-learning program was significantly more effective then either the milieu program or the traditional hospital programs. Its greater effectiveness was consistent across all classes of functioning in the intramural setting and in the production of institutional release . . . the social-learning program also maintained greater effectiveness over milieu and hospital programs in community stay. The improvement and releases within the social-learning program occurred . . . in the relative absence of psychotropic drugs. (Paul and Lentz, 1977, p. 432)

A number of these powerful behavior-change procedures were incorporated within the social learning treatment program that psychologist Gordon Paul and his colleagues tested at an Illinois state hospital in the mid-1970s. Some of their findings are discussed in the Research Box: A Comparison of Two Inpatient Treatments for Psychosis.

The Token Economy. Besides showing that many hitherto unmodifiable psychotic behaviors could be eliminated or reduced by simple behavior modification, Ayllon and Nathan Azrin (1965) advanced the concept further with another deceptively simple idea. They found that a **token economy** makes it possible to bring about desired behavioral changes more efficiently by employing tokens as rewards instead of direct praise or attention. The use of tokens, redeemable for material reinforcers like cigarettes and candy at the patient's discretion, made particularly good sense with schizophrenics because these patients often have trouble with verbal and social reinforcers. Furthermore, giving patients the responsibility for "spending" their tokens wisely in the token economy allowed them a sense of greater control over their lives than many of them had experienced for years. Patients became directly and explicitly responsible for their own rewards, and they loved it.

The success of the first token economy inspired other psychologists to experiment with more sophisticated systems. John Atthowe and Leonard Krasner, for instance, structured an ingenious system at a Veterans Administration Hospital in California. Tokens were given in return for specific desired behaviors and withheld when undesired behaviors were continued, but they were also handed out in extra quantities to those who performed more complex behavior and operated in more specialized ways (1968).

A patient whom we knew well lived for a time on a token economy ward in a large state hospital. She recalled the experience with pleasure: "The ward was much cleaner because patients were willing to keep it

---

Table 13.1 Common irrational ideas that cause us trouble

Albert Ellis, founder of rational-emotive therapy, believes that many of us get into emotional difficulty because we behave according to one or more irrational ideas about life and our pursuit of it. How many of the following irrational ideas do *you* live by? If you identify one or more self-defeating ideas specific to your way of life in this list of twelve, can you ever imagine yourself living by a more rational life schema?

1. It is a *dire* necessity to be loved and approved of.
2. I *should* be *thoroughly* competent, adequate and achieving in *all* possible respects.
3. Some people *are* bad, wicked or vile and *should* (or *must*) be punished.
4. If things do not go (or stay) the way I very much want them to, it would be *awful, catastrophic,* or *terrible!*
5. Unhappiness is *externally* caused and I *cannot* control it (unless I control the other person).
6. One *should* remain upset or worried if faced with a dangerous or fearsome reality.
7. It is *easier* to avoid responsibility and difficulties than to face them.
8. I have a *right* to be dependent and people (or someone) *should* be strong enough to rely on (or take care of me).
9. My early childhood experiences *must* continue to *control* me and determine my emotions and behavior!
10. I *should* become upset over my and other peoples' problems or behavior.
11. There is invariably *one* right, precise, and *perfect* solution and it would be *terrible* or *catastrophic* if this perfect solution is not found.
12. The world (and especially other people) *should* be fair and justice (or mercy) *must* triumph. (From Albert Ellis's books)

---

clean because they could earn tokens that way. And there was less noise because people took more pride in the place. And I did love being able to have candy and gum whenever I wanted—if I had the tokens to pay for them!"

Encouraged by the initial success of these token economy systems, clinicians and researchers have extended the reach of behavior modification programs in mental hospitals far beyond anything imaginable even as recently as ten years ago. Token economies have also begun to extend far beyond the wards of mental hospitals. They have been employed in public school classrooms to accelerate learning by normal children. Retarded children have also benefited because token systems make them more motivated and attentive. Similar results have been obtained in state institutions for juvenile delinquents where investigators report that they have been able, through token reinforcement, to channel hostile behavior into socially desirable behavior (Baer, 1982; Krasner, 1982).

Rational-Emotive Therapy

Rational-emotive therapy, developed by psychologist Albert Ellis (1962, 1973), *aims, above all, to help patients identify and challenge the irrational, self-defeating beliefs behind their troublesome behavior in order that they might take action to restore rational control over their emotions.* Rational-emotive therapists assume that most people are able to substitute reason for emotion in planning their own behavior as well as in changing it when it needs changing. The assumption is that the patient can learn how self-defeating such erroneous underlying beliefs as "I must be a perfect father, husband, and son to be a success in life" or "Everyone must love me or I am a social misfit" or "I must be at the top of my class or else I shouldn't be in college" are as guiding assumptions in life.

Can you think of any guiding assumptions in *your* life that are self-defeating? How many of those listed in table 13.1 do *you* live by?

GUIDED REVIEW

Learning Objectives 4, 5, and 6

1. _____ aims at direct change of learned maladaptive behavior.

2. _____ stems from Joseph Wolpe's conviction that bad habits, including neuroses, can be unlearned by inhibiting the anxiety that is often associated with them.

3. Along with_____ and_____ conditioning, _____ learning is a principal means by which maladaptive behavior is learned and, accordingly, can be unlearned.

4. _____ with psychotics and others requires the systematic and consistent manipulation of behavior with verbal praise and punishment, nonverbal signs of approval or disapproval, and selective attention.

5. Token economies substitute_____ reinforcers— tokens good for candy, cigarettes, and other reinforcers—for verbal reinforcement delivered by professional personnel.

ANSWERS

1. Behavior therapy 2. Systematic desensitization 3. classical, operant; observational 4. Behavior modification 5. material

Client-Centered Therapy

The first distinctly nonanalytic "talking therapy," client-centered therapy has been under continuous development by psychologist Carl Rogers and his colleagues since the 1940s (Rogers, 1961; Wexler and Rice, 1974). Today it is used mainly by counselors to deal with students' vocational and academic problems, since it appears most effective with persons faced with normal life problems rather than serious psychopathology.

Client-centered therapy *is based on the premise that people can solve their own problems if they can be helped to confront their own fears and self-deceptions and come to grips with what troubles them.* If you're not seriously disturbed and you haven't experienced a marked disruption in your daily routine, but are dissatisfied with your life and your capacity to honestly and completely own up to your own shortcomings, client-centered therapy may be for you.

According to Rogers, the troubled individual experiences conflicts between self-image and the objective facts. The function of the counselor, in his view, is to facilitate the client's resolution of these conflicts by contributing to a warm, human relationship. Rogers's belief that the client must take responsibility for his or her own treatment—and his conviction, accordingly, that the counselor must not assume control over the course of therapy—have led to another term of reference for client-centered therapy: nondirective therapy.

Client-centered therapy is based on the following core beliefs; all of them figure importantly in Rogers's theory of personality (see Chapter 11).

1. Therapy progresses best when the therapist and client share feelings of respect and affection for each other.
2. The client benefits most by passing from intellectual confrontation to an emotional sharing relationship.
3. Significant progress along the way is signalled when the client begins to be less self-condemning and defensive.
4. One of the counselor's prime functions is to convey genuine, empathic, and nonpossessive warmth and human concern—unconditional positive regard—for his or her clients.

In other words, the client-centered therapist encourages clients to talk freely about their problems and, without attempting to change their minds or to blame or criticize them, helps bring them to accept as genuine and worthwhile their feelings about themselves and others, whatever they are.

Learning Objective 7

1. Rogers's _____ is based on an emotional sharing relationship between client and therapist.

2. The counselor's job is to convey_____ for his/her clients.

ANSWERS

1. client-centered therapy 2. unconditional positive regard

Group Treatment Methods

All treatment methods discussed so far have focused on one therapist working with one patient. During recent years many therapists have concluded that there is value in seeing people in groups. Two of the methods, group therapy and family therapy, emphasize the therapeutic value of groups for troubled individuals. The third method, encounter groups, is designed for healthy people who are functioning normally but want to improve their capacity for living a full emotional life.

Group Therapy

Although the "active ingredients" of group therapy are not known for certain, the loneliness and isolation of many in our society are undoubtedly lessened in a group setting. In group therapy people come closer to one another; they learn the truth that misery loves company, the shared realization that their troubles are not unique to them. They also provide valuable insights to one another. After participating in a group long enough to learn its "rules" and the agreed-upon interpersonal relationships appropriate to it, group members are often surprisingly perceptive in their observations of their peers—surprisingly on target in their interpretations and the nature of their feedback. It is almost as though the therapist has several "cotherapists" helping each other achieve the kind of insight that takes so long to achieve in individual therapy. An additional benefit of

group therapy is that it gives patients the opportunity to "try out" socialization skills within an accepting, often nonjudgmental, framework before using them outside the group (Lubin, 1983; Rose and LeCroy, 1983).

For many years, both group and individual therapy was undertaken almost entirely from the psychoanalytic perspective; more recently, other approaches to group therapy, including Gestalt methods, have been proposed.

Patients in psychoanalytic group therapy are encouraged to share dreams, fantasies, and memories from the past in the group session so they can be interpreted and better understood, transference phenomena (both among group members and with the group therapist) are interpreted, as are resistances to therapy. The aim of psychoanalytic group therapy, like psychoanalysis and psychoanalytic psychotherapy, is to enable the individual to deal with life's realistic problems and challenges free from the psychological residuals of unresolved difficulties from the past.

Developed largely by Frederick (Fritz) Perls (1969), whose own early training was in psychoanalysis, **Gestalt therapy** *is a group therapy designed to provide a group experience in attending to immediate feelings and impulses and expressing and acting upon them.* Perls emphasized the importance of living in the here and now rather than either in the past or the future.

Gestalt therapy stems indirectly from the Gestalt psychology tradition, which teaches the necessity of attending both to a figure or foreground (the part of the environment to which we are currently attending), as well as to the background against which the figure is seen. In the Gestalt group, the group members try to help each other experience as fully as possible their feelings toward currently experienced problems and concerns—but not by excluding from current experience the emotional background within which they place the current distress.

A controversial approach to therapy because it deviates so markedly from more traditional individual and group therapy procedures, Gestalt therapy remains without strong empirical support. However, numerous adherents argue that it works where other more conventional therapies do not. The Gestalt philosophy and the model that Gestalt group therapy espouses is exemplified by the following quotation from Perls (1969):

> I do my thing, and you do your thing.
> I am not in this world to live up to your expectations.
> And you are not in this world to live up to mine.
> You are you and I am I,
> And if by chance we find each other, it's beautiful.
> If not, it can't be helped. (Perls, 1969, p. 4. © 1969 Real People Press. All Rights Reserved. Reprinted by permission.)

Family Therapy

Family therapy has grown considerably during the past decade (Gurman and Kniskern, 1981; Minuchin, 1978; Palazzoli–Selvini, et al., 1978). This growth began after psychologists and psychiatrists observed that it was extremely difficult to translate therapeutic gains made by a troubled child in the consulting room into equivalent gains at home. For instance, a child might learn to understand and control aggressive impulses in therapy, but he or she might blow up at the slightest provocation at home. When the therapist saw the child with his or her parents, the gains tended to last longer and to persist beyond the walls of the consulting room. We might suppose that one reason family therapy works in this way is that it permits all members of the family—parents and children alike—to "try out" new responses in the precise family setting in which they are to be maintained. In so doing, they can practice the new behavior in the presence of the parents, siblings, and children, in whose presence they can expect to be reinforced— or punished—at home.

Family therapy *allows both the therapist and patients (the entire family) to observe and deal with the complex set of interactions that precipitates and maintains the child's maladaptive behavior.* It does little good to help an aggressive child reduce the tendency to strike out in anger at every adult unless a parent (originally involved in the development of that behavior, perhaps even responsible for it) is also helped at the same time to understand the reasons why his or her own behavior precipitates this behavior in the child.

Figure 13.3 An encounter group

Encounter Groups

Members of encounter groups who meet as strangers are supposed to let down their inhibitions and defenses, touch each other (emotionally and, sometimes, physically), and tell what they like and what they don't like about one another (fig. 13.3). Why do they do it? Psychologists suggest that it is the great need of our times— to find someone to talk to, someone who cares, responds, and can help one be a fuller person. Although encounter groups experienced their greatest growth during the tumultuous early 1970s, when their unorthodoxy appealed to a society bent on rejecting everything from the past, they remain a component of current psychological practice.

Encounter groups continue to be organized, in part, because they may have advantages over both individual and group therapy. *In the* **encounter group,** *an individual can freely express both negative and positive feelings toward other group members and, at the same time, exchange understanding or emotion that might not be possible under life's normal rules of interpersonal behavior.*

The ever-present danger in encounter groups is that they may be conducted by untrained or poorly trained individuals who cannot or will not screen disturbed patients out of the group or who will permit the group to become punitive or accusatory in ways that could cause harm to group members whose adjustment is marginal.

The following excerpt from the sixth (of ten) meetings of a client-centered encounter group illustrates some of the group interaction one might expect to observe in such a setting:

> *Jack:* I've just been going through my mind a couple of thoughts about Nancy and Brian and I thought about some other things . . . About Barry's trip—the time he was attacking both of you . . . and I've worried that if I come out now and said that, you're obviously going to immediately react . . . (to Brian): I feel bad about you

because you seem—I see you giving almost as a game. I can see you, like you give to people *and that is the way of getting something back.* Giving to get. And I'm sure that envy enters into it somewhat . . . *Brian:* I think that—I have a problem taking things for myself but I resent you saying that I'm too smooth—that pisses me off. I don't know what I have together . . . I feel I have a lot of stuff to give. And I feel good about it. It helps me get through a lot of shit. (Bebout, 1974, pp. 385–386)

Though dangerous if not monitored carefully by an experienced and ethical group leader who will ensure that group members do not overwhelm each other with emotional burdens too heavy to carry, feedback like the kind Brian and Jack exchange in this excerpt, especially when conveyed with human concern, empathy, and warmth, can be quite constructive and helpful.

GUIDED REVIEW

Learning Objective 8

1. _____ enables many patients to experience a lessening of the loneliness and isolation of our society.

2. _____ developed from the widespread frustration of child therapists at the difficulty in translating therapeutic gains made by a troubled child in the consulting room into equivalent gains at home.

3. _____ are designed to help people who are functioning normally to get more from their lives by helping them become more open to new experiences.

ANSWERS

1. Group therapy 2. Family therapy 3. Encounter groups

The Somatic Therapies

Some forms of mental disorder, particularly those involving psychosis, must be treated by physical or somatic treatment methods. **Somatic treatment** methods *modify behavior by altering brain functions,* either temporarily or permanently. Sometimes these methods are used alone, but often they are used along with psychotherapy or behavior therapy.

Psychosurgery

In the 1930s and 1940s, before the discovery of the major tranquilizers, uncontrollably violent psychotic patients who were constant dangers to themselves or others were often referred for psychosurgery. This surgery took several forms, but the most common, called **prefrontal lobotomy,** involved *surgical destruction of the neural pathways from portions of the frontal lobes to the rest of the brain.*

Although patients receiving this surgery typically showed marked reductions in violence and anger, they also commonly suffered from serious, irreversible side effects. These included a loss in intellectual abilities, a reduction in emotional responsiveness, or both. As a result, when the major tranquilizers were discovered to be effective in alleviating many of the symptoms of major psychiatric disorder, psychosurgery was no longer used. However, some psychosurgeons continue to employ the surgery to control severe obsessions, compulsions, depression, and violent behavior when they cannot be treated effectively by other means.

Always a controversial treatment method, some clinicians still consider psychosurgery to represent a destructive treatment, and one that is used only as a last resort.

Electroconvulsive Therapy

Psychotic patients are sometimes given **electroconvulsive therapy** (**ECT**), *in which a brief electrical current is passed across the brain.* In the past, the shock was delivered with sufficient intensity to induce a grand mal seizure and unconsciousness. Today, following research indicating that a grand mal seizure is not necessary for good clinical results, the level of shock given to patients is less intense and rarely induces a grand mal seizure.

Once widely used for patients in almost every psychotic state, *ECT is now reserved almost entirely for sufferers from affective disorders, particularly those who have become psychotically depressed, uncontrollably agitated, or suicidal.* Enough empirical research on ECT has been done to justify the belief that it alleviates serious depressive conditions more quickly than any other treatment, including psychotherapy and antidepressant drug therapy (Avery and Winokur, 1978). On the other hand, additional data suggest that psychotic depressions terminated by ECT are apt to recur within a shorter period of time than depressions that end on their own.

ECT is almost as controversial a treatment as psychosurgery. Like psychosurgery, it is a "radical" treatment that has, at least in the past, been somewhat dangerous. And, again like psychosurgery, ECT had irreversible side effects, including broken bones from the

induced grand mal seizure and a loss in intellectual abilities from destruction of brain tissue. Current ECT methods, involving less intense electrical stimulation and fewer ECT treatments, rarely yield side effects that last beyond an hour or two.

ECT differs from psychosurgery in that substantial empirical data has been reported justifying its use in conditions that have failed to respond to other, less drastic treatments.

Drug Therapy

If there has been a revolution in the field of mental health, it can truly be credited to the development during the 1950s of drugs to treat schizophrenia, which had been largely untreated to that time. Drug therapy (also called chemotherapy) has made it possible to treat acute schizophrenia and to calm other psychotic patients so they are able to benefit from other forms of therapy.

The drugs now in widest use fall into four distinct categories (Davis and Greenblatt, 1979; Kessler and Waletzky, 1981). The **major tranquilizers** *are used most often to treat psychotic patients whose behavior is seriously disturbed.* The **minor tranquilizers** *are designed for patients suffering from disorders involving moderate anxiety.* The **antidepressant drugs** *are used to ease the pain and suffering of moderate and severe depression,* and **lithium carbonate** *is used to treat mania and decrease the likelihood of depression in bipolar affective disorder.* A summary of these families of drugs is provided in table 13.2.

The major tranquilizers include the large family of **phenothiazine** drugs. *The phenothiazines dramatically reduce the delusions, hallucinations, and violent behavior of many schizophrenic patients* and, in so doing, permit them to benefit from "talking" or activity therapies, which may hasten their return to society. As a result, the chaos and bedlam of hospital "back wards" is lessened, and patients who must continue to be institutionalized have a chance for a more serene life

---

Table 13.2 Drugs used to treat mental disorders

Major tranquilizers: Treatment for schizophrenia. (Decrease psychotic thinking, suspiciousness, perplexity, normalize psychomotor behavior, and lessen the impact of hallucinations and delusions.)
Examples: Chlorpromazine (Thorazine); Perphenazine (Trilafon); Haloperidol (Haldol).
Caution: Side effects can be formidable and irreversible.

Minor tranquilizers: Treatment for anxiety. (Cause sedation, reduce anxiety, may enhance mood and increase vigor.)
Examples: Chlordiazepoxide (Librium); Diazepam (Valium); Meprobamate (Equinil, Miltown).
Caution: These drugs are dependency inducing and may cause life-threatening withdrawal symptoms.

Antidepressant drugs: Treatment for moderate to severe depression. (Produce slight sedation, a lessening of depression, an increase in motor activity, and an increase in optimism for the future.)
Examples: Imipramine (Tofranil); Doxepin (Sinequan); Tranylcypromine (Parnate).
Caution: Imipramine and Doxepin and the other tricyclic antidepressants can cause dry mouth, rapid heart beat, and other autonomic effects; Tranylcypromine and the other MAO inhibitors can also precipitate manic or hypomanic episodes as well as, very rarely, dramatically increased blood pressure.

Lithium carbonate: A naturally occurring compound that reduces the intensity of manic episodes in bipolar affective disorder and may also reduce the likelihood that a period of depression will follow the mania.
Caution: The difference in a therapeutic and a toxic dose of lithium carbonate is small, so careful monitoring of blood levels of lithium are necessary as long as the patient is taking the drug.

---

during the period of their hospitalization. The same drugs, unfortunately, have also been given in massive quantities to sedate patients, without regard for their welfare, in order to make caring for them easier. Some of the patients treated in this way with these drugs have suffered from serious, irreversible side effects (see table 13.2).

The minor tranquilizers, including **Librium** and **Valium,** *enable moderately anxious patients to deal more effectively with normal life stresses.* Whereas many of the patients treated with these drugs carry the diagnostic label of anxiety or dysthymic disorder, the minor tranquilizers are also used successfully to help essentially healthy individuals deal with extraordinary tensions in their lives. Unfortunately, these drugs have also been subject to abuse since they are both addictive and capable of inducing desirable "highs."

Antidepressant drugs, including the tricyclic antidepressants, are effective in lessening the feelings of foreboding, worthlessness, and hopelessness that may overwhelm a depressed person. In general, seriously depressed patients are first given a trial of antidepressant drugs before ECT, a less conservative and more controversial treatment, is considered.

Many bipolar affective disorders are responsive to **lithium carbonate,** *a naturally occurring compound. The drug can terminate manic episodes and also appears to increase the interval between mania and depression in bipolar affective disorder.*

GUIDED REVIEW

Learning Objective 9

1. _____ , used to treat uncontrollable psychotic behavior, is now used rarely because drugs as effective as it can be utilized for the same purpose.

2. _____ is a widely used treatment for severe depression that is unresponsive to antidepressant medication.

3. The _____ tranquilizers, including the _____ , are effective in reducing the delusions, hallucinations, and violent behavior of some schizophrenic patients.

4. The _____ tranquilizers, including _____ and _____ , enable moderately anxious patients to deal more effectively with normal life stresses.

5. _____ drugs, including the _____ antidepressants, are effective in reducing some of the most distressing symptoms of depression.

6. _____ terminates _____ episodes and reduces the likelihood of depression in bipolar affective disorders.

7. The _____ therapies, including the phenothiazine drugs for schizophrenia, ECT for the serious psychotic depressions, and lithium carbonate for mania, are almost certainly the _____ effective treatments for these conditions.

ANSWERS

6. *Lithium carbonate; manic 7. somatic; most*
phenothiazines 4. minor; Librium; Valium 5. Antidepressant; tricyclic
1. Psychosurgery 2. Electroconvulsive therapy (ECT) 3. major;

What Treatment for Which Disorder?

At this point it is fair to ask, How do the different treatment methods we have described compare in effectiveness?

A single answer to this all-important question is impossible because of the profound measurement difficulties posed by outcome research of this kind. Among these difficulties are diagnostic unreliability (patients in a single diagnostic group may not actually demonstrate the same symptomatology), problems of treatment standardization (all patients in a single treatment group may not actually receive the same treatment in the same intensity), and lack of agreement on what constitutes treatment effectiveness (Luborsky, et al., 1971). Nonetheless, we will review some comparative treatment outcome studies to put into perspective what is and is not known about the outcome of treatment for the emotional disorders.

One of the few conclusions on which almost everyone agrees is that psychotherapy alone is clearly less effective in modifying the behavior of schizophrenic patients than are the major tranquilizers alone (Grinspoon, et al., 1968). Psychotherapy may help the patient achieve some insight into some of the causes of his or her psychosis, but it is the phenothiazines that enable the schizophrenic patient to achieve enough control over the psychotic symptoms to return to greater or lesser adjustment to the world. Most clinicians also agree that electroconvulsive therapy is often the most effective treatment for severe, intractable, life-threatening depressions (Avery and Winokur, 1978) and that lithium carbonate is the most effective treatment for mania (Quitkin, 1978).

What is not known and, for that reason, continues to be debated is how effective psychotherapy, psychoanalysis, behavior therapy, the other "talking therapies," and the minor tranquilizers are in treating the psychological disorders that do not involve psychosis. Answers to this question would be an inestimable boon to patients and therapists alike.

Controversy over the merits of psychotherapy began in 1952, shortly after the publication of a review of the effects of psychotherapy for anxiety and moderate depression, the most common reasons psychotherapy is sought. The review, written by Hans Eysenck, an influential English psychologist, was followed by similar reviews by Eysenck in 1960 and 1965 that made essentially the same point. In all reviews, Eysenck restricted his use of the word psychotherapy to the techniques and procedures of psychoanalytic psychotherapy. Eysenck's conclusion was that "there appears to be an inverse correlation between recovery and psychotherapy; the more psychotherapy, the smaller the recovery rate" (1952, p. 324). In other words, Eysenck claimed that psychotherapy makes patients worse. He bolstered his argument by citing data that the spontaneous remission rate for these disorders (the proportion of patients who shed these symptoms without therapy), is about the same as the rate for those helped by psychotherapy: roughly one out of three.

Though other researchers responding to Eysenck's reviews pointed out shortcomings in his logic, statistics, and objectivity, no one has yet been able to prove convincingly that psychotherapy or psychoanalysis have more than a moderately positive effect on the behavior of anxious and depressed patients (Imber, et al., 1983).

Much of the reason for this failure to confirm what many psychotherapists and their patients firmly believe is the nature of the proof: therapeutic benefit from psychotherapy and psychoanalysis, these advocates of psychotherapy say, simply cannot be measured reliably because it is impossible to quantify the global changes in functioning that result.

Controlled comparisons of psychotherapy versus drugs for the treatment of these disorders have been few. One of the best of these studies (Koegler and Brill, 1967) concluded that neither treatment is terribly effective, though one minor tranquilizer did seem to the patients themselves to be most effective. Studies of drugs in combination with psychotherapy are similarly unimpressive. As a result, conscientious students of the field disagree on whether drugs and psychotherapy are preferable to either alone in treating anxiety and depression that do not involve psychosis.

The best designed, best-controlled comparative study of psychotherapy and behavior therapy (Sloane, et al., 1975) suggests that behavior therapy may work faster than and be as effective as psychotherapy with symptoms like anxiety, phobias, and obsessive-compulsive behavior. The comparative longevity of these improvements remains in question, however, in view of the widespread belief that psychotherapy and psychoanalysis exert their unique impact long-term.

GUIDED REVIEW

Learning Objective 9

1. While _____ and _____ appear to exert a positive impact on the behavior of patients experiencing moderate but troublesome anxiety and depression, the extent and longevity of this improvement remains in question.

2. _____ seems to work as effectively—and more rapidly—on certain symptomatic behaviors than psychotherapy. Whether the greater speed of its effect results in greater or lesser maintenance of that effect, however, is not yet known.

ANSWERS
1. psychotherapy, psychoanalysis 2. Behavior therapy

Prevention and Community Psychology

In an office in Los Angeles the phone rings. "I'm going to kill myself," the voice says tensely. "I'm sitting here with a loaded gun." The person at the other end has heard such cries for help many times before. She knows the call may give her a chance to prevent a suicide attempt, but she can't be sure. Her voice calm, she says, "Why don't you tell me what happened. Why do you want to take your life?"

As the would-be suicide, sensing a friend, pours out his troubles, his fears, his utter desperation, the woman listening at the other end of the line has already gestured to a colleague to trace the call. In moments, while the caller is still talking in a voice sometimes troubled, sometimes deliberate, an unmarked police car is on its way to the scene, where the police hope to intervene.

Suicide prevention is a particularly dramatic example of community mobilization to abort a crisis. Ever since the end of World War II, when it was discovered that mental disease affects perhaps two out of seven people in the United States, large and small communities have directed efforts at preventive methods to help stop the rise of psychopathology. At first these efforts were undertaken largely by social workers, but in recent years community psychologists and psychiatrists have begun to develop programs to control the biological, interpersonal, and social factors that jeopardize mental health.

Psychiatrist Gerald Caplan, considered by many to be the father of the community mental health movement in the United States, believes that prevention operates on three levels, which he calls primary, secondary, and tertiary.

Primary Prevention

The essence of **primary prevention** is *the use of resources in the community to establish an environment more likely to nourish mental health and prevent the development of serious psychopathology.* For example, effective mental health consultants—specially trained psychologists, psychiatrists, social workers, and psychiatric nurses—working on this level may advise school systems on how to facilitate race relations among students and faculty. They may work with the police to help them present a more positive image of their functions to the citizens they serve. They may consult with city government to enable it to be more responsive to the needs of the people. Or they might help establish health education, preschool and old-age programs, and genetic counseling (to alert parents-to-be to potential birth defects) through existing community health centers.

In all cases the intent of primary prevention is to mobilize existing community resources to create an environment that heads off problems and conflicts and stimulates constructive growth.

Secondary Prevention

Secondary prevention *involves early detection of persons or institutions that have begun to exhibit preliminary signs of psychopathology.* The goal of prevention at this level is to minimize the harmful effects of the potential psychopathology on those who demonstrate it and on those with whom they come in contact. Marital counseling, family therapy, vocational guidance, crisis intervention, "hot lines" that bring help to youths troubled by drug abuse, and vocational guidance are examples of efforts to deal with problems before they become so disruptive of personal functioning that they cause serious difficulties in the community.

Tertiary Prevention

Tertiary prevention is the most expensive and least effective form of prevention. *It provides treatment for individuals who have actually developed psychopathology that is serious enough to cause disruption of functioning.* Psychotherapy, somatic therapy, or behavior therapy are forms of intervention that not only aim at modifying existing psychopathology but at preventing its further development. The aim of community psychology and psychiatry is largely to reduce as much as possible the need for tertiary prevention.

GUIDED REVIEW

Learning Objective 10

1. _____ aims to use the community to nourish mental health and prevent development of mental illness.

2. _____ involves early detection and treatment of persons who show early signs of mental disorder.

3. _____ provides treatment for individuals who have developed mental disorder. It is the most expensive and least effective form of prevention.

ANSWERS
1. Primary prevention 2. Secondary prevention 3. Tertiary prevention

SUMMARY

I. Psychoanalysis is the set of treatment procedures developed by Sigmund Freud. (p. 444)

A. Free association is the most important psychoanalytic technique because it enables the patient to recall unconscious determinants of behavior. (p. 444)

B. Resistance virtually always accompanies the psychoanalytic process as well as psychotherapy. It is caused by the erection of various defense mechanisms designed to protect the patient's ego from disturbing memories. (p. 445)

C. Transference is the means by which patients distort their perception of the psychoanalyst; this distortion is frequently a function of the patient's own experience with parents and other important figures in their early lives. (p. 445)

D. Interpretation brings the transference to the patient's attention and, it is hoped, to his or her understanding. (p. 445)

II. Psychoanalytic psychotherapy helps patients come to terms with their environments, rather than to bring about the total self-understanding that is the goal of psychoanalysis.   (p. 446)

III. Behavior therapy is designed to directly change learned maladaptive behavior.   (p. 447)

    A. Systematic desensitization is a behavior therapy technique developed by Wolpe that is designed to inhibit the anxiety that is often associated with bad habits.   (p. 447)

    B. Classical and operant conditioning and observational learning, which are basic mechanisms of learning, are all thought by social learning theorists to play a role in the development of both adaptive and maladaptive behavior.   (pp. 448–50)

    C. The systematic, consistent manipulation of behavior with verbal praise and punishment, nonverbal signs of approval or disapproval, and selective attention are all behavior modification techniques. They are most useful for the modification of psychotic and other behavior.   (pp. 450–51)

    D. Token economies involve the substitution of tangible or material reinforcers (for example, tokens that can be exchanged for candy, cigarettes, and other rewards) for verbal reinforcement given by professional personnel.   (pp. 451–52)

IV. Client-centered therapy is a nonanalytic therapy developed by psychologist Carl Rogers.   (p. 453)

    A. Client-centered therapy is based on an emotional sharing relationship between client and counselor.   (p. 453)

    B. The counselor's most important task in client-centered therapy is to demonstrate unconditional positive regard for his/her client.   (p. 455)

V. Group treatment methods help some patients lessen the loneliness and isolation they feel in our society.   (p. 454)

    A. Family therapy, a group treatment method, is designed to help the family understand its role in the disordered behavior of one or more of its members.   (p. 455)

    B. Encounter groups bring essentially normally functioning people into a group setting, where they can learn how to become more open to new emotional experiences.   (pp. 455–56)

VI. The somatic therapies change behavior by altering brain functioning.   (p. 456)

    A. Psychosurgery is employed only rarely today, generally to treat uncontrollable psychotic behavior.   (pp. 456–57)

    B. Electroconvulsive therapy (ECT) is widely used for severe depressions that do not respond to antidepressant medication.   (p. 457)

    C. The major tranquilizers, consisting primarily of the phenothiazines, are used to lessen the intensity of the hallucinations and delusions of schizophrenia.   (p. 457)

    D. Librium and Valium, which are minor tranquilizers, are effective in enabling moderately anxious patients to deal more competently with normal stresses in life.   (p. 458)

    E. The tricyclic antidepressants are designed to lessen the intensity of mild to moderate depression.   (p. 458)

    F. Lithium carbonate terminates manic episodes and decreases the likelihood of progression to depression in bipolar affective disorder.   (p. 458)

VII. The long-term effectiveness of psychoanalysis, psychotherapy, and behavior therapy remains essentially unproven.   (pp. 459–60)

VIII. Prevention is generally considered more cost-effective than treatment.   (p. 460)

    A. Primary prevention helps communities nourish the mental health of their citizens and thus prevent the development of mental illness.   (pp. 460–61)

    B. The early detection and treatment of persons showing signs of early mental disorder is called secondary prevention.   (p. 461)

    C. Least cost-effective and most expensive is tertiary prevention, in which individuals who have developed mental disorders receive treatment.   (p. 461)

ACTION GLOSSARY

Match the terms in the left column with the definitions in the right column.

___ 1. Psychoanalysis (p. 444)
___ 2. Free association (p. 444)
___ 3. Dreams (p. 445)
___ 4. Resistance (p. 445)
___ 5. Transference (p. 445)
___ 6. Interpretation (p. 445)
___ 7. Psychoanalytic psychotherapy (p. 446)
___ 8. Behavior therapy (p. 447)

A. According to Freud, symbolic representations of unconscious conflicts rearoused by the previous day's activities and events.
B. The means by which transference phenomena and other resistances are brought to the patient's attention.
C. A term that encompasses a number of methods designed to change maladaptive behavior directly.
D. A therapy that seeks to help patients come to terms with their environments and face their specific life problems.
E. The personality theory and related therapeutic approach designed by Sigmund Freud. The therapist attempts to help the patient to uncover repressed feelings so they can be faced and dealt with by the conscious mind.
F. A psychoanalytic technique in which the stream of one's thoughts are unburdened or "talked out."
G. A phenomenon common to most psychotherapy whereby the patient tends to attribute to the therapist many of the thoughts, feelings, and behaviors that actually belong to other important persons in his/her life.
H. A phase of therapy in which the patients find areas in which they feel blocked; they cannot talk anymore; they find it difficult to recollect crucial events from the past; they start forgetting appointments.

___ 9. Systematic desensitization (p. 447)
___ 10. Progressive relaxation training (p. 447)
___ 11. Assertive training (p. 447)
___ 12. Positive reinforcement (p. 448)
___ 13. Extinction (p. 448)
___ 14. Anorexia nervosa (p. 448)
___ 15. Agoraphobia (p. 448)
___ 16. Claustrophobia (p. 448)

A. A technique of behavior therapy that involves rewarding desirable behavior.
B. A behavior therapy technique in which the patient and the therapist role play situations that require assertive responses that many people have trouble making.
C. A behavior therapy procedure for dealing with distressing levels of anxiety.
D. Training in relaxation helps patients deal more effectively with anxiety.
E. Fear of closed places.
F. A technique of behavior therapy that involves not rewarding, or punishing, undesirable behavior.
G. Fear of open spaces.
H. An eating disorder characterized by rapid, life-threatening weight loss associated with uncontrollable vomiting that has no apparent physical cause.

___ 17. Role playing (p. 449)
___ 18. Cognitive behavior therapy (p. 449)
___ 19. Self-instructional training (p. 449)
___ 20. Token economy (p. 451)
___ 21. Rational-emotive therapy (p. 452)
___ 22. Client-centered therapy (p. 453)
___ 23. Gestalt therapy (p. 454)
___ 24. Family therapy (p. 455)

A. A therapeutic method developed by Albert Ellis. Aims to help patients identify the irrational, self-defeating beliefs behind their troublesome behavior in order that they might take action to restore rational control over their emotions.
B. A group therapy approach, developed by Frederick Perls, that was designed to provide a group experience in attending to immediate feelings and impulses and expressing and acting upon them.
C. A behavior modification approach that makes it possible to bring about desired behavioral changes more efficiently by employing material rewards rather than direct praise or attention.
D. A technique of behavior therapy that aims to teach the use of self-instruction as an aid to more adequate behavior.
E. An approach to behavior therapy through which the therapist changes the patient's attitudes and expectations in order to change the behaviors influenced by them.
F. Developed by psychologist Carl Rogers, this treatment is based on the premise that people can solve their own problems if they can be helped to confront their own fears and self-deceptions and come to grips with what troubles them.
G. A group therapy approach in which both the therapist and the patient are allowed to observe and deal with the complex set of interactions that precipitates and maintains a child's maladaptive behavior.
H. A behavior therapy method in which the therapist and the patient act out potentially more effective behavior.

___ **25. Encounter group (p. 455)**
___ **26. Somatic therapy (p. 456)**
___ **27. Prefrontal lobotomy (p. 456)**
___ **28. Electroconvulsive therapy (ECT) (p. 457)**
___ **29. Major tranquilizers (p. 457)**
___ **30. Minor tranquilizers (p. 458)**
___ **31. Phenothiazines (p. 457)**
___ **32. Librium (p. 458)**
___ **33. Valium (p. 458)**

A. *Methods of treatment that modify behavior by physically altering brain functions.*
B. *A method of treatment in which a brief electrical current is passed across the patient's brain.*
C. *A minor tranquilizer effective in reducing high levels of anxiety. It is also highly dependency inducing.*
D. *Drugs that are used to reduce the delusions, hallucinations, and violent behavior of many schizophrenic patients.*
E. *Drugs used most often to treat psychotic patients whose behavior is seriously disturbed.*
F. *An approach to therapy in which an individual can freely express both negative and positive feelings toward other group members and, at the same time, exchange understanding or emotion that might not be possible under life's normal rules of interpersonal behavior.*
G. *Drugs used to treat patients suffering from disorders involving moderate anxiety.*
H. *A type of psychosurgery that destroys the neural pathways from portions of the frontal lobes to the rest of the brain.*
I. *A minor tranquilizer effective in reducing high levels of anxiety, though it is also subject to abuse because it is dependency inducing.*

___ **34. Antidepressant drugs (p. 458)**
___ **35. Lithium carbonate (p. 458)**
___ **36. Primary prevention (p. 460)**
___ **37. Tertiary prevention (p. 461)**
___ **38. Secondary prevention (p. 461)**

A. *A naturally occurring compound that is used to terminate manic episodes and also to increase the interval between mania and depression in bipolar affective disorder.*
B. *Early detection of persons or institutions that have begun to exhibit preliminary signs of psychopathology.*
C. *Drugs used to ease the pain and suffering of moderate and severe depression.*
D. *The use of resources in the community to establish an environment more likely to nourish mental health and prevent the development of serious psychopathology.*
E. *Providing treatment for individuals who have actually developed psychopathology that is serious enough to cause disruption of functioning.*

ANSWERS

34. C, 35. A, 36. D, 37. E, 38. B

18. E, 19. D, 20. C, 21. A, 22. F, 23. B, 24. G, 25. F, 26. A, 27. H, 28. B, 29. E, 30. G, 31. D, 32. C, 33. I,

1. E, 2. F, 3. A, 4. H, 5. G, 6. B, 7. D, 8. C, 9. C, 10. D, 11. B, 12. A, 13. F, 14. H, 15. G, 16. E, 17. H,

SELF-TEST

1. The most important psychoanalytic technique is
   (a) dream interpretation.
   (b) interpretation of resistance.
   (c) free association.
   (d) systematic desensitization.
       (LO 1; p. 444)

2. One of the most common accompaniments of psychoanalysis is
   (a) resistance.
   (b) regression.
   (c) fixation.
   (d) poverty.
       (LO 2; p. 445)

3. The psychoanalytic phenomenon by which patients distort reality as a function of their earlier experience with parents is called
   (a) parentification.
   (b) identification.
   (c) introjection.
   (d) transference.
       (LO 2; p. 445)

4. Above all, psychoanalytic psychotherapy differs from psychoanalysis in its
   (a) rejection of the couch.
   (b) methods.
   (c) basic goals.
   (d) rejection of interpretation as a prime mode of therapeutic gain.
       (LO 3; p. 446)

5. Behavior therapy aims at direct change of
   (a) all behavior.
   (b) behavior acquired by classical and operant conditioning.
   (c) all maladaptive behavior.
   (d) learned maladaptive behavior.
   (LO 4; p. 447)

6. Joseph Wolpe developed
   (a) vicarious reinforcement.
   (b) systematic desensitization.
   (c) client-centered therapy.
   (d) positive reinforcement and extinction.
   (LO 4; p. 447)

7. Which of the following is *not* one of the three principal modes of learning?
   (a) vicarious reward.
   (b) classical conditioning.
   (c) observational learning.
   (d) operant conditioning.
   (LO 5; p. 449)

8. The counselor's principal job in client-centered therapy is to convey
   (a) thoughtful interpretations.
   (b) unconditional positive regard.
   (c) conditional positive regard.
   (d) a critical attitude toward the patient's symptomatic behavior.
   (LO 7; p. 453)

9. Family therapy
   (a) works best when the patient is a child.
   (b) enables generalization of treatment gains.
   (c) is generally based on social learning principles.
   (d) is a variant of encounter groups.
   (LO 8; p. 455)

10. Essentially normal persons can benefit from
    (a) somatic treatments.
    (b) family therapy.
    (c) exploration of transference phenomena.
    (d) encounter groups.
    (LO 8; p. 454)

11. Psychosurgery is designed for patients who show
    (a) delusions and hallucinations.
    (b) uncontrollable psychotic behavior.
    (c) seizures.
    (d) organic brain disorders.
    (LO 9; p. 457)

12. ECT is a treatment that is specific for
    (a) severe depression.
    (b) severe anxiety.
    (c) uncontrollable agitation.
    (d) psychomotor seizures.
    (LO 9; p. 457)

13. The phenothiazines reduce the hallucinations and delusions of
    (a) the manic depressive.
    (b) the severely depressed.
    (c) the schizophrenic.
    (d) all of the above.
    (LO 9; p. 457)

14. Librium and Valium are
    (a) phenothiazines.
    (b) forms of lithium carbonate.
    (c) tricyclic antidepressants.
    (d) minor tranquilizers.
    (LO 9; p. 458)

15. Lithium carbonate
    (a) terminates manic episodes.
    (b) reduces the likelihood of future depressive episodes.
    (c) is a treatment for bipolar affective disorder.
    (d) all of the above.
    (LO 9; p. 458)

16. The most effective treatment for schizophrenia and bipolar affective disorder is
    (a) psychoanalysis.
    (b) the phenothiazines.
    (c) lithium carbonate.
    (d) the somatic therapies.
    (LO 9; p. 459)

17. Psychotherapy and psychoanalysis are
    (a) still questioned as treatments for patients experiencing anxiety and depression.
    (b) the treatments of choice for most nonpsychotic individuals.
    (c) not as effective as the somatic therapies.
    (d) the most expensive forms of treatment.
    (LO 3; p. 459)

18. The most cost-effective kind of prevention is
    (a) tertiary prevention.
    (b) secondary prevention.
    (c) initial prevention.
    (d) primary prevention.
    (LO 10; p. 460)

19. Tertiary prevention is
    (a) cost-effective.
    (b) ineffective.
    (c) treatment.
    (d) community-based.
       (LO 10; p. 461)

20. Secondary prevention requires
    (a) early detection and treatment.
    (b) well-trained personnel.
    (c) cooperation from the community.
    (d) all of the above.
       (LO 10; p. 461)

ANSWERS

1. c, 2. a, 3. d, 4. c, 5. d, 6. b, 7. a, 8. b, 9. b, 10. d, 11. b, 12. a, 13. c, 14. d, 15. d, 16. d, 17. a, 18. d, 19. c, 20. a

SUGGESTED READINGS

Ayllon, T., and J. Michael. "The psychiatric nurse as a behavioral engineer." *Journal of the Experimental Analysis of Behavior* (2) (1959): 323–334. The first report on behavior modification of psychotic patients.

Bandura, A. *Principles of behavior modification.* New York: Holt, Rinehart, & Winston, 1969. Still the best introduction to behavioral views on the etiology of mental disorder.

Bandura, A., E. B. Blanchard, and B. Ritter. "Relative efficacy of desensitization and modeling approaches for inducing behavioral, affective, and attitudinal changes." *Journal of Personality and Social Psychology* 13 (1969): 173–199. One of the most important early papers on use of modeling procedures to induce behavior change in children.

Freud, S. "Analysis of a phobia in a five-year-old boy" (1909). In *Collected Papers,* Volume III. New York: Basic Books, 1959. The classic psychoanalytic description of childhood phobia, this paper also reveals Freud's views on the natural development of neurotic behavior and the prime etiological significance of the Oedipal period of psychosexual development.

Freud, S. "The dynamics of the transference" (1912). In *Collected Papers,* Volume II. New York: Basic Books, 1959. One of Freud's classic papers on technique, this one deals with the phenomenon of transference as it relates to behavior change during the psychoanalytic relationship.

Fromm-Reichman, F. *Psychotherapy with schizophrenics.* New York: International Universities Press, 1952. One of the very best descriptions of the trials and triumphs experienced by the psychoanalytic therapist who chooses to work with schizophrenics.

Rogers, C. R. *Client-centered therapy.* Boston: Houghton-Mifflin, 1951. The classic description of how to do client-centered therapy, written by its developer. A most informative book for those who develop almost any kind of counseling relationship with patients or clients.

Watson, J. B., and R. Rayner. "Conditioned emotional reactions." *Journal of Experimental Psychology,* 3 (1920): 1–14. The case of Little Albert demonstrated that so-called neurotic behavior could be learned, thus paving the way for more elaborate behavioral explanations of a wider variety of neurotic and psychotic behavior.

p a r t

V

SOCIAL PSYCHOLOGY AND APPLICATIONS

c h a p t e r

14

Social Behavior

LEARNING OBJECTIVES

After reading this chapter, you should be able to

1. understand the functions of social interaction. **(pp. 470–71)**

2. know why we spend time with the particular individuals we do. **(p. 470)**

3. recognize the differences between perceiving objects and perceiving other people. **(p. 471)**

4. identify the nature of implicit theories of personality. **(pp. 471–72)**

5. distinguish between external and internal attributions. **(p. 473)**

6. understand the bases of interpersonal attraction. **(pp. 474–77)**

7. identify basic conceptualizations of emotions, including love. **(pp. 476–77)**

8. understand the principal means of social influence. **(pp. 478–80)**

9. identify the nature of attitudes and attitude change. **(pp. 478–80)**

10. discuss the nature of prejudice. **(p. 480)**

11. recognize the role played by assumed differences in racial prejudice. **(p. 483)**

12. describe the Milgram experiments on obedience. **(pp. 484–85)**

13. realize the role played by situational, rather than personality, variables in prosocial and antisocial behavior. **(pp. 484–89)**

14. understand the concept of diffusion of responsibility. **(p. 487)**

15. trace the development of frustration-aggression and arousal theories. **(pp. 489–95)**

16. apply social learning theory to the understanding of family violence and mass media effects. **(pp. 494–95)**

Figure 14.1 *Social psychology deals with the behavior of human beings in groups*

Social Psychology *is that branch of the study of behavior concerned with the effects that people have on one another.* It is concerned with social interaction and groups, the topics covered in this and the next chapter. Human beings are perhaps the most social of all animals (fig. 14.1). Who you are and what you think depend to a surprising extent on your contacts with other people. Being with others is so basic that one of the most severe penalties a society can enact against a criminal is to isolate him from other people. Why should solitary confinement be such an extreme form of punishment? As we will see in our discussion of social psychology, being with others helps us to define ourselves and the world we live in. To isolate a person from others is to remove an important source of information and stability. Prisoners frequently fear solitary confinement because they lose their hold on reality and quickly come to question their own sanity. Why should this be so?

Social Comparison

Many of the questions people ask about themselves and about others cannot be answered objectively. There are no machines to measure how friendly or how trustworthy someone is, or whether classical music is better than hard rock. We arrive at answers to such questions by discussing them with other people, by listening to or reading about what others have to say about them, and by observing the reactions of people to ourselves and to different situations. The answers to these questions, in other words, are socially constructed. We engage in a process of **social comparison** *in which we compare ourselves and our experiences with those of other people in order to arrive at judgments about the social and physical world, and even about ourselves.* This does not mean that we simply adopt the beliefs and opinions of everyone around us but that to some extent we base our beliefs and opinions on those of others.

Festinger's Social Comparison Theory

In 1954, Leon Festinger proposed that people have a need to evaluate their own opinions and abilities. They prefer objective evaluations of these traits, but when objective methods are unavailable, they compare themselves to other people. They do not compare themselves to just anyone, however, but to those whom they expect to be somewhat similar on the trait in question. For example, if you wish to know how intelligent you are, you do not compare yourself to grade school children or to your physics professor, but most likely to other students at your college.

What happens if, after comparing yourself to others, you find that your opinion or ability is very different from theirs? According to the theory (and a good deal of supportive research [e.g., Suls and Miller, 1977]), a person will either change to conform to the opinion or ability of the others or will withdraw from further contact with that person or group. The stronger the initial attraction to the other person or group, the greater will be the pressure on the individual to conform.

Social comparison theory helps us to understand why people belong to so many different groups and tend to associate so often with others. It is because others help us understand our own abilities and opinions. Social interaction is basic to human functioning because it allows us to form and hold opinions about the world that cannot be assessed in any objective way. By comparing ourselves with others, we arrive at socially agreed-upon ways of viewing ourselves, other people, and our world (Berger and Luckman, 1969).

Some Applications of the Theory

Social comparison helps to reduce the ambiguity of uncertain events. When we hear a sudden noise, our first response is to turn to someone else and ask, "What was that?" Before undergoing surgery a patient will frequently wish to talk with other patients who have undergone similar treatment (Wood, Taylor, and Lichtman, 1985). Social comparison processes are also useful in helping people reduce their fear of threatening events, such as natural disasters. In a study of people living in an area threatened by floods, those who had no previous experience with floods engaged in social comparison. They discussed floods with their neighbors, which had the effect of calming them, building confidence in their ability to cope with flooding, and increasing their commitment to taking preventive measures (Hansson, Noulles, and Bellovich, 1982).

GUIDED REVIEW

Learning Objectives 1 and 2

1. We often evaluate our own opinions and abilities by comparing ourselves with _____ .

2. This process is referred to as _____ .

3. We prefer to compare ourselves to others whom we expect to be _____ to ourselves.

4. Two additional functions of social comparison are to _____ and _____ .

ANSWERS

1. others 2. social comparison 3. similar 4. cope with threat, reduce ambiguity

---

Social Perception

How do we form judgments of other people? There are some people we admire, some we love, and some we would not wish to emulate. How do we arrive at such distinctions? In this section we consider how we form impressions of individuals whom we do not know; then we consider how we assess the causes of their behavior. Finally, we discuss how we form attachments to others in the form of friendships and romantic involvements.

Perception, which we discussed in Chapter 4, deals with judgments of the physical world. **Social perception** deals with *judgments of people*. The difference between perceiving people and perceiving objects is that in the former case we have to take into account the motives, intentions, and feelings of individuals—characteristics that mere objects do not possess.

Implicit Theory of Personality

Your perception of people—including your view of yourself—is influenced by your expectations and by the information you have about them. We learn an **implicit theory of personality**, *a general belief that certain traits of personality somehow "belong" together,* such as a sense of humor and intelligence, or low self-esteem and hostility toward others. If you meet a man who is reputed to have a good sense of humor, you might also expect him to be intelligent. This is not necessarily so, but it is a belief that enables you to form a unified and fairly well-rounded impression of him based only on a limited amount of first-hand information. Our implicit theories of personality are not necessarily correct. They enable us to form consistent and fairly comprehensive impressions of others. Of course, different people learn different implicit theories of personality, depending on the kinds of beliefs their parents and friends hold and on their experiences with others.

First Impressions

In an early study of **impression formation,** *or, how we develop opinions of others,* Solomon Asch (1952) described a fictitious male to college students. The students were told that the person was intelligent, skillful, industrious, determined, practical, and cautious. Some also heard him described as "warm," whereas others heard him described as "cold." After reading one of these two lists of traits, each student was asked to form an impression of him and to describe him in a brief essay. Asch found that students were able to describe the person in a complex, fairly complete way, based only on a very limited amount of information about him. In other words, there is a tendency to use an implicit theory of personality, to go beyond the information given, in forming impressions of others. Asch also reported that varying one adjective—"warm" or "cold"—influenced the overall impressions formed by the students. He noted that changing one adjective probably modified how each of the others was interpreted. For example, the term *intelligence* may mean one thing when it is paired with the adjective "warm" and something different when it is paired with "cold." Because some trait descriptions, such as "warm-cold," influence how other traits are interpreted, they have been referred to as "central traits." You can see in table 14.1, for example,

Table 14.1 Percent of subjects choosing each adjective		
Adjective	Warm (%)	Cold (%)
Generous	91	8
Wise	65	25
Good-natured	94	17
Happy	90	34
Humorous	77	13
Sociable	91	38
Popular	84	28
Important	88	99
Humane	86	31
Restrained	77	89
Altruistic	69	18
Imaginative	51	19

From Solomon E. Asch, Social Psychology, *1952, p. 209. Reprinted by permission of Solomon E. Asch.*

that a person described as "warm" is thought to be "generous" by ninety-one percent of the subjects, whereas only eight percent who heard him described as "cold" believed he would also be generous.

There is a tendency, stronger in some people than in others (O'Neal, 1971), to see people as either good or bad. For instance, if you learned that Bob was intelligent and friendly, had a good sense of humor, was warm, and frivolous, you would be most apt to discount, or even to forget, the last characteristic when forming an impression of him. The **halo effect** refers to this *tendency to form positive impressions when we know a few positive traits about a person.* It is more difficult to form an impression of another person that is complex, including both good and bad traits, and that is not necessarily consistent. Of course, individuals whom we know well appear to us to be more complex than casual acquaintances and strangers.

Impression formation research examines the ways in which we form evaluative judgments of people whom we don't know very well. We are often in a position to make judgments about *why* a person acted in a certain way, and this is the province of attribution theory.

Attribution

It is nearly Mother's Day and you have not yet bought a present for your mother. What will you get her? What would she like? You recently saw her reading a book of poetry; maybe she'd like a book of poems. But perhaps that was only because there was nothing else around for her to read; you've never known her to read poetry before. How about something for the kitchen? She is a terrific cook, and she spends a lot of time preparing meals. But perhaps she feels trapped there and would be insulted if you bought her such a sex-stereotyped gift that implied she was primarily a cook.

We spend much of our time trying to unravel the likes and dislikes of others, attempting to find out why they do what they do. **Attribution** *is the study of how we explain the underlying causes of a person's behavior.*

Fritz Heider (1958) suggests that we analyze another person's behavior to determine whether it is caused by some internal state of the person, such as personality or attitudes, or by external forces, such as the demands of a job or family situation. We base our attributions on such considerations as the person's ability to perform an act, the person's motivation for performing it, and the difficulty of the act itself before deciding whether the person performed it for internal reasons (e.g., saying that mother likes to cook) or for external reasons (e.g., saying that mother feels she must feed her family and makes the best of it by turning cooking into an art).

If you ask your dad and your brother why your mom spends so much time in the kitchen, they are apt to say that she enjoys cooking and has a talent for it. This is an "internal" explanation of her behavior. However, if you ask your mom why she spends so much time cooking, she might tell you that it is part of being a good mother—that her family deserves to eat well. This is an "external" attribution, based on demands and pressures from her family. Whose explanation is correct? Perhaps there is no one interpretation of someone's behavior that is completely correct. The study of attribution examines what types of explanations people give for events and what types of information are taken into account when explaining someone's behavior.

The attributions of mother and her family serve as examples of the **attributional bias,** *the tendency to see other people's behavior as internally caused and to see our own behavior as externally caused.* Mom explains her own behavior by reference to the external situation, whereas Dad and your brother interpret her behavior as internally motivated.

The attributional bias is self-serving. A person tends to deny being responsible for actions that have unfavorable consequences (Carver, DeGregoria, and Gillis, 1980). For example, the coaches of winning and losing teams often make different attributions in explaining the outcome of a game. The winning coach believes that his coaching decisions with regard to plays and players were responsible for the victory. The coach of the losing team is more apt to refer to the lucky break of the opposing team, to the bad officiating, and the difficult journey on the way to the game (Kelley, 1973; Mummendey and Mummendey, 1983). This attribution bias is a way of avoiding personal responsibility for unfavorable outcomes and of taking credit for favorable occurrences. The net effect of these attributions is that they enhance the person's self-esteem (Weary, 1980). Occasionally, there is social pressure on an individual to take responsibility for failure or to deny personal responsibility for success. For example, someone accepting an Academy Award frequently thanks the director, producer, and others without whom she would not have won the award. Even this, however, may be interpreted as a way for the person to enhance the views that others have of her.

Attribution studies explore the ways people form judgments about the causes of behavior. On what basis do we decide whether we like someone else? This question is addressed in the next section.

Learning Objectives 3, 4, and 5

1. The perception of people, unlike the perception of objects, must take into consideration their _____ , _____ , and _____ .

2. We learn to associate certain personality traits with one another. This basis for forming impressions of others is referred to as _____ .

3. The tendency to assume that the presence of some positive personality traits is accompanied by other positive traits is known as the _____ .

4. _____ is concerned with explaining the causes of our own and other people's behavior.

5. Attributions about another's behavior may be _____ or _____ . Internal attributions refer to the personality, needs, wishes, and motives, while external attributions refer to the situation in which behavior takes place.

6. People tend to take credit for positive effects and deny responsibility for unpleasant effects, a process known as the _____ .

ANSWERS

1. motives, needs, desires 2. implicit theory of personality 3. halo effect 4. Attribution theory 5. internal, external 6. fundamental attribution bias

Interpersonal Attraction

Friendship is commonly overlooked by psychologists as an important and influential aspect of social life. We often hear of the influence that parents, siblings, and peers have on our personalities, but of these important relationships, only our friends (peers) are freely chosen. Who are your closest friends, and why are they your friends? Of all the relationships a person has in a lifetime, perhaps none is more important or more carefully considered than the choice of a spouse. What psychological and social forces enter into the decision to marry someone? **Interpersonal attraction** *is the area of study that looks at the social and psychological bases of friendship and love.*

The simplest and most frequent finding in interpersonal attraction studies is that people form attachments most readily and most often to others who live or work nearby. This is the notion of *propinquity,* which means proximity or nearness. For example, people living in a campus housing project at MIT tended to form friendships with those who lived closest to them (Festinger, Schachter, and Back, 1950), and an early study of couples filing for marriage licenses in Philadelphia found that in the majority of cases the man and woman

lived in the same neighborhood (Bossard, 1945). People who live in a multiunit housing development tend to form friendships with others who live nearby, but they also take into account the age, race, and sex of the person. Friends tend to live in close proximity but also share other features in common (Nahemow and Lawton, 1975). This raises the issue of the degree to which friends are similar to one another in personality and interests.

Similarity and Attraction

The oldest and most widely recognized theory of attraction is based on the saying that "birds of a feather flock together." As early as 300 B.C., Aristotle noted that "they are friends who have come to regard the same things as good and the same things as evil, they who are friends of the same people, and they who are the enemies of the same people. . . . We like those who resemble us, and are engaged in the same pursuits." More than 2000 years later, Aristotle's theory is still useful for understanding interpersonal attraction. Of course, in the hands of psychologists the theory has been expanded and modified, but similarity of attitudes and interests still lie at the core of many psychological theories of attraction.

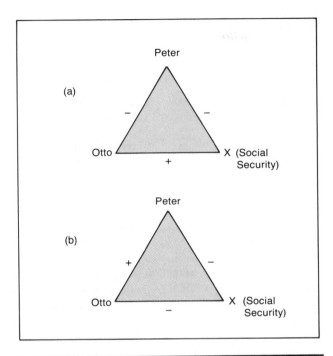

*Figure 14.2 Heider's balance theory. (a) Peter dislikes the
Social Security system, whereas Otto likes it. The tendency will
be for Peter not to be attracted to Otto. (b) If both Peter and Otto
hold a common attitude toward Social Security, there will be a
tendency for Peter to like Otto.*

In many theories of attraction (e.g., Berscheid and Walster, 1978; Byrne, 1971; Heider, 1958; Newcomb, 1956), a person is said to be most attracted toward someone whose attitudes, behaviors, interests, or personality traits are most similar to the person's own. The theories differ in their views of *why* similarity leads to attraction, but they agree that it does. Heider's balance theory, presented in figure 14.2, shows that Peter, who holds an unfavorable attitude toward some object or issue, such as Social Security (X), would like Otto, who holds a similar attitude toward X. This would produce a tension-free or balanced relationship. If an unbalanced state exists, such as learning that someone you like holds a different attitude from you, then there is a state of tension, and pressure exists to change your attitude or to change your relationship with the other person.

Donn Byrne (1971) looks at the relationship between similarity and attraction in behavioral terms. If a person holds the same attitude as you, that serves as a positive reinforcement for your position, and Byrne's theory holds that we like those people who provide us with the greatest amount of positive reinforcement. Byrne distinguishes between the *number* of similar traits that two people share and the *proportion* of similar traits they share. According to the theory, you will be most attracted to someone who shares the greatest proportion of similar traits to your own. For example, suppose you are familiar with ten of Joe's attitudes and believe that seven of them are the same as your own attitudes. You know twenty of Fred's attitudes, and seven of them are the same as your own. The theory predicts that you will be more attracted to Joe than to Fred because Joe's attitudes are seventy percent similar to your own, whereas Fred's are only thirty-five percent similar.

In a cross-cultural study of similarity and attraction, students in Hawaii, Japan, India, Mexico, and the continental United States were presented with attitude questionnaires presumably filled out by another student (Byrne, et al., 1971). The students completed the same questionnaire, which enabled the researchers to determine the degree of similarity between the two. The students were then asked to indicate how much they thought they would like the other person. The results, which are summarized in table 14.2, indicate that as the proportion of responses similar to the subjects' increased, attraction also increased. These results were obtained in each of the five groups studied.

According to one controversial theory of attraction, the ability of another person to validate or confirm the correctness of your beliefs and attitudes is only the basis of initial attraction. Only in beginning stages of a relationship is similarity important (Kerckhoff and Davis,

Table 14.2 Attraction toward others in five groups				
	Proportion of similar responses			
	.00–.40	*.47–.60*	*.67–1.00*	*Total*
Hawaii	7.03	8.27	8.46	7.92
India	7.19	8.34	9.40	8.31
Japan	6.27	6.94	7.53	6.91
Mexico	7.31	8.55	9.11	8.32
U.S.	6.00	7.33	7.38	6.90
Total	6.76	7.89	8.37	

Note: The higher the score, the greater the attraction.

Adapted from D. Byrne, C. Gouaux, W. Griffitt, J. Lamberth, N. Murakawa, M. B. Prasad, A. Prasad, and M. Ramirez, III, "The ubiquitous relationship: Attitude similarity and attraction. A cross-cultural study," Human Relations, 24, 201–207. Copyright © 1971 by Plenum Publishing Corporation.

1962). Once a certain degree of similarity has been established, other characteristics of a person become important. The ability of another person to satisfy social and psychological needs has been proposed as the basis for long-lasting relationships (Winch, 1958). *The ability of each person to satisfy the needs of the other is referred to as* **need complementarity.** For example, if Wayne has a high need to be mothered and Joan has a need to be nurturant and protective, then Wayne and Joan should be attracted to one another. There is only a minimum of empirical evidence to support this theory, partly because we do not have satisfactory ways to measure people's needs (Levinger and Snoek, 1972).

Romantic Love

We have briefly discussed the nature of attraction by noting the roles played by similarity and complementarity. Though these are also the bases of romantic attraction, they do not explain what we generally think of as love. One of the difficulties in discussing love is that it means so many things to so many people. There is the love of a mother for her child and of a brother for his sibling; people say they love a sport, and some would die for love. Can all of these uses of the word mean the same thing? Probably not. This is an instance in which language limits our ability to understand. The ancient Greeks, for instance, had a separate word for each of these types of love. In this brief section we discuss the love that occurs between a man and a woman.

Love as an Emotion. Love is an emotion and, like other emotions, may be seen as having both physiological and psychological components (see Chapter 8). One theory (Schachter, 1964) states that any source of physiological arousal may be interpreted as love (or any other emotion) if the circumstances are compatible with that interpretation. According to this theory, passionate love is likely to be experienced when a person is nervous or otherwise aroused and when a member of the opposite sex is present and expresses some interest in the person (Berscheid and Walster, 1978; Walster and Walster, 1978). In one study based on this theory (Dutton and Aron, 1974), males who had just crossed a dangerous, narrow bridge over a canyon were more likely to be attracted to a female who spoke with them than were males who had not yet been aroused by the dangerous crossing. In other words, a slight amount of anxiety, fear, or other source of arousal may be related to attraction because it may be (mis)interpreted as the emotion of love.

How does loving a person differ from liking that person? Zick Rubin (1970) asked lovers to write descriptions of love and friends to write descriptions about liking. The analysis of these descriptions led Rubin to conclude that love involves an idealization of the lover, sexual attraction, and a longing to be with the other. Liking involves attraction, similarity, and respect. Rubin developed a measuring instrument to distinguish these two types of close relationships. One of the items that measures liking is "I have great confidence in _____'s good judgment;" one from the "Love scale" is "I feel responsible for _____'s well-being." According to Rubin's analysis, loving and liking differ with respect to both attitudes and behaviors.

Sternberg and Grajek (1984) examined the ability of a number of factors, including similarity, complementarity, physical attractiveness, and liking, to predict the success of a romantic relationship. They found that romantic love cannot be considered a single factor, but rather a cluster of positive feelings involving liking, complementary personalities, and similarity.

Love as a Social Role. The traditional Western view of romantic love is that it is a passion. In this perspective, love has a number of "symptoms." It is viewed metaphorically as something a person "falls" into. In many parts of the world, however, people marry for reasons having little to do with falling in love. This is true of traditional Oriental and Arab cultures. Here marriages are typically arranged. Yet these marriages appear to be satisfying and stable. When we have spoken with people whose marriages were arranged,

they reported that love would emerge over time; it was not necessary, indeed it was not possible, for love to be present prior to marriage. That would come as the couple shared experiences and came to know and appreciate one another. This suggests that love is not so much an emotional state as a set of behaviors that a person learns in his or her culture—a social role. Like any other social role, the role of lover carries with it rights and responsibilities: the right to intimacy, to raise a family, to buy a house, and to file a joint tax return, and the responsibilities of loyalty, openness, of being a good spouse, and so on.

In our culture, we learn about love from childhood on. We learn from children's stories, television and films, song lyrics, and novels that love is an intense often indefinable and irrational emotion. But love is not something that "just happens" to us. In fact, people fall in love when they are ready and willing to assume the role of lover, usually when they have undergone a change in status, such as graduating from school, moving to a new city, or changing jobs. In many nonwestern cultures, love is perceived as a process emerging out of understanding, sharing, mutual respect, and common background. (Even arranged marriages are based on similarity of social class or caste and family background.) The view of love as a social role is one that social psychologists have not yet studied in depth, though it is gaining theoretical ground (Averill, 1982; Levinger and Raush, 1977).

GUIDED REVIEW

Learning Objectives 6 and 7

1. Many theories of interpersonal attraction are based on the belief that individuals are attracted to someone who is _____ to them.

2. In some theories of romantic attraction, similarity is believed to be important in early stages of a relationship, but _____ is seen as important in subsequent stages.

3. Romantic love has been viewed as an emotion by most psychologists, but can also be seen as a learned _____ , carrying rights and responsibilities.

ANSWERS
1. *similar* 2. *complementarity* 3. *social role*

Social Influence

When a lawyer argues a case before a jury, he is trying to influence their attitudes and behaviors. In fact the purpose of many forms of social interaction is to influence other people's beliefs, attitudes, and actions. All are forms of social influence. We discuss three types of social influence here: direct persuasion, the development and reduction of prejudice, and obedience to the commands of an authority figure.

Attitudes and Persuasion

Parents and teachers, clergymen and politicians, lawyers and advertisers are all interested in attitudes. In most cases, they would like others to come around to their way of seeing things, and they expend a great deal of time and energy in trying to persuade people. The reason so much attention is devoted to attitudes is that it is believed that attitudes are related to behavior. Change a person's attitude, and you may also change his or her behavior. But what are attitudes, and what is their relationship to behavior?

Social psychologists define **attitude** as *a tendency to respond in a consistently favorable or unfavorable way to a class of objects.* Attitudes are believed to have three components. The first is beliefs or cognitions about an object; the second is liking or disliking of an object; and the third is the tendency to seek or avoid the object. These are called, respectively, the *cognitive,* the *emotional,* and the *behavior-tendency* components of an attitude. Let us use Judy's attitude toward communism as an example. She believes it is a stifling and unfair distribution of goods and services and that it often goes hand in hand with nondemocratic government (her cognitive component). Because of these beliefs she does not like communism (emotional component), and when she has an opportunity to do so, she is inclined to speak out against communism (behavior tendency component).

Attitudes and Behavior. The reason there is so much interest in attitudes is that they presumably bear some relationship to an individual's behavior. However, behavior is influenced by many factors, and attitudes represent only one of these. Therefore, although attitudes are indeed positively related to behavior, they do not allow a person to predict behavior perfectly (Fishbein and Ajzen, 1980). For example, although you may have a negative attitude toward strawberries, you may eat strawberries under certain circumstances, such as when you are a guest in someone's home and are offered strawberries for dessert. In most situations, however, when given a choice you avoid eating strawberries. So although your attitude may not predict each specific behavior, it will allow one to predict in general how you will act toward the class of objects, strawberries.

Cognitive Dissonance Theory. Behavior tends to follow from attitudes, but attitudes also result from behavior. This is most clearly seen in Leon Festinger's (1957) theory of cognitive dissonance. Festinger argues that a person has a natural tendency to maintain consistency among his or her cognitions, which include attitudes, beliefs, and perceptions. *When two or more cognitions are logically inconsistent with one another,* a state of **cognitive dissonance** arises. This is a psychologically uncomfortable state that motivates a person to act in such a way as to reduce the dissonance. This may be done by changing a cognition or a behavior. Suppose that someone who smokes cigarettes believes that smoking is bad for her health. This inconsistency produces cognitive dissonance that can be reduced by (1) changing a behavior (stop smoking), (2) changing a cognition (distort the extent of the health hazard, for example, by saying that smoking isn't very dangerous), or (3) adding other cognitions to reduce the extent of dissonance (e.g., "Smoking may be hazardous but it relaxes me.").

People act to reduce dissonance once it is aroused, but they also try to avoid it wherever possible. In this way, a person who engages in some public behavior, such as smoking a cigarette, is unlikely to hold an attitude incompatible with that behavior. The behavior, in other words, comes to influence the person's attitudes. In research on this issue carried out over a period of two decades, we have learned that attitudes tend to form in a manner consistent with behavior when that behavior is engaged in freely, without coercion, and if it is performed publicly; that is, when other people are aware of it (Baumeister and Tice, 1984; Calder, Ross and Insko, 1973; Linder, Cooper, and Jones, 1967). If, on the other hand, a person feels pressure to perform a behavior, such as eating a disliked food, or if the behavior takes place privately, then the person's attitude will not necessarily follow logically from the behavior. The dinner guest who eats strawberries because his host has raved about them is not likely to come to like strawberries, even though he is willing to eat them in this case.

Attitude Change: Persuasion and Propaganda. Advertisers, politicians, and others interested in influencing your behavior either wish to establish a new attitude, such as toward a new product or a candidate running for first-time election, or hope to change an already existing attitude, as in trying to get you to switch from one soft drink to another or to re-elect someone for whom you did not vote before. In these cases, they are trying to persuade you to change your attitude and, presumably as a result of this changed attitude, to influence your behavior. Almost all persuasion attempts use some form of communication, which involves a *source* who delivers a *message* through some *medium* to an *audience*. In other words, the process of communication involves who says what to whom through which medium (Lasswell and Casey, 1946). Because much of the early work on persuasion was conducted by learning theorists, a great deal of attention was focused on the source and the message, since these comprise the "stimuli" to which attitude change is the "response" (Hovland, Janis, and Kelley, 1953). We discuss those aspects on which the most research has been conducted: source, message, and medium.

The Source. According to learning theory, the recipient must perceive the stimulus, or, pay attention to the communication, understand it, and adopt the attitude suggested in the message. This will be done if the new attitude is seen as more rewarding than the recipient's initial attitude. Among the rewards for paying attention to and accepting a message are the personal benefits that result from adopting the new attitude. For example, if you use Snuggle-up toothpaste, the love of your life will suddenly notice how attractive you are, and love and beauty, not to mention sparkling teeth, will be yours.

According to learning theory, we attend to and are influenced by a message stemming from a **high-credibility source,** *one thought to be expert, trustworthy, and having relevant experience* (Berscheid, 1966; Hovland and Weiss, 1951). If the source takes a stand that is seen to be against his own best interest, for example, a criminal arguing that judges are too lenient, then that will increase the perceived credibility of the source (Walster, Aronson, and Abrahams, 1966).

The Message. Suppose a political lobbyist wishes to persuade a politician to reduce the size of the military budget. How extreme should her position be? Should she ask for a reduction of one percent, ten percent, or fifty percent of the military appropriation? While she might regard a cut of one percent as meaningless, the politician may see it as a threat to the security of the nation. If the lobbyist takes a stand very different from the politician's own view, there is an increased risk that the politician will misperceive her position. If the lobbyist has high credibility to the politician, for example, as someone who is informed and who has proven reliable in the past, then taking a more extreme stand will result in more attitude change. If the lobbyist is low in credibility, then taking an extreme position will result in less change than a more moderate position (Bochner and Insko, 1966). If the issue is a highly controversial one, as military funding is, then taking an extreme stand will produce less change than taking a moderate stand (Freedman, 1964). Indeed, even the perception of the lobbyist's position may depend on one's initial attitude toward military appropriations (Vallone, Ross, and Lepper, 1985). In the preceding example, the lobbyist is well advised to take a moderate stand, asking for a ten percent reduction in funding.

Should the lobbyist discuss the horrible aftermath of nuclear war and appeal to the politician's emotions, or would a more reasoned approach be effective? According to research on rational versus emotional appeals, the former are more effective with a highly educated audience. Emotional appeals, specifically those based on fear, can be effective providing they are accompanied by specific recommendations on how to reduce the fear (e.g., Leventhal, 1970).

The relationship between fear and persuasion is complex because different processes are involved (McGuire, 1969). The greater the amount of fear that is aroused, the greater the likelihood that the audience will be "tuned in to" their own emotions and thus less likely to pay attention to the communication. So, high fear may interfere with receiving the message. Among those who do receive the message, high fear will produce insecurity and a motivation to try to reduce the fear, increasing compliance with the recommendations of the message.

One form of advertisement involves an emotional appeal in that it refers to a product's image, rather than to its quality. Other ads stress the quality of the product. Research has shown that for individuals who are concerned with image, or with "being the right person in the right place at the right time" (sometimes called high self-monitoring individuals), these image-based ads are most effective. For low self-monitors, or those who do not typically mold their behavior to fit the situation, appeals to the product's quality are apt to be most effective (Snyder and DeBono, 1985).

The Medium. Communication must occur through some channel or medium, such as face-to-face speech, the written word, radio, or television. In an age of satellite communications, we do not often think of face-to-face communication as particularly effective. However, personal communication is more frequent and may

sometimes be more influential than mass media communications. It is often the two together that result in attitude change. There are some people, called **opinion leaders,** who *pay particular attention to the mass media.* In the **two-step flow of communications** (Lazarsfeld, Berelson, and Gaudet, 1948; Oskamp, 1977), *opinion leaders tell their friends and colleagues in face-to-face communications what new information they have acquired through the mass media.* In this way, most people are influenced by the mass media indirectly, through opinion leaders, and personal communication has the greatest and most immediate impact on their attitudes and behavior.

Prejudice

There are different names for the group we are about to describe, some of them unflattering. We will call them Eta, which is what they are sometimes called in their native land. The Eta are not a genetically distinct group; they are not a race and do not have any particular identifying physical characteristics. If differences between the Eta and the rest of the population exist, these differences were created by generations of segregation and inferior social status. Because the Eta are forced to spend so much of their time only with one another (non-Eta will not associate with them), and because their education is minimal, they have developed distinctive speech patterns that immediately identify them as Eta, much as the lower-class Cockney of London developed distinctive habits of speech.

The Eta are a sizable minority in their land, numbering in the millions. They are scattered throughout the country, where they live in slums or ghettos. They are regarded as unclean and fit only for the most undesirable occupations. Intermarriage with the Eta is taboo. The average IQ of an Eta is about sixteen points lower than that of the general population (88 compared with 104). Measures of school achievement show the Eta to be considerably below others, with more truancy and with a delinquency rate over three times as high as that found among other youth.

APPLICATION BOX

The Foot in the Door

Social psychologists have long known that people have a need for consistency. We tend to act in ways that give others the impression that we are reliable and that convince ourselves that we act in consistent ways from one moment to another. Festinger's theory of cognitive dissonance (1957) makes explicit the consequences of inconsistency and the ways in which we seek to maintain consistency.

Self-perception theory (Bem, 1972) also sees individuals as seeking to maintain consistency in their behavior. If a person does something once, he or she is likely to repeat the behavior in order to be consistent. If a child can be induced to eat spinach once, he or she may decide that spinach isn't so bad and may eat it again. After all, why would the child have eaten it the first time if it weren't good?

Salespeople seem to have known of these basic processes for many years. They often attempt to get a prospective client to engage in some trivial act, such as completing a form, mailing back a prepaid card, or simply allowing the salesperson to perform some simple demonstration. Then they try to sell their product or service to the client, believing that because the client complied with the first request, the likelihood of complying with the second request is greater. As it turns out, research by social psychologists supports this belief. If the salesman can only get his foot in the door, he believes he is more likely to make the sale. And, research shows, he is right.

The earliest psychological study of this "foot-in-the-door" phenomenon was conducted by Freedman and Fraser (1966). They found that complying with a small request was related to complying with a later, larger request. Those who were simply asked the larger request were less likely to comply than those first asked a simpler one. A review of all the studies investigating this phenomenon finds that the effect is a reliable one, regardless of the types of request made (Beaman, et al., 1983).

The many studies investigating the foot-in-the-door phenomenon do not always find greater compliance following a small request, but, overall, the results do support the validity of the phenomenon. Such additional variables as the length of time between requests and the sex of the person making the request appear to influence compliance with the larger request. If one or more days elapse between requests, compliance is greater. Likewise, it is greater if the person making the requests is male.

These differences between Eta and others are generally regarded as signs of "innate racial inferiority" and are used to justify further discrimination. Yet these differences arose only as a result of centuries of discrimination, and they are cultural and historical, rather than biological, in origin.

The Eta exist as a group in Japan—the Burakumin (DeVos and Wagatsuma, 1966; Klineberg, 1971). Prejudice and the consequences of discrimination are strikingly similar to that found for blacks in the United States and to minority groups in many other countries.

CAREER BOX

Salesperson

Nearly seven million Americans are employed as salespersons. Although many of them receive a salary, the income of most depends upon performance; the more goods they sell, the greater their incomes. What makes for a successful salesperson? The best-seller lists are filled with books on how to be a business success, and though they often disagree as to the specific details, they all agree that the following social psychological processes are critical:

> making a good first impression
> being perceived positively by others
> being an effective communicator
> filling a need of the client's.

Do salespeople know social psychology? Do they use cognitive dissonance theory or social comparison theory? It appears that they do. Some undoubtedly studied social psychology as students, but many have "invented" social psychology as a result of their experiences with clients, supervisors, and coworkers.

An effective salesperson takes into consideration the needs, experiences, and attitudes of his or her prospective clients. The similarity of experiences and interests between salesperson and client may be stressed, and in order to do this the salesperson must first learn something about the client. Although this may lead to initial attraction, it is also important to be a credible communicator if attitude change in favor of the salesperson's product or service is to be achieved. Credibility may be enhanced by being an expert in the field and by being a reliable and trustworthy communicator. This can be accomplished by knowing as much as possible about the product or service offered, about competitors' products, and about the specific needs of the prospective client.

In recent years, schools of business have begun to offer courses in social psychology for their students. Marketing, advertising, and sales are all processes involving social influence, and the principles of social influence studied by social psychologists are applied by effective salespeople in their everyday business lives.

What is Prejudice?   **Prejudice** is most often regarded as an attitude. While it can refer to any irrational like or dislike, it is used by social psychologists to refer to *negative views and actions toward groups of people and the members of these groups* (Ashmore, 1981). **Discrimination,** *behavior that arises from prejudiced attitudes, prevents a person from acting freely because of his or her membership in a group.*

The example of the Burakumin serves to point out several important issues. First, that prejudice is a complex process involving attitudes and behaviors, and second, that prejudiced individuals are not generally openminded about correcting their prejudices. They tend to stereotype members of the minority, so that once a person is identified as a Burakumin, he is believed to be "different," to be intellectually inferior, and to prefer associating only with other Burakumin. A **stereotype** *is a generalization about a person or group in which* *all members of the group are incorrectly assumed to have some trait in common other than the one defining the group.*

Much of what we know about prejudice was summarized in a classic book by Gordon Allport (1954). Allport discusses the development of prejudice as stemming from rigid and authoritarian parents. These parents are hostile, intolerant, and show strict adherence to middle-class morals. But prejudice is also a cultural phenomenon, with stereotypes and negative portrayals of minority groups pervading the mass media, textbooks, and the arts.

Race versus Belief Prejudice. In many parts of the world, prejudice and discrimination center on issues of race. Some psychologists have proposed that racial prejudice is not primarily a result of physical differences between races but of the assumption of differences in beliefs and values (Rokeach, Smith, and Evans, 1960; Smith, Williams, and Willis, 1967). We have seen in our discussion of attraction that individuals who hold dissimilar attitudes do not like each other as well as those who are similar. What about people who are *assumed* to be dissimilar? Whites, for example, may believe that blacks hold different values and beliefs than they do and may have unfavorable attitudes toward them solely on this basis. This implies that blacks who are known to hold similar beliefs and values to whites will not be viewed unfavorably, and whites known to hold dissimilar beliefs and values will be disliked.

In research testing these ideas, college students meet a person of the same or a different race who, during the course of conversation, indicates that he holds beliefs that are either the same as or different from the subject's. Such studies typically find that *both* the person's race and the person's belief are related to liking. If a person is known to differ in his views on important issues, then, regardless of race, subjects tend not to like that person. On the other hand, if the person holds similar beliefs on these issues, then students are apt to like him. The evidence shows that although belief similarity is the most important determinant of attraction in these studies, attraction is further enhanced if the other person is the same race as the subject (Insko and Robinson, 1967; Kidder and Steward, 1975; Moe, Nacoste, and Insko, 1981).

Reducing Prejudice. It is one thing to study a problem and quite another to solve it. Psychologists are decidedly better at the former, but in the case of prejudice and discrimination they have devoted a good deal of attention to devising methods for the reduction of prejudice. In numerous studies, increased contact between members of different groups has been found to reduce prejudice, if that contact involves individuals who are acting as equals, such as members of the same athletic team or coworkers on a job (Amir, 1976). Working on a common task also reduces stereotypic thinking and prejudicial attitudes, particularly among children (Aronson, et al., 1975; Eaton and Clore, 1975).

Some tasks, called **superordinate goals,** *require members from antagonistic groups to work together.* In a study by Muzafer Sherif and his colleagues (1961), a series of superordinate goals was introduced after different groups had engaged in hostile and violent exchanges. Boys who had recently arrived at a summer camp quickly formed cohesive groups based on the location of their bunks. The boys formed friendships only within their own group. Within days they had staged raids on the other group's bunkhouse. Sherif and colleagues then introduced a task that required the cooperation of all the boys. The camp's water supply was said to be in danger, and all campers were required to work together to restore the water supply; if they cooperated, they would see a movie that evening. This superordinate goal, the restoration of the water supply, forced the boys to work together in their common interest. This equal-status cooperation broke down animosities and stereotypes and reduced conflict between groups. Recent research has also supported the notion that superordinate tasks increase intergroup cooperation (Tyerman and Spencer, 1983).

Obedience to Authority

Social influence is often subtle and indirect, as much prejudice and discrimination are. Parents do not directly teach their children to be prejudiced, but prejudice can easily be acquired through a variety of learning experiences. Social influence can also be straightforward and direct, as when one person voluntarily agrees to be influenced by an authority figure. For example, a professor tells his students to read chapters five and six in the textbook, and they obediently do so. A captain issues orders to a private, who dutifully carries them out. A parent tells her child to go to bed, and the child, however reluctantly, does so. These are all examples of obedience to authority. In many cases, the authority is seen as legitimate and as taking into consideration the actor's welfare. On some occasions, however, the authority figure urges actions that are destructive and morally reprehensible, as when the Nazis urged the destruction of Jews and other groups. How could ordinary citizens obediently follow such commands?

Stanley Milgram (1974) wished to conduct research to determine whether Germans were more obedient than other people to orders from authority figures. His intention was to gain insight into the blind obedience that seemed to characterize the Nazis during the years of World War II. His research was perhaps the most publicized of any social psychological studies, becoming the subject of a play, a television drama, at least two educational films, and many magazine articles. It was also the impetus for a research code of ethics. The research that brought all this about was fairly simple in design and was based on no particular psychological theory. And Milgram never did conduct his experiments in Germany; he found obedience of a surprisingly high level in the United States.

The Milgram Experiments.   A subject enters an experimental laboratory, is introduced to another subject (actually an assistant of the experimenter), and is told that his job is to teach the other person a verbal task.

For example, the subject reads pairs of words to the learner, such as "blue box, nice day, wild duck," and in the testing sequence reads the word "blue," for example, along with four other words: "sky, ink, box, lamp." The learner is to decide which of these four words was originally paired with the first word. Each time the learner fails to give the correct answer, the subject is to administer an electric shock to him. Of course, the accomplice, who is usually in an adjoining room, actually receives no shock, but the subject does not know this. There are thirty levers on the shock machine, labeled from 15 to 450 volts. On every fourth switch there is a verbal designation from "Slight shock" to "Danger: Severe shock." The label at the extreme right end simply reads "XXX."

Each time the learner made an error, the subject was to administer a shock of greater intensity than the previous shock. The learner, of course, made a prearranged number of errors on the task, and the conflict confronting the subject was whether to continue to administer increasingly painful shocks, as the experimenter requested, or to disobey the experimenter and refuse to shock the learner.

Before conducting these experiments, Milgram asked a group of psychiatrists, a class of Yale University students, and a sample of middle-class adults what they would do if they were the subjects in such an experiment. Not one of the more than 100 people who were questioned thought they would continue to shock the learner to the end of the shock scale. This is just one of several instances in which people are unable to predict how they will perform in a psychological experiment. What actually happened is that a majority of subjects administered the maximum "XXX" shock.

Despite the repeated protests of the learner, which began with several grunts at 75 volts and shouts of "I can't stand the pain!" at 270 volts, sixty-five percent of the subjects in the first experiment administered the maximum shock. Even when the experiment was transferred from the prestigious laboratories of Yale to a rundown office in the working-class city of Bridgeport, Connecticut, nearly half the subjects continued to administer what they thought were 450 volt shocks.

Disobedience and Personal Responsibility. Over a dozen variations on the basic obedience procedure were made to determine under which conditions obedience would diminish. Among the findings were that the closer the subject was to the victim (learner), the less likely the subject was to administer strong shocks. Obedience was reduced to thirty percent when the subject was required to place the victim's hand on the shock plate. Likewise, if two experimenters disagreed in the presence of the subject over the subject's obligation to continue to administer shock, obedience completely disappeared. None of the twenty subjects receiving contradictory orders shocked the victim to the end of the shock scale.

Here is a portion of the transcript in which one subject, a thirty-two-year old industrial engineer who emigrated from Holland after World War II, refuses to continue in the experiment:

At 250 volts, he pushes the chair away from the shock generator and turns to the experimenter.
Subject: Oh, I can't continue this way; it's a voluntary program, if the man doesn't want to go on with it. . . .
Experimenter: Please continue.
Subject: No, I can't continue, I'm sorry.
Experimenter: The experiment requires that you go on.
Subject: The man, he seems to be getting hurt.
Experimenter: There is no permanent tissue damage.
Subject: Yes, but I know what shocks do to you. I'm an electrical engineer, and I have had shocks . . . and you get real shook up by them—especially if you know the next one is coming. I'm sorry.
Experimenter: It is absolutely essential that you continue.
Subject: Well, I won't—not with the man screaming to get out.
Experimenter: You have no other choice.
Subject: I *do* have a choice. Why don't I have a choice? I came here on my own free will. I thought I could help in a research project. But if I have to hurt somebody to do that, or if I was in his place, too, I wouldn't stay there. I can't continue. I'm very sorry. I think I've gone too far already, probably.

How can we distinguish between those people who agree to obey the experimenter's demands to administer increasing shock and those who refuse to obey? Studies examining personality traits have failed to find any differences between obedient and disobedient subjects (Elms and Milgram, 1966; Kilham and Mann, 1974). Nor do there appear to be any differences in the level of obedience in different countries (Mantell, 1971). For reasons that are not yet clear to social psychologists, there are some people—the disobedient subjects—who refuse to relinquish personal responsibility for their actions to someone else. Obedient subjects, on the other hand, appear willing to let the experimenter take responsibility for what they, the subjects, are doing. Subjects reason that the experimenter must know what he is doing and that they aren't responsible if they are merely acting as his agents or assistants. Therefore, believing they are not personally responsible for what happens to the learner, obedient subjects administer what could be a lethal electric shock.

We will see in the following section that the same issue of denying personal responsibility for one's own actions can also impede helping another person in an emergency.

GUIDED REVIEW

Learning Objectives 8, 9, 10, 11, and 12

1. Changes in attitudes, emotions, or behaviors resulting from the actions of others is referred to as _____ .
2. An attitude consists of three components: _____ .
3. Attitudes are positively, though imperfectly, correlated with _____ .
4. A persuasive communication is apt to have a greater effect on attitude change if the communicator is high in _____ .

5. Mass media are often influential only indirectly. _____ , who pay particular attention to the mass media, communicate the information they have acquired in face-to-face interaction with others, a process called _____ .

6. _____ involves judging someone on the basis of membership in a group. It is often accompanied by _____ , beliefs about members of a group that are resistant to change.

7. Racial prejudice can be viewed as an _____ .

8. The assumption that individuals who differ in race are also different in their beliefs is known as _____ .

9. _____ and increased _____ can reduce prejudice and stereotyping.

10. Individuals may relinquish personal responsibility for their actions by following the orders of an authority figure, according to Milgram's studies on _____ .

11. Disobedience can be increased by bringing the subject and learner _____ and by including a second experimenter who _____ with the first.

ANSWERS

1. *social influence* 2. *cognitive, emotional, and behavior tendency* 3. *behavior* 4. *credibility* 5. *Opinion leaders; the two-step flow* 6. *Prejudice; stereotypes* 7. *attitude* 8. *belief prejudice* 9. *Familiarity; contact with others on an equal basis* 10. *obedience to authority* 11. *closer together; disagrees*

Prosocial and Antisocial Behavior

Among the most fascinating puzzles of human behavior is why it is that people can be so compassionate and loving toward one another and at other moments be so cruel and inhumane. Milgram's research on destructive obedience to authority was designed to deal with one small piece of this puzzle. Psychologists have addressed the larger issues of kindness and cruelty more directly by studying the willingness or unwillingness of people to help or harm others. We begin with a discussion of people's willingness to offer assistance to others in need, also known as prosocial behavior. We then consider studies of aggression, or antisocial behavior. In each section we see the importance, not of an individual's personality as a determinant of helpfulness or violence, but of the immediate situation in which an act of kindness or cruelty seems appropriate to the individual actor.

Helping Behavior

In 1982, Americans contributed more than $59.9 billion to charitable organizations. Over 300,000 charities exist in the United States, according to the American Association of Fund-Raising Council, and these charities receive much of their support from voluntary contributions and volunteer workers. It would seem that we are altruistic, caring people.

Kitty Genovese was a young woman who was murdered on the streets of New York one night in 1964 in view of at least thirty-eight of her neighbors. Not a single person tried to intervene or help in other ways, despite the fact that the slaying took about thirty minutes. The case, which has become a classic example of people's indifference toward others, implies we are uncaring, unhelpful people.

How can we explain this paradox, which on the one hand suggests that we are helpful and on the other hand that we are uncharitable and reluctant to help? When *The New York Times* investigated the slaying of Kitty Genovese, it reported the wisdom of social scientists, philosophers, and clergymen about the unwillingness of her neighbors to offer assistance: New Yorkers are apathetic, some suggested. They don't care about anyone but themselves, suggested others. We are all alienated from society, or from God, or from our neighbors, said still others. A psychiatrist reported that television has turned us into passive spectators, rather than actors. Among the many explanations offered were that people are afraid to get involved; they have no sense of social responsibility; and they are fascinated by violence. If any of these answers are correct, how can we explain the remarkable degree of sacrifice and philanthropy reported by charitable organizations?

One common element in the answers of experts that were reported by the *Times* is that the failure to help in an emergency stems from some characteristic of individuals: apathy, fear, or a feeling of isolation, for example. As we have seen in our discussion of attribution, when people are asked to explain the causes of another person's actions, or in this instance inaction, they often do so by referring to some characteristic of the other's personality. However, research on this topic demonstrates that personality traits may have little to do with action or inaction in such cases. Instead, attention must be given to the situation in which the event occurs. Perhaps there are certain situations in which a person is more or less likely to offer help.

The Good Samaritan Often Acts Alone: Diffusion of Responsibility.   Two social psychologists began a series of studies shortly after the Kitty Genovese slaying to explore why so many people failed to intervene on her behalf (Latané and Darley, 1970). They found that New Yorkers would often respond to simple requests for help, such as giving directions or change for a dollar, so it was not the case that they were unconcerned or apathetic about their fellow citizens.

The researchers noted that people were most likely to respond to a request for aid when they were alone, rather than with others. In one study, students were participating in what they thought was a market research survey being conducted by a young woman. Subjects were filling out questionnaires alone or with another person while the young woman was on the other side of a sliding partition. As they worked on their questionnaires, they heard her moving around in her "office" and eventually heard her climb up on a chair to get a book from the top shelf of her bookcase. Then they heard a loud crash, a woman's screams, and "Oh, my God, my foot . . . I . . . I . . . can't move. . . ." This tape-recorded sequence was the "emergency" to which subjects could respond.

In all, there were four different groups in this experiment: students alone in the testing room, two strangers in the room, two strangers, one of whom was passive during the emergency, and two friends in the

Table 14.3 Percent of subjects helping in the emergency

Condition	Percent offering help
Alone	70
With passive stranger	7
With another stranger	40
With friend	70

From Bibb Latané and John Darley, The Unresponsive Bystander: Why Doesn't He Help?, © 1970, pp. 60 and 62. Adapted by permission of Prentice-Hall, Inc., Englewood Cliffs, New Jersey.

room. The results, shown in table 14.3, indicate that a person alone or one with a friend is more likely to respond to the emergency by seeking help or offering help than in the other conditions.

Bibb Latané and John Darley explain this as a **diffusion of responsibility;** that is, *feelings of responsibility to help are spread across all the individuals present.* If there is only one witness to an emergency, that person is apt to feel fully responsible for helping the victim, and so is most likely to help. If there are several people present, each of them feels somewhat less responsibility for helping the victim. After all, each of them can ask "Why should I help when there are all these other people around? Why me?" and so each of them is less apt to help.

In a study designed to test the importance of personality in helping, Latané and Darley gave students a wide variety of personality tests, including measures of authoritarianism, alienation, need for social approval, and social responsibility. Later on in the semester, some of the students were gathered together to discuss problems of college life, and one of these students (actually working with the researchers) noted that he was an epileptic. During the course of the discussion, the epileptic began to have a seizure. Latané and Darley were interested in correlating the students' scores on personality scales with the speed of helping. (For an explanation of correlation, see Appendix A.) As can be seen in table 14.4, the correlations are all low, the

Table 14.4 Correlates of speed of reporting the seizure	
Personality item	Correlation
F Scale (authoritarianism)	+.20
Number of siblings	+.18
Age	+.14
Machiavellianism	+.08
Need for social approval	+.04
Birth order	.00
Social responsibility	−.02
Alienation	−.10
Father's education	−.12
Church attendance	−.17
Length of stay in New York City	−.18
Father's occupation	−.24
Size of community in which subject grew up	−.26

From Bibb Latané and John Darley, The Unresponsive Bystander: Why Doesn't He Help?, *© 1970, pp. 115–117. Adapted by permission of Prentice-Hall, Englewood Cliffs, New Jersey.*

strongest one being −.26 between speed of helping and the size of the community in which the student was raised. In other words, personality does not predict who will offer help or how quickly.

Further studies on personality and helping have pointed out that the type of emergency or request for help is important. If there are personality traits correlated with donating blood, for example, they may not be the same ones that are correlated with intervening in a violent crime (Gergen, Gergen, and Meter, 1972).

Imitation and Helping.   While the diffusion of responsibility explanation for helping (or failing to help) has been widely supported in studies by social psychologists, it is still true that some people do offer help, regardless of whether other people are present. These people are relatively uninfluenced by the social setting (the number of others present) and act on behalf of the victim. It is also true that for some types of emergency, such as an automobile crash, the most proper kind of help to offer is not always apparent. In many of these situations, people may want to help but not know what to do. In such cases people are likely to look to others for guidelines as to how to act. As in so many other ambiguous situations, we take our cues from other people. By their words and deeds, they help us to define the situation as one that does or does not require action. If others help, we are more likely to help. If they merely stand around, trying to figure out what to do, we are more likely to stand around doing the same (Bryan and Test, 1966; Shotland and Heinold, 1985). Thus, social comparison processes also play a role in emergency intervention.

In some cases it is possible to distort the nature of the emergency, to convince yourself that it isn't really an emergency, or even that the victim for some reason deserves to be a victim. This last possibility has been studied by Melvin Lerner (1980) as the *just-world phenomenon.*

The Just-World Phenomenon.   Nearly everyone learns to think of events in the world as meaningful, orderly, and caused. Every great religion teaches that God is fair and just. Therefore, if something happens, it must be fair and just or it would not have occurred. Events, in other words, don't just happen for no reason. If an emergency arises, it is not unreasonable to assume that it has some causes and that it is in some way explainable. The belief in a just world suggests that we look for, and are often able to find, some reason that will explain why an event occurs. Stereotypes of minority groups, for example, may be seen as justifications for why they may live in substandard housing, be in ill health, and often be unemployed. The just-world phenomenon suggests that stereotypes arise because we are able to see people as responsible for their own misfortunes. Likewise, when someone encounters an attack taking place on the street, the belief in a just world may enable them to justify the event by blaming the victim. This is particularly true of our reactions to strangers. If a person feels some emotional attachment to the victim, then the victim is less likely to be blamed for the misfortune (Aderman, Brehm, and Katz, 1974).

And sometimes an individual concludes that the world is not always just, as was the case with many of the individuals who rescued Jews from the Nazis.

Christians Who Saved Jews from the Nazis. An interesting study was conducted by Perry London (1970), whose purpose was to find out "if there are stable traits of character connected with extremely altruistic acts such as those in which the Christians in Nazi occupied Europe risked their lives trying to save Jews." Twenty-seven Christians who had rescued Jews during World War II were interviewed.

"The behavior of rescuers cannot easily be classified by any simplistic definition, however. Some were paid a great deal of money for their efforts, usually in connection with essential parts of their operations, such as buying forged papers, food, or arms, or bribing officials. Some spent fortunes or were left destitute as a result. Some who had almost nothing to begin with shared it with good grace—or without" (London, p. 244). There were almost no common themes in the rescuers' motives for helping Jews. Some of them had long been affiliated with Jews, others were anti-Semitic. Some began their operations out of kindness; others just seemed to fall into the role of rescuer.

For instance, rescuing Jews began for a wealthy German businessman when his secretary came to him, said that the Germans were going to kill her Jewish husband, and asked for help. At first he thought she was crazy, but she was convinced that they were going to kill all the Jews in town, so although he felt this was untrue, he agreed to let her husband stay in his office over the weekend. Through this act of compassion he found himself in the rescue business. Once he found that the Jews' fears were justified, he was pulled in deeper and deeper.

London points out that many rescuers began their operations not with forethought but out of circumstances. He did note that there seemed to be certain personality traits needed for persistent work in rescuing others: (1) a spirit of adventure; (2) a strong identification with a model of moral conduct, usually a parent; and (3) a sense of being on the margins of society, of not quite fitting into the mainstream.

One rescuer, a Seventh-Day Adventist minister, helped because he felt it was his duty as a Christian to do so, despite the fact that he was mildly anti-Semitic. In other words, people helped for a wide variety of reasons, mainly having to do with circumstances rather than with any particular set of personality traits.

Aggression

Because aggression is such a troubling and complex feature of human behavior, there are studies and interpretations of aggression from nearly every conceivable position in the social and behavioral sciences. There are many summaries of this varied literature (e.g., Blanchard and Blanchard, 1984; Geen and Donnerstein, 1983; Goldstein, 1986; Moyer, 1976; Zillmann, 1980). We focus here on social psychological interpretations of aggression, though some of them also involve biological and physiological variables.

Most social psychologists define **aggression** as *the intentional injury of another person,* and we will use this definition here, although it is not very precise. It is imprecise because it excludes the possibility that kicking the cat or smashing a glass against the wall is aggression, and because discovering the intention of an actor's behavior is no easy task. What, for example, is a father's intention when he spanks his child for lying? Is it his intention to injure the child? To prevent him from lying again? To teach the child how a father punishes a child? Most students of aggression agree that the motives for aggressive behavior are mixed, that the majority of instances of aggression are seen by the aggressor as *instrumental,* that is, helpful in the attainment of some goal. (See Research Box: Frustration and War.)

The study of human aggression has led to the development of many theories, some of which are reviewed here. Note how one theory led to modifications and revisions in later theories to make them more precise.

RESEARCH BOX

Frustration and War

Table 14.A Relationship between level of frustration and degree of internal violence

High degree of internal violence	High frustration (34)		Low frustration (6)
	Bolivia	Iran	Argentina
	Brazil	Iraq	Belgium
	Bulgaria	Italy	France
	Ceylon	Japan	Lebanon
	Chile	Korea	Morocco
	Colombia	Mexico	Union of South Africa
	Cuba	Nicaragua	
	Cyprus	Pakistan	
	Dom. Republic	Panama	
	Ecuador	Paraguay	
	Egypt	Peru	
	El Salvador	Spain	
	Greece	Syria	
	Guatemala	Thailand	
	Haiti	Turkey	
	India	Venezuela	
	Indonesia	Yugoslavia	

A theory of aggression, if it is sound, ought to be capable of explaining, and perhaps predicting, wars between nations. In addition, a good theory should carry implications for the reduction of violence. Of the theories reviewed in this chapter, frustration-aggression theory more than any other has been applied to aggression between nations.

In examining the frustration-aggression theory within the context of nations rather than individuals, it is necessary to distinguish between two types of political violence: revolutionary violence *within* a country and international warfare *between* two or more countries. Frustration-aggression theory has more often been applied to the former than the latter.

In perhaps the best studies of frustration and revolutionary violence, Ivo Feierabend, a political scientist, and Rosalind Feierabend, a social psychologist, examined various sources of frustration and their effects on violence within political entities (1966, 1972). They obtained information for eighty-four nations on such variables as the percent of the population that was literate; the number of radios, newspapers, and telephones per 1000 people; the number of phy-

Low degree of internal violence	High frustration (2)	Low frustration (20)	
	Philippines	Australia	New Zealand
	Tunisia	Austria	Norway
		Canada	Portugal
		Costa Rica	Sweden
		Czechoslovakia	Switzerland
		Denmark	United States
		Finland	Uruguay
		West Germany	
		Great Britain	
		Iceland	
		Ireland	
		Israel	
		Netherlands	

om Feierabend and Feierabend (1972). Data are for the period from 1948 to 1962.

sicians in the nation; per capita income and GNP; and the percent of population living in rural and urban areas. They also obtained information on the degree of aggression within the country. They determined the amount of aggression directed by individuals and groups within the political system against other groups or officeholders, as well as the amount of aggression directed by officeholders against others. Political violence includes strikes, riots, terrorist acts, mass political arrests, coups d'etat, and political executions.

In this research, frustration was defined as unsatisfied needs, expectations, or aspirations of many people. Feierabend and Feierabend reasoned that in countries with a largely urban population and a high degree of literacy, people would be aware of, and consequently would expect, more phones, newspapers, medical attention, money, and food. In one study, Feierabend and Feierabend (1972) found that those countries with the greatest frustration levels also had the highest rates of political violence (see table 14.A).

Does this way of conceptualizing frustration also account for international aggression? The Feierabends and Frank Scanland (1972) examined international hostility, including formal protests, accusations, expulsion of diplomats, troop movements, the severing of diplomatic relations, military actions, and declarations of war. For the period of 1955 to 1960, the relative amount of internal frustration for fifty-three nations is positively correlated with international aggression ($r = +.33$). Not surprisingly, those countries exhibiting greatest internal violence also were the most externally aggressive ($r = +.52$).

To the extent that the Feierabends' conception of frustration is similar to that of Dollard, et al. (1939) in their initial version of the theory, we can conclude that both revolutionary violence within a country and warfare between countries are positively related to frustration. Unfortunately, this analysis of war does not provide a detailed description of the particular mechanisms that operate to determine revolutions or wars. For example, it does not tell us whether a high degree of internal violence follows or precedes international violence. It is conceivable that international acts of aggression are instrumentally employed to undermine internal revolutions by providing the population with a common focus in the form of a foreign enemy. Also, the theory does not tell us which countries will be aggressed against. On the whole, however, the evidence indicates that the level of frustration of a nation's population is positively associated with both domestic and foreign aggression.

Frustration-Aggression Theory. The frustration-aggression theory is elegant in its simplicity (Dollard, et al., 1939). It states that "The occurrence of aggression always presupposes the existence of frustration and . . . the existence of frustration always leads to some form of aggression." Frustration was defined as any interference with ongoing behavior.

It was quickly pointed out by critics that interference with ongoing behavior is very common and rarely leads to aggression (Maslow, 1941). Each day people are frustrated by closed doors, waiting lines, and impossible or difficult tasks, and they are remarkably nonaggressive in the face of these persistent frustrations. We know, too, that people may be aggressive in the absence of frustration. Soldiers fighting a battle, children imitating aggressive scenes they have witnessed on television, and bullies picking a fight with a weaker individual are all examples of aggression that does not stem directly from frustration. So the theory as originally stated is incorrect. Frustration does not always lead to aggression and aggression is not always preceded by frustration.

To their credit, the original theorists conceded that many of these criticisms were valid, and they revised the theory. While frustration always leads to a *tendency* to aggress, they now said, the organism may learn other ways of responding to frustration. Neal Miller (1941) further stated that aggression may also be caused by factors other than frustration. But which frustrations lead to aggression, and when will aggression occur in the absence of frustration? These questions were not addressed in the revised frustration-aggression theory, thus making it difficult to test. What was needed was a theory that specifies when frustration will lead to aggression.

A Revised Frustration-Aggression Theory. That refinement was made by Leonard Berkowitz (1969; 1978), who borrowed from recent developments in biology. It had become increasingly obvious to students of animal behavior that animals often perform certain unlearned behaviors only in the presence of particular stimuli. For example, the male stickleback fish will perform a complicated mating ritual only when it first sees a swollen red belly on a female stickleback (Tinbergen, 1951). Thus, the "instinctive" behavior of fertilizing her eggs is accomplished only when a particular stimulus—the sight of a swollen red belly—triggers the behavior. Berkowitz suggested that in order for frustration to produce aggression, some triggering mechanism or releaser stimulus must be present. In humans this is the presence of an **aggressive cue,** *a target, situation, or object that is associated with aggression.* If a person is frustrated and there is an aggressive cue present, then aggression will result. If frustration occurs in the absence of an aggressive cue, then some other behavior will occur. In humans, unlike in stickleback fish, aggressive cues may be learned through a variety of processes, usually through classical conditioning (see Chapter 5).

Over the past twenty years, Berkowitz and his colleagues have published dozens of studies in support of this version of the frustration-aggression theory. Berkowitz further modified the theory to include anger, as well as frustration, as a prerequisite for aggression.

Arousal and Aggression. Why should just the two emotions of frustration and anger precede aggressive behavior? What is special about them, as distinct from other emotions, such as fear, jealousy, love, or anxiety? Dolf Zillmann (1971; 1979) has argued that it may not be the particular emotions of frustration or anger that lead to aggression but the fact that these and other emotions are accompanied by physiological arousal. Perhaps what is necessary for aggression is arousal, rather than a particular emotion, such as frustration or anger.

In order to test this theory, Zillmann (1971) showed groups of college males one of three films. One was a relatively boring story that contained no aggressive or sexual scenes that might arouse the students. A second group viewed a film that had been determined to be moderately arousing and highly aggressive in content. A third group saw a highly arousing film with explicit scenes of sexual activity. At various points in the experiment, arousal was measured by taking blood pressure readings. After viewing the films, students were incorrectly led to believe that they were teaching a list of words to someone and could express their approval or disapproval of his responses by administering various intensities of electric shock. As predicted, the students who were most aroused (those viewing the sexually explicit film) gave the most intense shock. Those who were least aroused (who viewed the boring film) gave the least aggressive responses.

More recently, numerous studies have examined both the role of arousal and of sexually explicit material in eliciting aggressive behavior (Donnerstein and Malamuth, 1985; Goldstein, et al., 1975; Malamuth, Feshbach, and Jaffe, 1977). When a person is aroused by whatever means—even by physical exercise—that arousal may dissipate slowly, and long after the initial arousal there may be some residual arousal remaining. This may be reinterpreted by the person as anger, which in turn may justify aggressive behavior. In other words, a person may attribute his arousal to another person and not to the film or exercise that actually produced it. This often happens in cases of child or spouse abuse, in which the victim is blamed for angering or frustrating the aggressor.

Social Learning Theory and Aggression. Despite the advances in our understanding of aggression, made possible by the various modifications of frustration-aggression and arousal theories, much violent behavior remains to be explained. In many instances of aggression, the aggressor does not appear to be frustrated or aroused. Where does seemingly spontaneous aggression come from? This question is particularly troubling when the aggressor is a youngster. Parents are often surprised to find their children acting aggressively when they have made every effort to suppress their aggression. Part of the answer is provided in research on modeling and observational learning, described in Chapters 11 and 12.

Albert Bandura (1973) proposed that children learn aggressive behaviors merely by being exposed to them. Seeing aggression performed on television or by parents and siblings is sufficient to cause the child to learn aggressive behaviors (fig. 14.3). Whether or not the child actually performs the learned behavior depends on whether the child has been, or has seen others, rewarded or punished for aggression. Even if the child has been punished, the aggressive behaviors will still have been learned and are, therefore, potentially capable of being expressed.

How much violence are people exposed to? According to ratings published in the Newsletter of the National Coalition on Television Violence (1983), there are about ten acts of violence per hour of television programming. The average child watches TV for six hours per day, thus viewing more than twenty thousand violent episodes per year.

Social learning theory has numerous implications for the understanding of aggression. Not only is it concerned with the acquisition and performance of aggressive behavior; it also has implications for the reduction of violence, for aggression in the mass media, sports, and even the criminal justice system. The foremost implication of social learning theory and its considerable empirical support is that witnessing violence on television, in sports, or in other people does not result in a decrease in the viewer's own level of violence.

Figure 14.3 *According to Albert Bandura, seeing aggression performed on T.V. is sufficient to cause children to learn aggressive behaviors*

Though there is very little evidence to support this position, known as the **catharsis hypothesis,** most people believe *that one somehow gets rid of anger or aggressiveness by watching other people engage in violence.* On the contrary, social learning theory and its accompanying research demonstrate that for most people, most of the time, exposure to violence increases a person's level of aggressiveness.

Child and Spouse Abuse. The incidence of child abuse and spouse abuse in the United States is not known, but it is estimated that over five children per 100,000 are physically assaulted by their parents each year, and that as many as ten percent of all married women are physically abused by their husbands (Gil, 1970; Green, 1980; Steinmetz and Straus, 1978).

Most studies of abusive parents have attempted to find the types of personality that are correlated with abuse (Spinetta and Rigler, 1977). The most common finding of such studies is that children who were abused often grow up to abuse their own children, a social learning view. Even so, most parents who abuse their children were not abused themselves, and many children who were abused grow up to be loving, nonabusive parents. A study of sixty abusive parents concluded that "If all the people we studied were gathered together, they would not seem much different than a group picked by stopping the first dozen people one would meet on a downtown street" (Steele and Pollock, 1968).

If abusive parents and spouses do not differ in any obvious psychological way from nonabusers, then perhaps the process of abuse is not different from aggressive behavior in general. A parent begins to punish a child, and the aggression escalates until it results in serious harm to the child. In laboratory studies, aggression escalates, as well (Zimbardo, 1969). College students who were placed in a situation in which they could punish another person for errors on a learning task became increasingly aggressive over time (Goldstein, Davis, and Herman, 1975).

GUIDED REVIEW

Learning Objectives 13, 14, 15, and 16

1. Individuals are more likely to help a person in distress when they are alone than when they are in groups of strangers. This is explained by the concept of _____ .

2. People often look to others to help them define what sort of response is appropriate in an emergency. They often _____ the helping or nonhelping response of those around them.

3. The tendency to justify a person's being a victim can be explained with Lerner's concept of the _____ .

4. In a study of Christians who saved Jews from the Nazis, _____ personality traits were found among the rescuers.

5. _____ has gone through several modifications, since its first appearance in 1939. A recent modification by Berkowitz states that frustration and _____ result in aggression only when an _____ is present.

6. Emotions, such as anger and frustration, also include _____ , which Zillmann says is necessary for aggression.

7. Exposure to violence is capable of teaching violence to observers, according to Bandura's _____ .

ANSWERS

1. diffusion of responsibility 2. imitate 3. just-world phenomenon 4. no common 5. Frustration-aggression theory; anger; aggressive cue 6. physiological arousal 7. social learning theory

SUMMARY

I. Social comparison is the process by which we obtain information about ourselves and our world by comparing ourselves with others.   (p. 470)

   A. We tend to choose others for social comparison whom we expect to be similar to ourselves in terms of the particular opinion or ability under examination.   (p. 470)

   B. Social comparison is often used to cope with stressful or ambiguous events, such as surgery or natural disasters.   (p. 471)

II. Social perception refers to the process of forming judgments and impressions of other people. (p. 471)

   A. Our impressions of others are typically uniform and consistent. We form beliefs about what personality characteristics belong together, which is our implicit theory of personality. (p. 472)

B. Impression formation is concerned with how we form opinions about others. First impressions are sometimes based only on simple adjective descriptions. In such situations some descriptions, such as "warm" or "cold," may influence how we evaluate other traits. (p. 472)

C. Attribution is the study of how we explain the causes of one's behavior. We tend to judge whether a behavior is internally or externally caused, that is, whether it is due to some characteristics of the actor or to situational pressures from the actor's environment. There is a tendency to see our own behavior as internally caused when the outcome of the behavior is desirable and as externally caused when the outcome of the behavior is undesirable. This is known as the attributional bias. (p. 473)

III. Interpersonal attraction research looks at the social and psychological bases of friendship and love. (p. 474)

A. The most frequent basis for attraction is theorized to be similarity of attitudes, values, beliefs, and experiences. Theories differ in their explanations of why similarity leads to attraction. (pp. 474–75)

B. Romantic love has most often been viewed by psychologists as an emotion, involving both physiological and cognitive components. (p. 476)

1. One theory of romantic love says that although similarity may be important early in a relationship, complementary personality traits are important at a subsequent stage. (p. 476)

2. Love can also be seen as a social role that we learn. As with any other social role, love carries with it certain obligations and rights, and individuals play this role when they believe it is appropriate or desirable to do so. (p. 477)

IV. Social influence is the effect that other individuals have on our beliefs, attitudes, and behaviors. (p. 478)

A. Attitude is a tendency to respond in a consistently favorable or unfavorable way to a class of objects. Attitudes consist of cognitive, emotional, and behavioral tendency components. (p. 478)

1. Attitudes are related to behavior but do not always correspond precisely to behavior. Attitudes are one of several determinants of behavior. (p. 478)

2. Cognitive dissonance theory helps explain the relationship between attitudes and behavior. The theory states that behavior also influences attitudes, as well as vice versa. (p. 478)

3. Attitude change may result from persuasive communications. All communication involves a source, message, channel, and audience. If sources are high in credibility, they are generally more effective than low-credibility sources. Persuasive messages tend to be most effective when they take into account the audience's own attitude. Mass media tend to influence people's attitudes indirectly by first influencing those who pay most attention to the media, who then influence their friends in face-to-face contact. (pp. 479–80)

B. Prejudice is often viewed as an attitude in which a person holds negative views about a person on the basis of that person's membership in a group. (pp. 480–82)

1. Prejudice is usually accompanied by stereotypes, or generalizations about a person or group in which all members of the group are incorrectly assumed to have some trait in common other than the one defining the group. (pp. 482–83)

2. People may assume that members of other races may hold different beliefs and values. This is known as belief prejudice. (p. 483)

3. Prejudice can be reduced by working together toward superordinate goals. (p. 483)

C. We are often influenced by the demands of authority figures to obey them. This process has been examined in classic experiments by Stanley Milgram. (pp. 484–85)

1. Obedience to authority can be reduced by bringing the teacher and learner closer together or by having a second experimenter who disagrees with the first in the presence of the teacher.   (p. 485)

V. Humans can be both very helpful and supportive or very cruel and violent toward one another. Psychologists study these seemingly contradictory tendencies in the areas of prosocial and antisocial behavior.   (p. 486)

A. Prosocial behavior examines the extent to which people offer assistance to others. (p. 486)

1. Studies of helping people in an emergency have led to the finding that people are more likely to help when they are alone, rather than with a group of strangers. This is explained with the concept of diffusion of responsibility.   (p. 487)

2. Because emergency situations are often ambiguous, there is a tendency to imitate the responses of others around us in deciding whether to help or what form of help to offer.   (p. 488)

3. Some people have a strong belief that things don't happen without a reason, and they are apt to justify a situation in which a person is victimized. This is Lerner's notion of the belief in a just world. (p. 488)

4. Studies of heroes do not often find that they have any personality traits in common.   (p. 489)

E. Aggression is the intentional injury of one person by another.   (p. 489)

1. Frustration-aggression theory is widely used in psychology and has been modified several times since it first appeared in 1939.   (pp. 490–92)

2. Berkowitz modified the theory to include anger as well as frustration, and he added the concept of an aggressive cue as a necessary condition for aggressive behavior. (p. 493)

3. Physiological arousal has been seen as a necessary condition for aggression in the theory proposed by Zillmann.   (p. 493)

4. Exposure to aggression may teach observers to act aggressively, according to social learning theory.   (p. 494)

5. Social learning theory helps explain the effects of television and film violence on the audience, as well as why aggression tends to be correlated between parents and their children. Social learning theory often contradicts the catharsis hypothesis, which presumes that observing violence is a healthy outlet for aggression. There is little empirical support for the catharsis hypothesis.   (p. 494)

6. Violence in the family, such as child and spouse abuse, does not often involve serious personality disorders but rather seems to be a gradually emerging process. (pp. 494–95)

ACTION GLOSSARY

Match the terms in the left column with the definitions in the right column.

____ 1. Social psychology (p. 470)
____ 2. Social comparison (p. 470)
____ 3. Social perception (p. 471)
____ 4. Implicit theory of personality (p. 471)
____ 5. Impression formation (p. 472)
____ 6. Halo effect (p. 472)
____ 7. Attribution (p. 473)
____ 8. Attributional bias (p. 473)

A. *The tendency to see other people's behavior as internally caused and to see our own behavior as externally caused.*
B. *A general belief that certain personality traits "belong" together.*
C. *The process by which individuals develop opinions of others.*
D. *The field of psychology concerned with the effects that people have on one another.*
E. *The study of how we explain the underlying causes of a person's behavior.*
F. *The process of comparing ourselves with others in order to arrive at judgments about the social and physical world.*
G. *Judgments of other people.*
H. *The tendency to form positive impressions when we know that a person has some positive traits.*

____ 9. **Interpersonal attraction** (p. 474)
____ 10. **Attitude** (p. 478)
____ 11. **Cognitive dissonance** (p. 478)
____ 12. **High-credibility source** (p. 479)
____ 13. **Two-step flow of communication** (p. 480)
____ 14. **Opinion leaders** (p. 480)
____ 15. **Prejudice** (p. 482)
____ 16. **Need complementarity** (p. 476)

A. *One who is thought to be expert, trustworthy, or having relevant experience.*
B. *Negative views and actions directed toward groups of people or members of these groups.*
C. *A tendency to respond in a consistently favorable or unfavorable way to a class of objects.*
D. *Individuals who pay particular attention to the mass media.*
E. *An uncomfortable psychological state that results when two or more cognitions are logically inconsistent.*
F. *The study of the social and psychological bases of friendship and romantic attachments.*
G. *The ability of each person in a relationship to satisfy the needs of the other.*
H. *The process by which individuals learn of mass media content from face-to-face contact with opinion leaders.*

____ 17. **Discrimination** (p. 482)
____ 18. **Stereotype** (p. 482)
____ 19. **Superordinate goal** (p. 483)
____ 20. **Diffusion of responsibility** (p. 487)
____ 21. **Aggression** (p. 489)
____ 22. **Aggressive cue** (p. 493)
____ 23. **Catharsis hypothesis** (p. 494)

A. *A common task that requires members from antagonistic groups to work together.*
B. *A target, object, or situation that is associated with aggression.*
C. *Tendency to spread responsibility for acting among all potential actors.*
D. *The intentional injury of another person.*
E. *The belief that one somehow gets rid of anger or aggression by watching other people engage in violence.*
F. *A generalization about a person or group in which all members are incorrectly assumed to have a trait in common.*
G. *Behavior that arises from prejudiced attitudes and prevents a person from acting freely because of his or her membership in a group.*

ANSWERS

18. F, 19. A, 20. C, 21. D, 22. B, 23. E

1. D, 2. F, 3. G, 4. B, 5. C, 6. H, 7. E, 8. A, 9. F, 10. C, 11. E, 12. A, 13. H, 14. D, 15. B, 16. G, 17. G.

SELF-TEST

1. According to Festinger's social comparison theory, people
   (a) have a need to evaluate their opinions and abilities.
   (b) prefer objective means of evaluating themselves, rather than social means.
   (c) compare themselves with others when objective measures of their opinions and abilities are unavailable.
   (d) All of the above.
   (e) None of the above.
   (LO 1; p. 470)

2. According to social comparison theory, one reason people interact with others is to
   (a) enhance their self-esteem.
   (b) receive positive reinforcement.
   (c) receive feedback about themselves.
   (d) All of the above.
   (e) None of the above.
   (LO 2; p. 471)

3. The study of social perception indicates that
   (a) object perception is just as complex as person perception.
   (b) perceiving people requires consideration of their needs and motives.
   (c) we view people and the causes of their behavior objectively and accurately.
   (d) All of the above.
   (LO 3; p. 471)

4. In Asch's early study of impression formation, in which students were presented with adjectives describing a person,
   (a) the warm-cold variable was a central trait.
   (b) the warm-cold variable was a peripheral trait.
   (c) impressions were based on the sum of all the individual traits.
   (d) people were very accurate in their impressions.
   (LO 3; p. 472)

5. Otto thinks that intelligent people are also friendly. This is an example of his

   (a) perceptual constancy.
   (b) implicit theory of personality.
   (c) halo effect.
   (d) accuracy of person perception.
   (LO 4; p. 472)

6. The relationship between similarity and attraction is

   (a) widely accepted, but disagreement exists as to its best explanation.
   (b) consistent only with a cognitive approach to attraction.
   (c) consistent only with a learning approach to attraction.
   (d) not as important in early stages of a relationship as in later stages.
   (LO 6; pp. 474–75)

7. According to Byrne, an individual will be most attracted to someone who is

   (a) similar on a large *number* of traits.
   (b) similar on a great *proportion* of traits.
   (c) different on some traits and similar on others.
   (d) intelligent, wealthy, and physically attractive.
   (LO 6; p. 475)

8. A person is more likely to form a friendship with someone who lives nearby than at a great distance. This is referred to as the principle of

   (a) residential similarity.
   (b) cognitive balance.
   (c) symmetry.
   (d) None of the above.
   (LO 6; p. 474)

9. According to Winch's notion of need complementarity, similarity is

   (a) unrelated to attraction.
   (b) related to early stages of attraction.
   (c) important only in later stages of a relationship.
   (d) None of the above.
   (LO 6; p. 476)

10. Love can be seen as a learned set of behaviors that is accompanied by rights and responsibilities. This perspective considers love as

    (a) an emotion.
    (b) a social role.
    (c) a form of psychopathology.
    (d) None of the above.
    (LO 7; p. 477)

11. The communication process includes which of the following?

    (a) source
    (b) channel
    (c) message
    (d) All of the above.
    (e) None of the above.
    (LO 8; p. 479)

12. An attitude consists of all but which of the following components?

    (a) cognitive
    (b) attributional
    (c) emotional
    (d) behavior tendency
    (LO 9; p. 478)

13. Attitudes

    (a) allow psychologists to predict behavior accurately.
    (b) are not always predictive of behavior.
    (c) do not concern behavior at all.
    (d) are negatively correlated with behavior.
    (LO 9; p. 478)

14. Research indicates that reducing prejudice between two groups may occur with

    (a) any contact between the two groups.
    (b) equal-status contact between the two groups.
    (c) educational programs aimed at correcting misconceptions.
    (d) engaging in competitive tasks.
    (LO 10; p. 483)

15. Conflict between groups can be reduced by working together on a task for their mutual benefit. This is referred to by Sherif as

    (a) cognitive dissonance.
    (b) equity.
    (c) a superordinate goal.
    (d) the culture assimilator.
    (LO 10; p. 483)

16. Belief congruence is Rokeach's notion that

    (a) we like people of the same race as ourselves who agree with us.
    (b) we like people of other races to disagree with us.
    (c) we like people who share our beliefs, regardless of race.
    (d) prejudice is a result of an authoritarian personality.
    (LO 11; p. 483)

17. According to Latané and Darley, the reason that people are unlikely to help someone in an emergency can be explained by

    (a) the personalities of the witnesses.
    (b) the tendency to devalue the victims of crime.
    (c) the situational variable of number of witnesses present.
    (d) None of the above.
    (LO 14; p. 487)

18. According to a social learning interpretation of the failure of a group of bystanders to help someone in distress, each individual

    (a) determines the relative costs and rewards for helping.
    (b) attempts to determine his or her responsibility for helping.
    (c) imitates the nonhelping response of others.
    (d) assesses the victim's blame for being in such a predicament.
    (LO 16; p. 488)

19. If something good happens to a person, we may conclude that the person deserved it. This is part of which theory?

    (a) diffusion of responsibility
    (b) social learning theory
    (c) imitation and modeling
    (d) just-world phenomenon
    (LO 13; p. 488)

20. A study of Christians who saved Jews from the Nazis found that the rescuers

    (a) had a high need for social reward.
    (b) all held positive attitudes toward Jews.
    (c) usually worked closely with Jews in their jobs.
    (d) All of the above.
    (e) None of the above.
    (LO 13; p. 489)

21. Milgram's research on obedience found that

    (a) in most studies, only one or two percent of subjects administered the most severe shocks.
    (b) even when subjects had to place the victim's hand on the shock plate, over half of them still administered the most intense shock.
    (c) the closer the subject was to the victim, the less likely the subject was to administer severe shock.
    (d) the more education a subject had, the less likely the subject was to obey the experimenter's demand for intense shock.
    (LO 12; p. 484)

22. The original frustration-aggression theory by Dollard, et al., states that

    (a) frustration always causes aggression.
    (b) aggression is always caused by frustration.
    (c) frustration is the interruption of ongoing behavior.
    (d) All of the above.
    (e) None of the above.
    (LO 15; p. 492)

23. Berkowitz proposed that frustration

    (a) always leads to aggression.
    (b) is not related to aggression.
    (c) leads to aggression only when an aggressive cue is present.
    (d) does not cause physiological arousal, which is necessary for aggression.
    (LO 15; p. 493)

24. According to Zillmann's theory, which of the following is a necessary condition for aggressive behavior?

    (a) an aggressive cue
    (b) physiological arousal
    (c) frustration
    (d) anger
    (LO 15; p. 493)

ANSWERS

24. b
13. b, 14. b, 15. c, 16. c, 17. c, 18. c, 19. d, 20. e, 21. c, 22. d, 23. c,
1. d, 2. c, 3. b, 4. a, 5. b, 6. a, 7. b, 8. d, 9. b, 10. b, 11. d, 12. b,

SUGGESTED READINGS

Aronson, E. *The social animal.* 4th ed. New York: Freeman, 1984. An excellent overview of the major topics in social psychology, including attraction, aggression, and persuasion.

Goldstein, J. H. *Aggression and crimes of violence.* 2d ed. New York: Oxford University Press, 1986. An overview of the psychological literature on human aggression and violence.

Levin, J., and W. Levin. *The functions of discrimination and prejudice.* New York: Harper & Row, 1982. A discussion of the development and maintenance of prejudice in American society.

Milgram, S. *Obedience to authority.* New York: Harper & Row, 1974. A summary of a dozen experiments on obedience, with fascinating excerpts from dialogue between subjects (both obedient and disobedient) and the experimenter.

Tavris, C. *Anger: the misunderstood emotion.* New York: Simon & Schuster, 1983. A highly readable and thoroughly up-to-date view of the social psychology of anger, emotion, and aggression. Tavris argues persuasively that anger is a controllable, but sometimes useful, emotion.

c h a p t e r

15

Group Processes

LEARNING OBJECTIVES

After reading this chapter, you should be able to

1. distinguish between large and small groups, primary and secondary groups, task-oriented and socio-emotional groups, ascribed and achieved groups. **(p. 504)**

2. indicate some of the ways in which individuals behave differently in groups than when acting alone. **(pp. 506–9)**

3. trace the development of social facilitation theory, and understand the ways in which the presence of others may influence learning and performance. **(pp. 507–8)**

4. specify the reasons that people join groups and the bases for their attraction to a group. **(pp. 510–12)**

5. identify two types of leadership theories: those that see leadership as a personality trait or set of traits of the leader, and those that emphasize that leadership is a product of the relationships among leader characteristics, group tasks, and group structure. **(pp. 514–15)**

6. recognize how norms develop in a group and how they are passed on from one "generation" to another. **(pp. 517–18)**

7. discuss the extent and reasons for conformity to group norms, beginning with the classic studies by Asch and Newcomb. **(pp. 519–21)**

8. indicate how group behavior differs from collective behavior. **(p. 522)**

9. outline the basic theories of collective behavior. **(pp. 524–25)**

Types and Characteristics of Groups

A **group** *is two or more people who are aware of having something meaningful in common.* Groups do not really exist: they are abstractions. Individuals are the tangible components of a group, but groups exist only when the individuals feel a sense of something shared. Even though groups are abstractions, they exert great force on us and may profoundly influence our lives, in much the same way that democracy and liberty do.

Most people gain a sense of themselves by being members of different groups. In answer to the question "Who am I?" group membership plays an important role. "I'm Hungarian. I'm a Catholic. I play the violin. I'm an engineering major. I belong to the theater club." We are unique in part because our group loyalties and memberships are unique (Simmel, 1955).

Types of Groups

Because groups are so numerous and ubiquitous, psychologists and sociologists have found it useful to divide them into various categories. The most frequent distinctions are made among types of groups based on their size, the amount of intimacy existing among members, their function, and their membership requirements.

Size: Large and Small Groups. In **small groups,** *those with thirty or fewer members, each member may have personal, face-to-face contact with the other members.* In **large groups,** *with more than thirty members,* such *personal contact is difficult or impossible* to achieve. Large groups are likely to have a formal organizational structure, such as a president and board of directors. Large groups also divide their labor into specific tasks. For example, one committee may take care of social functions and another may facilitate the business meetings. In small groups, formal organization is less common, and division of labor does not so often occur.

In a small group it is possible to maintain close, personal contact with other group members, and this is one of the prime sources of satisfaction in being a member of a small group. This can be seen in the tendency to form small subgroups within a large group. At a large party, for example, as the guests arrive, they tend to form a single group engaged in one conversation. Once ten or so people have arrived, the larger group will form smaller subgroups, perhaps with four or five people standing in one corner of a room talking about one thing and a second subgroup of a half dozen in the kitchen discussing something else. Once the party is in full swing, there will be a number of small groups, each consisting of from two to about six or seven members. When the party begins to break up, the process will reverse itself until the few remaining guests once again form a single interacting unit of five or six individuals.

Intimacy: Primary and Secondary Groups. Some groups are much more impersonal and formal than others. Our family and close friends clearly are different sorts of groups than the freshman class or the local stamp club. The sociologist Charles Horton Cooley (1909) proposed that primary groups, those in which face-to-face contact occurs, are basically different from **secondary groups,** *in which contact is formal and impersonal.* **Primary groups,** *especially family and peers, are fundamental to the formation and maintenance of our values, attitudes, goals, and sense of identity.* In secondary groups there is little sense of sharing a common fate, of what Cooley called a "we feeling." Participation in a primary group is often an end in itself. It is satisfying and meaningful and may serve no other purpose than allowing us to be with our friends and family. Secondary groups are not ends in themselves but are means to some personal, social, or professional goal. Examples of secondary groups are business organizations, the Democratic party, the Boy Scouts, a church, the Psychology club, and autograph collectors.

CAREER BOX

Leading a Self-Help Group

A great many behaviors that contribute to illness and death are a result of pressure from one's family and group of peers. Smoking, overeating, and lack of exercise are three examples of changeable behaviors that arise largely from conformity to the norms of one's reference groups. For example, teenagers begin to smoke cigarettes when they are exposed to parents and peers who smoke cigarettes. If group pressure can lead to smoking, why not use group pressure to change undesirable behavior?

Many self-help groups use basic principles of small-group study to change the health-related behavior of their members. For example, in a typical group designed to help members give up smoking cigarettes, new norms are presented. The connection between smoking and drinking coffee or talking on the telephone must be broken, and this is accomplished by providing the individual with new norms and with social support from the group for conforming to these norms. The member who violates these norms will feel like an outsider in the group.

In order to become a full-fledged member, the individual must quit smoking. Rewards and group support are provided for adherence to this new standard. Social comparison processes enable the new member to compare his or her reactions to giving up cigarettes with those of others who have undergone a similar experience. This reassures them that their reactions are typical and that they will adjust to this new norm. Loyalty to the group grows, particularly as the individual feels that giving up cigarettes is a difficult sacrifice to make. Most self-help groups encourage members to contact one another for support and encouragement. As a member goes without cigarettes for a longer and longer period of time, newer members may come to rely on him for support and advice, thus strengthening loyalty to the group and the commitment not to smoke.

Many former members of self-help groups subsequently come to lead such groups, perhaps the supreme measure of commitment. A knowledge of the principles by which groups develop and transmit norms and by which group cohesion and loyalty are strengthened allow a leader to run these groups effectively. What is essential for the effective functioning of self-help groups is to permit members to interact and reinforce commitment among one another.

Function: Task-Oriented and Socio-Emotional Groups. **Task-oriented groups** *form for the limited and specific purpose of attaining a goal:* to elect a candidate to office, to raise money for a charity, or to win a football game, for example. Other groups, called **socio-emotional groups,** have no such specific aim but *exist in order to satisfy the social and emotional needs of their members* (Bales, 1950). In socio-emotional groups it is the interaction itself that is the major purpose of membership. Fraternities, parties, and social clubs are all examples of socio-emotional groups. Of course, no single group is purely task-oriented or purely socio-emotional. A factory may hold an annual picnic, and a sorority may volunteer at a state hospital. So we speak of groups as being *primarily* one or the other type.

Figure 15.1   Group memberships may be ascribed or achieved

Membership Requirements.   We join some groups and are thrust at birth into others. Our nationality, religion, gender, and innate abilities are all **ascribed** to us; we do not choose them. Yet we are all members of what are called **ascribed groups** *based on involuntary traits and characteristics.* Other groups, such as social clubs and professional organizations, are **achieved groups;** *we voluntarily join* them, assuming we meet their membership requirements, such as being a student or having a medical degree. (See fig. 15.1.)

Not only may groups that we join or otherwise belong to influence our values, attitudes, and behavior, but groups we do not belong to may also have a profound influence on us if we identify strongly with them. *Groups that a person does not actually belong to but identifies with are called* **reference groups,** and these may have as strong an influence on behavior as membership groups. In Philadelphia on any spring or summer day one can see hundreds of people who are not members of the Phillies wearing Phillies caps or shirts, a sign of their identification. And when the Phillies win a game, even more people wear Phillies caps and shirts (Cialdini, Borden, Thorne, Walker, Freeman, and Sloan, 1976; Sloan, 1979). As a reference group, a sports team is often more influential than one's own membership groups.

How Does Group Behavior Differ from Individual Behavior?

Since a group consists only of individuals, one might think that the behavior of a group could be predicted from a detailed knowledge of its individual members.

Psychologists are divided in their opinions on this issue. Behaviorists tend to believe that a detailed knowledge of the individuals comprising a group will enable prediction of the group's behavior. Research has shown, however, that the behavior of groups and individuals do differ. This may be because a group presents additional stimuli that may affect its members. As one psychologist notes, "The group is not more than the sum of its parts, but rather it is *different* from the sum of its parts. An individual behaves differently in the group situation because he is experiencing a different set of stimuli" (Shaw, 1976). Therefore, people's behavior outside a group will not necessarily allow prediction of their behavior within a group. This can be seen clearly in studies of social facilitation and risk-taking.

Social Facilitation. Perhaps the most fundamental question we can ask about groups is *how the mere presence of other people influences the behavior of a single individual.* This is generally considered under the somewhat misleading heading of **social facilitation.**

In one of the earliest experiments in psychology, which involved bicycle racers, and in a later study of children winding fishing reels, subjects were observed while they performed either alone or in the presence of other people (Triplett, 1897). Cyclists racing only against time did less well than those who raced against another cyclist. Overall, children wound fishing reels better when they were in competition than when they performed the task alone. From this and several other early experiments (e.g., Dashiell, 1930), it appeared that the presence of other people facilitated or improved performance, thus the term social facilitation.

However, not all studies found an improvement in performance when others were present. In one study (Pessin, 1933), students learned lists of nonsense syllables either alone or in the presence of an audience. Learning a series of nonsense syllables was accomplished faster when students were alone than when they were in front of spectators. Here is a case in which the presence of others interfered with performance.

These inconsistent findings occurred not only with human subjects but also with various infrahuman species. Rats and chickens were found to eat more in groups than when alone (Harlow, 1932; Tolman and Wilson, 1965), and ants excavated more soil in the same amount of time when other ants were working simultaneously with them than when they worked alone (Chen, 1937). These animal experiments all point to a facilitation of behavior when others of the same species are present. In some animal experiments, however, notably those in which the animals were learning a maze or learning to make discriminations among different objects, the animals did better when alone (Gates and Allee, 1933; Klopfer, 1958).

The research on the effects of working alone versus working with others was thus truly contradictory. This state of confusion existed for over fifty years. In 1965, Robert Zajonc provided a clear theoretical explanation of all these seemingly contradictory effects. He noted that essentially two types of tasks were studied in social facilitation research: tasks that required the performance of well-learned responses and tasks that required the acquisition of new responses. This is the familiar distinction made by many learning theorists (e.g., Bandura, 1965; Tolman, 1932) between *learning* and *performance.*

If we divide all the tasks studied in social facilitation research into learning tasks and performance tasks, the results are not contradictory at all. When the task requires the subject to acquire some new response, such as learning nonsense syllables or learning to negotiate a maze, the task is accomplished better when the subject is alone than when others are present. When the task requires only the performance of some well-learned or instinctual response, such as riding a bicycle or eating food, performance is better when others are present.

Why should learning be impaired and performance enhanced by the presence of others? Zajonc borrowed two concepts from learning theory: response hierarchy and general drive. *The range of responses to a task or stimulus, from the most to the least probable is a* **response hierarchy.** If the task is well-learned, such as riding a bicycle or instinctive, the dominant or most probable response in the hierarchy of possible responses is correct. If the task requires learning, the most likely or dominant response is apt to be wrong. For example, when you first learn a task, such as typing, positioning your fingers on the keyboard is awkward, and your first efforts at typing are anything but correct. Once you have mastered the task of typing, the dominant response is likely to be correct. You no longer need to look at the keyboard while typing; you somehow "know" when you're doing it right.

We can now state that the presence of others enhances the emission of dominant responses. According to learning theory (Spence, 1956), one reason that dominant responses are likely to occur is that **general drive** level, or arousal, is high. Zajonc proposed that the presence of others increases drive, and this increase in arousal accounts for the increased emission of dominant responses. Thus, novel tasks are better learned alone, whereas performance tasks are better performed in the presence of others.

This elegant bit of detective work by Zajonc not only makes sense of scores of contradictory studies but also highlights the importance of theory as a tool in explaining behavior. There have been some modifications in the theory. Nicholas Cottrell (1968; Cottrell, et al., 1968) has argued that the presence of others is not an innate biological source of drive in humans but a learned source of arousal. He proposes that the presence of others increases arousal primarily when the audience is evaluating the individual. In one series of studies (Strube, Miles, and Finch, 1981), joggers were timed when there was either an attentive or an inattentive audience, or no audience at all. They ran faster when there was an interested spectator, but not when there was an uninterested spectator, thus confirming Cottrell's hypothesis. This theory has also been used to explain the home-team effect in sports. John Edwards (1979) argues that home teams tend to perform better than visiting teams partly because they play before supportive fans. These home-team fans increase the arousal of

the athletes, which in turn enhances the emission of dominant responses, accounting for their improved performance. (See Research Box: The Home-Field Disadvantage?)

Do Groups Make More Risky Decisions Than Individuals? Imagine that the social committee, of which you are a member, has raised $10,000 for the junior class. Most of that money will be used in eight or nine months for the annual Junior Class Bash, and so your committee must decide where to invest the money for the next several months. After discussing the possibilities for investment with the faculty advisor from the School of Business, your choices are most reasonably restricted to:

Savings account	Pays 5¼% interest
Blue-chip stock	Probably won't lose money; will make about 8% plus dividends
Money market fund	Variable interest, probably about 12%
Mutual fund	May lose money or make up to 20% with dividends and interest
Speculative stock	May lose money or make up to 100% with dividends and interest

What will the committee do? Research has shown that if the individual members of the committee vote on these alternatives independently, they will suggest a more conservative investment, such as the blue-chip stock, than if the group makes a single decision after discussing the alternatives as a group (Stoner, 1961; Kogan and Wallach, 1964; Dion, Baron, and Miller, 1970; Brown, 1986). This *greater risk-taking in groups, as compared to the decisions of individuals, is referred to as the* **risky shift.** (This should not imply that groups *always* make riskier decisions than individuals. When making group bets, such as on a horse race, group decisions tend to be more conservative [Knox and Safford, 1976; see also Fraser, Gouge, and Billig, 1971].)

There have been numerous explanations offered for the fact that groups and individuals differ in their decisions. The diffusion of responsibility interpretation (see Chapter 14) states that there is relative anonymity in a group and that this makes the individual in the group feel less responsibility for the quality of the group decision. Thus, individuals in a group are more willing to accept a decision that carries a lower probability of success (Wallach, Kogan, and Bem, 1964). But because we know that group decisions are not more risky than individual decisions in every instance, an alternative interpretation is that groups tend merely to *polarize* decisions. Whatever the initial tendency of the majority of group members is—toward risk or conservatism—will be the direction of the group decision (Doise, 1969; Laughlin and Earley, 1982; Zaleska, 1978). Group decisions may simply be more extreme than individual decisions, sometimes in the direction of more extreme caution and sometimes in the direction of more extreme risk.

The familiarization explanation argues that enhanced risk-taking in groups is a function of group discussion. A risky alternative might seem very extreme and therefore undesirable to an individual. However, in a group setting in which this alternative is widely discussed, it becomes more familiar and then seems less extreme.

Disinhibition, *a general lowering of restraints,* may also explain increased risk-taking in groups. When one group member argues for a risky alternative, others in the group may also become less inhibited about arguing for extreme positions (Pruitt, 1971).

The explanation most favored by social psychologists is risk as a cultural value (Brown, 1965; 1986). According to this view of decision making, for any given type of decision there is apt to be some general belief about the desire of risk in the culture. For example, risk is a positive value in discussing investments in a capitalist society, but in discussing certain health issues, risk is a negative value, and decisions concerning one's health tend to be more cautiously made.

GUIDED REVIEW

Learning Objectives 1, 2, and 3

1. Groups may be characterized along four dimensions: _____ , _____ , _____ , and _____ .

2. _____ are those groups with more than thirty members, while _____ are those with thirty or fewer. In _____ , face-to-face contact with all members is possible.

3. Intimate, face-to-face groups are called _____ , whereas _____ are more formal and structured.

4. Groups that exist primarily to accomplish a goal or perform a task are called _____ . Those that exist mainly for the pleasure of interacting with others are called _____ .

5. Groups to which we belong at birth are called _____ and those whose membership requirements we must meet in order to join are called _____ .

6. A group may influence us even if we are not technically one of its members. Such groups are referred to as _____ .

7. The mere presence of others may influence our behavior. This area of theory and research is called _____ .

8. We tend to _____ better alone and _____ well-learned responses better in the presence of others.

9. Learning and performance are influenced by others because the presence of others increases _____ .

10. Groups often make _____ decisions than the individuals would who comprise the group.

11. Explanations for the "risky shift" include _____ , and risk as a _____ .

ANSWERS

1. size, intimacy, function, membership requirements 2. Large groups; small groups; small groups 3. primary groups; secondary groups 4. task-oriented groups; socio-emotional groups 5. ascribed; achieved groups 6. reference groups 7. social facilitation 8. learn; perform 9. drive or arousal 10. more risky 11. diffusion of responsibility, familiarization, disinhibition; cultural value

RESEARCH BOX

The Home-Field Disadvantage?

It is generally assumed that playing a game at home is an important advantage to the individual athlete or team. There is some research in support of this belief (Edwards, 1979; Goldstein, 1979). The reasons given for this "home-team effect" are increased motivation and arousal among athletes engendered by supportive fans. But is playing before the home crowd always beneficial?

Roy Baumeister and Andrew Steinhilber (1984) reasoned that the desire to perform well before a home crowd might increase the athlete's self-awareness and that this, in turn, would interfere with athletic performance (because when you're busy paying attention to yourself you can't also be paying attention to the ball or concentrating on your performance). To test this hypothesis the researchers examined the records of baseball World Series games from 1924 to 1982 and National Basketball Association championship games from 1967 to 1982. For each of these games the location is determined by a simple formula without regard to win-loss records. (For example, in alternate years, the American and National baseball leagues host the first, second, sixth, and seventh World Series games.) As it becomes more critical to win (for example, in the last or seventh game of the World Series), self-awareness should increase, particularly among home teams, because the fans are judging them more critically. It is in just such circumstances that performance is apt to suffer.

As can be seen in table 15.A, home teams tend to win the vast majority of their games early in the series. But when it is crucial to win (in the last or seventh game), home teams win only about four times out of ten.

Why Are Groups Attractive to Individuals?

People belong to many groups. Why do they join the particular groups they do, instead of other groups? What social and psychological functions do groups serve for their individual members? We have already examined one reason for social affiliation in Chapter 14, namely social comparison. We join with others in order to obtain information about our own abilities, opinions, and beliefs (Festinger, 1954; Suls and Miller, 1977). We tend to affiliate with those individuals who are similar to us because they provide us with valuable feedback about ourselves.

Sometimes we join a group expecting its other members to be similar to us and find that in some way our opinion, ability, or belief is considerably different from theirs. In such a case, we would find that the group exerts pressure on us to conform to its standards. If, after a period of trying to conform to the group's norms, a deviant member is unable or unwilling to conform, he will cease to compare himself with other members of the group and may withdraw from the group.

Emotion and Affiliation

Although social comparison theory is concerned with feedback about one's opinions, abilities, and beliefs, Stanley Schachter (1959) has extended the theory to

Table 15-A Outcome for home and visiting teams as a function of game

World Series Games, 1924–82				NBA Championship Games 1967–82			
Games		Winners		Games		Winners	
	Home	Visitor	Home %		Home	Visitor	Home %
1 and 2	59	39	.602	1–4	115	49	.701
Last game	20	29	.408	Last game	19	22	.463
7	10	16	.385	7	5	8	.385

From Baumeister, R., and A. Steinhilber, "Paradoxical Effects of Supportive Audiences on Performance Under Pressure: The Home Field Advantage in Sports Championships," in Journal of Personality and Social Psychology, 1984, 47, 85–93. Copyright 1984 by the American Psychological Association. Reprinted by permission of the publisher and the author.

Does the home team "choke," or do visiting teams excel in these circumstances? Baumeister and Steinhilber examined fielding errors in World Series games and found that home teams make twice as many errors in the seventh game (1.31/game) as in the first two games (.65/game). Visiting teams make fewer errors in the seventh game (.81) than in the first two games (1.04/game). Thus, there is evidence that the home-team performance deteriorates at a greater rate (.65 − 1.31 = −.66) than visiting-team performance improves (1.04 − .81 = +.23).

include feedback about one's emotional state as well. Schachter studied the role of emotion in affiliation based on social comparison theory. In a typical study, college women were told that they were about to participate in an experiment that involved either severe or mild electric shock. The women were then given an opportunity to wait alone or with others while the equipment was being set up. Choosing to wait with others was considered a measure of affiliation.

Those expecting severe shocks preferred to wait with others, whereas those expecting only mild shocks preferred to wait alone or didn't care whether they waited alone or with others. In a series of such experiments, Schachter found that the tendency to affiliate with others was greatest for those experiencing high fear.

Furthermore, subjects preferred to wait with others who were undergoing the same emotional experience rather than with others who were not experiencing fear at the time. Schachter also found that the tendency to affiliate with others was influenced by birth order. Firstborns and only children are more likely to want to wait with others than are subjects who have older brothers or sisters (Davis, Cahan, and Bashi, 1977; Zajonc and Markus, 1975).

What do people in these experiments talk about once they have chosen to wait with others? One study (Morris, et al., 1976) examined the topics of discussion among subjects who chose to wait with others. Subjects in the study were awaiting either a fearful task (involving electric shock), an anxiety-arousing task (involving explicit sexual material), or an ambiguous task. (This study distinguishes between fear and anxiety. Anxiety, as described in Chapter 12, is an emotional state that has no objective cause, and fear is an equally unpleasant state that stems from a particular object or event. We may fear something, such as small spaces or electric shock; but we are anxious for no conscious specific reason.) When waiting with others, only those in the fear condition discussed the experiment in an attempt to clarify the situation and presumably to reduce their own level of fear. The presence of other people who are calm can reduce fear in experimental subjects because the subjects tend to direct their attention outward, toward others. On the other hand, anxious people tend to focus inward. Hence, waiting with others will not reduce anxiety in anxious people but will reduce fear in fearful people (Friedman, 1981; Hansson, Noulles, and Bellovich, 1982).

A Reinforcement/Exchange Theory of Affiliation

According to the **social exchange theory** of John Thibaut and Harold Kelley (1959, 1978), *individuals are attracted to groups to the extent that they receive from them social, material, or psychological satisfactions that exceed their own costs or inputs.* This social exchange theory of groups, which stems from a reinforcement learning position, hypothesizes that people assess the relative rewards and costs of participating in a group and evaluate the net profit (outcomes minus inputs) in terms of a personal comparison level, a general expectation of how rewarding a relationship with others should be. People also recognize that if they were not involved in a current relationship or group, they could be part of an alternative relationship or group: if you don't join the stamp club, you will have time for the softball league. They attempt to compare the profits from these alternative groups with those from their current relationships. If an alternative group is seen as more profitable than a current group, a change may occur, but only if one also considers the relative costs of leaving one group (such as losing friends, seeming selfish) and of joining another group (being a new member, having to prove yourself).

Group Cohesiveness

Cohesiveness *refers to the overall attractiveness of a group to its members.* There are two broad sources of cohesion: internal and external. Internal sources of group cohesion include the similarity of the group members (Terborg, Castore, and DeNinno, 1976), the opportunity to interact personally with others (Marshall and Heslin, 1975), the relaxation that sometimes accompanies social interaction (Kissel, 1965), and the opportunity to compare one's own feelings and abilities with similar others (Festinger, 1954; Suls and Miller, 1977). Then, too, we may gain relative anonymity in a group, *losing our sense of identity and individuality in a crowd—a state called* **deindividuation** (Festinger, Pepitone, and Newcomb, 1952; Zimbardo, 1969). There are also outside pressures that tend to keep groups together. Sometimes these external sources of cohesion take the form of social pressures, such as prejudice and discrimination, that force people to live together or work together.

In most large American cities there are homogeneous neighborhoods that consist mainly of a single group: blacks, Hispanics, Irish, Italians, Jews, Orientals, Poles, or yuppies, for instance. These neighborhoods exist because of both internal and external factors. There are sources of social and personal satisfaction in living among one's kinsmen: it is possible to speak the same language, obtain familiar foods, observe ethnic customs, and to engage in social and recreational activities consistent with one's experience and interests. In a homogeneous community, one need not be so concerned with prejudice from outsiders. But there are also external pressures contributing to such "nations within a nation." Economic, educational, occupational, and social institutions exert various kinds of pressure on individuals to remain in these segregated neighborhoods. It is the combination of support and satisfaction from members of one's own group and threats and pressures from outsiders that leads to maximum cohesiveness.

Cognitive Dissonance and Group Cohesion. In the early 1950s, publicity was given to a group that had predicted the destruction of the earth by flood. Mrs. Keech, the group's leader, said she was in contact with inhabitants of the planet Clarion. She received messages telling her that she and her followers would be saved. Members of her cult gathered around her in anticipation of the arrival of a spacecraft from Clarion. Among her followers were three social psychologists who were interested in studying members' responses to the failure of her prophecy (and perhaps to save themselves in the event that she was right?). What would members do if at the appointed hour the earth was not destroyed and no spaceship appeared? There were three possibilities: the group could disband, denouncing Mrs. Keech as a false prophet; they could remain intact and conclude that somehow Mrs. Keech had gotten her messages confused; or the group could become even more cohesive in order to protect itself from ridicule. Of course, the earth was not destroyed in the 1950s and Mrs. Keech's predictions were clearly false. Which of the three possible responses did the group take? Not only did members of the group refuse to admit that they were in error but they took credit for saving the earth from destruction! Rather than disbanding, the group began to recruit new members (Festinger, Riecken, and Schachter, 1956).

Cohesiveness increased because of both internal and external pressures. Members had sacrificed a great deal in preparing to leave earth. Festinger's (1957) theory of *cognitive dissonance* tells us that when great sacrifices are made, a person tends to justify them because it would be inconsistent to have to contradict a public statement. **Cognitive dissonance** *is an uncomfortable psychological state arising from the simultaneous presence of two or more logically inconsistent cognitions.* External forces also increased cohesion. Members of the group had been singled out by the mass media and would have been branded as lunatics by the public had they retracted their pronouncements. If unfulfilled prophecies are to lead to greater cohesion among members, it is essential that the members lend strong support to one another (Hardyck and Braden, 1962).

The effects of false prophecies may be culturally determined, at least in part. In 1974, the leader of a new religious sect in Osaka, Japan, predicted that an earthquake would occur on June 18 at 8 A.M. Members of his sect distributed 100,000 leaflets concerning the forthcoming disaster. When the earthquake failed to occur, the leader attempted suicide and later disbanded the sect (Sanada and Norbeck, 1975). It appears that in some cultures suicide is sometimes preferable to shame and public humiliation. Therefore, we must consider not only the group but also the larger social and cultural context in which groups, and prophecies, function.

Another early study designed to test Festinger's theory of cognitive dissonance also dealt specifically with group loyalty. Elliot Aronson and Judson Mills (1959) tested the hypothesis that we come to value a group to the extent that we make sacrifices and exert effort on its behalf. It would be inconsistent, and therefore produce dissonance, to work hard for something, such as membership in a group, and then conclude that the group was unattractive and hardly worth the effort. The researchers studied college women who had volunteered to participate in a series of group discussions about sex. A screening session was held to ensure that each of the women could frankly and openly discuss such a topic.

Three different "initiations" into the group were held. One-third of the women underwent no initiation or screening, serving as a control group. One-third of them underwent a mild initiation, in which they had to read aloud sex-related words. A third group of women, the severe initiation group, had to read obscene words and erotic passages to a male experimenter. After this "initiation," the women listened to one of the group discussions, and what they heard was a dull discussion of the sexual behavior of animals. After having been allowed to join the group, and then learning that it was boring, how would the three groups of women come to view the group? The women who had undergone the embarrassing severe initiation thought the group was more attractive and interesting than those who underwent a mild initiation or no initiation. Thus, attraction to a group may increase the more we suffer or sacrifice for it.

Leadership

Many groups hold elections to determine who their leaders will be. Two questions immediately arise. First, what are the qualities, if any, that a chosen leader must have, both to receive the endorsement of the group's members and to be effective in leading the group toward its goals? Second, is the nominal leader always the most important group member, the one who, more than any other, helps the group achieve its aims?

Despite such common phrases as "a natural-born leader" or "good leadership qualities," leadership is not a characteristic that exists within a person. Instead, it defines a particular type of relationship between two or more people. One person can sometimes force others to do something, but this is not what is meant by leadership (Gibb, 1969). Leadership is more than a personality trait of the individual. We can define **leadership** as *"the presence of a particular influence relationship between two or more persons."* (Hollander and Julian, 1969). In order for a person to be a leader, there must be one or more followers. It would be ridiculous for a person to claim to be the leader of an organization whose membership included only himself. A leader needs followers as much as followers need a leader. An effective leader can facilitate the group's goals.

Leaders sometimes emerge when the goals of a group are not well formulated. In ambiguous circumstances, in which goals are not defined clearly beforehand, a

Figure 15.2 *Is leadership due to personality, to social situations, or to both?*

leader helps shape and articulate those goals. It is this characteristic of leadership—the defining of goals—that so often gives the appearance that personality is important to leadership. This can be seen in our discussion of the "great man" view of leadership.

The "Great Man" Theory of Leadership: Are Leaders Born? A great deal of modern history has been written as if historical events were directly shaped by the personalities of leaders. Hitler, Gandhi, Churchill, and Nixon have all shaped the course of world events on the basis of their personal strengths and weaknesses (fig. 15.2). A popular pastime of contemporary historians is writing psychohistorical analyses of world leaders (see the *Journal of Psychohistory*). Whether such analyses of political leaders are at all capable of explaining complex international events is questionable. Instead, perhaps we must look to the historical, social, economic, and political circumstances surrounding a leader. Here are two characterizations of very different types of leaders.

There is nothing striking about Gandhi—except his whole expression of 'infinite patience and infinite love. . . .' He feels at ease only in a minority, and is happiest when, in meditative solitude, he can listen to the 'still small voice' within. This is the man who has stirred three hundred million people to revolt, who has shaken the foundations of the British Empire, and who has introduced into human politics the strongest religious impetus of the last two hundred years. (Eriksen, 1961, quoting R. Rolland)

Leaders, as we have emphasized, need followers. Having examined Hitler's rise to power, Hadley Cantril (1963) made the following observations of Hitler and the German social climate.

> When institutions and social values are disturbed and when people are disturbed they are anxious to regain mental stability. The easiest and most usual way of accomplishing this is to look for a leader, identify oneself with him, transfer one's troubles to him, and believe that he can always cope with things, that he always has another trick up his sleeve, that he can safely protect one against external dangers. . . . It is no wonder, then, that the message of Hitler, his own obvious belief in the righteousness of his program, his sincerity, and his faith in himself made an indelible impression on those who heard him. In a period of doubt and uncertainty, here was a speaker who did not argue the pros and cons of policies but who was fanatically self-confident; who did not quietly suggest that he and his program were possible solutions, but who actually shouted certainty at the top of his lungs. (pp. 233–236)

Would Gandhi have become a leader in the Germany of the 1930s, or Hitler have become one in India? The **Great Man theory** *assumes that it is the personal strengths and motives of individuals that makes them powerful figures, destined to lead.* And there do seem to be personality traits that make some people more predisposed to lead than others. Yet the situation must be appropriate, and followers must be ready to accept a leader who possesses those particular traits. It is not only the man, in other words, but the situation confronting him that best explains the rise to prominence of historical figures.

Leadership Style. Leaders vary in their style of leadership. For example, some are more democratic than others. In an early study of leader style, children were placed in groups with either an authoritarian leader who controlled and directed their activities, a democratic leader who allowed the children to play a role in deciding what they would do, or a laissez-faire leader who simply let the children do as they wished (Lewin, Lippitt, and White, 1939). The authoritarian leader produced the most aggressiveness among members, whereas the democratic leader produced more efficient and more satisfied groups. (See Meade 1967, for a failure to replicate this experiment in India.) In general, research on personality correlates of leadership has not yielded very reliable or consistent findings (Borgatta, Couch, and Bales, 1954; Stogdill, 1948). As Hollander (1985) has concluded:

> (O)n the matter of leader personality there do not appear to be broad and invariant characteristics that generally distinguish leaders from nonleaders, or "effective" from "ineffective" ones. . . . (p. 516)

An Interaction Model of Leadership: The Contingency Model. If the personality traits of leaders are generally not the primary determinant of effective leadership, then we must consider the group's situation in addition to (or instead of) personality. The contingency model of Fred Fiedler (1971; Fiedler and Chemers, 1974) examines the interaction between leadership and group situations.

The contingency model consists of three dimensions: leader-member relations, the leader's power, and task structure. Some leaders are very authoritarian and directive, but others are very much oriented toward the social and emotional needs of their followers. This is what is meant by poor or good leader-member relations. Leader power refers to the ability to influence group members. Furthermore, some tasks confronting a group are clearly defined and have a definite solution, whereas other tasks are ambiguous and require many

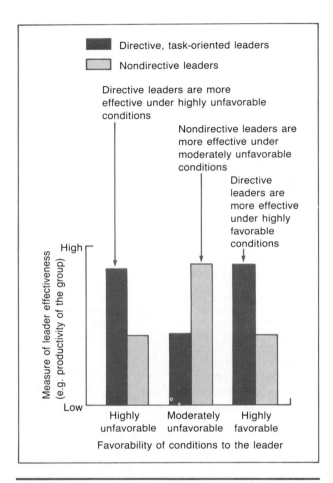

Figure 15.3 *The contingency model of leader effectiveness. According to Fiedler's theory, friendly, nondirective leaders are more effective than direct, task-oriented ones under moderately unfavorable conditions. However, directive leaders are more effective than nondirective ones under highly unfavorable and favorable conditions.*

or uncertain solutions (task structure). It is under conditions that are moderately favorable (defined as those in which there is low leader power and a structured task, or high leader power and an unstructured task) that people-oriented leaders are most effective. Under most other conditions, those that are very unfavorable, a directive leader would be most effective.

The primary predictions of the theory are presented in figure 15.3. For example, a well-liked sergeant who asks a group of privates to dig a ditch will be effective as a leader in this situation. His relationship with the others is good, the task is clearly structured, and the sergeant's power in the military structure is clear (Watson, de Bortali-Tregertham, and Frank, 1984). This theory emphasizes what leaders have known all along—simply being in the position of "leader" does not make one effective. One can be effective only with the proper combination of authority, appropriately good relations with group members, and with certain types of tasks. Even a leader who has strong power or authority but who does not get along well with group members will be ineffective if the task is an unclear one. Research on the contingency model has been supportive of its basic predictions, although some difficulties with the definition and measurement of these characteristics have been noted (Graen, Orris, and Alvares, 1971).

GUIDED REVIEW

Learning Objectives 4 and 5

1. According to _____ , people join groups to receive feedback about the quality of their own opinions, abilities, beliefs, and emotional states.

2. _____ are more affiliative than _____ .

3. _____ is the overall attractiveness of a group to its members.

4. Group cohesion may increase because of _____ attractions of the group and because of _____ pressure on the group.

5. According to _____ , the more we sacrifice for a group the more attractive it becomes to us.

6. The _____ theory explains leadership in terms of the personalities of leaders.

7. The _____ explains leadership in terms of the leader's relations with other members, the leader's power, and the task confronting the group.

ANSWERS

1. social comparison theory 2. First-born and only children; later-born children 3. Cohesiveness 4. internal; external 5. cognitive dissonance theory 6. Great Man 7. contingency theory

How People Behave in Groups

From a family to a fraternity to a government, groups are responsible for making decisions, formulating policy, and providing us with emotional support. Once individuals are assembled for the purpose of performing a task—whether it is something as simple as having a good time or as complex as formulating foreign policy—norms or standards for acceptable behavior begin to develop, and individuals influence one another in direct or subtle ways.

One of the characteristics of a group is that its members are aware of sharing something. What they often share in addition to a stated interest or skill is a set of standards for acting and for judging the behavior of members inside and outside of the group. These standards frequently emerge within the group and are taught indirectly to new members. That is why members of one fraternity may be conservative, dress well, and receive good grades, whereas those of another share a different set of standards for dress, grades, and politics. Not only are these standards developed and transmitted in a group; the group also enforces conformity to them, often in subtle ways. We will now consider how group standards develop and how groups bring about conformity to them.

The Development of Group Norms

The behavior of people in groups is guided not only by the personalities of group members and by sets of formal rules, such as Roberts' Rules of Order, but also by a set of standards or group norms that emerge within the group. The classic study of group norms was conducted by Muzafer Sherif (1936) using the **autokinetic effect,** *which refers to the fact that a point of light in a dark room appears to have movement,* as does a single star seen in the night sky.

Individual subjects were exposed to a point of light and asked to judge how far it moved. They were then tested in a group, and each subject in the group had to state his judgment of the movement of the light. In other conditions, the subjects first made their judgments as a group and were later tested individually. Sherif was

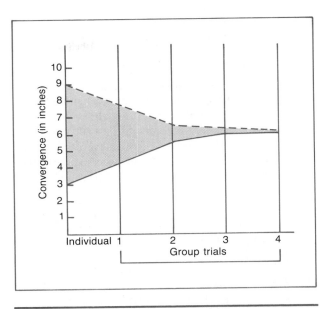

Figure 15.4 Distance judgments made by subjects alone and in a group experiment using a light (autokinetic phenomenon). Subject A, dotted line; subject B, solid line.

interested in whether the individuals would continue to use their own perceptions of distance movement once they were placed in a group, and he also wanted to find out whether those who were first tested in a group would continue to use the group standard or norm when they were later tested alone.

Sherif found that individuals tended to see a narrow range of distances in which light movement occurred. Although this range differed from one person to another, each individual was fairly consistent in his own perceptions of movement. When these individuals were then placed in a small group, the judgments of group members tended to converge, as shown in figure 15.4. For those who began their judgments in a group setting, rather than alone, there was also evidence of convergence. As each person called out the estimate of distance moved, others tended to modify their own estimates. The final result was a fairly narrow range of responses for all group members. The members of a group came to agree on the distance moved by the stationary light, indicating that they had formed an agreed-upon and shared social norm, a standard against which they evaluated their own perceptions. When group members were tested individually, they continued to perceive the movement of the light in terms of the group norm. The norm established in the group influenced the person's judgments even when the person was removed from the group. It should be noted that when subjects are told beforehand that the movement of the light is highly erratic, there is less of a tendency for judgments of group members to converge (Alexander, Zucker, and Brody, 1970; see Moscovici, 1974).

This does not imply that group norms are entirely arbitrary. Research suggests that the norms must be reasonably close to the actual perceptions of the members (Jacobs and Campbell, 1961). The researchers planted confederates in small groups. In the autokinetic situation, these confederates established norms that were considerably different from the perceptions of the actual group members. For example, a group member might judge the movement of the light to be four inches, whereas the judgments of the confederates were closer to fifteen inches. One by one, the confederates were removed from the group and replaced by naive subjects. Although the judgments of the confederates influenced the judgments of naive subjects for several "generations," there was a tendency for the judgments of the group to converge toward four inches and away from the arbitrary norm of fifteen inches. (See fig. 15.4.)

M. K. MacNeil and Muzafer Sherif (1976) have argued that the group norm "disintegrated" in the Jacobs and Campbell study because it was so divergent from the natural judgments of subjects. In their experiment, MacNeil and Sherif had confederates give highly arbitrary responses, somewhat different from those of the actual subjects. They found that the highly arbitrary norm tended to decay as the confederates were replaced by naive subjects but that the moderately arbitrary norm tended to be passed on for many generations of the group. Since new members quickly acquired the group norm when it was mildly arbitrary

and passed it on to still newer members, the norm was perpetuated even when there was a complete turnover in group membership. A very discrepant group norm is more likely to be passed on from generation to generation if the group's members are highly authoritarian in personality (Montgomery, Hinkle, and Enzie, 1976). (An authoritarian person is one who is rigid, conforms to rules obediently, and dislikes those who are different.)

This research indicates how groups are able to perpetuate their standards and beliefs over succeeding generations. It explains, for example, how a particular fraternity is able to maintain its conservative stance on political issues despite the fact that the members who originally adopted these norms have long since graduated.

This research on the formation of group norms is closely allied with studies of conformity and social influence. The research we have reviewed suggests that there are some conditions in which group members resist social pressure and some instances in which they conform to or adopt the judgments of others. To what extent does conformity occur in groups? That is a topic to which we turn next.

Conformity

Conformity *involves changing one's behavior to correspond more closely to the behavior of others.* The word *conformity* has a bad reputation. It suggests a certain amount of dependency, a loss of individuality, and mindless obedience. Yet society depends on conformity for its very existence. Without it, life would be chaotic and people unpredictable. We could not even drive a car from one place to another if motorists refused to conform to the local driving customs. Although not everyone drives precisely at the speed limit, most people do not differ from the posted speed by more than ten percent.

It is not easy to say why any particular driver adheres so closely to such rules, but there are three general explanations (Kelman, 1958). (1) *Compliance:* **Compliance** *is conformity that results from external* *rewards or punishments.* Since there are penalties, both legal and personal, for deviating very much from the speed limit, drivers may conform because of the pressure that the law and other individuals may bring to bear on deviant behavior. The sudden reduction in speed of cars is certainly noticeable when there is a police car ahead. People often comply with norms or customs because of the penalties for noncompliance. (2) *Identification:* **Identification** *is conformity that results from emulating an individual or a group whom one admires.* People may drive at or near the speed limit because they do not want to appear deviant. If they identify with someone who obeys the speed limit, such as their former driving instructor, then they will obey it too, particularly if that person is present as a passenger. (3) *Internalization:* **Internalization** *is conformity that results from one's own internal standards.* Some people drive at the speed limit because they have internalized the belief that the laws are meaningful and beneficial. Drivers may believe that the posted speed limit is indeed the safest or most efficient speed at which to drive. Some may believe that we live in a society of laws and that it is in the best interests of the society for each driver to obey the traffic laws. In these instances, the presence of a police car or the sudden change in speed of other drivers will have little effect on one's own driving speed.

The Asch Studies.   One of the basic statements of Gestalt psychology is that social groups exert pressure on our perceptions, emotions, and behaviors. Solomon Asch (1951) was concerned with the effects of group pressure on perceptual judgments. In one study, groups of from three to fifteen males were to choose which of several lines came closest to a standard line, a task shown in figure 15.5. All but one of the subjects in each group were accomplices of the experimenter. The real subject gave his judgment last, after hearing the judgments of the other group members. Asch arranged for the accomplices to give incorrect answers on certain trials.

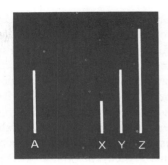

Figure 15.5   An experimental task employed in the Asch conformity study

Nearly one-third (32 percent) of the subjects, when confronted with an incorrect judgment by all other group members, gave incorrect responses themselves. Regardless of group size, if the judgments of accomplices were unanimous, the extent of conformity among naive subjects was the same. However, if one accomplice agreed with the real subject, the tendency to conform to the incorrect majority decreased to ten percent.

In interviews with the subjects following this judgment task, Asch found that there were three distinct motives for yielding to the pressure exerted by the incorrect majority: (1) wanting to appear the same as the others in the group; (2) a lack of confidence and doubts about their own perceptions; and (3) an unawareness of being incorrect. Some subjects actually perceived the incorrect response of other group members as the correct one. This is often interpreted to mean that conformity is not necessarily a conscious process.

Is conformity a particularly American trait? Cross-cultural research finds that conformity occurs to some degree in all cultures and that in Western societies the degree of conformity tends to be similar. Using variations of the Asch procedure, Stanley Milgram (1961) studied conformity in Norway and France. In five different types of situations, the Norwegians conformed to only a slightly greater extent than the French. In one study involving the judgment of tones, sixty percent of the Norwegian subjects and fifty-eight percent of the French subjects conformed to the majority. Considerable research has shown that people are more likely to conform when the judgment task is ambiguous and when members are uncertain of the correctness of their own judgments (Allen and Wilder, 1980; Mausner, 1954).

What if there is a minority of two instead of one? Researchers planted a minority of two confederates in groups of six people. The minority of two always gave incorrect responses on a perception task (judging colors). When the minority gave thoroughly consistent responses (saying "green" when the correct answer was "blue"), over eight percent of the true subjects said "green." In a control group with no confederates, fewer than half of one percent of the subjects said "green." When the two confederates were not consistent in their position, saying "green" on some trials and "blue" on others, naive subjects were not swayed by their judgments. Thus, when the minority is not consistent in its judgments, the majority is not at all influenced, but when the minority is consistent and persistent, a significant proportion of the majority is influenced (Moscovici, Lage, and Naffrechoux, 1969).

Bennington College Studies. We know from the studies of Sherif and Asch, reviewed above, that given fairly ambiguous perceptual tasks to perform in laboratory situations, individual group members are influenced by other members of the group. Theodore Newcomb (1952; 1978) extended research on group influence beyond the laboratory to a more convincing and complex setting. He studied the entire student body of over 600 students at Bennington College for a period of four years. He was particularly interested in "the manner in which the patterning of behavior and attitudes varied with different degrees of assimilation into the (college) community" (p. 215). Students at Bennington College came primarily from conservative and well-to-do homes, and as freshmen they entered college with the conservative attitudes of their parents. Seniors at Bennington, however, tended to be considerably more liberal than underclassmen (over half of them were Democrats, compared with twenty-nine percent of the freshmen). Parents, of course, are often appalled when their children return from a liberal arts college as liberals. How does this transformation occur?

The Bennington students generally identified strongly with their college. It served as a positive reference group (even though they were, technically, part of the group). There were rewards for being nonconservative. The students with the most prestige on campus were those who were most liberal.

Newcomb selected twenty-four nonconservative and nineteen conservative seniors for intensive study. Seniors who remained conservative throughout their four years at Bennington tended to be those who identified more strongly with "home and family" than with the college. They were not well-integrated into the college community and tended to return home on weekends. For them, the college community was not a positive reference group. Some of the conservative students were aware of the conflict between the values of the college and those of their parents and home communities, and they quite consciously decided to go along with the values of their parents. Those who did identify with the Bennington community gradually found that their attitudes converged toward the predominant and rewarded liberal attitudes of their peers.

When Newcomb conducted his studies at Bennington College, it was a school for women only. Do men conform to the same degree as women? There is considerable research with Americans that finds conformity to be more common among women than among men. Perhaps women conform more than men because conformity is taught as a feminine trait and because females attempt to focus their attention on others. In one study, both male and female students formed impressions of other group members and stated their opinions on several issues, such as whether there should be an extension of university library hours. Their opinions were either under surveillance by other group members or were not known by the others. The degree of conformity among females was unaffected by surveillance, but among males conformity was less when surveillance occurred (Eagly, Wood, and Fishbaugh, 1981). In other words, males may not conform in order to establish or maintain their independence in a group.

Conformity is not necessarily the sign of weakness and dependency that it is so often assumed to be. It is not necessarily synonymous with thoughtlessness, though mindless conformity does exist—for example, wearing the same style clothing as your peers or listening to the same kind of music just because they do. Instead, it is a sign of trust, of relying on others as valuable sources of information. Suppose you had a choice of eating in a dozen restaurants, all located on the same street. In several of them there are no customers, but in front of two or three of them are long lines of people waiting for tables. Where would you choose to eat? You might reasonably assume that the food or prices were not very attractive at the empty restaurants, and you would probably be correct. As social comparison theory suggests, we can obtain valuable information about the correctness of our opinions and actions from other people. In many situations, conformity is a sign of trust in the rationality and good judgment of others.

Task Performance

Bombs and the decision to use them, television sets and the programs they broadcast, and textbooks and the ideas they present are all products of group decisions and actions. How well a group performs a particular task or solves a certain problem depends on three sets of variables: task demands, resources, and interaction occurring within the group (Steiner, 1972).

Task demands consist of the requirements of the task and the rules under which the task must be performed. Tasks may be either unitary or divisible. Unitary tasks are those that cannot be easily or profitably broken into smaller subtasks. For unitary tasks, no division of labor within the group is possible. On divisible tasks there are specific subtasks that can be assigned profitably to some group members. For instance making an automobile is a divisible task in that it permits different people to perform different actions, some working on the engine block, others on the electrical system, and so on. Resources include all the relevant knowledge, abilities, skills, and tools possessed by the individuals who comprise the group. Task demands and resources together determine the maximum level of productivity that can be achieved. "If an individual or group possesses all the needed resources, it has the potential to perform the task" (Steiner, 1972, p. 8). If the group has the needed resources but fails to accomplish the task, then its actual productivity is less than its potential productivity. This may occur because of errors, inefficiency, or misuse of resources during the problem-solving process.

Social Loafing.   Groups often fail to achieve their maximum productivity because of **social loafing.** This is *the reduction of individual effort exerted when people work in groups, compared to when they work alone* (Latané, Williams, and Harkins, 1979). We saw in Chapter 14 that individuals may diffuse responsibility for acting in an emergency when other people are present. It appears they do something similar with regard to effort when working within a group. In a series of studies, groups of four people were found to do only about twice the work of the individuals acting alone. Groups of six did only about two and a half times as much work as six individuals working alone. This may be due to the fact that people are more deindividuated or less identifiable in groups.

Individuals were asked to shout as loudly as possible when they were alone, in groups of two, or in groups of six. Sometimes they were told that their individual performances would be recorded and that the experimenters would be able to identify their "output." Others were told that their individual output could not be identified by the experimenters (Williams, Harkins, and Latané, 1981). When people thought they were identifiable, social loafing disappeared. However, when they thought they were not identifiable in groups, social loafing resulted in a drastic reduction in their sound output.

There are also various pressures toward uniformity and conformity in a group that may diminish the quantity or quality of a group's performance (see Equity theory discussion, Chapter 16). Minority views are often discouraged, and it may be the minority view that is the most correct solution (Hoffman, 1965). Agreement may occur if people believe that by agreeing they will be more attractive to other group members. Some individuals in a group talk more than others, and this may also interfere with group productivity. The suggestion that receives the greatest number of favorable comments during group discussion tends to become the solution adopted by the group, even though most of these comments may come from only one or two members (Hoffman and Maier, 1964). The most talkative member is, therefore, likely to promote his or her solution. As the size of the group increases, fewer members contribute to the discussion, and so relatively few possible solutions are aired. (See the Application Box: Groupthink.)

According to social comparison theory and other analyses of group structure, there is a tendency for groups to be homogeneous in composition. This can interfere with problem solving, especially if the problem requires an unusual or highly creative solution. If group members tend to share the same attitudes and beliefs, then it is unlikely that one member will be able to arrive at a highly original solution to such a problem. Often more effective problem solving can be achieved by a heterogeneous group, but this requires being able to overcome the tendency for similar people to join groups.

Collective Behavior

On nearly any day we can read in the newspaper of strikes and riots, social, religious, and political movements, and the unfortunate consequences of panic during a fire, flood, or earthquake. Like so many seemingly patternless events, these behaviors are no more random than are problem solving or conformity. They are as amenable to study by traditional scientific methods as any other form of group phenomenon.

Collective behavior includes the study of crowds, riots, crazes, panics, fads, mass hysteria, protest movements, rebellions, revolutions, fashion, and social movements. **Collective behavior** *differs from other group processes in that it usually emerges spontaneously without a well-defined prior plan of action.* The study of collective behavior serves several purposes. First, it is a process that often involves a loss of life and property, and its study may help us reduce the heavy toll paid by panics, riots, and revolutions. Second, we may learn something about the normal social order if we have an understanding of collective behavior. Only when disorders occur do we have a very clear idea of the meaning of order and stability. Third, collective behavior highlights the dynamic relationship that exists between individuals and groups. You might be a passerby on the fringe of a large crowd, for example, and decide to stop to see what is going on. As others stop to do the same, you suddenly find yourself no longer on the fringes of the crowd but toward its center, being pushed this way and that and suddenly caught up in the pushing and shoving that so often is characteristic of large numbers of people in small spaces. Although there are interesting books and articles on various forms of collective behavior (Lurie, 1981; Milgram and Toch, 1969; Rosnow and Fine, 1977; Rudé, 1964; Turner and Killian, 1972), we will examine only two forms, panics and riots.

Panic. **Panic** *is a form of social disorganization in which individuals compete for access to limited resources, such as food or a doorway.* Panic, more than

Groupthink

Groups are often called upon to make complex and difficult decisions. Presidential advisory boards and cabinets, for example, must make decisions about foreign policy that have long-lasting and irreversible consequences. Many of these group decisions turn out to be ill-considered and disastrous. How do such unproductive decisions come to be made?

Irving Janis, a social psychologist at Yale University, has analyzed a number of American foreign-policy decisions that were less than successful, such as the Bay of Pigs invasion in the 1960s and the escalation of the war in Vietnam (1972; 1982). He calls the tendency of decision-makers to make irrational and uncritical decisions *groupthink.* Groupthink is characterized by the appearance of consensus or unanimous agreement within the group. Each member believes that all members are agreed on a particular decision or policy. Dissenting opinions are not expressed because of the belief that it would undermine the cohesion of the group or be unpopular. Thus, the number of alternatives considered by a cohesive group is minimal.

Some solutions to the problems caused by groupthink have been offered (Janis and Mann, 1977; Flowers, 1977; Tetlock, 1979). First, the leaders of a group must encourage the voicing of all positions on an issue. Longstanding beliefs of the group should be challenged so that new or innovative ideas might be expressed. Whenever a complex decision is to be made, a list of positive and negative factors should be drawn up in an effort to generate as many ideas and solutions as possible. Once a group decision seems to be reasonable, the group should think through all of the possible consequences of that decision. They can often do this by role playing, that is, by imagining themselves acting on the basis of the decision. Groups should encourage expert opinions from people outside the group whose involvement in the appearance of cohesion and consensus is minimal. Generally, if more alternatives are presented and considered, the group's decisions will be more creative and productive (Hackman and Morris, 1975).

any other form of collective behavior, has been studied experimentally by psychologists, perhaps because panics are so often responsible for the loss of lives at fires, sporting events, and rock concerts. The classic study of panic was conducted by Alexander Mintz (1951). He noted that because it normally takes only a few minutes for patrons to file out of a theater or restaurant, deaths that occur during fires are a result of nonadaptive behavior, such as blocking exits and pushing other people. Typically these panics had been explained by reference to such elements as emotional excitement, contagion of emotion among crowds, or suggestibility (LeBon, 1896). Mintz proposed that the decisive factor is not emotional excitement but rather the reward structure of the situation.

In most panic situations, there is a conflict of interest: if everyone cooperates, all can escape, but if a few individuals do not cooperate, if they push and shove, then anyone who does not push will be burned. Thus, when mutual cooperation breaks down, there is a conflict between self-interest and social interest, a conflict also found in analyses of the environment. For example, it may be to an individual's immediate advantage to pollute the atmosphere, but it is to the long-term disadvantage of everyone (Hardin, 1968; Stern, 1976). Mintz conducted experiments in which groups of people had the task of pulling cones out of a glass bottle. Each subject was given a piece of string attached to a cone. Cooperation on the part of subjects was required if the cones were to come out, since the neck of the bottle would permit only one cone at a time to pass. Mintz believed that this task was analogous to going out a theater exit that only one person could pass through at a time. Subjects could win or lose money depending on how much time elapsed before they pulled out the cone. In some experiments (Mintz conducted forty-two of them), water began to fill the bottle, and success was defined as retrieving a dry cone. In control groups, no rewards or fines were levied.

In order to test the various explanations of panic based on emotion, Mintz instructed some accomplices to scream, swear, and behave excitedly during the task. Results indicate that there were no "traffic jams" in the groups that received no reward or fine. Emotional excitement on the part of some subjects had little effect on group efficiency. However, in over half of the experiments involving rewards or fines, jams developed as soon as the bottleneck was temporarily blocked. The introduction of a screen to prevent subjects from seeing one another had no effect on traffic jams; thus, emotional facilitation as an explanation for panics was ruled out. According to Mintz's studies, panics occur when people are penalized for failure to escape and when they are rewarded for successful escape. As the penalties increase for failure to escape, nonadaptive panic behavior also increases (Kelley, et al., 1965; Klein, 1976; Kruglanski, 1969).

Riots.   Like panics, **riots** *are relatively spontaneous, uncoordinated collective phenomena that involve anger or violence.* They seem to be unpredictable and, for the most part, uncontrollable. The storming of the Bastille, the food riots in eighteenth-century Britain, the draft riots in New York during the Civil War, the race riots of the 1940s and 1960s, and riots that have occurred during fires, floods, and blackouts have all been analyzed by observers. Early explanations of riots centered on the immorality of participants, the spread of emotional excitement, and the individual's feelings of anonymity in the **crowd.** Gustav LeBon (1896) and Sigmund Freud (1921) proposed that rioters act on instinct and that emotional excitement spreads contagiously through a crowd. The belief was widespread that crowds engage in random acts of violence and destruction. So was the notion that there are no restraints or norms serving to inhibit the behavior of crowds.

Systematic research on riots, however, demonstrates that behavior is not random, that contagion does not spread indiscriminately among participants, and that there are norms that limit the extent of violence and destruction. Emotionality is passed from one person to another, but the pattern that this contagion takes is orderly and predictable. In a study of hysterical contagion in which workers at a small factory were "bitten" by insects (which in fact did not exist), the imaginary bug first infected those on the periphery of informal groups of friends, and only later did it spread through close circles of friends (Kerckhoff, Back, and Miller, 1965). The looting that often occurs during urban riots is not indiscriminate but shows a pattern of deliberate retaliation against shops and stores thought to be unfair to customers (Berk and Aldrich, 1972).

Riots are complex, dynamic entities. Collective behavior emerges gradually over time. Twenty people do not suddenly turn into a rioting mob. Certain conditions must exist before a particular incident, known as a precipitating event, turns a mass of individuals into a crowd. These conditions may be economic, social, or political.

One study correlated the occurrence of riots with a variety of economic, social, and political conditions (Lieberson and Silverman, 1965). In an analysis of over seventy-five racial disturbances in the United States up to 1916, demographic and housing conditions were found to have no effect on the probability of a riot, but the job situation for blacks and characteristics of local government did have a significant effect. Economic indices have fairly consistently been shown to relate to instances of collective violence. Carl Hovland and Robert Sears (1940) correlated the number of lynchings in the South for the years between 1882 and 1930 with the price of cotton and found that as the price of cotton fell, the number of lynchings increased. Blacks became scapegoats to Southern farmers who lost money on their cotton crops.

One theory of crowd behavior (Turner and Killian, 1957), **emergent norm theory,** *proposes that in ambiguous situations, in which the outcome is uncertain, communication in the form of passing rumors and mingling with others creates a sense that some action must be taken.* Rumors take on the function of norms, suggesting what actions might be undertaken. According to this theory, people in a crowd act the way they do because they believe it is appropriate or required. In other words, they conform to a norm. The initial impetus of this process is some number of individuals in an ambiguous and unstructured situation. A precipitating event, usually a rumor, a violent incident, or some other unusual occurrence, such as a blackout, triggers the rumor process, and ultimately a norm emerges calling for action.

A second theory of crowd behavior is based on the notion of deindividuation. According to this theory, an individual acts more violently in a crowd because he does not feel that he can easily be identified or singled out from the crowd. He feels less "like himself" and is apt to act more extremely. There is evidence that people whose identities are obscured are indeed more aggressive (Zimbardo, 1969). In a test of these two competing explanations for the aggressive behavior of crowds (Mann, Newton, and Innes, 1982), support was obtained only for the deindividuation theory and not for the emergent norm theory.

GUIDED REVIEW

Learning Objectives 6, 7, 8, and 9

1. Group _____ are guidelines for behavior.
2. Sherif used the _____ to study the formation of group norms.
3. Conformity to group norms may occur for three reasons: _____ , _____ , and _____ . Only in the case of _____ does the person conform regardless of whether others are present.
4. In Asch's experiments on conformity, about _____ of the naive subjects conformed to the incorrect judgments of the majority.
5. Newcomb's studies at Bennington College point to the importance of _____ in conformity.
6. Group performance on a task depends on _____ , _____ , and _____ .
7. Groups may perform at less than their potential level of productivity because of _____ , _____ of the abilities and opinions of the members, and the tendency for _____ to be withheld.

8. The emergence of a common focus and of common actions by a number of individuals is called _____ .
9. Collective behavior includes _____ , _____ , _____ , _____ , and _____ .
10. _____ theory suggests that a person is less inhibited in a crowd and is more apt to behave aggressively when immersed in a large group.
11. _____ often are a response to economic, social, and political conditions, rather than occurring spontaneously.

ANSWERS

1. norms 2. autokinetic effect 3. compliance, identification, internalization; internalization 4. one-third 5. reference groups 6. the nature of the task, the characteristics of group members, processes that occur in the group 7. social loafing, homogeneity; minority views 8. collective behavior 9. strikes, riots, crowds, social movements, panics 10. Deindividuation 11. Riots

SUMMARY

I. There are different types of groups with different effects on their individual members. (pp. 504–9)

  A. Groups vary in terms of size, intimacy, function, and membership requirements. (pp. 504–6)

    1. A large group is one in which personal contact with all other members is difficult; usually it consists of more than thirty members. A small group, with thirty or fewer members, is one in which face-to-face contact is feasible. (p. 504)

    2. A primary group is one in which personal contact occurs and from which we derive personal satisfaction. A secondary group is more formal and has less sense of "we feeling." (p. 504)

    3. Task-oriented groups exist primarily for the purpose of accomplishing a specific goal, whereas socio-emotional groups are those in which interaction itself is the primary purpose. (p. 505)

    4. Achieved groups are those whose membership requirements we meet and that we choose to join, and ascribed groups are those we belong to by virtue of our birth. (p. 506)

    5. A reference group is one with which we identify, even though we may not be an actual member of the group. Nevertheless, reference groups influence us because we identify with them. (p. 506)

  B. The behavior of an individual differs when he or she is alone or in a group. (pp. 506–9)

    1. Individuals learn and perform differently when in the presence of others, rather than when alone. This is known as social facilitation. Social facilitation effects may be explained in terms of physiological arousal or drive. (p. 507)

    2. The decisions of groups are often more risky than those of the individuals who comprise the group. This is referred to as the risky shift, which has been explained in terms of the diffusion of responsibility, polarization, familiarization, disinhibition, and risk as a cultural value. (pp. 508–9)

II. Groups are attractive to individuals primarily because they provide information or feedback about their individual members. (pp. 510–12)

  A. Social comparison theory, which states that individuals seek feedback about their opinions, abilities, and beliefs, has been supplemented by Schachter's work, suggesting that they also seek feedback about their emotional states, as well. Individuals who feel very fearful are more likely to affiliate with others than those experiencing less fear. Affiliation under conditions of fear is more pronounced among first- and only-born individuals than among those with older siblings. (pp. 510–11)

  B. Groups also provide social, material, and psychological satisfactions to their members, according to a social exchange theory of affiliation. (p. 512)

  C. Cohesiveness is the attractiveness of a group to its members. (p. 512)

    1. Cognitive dissonance theory states that individuals are most attracted to groups for which they have sacrificed. (p. 513)

  D. Leadership is the ability of one person to influence the behavior of others in a group. (p. 514)

    1. The "Great Man" theory argues that personality is of utmost importance in leadership ability. (pp. 514–15)

    2. Leadership style refers to the amount of control exerted by a leader, from none ("laissez-faire") to democratic, and authoritarian. These different styles are differentially effective, depending upon the task confronting the group and the composition of the group's members. (p. 515)

    3. Fiedler's contingency model of leadership stresses the interaction of the leader's relationship with the group's members, the amount of power possessed by the leader, and the type of task facing the group. All three must be considered in deciding who will be an effective leader in different situations. (pp. 515–16)

III. Groups possess norms and standards, and they demand a certain amount of conformity from their members.   (p. 517)

   A. Group norms emerge when individuals face an ambiguous situation, such as the autokinetic effect, and tend to be used by the individual even when he or she leaves the group. Group norms are passed along from one generation of group members to another.   (p. 517)

   B. Three types of or reasons for conformity are compliance, identification, and internalization.   (pp. 518–19)

      1. In Asch's studies of conformity, about one-third of the naive subjects gave the same judgment as the (incorrect) majority of group members.   (p. 519)

      2. Individuals gradually acquire the values or norms of their positive reference groups, as demonstrated in Newcomb's studies at Bennington College.   (p. 520)

   C. Group performance on a task depends on the demands of the task, the resources available to the group, and the amount and nature of interaction among group members.   (p. 521)

      1. Social loafing refers to the fact that groups sometimes exert less effort than the sum of their individual members acting alone.   (p. 521)

   D. Individuals may interact in response to an unusual or ambiguous event (called a precipitating event) and develop norms and plans for action. This is referred to as collective behavior and includes crowds, riots, panics, social movements, and revolutions.   (p. 522)

      1. Panic is a form of unorganized social behavior in which people compete for a scarce resource, such as an exit. Research indicates that panics are greatest when there are penalties for failure to obtain the scarce resource.   (p. 522)

      2. Riots are forms of collective behavior involving anger or violence. Crowd behavior has been explained by emergent norm theory and by the notion of deindividuation.   (p. 524)

ACTION GLOSSARY

Match the terms in the left column with the definitions in the right column.

_____ **1. Group** (p. 504)
_____ **2. Small group** (p. 504)
_____ **3. Large group** (p. 504)
_____ **4. Primary group** (p. 504)
_____ **5. Task-oriented group** (p. 505)
_____ **6. Socio-emotional group** (p. 505)

A. *An informal and personal group, such as family and peers, that is fundamental to the formation and maintenance of our values, attitudes, goals, and sense of identity.*
B. *A group with no specific aim other than the interaction of its members.*
C. *A group of thirty or fewer members, in which each member may have personal, face-to-face contact with other members.*
D. *A group of more than thirty members, in which personal contact is difficult or impossible.*
E. *Two or more individuals who are aware of having something in common.*
F. *A group formed for the limited and specific purpose of attaining a goal.*

_____ **7. Ascribed group** (p. 506)
_____ **8. Achieved group** (p. 506)
_____ **9. Reference group** (p. 506)
_____ **10. Social facilitation** (p. 507)
_____ **11. Response hierarchy** (p. 507)
_____ **12. General drive** (p. 508)

A. *A group with which an individual identifies but to which he or she does not actually belong.*
B. *A group to which an individual belongs by virtue of involuntary traits and characteristics.*
C. *A state of arousal or motivation to act, without any particular goal.*
D. *The range of responses to a task or stimulus from the most to the least probable.*
E. *A group that an individual may join voluntarily if its membership requirements are met.*
F. *The effect that the mere presence of others has on the learning and performance of an individual.*

____ 13. **Risky shift** (p. 508)
____ 14. **Disinhibition** (p. 509)
____ 15. **Social exchange theory** (p. 512)
____ 16. **Cohesiveness** (p. 512)
____ 17. **Deindividuation** (p. 512)
____ 18. **Cognitive dissonance** (p. 513)

A. *A general lowering of restraints.*
B. *The theory that individuals are attracted to groups to the extent that they receive from them satisfactions that exceed their own costs or outputs.*
C. *The psychological state that results from the simultaneous presence of two or more cognitions that are logically incompatible.*
D. *The state of losing one's sense of identity and individuality, especially in a large group.*
E. *The overall attractiveness of a group to its members.*
F. *The tendency for groups to take more risk when making certain decisions than would the individual group members acting alone.*

____ 19. **Leadership** (p. 514)
____ 20. **Great Man theory** (p. 514)
____ 21. **Autokinetic effect** (p. 518)
____ 22. **Conformity** (p. 518)
____ 23. **Compliance** (p. 518)
____ 24. **Identification** (p. 519)

A. *Changing one's behavior to correspond more closely to the behavior of others.*
B. *Conformity that results from external rewards or punishments.*
C. *The theory that assumes that it is the personal strengths and motives of individuals that makes them powerful leaders.*
D. *The presence of a particular influence relationship between two or more persons.*
E. *Conformity that results from emulating an individual or group whom one admires.*
F. *The tendency to perceive movement in a stationary light when there is no other reference point. Used by Sherif in his studies of the development of group norms.*

____ 25. **Internalization** (p. 519)
____ 26. **Social loafing** (p. 521)
____ 27. **Collective behavior** (p. 521)
____ 28. **Panic** (p. 521)
____ 29. **Riot** (p. 524)
____ 30. **Emergent norm theory** (p. 525)

A. *Conformity that results from one's own internal standards.*
B. *Relatively spontaneous, uncoordinated collective phenomena involving anger or violence.*
C. *A form of social disorganization in which people compete for access to limited resources, such as food or a doorway.*
D. *Proposes that in ambiguous situations, in which the outcome is uncertain, communication in the form of passing rumors and mingling with others creates a sense that some action must be taken.*
E. *Behavior of individuals in a crowd that emerges spontaneously without a well-defined prior plan of action.*
F. *The reduction of individual effort exerted when groups of people work on the same task, compared to the same individuals acting alone.*

ANSWERS

18. C, 19. D, 20. C, 21. F, 22. A, 23. B, 24. E, 25. A, 26. F, 27. E, 28. C, 29. B, 30. D

1. E, 2. C, 3. D, 4. A, 5. F, 6. B, 7. B, 8. E, 9. A, 10. F, 11. D, 12. C, 13. F, 14. A, 15. B, 16. E, 17. D,

SELF-TEST

1. Which of the following is *not* an integral part of the definition of *group?*
   (a) four or more people
   (b) interpersonal contact
   (c) meaningful interaction with others
   (d) a shared goal, attitude, or purpose
       (LO 1; p. 504)

2. Groups differ along four dimensions. Which of the following is *not* one of them?
   (a) function   (c) personality
   (b) intimacy   (d) membership requirements
                       (LO 1; pp. 504–6)

3. All but which of the following is an example of a primary group?
   (a) family
   (b) sorority sisters
   (c) friends
   (d) residents of the same county
       (LO 1; p. 504)

4. A person may identify with a group that the person does not actually belong to. Such a group is called
   (a) an achieved group.
   (b) a reference group.
   (c) a socio-emotional group.
   (d) an ascribed group.
       (LO 1; p. 506)

5. The effects of the mere presence of people on an individual's task performance is termed
    (a) the autokinetic effect.
    (b) social comparison.
    (c) social facilitation.
    (d) reference group function.
    (LO 2; p. 507)

6. Zajonc's theory of social facilitation
    (a) distinguishes between learning and performance.
    (b) notes that the presence of others enhances the emission of dominant responses.
    (c) states that the presence of others increases drive or arousal.
    (d) all of the above.
    (e) none of the above.
    (LO 3; pp. 507–8)

7. The overall attractiveness of a group to its members is the group's
    (a) affiliative tendency.
    (b) cohesiveness.
    (c) comparison level.
    (d) evaluative function.
    (LO 4; p. 512)

8. The text discusses leadership as a(n)
    (a) innate ability.
    (b) characteristic that some people have.
    (c) particular influence relationship between people.
    (d) all of the above.
    (e) none of the above.
    (LO 5; p. 514)

9. Sherif used the autokinetic effect to study
    (a) visual perception.
    (b) the development of social norms.
    (c) group conflict.
    (d) emergent leadership.
    (LO 6; p. 517)

10. People conform to a social norm because
    (a) there are penalties for violating social norms.
    (b) that is what other people do.
    (c) they want to.
    (d) all of the above.
    (e) none of the above.
    (LO 7; pp. 518–19)

11. What percent of subjects in the Asch studies conformed to the incorrect judgments of the group?
    (a) 5   (c) 75
    (b) 33   (d) 95
    (LO 7; p. 519)

12. Newcomb's Bennington College study demonstrated that students became more liberal if
    (a) Bennington was a positive reference group for them.
    (b) they maintained strong home and family ties.
    (c) they went home every weekend.
    (d) their roommates were liberal.
    (LO 7; p. 520)

13. Groups do not always produce as much as their individual members working separately. This is referred to as
    (a) social comparison.   (c) social loafing.
    (b) social learning.   (d) cognitive dissonance.
    (LO 7; p. 521)

14. Riots and crowds
    (a) exist because emotional contagion spreads through the group.
    (b) break out in random places at unpredictable times.
    (c) exist without norms or other regulatory mechanisms.
    (d) all of the above.
    (e) none of the above.
    (LO 8; pp. 522–23)

ANSWERS

1. a, 2. c, 3. d, 4. b, 5. c, 6. d, 7. b, 8. c, 9. b, 10. d, 11. b, 12. a, 13. c, 14. e

SUGGESTED READINGS

Brown, R. W. *Social psychology.* 2d ed. New York: Macmillan, 1986.

Davis, J. H. *Group performance.* 2d ed. Reading, MA: Addison-Wesley, 1979. An overview of research and theories on group problem solving and decision making.

Janis, I. L. *Victims of groupthink.* 2d ed. Boston: Houghton, Mifflin, 1982. A well-written and generally fascinating examination of how political decisions are made and why they are so often poor ones.

Paulus, P. B. *Basic group processes.* New York: Springer-Verlag, 1983. A detailed study of group structure and functioning, including discussions of leadership, decision making, and problem solving.

Weick, K. E. *The social psychology of organizing.* 2d ed. Reading, MA: Addison-Wesley, 1979. A brief examination of the nature, functioning, and functions of large organizations.

c h a p t e r

16

Applied Psychology

LEARNING OBJECTIVES

After reading this chapter, you should be able to

1. specify three of the basic areas of applied psychology: industrial/organizational psychology, human factors, and environmental psychology. **(p. 532)**

2. understand the functions and importance of work and the effects of unemployment on the individual. **(pp. 532–38)**

3. recognize relationships and distinctions between work and leisure. **(p. 532)**

4. outline the basic theories of work motivation: the valence-instrumentality-expectancy theory, and equity theory. **(pp. 533–35)**

5. realize that large organizations have formal structures and networks of communication but that informal social structures and communication networks also exist. **(pp. 539–43)**

6. indicate the roles that psychology has played in industry and business, for example, in personnel selection. **(p. 543)**

7. recognize the different areas of psychology that have been applied to man-machine systems, an area of research known as human factors. **(pp. 543–50)**

8. appreciate the importance of psychological considerations to reduce accidents and increase the efficiency of human-operated equipment. **(pp. 543–50)**

9. distinguish between personal space and territoriality. **(p. 553)**

10. see how personal space alters with circumstances and the ways in which people "defend" their personal space. **(p. 553)**

11. understand the effects that environmental stressors, such as noise, may have on behavior. **(pp. 555–57)**

Table 16.1 Principal work settings of industrial/ organizational psychologists	
Universities	31%
Industrial settings	27
Consulting firm	13
Government and military settings	11
Individual consulting	0.8
Research organizations	0.5
Other	0.5

Source: American Psychological Association

Table 16.2 Principal work activities of industrial/ organizational psychologists	
Management	57%
Applied research	12
Teaching	0.9
Basic research and test development	0.8
Training	0.7
Implementing personnel programs	0.5
Engineering/human factors design	0.2

Source: American Psychological Association

In this chapter, we consider the meanings and functions of work as well as individuals' motivations for working. These extend beyond wages and benefits to include social and psychological motives.

We then examine three distinct areas in which psychology has been applied: business and large organizations, the design and use of equipment, and environmental psychology.

Work and the Individual

The marriage between psychology and industry took place near the turn of the century when F. W. Taylor (1911) launched a movement called **scientific management.** Taylor *focused on the details of a worker's behavior, on his motivation for work, and on the precise measurement and description of jobs.* Since that time both psychology and industry have matured, and the growing process has not been without its pains and quarrels. Today we find industrial and organizational psychologists doing a variety of tasks in many different work settings, as can be seen in tables 16.1 and 16.2.

Industrial psychology *is the application of psychological principles and findings to the world of work (Encyclopedia of psychology* 1981*).* **Organizational psychology,** which *studies the behavior of and within a large bureaucratic business system,* is a branch of industrial psychology. Among the tasks performed by industrial and organizational psychologists are selecting and training personnel, analyzing jobs, developing useful research strategies for industry, and developing procedures for increasing the efficiency of decision making within organizations.

Some Meanings of Work and Leisure

In physics, "work" is a force that acts against resistance, resulting in movement or change. In psychology, **work** *is the expenditure of energy to accomplish a task or goal,* usually in exchange for compensation. In an organization, work consists of those activities whose goals are set not by the individual performing the work but by the worker's employer. **Leisure,** on the other hand, is defined as *activities, excluding essential maintenance functions* (such as shopping, cleaning, eating), *that are performed outside of the work context and whose goals are personally defined and individualistic* (Kabanoff, 1983). These formal definitions, however, do not fully convey the richness of either work or leisure experiences, their social and psychological functions, their interconnectedness, and their importance for day-to-day living.

The Motivation to Work

Why do people work? Would they continue to work if they did not have to earn money to support themselves and their families? Even if people feel they must work, why are some more satisfied with their jobs than others, and how can satisfaction with work be increased? These are some of the questions that industrial and organizational psychologists have addressed. Some psychologists believe that the motivation to work comes strictly from the external environment: a person works because of the rewards that work brings. To other psychologists, work is one method of fulfilling the individual's needs for creativity and productivity; that is, the motivation to work arises from within the individual, from the need to feel a sense of competence and mastery. Still others see work as stemming from deep-seated and unconscious motives.

In this section we consider the three primary explanations for work. The theories and research presented here are not incompatible with one another. Rather than seeing them as competing with one another, you should come to think of them as alternative perspectives, each with something to contribute to an understanding of work.

Herzberg's Two-Factor Theory. Theodore Herzberg and his associates, like many personality theorists, assume that individuals are born with different sets of needs that can be arranged in a hierarchy (Herzberg, 1966; 1976; Herzberg, Mausner, and Snyderman, 1959). Closest to Herzberg's two-factor theory of work motivation is Abraham Maslow's notion of a need hierarchy (see Chapter 8). It is assumed that there are basic biological needs, which, once satisfied, are replaced by more abstract and higher-order needs. Herzberg proposes that *the basic needs,* which he calls **hygiene needs,** include such things as pay, job security, relations with co-workers, general working conditions, and company policies. The *higher-order needs, called* **motivator needs,** *require people to seek challenge, creativity, stimulation, and independence.* They are satisfied by responsible work, by being able to make independent decisions on the job, and by recognition for one's accomplishments. They are satisfied by things that are part of the work itself, rather than by the context in which the work gets done.

Herzberg believes that work undertaken for motivation seeking is preferable to work undertaken for hygiene seeking because it yields productive activity on the part of the worker and few "control" problems for management (Landy and Trumbo, 1980). The theory suggests that if a manager can move individuals from hygiene-seeking levels to motivation-seeking levels, the workers will be self-motivated and not require as much supervision. Motivation-seekers are people who love their work. In order to move individuals from working under a hygiene-seeking to a motivation-seeking level, Herzberg proposes what he calls "job enrichment." This means attempting to make the work more interesting so that workers will derive greater satisfaction from it (Hackman and Oldham, 1975).

Valence-Instrumentality-Expectancy (V-I-E) Theory. Victor Vroom (1964) has proposed a cognitive model of worker motivation and satisfaction, called the V-I-E theory of work motivation, that includes not only the benefits of work, such as pay and fringe benefits, but also considers the individual's perceptions of the value and probability of receiving these benefits. The basic concepts in this expectancy theory are valence, instrumentality, and expectancy.

Valence refers to the emotional reaction to the anticipated consequences of one's behavior. If a person expects that his behavior on a job will lead to positive emotional consequences, then the behavior has a positive valence. Note that this involves the individual's anticipated or expected consequences, and not the actual consequences. *Expectancy* refers to the odds of receiving a particular payoff. An action may have a positive valence because the individual believes he will receive money as a consequence. His view of the probability of actually receiving this money is the expectancy. *Instrumentality* involves the relationship between a particular action and a particular outcome. For example, a promotion may be valued because it is related to other outcomes, such as more money. The relationship between the promotion and the increased money is called an instrumentality relationship. It answers the question, "Is the promotion instrumental in providing me with more money, which I value?"

Thus, the theory focuses not merely on an individual's actual experiences on the job but on the anticipation of events that lie in the future. It refers to the expectations of what will happen as a consequence of a given action. The theory states that individuals ask themselves whether (1) the action has a high probability of leading to an outcome (expectancy); (2) that outcome will yield other outcomes (instrumentality); and (3) those other outcomes are valued (valence).

The basic model of Vroom has been modified and expanded by Lyman Porter and Edward Lawler (1968) and has become the most popular approach to motivation among industrial researchers (Locke, 1975; Lawler, 1973). Research on the theory indicates that the various V-I-E models are better able to predict the *effort* of individuals than their actual job *performance*. It also finds that valence predicts individual effort better than does instrumentality or expectancy, and, furthermore, that the relationship among the three components (V-I-E) is not very strong (the correlations tend to be around .3).

Equity Theory.   In the 1960s, J. Stacy Adams and his colleagues startled the business community by proposing the unthinkable: that workers would be uncomfortable earning too much money, as well as too little. He formulated **equity theory,** which *states that one attempts to make one's inputs and outcomes in a situation comparable to those of one's peers* (1965). Adams represents the theory in the following manner:

$$\frac{O_p}{I_p} = \frac{O_a}{I_a}$$

where O is outcome
   I is input
   p is the person we are discussing
   a is a peer or co-worker of the person.

When this outcome-input ratio is not equal, a state of inequity exists. This, like cognitive dissonance (see Chapter 15), is an uncomfortable psychological motivational state that causes the individual to attempt to reduce the discomfort. When inequity exists, the individual will alter either the inputs (for example, by working harder or less hard or by changing the quality of his or her work), or by altering the outcomes (for example, asking for a raise, quitting, or striking for a better contract). It suggests that overcompensating or undercompensating workers diminishes productivity or job satisfaction.

Of course, the belief that underpayment lowers productivity and morale of workers is widespread and does not require equity theory to make this point. On the other hand, the notion that overcompensation also diminishes the quantity and quality of work was startling. In one test of equity theory (Pritchard, Dunnette, and Jorgenson, 1972), researchers hired more than 250 men to work as clerks. The men were led to believe either that they were being overpaid for their work (by being told that they were underqualified for the job), equitably paid, or underpaid (because they were overqualified). They found that the equitably paid men were more satisfied with their jobs than were either the overpaid or the underpaid workers.

How do inequitably paid workers handle the inequity? According to Adams and other equity theorists (e.g., Walster, Walster, and Berscheid, 1978), equity may be restored in at least four ways: by actually altering one's inputs or altering one's outcomes, or by psychologically distorting the perception of one's own or one's co-worker's inputs or outcomes. For example, an underpaid worker might restore equity by (a) reducing the quantity or quality of his work; (b) seeking a raise; (c) emphasizing the nonpay benefits of the work, such as sick days, vacation time, or the value or interest of the work; or (d) distorting the inputs or outcomes of fellow workers, such as believing they are overqualified for the job or that they find it uninteresting. Of course, the research generated by equity theory has focused primarily on the effects of overcompensation and its effects on work.

Many researchers have included other incentives in addition to wages and have reported that other motives, such as status and prestige, power, job security, novelty, and excitement may overpower equity effects (Andrews and Valenzi, 1970; Machuagwa and Schmitt, 1983). One study (Weick, Bougon, and Maruyama, 1976) found that in the Netherlands people place a high value on inputs, regardless of outcomes. It is doubtful that the input/outcome ratio would play a very significant role in the motivation of Dutch workers.

Support for equity theory has been considerable. When workers are given an opportunity to allocate rewards for work among themselves, for example, they tend to prefer an equitable distribution (Leventhal, Michaels, and Sanford, 1972). This and other research suggests that workers are most comfortable when they are equitably treated. "Research conducted specifically in business settings indicates that the norms of the marketplace are not so very different from those of the rest of life" (Walster, Walster, and Berscheid, 1978, p. 118).

Overcompensation and Intrinsic Motivation. Equity theory states that workers who are overcompensated for their inputs will experience inequity and will attempt to restore equity, probably by altering their performance on the job or their satisfaction with their job. Edward Deci (1975) has offered a theory of **intrinsic motivation,** *the extent to which a person wants to do something for its own sake.* The theory states that a task will lose some of its inherent interest or value if an external motivation, such as a reward, is introduced. If a task is interesting to an individual, then it will be undertaken for its own sake. That is, the motivation for the task is intrinsic; it lies within the individual. (This is similar to Herzberg's notion of motivation-seeking tasks.) If the individual is now paid for performing the task, it will lose some of its inherent interest. Perhaps the clearest example of this is in professional sports. Here, individuals initially played a sport, such as football, because it was enjoyable and they were skilled at it. They played football because they loved the game and would play even under adverse conditions, such as snow or rain, because they chose to.

Once players become compensated for playing football, some of the intrinsic motivation for playing is replaced by the external condition of payment. At some point, they become extrinsically motivated: they play because they are paid and not because they love to play.

In a study to test this hypothesis, Deci (1971) had two different campus newspaper staffs write headlines over a period of several weeks. Production records were kept for each worker. During one period, workers in one group were offered fifty cents for each headline they wrote and were told that their pay represented an effort to spend surplus funds before the end of the semester. They were told they would no longer be paid once the funds were exhausted. After this period of compensation, they returned to the no-pay system. Although there were no initial differences between the groups prior to the introduction of compensation, once the compensation was withdrawn, the experimental group began to work at a significantly slower pace than the group that never received compensation.

The effects of compensation in reducing intrinsic motivation for a task is limited to those tasks that are initially interesting to the individual (Daniel and Esser, 1980). If a task is not interesting, then paying increasing amounts of money to perform the task does not influence the workers' perception of the task or their motivation to perform it.

The degree to which incentives undermine performance and interest is likely to differ depending on whether the skills under consideration are well learned or in the process of being learned. Well-learned skills are probably less undermined by extrinsic incentives, but this is not yet proven (Condry, 1977, p. 472).

Effects of Unemployment

The importance of work in Western culture is never so clearly seen as when people are out of work. Children are asked what they are going to be when they grow up; adults are asked what they do for a living. When students are asked what they are majoring in, it is usually with the aim of judging their future careers. Work

Motivating Economic Achievement

Much work by industrial psychologists is limited to small-scale changes in a single industry or organization. An exception to this is the work of David McClelland and David Winter (1969; 1971), who attempted to influence economic productivity in underdeveloped countries by changing people's motivations and aspirations.

McClelland and his colleagues have found that individuals who have high achievement needs, that is, strong drives to succeed, tend to be more enterprising and to set moderately difficult goals for themselves, are interested in success for its own sake rather than for money or power, are more interested in concrete feedback on how well they perform a task, and have a greater future time perspective than those with low achievement needs. McClelland and Winter wanted to test this theory by trying to influence the achievement-motivation levels of businessmen in economically underdeveloped areas. They reasoned that an increase in the levels of achievement need among some businessmen would lead to more enterprising behavior, which in turn would lead to the opening of more businesses and the hiring of more workers, all to the economic benefit of the community.

They gave a course in increasing the need for achievement in a city in Andhra Pradesh, India. The course was given to some businessmen, and others in the town constituted a control group. Businessmen in a comparable town in the same state served as a second control group. Data from the experimental town of Kakinada and the control town of Rajahmundry were collected over a period of five years, be-

ginning two years before the training commenced.

The course consisted of about ten days of training in four specific types of behavior.

1. *Achievement syndrome.* The participants were trained to recognize and produce fantasies and stories that were related to a high need for achievement. It is through an analysis of such stories that a person's level of achievement need is measured. In short, participants learned how to score high on need for achievement tests.
2. *Self study.* The participants were given various homework assignments in which they had to relate the material from the classroom to their own personal and business lives. As McClelland and Winter note, "The scientific implication of the research findings is inescapable. If they want to do a better entrepreneurial job, then the scientific evidence shows that the means to that end is to learn to think, talk, and act like a person with high need achievement." (p. 59)
3. *Goal setting.* Participants learned to set goals for themselves that reflected a high need for achievement; that is, goals that were moderately difficult to attain. The goal setting included training in various types of games, such as ringtoss, in which an individual could make the task easy by standing close to the pegs or make it difficult by standing a great distance away. (See Chapter 8.) Participants in the course learned to set moderately difficult goals in this and other tasks.

Table 16.A Some economic effects of training in achievement motivation

	Before the course	After the course
Percent working longer hours		
Trained (n = 61)	7	20
Controls (n = 44)	11	7
Percent starting new businesses		
Trained (n = 51)	6	27
Kakinada controls (n = 22)	5	5
Other controls (n = 35)	9	14
Percent in charge of firm		
Trained (n = 33)	32	58
Kakinada controls (n = 14)	23	21
Other controls (n = 24)	35	42

4. *Interpersonal supports.* The course participants quickly formed a close-knit group in which they reinforced and supported one another.

What were the effects of this ten-day training? There were two types of dependent measure in this study: individual measures of the participants' behavior, and economic measures of the impact of the course on the town of Kakinada. The participants in achievement-motivation courses showed significant improvement in many aspects of entrepreneurial performance, both as compared with themselves before the course and as compared with the control groups. Course participants showed more active business behavior. Participants in the training course worked longer hours, made more investments in new and fixed capital, employed more workers, and had increased gross income in their firms. About 135 new jobs were created in Kakinada. Some of the economic effects of the training are shown in table 16.A.

In a note in their 1971 book, McClelland and Winter note that in general, the effects of this fairly brief training in need for achievement persisted for several years and thus had a lasting impact on the economic well-being of the town of Kakinada. They also point out that training in achievement motivation is not a panacea for economic ills. The training was more effective for participants who were initially most dissatisfied with themselves and who believed that they might be able to solve some of their own economic problems. The course provided them with some of the skills and attitudes necessary to solve these problems. Training in achievement motivation would not be as effective in places where there was little opportunity or incentive for entrepreneurial behavior.

is an important part of our self-concept. When we are out of work as a result of a reduction in the labor force— as millions of Americans currently are—our view of ourselves may change dramatically. Only recently, perhaps since the mid–1970s, have social scientists explored in depth the effects of joblessness.

In studying the effects of unemployment, it becomes clear that joblessness influences not only the individual who is without work but the person's family and even the community in which the person lives. Unemployment touches nearly every aspect of family and community life, "resulting in higher divorce rates, increased incidence of alcoholism and drug abuse, child and spouse abuse, and juvenile delinquency," according to Senator Donald Riegle of Michigan (1982). A 1 percent rise in long-term unemployment is related to a 4.1 percent increase in suicides, a 5.7 percent increase in homicides, an almost 2 percent increase in heart disease and other stress-related disorders, and to an increased rate of psychiatric hospital admissions of 4.3 percent for men and 2.3 percent for women (Brenner, 1973, 1976).

Rapid upturns in the economy as a whole are also related to increased rates of mortality from various causes, probably due to the demands for change and readjustment (Brenner, 1976). We have already seen in our discussion of stress (Chapter 12) that any change in the environment that requires adaptation may be stressful, whether the change is seen as good or bad.

Two projects followed unemployed workers over fairly long periods of time (Liem and Liem, 1979; Liem and Rayman, 1982). This afforded the researchers an opportunity to examine the effects of reemployment as well as of long-term unemployment. In one study (Liem and Liem, 1979), the researchers studied forty blue-collar and forty white-collar families in which the husband was involuntarily without work. Each family was matched with an employed control in terms of occupation, the working status of the wife, locality, and number of children. Being without work was strongly associated with higher levels of psychiatric symptoms, relative to controls who were employed. Following reemployment, these symptoms diminished to a level below that of the controls. Interestingly, the researchers reported that the wives of unemployed husbands also suffered severe symptoms. They were significantly more depressed, anxious, phobic, and sensitive about their personal relationships than were the wives of working spouses.

A study called The Hartford Project examined the aircraft industry (Rayman and Bluestone, 1982). The majority of workers who experienced joblessness during any portion of a ten-year period showed signs of serious physical or emotional strain. "High blood pressure, alcoholism, increased smoking, insomnia, neurasthenia, and worry and anxiety were among the more commonly reported forms of strain. Middle-aged heads of households with young dependents experienced more intense stress effects than younger, single workers" (p. 1120). This last finding makes it clear that the impact of joblessness may depend upon one's age and marital and family status.

GUIDED REVIEW

Learning Objectives 1, 2, 3, and 4

1. _____ is the performance of tasks in exchange for compensation. The goals of work, unlike those of leisure, are not set by the individual.

2. Three theories of _____ are presented: Herzberg's two-factor theory, Vroom's valence-instrumentality-expectancy theory, and equity theory.

3. _____ states that there are two innate sets of needs, _____ and _____ . The former consist of external factors, such as pay and work conditions. The latter stem from within the individual and include the need for creativity and independence.

4. _____ includes the individual's expectations of future satisfactions and experience. Individuals are said to ask themselves whether a particular job or behavior will lead to some outcome (expectancy), whether that outcome will yield other outcomes (instrumentality), and whether those outcomes are valued by the individual (valence).

5. _____ states that a person makes a comparison between his output/input ratio and the output/input ratios of others in similar positions. When these two ratios are not equal, inequity exists. This motivates the individual to attempt to restore equity. This can be accomplished by altering inputs (working more or less hard) or outcomes (asking for a raise, going on strike).

6. Equity theory leads to the interesting hypothesis that _____ creates inequity just as undercompensation does. Overcompensation may undermine the _____ to perform a task.

7. _____ influences people's emotional and physical well-being, and even rates of homicide, family violence, and hospital admission rates.

8. The effects of unemployment depend to some extent on _____ and _____ and _____ status.

ANSWERS

The Nature of Organizations

IBM, Mitsubishi, the University of Oklahoma, the National Football League, the FBI, and the Catholic church are all formal organizations that have in common a variety of features: organizational structure or bureaucracy; formal and informal systems and channels of communication; a division of labor; methods for recruiting new members and replacing old ones; and goals to be accomplished and means for accomplishing them. Although the focus in this chapter is on industry and work organizations, the principles apply as well to those organizations that have little or nothing to do with business.

Prior to the rise, during the Industrial Revolution, of the formal organization, with its bureaucratic structure and chain of command, tasks were accomplished in traditional groups in which one advanced on the basis of who he knew, how much he was willing to pay for a particular position, and inheritance. The idea of holding a position in an organization purely on the basis of one's skills and experience was unheard of. In this respect, bureaucratic organizations contributed greatly to the spread of democracy in the workplace. We may criticize them, as Karl Marx and many others have, on the basis of their boring and routinized work and on their alienating effects on the worker; however, large-scale organizations are, theoretically at least, institutions in which a person is evaluated solely on the basis of his or her ability to perform a clearly described job.

Organizations are artificial structures in the sense that they are deliberately planned for the purpose of reaching particular objectives. An organization is designed to permit smooth functioning independent of the feelings of its individual members. In fact, many organizations discourage the formation of friendships among their members because they fear that such emotional ties will undermine both judgment and discipline. For example, they often have separate dining facilities for different levels of employees, base decisions on interpersonal criteria, and so on (Collins, 1983). Even though organizations discourage emotional bonds among its members, informal social attachments still form, and friendship groups and social cliques can be found in all large organizations. It is therefore important to examine the formal organization as well as the informal social groups that exist within it.

Bureaucracy: Formal Structure

One of the features of formal organizations is **bureaucracy,** which is *the recruitment of and relationships among individuals who are responsible for attaining the goals of the organization and for maintaining the organization itself.* The German sociologist Max Weber (1957), believed that modern bureaucracy was the most efficient way of organizing large numbers of people for the attainment of complex tasks. (See Table 16.2.) By making human activity regular, orderly, and predictable, bureaucracy is a means of ensuring the conditions necessary for efficient work. Of course, whether or not this efficiency is achieved depends on factors of the informal as well as the formal organization (*Society Today,* 1971).

The formal bureaucratic structure of an organization, whether it is a business organization, an educational or governmental organization, or even a social organization, ensures that individuals have specialized jobs to perform. When each individual performs his or her job, the goals of the organization are reached. This *specialization of roles is referred to as a* **division of labor.** The work of the organization is divided into smaller tasks, and each individual becomes responsible for performing only one or a few tasks. Instead of needing a variety of skills that would enable a person to do all the tasks required to reach the organization's goals, an individual needs only to be able to perform a single specialized task to fit into the modern organizational structure. In a small, traditional business, in contrast to the bureaucratic organization, a person would have to purchase the raw material, shape it into a new product, market the new product, keep records of these transactions, and be able to maintain the facilities and equipment of the business. In the modern bureaucracy, an individual is apt to specialize in marketing, purchasing, accounting, maintenance, or personnel, for example, requiring no knowledge of the other specialties. There are obvious drawbacks to this specialization, such as monotony and inability to change jobs without retraining, but it does enable one to train for a specific job, such as accountant (Argyris, 1964).

Informal Social Structure

Whereas the formal organization specifies the requirements and tasks of its members, there exists a parallel and often unseen informal organization that sets its own requirements and standards. There are informal groups, friends and cliques, that do not have a formal organizational structure within a large organization; for example, co-workers who always eat lunch together constitute an informal social group. They do not have anything resembling an "organizational chart," such as the one shown in Table 16.2. Probably the first recognition that informal groups exist within large organizations and exert considerable influence on worker activity came from what are known as the Hawthorne experiments.

The Hawthorne Experiments. Beginning in the mid-1920s and continuing for ten years, a group of psychologists from Harvard University studied productivity and worker morale at the Western Electric plant in Chicago. The human relations movement in industry and the now-famous "Hawthorne effect" developed as a result of these studies.

The researchers conducted a variety of studies (Roethlisberger and Dickson, 1939; Mayo, 1945). In one study, the researchers examined how changes in illumination influenced worker output. Sometimes lighting in the workplace was increased, and sometimes it was diminished. Each time the lighting changed, whether it became brighter or dimmer, productivity was found to increase. In other studies, women who assembled electrical relays, or men who wired equipment, were studied intensively over a period of months. Their rest periods, hours of working, days off, and pay incentives were systematically varied to determine the optimum work-rest ratios. Sometimes changes were made in worker-management relations, varying worker participation in decisions affecting their work. Regardless of the type of change made, Elton Mayo and his colleagues reported that productivity tended to increase as the studies progressed.

Changes in productivity were interpreted as due not to the physical changes that took place in working conditions but to social and psychological changes that occurred. Mayo and his colleagues concluded that workers wanted to please the researchers, so they worked harder. They concluded that this increase in productivity was due to the fact that the workers were observed and not to the other changes that took place. This is referred to as the **Hawthorne effect;** that is, *that the research* *itself was responsible for the results.* Furthermore, there were found to be subjective norms among the workers that set the standards for productivity.

The researchers concluded that one must pay attention to the social conditions and social relations of the workers. These beliefs form the foundation of the **human relations movement** in industry, *the notion that the informal social and psychological conditions of the workers, in addition to pay, benefits, and physical conditions, influence worker productivity.*

Despite the revolution in industry that resulted from the Hawthorne studies, the studies themselves and the investigators who conducted them increasingly have come under attack. The researchers appear to have ignored the resistance of many workers at the Western Electric plant to attempt to increase their productivity; instead, they reported that the workers were cooperative with respect to each change in working conditions (Bramel and Friend, 1981). Furthermore, upon closer scrutiny some of the studies in which increased productivity was reported do not show increased productivity at all (Franke and Kaul, 1978). For example, in one study the workers were required to work longer hours over a period of a few weeks. It was reported that their productivity increased, but that is true only for their total work output. If one examines output *per hour,* productivity is actually found to have decreased. Despite such criticisms, the fact remains that Mayo and his colleagues pointed to the existence and importance of informal structures, such as friendship groups, within the formal organization and thus changed forever our perception of large formal groups. It is now routine among researchers to pay attention to the informal social groups as well as to the formal structure of the organization.

Communication in Organizations

The larger an organization is, the more complex and elaborate communication between members becomes. To facilitate communication, formal **communication networks** may be established *in which each individual is permitted to communicate only with specified other*

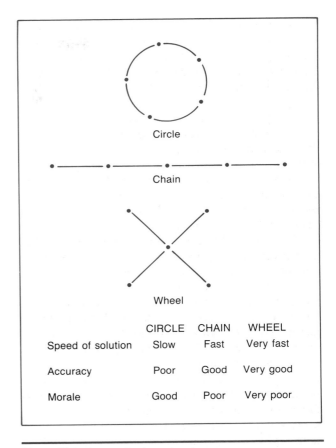

Figure 16.1 Communication networks

members of the organization. For example, an assembly-line worker in a plant can easily communicate with other assembly-line workers and may communicate with the shop steward and the foreman. However, communications with the company vice-president or with workers in the marketing department may be difficult, impossible, or prohibited. In the military, for instance, an official chain of command establishes channels of communication.

Various versions of communication networks, as diagrammed in figure 16.1, have been studied (Bavelas, 1948; Shaw, 1964). In some networks, an individual may be central; that is, many people may have to go through him or her to reach a particular other individual. The "wheel" network has a highly central individual and four dependent peripheral individuals. In a circle, individuals are more independent in that they each may communicate with two individuals. To study the effects of these networks, a task is given to a small group with instructions on how communications may be passed. Typically, each individual is given four symbols, and by passing notes to other members in accordance with the requirements of their communication network, they must determine what one symbol all members have in common. They then rate their satisfaction with the group.

The solution to such a problem tends to be fastest in centralized networks, such as the wheel; fewer notes must be passed back and forth to solve the problem. It should be noted that a problem such as determining a common symbol is a fairly simple one, having a single correct solution and having available all the needed information for a solution. For more complex tasks, such as those having multiple solutions or having some vital information unavailable, centralized networks lose their superiority, probably because the central members suffer from "information overload." Satisfaction with the group, tends to be highest in networks in which individuals are free to communicate with many others (Shaw, 1964).

Informal Social Communication.   Communications in organizations do not always follow the formal structure of the communication network. Instead, communications often have nothing directly to do with the purposes of the organization. Whereas formal communications tend to be concerned with improved productivity, solutions to organizational problems, or the enhancement of the communicator's status, informal communications are frequently about personal events, "small talk", and joking. Informal communications tend to occur in small, face-to-face groups, such as staff conferences, work groups, and board meetings. Hearing something "through the grapevine" attests to the importance of such informal communication channels.

R. F. Bales (1955, 1970) developed a procedure called "Interaction Process Analysis" that enables trained observers to categorize every communication act that takes place during a group meeting. In his research, Bales arranges for several people to discuss a complex problem while being observed through a one-way screen. Each statement, question, or gesture (termed an *act*) is recorded. Acts are divided into task relations (those concerned with solving the problem at hand) and social-emotional relations (those unrelated to the task).

In a typical group session, there are between fifteen and twenty acts per minute. About half of these are pertinent to the problem, and half are not. Typically, during the first one-third of the meeting, the most frequent act tends to be giving information about the problem. During the middle portion of the meeting, opinions tend to be given concerning the problem and possible solutions. Suggestions for solving the problem are most common in the last one-third of a session. Acts tend to alternate between socio-emotional and task-related communications. When too much emphasis is given to the problem, socio-emotional relations become strained, and emphasis is then placed on these interpersonal relations. The group returns to the problem later.

Many groups have a "wise guy" who injects jokes and unrelated comments throughout the course of a meeting. Rather than being an irrelevant distraction, however, such people actually help the group move closer to its goal of solving a problem with the least amount of conflict. These "socio-emotional specialists" are important parts of an effective group, and their wisecracks are ways of smoothing over interpersonal relations in the group. In studies of staff conferences at psychiatric hospitals, joking has been found to occur frequently, about once every ten minutes (Goodrich, Henry, and Goodrich, 1954). These jokes are usually directed at colleagues and tend to be made at the expense of a subordinate. The jokes reflect and serve to reinforce the structure of the group, so that psychiatrists joke about nurses, who joke about the volunteer staff, who joke about patients (Coser, 1960).

Many informal communications, whether in the form of jokes or nonhumorous comments, serve to enforce group standards. When a group member deviates too far from group norms, criticism, often in the form of a joke, may serve to bring the person into line. These informal remarks may also serve simply as a "time out" from the serious business of the group, a way of taking a ten-second vacation from work. In either case, informal social communications seem to improve group effectiveness and make the work of the group more enjoyable.

GUIDED REVIEW

Learning Objective 5

1. Organizations are characterized by a _____ , formal and informal systems of communication, division of labor, and goals and means for achieving them.

2. Within every large formal organization there are cliques and groups of friends. These _____ exert considerable influence on the overall functioning of the organization.

3. _____ gave rise to the focus on social relations in industry. The mere act of studying workers was found by Mayo and his colleagues to increase productivity. This is known as the _____ .

4. Organizations may have formal _____ , which differ in the _____ of each member and the _____ of each member. For simple problems, centralized networks, such as the wheel, are superior. Satisfaction is highest in networks that maximize individuals' independence.

5. _____ are important for the morale of a group and may strengthen the group's structure and enforce its norms.

ANSWERS

1. bureaucratic structure 2. informal social groups 3. The Hawthorne experiments; Hawthorne effect 4. communication networks; centrality; independence 5. Informal communications

Human Factors

Since the early twentieth century, psychologists have been involved in the world of business and industry. They have often helped organizations to select and train personnel, to market goods and services, and have worked with engineers to design more efficient products.

Personnel Selection

When people apply for jobs, they have already done some preliminary assessment of the requirements of the jobs and of their ability to fulfill those requirements. Generally there are more applicants for a position than there are openings, so additional screening must occur before filling a post. The purpose of various employee selection methods is to collect information at the time of hiring that has been shown to be related to job performance.

The use by psychologists of reliable and valid tests and measures for the selection, training, and assessment of personnel has improved both workers' satisfaction with their jobs and their productivity (Tornetsky and Solomon, 1982). Psychological assessment methods are able to predict performance well enough to have practical value for an employer (Ghiselli, 1966). One study found that the use of a test to select computer programmers could result in greater productivity equivalent to hundreds of millions of dollars (Schmidt, et al., 1979).

Human Factors

The primary aim of the field known as **human factors** *is to design equipment and systems that increase the effectiveness, comfort, safety, and productivity of the people using them.* The reduction of human error through proper design is an important goal. A favorite

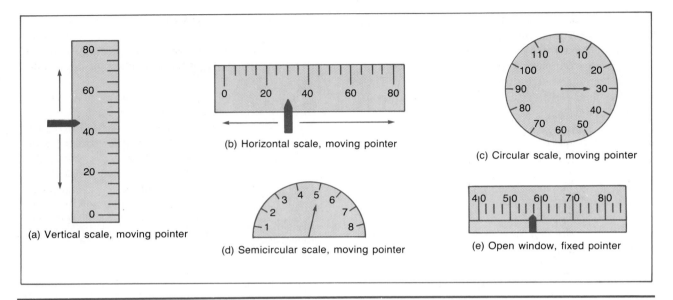

Figure 16.2 Possible speedometers

saying among human factors researchers is, "To err is human; to forgive, design." A large amount of human factors research is conducted after it is clear that a system has design problems (because of frequent accidents or a single major mishap, for instance).

Before equipment or complex systems that reduce human error can be designed, we need to know a great deal about human beings: their sensory systems, their cognitive abilities, their motor systems, and especially their limitations. We need to have some understanding of their psychological and social needs as well. In the past, engineers used their own abilities and inclinations as guides for the design of equipment, but this approach produced much equipment that was unsuitable for a large number of workers. A more appropriate approach is to study the capabilities and limitations of human workers and design equipment to their needs and specifications.

Information Input.   Human beings have five senses through which they can receive information. To design an effective system, such as a control panel, one needs to know more than just the basics about the sensory systems. It is important to know the capacity of each

system and the capability each one has to discriminate between similar stimuli, for instance. Most of the information supplied in complex systems comes through the visual and auditory channels, so most human factors research is concentrated on those topics.

Visual Information.   The speedometer of a car offers visual information, but a designer might choose to design one with another sensory mode. For example, the speedometer might have an auditory channel that produces a tone that varies in pitch for different speeds. When the car goes faster, the pitch becomes higher and higher. Even without field testing this hypothetical piece of equipment, you can probably spot some deadly flaws. For one thing, the noise would be annoying to any driver and might mask honking horns, police sirens, or just the music on the radio. Also, the driver would know when the speed of the car was changing, but she would not know precisely what her speed was if it was constant. A visual display of some kind is probably a better solution.

Figure 16.2 shows some possible speedometers. An engineer might simply arbitrarily choose one that seems "best," but a human factors researcher would test each

Table 16.3 Percent errors made in trying to read various kinds of dials

Type of dial	Percent error
Vertical	35.5
Horizontal	27.5
Circular	10.9
Semicircular	16.6
Open window (fixed pointer)	0.5

(From Sleight, R. B. The effect of instrument dial shape on legibility. Journal of Applied Psychology, 1948, vol. 32, 170–188.)

design before making any decisions. In an actual study that tested the usefulness and "readability" of these different kinds of speedometers, sixty subjects read each of the five types of dials seventeen times. For each reading the subject could look at the dial for only 0.12 seconds, a short but not unreasonable amount of time (Sleight, 1948). The average errors of the subjects are shown in table 16.3. The open window design clearly had the advantage; subjects made far fewer errors when they read this kind of dial in this experiment. (If you drive, you know that the engineers who designed your speedometer probably did not read this study.)

The error you might make in reading your car's speed would probably not be a large one and might earn you only a speeding ticket. However, the type of dial that is used in cockpits to display the altitude of a plane has probably been misread many times. Pilots believe it presents a dangerous hazard and should be redesigned.

Figure 16.2d shows the commonly used three-pointer dial. This circular display has three hands, like those of a clock. The hands represent altitudes of 10,000, 1000, and 100 feet, much as the hands of a clock represent hours, minutes, and seconds. Studies of this dial have shown over and over again that pilots take longer to read it than other types of dials (fig. 16.2a–c), and they make many more errors (Hill and Chernikoff, 1965). Of the four models shown, the three-pointer model was always last, measured in terms of accuracy, time to read, and pilot's preferences. The most desirable altimeter is the one in the upper left corner. The

counter reveals thousands of feet, whereas the pointer shows hundreds. Pilots have registered many complaints about these cumbersome and dangerous three-pointer altimeters, but improvements have been made very slowly.

The display of visual information has also become an increasingly important issue because people who speak different languages must interact with one another rather frequently in these days of global travel. Subway ticket vendors, people who design signs for airports, and tourist information booths, for example, must choose symbols carefully to ensure that speakers of other languages can understand them as easily as a native English speaker can. The Research Box: Research on Symbols, describes how some of these signs are developed.

Auditory Displays. In complex systems, auditory displays can be particularly appropriate for certain functions. For example, they can emit warning signals to attract attention, and they can be useful when the operator is moving from one place to another. They have certain advantages over visual displays, such as their discriminability in low lighting. They also have some disadvantages: they transmit sequential, rather than spatial information, and because of this they cannot easily provide the operator with changing information over time.

Examples of auditory displays in common use are not difficult to find: sirens on ambulances, police cars, and fire engines; ringing noises at railroad crossings; beeping sounds made by trucks in reverse gear; and smoke-alarm signals in homes. Although auditory signaling is frequently and effectively used for warnings, it can also be used to transmit nonemergency information. Sonar equipment, for example, transmits high-frequency sounds underwater, and operators listen for the returning signal. Whether the frequency of the return signal is higher, lower, or the same as the one originally transmitted will depend on whether the object it intercepted is moving closer, moving away, or remaining at the same distance as the transmitting source.

RESEARCH BOX

Research on Symbols

One of the important functions of research in human factors is to assess the usefulness of international symbols designed to communicate information to people who speak different languages. Ideally, this research is conducted before the symbols are adopted. Then when they are adopted, they will communicate the correct message to the most people, and they will be uniform across countries.

The understandability and meaningfulness of symbols has been assessed in a variety of ways. Some experiments show subjects a series of symbols, perhaps on slides or in a booklet, and ask them to provide short definitions for each one. This method is useful because it can provide insight into the kinds of misunderstandings likely to arise from each kind of symbol. Another way to assess understandability is simply to show subjects a variety of symbols for a specific message and ask them which one they prefer. A third approach is to let subjects choose the meanings for a particular symbol from a list, a kind of multiple-choice test.

An example of this kind of research on symbols was conducted at the National Bureau of Standards (Collins and Lerner, 1982), using symbols that relate to fire safety. (See fig. 16.A.) The researchers used several approaches to assess the usefulness of various symbols, including asking subjects to write short definitions and asking them to choose the correct definition from a short list. Some subjects were also asked to provide their own symbols for specific fire-safety messages, such as "Fire Extinguisher," "No Smoking," "Do Not Lock," and "Fire Exit."

The results of the study demonstrated that the symbols varied considerably in understandability. Some symbols, like the one for "Do Not Block," were misunderstood by practically everyone. Others, like the symbol for "Fire Extinguisher," were understood by nearly everyone. (The percent correct on the multiple-choice test is given below each of the symbols.) Studies like this point to the importance of testing symbols for understandability *before* they are widely adopted.

One set of studies for the Air Force suggested that auditory signals could transmit more information than most people believed (Licklider, 1961). Most Air Force warning signals were simply one loud noise, repeated over and over. The research, however, sought to determine whether the signal could incorporate two or three pieces of information: one that said "emergency," a second that signaled the type of emergency, and a third that signaled what action should be taken. This research found that one loud noise to attract attention and to identify the type of emergency, followed by a second noise that directed action, would be easily understood and would communicate more information.

Fire extinguisher
(white on red)
100

Hose and reel
(white on red)
96

Fire ladder
(white on red)
20

Fire bucket
(white on red)
96

Fire fighter's
equipment
(white on red)
0

Break glass for
access
(white on green)
28

Slide door
to right
(white on green)
57

Do not use water
to extinguish
(black on white,
red circle & slash)
76

Do not lock
(black on white,
red circle
& slash)
89

No smoking
(black on white,
red circle
& slash)
100

No open flame
(black on white,
red circle
& slash)
87

Do not block
(black on white,
red circle
& slash)
2

Figure 16.A Symbols for fire-safety alerting

Smell, Taste, and Touch. Studies on information input through these channels are very scarce, but they should probably receive more attention. Tactual information, in particular, is probably underused in complex systems. Knobs that control several different functions are often the same size and shape, differing only in their visual label. However, accident reports from aircraft sometimes indicate that the pilot mistook one control, such as the landing gears, for another, such as the flaps lever. Controls can be coded by color, of course, but often a pilot or other equipment operator has little time for a visual search or is concentrating on visual displays elsewhere on the control panel. Errors might be reduced if frequently confused controls were given different shapes (triangles, squares) or textures

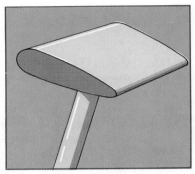

Landing flap   Landing gear

Figure 16.3   Controls that are related in form to their function and designed to be easily distinguished by touch. (From Ernest J. McCormick and Daniel Ilgen, Industrial Psychology, *Seventh Edition, © 1980, p. 353. Reprinted by permission of Prentice-Hall, Inc., Englewood Cliffs, New Jersey.)*

(bumpy, smooth, or perhaps saw-toothed). In a nuclear power plant, for example, all the knobs that affect the coolant system might be square, and those that affect the steam generators might be oval.

Research on tactual discriminability has been conducted on blindfolded subjects in an effort to improve the design of complex control panels (e.g., Jenkins, 1947). Handles and knobs for different levers and controls are given different shapes. Some control panels of aircraft take this concept one step further by having the control knob bear some relationship to its function. The control for the flaps is shaped like a flap, and the control for the landing gear resembles a wheel. (See fig. 16.3.) The transmission of information through the sense of touch offers the potential for correct identification without asking the operators to take their eyes away from other displays, but it does take longer than visual identification. It also requires bare hands that are not too cold.

Information Processing.   Between the input of information and the output of a motor response lies an information processing stage. Perception, reasoning, thinking, decision making, remembering, and forgetting all occur in the human brain, and are all affected (and affect) the system with which the human being is

working. The information processing capacities and limitations of the human being should be an important consideration in the design of any complex system.

Motor Output.   Designing equipment and environments so that they take advantage of human motor skills, and also make up for our deficiencies, is an important subfield of human factors research. Most pieces of equipment evolve through many generations, their usefulness being improved by trial and error. The hammer, for example, probably began as nothing but a heavy weight on a stick. As humans used the tool, they modified it to accommodate to the average strength of ordinary humans as well as to the size and contrariness of nails.

The design of a child's schoolbag can illustrate the importance of considering human motor output. An early study compared the amount of oxygen consumed by children carrying six pounds of weight in a schoolbag in one of four slightly different ways: a knapsack carried across the upper back; a bag carried across the lower back; a bag carried across the shoulder; and a bag carried by the hand. The knapsack carried across the upper back was clearly superior. Compared to carrying the knapsack, children consumed 37% more oxygen when carrying a bag across the lower back, 82% more oxygen when carrying a shoulder bag, and 141% more oxygen when carrying a schoolbag by the hand

(Malhotra and Sengupta, 1965). A simple study like this one could mean the difference between a child who is too tired to do homework at night and one who has enough energy to do homework, dry the dishes, and play baseball.

The design of computers also illustrates the importance of considering human motor skills. As computers enter every phase of human life, the ability to type becomes more important. The most common arrangement for letters on the keyboard is the "qwerty" style, originally designed by the Sholes brothers in 1873. Their aim was to keep frequently used keys far apart and thereby *slow down* the typist to minimize the jamming of type bars in their early primitive typewriter design. Unlike the Sholes model, the Dvorak keyboard was designed with human factors principles in mind; the layout of keys minimizes hand and finger motion (Dvorak, 1943). A recent study compared the efficiency of alphabetically arranged keyboard layouts to those that are randomly arranged for nontypists (Norman and Fisher, 1982). After a pretest on the Sholes board to ensure they really could not type more than twenty-five words per minute, the subjects were tested for ten minutes on two alphabetic and one random keyboard layouts, using some text material from *Reader's Digest*. The number of words typed, the number of errors, and the subjects' preferences for each keyboard were recorded. In terms of the number of words typed, the subjects performed about ten percent better on the alphabetic keyboard arrangements than on the random keyboard.

Testing other keyboard arrangements for expert typists is very difficult because it would require months of training (and then retraining on the "qwerty"). However, a computer simulation program of the hand and finger movements of typists is available (Rumelhart and Norman, 1982). Using the same *Reader's Digest* text, the program was tested on several keyboard arrangements, including the Dvorak. Overall, the program estimated that the Dvorak arrangement would result in an improvement of 5.4% in typing speed, compared to "qwerty." Alphabetic keyboard arrangements would all produce decreases in typing speed from "qwerty."

Human Limitations. Human beings have a wide variety of limitations as well as abilities. They can carry fairly heavy loads, provided the loads are positioned properly on the body. They can read dials and manipulate controls that are designed with human sensory systems and information processing abilities in mind. They can work long hours, but they must sleep. The design of equipment and jobs must take into account both human abilities and human limitations.

In addition to physical limitations, human beings have an almost infinite variety of psychological and social characteristics that can affect their ability to function within a technical system. They need privacy at some times and social interaction at other times. They need social approval from their friends and rewards from their bosses. One might suppose, for example, that two people working at adjacent desks should perform equally well whether their desks are facing one another or facing away from one another. Depending on the jobs they are performing, however, these two different desk arrangements could have vastly different impacts on efficiency and productivity. Their needs for privacy and social interaction should be considered.

Case Study: Three Mile Island. The tragedy at Three Mile Island preceded the Chernobyl nuclear reactor disaster and captured the attention of nearly everyone in the world. The incident was a sobering reminder that human beings make mistakes and that some systems are more "accident-provocative" than others. The more complicated and the more poorly designed the system in which humans are working, the more mistakes the operators are likely to make.

Much human factors research is based on the analysis of accidents. Most complicated systems are designed by engineers, and human factors specialists are usually not consulted—until humans begin making mistakes in the system. Especially when the error costs many lives, everyone wonders why the system wasn't better designed in the first place.

The review team's evaluation of the Three Mile Island incident listed several human errors, most of which could have been prevented, or at least reduced, by appropriate design of the system. One major error occurred because the indicator light for a relief valve, which was actually open, showed that the valve was closed throughout the accident. The operators wrongly assumed that the valve was closed. They should have checked other indicators, which would have told them the indicator light was malfunctioning.

Another important error occurred when the steam generators boiled dry. This dangerous event went unnoticed in the general confusion. The operators at Three Mile Island generally failed to diagnose the problem until it became a major accident. Their failure was partly due to their lack of training, particularly in nuclear power technology. At that time, operators needed only a high-school degree and minimal training to enter the control room. Instead of being trained to diagnose trouble and solve problems, they simply learned to follow a "cookbook" list of emergency procedures.

When the accident started, more than one hundred alarms went off. But even under "normal" conditions, as many as fifty alarms might be ringing. This circumstance first created confusion, but it also might have engendered some complacency in the face of constant alarms. The operators may have been legitimately confused about whether the emergency were truly an emergency.

Many important control panels were mounted on the back of the consoles, facing *away* from the operators. The critical dials were not grouped together; they were scattered all over the room. An important valve in the steam cooling system had to be adjusted manually by the senior operator. This task removed him from the control room for more than forty-five minutes during the accident.

Review teams have since visited other nuclear plants and have found many design problems that make it more likely that the human operators could make mistakes. In some places a red light meant that a valve was open, and in others it meant that it was closed. A lever pulled down in one system closed a valve; in another it opened it.

An important development in nuclear power plant technology is the use of simulators to test both equipment and operators. During simulated emergencies, operators must diagnose problems and develop solutions. This kind of simulation not only gives the operators a chance to develop their problem-solving skills but trains them to do it under some stress, which they would face in a real emergency.

GUIDED REVIEW

Learning Objectives 6, 7, and 8

1. The use of scientifically developed tests to _____ is one contribution of psychology to organizational effectiveness.

2. The field of _____ attempts to improve the efficiency, productivity, comfort and safety of human beings operating in complex man-machine systems. Its main approach to design takes the abilities and limitations of humans into account.

3. Human factors assumes that people will make mistakes, but that they will make fewer mistakes in systems that recognize the nature of the _____ .

4. Aspects of _____ capabilities, such as perception, reasoning, thinking, decision-making, and memory all affect the efficiency with which humans interact with equipment.

5. The design of technological systems also considers human _____ . Long work shifts, and shift work are not conducive to optimal human performance. Psychological and social factors should also be considered in the design of these systems.

ANSWERS

1. select personnel 2. human factors 3. human operator 4. human information processing 5. limitations

Environmental Psychology

Environmental psychology is *the study of the relationship between behavior and the natural and constructed environment.* It examines the concept of space, as well as the effects of noise, temperature, pollution, and crowding on human behavior. It is also concerned with the ways in which organisms adapt to their environments. Researchers in environmental psychology study how environmental design may alter attitudes, perceptions, and behavior. Another concern in the field is the preservation of the environment (Proshansky, Ittelson, and Rivlin, 1970).

Personal Space

Human beings are highly social creatures. They tend to congregate in cities and can almost always be found more or less close together on small plots of land. Despite this tendency to huddle together, people also enjoy a certain amount of privacy and solitude (Altman, 1975). One of the ways to maintain some privacy while still in the company of others is to prevent them from getting too close, to regulate both psychological and physical distance by means of personal space.

The term **personal space** was popularized by the psychologist Robert Sommer (1959, 1967). It refers to *"the area individual humans actively maintain around themselves* into which others cannot intrude without arousing discomfort" (Hayduk, 1978, p. 118). Personal space may be thought of as an "invisible bubble" surrounding a person that encloses space regarded as "private." The individual engages in a good deal of distance regulation, changing the shape and size of this bubble depending on the circumstances. If you are walking down a crowded city street during lunch hour, you contract your personal space and may tolerate intrusions as close as a few inches on either side. If you are sitting in a public library, your personal space may consist of several feet in all directions.

Personal space expands or contracts with the circumstances; it also differs from one culture to another (Hall, 1966; Jones and Aiello, 1973). There is some evidence (albeit controversial) that certain individuals,

such as violent prisoners, have larger personal spaces than others under similar conditions (Kinzel, 1971; Lothstein, 1974). It is worth noting that personal space is a matter of ongoing distance regulation and, as such, moves with the person. Territory, on the other hand, is an area of space that a person regards as his own and that is used fairly regularly over a period of time (Edney, 1974). A person can leave his territory to return to it later; he cannot leave his personal space because it is "part" of him.

Intrusion of personal space leads to feelings of discomfort; individuals try to reduce this discomfort by defending or reestablishing their personal space from intruders. Most of us learn quite early to respect the privacy of others (Eberts and Lepper, 1975; Guardo, 1969; Scherer, 1974). As early as age ten, most American children recognize that they should not encroach upon the personal space of others either in public or private. Children are repeatedly told by their parents to leave people alone, even when they are clearly not imposing on others but are merely in close proximity to them.

The anthropologist E. T. Hall (1959, 1966) has categorized various spatial distances between individuals into four types: intimate, personal, social, and public. "Intimate distance" between two individuals ranges from physical contact to about eighteen inches. Hall notes that "This is the distance of love-making and wrestling, . . ." for in purely spatial terms both are highly intimate behaviors. A distance of from about one and one-half to four feet (0.3 to 1.3 meters) is the "personal distance" at which the other is at "arm's length" but still near enough to provide a sense of closeness.

"Social distance" ranges from four to twelve feet (1.3 to 3.5 meters). It is more impersonal than either intimate or personal distances, and it commonly regulates the distance between people working cooperatively on a task or engaged in social conversation. Hall refers to a distance of twelve feet and beyond (3.5 meters) as "public distance." Here, one's field of vision includes not only the other person but also people in the general vicinity. One person is psychologically, and literally, keeping his distance from the other.

Personal Space and Culture. Hall is responsible for popularizing the notion that spatial behavior varies among peoples of different cultures. There is a cultural norm of appropriate distance between two individuals, depending on the circumstances. When people stand too close or too far away while we are speaking with them, we have a feeling that something is wrong. For example, consider an informal social conversation between two individuals, one of whom is British, the other American. Because of her cultural norms, the British person tends to feel most comfortable with greater distance between herself and the other speaker. The American might feel that the British person is moving away, being "aloof" or "cold." In attempting to establish a closer, more comfortable personal distance, the American may appear rude and aggressive to the British person.

Studies on spacing behavior have revealed differences between many cultures. In one study, over 20,000 pedestrians were observed in cities in the United States, Europe, and several Middle Eastern countries. Table 16.4 shows the percentage of those who had physical contact with their companions (Berkowitz, 1971). Clearly, there is considerable variation in the extent to which companions engage in contact. It should be noted that these results are not entirely consistent with the observations of Hall on speaking distance in Arab cultures. A higher percentage of English pedestrians had contact with their companions, compared to Middle Easterners (referred to as Moslem in table 16.4). Probably, the two measures—speaking distance and contact with pedestrian companion—have different cultural meanings, accounting for these differences.

Theories of Personal Space. It is not always possible to maintain the optimum distance for every occasion. Sometimes circumstances force people into close contact or prevent them from achieving the desired levels of intimacy. What do people do in such circumstances? Two theories of personal space, the equilibrium theory and the stimulation theory, are concerned with the reasons for maintaining personal space and reactions to intrusions.

Table 16.4 Percentage of pedestrians in groups who were also in contact

Country	Percent in contact
Sweden	18.1
United States	19.4
"Moslem"	15.4
England	24.1
W. Germany	26.4
Italy	29.8

From Berkowitz, 1971, Table 4.

Equilibrium theory *maintains that personal space or distance between individuals is a component of intimacy* (Argyle and Dean, 1965). The greater the intimacy between two people, the more likely they are to discuss personal topics, maintain eye contact, and minimize personal distance. If something interferes with any of these mechanisms for expressing intimacy, there will be a tendency to compensate by changing other aspects of the situation. For example, if a person is prevented from having eye contact with an intimate acquaintance, compensation might take the form of standing closer to that person. Thus, the same level of intimacy is expressed by striking a balance between distance, eye contact, and discussion topic.

Stimulation theory *emphasizes the relationship between personal space and other behaviors* that have to do with spacing between people, such as crowding (Desor, 1972). A person is crowded when he or she *feels* crowded (Stokols, 1972), and that usually occurs when a person receives excessive stimulation from other people. The differences in personal space found under various circumstances are mechanisms for regulating the amount of stimulation a person receives from others. This, of course, can be closely related to intimacy. Stimulation theory proposes that it is not intimacy per se but social and sensory stimulation that is regulated by variations in space.

Figure 16.4 Personal space expands and contracts depending on how much space is available

Violations of Personal Space.   By definition, personal space is that distance whose violation by another causes feelings of discomfort. If this discomfort occurs, we naturally expect a person to attempt to reduce the discomfort. This can be done by withdrawing, by standing one's ground and attempting to drive off the intruder, or by avoiding situations in which personal space might be violated by others.

In studies conducted at a university library, people took certain defensive actions to prevent spatial invasion (Sommer, 1969). When asked where a person would sit at a rectangular table with six, eight, or ten chairs, students predicted they would sit in a location that would discourage others from sitting at the same table (fig. 16.4). When the students left their chairs temporarily, they placed various kinds of "markers" to signal that the chairs were occupied. For example, people left sweaters draped over the backs of their chairs

or open books in front of them. When such markers were used in a library, the chairs were never occupied by someone else.

Individuals feel uncomfortable not only when their personal space has been invaded by others but also when circumstances force them to violate the personal space of others (Efran and Cheyne, 1974). Imagine how you would feel if an usher told you to sit right next to a stranger in an almost-empty theater. There are potent norms for the preservation of one's own and another's personal space.

Human Territoriality

Territoriality is a concept closely related to personal space. Unlike personal space, which moves with the person and is constantly regulated, **territoriality** *refers to behavior designed to preserve a particular geographic space,* such as one's home. Many animal species are territorial. They establish home territories, nesting territories, and hunting territories, and they often defend them from intruders under certain circumstances. Animals often use territorial markers to individualize their territories, and these markers sometimes ward off intruders. Rabbits, for example, urinate around the perimeter of their territories; the odor signals to other rabbits that the territory is occupied.

There are some striking parallels between animal and human territorial behavior. Humans also appear to "mark" their territories. They put fences around their yards to delineate the boundaries, names on their mailboxes, numbers on their doorposts, and distinctive and personal decorations in their houses. However, these similarities between animal and human territorial behavior should not be interpreted as meaning the same thing. The evolutionary trends that culminated in rabbits urinating around their territories are not likely to be similar to the forces that cause humans to write their names on their mailboxes. "It is virtually undisputed that humans exhibit territoriality, at the national, family, home, or temporary (my-seat-on-the-bus) level, but the question remains how meaningful the similarities are to animal territoriality" (Edney, 1974, p. 961).

Although human and animal territorial behaviors appear to be similar under some conditions, there are many differences. For example, unlike animals, the human defense and use of territories is quite flexible. Territories seem to serve largely biological purposes for animals; they provide them with places to hide from predators, to rear offspring, and to search for food. In humans, territories are often used for social and recreational purposes. Humans may be the only species that uses the home territory for entertaining others without antagonism (Edney, 1974). Humans also engage in many behaviors in which they share territories with one another, such as dining at a table in a restaurant and then leaving it for others to use.

Crowding and Population Density. Because a number of animal studies demonstrate that high population density may have negative social and physiological effects, there is a widespread belief that crowding might be deleterious to human beings as well (Calhoun, 1962). Nevertheless, it is far from clear that for humans "density is destiny."

What do the terms *crowded* or *overpopulated* mean? Tokyo is more densely populated than New York City. The Netherlands is more densely populated than the United States. Do these facts explain any of the differences in behavior that may exist between the people who live in these locations? We should begin by clarifying some terms. First, we must distinguish between **population density,** *the number of people living in a given area* (such as 100 people per square mile), and **crowding,** *the subjective feeling that there are too many people present* for one's comfort or freedom of movement (Schopler and Stockdale, 1977). Second, we must distinguish between short-term crowding, such as being in an elevator with many other people for a few minutes, and long-term crowding, such as living in Tokyo for years.

Crowding in Animals. Jonathan Freedman (1975) has summarized and criticized much of the research on crowding in animals. There is evidence that animals housed for many generations in densely populated conditions display increased aggressiveness or increased passivity, deterioration in normal social and sexual behavior, increased infant mortality, and other abnormalities. However, these effects are not likely to be caused solely or directly by increased density. Freedman suggests that the presence of additional animals intensifies certain physiological responses and social interactions, and this intensification may account for these effects in animals. In other words, the evidence that increased density per se has deleterious effects on animal species is inconclusive at best.

Crowding in Humans. In much of his own research, Freedman and his colleagues (Freedman, Klevansky, and Ehrlich, 1971; Freedman, Levy, Buchanan, and Price, 1972) have examined the behavioral and emotional effects of short-term increases in population density in human beings. The findings indicate no straightforward effect of high density on creativity, memory, performance of various tasks, or aggressiveness. When one considers the sex of the subjects, however, Freedman, among others (Ross, et al., 1973) reports that high density may produce a heightening of emotion. Males, who are generally more aggressive than females, become even more aggressive under densely populated conditions. Females become less aggressive. In other words, there does not appear to be any unidirectional effect of short-term increases in population density. Rather, we must consider additional variables in evaluating the effects of density on behavior and emotion, such as the initial emotional state of the person.

Studies of long-term crowding are difficult to conduct with acceptable degrees of scientific rigor. Comparing mood and behavior in people who live in densely populated areas, such as the Bronx, and sparsely populated areas, such as rural Connecticut, can tell us little about the effects of density since there are so many differences between these two areas and their inhabitants. It is generally true that various indices of behavior, such as the Uniform Crime Reports of the FBI, indicate more criminal behavior in densely populated areas, but such studies cannot help us determine the effects of density on crime. The fact is that we know very little about the consequences of long-term crowding on humans, and what we do know suggests that factors other than density per se are most strongly associated with illness, psychopathology, aggression, and crime (Bell, Fisher, and Loomis, 1978; Freedman, Heshka, and Levy, 1975; Giel and Ormel, 1977; Levy and Herzog, 1974).

Subjective Feelings of Crowding. The subjective feeling of crowding is only loosely related to the level of density. Feelings of crowding can be increased or decreased within the same geographic space by many means. For example, techniques like keeping room area constant but varying architectural features such as partitions and number of doors can minimize discomfort (Desor, 1972). For instance, Tokyo is filled with tiny restaurants with no more than three or four tables separated by sliding shoji screens, making the patrons feel they are eating in a very private setting.

Since crowding is assumed to be an uncomfortable subjective state, individuals will avoid feeling crowded, if possible, or attempt to reduce the feeling when it arises. This may explain why so many people in elevators watch the floor numbers change as the elevator moves. By varying the visual environment and avoiding eye contact with others, they may reduce their feelings of crowding.

Under conditions of high population density, cultures appear to establish social norms that help reduce feelings of crowding. This has been confirmed in studies in the United States and elsewhere (Baum, Harpin, and Valins, 1975; Tucker and Friedman, 1972). For example, researchers investigated the behavior of people in three African societies that differed in population density (Munroe and Munroe, 1972). The three societies included the Logoli, at 1440 people per square mile, the Gusii, at 691 per square mile, and the Kipsigis, at 253 per square mile. The researchers predicted that the people in the most densely populated societies would exhibit less touching during casual encounters, such as handholding by friends, and would place less value on group affiliation. They measured the latter by asking their subjects to remember a list of words, some

of which were affiliation words such as "friend" or "party." People from the most densely populated group, the Logoli, were indeed the least likely to hold hands and were also least able to remember affiliation words on a short-term memory test, as the hypothesis predicted. Therefore, it appears that when population density is great, social norms and psychological mechanisms may begin to operate to minimize additional contact with others.

Environmental Stressors

An important part of the field of environmental psychology investigates the effects of various environmental stressors, such as noise, air pollution, and extreme temperatures. Noise, in particular, has received a great deal of attention. In the laboratory, loud noise produces quite a range of effects on cognitive processes, motivation, and general physiological processes. It is associated with changes in performance, decreased sensitivity to others, and physiological changes such as higher blood pressure and increased adrenalin secretion (Broadbent, 1978; Glass and Singer, 1972; Cohen and Lezak, 1977). A critical factor in the effects of noise on behavior and physiology is whether the noise is unpredictable and uncontrollable. If it is, the effects of noise are much greater.

These lab studies would suggest that noise constitutes a serious hazard and that allowable levels should be regulated. However, in order to make reasonable policies it is necessary to conduct both laboratory and field studies on the effects of noise. A field study examined the effects of aircraft noise on children attending elementary schools in the air corridor of Los Angeles International Airport (Cohen, et al., 1980). Noise levels in these areas reach peaks as high as ninety-five decibels, and planes fly overhead about every two and one-half minutes during school hours. The behavior of the children attending these "noisy" schools was compared to the behavior of other children in three control "quiet" schools, matched for grade level, ethnic and racial distribution, and other variables.

The children from the "noisy" and "quiet" schools differed on several physiological and behavioral measures. For example, the children from the "noisy" schools had higher blood pressure. On one test designed to measure "distractability," the children were asked to cross out the letter "e" each time it appeared in a two-page passage from a sixth-grade reader, moving from left to right and top to bottom, as if they were reading. Some of the children were in the "distraction-condition" and heard a taped story while they were trying to perform the task. The others were not distracted by any tape recordings. The children who had been at the "noisy" school only a short time did better at crossing out the letters than did the children from the "quiet" school, suggesting that they were good at "tuning out" the distracting noise. However, those who had been at the "noisy" school for several years performed poorly. Perhaps the strategy of "tuning out" distracting noise is only successful for a short time, after which the children give up.

The notion that children exposed to unpredictable and uncontrollable noise eventually "give up" is an intriguing one. Their behavior may represent learned helplessness. This theory (Seligman, 1975) predicts that people enter a psychological state of helplessness when they continually encounter unpleasant events about which they can do nothing. They soon quit trying to prevent unpleasant happenings in their lives, even though the circumstances might change and the events become controllable. They perceive a lessening of control over things, depression, and a decrease in motivation. Another test given to the children at the "noisy" and "quiet" schools attempted to determine whether the children were indeed learning to be helpless. Half the children from each school were given puzzles they could solve, and the other half worked on unsolvable puzzles. Then all were given a solvable puzzle. The children from the "noisy" schools were more likely to fail the second puzzle or to give up trying to solve it before the allotted amount of time had passed. This suggests that the children from the "noisy" schools had greater feelings of helplessness than did the "quiet" school children.

Environmental Planning and Design

One of the major goals of environmental psychology is to assist in the design of environments so that they meet the needs of the humans who will be using them. Proper environmental design can improve productivity, efficiency, safety, comfort, social interactions, and general satisfaction. Poorly thought out environmental design can hinder all of these things.

Consider the design of a hospital (Lindheim, 1970; Souder, et al., 1970). Historically, hospitals were built to isolate the sick from the healthy, particularly because of contagion problems; they looked like fortresses that were more appropriate for dying than for living. Today hospitals have different goals and functions. They should do some good for both ambulatory and bedridden patients, as well as outpatients. They should also provide preventive services for the healthy.

Incorporating new functions into the design of the hospital requires the expertise of a great many people, not least of whom are the people who work in or use the hospital. The design of a radiology department offers an example. Planning advice is usually offered by the manufacturers of the radiology equipment, even though they may have little understanding of the hospital's total needs. Most hospitals have tended to group radiology-related items together, such as film-processing labs, radiologists' offices, and filing cabinets. Also, radiology is placed near surgery, emergency, and lab facilities, since these departments use radiology tests most frequently. However, spatial proximity of these departments and areas is not necessary. According to one study (Lindheim, 1970), there are only three sets of the system that need to come into contact: (1) the patient, the machine, and the technician; (2) the film and the film processing lab; and (3) the radiologist and the X-ray machine. Thus, for example, an efficient radiology department might be designed with the film processing lab on another floor and a "dumbwaiter" to send the film between floors.

The kind of research needed for environmental planning and design, whether it is for a hospital, a national park, a nursing home, a restaurant, a child's bedroom (as described in the Career Box: Interior

Interior Designer

The creative work of interior designers helps make our environments both more attractive and more useful. These people plan and supervise the arrangement of building interiors and furnishings, working in private homes, department stores, offices, and civic buildings. Their work can benefit enormously from the research in environmental psychology, a field that examines the relationship between the behavior of human beings and their surroundings.

One example of how psychology is contributing to the work of an interior designer involves the design of a child's room. Psychologists do not believe there is a single, best design for a child's room, and no environment can substitute for a loving, caring home, but there is, nevertheless, a vast difference between a room that resembles an army barracks and one that is more like an adventure playground.

Researchers in child development especially stress three features of the room that should be considered. First, the room should offer stimulation, but not overstimulation. The patterns and textures in the room should be diverse, but the room should also be a kind of "stimulus shelter" to which the child can escape from noise and distractions. Secondly, the room should offer privacy, especially for children entering puberty. Even in cases where children share a room, it should be possible to create personal spaces with bookcases, room dividers, or other physical structures. A third important consideration concerns the TV. The placement of the television affects how the child interacts with family and friends, and also affects the child's general use of time. If the child has a TV in his room, he will probably spend more time watching it even if his friends are present, limiting his social interactions and reading time.

Children like to be consulted about the design of their rooms, although their suggestions are not always very useful. One six-year-old girl said, "I'd like my whole room to be one big bed, so then I could crawl all over it and everyone could sleep in it." Some psychologists suggest that a better approach is to observe children and note their preferences for various kinds of furnishings, furniture heights, room arrangements, and designs at different ages.

Designer), or an entire city, is very extensive. Designers need to know what the objectives are and what the environment will be used for. They need to know which behaviors should be encouraged and which ones discouraged. They need to have all the basic research information that helps them decide *how* to meet the needs of the group that will be using the environment under design. Environmental psychology is a young discipline but one that is making important contributions to the quality of life.

GUIDED REVIEW

Learning Objectives 9, 10, and 11

1. _____ is the study of the relationship between behavior and the environment. Topics include human spatial behavior (personal space, territoriality, and crowding), the effects of environmental stressors such as noise or pollution, and the design of environments.

2. The term _____ refers to an area around an individual into which others cannot intrude without arousing discomfort. Individuals engage in distance regulation, changing the size and shape of the personal space, depending on the circumstances.

3. Spatial distances between people can fall into four categories: _____ , _____ , _____ , and _____ . These distances are increasingly large, and they regulate different interactions between people.

4. Some of the dimensions and characteristics of _____ differ among people from different cultures. Contact between pedestrian companions is more common among some cultures. However, while working on cooperative tasks, people from different cultures seem to maintain similar spacing.

5. Two theories of personal space include _____ and _____ . Equilibrium theory proposes that personal space is a component of intimacy; two people who are intimate will regulate their distance accordingly, and if this is not possible, will engage other mechanisms to compensate.

6. _____ hypothesizes that differences in personal spacing under different circumstances are actually mechanisms for regulating the amount of social and sensory stimulation an individual receives from others.

7. People try to _____ in a variety of ways. For example, they erect physical barriers around their chairs or leave markers when they leave temporarily.

8. _____ behavior refers to behavior designed to preserve and defend from intruders a particular geographic area, such as one's home.

9. High population density seems to have many negative effects on behavior and physiology in animals, although it is not clear whether density, per se, is the cause. _____ refers to the number of individuals per unit area; _____ refers to a subjective feeling that there are too many others present.

10. People try to reduce feelings of _____ in many ways. For example, people who live in high-density societies engage in less friendly touching, and they also place less value on group affiliation, perhaps to reduce the feelings of crowding.

11. _____ is an important environmental stressor that can have deleterious effects on behavior and physiology, particularly if it is uncontrollable and unpredictable.

12. _____ can improve productivity, efficiency, safety, comfort, social interactions, and general satisfaction.

ANSWERS

1. Environmental psychology 2. personal space 3. intimate, personal, social, public 4. spatial behavior 5. equilibrium theory, stimulation theory 6. Stimulation theory 7. prevent violations of personal space 8. Territorial 9. Density; crowding 10. crowding 11. Noise 12. Environmental planning

SUMMARY

I. Work is such an integral part of people's lives that they often overlook its contribution to health and well-being and its relationship to nonwork activities, such as recreation and leisure.   (p. 532)

   A. There are several different theories about people's motivation to work.   (pp. 533–35)

      1. Herzberg's two-factor theory distinguishes between a person's basic needs, such as pay and job security, and higher-order "motivator needs," such as the need for challenge, stimulation, and creativity. Herzberg proposes that jobs can be enriched to make them more meaningful and satisfying to workers.   (p. 533)

      2. Vroom's valence-instrumentality-expectancy theory is a cognitive model of motivation and satisfaction that focuses on the individual's expectations and perceptions of work and the outcomes resulting from work.   (pp. 533–34)

3. Adam's equity theory states that people attempt to make their inputs and outcomes comparable to those of others in similar positions. When this outcome/input ratio is not comparable to similar others, there exists a state of inequity, which a person will attempt to reduce either by altering inputs (work or the quality of work) or outcomes (asking for a raise or going on strike). (p. 534)

Equity theory also leads to the prediction that overcompensation results in inequity, just as undercompensation does. Overcompensation may lower the intrinsic motivation to perform a task. (p. 535)

B. Unemployment can be seen as a source of stress that, like other stressors, influences an individual's health as well as that of his family. (pp. 535–38)

II. Large organizations are characterized by a division of labor, a formal structure, methods for recruiting and replacing members, and means for setting and accomplishing specific goals. (p. 539)

A. Bureaucracy refers to the formal structure of relationships within an organization. Such a structure makes for predictable and orderly activity and is presumed to increase the organization's efficiency by assigning specific tasks to each individual. This is known as a division of labor. (pp. 539–40)

B. Within any large bureaucratic organization, however, informal social groups form. These are groups of friends or co-workers who often establish norms that are at variance with those of the organization itself. (p. 540)

1. Early psychological studies of productivity in a plant, known as the Hawthorne experiments, found increases in productivity with both increased and decreased lighting. It was believed that the act of studying workers itself resulted in these productivity changes, and it is referred to as the "Hawthorne effect." The Hawthorne studies led to the human relations movement in industry; that is, to a concern with the informal social structure of organizations. (pp. 540–41)

C. Large organizations often have formal networks of communication specifying who may communiate with whom. These "communication networks" vary each individual's centrality and independence. For simple problems, centralized networks such as the wheel are most efficient, though individual's satisfaction tends to be greatest when they are most independent. (pp. 541–42)

1. Even though organizations may have formal communication networks, informal networks usually develop. Informal communication, such as company gossip and "small talk," is related to efficient group functioning. (p. 542)

III. Psychologists have developed personnel selection and training procedures and worked with engineers to enhance equipment design. (pp. 543–50)

A. Personnel selection is made more efficient by the use of psychological tests and measures. (p. 543)

B. Human factors research involves the design of equipment and systems to increase effectiveness, comfort, safety, and productivity of the individuals who use them. (pp. 543–44)

1. It is important to take into account the characteristics and limitations of individuals who will operate or use equipment. Research has examined each of the five sensory modalities in helping to design equipment. This was discussed as "information input." (pp. 544–50)

2. The design of equipment to enhance error-free and efficient operation must consider the operators' capabilities and habits. (p. 544)

3. The limits on people's abilities to perform tasks, their sensory apparatus, their sleep cycles, and their need to interact with others must all be considered when designing equipment and complex systems. (p. 544)

4. Many design problems stemming from the failure to consider human factors may be seen in the case of the nuclear accident at Three Mile Island. (pp. 549–50)

IV. Environmental psychology is the study of the relationship between the environment (both the natural and the constructed environment) and behavior.   (p. 551)

   A. The area around an individual that is considered private is referred to as personal space.   (p. 551)

      1. The size of an individual's personal space and the individual's reactions to violations of this space varies from one culture to another.   (p. 552)

      2. Equilibrium theory maintains that personal distance between individuals varies with their intimacy. As intimacy increases, interpersonal distance diminishes, eye contact increases, and topics of conversation become more personal. When one of these characteristics is restricted, individuals compensate by altering one or both of the others.   (p. 552)

      3. Stimulation theory states that variations in interpersonal distance is a means of regulating the extent of an individual's sensory and social stimulation.   (p. 552)

      4. When an individual's personal space is invaded, the person attempts to reestablish it, perhaps by moving or by erecting barriers to further encroachment. (p. 553)

   B. Territoriality is behavior designed to identify and preserve a particular geographic space, such as one's home or office.   (p. 553)

      1. Many species of animal are territorial. They mark and defend their territories from intrusion.   (p. 554)

      2. The behavior of human beings in marking and defending territories bears some resemblance to animal territoriality, but it is clear that human territoriality is much more variable and flexible than animal territoriality.   (p. 554)

      3. Although many species of animal appear to suffer from overcrowding, there is little evidence that humans inevitably suffer from densely populated situations. (p. 554)

         For humans, it is not so much population density as psychological factors that lead to feelings of being crowded. (pp. 554–55)

   C. Noise and environmental pollution may be seen as a source of stress. Like other stressors, noise, particularly if it is unpredictable and uncontrollable, interferes with cognitive functioning and may lead to feelings of helplessness. Noise also has physiological effects, such as increasing a person's blood pressure.   (pp. 555–56)

   D. Environmental psychologists assist architects in designing buildings and other environments to improve efficiency and the behavioral and social effects of the constructed environment. (pp. 556–57)

ACTION GLOSSARY

Match the terms in the left column with the definitions in the right column.

____ **1. Scientific management (p. 532)**
____ **2. Industrial psychology (p. 532)**
____ **3. Organizational psychology** (p. 532)
____ **4. Work (p. 532)**
____ **5. Leisure (p. 532)**
____ **6. Hygiene needs (p. 533)**
____ **7. Motivator needs (p. 533)**

A. *Activities that are performed outside the work context and whose goals are personally defined.*
B. *In Herzberg's theory, "higher order" needs, such as creativity and stimulation.*
C. *Empirical focus on worker behavior, motivation for work, and precise measurement and description of jobs.*
D. *Expenditure of energy to accomplish a task or goal.*
E. *Study of behavior of and within large organizations.*
F. *Application of psychological principles and findings to work.*
G. *In Herzberg's theory, basic needs, such as pay and job security.*

____	8. Equity theory (p. 534)	A. Extent to which a person wants to do something for its own sake.
____	9. Intrinsic motivation (p. 535)	B. The finding that the act of research may alter the behavior of its subjects.
____	10. Bureaucracy (p. 539)	C. States that one attempts to make inputs and outcomes in a situation comparable to those of one's peers.
____	11. Division of labor (p. 540)	
____	12. Hawthorne effect (p. 541)	D. Formal structures in which individuals may communicate only with specified others.
____	13. Human relations movement (p. 541)	E. Specialization of roles within an organization.
____	14. Communication networks (p. 541)	F. The belief that informal social conditions influence worker productivity.
		G. The recruitment of and relationships among individuals who are responsible for attaining the goals of an organization and for maintaining the organization itself.

____	15. Human factors (p. 543)	A. The subjective feeling that there are too many people present.
____	16. Environmental psychology (p. 551)	B. Behavior designed to preserve a particular geographic space, such as one's home.
____	17. Personal space (p. 551)	C. The study of the relationship between behavior and the natural and constructed environment.
____	18. Equilibrium theory (p. 552)	D. Emphasizes the relationship between personal space and social and sensory stimulation.
____	19. Stimulation theory (p. 552)	
____	20. Territoriality (p. 553)	E. The field that aims to design equipment and systems that increase the effectiveness, comfort, safety, and productivity of the people using them.
____	21. Population density (p. 554)	F. States that personal distance between individuals is a component of intimacy.
____	22. Crowding (p. 554)	G. The number of people living in a given area.
		H. The area an individual actively maintains around him or herself into which others cannot intrude without arousing discomfort.

ANSWERS

1. C, 2. F, 3. E, 4. D, 5. A, 6. G, 7. B, 8. C, 9. A, 10. G, 11. E, 12. B, 13. F, 14. D, 15. E, 16. C, 17. H, 18. F, 19. D, 20. B, 21. G, 22. A

SELF-TEST

1. Leisure activity differs from work primarily in that
   (a) it is more enjoyable.
   (b) its goals are personally defined.
   (c) it is unrelated to maintenance functions, such as biological needs.
   (d) it is voluntary, whereas work is not.
   (LO 2; p. 532)

2. The fact that there are different theories of motivation to work indicates that
   (a) psychologists don't know why people work.
   (b) the motivation to work involves many different needs.
   (c) psychologists disagree among themselves about work motivation.
   (d) all of the above.
   (e) none of the above.
   (LO 2, 3; pp. 532–33)

3. Seeking a challenge in one's work, the need for stimulation, the need for creativity, and the desire for independence are regarded in Herzberg's two-factor theory as
   (a) basic needs.
   (b) hygiene needs.
   (c) job enrichment.
   (d) motivator needs.
   (LO 4; p. 533)

4. An employee thinks that a promotion will be accompanied by a raise that will enable him to buy a new piano. This indicates what Vroom's V-I-E theory would consider
   (a) valence.
   (b) instrumentality.
   (c) expectancy.
   (LO 4; p. 533)

5. Research indicates that Vroom's V-I-E theory predicts
   - (a) an individual's job performance better than his or her effort.
   - (b) an employee's effort better than his or her job performance.
   - (c) both effort and job performance.
   - (d) predicts neither job performance nor effort.
   (LO 4; p. 534)

6. If a person's job outcomes, relative to his inputs, are not comparable to those of a co-worker in the same job,
   - (a) the individual experiences inequity.
   - (b) the individual will alter either his inputs or his outcomes.
   - (c) the individual will feel psychological discomfort.
   - (d) all of the above.
   - (e) none of the above.
   (LO 4; p. 534)

7. According to equity theory, being overpaid for a task may result in
   - (a) lowered intrinsic motivation.
   - (b) raised intrinsic motivation.
   - (c) increased liking for the task.
   - (d) more effort expended in completing the task.
   (LO 4; p. 535)

8. Losing one's job influences
   - (a) not only the former worker but his or her family as well.
   - (b) the person's physical health.
   - (c) the person's emotional well-being.
   - (d) all of the above.
   - (e) none of the above.
   (LO 2; p. 538)

9. In a bureaucracy, individuals perform specialized tasks. This is referred to as
   - (a) intrinsic motivation.
   - (b) equity.
   - (c) division of labor.
   - (d) none of the above.
   (LO 5; p. 540)

10. A small group of friends who always eat lunch together at the same large company is an example of
    - (a) division of labor.
    - (b) bureaucracy.
    - (c) a communication network.
    - (d) an informal social structure.
    (LO 5; p. 540)

11. Which of the following communication networks would produce the most efficient solution to a simple problem?
    - (a) One in which all members can communicate with all other members.
    - (b) One in which there is a central member through whom everyone else must communicate.
    - (c) One in which every member is independent.
    - (d) They would all produce efficient solutions to simple problems.
    - (e) Not enough information is given to answer the question.
    (LO 5; p. 542)

12. Human factors research is concerned with
    - (a) the design of equipment and complex systems.
    - (b) the comfort of workers and safety of equipment.
    - (c) interactions between humans and machines.
    - (d) all of the above.
    - (e) none of the above.
    (LO 7; p. 543)

13. The area a person maintains around him- or herself, into which others may not intrude without arousing discomfort, is
    - (a) personal space.
    - (b) territoriality.
    - (c) cognitive map.
    - (d) human factors.
    (LO 9; p. 551)

14. According to E. T. Hall, the distance of 1.3 to 3.5 meters, at which people work cooperatively or engage in social conversation, is referred to as
    - (a) intimate distance.
    - (b) social distance.
    - (c) personal space.
    - (d) public distance.
    (LO 9; p. 551)

15. Cross-cultural studies of personal space indicate that
    - (a) people use space in much the same way everywhere in the world.
    - (b) people in the twentieth century use space in similar ways, but it differs from the use of space in the eighteenth and nineteenth centuries.
    - (c) personal contact among pedestrians varies considerably by country.
    - (d) comfortable speaking distance is the same in the Middle East as in England.
    (LO 9; p. 552)

16. Equilibrium theory concerns intimacy as a function of all but which of the following?

    (a) eye contact
    (b) topic intimacy
    (c) personal distance
    (d) nationality
        (LO 10; p. 552)

17. According to stimulation theory of personal space, different interpersonal spatial distances help to regulate

    (a) noise.
    (b) social and sensory input.
    (c) intimacy.
    (d) odor.
    (e) none of the above.
        (LO 10; p. 552)

18. The difference between the concepts of personal space and territoriality is that the latter

    (a) is larger.
    (b) applies only to animals.
    (c) does not move with the person or organism.
    (d) all of the above.
    (e) none of the above.
        (LO 9; p. 553)

19. The difference between population density and crowding is that the latter refers to

    (a) the number of people in a given spatial area.
    (b) physiological arousal due to the presence of too many others.
    (c) an uncomfortable feeling resulting from the presence of too many others.
    (d) the amount of resources available for a given number of people.
        (LO 9; p. 554)

20. Cross-cultural studies of population density and personal space show that in densely populated countries

    (a) people are less likely to hold hands while walking.
    (b) the birthrate is lower than it is when density is lower.
    (c) there are rules to prevent early marriages.
    (d) all of the above.
    (e) none of the above.
        (LO 9; p. 555)

ANSWERS

1. B, 2. B, 3. D, 4. B, 5. B, 6. D, 7. A, 8. D, 9. C, 10. D, 11. B,
12. D, 13. A, 14. B, 15. C, 16. D, 17. B, 18. C, 19. C, 20. A

SUGGESTED READINGS

Dunnette, M. D., *Handbook of Industrial and Organizational Psychology*. New York: Wiley, 1983. Thirty-seven chapters on all aspects of the application of psychology to industrial and other organizations.

Fisher, J. D., P. A. Bell, and A. Baum. *Environmental Psychology,* 2d ed. New York: Holt, Rinehart & Winston, 1984. An introductory text on the relationship between human behavior and the environment.

Kanter, R. M. *Men and Women of the Corporation.* New York: Basic Books, 1977. An important contribution on the effect of gender on the functioning of the organization.

Kantowitz, B. H., and R. D. Sorkin. *Human Factors: Understanding People-System Relationships.* New York: Wiley, 1983. A text that emphasizes the theoretical aspects of research on human factors. It covers areas such as the human factors of data entry in computer systems, human sensory-motor abilities, and workspace design.

Scientific American (1982, September). An entire issue devoted to the mechanization of work, with an especially interesting article on the mechanization of office work by Vincent Giuliano.

Varela, J. A. *Psychological Solutions to Social Problems.* New York: Academic Press, 1971. An engineer applies social psychology to various problems in industry, from job design to social relations among workers and management.

Wickens, C. D. *Engineering Psychology and Human Performance.* Columbus, OH: Charles E. Merrill, 1984. A text that relates the principles of cognitive psychology to the design of systems and machines.

a p p e n d i x

Statistical Methods

A survey on the way people feel about health and illness reported some fascinating findings (Rubenstein, 1982):

Forty-two percent of the sample think about their health more often than just about anything else, including love, work, and money.

Men and women whose parents were divorced feel less healthy than adults who grew up in intact families.

Four out of ten reported avoiding salt; one-third said they did not use sugar.

Women reported an average of nine symptoms; men an average of seven.

Nine percent complained about being given too many drugs.

Twenty-five percent said they experienced and were bothered by the doctor's uncaring or condescending attitude.

Thirty-four percent of the men reported having trouble falling asleep; 40% of women reported sleeping problems.

These findings say a great deal about how extremely health-conscious humans are. Or do they? Surveys like this one appear regularly in magazines on topics ranging from "Who has a happy sex life?" to "How do people spend their money?" They obviously help sell magazines, but do they tell us anything about human behavior?

To understand and evaluate these numerous psychological reports, it is necessary to have a basic understanding of statistics. Three of the most important topics are descriptive statistics, statistical inference, and correlation.

Descriptive Statistics

One of the most valuable uses of statistics is to describe and make sense out of mounds of data. A stack of computer printouts is almost useless to people who need information, unless the printouts are described and summarized. Descriptive statistics accomplishes this purpose, using frequency distributions, measures of central tendency, and measures of variation.

Betty	2.6	Bob	5.1	Barb	3.5
Joe	4.8	Lisa	2.1	Wendell	2.6
Helga	5.6	Pam	2.6	Brian S.	2.2
Tom	2.1	Laura	4.2	Brian J.	1.7
Bill A.	3.6	Dennis	4.1	George	3.0
Bill P.	0.7	Wes	2.9	Alice	3.4
Jenny	3.7	Greg	1.1	Callie	4.2
John	6.1	Lou	1.6		

Figure A.1   A list of the number of cups of coffee consumed by each member of a psychotherapy group

Interval	Frequency
0 — 0.9	1
1.0 — 1.9	3
2.0 — 2.9	7
3.0 — 3.9	5
4.0 — 4.9	4
5.0 — 5.9	2
6.0 — 6.9	1
7.0 — 7.9	0

Figure A.2   A frequency distribution of the data in figure A.1

Frequency Distributions

Figure A.1 lists the number of cups of coffee drunk by each member of a psychotherapy group during a session. This list becomes comprehensible when it is grouped into a frequency distribution, which is a set of scores assembled according to size and grouped into intervals (fig. A.2). The numbers from figure A.1 are arranged into intervals (0–0.9, 1.0–1.9, 2.0–2.9, etc.), and then the number of people who drank an amount of coffee that fell within each interval is tabulated. For example, three people drank between 1.0 and 1.9 cups of coffee. We can see how much coffee the clients are drinking simply by glancing at this frequency distribution.

A graph would express the data even more clearly than the table. Figure A.3 shows a frequency histogram, one of the most common means to graphically display a frequency distribution. The vertical axis is labeled *frequency,* a general term that means the number of cases, and the horizontal axis is "number of cups of coffee." The intervals are shown across the horizontal axis, and above each one is a bar showing the number of people who drank an amount of coffee that fell within that interval.

A frequency polygon is another common graphing technique (fig. A.4). The axis labels are the same, but the frequencies are plotted with points and connecting straight lines. In this example there were only eighteen

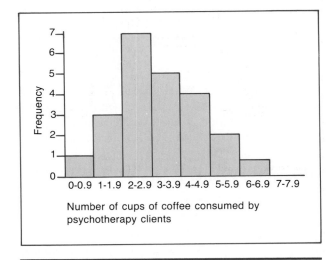

Figure A.3   A frequency histogram

people in the psychotherapy session, so the polygon appears rather angular. If there were many more people and much smaller intervals, the frequency polygon would begin to look more like a bell-shaped curve. When researchers measure variables in large samples and graph them on a frequency polygon, the result is much like the curve shown in figure A.5. Most scores tend to lie in the middle of the variable, and a few lie

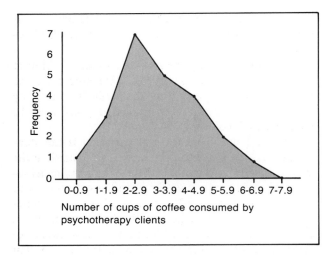

Figure A.4 A frequency polygon

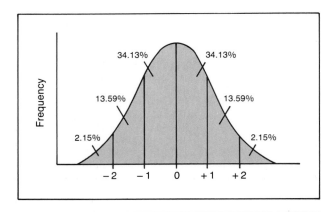

Figure A.5 The normal distribution

at the extreme ends. When the curve is symmetrical and bell shaped, as it often turns out to be, it is called a normal distribution. If it is asymmetrical, with a long "tail" on one side or the other, it is called skewed.

Measures of Central Tendency

Another way to describe a list of figures like those in figure A.1 is to provide a single number or average of some kind. Statisticians actually use three different procedures to arrive at an average, each of which may yield a slightly different value. These three measures of central tendency are the mean, mode, and median.

The mean is what most of us refer to when we use the word "average." It is simply the sum of the scores divided by the number of scores. In the psychotherapy group, the mean number of cups of coffee consumed by the clients was 3.2. The statistical symbol for mean is $\overline{X}$.

The mode is the most frequent score in a distribution. In the psychotherapy group, the mode was 2.6 cups of coffee. If you did not have the list of scores, you could

obtain the mode simply by looking at the frequency histogram. The highest frequency occurs in the 2.0–2.9 interval, and the mode would simply be the midpoint of that interval (2.5).

The median is the score below which 50% of the scores in the distribution fall. It is the middle score, and in that sense it is like a percentile rank. The median is the score at the 50th percentile. In the example the median is 3.0, since eleven scores fall below that and eleven fall above it.

In a normal distribution, the mean, mode, and median are all about the same value. However, the three measures of central tendency diverge when the distribution is skewed. The distribution of the amount of coffee the clients drank is skewed, with most people drinking between 1 and 4 cups and a few heavy caffeine users drinking 5 or 6. In this case the mean, median, and mode are different. Of all the measures of central tendency, the mean is most affected by extreme scores like the 5.6 and 6.1, so it is pushed higher. In a skewed distribution like this one, the median usually falls between the mean and the mode.

For most distributions, the mean is the preferred measure of central tendency; however, in some highly skewed cases the mean is very misleading. For instance, suppose you are an employee of a company with

San Francisco	Phoenix
32	65
55	65
61	67
66	68
78	73
81	76
84	76
89	78
94	84
100	88
$\bar{x}$ = 74	$\bar{x}$ = 74
s = 19.6	s = 7.5

Figure A.6   Scores on a statistics pretest from two different

ten people earning around $12,800 per year and a president earning $70,000. The mean salary at this company is almost $18,000, a figure that would look very attractive in quarterly reports and employee newsletters. But none of the employees actually earn anywhere near that.

Measures of Variation

Figure A.6 shows the scores that people in two different classes received on a statistics pretest. The test was designed to determine whether the students have the background for a course in probability. The means of the scores of the two classes are the same: 74, but the scores of the San Francisco class are scattered much more widely. Some students did very poorly, and others did quite well. In contrast, the scores of the Phoenix group were more tightly clustered around the mean. Their scores were more homogeneous.

A teacher would certainly want to know the means of the classes, but he or she would also want to know something about variation, or scatter, about the mean. The San Francisco class will be much harder to work with because some students have so little preparation and others have so much. The two most common measures of variation are the range and the standard deviation.

The range is simply the spread between the highest and the lowest score. In the San Francisco class, for example, the range was from 32 to 100. It is certainly easy to provide, but it does not tell very much about the scatter of scores.

The most useful measure of variation is the standard deviation, a statistic that is actually based on the distance of each score from the mean of the distribution. For each score, the difference between the mean and the score is squared, and then all the squared deviations are summed together. (In statistical notation, Σ means "sum together.") The sum of the squared deviations is divided by N, the number of scores, to obtain an average of the squared deviations. Then to return to the original unsquared scale of numbers, the square root is taken. The more that the scores are scattered away from the mean, the higher the standard deviation will be. The value will be lower when the scores are tightly clustered about the mean. Notice that the standard deviation, or *s*, for the Phoenix group was 7.5. For the more widely scattered scores in the San Francisco class, the standard deviation was nearly 20.

In a normal distribution, about 34% of the cases fall between the mean and one standard deviation above the mean, and also between the mean and one standard deviation below. About 13.59% of the cases fall between one and two standard deviations, either above or below the mean. And 2.15% of the cases fall more than two standard deviations away from the mean (figure A.5). This means that it is possible to determine approximately where in the distribution any particular score falls, provided the distribution is normal. If the mean on a test with normally distributed scores is 100 and the standard deviation is 10, then about 34% of the people got between 100 and 110. A person who got 110 on the test would be at about the 84th percentile.

Statistical Inference

Describing a set of data and drawing conclusions from it can be two very different things. A number of procedures are available that permit researchers to draw sound conclusions from data, even when they only have a chance to observe the behavior of a small group of people. The first step is to collect data on people who are generally representative of the total group that the researchers would have been interested in.

Populations and Samples

When researchers want to learn something about human behavior, they never try to observe everybody in the population of individuals with whom they are concerned; instead, they observe a small *sample* or subset of the population. For example, a researcher who is interested in the voting preferences of residents of Vermont would not try to telephone everyone in the population of registered voters in the state and ask questions. Instead, she would obtain a list of registered voters in the state and randomly choose a small subset. If the sample is randomly chosen, each member of the population has an equal chance of being included. As long as the random sample is not too small, it should be representative of the larger population. Therefore, measures of the voting preferences of this sample should indicate fairly closely the preferences of the entire population. If 60% of the sample say they intend to vote for a particular candidate, one can assume that approximately 60% of all the registered voters in Vermont have the same preference.

In psychological research it is not always possible to obtain a random sample. In an investigation of short-term memory processes, for example, the population that interests the researcher probably includes all adult human beings. Getting a random sample would mean obtaining a list of all adults on earth and randomly choosing a sample of perhaps fifty of them. The sample would probably include several Chinese, Indians, Africans, and many others who do not speak English. Since this is not really an option, most researchers use the available sample, a group that includes, basically, whomever they can get. Since psychologists are often college or university professors, the sample often includes college students who earn money or extra credit by participating in experiments. For much psychological research, the results obtained from an available sample are probably reasonably close to what would be obtained from a sample that is more representative of all adult humans. It would be very surprising, for example, to learn that the short-term memories of Chinese young adults was profoundly different from Americans. However, probably no one would argue that a survey of the sexual practices of American college students would tell us very much about all adult Americans, as well as adult Chinese.

The magazine surveys referred to earlier always have difficulty generalizing to all adult Americans because their samples are rarely representative of the population. It is usually limited to readers of the magazine since that is often where the survey questions appear. For the health survey in *Psychology Today,* 31% of the respondents were men and 68% were women—hardly a balance that represents what actually exists in the United States. Furthermore, the largest proportion were never married. (In the United States, more than three-fourths of the adult population have been married.) More than half of the sample had at least a college degree and an annual family income over $25,000. Thus, we were learning something about the young, well-educated readers of *Psychology Today* who have time to spend and some interest in filling out a questionnaire about health. People who spare the time are often those who are unusually interested in the topic, making it unremarkable that the respondents seemed very health-conscious. In fact, one in five of the respondents enclosed a personal letter describing their own approach to health.

Before drawing any conclusions about the results of a study, it is important to consider the sample. Was it all men? Did it include people from all socioeconomic groups? Were older and younger people included? If the sample was a narrow one, the conclusions must be very cautious; most studies will mention a caveat about the nature of the sample. The health survey stated, "These conclusions are based on a young, well-educated sample, and thus may not be applicable to all Americans." In the beginning of the report, however, the sample problem is ignored: "Our findings confirm that physical health has taken on great importance in our lives and that many of us think about it almost to the point of obsession these days."

Significant Differences

A great deal of statistical inference is involved with determining whether differences between the means of two or more groups are significant. In statistical jargon, the word *significant* has very little to do with "important" or "noteworthy." The word simply reflects whether it is a reliable difference that did not occur simply by chance. In some cases, significant differences can actually be quite small and be of little practical interest.

The health survey mentioned that women checked an average of nine symptoms and men an average of seven. One might hastily draw some conclusions from this finding, such as that women are less healthy than men, that women *think* they are less healthy than men, or that men are reluctant to talk about their physical complaints. Before drawing any conclusions at all, however, one should determine whether the difference is a significant one. After all, whenever you measure two groups of people on any test, it is extremely *un*likely that the mean would be exactly the same, even if there is no difference at all between the populations from which the two samples were drawn.

Figure A.7 shows two sets of data, both of which have two groups with means of 7 and 9. In the first set the scores are tightly clustered around the means, and there is hardly any overlap between the scores of the men and the women. In the second, there is considerable overlap. Notice that the standard deviations of the distributions in the first set are much smaller than those in the second set.

A statistical test of significance would show that the probability that the two-point difference between the means in the first set occurred by chance is extremely

I.		II.	
Men	Women	Men	Women
6	8	1	3
6	8	3	5
7	9	5	7
7	9	7	9
7	9	9	11
8	10	11	13
8	10	13	15
$\bar{x} = 7$	$\bar{x} = 9$	$\bar{x} = 7$	$\bar{x} = 9$
$s = .8$	$s = .8$	$s = 4.0$	$s = 4.0$
$p < .001$		p is about .2	

Figure A.7 Two hypothetical sets of data in which the mean number of symptoms reported by women was 9 and the mean for men was 7. The difference between the means for set I is significant. For set II the difference between 7 and 9 is not significant.

low. There seems little likelihood that we could have accidentally obtained such a large difference between the means, given that the populations of men and women do not differ very much. We can be quite confident that the populations of men and women who are represented by the samples do indeed differ in the number of symptoms they report. In contrast, we cannot be confident at all about the difference between men and women if we obtained the data in the second set. The probability that the two-point difference between the means occurred by chance alone is rather high.

There are many different kinds of tests of significance, each of which is appropriate in different experimental designs. However, the end result of all of them is a probability figure that describes the likelihood that the difference obtained between the means of two or more groups was due to chance, rather than to any real difference between the means of the populations from which the samples were drawn. It is usually abbreviated p, and it might read "$p < .05$," or "$p < .001$." This means that the probability that the difference between the means occurred by chance is less than .05, or one out of twenty, or .001, one out of 1000. Psychologists usually use a p of .05 as a kind of cutoff point.

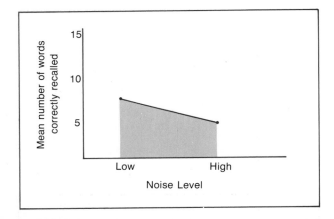

Figure A.8 *Graphing data from an experiment*

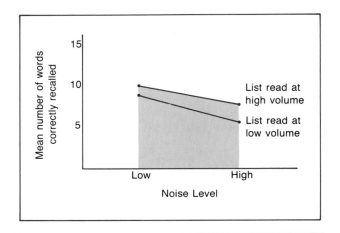

Figure A.9 *Graphing data from an experiment with two independent variables*

If there is less than .05 chance that the difference occurred by chance, psychologists assume it did *not* occur by chance and that it represents a significant difference. If p is greater than .05, we assume the two groups probably were drawn from populations that have very similar or identical means, and thus there is no significant difference between them.

In our hypothetical results from the health survey, the data in set I would have resulted in a p value that was less than .001. We would therefore conclude that the difference between the mean number of symptoms reported by the men and women was significant. In set II, the p value was about .2, meaning that there was a one in five chance that the difference occurred simply by chance. For psychologists, this difference is not reliable enough. The p value is too large, and we would call the difference between the means of the two groups "nonsignificant." (Although the survey did not actually report the p values, we guess that the difference between the mean number of reported symptoms for men and women was significant. If it were not, a responsible psychologist would not have mentioned them.)

Graphing the Results of Experiments

The graphs that are used to illustrate data from experiments usually place the independent variable along the horizontal axis and the dependent variable along the vertical axis. For example, a study that explored the effects of noise on short-term memory processes might ask twenty subjects to listen to a list of words and, afterwards, to write down as many as possible. The twenty subjects would be randomly divided into two groups, one of which listened to the list under low-noise and the other under high-noise conditions (fig. A.8). Experiments often have more complex designs using many more groups, such as the one in figure A.9. This design has *two* independent variables: amount of noise (shown across the horizontal axis) and the volume at which the word list was read to the subjects.

Correlation

Correlation refers to the degree of relationship or association between two variables. It provides a method to determine whether changes in one variable are related to changes in another. For example, there would probably be a strong correlation between height and weight because tall people tend to be heavier than short people.

Student	Number of Absences	Grade
Ames, S.	2	3.6
Barnes, C.	5	2.1
Bennetti, T.	6	2.7
Collins, D.	1	2.9
Davidson, B.	7	1.6
Eggars, K.	6	3.2
Frye, A.	14	1.0
Holland, K.	0	3.6
Jackson, B.	1	3.9
Moore, T.	2	3.0
Thomas, G.	10	1.9
Toras, J.	3	3.3
Wachal, N.	8	2.0
West, B.	12	0.5
Zwink, M.	4	1.2

Figure A.10   The number of absences and grades of the students in a psychology class

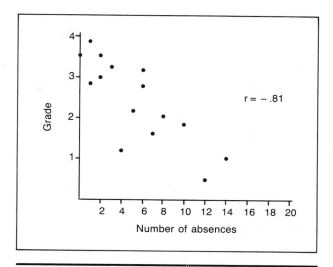

Figure A.11   A scatter diagram showing the relationship between grades and number of absences from class

The Scatter Diagram

The scatter diagram is the graph that is used to illustrate a correlation. The data in figure A.10 represent the number of absences of each student in a psychology class, and next to it is each student's grade, converted to a four-point scale. These data can be graphed by using a single point for each person (fig. A.11).

In general, the more absences a person has, the lower the grade is. The scatter diagram shows a general trend from the upper left to the lower right.

The Correlation Coefficient

A statistical measure of the direction and degree of association between two variables is obtained by the correlation coefficient. The most common coefficient is the product-moment correlation, or r, which ranges in value from -1 to $+1$. The direction of the relationship is shown by the sign. A minus indicates a negative correlation and means that as one variable increases, the other decreases. The relationship between number of absences and the student's grade is negative because as the number of absences increases, grade decreases. A positive r means that as one variable increases, the other also increases. The relationship between height and weight would be positive, for example.

The strength of the association between the two variables is indicated by the absolute value of the correlation coefficient. An r of .9 would indicate a very strong relationship, and an r of $-.95$ would indicate an even stronger relationship.

The strength of the association between two variables can be computed using a formula described in any introductory statistics text, or it can be estimated by looking at the scatter diagram. If the trend of the scores is from the lower left to the upper right, then the relationship is positive. If the trend is from the upper left to the lower right, it is negative. If there seems to be no trend at all, r is probably close to zero. If the dots cluster tightly around an imaginary line going through the center of the scores, the correlation is probably very strong, and the absolute value of r is high. However, if they are scattered widely throughout the scatter diagram, r will be low. The correlation coefficient for the relationship between grade and number of absences was negative and rather strong: $-.81$.

Correlation and Causation

It is a common mistake to assume that if two variables are correlated, one probably is the cause of the other. A newspaper might report that most people who commit crimes come from homes with a history of alcohol abuse. This might lead one to suppose that a criminal's early childhood experiences with alcoholic parents led to a life of frustration, anger, and crime. Correlation, however, is not necessarily causation, and other possibilities exist. Perhaps the criminal began a life of crime early, driving the parents crazy and straight to the bottle. Or a third variable, such as poverty, is the main cause of both the alcohol abuse in the home and the criminal behavior of the children.

One might assume at first glance that the students in the psychology class were getting low grades because they missed so many classes, and those getting high grades did so because of good attendance. It could also be the other way around. Perhaps the students whose grades were poor began losing interest in the class and thus failed to attend.

Statistics and Anxiety

Statistics is one of the courses that many students approach with trepidation, perhaps because it seems remote, extremely difficult, and complicated. Some fear that it will be a grueling exercise in memorizing horrifying formulas. Skeptical students think it will be a course in learning how to conjure with figures. It does require a certain facility with math, something that many people feel they do not have.

The approach to statistics is very important. It is not like introductory psychology, in which you can read Chapter 12 first and then read Chapter 6 later. You must start from the beginning, mastering each step before proceeding to the next one. Some sections will take two or three readings and much homework time before complete mastery. As you succeed on each level, however, your confidence will increase and your anxiety will eventually decrease.

B

Computer Applications in Psychology

Carl Sagan (1977) told a possibly apocryphal story about a U.S. senator enjoying a tour of a computer system that included an advanced translation program. The program could take text from one language, English, for instance, and translate it into another. The senator was asked to provide an English phrase for translation into Chinese, and he came up with "out of sight, out of mind." The computer quickly produced a piece of paper with a few Chinese characters on it that presumably represented the translation of the senator's proverb. To complete the test, the Chinese characters were fed back into the machine to be translated into English. The computer produced a piece of paper that read, "invisible idiot."

Computers are enormously powerful machines that are extremely capable in some areas and rather obtuse in others. A computer can calculate the most complex mathematical formulas in microseconds but is not yet able to understand a simple proverb. Nevertheless, it is having important effects on all areas of life, including the world of psychology.

The field of psychology has been affected by the current technological revolution in many ways, and this appendix examines a few of them. For example, the computer is used to produce stimuli for experimental work and to collect and analyze the data. It administers, scores, and interprets psychological tests, conducts interviews with patients, and even assists in some kinds of therapy. In the field of artificial intelligence, psychologists compare the thinking processes of humans to those of the machine, partly in an attempt to make the computer "smarter" and thus more useful. Computer-assisted instruction is being developed by and for psychology professors, incorporating the principles of learning and motivation that apply in education.

The computer has also provided psychologists with a new perspective with respect to their ideas about the way humans think and behave. In some ways, the computer operates like the human brain, receiving input, analyzing it, and constructing output. The approach in psychology called "information processing" uses this analogy between the human brain and the computer to learn more about cognitive processes. Although there are many important differences between the way humans think and the way computers "think," the analogy has provided some important insights into human behavior.

The applications that follow are only a few that exist in the field of psychology, though they generally represent the directions that computer applications are currently taking. However, it is dangerous to make predictions in either computer science or in psychology, and the applications that exist even five years from now may be quite surprising.

Computers in the Laboratory

The application of computer technology in the psychological laboratory has had a long and successful history. As early as the 1960s, a computer called the LINC (Laboratory Instrument Computer) was under development and eventually used in a variety of psychological applications, such as investigations of operant conditioning, speech synthesis, and the preparation of stimulus material for studies in sensation and perception (Bird, 1981).

An important advantage of the computer is that it has the ability to precisely determine and control the stimulus, particularly in studies that require a visual or auditory display of some kind. The computer can generate simple or incredibly complex visual patterns, and it can display them as stationary or moving forms. Displays can appear for a brief fraction of a second, or they can flicker on and off at varying speeds. The potential variety is virtually limitless.

Using speakers, the computer can generate and control simple or complex auditory stimuli, including speech sounds. Although synthetic speech is still not as intelligible as normal human speech, it probably will be as advances are made. In the meantime, the computer can precisely control the frequencies and amplitudes of sounds for studies of audition.

A computer program can control the presentation of stimuli just as it controls the stimuli themselves. For example, a particular study might call for the presentation of five lists of twenty nonsense syllables, and the syllables must be "shuffled" for each of the five lists.

A computer can randomly arrange the twenty syllables for each of the five lists and do it over and over for each new subject taking the memory test. The program might also make the presentation of stimuli contingent upon the behavior of the subject. It might "wait" for the subject to demonstrate that he is ready before presenting the next trial, perhaps by pressing a specific key on the keyboard. More involved programs might make the presentation of specific sets of stimulus material dependent upon the subject's performance on earlier trials. A computerized IQ test, for example, might select questions based on whether the testee had answered previous questions correctly.

Responses can also be measured by the computer, and quite detailed and accurate information about the nature of each response can be accumulated. In a simple case, the subject of an experiment might just be asked to press a key when a visual stimulus appeared, and the computer would measure the subject's reaction time. Or, the experiment might be one that required the subject to choose between two or more alternatives, and the computer would record the subject's accuracy on each trial, and perhaps his reaction time as well.

Anything that can be typed on the keyboard can be monitored, and many computers receive input through light pens or graphics tablets. As more sophisticated programs are written that enable computers to understand original English sentences, either spoken or typed into the keyboard, the possibilities for data collection will grow enormously.

One example of a study in which a computer was used to present stimuli and monitor the responses of the subjects dealt with cognition (Ratcliff and McKoon, 1982). The study was designed to assess how people process and verify semantic information contained in simple sentences, such as, "A robin is a bird." There are several theories that attempt to explain how semantic information in the brain is accessed and used to process incoming information. (See Chapter 6.) The aim of the researchers in this study was to evaluate several of the theories and determine whether the data they collected could be used to support or refute any of them.

Each subject sat in front of a terminal with a keyboard, and a series of sentences were presented. The sentences were of various kinds, including some in which the two concepts were opposites (A mother is a father), and some in which they were synonyms (A carpet is a rug). Some sentences, called "category-member sentences," included the title of a category and a member of the category (A bird is a robin). These kinds of sentences were false because not all birds are robins. Other sentences mentioned the member of the category first, making the sentence true (A robin is a bird). "Anomalous" sentences mentioned two totally unrelated concepts (A problem is a swallow), and "description" sentences included an adjective as one of the concepts (A razor is sharp).

The researchers programmed the computer to control the experimental procedure in several ways. The first part of the sentence, for example, "Is a robin," was presented for 500 msec. Then the second part, "a bird," was presented. A signal (a row of asterisks) that told the subject to respond as quickly as possible was displayed at varying intervals after the presentation of the second part of the sentence. The signal was given at 50, 150, 300, 600, 1000, or 1500 msec after the second part of the sentence appeared on the screen, and the computer program randomly chose one of the six time lags for each trial. Subjects were instructed to respond as quickly as possible when they saw the row of asterisks, even if they were not sure of the answer. The researchers were especially interested in how the accuracy of the subjects would be affected on the different kinds of sentences when they were forced to respond quickly. After a subject responded by pressing the ? key for yes and the z key for no, the reaction time was displayed on the screen, and the program waited until the subject pressed the space bar to begin the next trial.

In this experiment, the computer controlled the timing for the presentation of each of the stimuli and randomly varied the timing for presenting the asterisk signal to respond. It also monitored and recorded the accuracy and reaction time of the subject on each trial, and it provided immediate feedback about the subject's reaction time. Further, the computer generated a new random order for the presentation of sentences for every two subjects who were tested. One of the findings from this study was that the processing of a sentence like "A bird is a robin" is rather different from the processing of other kinds of sentences. When the subjects are encouraged to respond after very short time lags, they have a tendency to say "yes," even though that answer is incorrect. The researchers suggested that the subject might simply be assessing the overall similarity of the two nouns. After the longer response time lags, the subjects showed a bias toward answering "no," perhaps because the subjects had more time to evaluate the exact nature of the relationship between the two nouns.

The complexity of the stimulus presentations, as well as the need for precision timing in this experiment, would make it an almost impossible task without the aid of the computer. With computer technology, however, researchers studying information processing are able to measure the most minute differences in processing times.

Computer applications in the laboratory can be extended by using the computer to control the operation of ordinary equipment commonly used in psychological laboratories. For example, the computer can be used to program the apparatus that delivers food pellets to a rat in an operant conditioning chamber. The computer receives information about the rat's lever pressing behavior and controls the delivery of reinforcement, the lighting or noises in the chamber, electric shocks on the floor grid, or any number of other conditions. Equipment like slide projectors, videotape machines, tape recorders, or electrical stimulators can all be controlled and timed by computer programs.

The measurement of responses can also be expanded by connecting the equipment to other monitoring devices, such as physiological recorders, microphones, videocameras, photoelectric light beams, electronic scales, and many other kinds of equipment. Physiological information, for example, can be monitored with temperature probes, ohmmeters, voltmeters, or other kinds of equipment; it can then be converted into the digital signals required by the computer, making it possible for the computer to analyze complex waveforms typical of heartbeats, galvanic skin responses, or muscular contraction. The computer can analyze the frequency patterns in human speech or animal sounds. In conjunction with videocameras, it can analyze movements of the whole body or of tiny parts like the eyelid.

The computer offers quite a number of advantages in the experimental laboratory. It gives the researcher better control over stimulus presentations and permits more detailed and accurate monitoring of responses. It also relieves the researcher from the repetitive, time-consuming aspects of data collection. The computer can be programmed to individualize the presentation of materials for each subject, relying on randomization or feedback from each subject.

The use of the computer also removes the possibility of "experimenter effects" (Rosenthal, 1963; 1976). A variety of studies have shown that the experimenter can influence the results of that study he or she is conducting in unpredictable and usually unconscious ways. The experimenter who thinks that the subjects should react faster to a certain kind of sentence in the study discussed earlier, for example, might have provided a tiny bit more encouragement to the subject during those trials without even being aware of it.

Another advantage of the computer in the laboratory is its ability to assist in data analysis. The days when an analysis of variance or a multiple regression had to be computed on an adding machine, or even on an electronic calculator, are just about over.

Despite the many advantages it offers to researchers in psychology, the computer can present some problems. One is the time and expense of programming. Although the hardware needed for computers is becoming less and less expensive, software is still very expensive, particularly when it must be designed individually for each experiment. Another drawback is that experimenters spend much less time observing the behavior of people (or animals). This is partly an advantage, but it may also deprive researchers of the chance to observe serendipitous events that often happen during the course of an experiment.

A final drawback involves the effects that such a powerful research tool can have on the direction of research. There is an old proverb: "When you have a hammer in your hand, everything looks like a nail." When you have something as powerful as a computer, you may begin to design experiments that take advantage of the computer's capabilities, rather than experiments that solve important problems. Fortunately, the computer's capabilities can be applied to important problems like cognition, vision, and problem-solving, for example. However, problems that are not easily approached with this research tool may receive less emphasis than they deserve.

Psychological Testing and Assessment

Computers are very rapidly becoming standard equipment in clinics and offices in which psychological testing is conducted. They are well suited to a number of applications in such settings. For example, they can be programmed to directly collect background information about the client, a task that is normally done either with paper-and-pencil forms or by interviews with the clinician. In some ways, the computer is a superior "interviewer" because it can make sure all questions are answered, skip over questions that do not apply, and ask for elaboration on those that do. For example, a background information form might ask "Are you married?" and then, "If so, for how long?" A computer can skip the second question. Also, unlike a human interviewer, the computer's attention does not wander.

Some computer interviews can collect very sensitive and detailed information that can help the clinician make diagnostic decisions. One, for example, in use at the Institute of Psychiatry in London, includes questions that comprise an assessment of depression based on the Hamilton Depression Scale (Carr, et al. 1981). Patients appearing at the emergency clinic who showed some signs of depression were asked to take the ten-minute interview, which contains items like those in figure B.1.

How depressed are you?
    answer 0 if not at all
    answer 1 if a little
    answer 2 if a lot
    answer 3 if extremely so

Do you feel guilty about things you have done
or thought?
    answer 0 if not at all
    answer 1 if a little
    answer 2 if a lot
    answer 3 if extremely so

Is it taking you longer to get off to sleep?
    answer 0 if no
    answer 1 if sometimes
    answer 2 if always

Do you sleep fitfully, often awakening?
    answer 0 if no
    answer 1 if sometimes
    answer 2 if always

Do you waken earlier than usual and then find
yourself unable to get back to sleep?
    answer 0 if no
    answer 1 if sometimes
    answer 2 if always

Figure B.1 Some items used in computerized assessment of depression

Computer programs are an ideal way to administer and score the lengthy psychological inventories that measure vocational interests, personality traits, cognitive abilities, and other psychological variables. For example, a personality inventory might contain questions like, "I think of myself as a forgiving person," each of which would appear individually on the terminal screen. The test taker would respond to each item by pressing one of several keys indicating "strongly agree," "agree," "disagree," or "strongly disagree." The software would automatically score the test, giving the clinician and the test taker immediate feedback about his or her performance on each of the scales of the test. A typical personality test, for example, might provide scores on a number of personality traits, such as nervousness, depression, extroversion, hostility, and self-discipline.

Many programs are being developed that provide computerized interpretations of the test as well as raw scores. Some of these programs simply compare the individual's scores on each scale to norms for specific populations and provide the percentile rank of the test taker's score on each scale of the test. There are also programs that provide more sophisticated interpretations. For example, computerized interpretations of one of the most widely used psychological tests, called the MMPI, provide a detailed analysis of the patient's profile, as discussed in Chapter 11. The analysis compares the patient's overall responses to those made by large numbers of people with disorders such as schizophrenia, bipolar depression, or hysteria. One study (Goldberg, 1970) found that the computer, programmed with the assessment strategies used by twenty-nine clinical psychologists, was more proficient than the individual clinicians in differentiating between certain behavioral disorders on the basis of MMPI profiles.

Another program (Vincent, 1982a; 1982b), attempts to administer, score, and interpret the Holtzman Inkblot Technique. This is a projective test that displays an ambiguous inkblot shape, either in color or in black and white, and asks the subject to tell what the blot could represent. When clinicians administer this test, they usually take into account variables like the content of the answer, the location of the part of the blot to which the patient is responding, the amount of movement in the patient's perception, and the patient's response to color. However, the software program concentrates on the content of the response only. The inkblot is displayed on a monitor by means of a laser video disk, and the patient types his or her response on the computer's keyboard.

Computerized psychological testing offers some important advantages. First, many clients seem to prefer taking these tests by computer because they feel freer to answer the questions honestly. They perceive their answers to be somehow more anonymous. Second, a computer can be programmed to insist that each question is answered completely, thereby eliminating the problem of missed items. And third, computerized testing makes obsolete the time-consuming, hand-scoring process.

Despite the many advantages of computerized testing and assessment, a number of psychologists are concerned about the confidentiality of test scores, the interpretation of the tests, the validity and reliability of computerized versions of psychological tests, copyright infringements, and other potential problems associated with their use. The ease with which these programs are used, and the growing sophistication of the programs that provide interpretations of psychological tests, are creating some troubling concerns about possible testing abuses (Turkington, 1984).

An important problem is that the interpretation of a test is not easily accomplished by a computer, despite the official-looking computerized printout that might be produced by any software package. A psychologist is trained to assess motivational variables and to interpret the test scores against a background of other observations of the client. In that sense, a computerized interpretation of a client's scores is no more a psychological assessment than a laboratory printout is a complete medical examination (Matarazzo, 1983). It is possible that many people who have little or no training in psychological testing will begin using these programs, simply because they are so easy to purchase and use.

Computers in Therapy

In addition to administering, scoring, and interpreting psychological tests, the computer is helping the practicing psychologist by assisting in the therapeutic process. One application in the area of therapy involves cognitive rehabilitation.

After a stroke or other brain injury, a patient may require extensive therapy in simple cognitive skills, such as pattern recognition, eye-hand coordination, reaction time, free recall, memory span, and vocabulary. One set of programs, developed by Rosamond Gianutsos and Carol Klitzner, is intended for the diagnosis and treatment of the kinds of cognitive deficits typically associated with stroke and traumatic head injuries (Harley, 1984). For example, one program asks the patient to read aloud from left to right, and then from right to left. A visual matching task shows the patient an array of sixteen distinct nonsense shapes, with a target stimulus located in the center. The patient searches for a match and presses the space bar when one is found to stop the internal timer. The programs can store data on each patient's progress. Programs like these provide an enormously useful adjunct to traditional therapy in cognitive rehabilitation.

Psychologists are attempting to use the computer in other areas of therapy as well. One therapist designed a simple program that generates the sound of ocean waves to induce hypnosis in susceptible subjects, for example (Edelman, 1983). Another group of psychologists uses the computer to help people stop smoking by mail (Schneider, 1982). Each week clients mail in their smoking diary sheets, their responses to smoking questionnaires, and other "homework," and the data are entered. The computer is programmed to generate individualized feedback for each smoker and instructions for each week.

Some programs have been developed that represent attempts to actually interact with the patient, asking questions that might be asked by a therapist. For example, Morton Wagman has developed a program to offer the "Dilemma Counseling System" through the extensive network of computers in the PLATO system, which links hundreds of terminals across the country to a main Control Data Corporation Cyber 73 computer at the University of Illinois (Wagman, 1982a; 1982b). Clients who have a dilemma involving dating, occupational choice, study habits, or some other problem, are taught the dilemma counseling method, which involves learning how to generate and evaluate a variety of alternate solutions. The program teaches the method, provides praise and encouragement, remembers the client's solutions, and even suggests new ones based on its own library.

Another program, developed at the Artificial Intelligence Laboratory at Stanford University, had a "conversation" that went like this:

> Patient: Hello
> Computer: How do you do? Please state your problem.
> Patient: I feel depressed all the time.
> Computer: Tell me more about such feelings.
> Patient: I am just unhappy and I want your help.
> Computer: You believe I can help you, don't you?
> Patient: I am not sure.
> Computer: Is it because you are not sure that you came to me?
> Patient: I think that I hate you.
> Computer: Perhaps in your fantasy, we do not like each other.
> Patient: You are nothing but a dumb machine.
> Computer: Do computers worry you? (Adapted from Zimbardo, P., *Psychology and Life,* 10th ed., p. 134. Scott, Foresman and Company, 1979.

Artificial Intelligence

According to one recent textbook in the field of artificial intelligence, the definition of the term is "the study of ideas that enable computers to be intelligent" (Winston, 1984). That succinct definition, however, relies on the assumption that we know what the word "intelligent" means. As we discussed in Chapter 7, the term is very difficult to define.

We generally think of "intelligence" as the ability to adapt to the environment, to reason, to learn, to solve problems, to understand and acquire concepts, to use language fluently and precisely, to deal with abstractions, to learn from mistakes, and to perform any number of intellectual feats. One goal of workers in the field of artificial intelligence is to make computers more useful by making them more capable of performing these kinds of cognitive tasks. However, the artificial intelligence that a computer demonstrates is not necessarily the same, or even similar to, the intelligence demonstrated by human beings. A computer chess player, for example, might play an excellent game of chess by using techniques quite different from those used by a human master. The computer might approach a chess problem by a sequential and orderly search through a defined range of possible moves. A human, however, might rely on heuristic strategies developed over years of playing the game, winning some games and losing others. Thus, another goal of those in the field of artificial intelligence, one of particular interest to psychology, is to gain a better understanding of human intelligence by simulating it on the computer—mistakes, insights, and irrational leaps of logic included.

Intelligence is a very broad concept, but scientists in the field of artificial intelligence have tended to focus their research efforts on a few major areas. These include problem solving and decision making, understanding language, understanding and interpreting images, logic and theorem proving, and learning from experience. More recently, researchers have been trying to program more "common sense" into computers. A typical computer program might determine whether a cup of coffee is about to spill on the lap of the drinker by computing complex formulas involving variables like gravity, momentum, velocity. A human would make the judgment without such calculations, relying on previous experience with coffee cups and a general knowledge of the movements of liquids.

Encouraging a computer to behave intelligently requires a substantial knowledge of both computers and intelligence. A problem that may not seem too difficult to a human requires an enormous amount of programming for a computer-generated solution. Figure B.2, for example, shows the "8-puzzle." The problem is to move the blank space, one space at a time, to arrive at figure B.2b. For a computer to solve the problem, the program must begin with a description of the initial state of affairs and the kinds of moves or manipulations that can be made to reach the goal. In the next step, the program begins to employ some strategy that will direct the movement or manipulation of the pieces in the puzzle. Most of these strategies will not be useful, and the program should discard them.

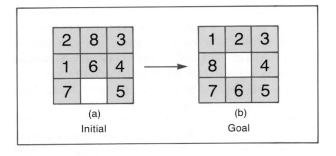

Figure B.2 Initial and goal configurations for the 8-puzzle

One of the fascinating areas of artificial intelligence involves research on the strategies that can be used to solve problems, called "control strategies." One such strategy is the search tree, shown in figure B.3. The root of the tree at the top shows the initial state of the problem, and the first set of branches shows the states that could be reached with a single move of the blank space. The program continues to "grow" a tree like this until it reaches a state that corresponds to the goal.

Researchers in artificial intelligence design programs that enable computers to solve many kinds of problems, some of which are much more complicated

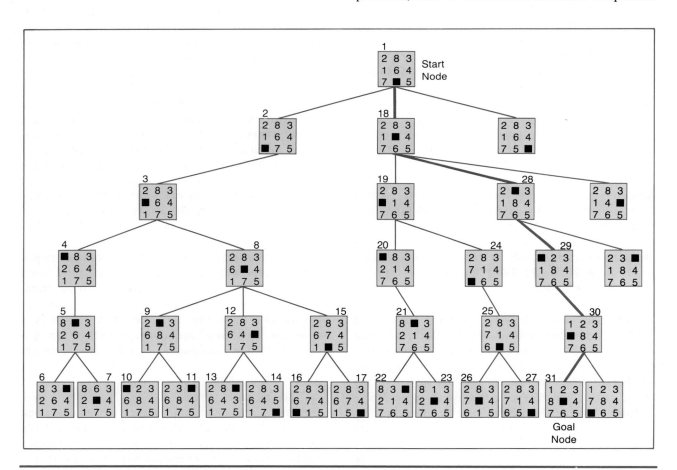

Figure B.3 A search tree for the 8-puzzle

than the 8-puzzle. The control strategies are necessarily more complex. For example, a search tree that defined all the possible moves that might result from an opening play in checkers would be astronomically large, and even a very large computer would not be able to investigate all the possibilities and discard those that led to defeat. Instead, the program uses other control strategies, ones that attempt to narrow the search. One strategy, for example, evaluates the "promise" of each branch near the top before it begins to search more deeply. Then it selects the branches that have the greatest likelihood of resulting in an optimal solution.

A widely used computer program, MYCIN, designed by Edward Shortliffe, solves problems in the area of medicine. The goal of the program is to help physicians treat bacterial infections by beginning a course of antibiotic treatment before all the laboratory tests have been conducted to determine the specific bacterium involved. Without the program, the physician would probably begin treatment with a broad-spectrum antibiotic to cover all the possible organisms, but the program helps the physician narrow the possibilities so a more effective, disease-specific drug can be prescribed. Figure B.4 shows an excerpt from a sample session.

Researchers in artificial intelligence are developing programs in other areas besides problem solving. For example, there are many programs that enable the computer to understand and handle questions expressed in English. This may seem to be a simple task, but a natural language is incredibly complex, and most sentences that an individual expresses are original. A computer must store an immense amount of knowledge in the form of vocabulary and rules that govern sentence construction in order to understand even very simple sentences. A program called INTELLECT, developed by Larry R. Harris, can understand a question like, "I wonder how actual sales for last month compared to the forecasts for people under quota in New England?" (Winston, 1984).

Another important component of artificial intelligence research deals with understanding images. Determining the rules that apply to three-dimensional space are extraordinarily difficult, however, especially when the image is real and not just a drawing.

To psychologists, designing programs that mimic human reasoning is one of the most interesting applications. One technique that is used to assess the way humans solve a problem is called "protocol analysis" (Newell and Simon, 1972). The procedure involves asking subjects to comment aloud on the thoughts that pass through their minds as they attempt to solve a problem. For example, one subject was given the following "cryptarithmetic problem," in which the letters are substituted for numbers. The task is to find out what number each letter stands for:

$$\begin{array}{r} \text{DONALD} \\ + \text{GERALD} \\ \hline \text{ROBERT} \end{array}$$

The solver is told that D = 5 and then is asked to solve the problem. Following is a small part of one subject's protocol: "If we assume that L is, say, 1. . . ." After working out a series of steps, he says "Of course, this is all going on the assumption that R is 7." After trying E = 9, he said, "I seem to be running into trouble the way I am here. Having trouble with this E. . . . I can't make E a 9." (The answer to ROBERT is 723970.)

After analyzing these protocols, researchers try to design computer programs that simulate the reasoning processes and strategies that were used to determine the answer. The processes are not necessarily logical, nor are they necessarily the ones that are most likely to lead to a solution; however, they are very instructive in learning about how humans actually solve problems.

Computer-Assisted Instruction (CAI)

Computers are now part of many classrooms. Teachers in elementary schools, junior and senior high schools, colleges, universities, and vocational schools appreciate the usefulness of the computer as an aid to instruction.

```
1.   PATIENT'S NAME:  PT538
2.   Age:  45
3.   Sex:  Male
4.   Race:  Caucasian
5.   Are there any cultures for PT538 which may be related to the present
illness, and from which organisms have been grown successfully in the
microbiology laboratory?  No
6.   Are there any pending cultures?  Yes
7.   From what site was the specimen for CULTURE-1 taken?  CSF
(Cerebrospinal fluid)
8.   Please give the date and time when the pending csf culture
(CULTURE-1) was obtained.  11/28/78
9.   Was a smear examined at the time that the specimen for the pending csf
culture (CULTURE-1) was obtained?  Yes
10.  Were any organisms seen on the smear of the specimen submitted as the
pending csf culture (CULTURE-1)?  Yes
     .  .  .  .  .
     .  .  .  .  .
     .  .  .  .  .
My therapy recommendations will be designed to treat for organisms that
either are very likely or, although  less likely, would have a significant
effect on therapy selection if they were present.  It is important to cover
for the following probable infection(s) and associated organisms(s):


INFECTION 1 is MENINGITIS

   +  <ITEM-1>   E.COLI
   +  <ITEM-2>   PSEUDOMONAS-AERUGINOSA
   +  <ITEM-3>   KLEBSIELLA-PNEUMONIAE
   +  <ITEM-4>   DIPLOCOCCUS-PNEUMONIAE

41.  Does PT538 have a clinically significant allergic reaction to any
antimicrobial agent?  No

42.  Do you have reason to suspect that PT538 may have impaired renal
function?  No

43.  PT538's weight in kilograms:  70

(REC-1)  My preferred therapy recommendation is:
   In order to cover for Items <1 2 3 4>:
   Give the following in combination:
    1)  AMPICILLIN
    Dose:  3.5g (28.0 ml) q4h IV
      (calculated on basis of 50 mg/kg)
    2)  GENTAMICIN
    Dose:  119 mg (3.0 ml, 80 mg/2ml ampule)
       q8h IV  (calculated on basis of 1.7 mg/kg)
       plus consider giving 5 mg q24h intrathecally.

    Since high concentrations of penicillins can inactivate aminoglycosides,
do not mix these two antibiotics in the same bottle.
```

Figure B.4   Portions of a sample consultation using MYCIN

The computer seems to offer three main advantages over other kinds of technological instructional tools such as videotapes, film strips, or audio cassettes.

1. Active participation. The computer program can require the learner to respond at any point in the program. As computer programs become more sophisticated, they will eventually be able to parse natural language that is either typed into a keyboard or spoken aloud.
2. Feedback. An educational program can be designed to assess the learner's responses and provide either immediate or delayed feedback about performance at each step of the learning process. It can also monitor overall progress through one session or through a series of sessions and display the results in a simple graph or in more creative ways.
3. Individualization. A program can be designed to allow each student to proceed at his or her own pace. Through an evaluation of the student's responses, the program might branch to remedial work or faster-paced lessons. Specific learning deficits can be assessed, and the program could branch to learning material designed to make up the deficit. Thus, students who learn quickly will not be bored by a slow pace, and students who need more time, examples, and practice to grasp certain concepts can receive it.

Psychologists are involved in computer-assisted instruction primarily because of their expertise in learning, motivation, memory, and perception, and also because of their work in artificial intelligence. Although computers have tremendous potential as aids to instruction, they will not fulfill that potential unless programs are designed that are sensitive to the cognitive processes and motivation of the student. Much of the early educational software simply used the computer screen as a device to present material to read, and then asked the user to respond to multiple-choice questions to demonstrate that she had understood it. However, recent programs take advantage of more of the computer's capabilities, including branching, simulations, graphics, modeling, and interfaces with videodiscs or laser disc equipment, for example. Programs under development utilize much more artificial intelligence as well, enabling the computer to adapt to the learner, rather than the other way around.

One example of a technique becoming widely used in CAI is simulation. Students learn by being placed into a situation in which they are expected to make decisions, based on their own knowledge, in order to reach certain goals. The technique is quite different from the lecture method of instruction. Students become very involved because they have a chance to directly manipulate variables and assess the consequences of their own decisions. The simulation technique emphasizes active learning, rather than the passive learning that characterizes many classroom settings.

A simulation program called ASTRO, developed in Connecticut by the Talcott Mountain Science Center, simulates a lunar landing to help students learn basic principles of physics. The object of the program is to land a spacecraft safely, and it begins with the craft traveling at a velocity of 3600 miles per hour at an altitude of 120 miles above the moon. Every ten seconds a "radar" check is made, and measurements are taken of velocity and remaining fuel. The calculations needed to safely land the craft require students to understand gravitational effects and Newton's laws of motion.

A set of computer simulations called MESS (Stout, 1974; Anderson, 1982), introduces students to the principles of research. Using the vast storehouse of data contained in the program, students are confronted with the problem of unscrambling the genetic and social roots of schizophrenia. The program offers six different independent variables around which the student can design studies, but the investigator's budget is limited, and each study "costs," depending on the number of variables investigated and the number of subjects involved. Although the programs are basically designed to teach students the principles of experimental design, the data contained in them is at least loosely based on data that has been obtained by actual studies of psychological phenomena. Other simulations in the MESS series include marijuana and reaction time, classical conditioning, imprinting in baby chicks, and the effect of social facilitation on both cockroaches and college freshmen.

A program called PARRY, developed by Kenneth M. Colby at the UCLA Neuropsychiatric Institute and his coworkers, assists in the training of clinical psychologists by simulating paranoid thought processes. Psychiatrists communicating with the program found it difficult to distinguish its responses from a real patient's responses (Freiherr, 1982). PARRY is used to teach students about the characteristics of a patient suffering from paranoia.

Combining the power of a computer with a videotape recorder or a laser disc enhances the potential for effective computer-assisted instruction. For example, the computer can be programmed to control the selection of frames or video sequences depending on the responses of the student. This capability is particularly important in psychology because the subject matter involves human behavior, much of which is nonverbal and cannot easily be simulated on a computer screen. One program that is used to train psychology students shows a video of an interview with a depressed patient. Each segment is followed by a frame of computer text that asks the student to provide some psychological analysis of what the patient appeared to be saying. If the answer is incorrect, the program rewinds the videoplayer to the particular sequence that was misunderstood (Schwartz, 1984).

Current approaches in computer-assisted instruction are partly based on the "teaching machine" developed within the theoretical context of behaviorism by B. F. Skinner. These machines, and the material that was presented with them, were designed around the principle that if a learner emits a correct response, an immediate reinforcement maximizes the likelihood that the response will be learned. The materials used by the teaching machine are arranged so that the questions or tasks proceed from material that is well understood by the learner to more complex material in a series of small, preplanned steps. Each question and answer is called a "frame," and the frames are arranged so that each one adds a tiny amount to the user's storehouse of knowledge. The learner must do something for each frame so the learning process is an active one. The frames are arranged so that the learner makes few if

any errors, and the machine shows the learner the correct answer after each frame so that the learner is rewarded.

Although the teaching machines and the behavioristic approach to learning have had an important influence on current educational computer programs, they have not been the single guiding factor. More cognitive approaches to the learning process characterize programs like ASTRO and PARRY. In some of the simulation programs or modeling programs, the learner must perform rather complex cognitive tasks successfully before any reward is forthcoming.

The computer became widely used in business, government, and science well before it became standard in the schools. Although most educators and psychologists believe that CAI can be a tremendously useful adjunct to traditional educational techniques, most do not believe it will supplant the teacher. The usefulness of CAI will depend heavily on whether a great variety of programs can be designed that take advantage of the things psychologists have learned about learning, motivation, memory, and perception.

Computer Applications in Psychology: Future Prospects

Computer applications have increased dramatically over the past decades in most fields, including psychology. More and more innovative applications will undoubtedly be designed in the future, especially as more psychologists have access to terminals in their own offices and laboratories.

Psychologists will develop more therapeutic tools for their patients, tools that incorporate more intelligence and decision-making capabilities. They will probably develop an overall diagnostic program for behavioral disorders along the lines of MYCIN. They will use their home or office computers to communicate new findings to their colleagues across the globe. Psychologists, along with many other professionals in the United States, will easily do literature searches in *Psychological Abstracts* and other data banks from their own homes or offices. They will develop more and better aids for the handicapped, enabling the blind, the deaf, the paralyzed, and the brain damaged to better communicate with and enjoy the world. They will participate in the enormous amount of research and development required to produce computers that can understand and speak natural languages. The future of computer applications in psychology holds much promise, in these areas and in a long list of others.

The growing sophistication of modern computers is a welcome trend to many people but an ominous one to others. The computer is becoming more and more intelligent, both in the sense that humans are intelligent and in their overall abilities to perform cognitive tasks.

One concern over the growth of computer applications comes from some educators who wonder whether the use of computers, especially in the early grades, will make people very dependent on them. Students will not learn fundamentals of mathematics because they will have machines that can do these tasks much more efficiently.

In a dialogue written by a philosopher, such fears about the effects that new technology can have on human behavior are expressed:

> This discovery of yours will create forgetfulness in the learners' souls, because they will not use their memories; they will trust to the external written characters and not remember of themselves. The specific which you have discovered is an aid not to memory, but to reminiscence, and you give your disciples not truth, but only the semblance of truth; they will be hearers of many things and will have learned nothing; they will appear to be omniscient and will generally know nothing; they will be tiresome company, having the show of wisdom without its reality.

The dialogue was in *Phaedrus,* the philosopher is Plato, and the "discovery" is writing.

references

A

Adam, B. O. (1983). Tracking . . . the instinct and dedication. *Dog World, 68*(6), 19–20.

Adams, J. S. (1965). Inequity in social exchange. In L. Berkowitz (Ed.), *Advances in social psychology* (Vol. 2). New York: Academic Press.

Aderman, D., Brehm, S. S., & Katz, L. B. (1974). Empathic observation of an innocent victim: The just world revisited. *Journal of Personality and Social Psychology, 29,* 342–347.

Agras, W. S., Leitenberg, H., & Barlow, D. H. (1968). Social reinforcement in the modification of agoraphobia. *Archives of General Psychiatry, 19,* 423–427.

Ainsworth, M. D. S., & Bell, S. M. (1970). Attachment, exploration, and separation: Illustrated by the behavior of one-year-olds in a strange situation. *Child Development, 41,* 49–67.

Ainsworth, M. D. S., Blehar, M. C., Waters, E., & Wall, S. (1978). *The strange situation: Observing patterns of attachment.* Hillsdale, NJ: Erlbaum.

Al-Issa, I. (1977). Social and cultural aspects of hallucinations. *Psychological Bulletin, 84,* 570–587.

Alexander, C. N., Zucker, L. G., & Brody, C. L. (1970). Experimental expectations and autokinetic experiences: Consistency theories and judgmental convergence. *Sociometry, 33,* 108–122.

Alexander, F. (1935). The logic of emotions and its dynamic background. *International Journal of Psychoanalysis, 16,* 339–413.

Alexander, F. (1948). Emotional factors in essential hypertension. *Psychosomatic Medicine, 1,* 173–179.

Alexander, F. (1962). The development of psychosomatic medicine. *Psychosomatic Medicine, 24,* 13–24.

Allen, M. J. (1984). Experimental neurosis. In R. J. Corsini (Ed.), *Encyclopedia of Psychology* (Vol. 1). New York: John Wiley and Sons.

Allen, V. L., & Wilder, D. A. (1980). Impact of group consensus and social support on stimulus meaning: Mediation of conformity by cognitive restructuring. *Journal of Personality & Social Psychology, 39,* 1116–1124.

Allport, G. W. (1954). *The nature of prejudice.* Boston: Addison-Wesley.

Altman, I. (1975). *The environment and social behavior.* Monterey, CA: Brooks/Cole.

American Psychiatric Association. (1980). *Diagnostic and statistical manual of mental disorders* (3rd ed.). Washington, DC: Author.

Amir, S., Brown, Z. W., & Amir, Z. (1980). The role of endorphins in stress: Evidence and speculations. *Neuroscience and Biobehavioral Reviews, 4,* 77–86.

Amir, Y. (1976). The contact hypothesis revisited. *Psychological Bulletin.*

Anastasi, A. (1982). *Psychological testing.* New York: Macmillan.

Anastasi, A. (1983). Psychological testing. In C. E. Walker (Ed.), *Handbook of clinical psychology.* Homewood, IL: Dorsey.

Anderson, D. E. (1982). Computer simulations in the psychology laboratory. *Simulations and Games, 13*(1), 13–36.

Anderson, J. R. (1983). Retrieval of information from long-term memory. *Science, 220,* 25–30.

Anderson, J. R., & Bower, G. H. (1973). *Human associative memory.* Washington, DC: Hemisphere Press.

Andrews, I. R., & Valenzi, E. R. (1970). Overpay inequity and/or self-image as a worker: A critical examination of an experimental induction procedure. *Organizational Behavior and Human Performance, 5,* 266–276.

Argyle, M., & Dean, J. (1965). Eye-contact, distance and affiliation. *Sociometry, 28,* 289–304.

Argyris, C. (1964). *Integrating the individual and the organization.* New York: Wiley.

Aronson, E., Blaney, N., Sikes, J., Stephan, C., & Snapp, M. (1975). Busing and racial tension: The jigsaw route to learning and liking *Psychology Today, 8,* 43–50.

Aronson, E., & Mills, J. (1959). The effect of severity of initiation on liking for a group. *Journal of Abnormal and Social Psychology, 59,* 177–181.

Asch, S. E. (1951). Effects of group pressure upon the modification and distortion of judgments. In H. Guetzkow (Ed.), *Groups, leadership, and men.* Pittsburgh: Carnegie Press.

Asch, S. E. (1952). *Social psychology.* Englewood Cliffs, NJ: Prentice-Hall.

Aschoff, J. (1969). *Aerospace Medicine, 40,* 844.

Ashmore, R. D. (1981). Prejudice. In *Encyclopedia of psychology.* Guilford, CT: DPG Reference Publishers.

Atkinson, J. W., & Feather, N. T. (1966). Review and appraisal. In J. W. Atkinson & N. T. Feather (Eds.), *A theory of achievement motivation.* New York: Wiley.

Atkinson, J. W., & Litwin, G. H. (1960). Achievement motive and test anxiety conceived as motive to approach success and motive to avoid failure. *Journal of Abnormal and Social Psychology, 60,* 52–63.

Atkinson, R. C., & Shiffrin, R. M. (1968). Human memory: A proposed system and its control processes. In K. W. Spence & J. T. Spence (Eds.), *The psychology of learning and motivation: Advances in research and theory* (Vol. 2). New York: Academic Press.

Atthowe, J. M., & Krasner, L. (1968). Preliminary report on the application of contingent reinforcement procedures (token economy) on a "chronic" psychiatric ward. *Journal of Abnormal Psychology, 73,* 37–43.

Au, T. K. (1983). Chinese and English counterfactuals: The Sapir-Whorf hypothesis revisited. *Cognition, 15*(1–3), 155–187.

Au, T. K. (1984). Counterfactuals in reply to Alfred Bloom. *Cognition, 17*(3), 289–302.

Averill, J. R. (1982). *Anger and aggression.* New York: Springer-Verlag.

Avery, D., & Winokur, G. (1978). Suicide, attempted suicide, and relapse rates in depression. *Archives of General Psychiatry, 35,* 749–753.

Ayllon, T., & Azrin, N. H. (1965). The measurement and reinforcement of behavior of psychotics. *Journal of the Experimental Analysis of Behavior, 8,* 357–383.

Ayllon, T., & Michael, J. (1959). The psychiatric nurse as a behavioral engineer. *Journal of the Experimental Analysis of Behavior, 2,* 323–334.

Ayoub, D. Y., Greenough, W. T., & Juraska, J. M. (1983). Sex differences in dendritic structure in the preoptic area of the juvenile Macaque monkey brain. *Science, 219,* 197–198.

B

Baer, D. M. (1982). Applied behavior analysis. In G. T. Wilson & C. M. Franks (Eds.), *Contemporary behavior therapy.* New York: Guilford.

Bakan, P. (1973). Left-handedness and alcoholism. *Perceptual and Motor Skills, 36,* 514.

Baker, R. K., & Ball, S. J. (1969). *Mass media and violence* (Vol. 9). Washington, DC: U.S. Government Printing Office.

Bales, R. F. (1950). *Interaction process analysis.* Cambridge, MA: Addison-Wesley.

Bales, R. F. (1955). How people interact in conferences. *Scientific American, 192*(3), 31–35.

Bales, R. F. (1970). *Personality and interpersonal behavior.* New York: Holt, Rinehart, & Winston.

Baltes, P. B., & Schaie, K. W. (1977). Aging and IQ: The myth of the twilight years. In S. H. Zarit (Ed.), *Readings in aging and death: Contemporary perspectives.* New York: Harper and Row.

Bandura, A. (1965a). Influence of models' reinforcement contingencies on the acquisition of imitative responses. *Journal of Personality and Social Psychology, 1,* 589–595.

Bandura, A. (1965b). Vicarious processes: A case of no-trial learning. In L. Berkowitz (Ed.), *Advances in experimental social psychology* (Vol. 2). New York: Academic Press.

Bandura, A. (1971). Analysis of modeling processes. In A. Bandura (Ed.), *Psychological modeling.* New York: Lieber-Atherton.

Bandura, A. (1973). *Aggression: A social learning analysis.* Englewood Cliffs, NJ: Prentice-Hall.

Bandura, A. (1974). Behavior therapy and the models of man. *American Psychologist, 29,* 859–869.

Bandura, A. (1977). *Social learning theory.* Englewood Cliffs, NJ: Prentice-Hall.

Bandura, A. (1982). The psychology of chance encounters and life paths. *American Psychologist, 37*(7), 747–755.

Bane, M. J. (1978). *HEW policy toward children, youth, and families.* (Order # SA-8139-77). Cambridge, MA: Office of Assistant Secretary for Planning and Evaluation.

Banks, M., & Salapatek, P. (1981). Infant pattern vision: A new approach based on contrast sensitivity function. *Journal of Experimental Child Psychology, 31*(1), 1–45.

Barahal, R. M. (1978). A comparison of parent-infant attachment and interaction patterns in day care and non-day-care family groups (Doctoral dissertation, Cornell University, 1977). *Dissertation Abstracts International, 38,* 5639B.

Barber, T. X. (1965). The effect of "hypnosis" on learning and recall: A methodological critique. *Journal of Clinical Psychology, 21,* 19–25.

Barber, T. X. (1969). *Hypnosis: A scientific approach.* New York: Van Nostrand Reinhold Co.

Baron, R. A. (1977). *Human aggression.* New York: Plenum.

Barron, F., & Harrington, D. M. (1981). Creativity, intelligence, and personality. *Annual Review of Psychology, 32,* 439–476.

Bartholomeus, B. (1974). Effects of task requirements on ear superiority for sung speech. *Cortex, 10,* 215–223.

Bartus, R. T., Dean, R. L., III, Beer, B., & Lippa, A. S. (1982). The cholinergic hypothesis of geriatric memory dysfunction. *Science, 217,* 408–417.

Baskett, L. (1974). *The young child's interactions with parents and siblings: A behavioral analysis.* Unpublished doctoral dissertation, University of Oregon.

Baum, A., Harpin, R. E., & Valins, S. (1975). The role of group phenomena in the experience of crowding. *Environment and Behavior, 7,* 185–198.

Baumeister, R., & Steinhilber, A. (1984). Paradoxical effects of supportive audiences on performance under pressure: The home field advantage in sports championships. *Journal of Personality & Social Psychology, 47,* 85–93.

Baumeister, R. F., & Tice, D. M. (1984). Role of self-presentation and choice in cognitive dissonance under forced compliance: Necessary or sufficient causes? *Journal of Personality and Social Psychology, 46,* 5–13.

Baumrind, D. (1971). Current patterns of parental authority. *Developmental Psychology Monographs, 4*(1, Pt. 2).

Bavelas, A. (1948). A mathematical model for group structures. *Applied Anthropology, 7,* 16–30.

Beach, F. A. (1942). Effects of testosterone propionate upon the copulatory behavior of sexually inexperienced male rats. *Journal of Comparative Psychology,* 227–247a.

Beaman, A. L., Cole, C. M., Preston, M., Klentz, B., & Steblay, N. M. (1983). Fifteen years of foot-in-the-door research: A meta-analysis. *Personality and Social Psychology Bulletin, 9,* 181–196.

Bebout, J. (1974). It takes one to know one: Existential-Rogerian concepts in encounter groups. In D. A. Wexler & L. N. Rice (Eds.), *Innovations in client-centered therapy.* New York: Wiley-Interscience.

Becker, P. T., & Thoman, E. B. (1981). Rapid eye movement storms in infants: Rate of occurrence at 6 months predicts mental development at 1 year. *Science, 212,* 1415–1416.

Begleiter, H., & Porjesz, B. (1975). Evoked brain potentials as indicators of decision making. *Science, 187,* 754–755.

Bell, P. A., Fisher, J. D., & Loomis, R. J. (1978). *Environmental psychology.* Philadelphia: Saunders.

Bem, D. J. (1972). Self-perception theory. In L. Berkowitz (Ed.), *Advances in experimental social psychology* (Vol. 6). New York: Academic Press.

Benbow, C. (1985). Paper presented at the Conference on Neurobiology of Intellectual Giftedness, New York. Reported by Bower, B. (1985). The left hand of math and verbal talent. *Science News, 127,* 263.

Benderly, B. L. (1980). *Dancing without music: Deafness in America.* New York: Anchor Press.

Bennett, E. L., Diamond, M. D., Krech, D., & Rosenzweig, M. R. (1964). Chemical and anatomical plasticity of brain. *Science, 146,* 610–619.

Bennett, W., & Gurin, J. (1982, March). Do diets really work? *Science 82,* pp. 42–50.

Benton, A. L. (1980). The neuropsychology of facial recognition. *American Psychologist, 35*(2), 176–186.

Berger, P., & Luckmann, T. (1966). *The social construction of reality.* Garden City, NY: Doubleday.

Berger, R. J. (1969). Oculomotor control: A possible function of REM sleep. *Psychological Review, 76,* 144–164.

Berk, R. A., & Aldrich, H. E. (1972). Patterns of vandalism during civil disorders as an indicator of selection of targets. *American Sociological Review, 37,* 533–547.

Berkowitz, L. (1969). *Roots of aggression: A re-examination of the frustration-aggression hypothesis.* New York: Atherton.

Berkowitz, L. (1978). Whatever happened to the frustration-aggression hypothesis? *American Behavioral Scientist, 21,* 691–708.

Berkowitz, L. (1983). Aversively stimulated aggression: Some parallels and differences in research with animals and humans. *American Psychologist, 11,* 1135–1144.

Berkowitz, W. R. (1971). A cross national comparison of some social patterns of urban pedestrians. *Journal of Cross-Cultural Psychology, 2,* 129–144.

Berkun, M. M. (1964). Performance decrement under psychological stress. *Human Factors, 6,* 21–30.

Berkun, M. M., Bialek, H. M., Kern, R. P., & Yagi, K. (1962). Experimental studies of psychological stress in man. *Psychological Monographs, 76*(15, Whole No. 534).

Berlin, B., & Kay, P. (1969). *Basic color terms: Their universality and evolution.* Berkeley: University of California Press.

Berscheid, E. (1966). Opinion change and communicator-communicatee similarity and dissimilarity. *Journal of Personality and Social Psychology, 4,* 670–680.

Berscheid, E., & Walster, E. H. (1978). *Interpersonal attraction* (2nd ed.). Reading, MA: Addison-Wesley.

Bevan, W. (1982). A sermon of sorts in three plus parts. *American Psychologist, 37,* 1303–1322.

Bird, R. J. (1981). *The computer in experimental psychology.* New York: Academic Press.

Birnholz, J. C. (1981). The development of human fetal eye movement patterns. *Science, 213,* 679–681.

Bjerner, B., Holm, A., & Swensson, A. (1955). Diurnal variation in mental performance: A study of three-shift workers. *British Journal of Industrial Medicine, 12,* 103–110.

Blanchard, R. J., & Blanchard, D. C. (Eds.). (1984). *Advances in study of aggression*. Orlando, FL: Academic Press.

Bland, J. (1982, January). The junk-food syndrome. *Psychology Today*, p. 92.

Bleuler, E. (1950). *Dementia praecox or the group of schizophrenias*. New York: International Universities Press. (Original work published 1911)

Bloom, F. (1985). Paper presented at the meeting of American Association for the Advancement of Science, Los Angeles.

Bochner, S., & Insko, C. A. (1966). Communicator discrepancy, source credibility, and opinion change. *Journal of Personality and Social Psychology, 4*, 614–621.

Bogen, J. E. (1969). The other side of the brain: An appositional mind. *Bulletin of the Los Angeles Neurological Societies, 34*(3), 135–162.

Bolles, R. C., & Fanselow, M. S. (1982). Endorphins and behavior. *Annual Review of Psychology, 33*, 87–101.

Borgatta, E. F., Couch, A. S., & Bales, R. F. (1954). Some findings relevant to the great man theory of leadership. *American Sociological Review, 19*, 755–759.

Bossard, J. H. S. (1945). Law of family interaction. *American Journal of Sociology, 50*, 292–294.

Bower, G. H. (1981). Mood and memory. *American Psychologist, 36*(2), 129–148.

Bowerman, M. (1973). Structural relationships in children's utterances: Syntactic or semantic? In T. Moore (Ed.), *Cognitive development and the acquisition of language*. New York: Academic Press.

Bramel, D., & Friend, R. (1981). Hawthorne, the myth of the docile worker, and class bias in psychology. *American Psychologist, 36*, 867–878.

Bransford, J. D., & Johnson, M. K. (1973). Considerations of some problems of comprehension. In W. G. Chase (Ed.), *Visual information processing*. New York: Academic Press.

Breland, K., & Breland, M. (1966). *Animal behavior*. New York: Macmillan.

Brenner, M. H. (1976). *Estimating the social costs of national economic policy*. Washington, DC: Joint Economic Committee of Congress. (In Liem & Rayman, 1982)

Brenner, M. H. (1973). *Mental illness and the economy*. Cambridge, MA: Harvard University Press.

Brobeck, J. R., Tepperman, J., & Long, C. N. H. (1943). Experimental hypothalamic hyperphagia in the albino rat. *Yale Journal of Biology and Medicine, 15*, 831–853.

Brown, J. (1958). Some tests of the decay theory of immediate memory. *Quarterly Journal of Experimental Psychology, 10*, 12–21.

Brown, N. R., Rips, L. J., & Shevell, S. K. (1985). The subjective dates of natural events in very-long-term memory. *Cognitive Psychology, 17*, 139–177.

Brown, R. (1986). *Social psychology* (2d ed.). New York: Macmillan.

Brown, R. T. (1968). Early experience and problem-solving ability. *Journal of Comparative and Physiological Psychology, 65*, 433–440.

Brown, R. W. (1965). *Social psychology*. Boston: Little, Brown.

Brown, R. W. (1973). *A first language: The early stages*. Cambridge: Harvard University Press.

Bruner, J. S. (1977). Early social interaction and language acquisition. In H. R. Schaffer (Ed.), *Studies in mother-infant interaction*. London: Academic Press.

Bruner, J. S., Goodnow, J., & Austin, G. A. (1956). *A study of thinking*. New York: Wiley.

Bryden, M. P. (1982). *Laterality: Functional asymmetry in the intact brain*. New York: Academic Press.

Buck, R. (1980). Nonverbal behavior and the theory of emotion: The facial feedback hypothesis. *Journal of Personality and Social Psychology, 38*, 811–824.

Buck, R. (1984). *The communication of emotion*. New York: Guilford Press.

Byrne, D. (1971). *The attraction paradigm*. New York: Academic Press.

Byrne, D., Gouaux, C., Griffitt, W., Lamberth, J., Murakawa, N., Prasad, M. B., Prasad, A., & Ramirez, M., III. (1971). The ubiquitous relationship: Attitude similarity and attraction. A cross-cultural study. *Human Relations, 24*, 201–207.

C

Calder, B. J., Ross, M., & Insko, C. A. (1973). Attitude change and attitude attribution: Effects of incentive, choice, and consequences. *Journal of Personality and Social Psychology, 25*, 84–99.

Calhoun, J. B. (1962). Population density and social pathology. *Scientific American, 206*, 139–148.

Cantril, H. (1963). *The psychology of social movements*. New York: Wiley. (Original work published 1941)

Carr, A. C., Ancill, R. J., Ghosh, A., & Margo, A. (1981). Direct assessment of depression by microcomputer. *Acta Psychiat. Scand., 64*, 422–429.

Carter, R. C. (1982). Search time with a color display: Analysis of distribution functions. *Human Factors, 24*, 203–212.

Carter-Saltzman, L. (1980). Biological and sociocultural effects on handedness: Comparison between biological and adoptive families. *Science, 209*, 1263–65.

Cartwright, R. (1977). *A primer on sleep and dreaming*. Reading, MA: Addison-Wesley.

Carver, C. S., DeGregoria, & Gillis. 1980.

Cazden, C. (1972). *Child language and education*. New York: Holt, Rinehart and Winston.

Chamberlain, H. D. (1928). The inheritance of left-handedness. *Journal of Heredity, 19*, 557–559.

Charney, D. S., Heninger, G. R., & Jatlow, P. I. (1985). *Archives of General Psychiatry*.

Chein, I., Gerard, D.L., Lee, R.S., & Rosenfeld, E. (1964). *The road to H*. New York: Basic Books.

Chen, S. C. (1937). The leaders and followers among the ants in nest building. *Physiological Zoology, 10*, 437–455.

Cheng, P., & Casida, L. E. (1949). Effects of testosterone propionate upon sexual libido and the production of semen and sperm in the rabbit. *Endocrinology, 44*, 38–48.

Chermol, B. H. (1983, July). Psychiatric casualties. *Military Review*, pp. 27–32.

Cherry, E. C. (1953). Some experiments on the recognition of speech, with one or with two ears. *Journal of the Acoustical Society of America, 25*, 975–979.

Chomsky, N. (1959). Review of "Verbal behavior" by B. F. Skinner. *Language, 35*, 26–58.

Chomsky, N. (1972). *Language and mind*. New York: Harcourt, Brace & World.

Chomsky, N. (1975). *Reflections on language*. New York: Pantheon.

Chomsky, N. (1979). Species of intelligence. Encounter, a dialogue with Noam Chomsky and David Premack. *The Sciences, 19*, 6–11, 23.

Cialdini, R. B., Borden, R. J., Thorne, A., Walker, M. R., Freeman, S., & Sloan, L. R. (1976). Basking in reflected glory: Three (football) field studies. *Journal of Personality and Social Psychology, 34*, 366–375.

Cimmerman, A. (1981). The Fay case. *Criminal Defense, 8*, 7.

Clark, H. H., & Clark, E. V. (1977). *Psychology and language*. New York: Harcourt Brace Jovanovitch.

Clark, W. C., & Clark, S. B. (1980). Pain responses in Nepalese porters. *Science, 209*, 410–412.

Clarke, P. G. H., & Whitteridge, D. (1978). A comparison of stereoscopic mechanisms in cortical visual areas V1 and V2 of the cat. *Journal of Physiology, London, 275*, 92–93.

Coch, L., & French, J. R. P., Jr. (1948). Overcoming resistance to change. *Human Relations, 1*, 512–532.

Cohen, S., Evans, G. W., Krantz, D. S., & Stokols, D. (1980). Physiological, motivational, and cognitive effects of aircraft noise on children. *American Psychologist, 35*(3), 231–243.

Cohen, S., & Lezak, A. (1977). Noise and inattentiveness to social cues. *Environment and Behavior, 9*, 559–572.

Colby, A., Kohlberg, L., Gibbs, J., Candee, D., Speicher-Dubin, B., Hewer, A., & Power, C. (1983). *The measurement of moral development: Standard issue scoring manual.* New York: Cambridge University Press.

Cole, M., & Scribner, S. (1977). Cross-cultural studies of memory and cognition. In R. V. Kail & J. H. Hagen (Eds.), *Perspectives on the development of memory & cognition.* Hillsdale, NJ: LEA.

Coleman, J. (1972). *Abnormal psychology and modern life.* Glenview, IL: Scott, Foresman.

Coles, M. G., Gale, A., & Kline, P. (1971). Personality and habituation of the orienting reaction: Tonic and response measures of electrodermal activity. *Psychophysiology, 8*, 54–63.

Collins, A. M., & Quillian, M. R. (1969). Retrieval time from semantic memory. *Journal of Verbal Learning and Verbal Behavior, 8*, 240–247.

Collins, E. (1983, September). Managers and love. *Harvard Business Review.*

Colvin, R. H., & Olson, S. B. (1983). A descriptive analysis of men and women who have lost significant weight and are highly successful at maintaining the loss. *Addictive Behaviors, 8*, 287–296.

Condry, J. (1977). Enemies of exploration: Self-initiated versus other-initiated learning. *Journal of Personality and Social Psychology, 35*, 459–477.

Conger, J. C., & Keane, S. P. (1981). Social skills intervention in the treatment of isolated or withdrawn children. *Psychological Bulletin, 90*, 478–495.

Cooley, C. H. (1909). *Social organization.* New York: Scribner's.

Corballis, M. C., & Beale, I. L. (1976). *The psychology of left and right.* Hillsdale, NJ: Erlbaum Associates.

Coren, S., Porac, C., & Ward, L. M. (1979). *Sensation and perception.* New York: Academic Press.

Corsaro, W. A. (1981). Friendship in the nursery school: Social organization in a peer environment. In S. R. Asher & J. M. Gottman (Eds.), *The development of children's friendships.* Cambridge: Cambridge University Press.

Coser, R. L. (1960). Laughter among colleagues. *Psychiatry, 23*, 81–95.

Cottrell, N. B. (1968). Performance in the presence of other human beings. In E. Simmel, R. Hoppe, & G. Milton (Eds.), *Social facilitation and initiative behavior.* Boston: Allyn and Bacon.

Craik, F. I. M., & Lockhart, R. S. (1972). Levels of processing: A framework for memory research. *Journal of Verbal Learning and Verbal Behavior, 11*, 671–684.

Cross, T. G. (1978). Mothers' speech and its association with rate of syntactic acquisition in young children. In N. Waterson & C. Snow (Eds.), *The development of communication.* New York: Wiley.

Curry, F. K. W. (1967). A comparison of left-handed and right-handed subjects on verbal and non-verbal dichotic listening tasks. *Cortex, 3*, 343–352.

Curtiss, S. (1977). *Genie: A psycholinguistic study of a modern-day "wild child."* New York: Academic Press.

Czeisler, C. A., Moore-Ede, M. C., & Coleman, R. M. (1985). Rotating shift work schedules that disrupt sleep are improved by applying circadian principles. *Science, 217*, 460–463.

D

Dahlberg, C., & Jaffe, J. (1977). *Stroke.* New York: Norton.

Dahlstrom, W. G., & Dahlstrom, L. E. (1979). *Basic readings on the MMPI: A new selection on personality measurement.* Minneapolis: University of Minnesota Press.

Dainoff, M. J., Happ, A., & Crane, P. (1981). Visual fatigue and occupational stress in VDT operators. *Human Factors, 23*(4), 421–438.

Daniel, T. L., & Esser, J. K. (1980). Intrinsic motivation as influenced by rewards, task interest, and task structure. *Journal of Applied Psychology, 65*, 566–573.

Darwin, C. J., Turvey, M. T., & Crowder, R. G. (1972). An auditory analogue to the Sperling partial-report procedure: Evidence for brief auditory storage. *Cognitive Psychology, 3*, 255–267.

Dashiell, J. S. (1930). An experimental analysis of some group effects. *Journal of Abnormal and Social Psychology, 25*, 190–199.

Davenport, W. H. (1977). Sex in cross-cultural perspective. In F. A. Beach (Ed.), *Human sexuality in four perspectives.* Baltimore: Johns Hopkins University Press.

Davidson, J. M. (1966). Characteristics of sex behavior in male rats following castration. *Animal Behaviour, 14*, 266–272.

Davis, D., Cahan, S., & Bashi, J. (1977). Birth order and intellectual development: The confluence model in the light of cross-cultural evidence. *Science, 196*, 1470–1471.

Davis, J. M., & Greenblatt, D. (1979). *Psychopharmacology update.* New York: Grune & Stratton.

Deaux, K. (1985). Sex and gender. *Annual Review of Psychology, 36*, 49–81.

DeCasper, A. J., & Fifer, W. P. (1980). Of human bonding: Newborns prefer their mothers' voices. *Science, 208*, 1174–1176.

Deci, E. L. (1971). Effects of externally mediated rewards on intrinsic motivation. *Journal of Personality and Social Psychology, 18*, 105–115.

Deci, E. L. (1975). *Intrinsic motivation.* New York: Plenum.

Dee, H. L. (1971). Auditory asymmetry and strength of manual preference. *Cortex, 7*, 236–245.

deFleur, M., & Westie. (1956).

Deikman, A. J. (1971). Bimodal consciousness. *Archives of General Psychiatry, 25*, 481–489.

Dennis, W. (1966). Creative productivity between the ages of 20 and 80 years. *Journal of Gerontology, 21*, 1–8.

Descartes, R. (1960). *Discourse on method and meditations* (L. Lafleur, Trans.). Indianapolis: Bobbs-Merrill. (Original work published 1637)

Desor, J. A. (1972). Toward a psychological theory of crowding. *Journal of Personality and Social Psychology, 21*, 79–83.

Deutsch, D. (1980). Handedness and memory for tonal pitch. In J. Herron (Ed.), *Neuropsychology of left-handedness.* New York: Academic Press.

Deutsch, J. A., & Deutsch, D. (1963). Attention: Some theoretical considerations. *Psychological Review, 70*, 80–90.

DeValois, R. L., Abramov, I., & Jacobs, G. H. (1966). Analysis of response patterns in LGN cells. *Journal of the Optical Society of America, 56*, 966–977.

DeValois, R. L., & DeValois, K. K. (1980). Spatial vision. *Annual Review of Psychology, 31*, 309–341.

DeVos, G., & Wagatsuma, H. (1966). *Japan's invisible race.* Berkeley: University of California Press.

Dienstbier, R. A., & Munter, P. O. (1971). Cheating as a function of the labeling of natural arousal. *Journal of Personality and Social Psychology, 17*, 208–213.

Dillon, J. T. (1981). The emergence of the colon: An empirical correlate of scholarship. *American Psychologist, 36*(8), 879–884.

Dimond, E. G. (1971). Acupuncture anaesthesia: Western medicine and Chinese traditional medicine. *J. Amer. Med. Assoc., 218*, 1558–1563.

Dion, K. L., Baron, R. S., & Miller, N. (1970). Why do groups make riskier decisions than individuals? In L. Berkowitz (Ed.), *Advances in experimental social psychology* (Vol. 5). New York: Academic Press.

Doise, W. (1969). Intergroup relations and polarization of individual and collective judgments. *Journal of Personality and Social Psychology, 12*, 136–143.

Dollard, J., Doob, L., Miller, N. E., Mowrer, O. H., & Sears, R. R. (1939). *Frustration and aggression.* New Haven, CT: Yale University Press.

Dornbusch, S. M. et al. (1985). Single parents, extended households, and the control of adolescence. *Child Development, 56*(2), 326–341.

Duncan, C. P. (1949). The retroactive effect of electroshock on learning. *Journal of Comparative and Physiological Psychology, 42,* 32–44.

Dunn, A. J. (1980). Neurochemistry of learning and memory: An evaluation of recent data. *Annual Review of Psychology, 31,* 343–390.

Dunn, A. J., & Bondy, S. C. (1974). *Functional chemistry of the brain.* New York: Spectrum Publications.

Dutton, D. G., & Aron, A. P. (1974). Some evidence for heightened sexual attraction under conditions of high anxiety. *Journal of Personality and Social Psychology, 30,* 510–517.

Dvorak, A. (1943). There is a better typewriter keyboard. *National Business Education Quarterly, 11,* 58–66.

E

Eagly, A. H., Wood, W., & Fishbaugh, L. (1981). Sex differences in conformity: Surveillance by the group as a determinant of male nonconformity. *Journal of Personality and Social Psychology, 40,* 384–394.

Eaton, W. O., & Clore, G. L. (1975). Inter-racial imitation at a summer camp. *Journal of Personality and Social Psychology, 32,* 1099–1105.

Ebbinghaus, H. (1964). *Memory* (H. A. Ruger & C. E. Bussenius, Trans.). New York: Dover. (Original work published 1885).

Eberts, E. H., & Lepper, M. R. (1975). Individual consistency in the proxemic behavior of preschool children. *Journal of Personality and Social Psychology, 32,* 841–849.

Edelman, S. (1983). Therapeutic computer applications: Hypnosis. *Computers in Psychiatry/Psychology, 5*(4), 19–20.

Edney, J. J. (1974). Human territoriality. *Psychological Bulletin, 81,* 959–975.

Edwards, J. D. (1979). The home-field advantage. In J. H. Goldstein (Ed.), *Sports, games, and play.* Hillsdale, NJ: Erlbaum (Wiley).

Efran, M. G., & Cheyne, J. A. (1974). Affective concomitants of the invasion of shared space: Behavioral, physiological, and verbal indicators. *Journal of Personality and Social Psychology, 29,* 219–226.

Egan, J. P. (1975). *Signal detection theory and ROC analysis.* New York: Academic Press.

Egel, A. L., Richman, G. S., & Koegel, R. L. (1981). Normal peer models and autistic children's learning. *Journal of Applied Behavior Analysis, 14,* 3–12.

Ehrhardt, A. A., & Meyer-Bahlburg, H. F. L. (1981). Effects of prenatal sex hormones on gender-related behavior. *Science, 211,* 1312–1317.

Ekman, P., & Friesen, W. V. (1975). *Unmasking the face.* Englewood Cliffs, NJ: Prentice-Hall.

Ekstrom, R. B., French, J. W., Harman, H. H., & Derman, D. (1976). *Manual for kit of factor-referenced cognitive tests.* Princeton, NJ: Educational Testing Service.

Ellis, A. (1962). *Reason and emotion in psychotherapy.* New York: Lyle Stuart.

Ellis, A. (1973). *Humanistic psychotherapy: The rational-emotive approach.* New York: Julian.

Ellis, H. C., Thomas, R. L., McFarland, A. D., & Lane, J. W. (1985). Emotional mood and retrieval in episodic memory. *Journal of Experimental Psychology, 11*(2), 363–370.

Elms, A. C., & Milgram, S. (1966). Personality characteristics associated with obedience and defiance toward authoritative command. *Journal of Experimental Research in Personality, 2,* 282–289.

Emde, R. N. (1985). Adult judgments of infant emotions: Replication studies within and across laboratories. *Infant Behavior and Development, 8*(1), 79–88.

Epstein, S. (1979). Explorations in personality today and tomorrow: A tribute to Henry A. Murray. *American Psychologist, 34,* 649–653.

Epstein, S. M. (1967). Toward a unified theory of anxiety. In B. A. Maher (Ed.), *Progress in experimental personality research* (Vol. 4). New York: Academic Press.

Ericsson, K. A., Chase, W. G., & Faloon, S. (1980). Acquisition of a memory skill. *Science, 208,* 1181–1182.

Ericsson, K. A., & Simon, H. A. (1984). *Protocol analysis: Verbal reports as data.* Cambridge, MA: MIT Press.

Erikson, E. H. (1961). *Gandhi's truth.* New York: Norton.

Erikson, E. H. (1972). Eight stages of man. In C. S. Lavatelli & F. Stendler (Eds.), *Readings in child behavior and child development.* New York: Harcourt Brace Jovanovich.

Eron, L. D. (1982). Parent-child interaction, television violence, and aggression of children. *American Psychologist, 37*(2), 197–211.

Etaugh, C. (1980). Effects of nonmaternal care on children: Research evidence and popular views. *American Psychologist, 35,* 309–319.

Eysenck, H. J. (1967). *The biological basis of personality.* Springfield, IL: Thomas.

F

Fagot, B. I. (1974). Sex differences in toddlers' behavior and parental reaction. *Developmental Psychology, 10,* 554–558.

Fancher, R. E. (1979). *Pioneers of psychology.* New York: W. W. Norton.

Fantz, R. L. (1961). The origin of form perception. *Scientific American, 204,* 66–72.

Fantz, R. L., Fagan, J. F., & Miranda, S. B. (1975a). Early visual acuity. In L. B. Cohen & P. Salapatek (Eds.), *Infant perception: From sensation to cognition* (Vol. 2). New York: Academic Press.

Fantz, R. L., Fagan, J. F., & Miranda, S. B. (1975b). Early visual selectivity. In L. B. Cohen & P. Salapatek (Eds.), *Infant perception: From sensation to cognition* (Vol. 1). New York: Academic Press.

Farberow, N. L. (Ed.). (1980). *The many faces of suicide: Indirect self-destructive behavior.* New York: McGraw-Hill.

Farley, J., & Alkon, D. L. (1985). Cellular mechanisms of learning, memory, and information storage. *Ann. Rev. Psychology, 36,* 419–494.

Fawl, C. L. (1963). Disturbances experienced by children in their natural habitats. In R. G. Barker (Ed.), *The stream of behavior.* New York: Appleton.

Fawzy, F. I., Coombs, R. H., & Gerber, B. (1983). Generational continuity in the use of substances: The impact of parental substance use on adolescent substance use. *Addictive Behaviors, 8,* 109–114.

Feather, N. T. (1962). The study of persistence. *Psychological Bulletin, 59,* 94–115.

Feierabend, I. K., & Feierabend, R. L. (1966). Aggressive behavior within politics, 1948–1962: A cross-national study. *Journal of Conflict Resolution, 10,* 249–271.

Feierabend, I. K., & Feierabend, R. L. (1972). Systemic conditions of political aggression: An application of frustration-aggression theory. In I. K. Feierabend, R. L. Feierabend, & T. R. Gurr (Eds.), *Anger, violence, and politics: Theory and research.* Englewood Cliffs, NJ: Prentice-Hall.

Feierabend, I. K., Feierabend, R. L., & Scanland, F. (1972). The relation between sources of systemic frustration, international conflict, and political instability. Study 5. In I. K. Feierabend, R. L. Feierabend, & T. R. Gurr (Eds.), *Anger, violence, and politics: Theory and research.* Englewood Cliffs, NJ: Prentice-Hall.

Feinberg, I., Fein, G., Walker, J. M., Price, L. J., Floyd, T. C., & March, J. D. (1977). Flurazepam effects on slow-wave sleep: Stage 4 suppressed but number of delta waves constant. *Science, 198,* 847–848.

Feldman, H., Goldin-Meadow, S., & Gleitman, L. R. (1978). Beyond Herodotus: The creation of language by linguistically deprived children. In A. Lock (Ed.), *Action, gesture, and symbol: The emergence of language.* London: Academic Press.

Ferguson, C. A., & Slobin, D. I. (Eds.). (1971). *Studies of child language development.* New York: Holt, Rinehart and Winston.

Festinger, L. (1954). Theory of social comparison processes. *Human Relations, 7,* 117–140.

Festinger, L. (1957). *A theory of cognitive dissonance.* Stanford, CA: Stanford University Press.

Festinger, L., Pepitone, A., & Newcomb, T. M. (1952). Some consequences of deindividuation in a group. *Journal of Abnormal and Social Psychology, 47,* 382–389.

Festinger, L., Riecken, H. W., & Schachter, S. (1956). *When prophecy fails: A social and psychological study of a modern group that predicted the destruction of the world.* Minneapolis: University of Minnesota Press.

Festinger, L., Schachter, S., & Back, K. (1950). *Social pressures in informal groups: A study of human factors in housing.* New York: Harper.

Fiedler, F. E. (1971). *Leadership.* New York: General Learning Press.

Fiedler, F. E., Chemers, M. M., & Mahar, L. (1976). *Improving leadership effectiveness.* New York: Wiley.

Field, T. M., Woodson, R., Greenberg, R., & Cohen, D. (1982). Discrimination and imitation of facial expressions by neonates. *Science, 218,* 179–181.

Fine, R. (1979). *A history of psychoanalysis.* New York: Columbia University Press.

Fischer, K. W., & Silvern, L. (1985). Stages and individual differences in cognitive development. *Annual Review of Psychology, 36,* 613–648.

Fishman, J. A. (1982). Whorfianism of the third kind: Ethnolinguistic diversity as a worldwide societal asset (The Whorfian Hypothesis: Varieties of validation, confirmation, and disconfirmation II). *Language & Society, 11,* 1–14.

Fitzsimons, J. T. (1961). Drinking by rats depleted of body fluid without increase in osmotic pressure. *Journal of Physiology* (London), *159,* 297–309.

Fitzsimons, J. T. (1972). Thirst. *Physiological Reviews, 52,* 468–561.

Flowers, M. L. (1977). A laboratory test of some implications of Janis' group-think hypothesis. *Journal of Personality and Social Psychology, 35,* 888–896.

Fodor, J. A., Bever, T. G., & Garrett, M. F. (1974). *The psychology of language.* New York: McGraw-Hill.

Ford, C. S., & Beach, F. A. (1951). *Patterns of sexual behavior.* New York: Harper.

Franco, L., & Sperry, R. W. (1977). Hemispheric lateralization for cognitive processing of geometry. *Neuropsychologia, 15,* 107–114.

Franke, R. H., & Kaul, J. D. (1978). The Hawthorne experiments: First statistical interpretation. *American Sociological Review, 43,* 623–643.

Fraser, S., Gouge, C., & Billig, M. (1971). Risky shifts, cautious shifts and group polarization. *European Journal of Social Psychology, 1,* 7–29.

Frederiksen, N., & Ward, W. C. (1978). Measures for the study of creativity in scientific problem-solving. *Appl. Psychol. Meas., 2,* 1–24.

Freed, W. J., de Medinaceli, L., & Wyatt, R. J. (1985). Promoting functional plasticity in the damaged nervous system. *Science, 227,* 1544–1552.

Freedman, J. L. (1964). Involvement, discrepancy, and change. *Journal of Abnormal and Social Psychology, 69,* 290–295.

Freedman, J. L. (1975). *Crowding and behavior.* San Francisco: Freeman.

Freedman, J. L., & Fraser, S. C. (1966). Compliance without pressure: The foot-in-the-door technique. *Journal of Personality and Social Psychology, 4,* 195–202.

Freedman, J. L., Heshka, S., & Levy, A. (1975). Population density and pathology: Is there a relationship? *Journal of Experimental Social Psychology, 11,* 539–552.

Freedman, J. L., Klevansky, S., & Ehrlich, P. R. (1971). The effect of crowding on human task performance. *Journal of Applied Social Psychology, 1,* 7–25.

Freedman, J. L., Levy, A., Buchanan, R. W., & Price, J. (1972). Crowding and human aggressiveness. *Journal of Experimental Social Psychology, 8,* 528–548.

Freiherr, G. (1982). Studies of artificial intelligence in psychology and psychiatry. *Computers in Psychiatry/Psychology, 4*(1), 7–11.

French, J. R. P., Jr., Israel, J., & As, D. (1960). An experiment in participation in a Norwegian factory. *Human Relations, 13,* 3–19.

Freud, A. (1936). *The ego and the mechanisms of defense.* New York: International Universities Press.

Freud, S. (1945). *Group psychology and the analysis of the ego.* London: Hogarth. (Original work published 1921)

Freud, S. (1949). *Three essays on the theory of sexuality.* In *Standard edition* (Vol. 7). London: Hogarth. (Original work published 1905)

Freud, S. (1950). *The ego and the id.* In *Standard edition* (Vol. 19). London: Hogarth. (Original work published 1932)

Freud, S. (1959). *Further reflections on the technique of psychoanalysis, recollection, repetition and working through.* In *Collected papers* (Vol. 2). New York: Basic Books. (Original work published 1914)

Freud, S. (1959). *Neurosis and psychosis.* In *Collected papers* (Vol. 2). New York: Basic Books. (Original work published 1924)

Friedman, L. (1981). How affiliation affects stress in fear and anxiety situations. *Journal of Personality and Social Psychology, 40,* 1102–1117.

Friedman, M., Rosenman, R. H., & Carroll, V. (1958). Changes in serum cholesterol and blood clotting time in men subjected to cyclic variations of occupational stress. *Circulation, 17,* 852–861.

Friedman, M. I., & Stricker, E. M. (1976). The physiological psychology of hunger: A physiological perspective. *Psychological Review, 83,* 409–431.

Fromm, E. (1941). *Escape from freedom.* New York: Rinehart & Co.

Fromm, E. (1970). Age regression with unexpected reappearance of a repressed childhood language. *International Journal of Clinical and Experimental Hypnosis, 18,* 79–88.

Fry, P. S. (1985). Relations between teenagers' age, knowledge, expectations and maternal behaviour. *British Journal of Developmental Psychology, 3*(1), 47–55.

G

Gage, D. F., & Safer, M. A. (1985). Hemispheric differences in the mood state-dependent effect for recognition of emotional faces. *Journal of Experimental Psychology: Learning, Memory and Cognition, 11*(4), 752–763.

Galbraith, R. C. (1982). Just one look was all it took: Reply to Berbaum, Markus, and Zajonc. *Developmental Psychology, 18*(2), 181–191.

Garcia, J., & Koelling, R. A. (1966). Relation of cue to consequence in avoidance learning. *Psychonomic Science, 4,* 123–124.

Garcia, J., Rusiniak, K. W., & Brett, L. P. (1977). Conditioned food illness aversion in wild animals: Caveant canonici. In H. Davis & H. M. B. Hurwitz (Eds.), *Operant-Pavlovian interactions.* Hillsdale, NJ: Erlbaum.

Gardner, B. T., & Gardner, R. A. (1971). Two-way communication with an infant chimpanzee. In A. M. Schrier & F. Stollnitz (Eds.), *Behavior of nonhuman primates* (Vol. 4). New York: Academic Press.

Gaston, S., & Menaker, M. (1968). Pineal function: The biological clock in the sparrow? *Science, 160,* 1125–1127.

Gates, M. J., & Allee, W. C. (1933). Conditional behavior of isolated and grouped cockroaches on a simple maze. *Journal of Comparative Psychology, 15,* 331–358.

Gazzaniga, M. S. (1967). The split brain in man. *Scientific American, 217,* 24–29.

Geen, R. G., & Donnerstein, E. I. (1983). *Aggression* (Vols. 1–2). New York: Academic Press.

George, W. C., Cohn, S. J., & Stanley, J. C. (Eds.). (1979). *Educating the gifted.* Baltimore: Johns Hopkins University Press.

Gergen, K. J., Gergen, M. M., & Meter, K. (1972). Individual orientations to prosocial behavior. *Journal of Social Issues, 28,* 105–130.

Getzels, J. W. (1975). Problem finding and inventiveness of solutions. *Journal of Creative Behavior, 9,* 12–18.

Ghiselli, E. E. (1966). *The validity of occupational aptitude tests.* New York: Wiley.

Gibb, C. A. (Ed.). (1969). *Leadership.* Baltimore: Penguin.

Gibbs, J. C., & Schnell, S. V. (1985). Moral development "versus" socialization: A critique. *American Psychologist, 40*(10), 1071–1080.

Gibson, H. B. (1977). *Hypnosis: Its nature and therapeutic uses.* New York: Taplinger Publishing Co.

Giel, R., & Ormel, J. (1977). Crowding and subjective health in the Netherlands. *Social Psychiatry, 12,* 37–42.

Gil, D. (1970). *Violence against children.* Cambridge, MA: Harvard University Press.

Gilligan, C. (1982). *In a different voice.* Cambridge, MA: Harvard University Press.

Glaser, R. (1981). The future of testing: A research agenda for cognitive psychology and psychometrics. *American Psychologist, 36,* 923–936.

Glaser, R. (1982). Instructional psychology: Past, present and future. *American Psychologist, 37,* 292–305.

Glass, A. L., Holyoak, K. J., & Santa, J. L. (1979). *Cognition.* Reading, MA: Addison-Wesley.

Glass, D. C., & Singer, J. E. (1972). *Urban stress: Experiments on noise and social stressors.* New York: Academic Press.

Glick, P. C. (1979). Children of divorced parents in demographic perspective. *Journal of Social Issues, 35*(4), 170–182.

Glucksberg, S., & Cowen, G. N., Jr. (1970). Memory for nonattended auditory material. *Cognitive Psychology, 1,* 149–156.

Gold, P. E., Macri, J., & McGaugh, J. L. (1973). Retrograde amnesia gradients: Effects of direct cortical stimulation. *Science, 179,* 1343–1345.

Gold, P. E., & van Buskirk, R. (1975). Enhancement of time-dependent memory processes with post-trial epinephrine injections. *Behavioral Biology, 13,* 145–153.

Gold, P. E., & van Buskirk, R. (1978). Effects of alpha and beta adrenergic receptor antagonists on post-trial epinephrine modulation of memory: Relationship to posttraining brain norepinephrine concentrations. *Behavioral Biology, 24,* 168–184.

Goldberg, L. R. (1970). Man versus model of man. *Psychological Bulletin, 73*(6), 422–432.

Goldstein, J. H. (1979). Outcomes in professional team sports: Chance, skill and situational factors. In J. H. Goldstein (Ed.), *Sports, games, and play.* Hillsdale, NJ: Erlbaum (Wiley).

Goldstein, J. H. (Ed.). (1979). *Sports, games, and play.* Hillsdale, NJ: Lawrence Erlbaum Associates.

Goldstein, J. H. (1986a). *Aggression and crimes of violence* (2nd ed.). New York: Oxford University Press.

Goldstein, J. H. (1986b). *Reporting science: The case of aggression.* Hillsdale, NJ: Lawrence Erlbaum Associates.

Goldstein, J. H., Davis, R. W., & Herman, D. (1975). Escalation of aggression: Experimental studies. *Journal of Personality and Social Psychology, 31,* 162–170.

Goldstein, J. H., Davis, R. W., Kernis, M., & Cohn, E. S. (1981). Retarding the escalation of aggression. *Social Behavior and Personality, 9,* 65–70.

Goldstein, J. H., Rosnow, R. L., Raday, T., Silverman, I. W., & Gaskell, G. D. (1975). Punitiveness in response to films varying in content: A cross-national field study of aggression. *European Journal of Social Psychology, 5,* 149–165.

Gomersall, E. A., & Myers, M. S. (1966). Breakthrough in on-the-job training. *Harvard Business Review, 44*(4), 62–72.

Goodall, J. (1963). My life among the wild chimpanzees. *National Geographic, 124,* 272–308.

Goodrich, A. J., Henry, J., & Goodrich, D. W. (1954). Laughter in psychiatric staff conferences: A sociopsychiatric analysis. *American Journal of Orthopsychiatry, 24,* 175–184.

Goodwin, D. W. (1979). Alcoholism and heredity. *Archives of General Psychiatry, 36,* 57–61.

Goodwin, D. W. (1983). The genetics of alcoholism. In E. Gottheil, K. A. Druley, T. E. Skoloda, & H. M. Waxman (Eds.), *Etiological aspects of alcohol and drug abuse.* Springfield, IL: C. C. Thomas.

Goodwin, D. W., Guze, S., & Robins, E. (1969). Follow-up studies in obsessional neurosis. *Archives of General Psychiatry, 20,* 182–187.

Gordon, H. W. (1980). Degree of ear asymmetries for perception of dichotic chords and for illusory chord localization in musicians of different levels of competence. *Journal of Experimental Psychology: Human Perception and Performance, 6,* 516–527.

Gorman, A. N. (1961). Recognition memory for names as a function of abstractness and frequency. *Journal of Experimental Psychology, 61,* 23–29.

Graen, G., Orris, J., & Alvares, K. (1971). The contingency model of leadership effectiveness: Some experimental results. *Journal of Applied Psychology, 55,* 196–201.

Gratch, G. (1982). Responses to hidden persons and things by 5-, 9-, and 16-month-old infants in a visual tracking situation. *Developmental Psychology, 18*(2), 232–237.

Gray, J. A., & McNaughton, N. (1983). Comparison between the behavioural effects of septal and hippocampal lesions: A review. *Neuroscience and Biobehavioral Reviews, 7,* 119–188.

Green, M. R. (1980). *Violence and the family.* Boulder, CO: Westview.

Greeno, J. G. (1978). A study of problem solving. In R. Glaser (Ed.), *Advances in instructional psychology* (Vol. 1). Hillsdale, NJ: Erlbaum Associates.

Greenough, W. T. (1975). Experiential modification of the developing brain. *American Scientist, 63,* 37–46.

Griffin, G. R. (1980). Hypnosis: Towards a logical approach in using hypnosis in law enforcement agencies. *Journal of Police Science and Administration, 8*(4), 385–389.

Grinspoon, L., Ewalt, J. R., & Shader, R. (1968). Psychotherapy and pharmacotherapy in chronic schizophrenia. *American Journal of Psychiatry, 124,* 1645–1652.

Gross, C. G., Rocha-Miranda, C. E., & Bender, D. B. (1982). Visual properties of neurons in inferotemporal cortex of the macaque. *Journal of Neurophysiology, 35,* 96–111.

Grotevant, H. D., & Thorbecke, W. L. (1982). Sex differences in styles of occupational identity formation in late adolescence. *Developmental Psychology, 18*(3), 396–405.

Guardo, C. J. (1969). Personal space in children. *Child Development, 40,* 143–151.

Guilford, J. P. (1967). *The nature of human intelligence.* New York: McGraw Hill.

Guilford, J. P. (1984). Humanistic psychology. In R. J. Corsini (Ed.), *Encyclopedia of psychology* (Vol. 2). New York: Wiley.

Guilford, J. P., & Hoepfner, R. (1971). *The analysis of intelligence.* New York: McGraw Hill.

Gurman, A., & Kniskern, D. (Eds.) (1981). *Handbook of family therapy.* New York: Brunner/Mazel.

H

Hackman, J. R., & Morris, C. G. (1975). Group tasks, group interaction process, and group performance effectiveness: A review and proposed integration. In L. Berkowitz (Ed.), *Advances in experimental social psychology* (Vol. 8). New York: Academic Press.

Hall, D. T., & Nougaim, K. E. (1968). An examination of Maslow's need hierarchy in an organizational setting. *Organizational Behavior and Human Performance, 3,* 12–35.

Hall, E. T. (1959). *The silent language.* Garden City, NY: Doubleday.

Hall, E. T. (1966). *The hidden dimension.* Garden City, NY: Doubleday.

Hamilton, J. O. (1974). Motivation and risk-taking behavior: A test of Atkinson's theory. *Journal of Personality and Social Psychology, 29,* 856–864.

Hansel, C. E. M. (1980). *ESP and parapsychology: A critical re-evaluation.* Buffalo, NY: Prometheus Press.

Hansson, R. O., Noulles, D., & Bellovich, S. J. (1982). Social comparison and urban-environmental stress. *Personality and Social Psychology Bulletin, 8,* 68–73.

Hardin, G. (1968). The tragedy of the commons. *Science, 162,* 1243–1248.

Hardyck, C., & Petrinovitch, L. F. (1977). Left-handedness. *Psychological Bulletin, 84,* 385–404.

Hardyck, C., Petrinovitch, L. F., & Goldman, R. D. (1976). Left-handedness and cognitive deficit. *Cortex, 12,* 266–280.

Hardyck, J. A., & Braden, M. (1962). Prophecy fails again: A report of a failure to replicate. *Journal of Abnormal and Social Psychology, 65,* 136–141.

Harley, J. P. (1984). Software review: "COGREHAB" cognitive rehabilitation programs. *Computers in Psychiatry/Psychology, 6*(1), 15–17.

Harlow, H. F. (1932). Social facilitation of feeding in the albino rat. *Journal of Genetic Psychology, 43,* 211–221.

Harlow, H. F. (1962). The heterosexual affectional system in monkeys. *American Psychology, 17,* 1–9.

Harlow, J. M. (1848). Passage of an iron rod through the head. *Boston Medical and Surgical Journal, 39,* 389–393.

Harlow, J. M. (1868). Recovery from passage of an iron bar through the head. *Massachusetts Medical Society, 2,* 327–346.

Hart, R. D. A. (1960). Monthly rhythm of libido in married women. *British Medical Journal, 1,* 1023–1024.

Hayden, A. H., & Haring, N. G. The acceleration and maintenance of developmental gains in school-aged Down's syndrome children. In R. I. Jahiel, J. Byrne, R. Lubin, & J. Gorelick (Eds.), *Handbook of prevention of mental retardation and developmental disabilities.* New York: Van Nostrand Reinhold.

Hayduk, L. A. (1978). Personal space: An evaluative and orienting overview. *Psychological Bulletin, 85,* 117–134.

Hayes, K. J., & Hayes, C. (1951). The intellectual development of a home-raised chimpanzee. *Proceedings of the American Philosophical Society, 95,* 105–109.

Heath, R. G. (1964). Pleasure response of human subjects to direct stimulation of the brain: Physiologic and psychodynamic considerations. In R. G. Heath (Ed.), *The role of pleasure in behavior.* New York: Harper and Row.

Hebb, D. O. (1949). *The organization of behavior.* New York: Wiley.

Hecaen, H., & Ajuriaguerra, J. (1964). *Left-handedness: Manual superiority and cerebral dominance.* New York: Grune and Stratton.

Heider, F. (1958). *The psychology of interpersonal relations.* New York: Wiley.

Herron, J. (Ed.). (1980). *Neuropsychology of left-handedness.* New York: Academic Press.

Herzberg, T. (1966). *Work and the nature of man.* Cleveland: World.

Herzberg, T. (1976). *The managerial choice.* Homewood, IL: Dow-Jones/Irwin.

Herzberg, T., Mausner, B., & Snyderman, B. (1959). *The motivation to work.* New York: Wiley.

Hetherington, E. M. (1972). Effects of father absence on personality development in adolescent daughters. *Developmental Psychology, 7,* 313–326.

Hetherington, E. M. (1977). *My heart belongs to daddy: A study of the remarriages of daughters of divorcees and widows.* Unpublished manuscript, University of Virginia.

Hetherington, E. M. (1979). Divorce: A child's perspective. *American Psychologist, 34,* 851–858.

Higgins, E. A., Chiles, W. D., McKenzie, J. M., Iampietro, P. F., Winget, C. M., Funkhauser, G. E., Burr, M. J., Vaughan, J. A., & Jennings, A. E. (1975, October). *The effects of a 12 hour shift in the wake-sleep cycle on physiological and biochemical responses and on multiple task performance* (FAA-AM-75-10). Washington, DC: U.S. Dept. of Transportation, Federal Aviation Administration.

Hilgard, E. R. (1977). *Divided consciousness: Multiple controls in human thought and action.* New York: Wiley-Interscience.

Hilgard, E. R. (1980). Consciousness in contemporary psychology. *Ann. Review of Psychology, 31,* 1–26.

Hilgard, E. R., & Hilgard, J. R. (1975). *Hypnosis in the relief of pain.* Los Altos, CA: William Kaufmann, Inc.

Hilgard, J. R. (1970). *Personality and hypnosis: A study of imaginative involvement.* Chicago: University of Chicago Press.

Hill, J. H., & Chernikoff, R. (1965, January 26). *Altimeter display evaluations: Final report* (USN, NEL Report 6242).

Hinton, J. (1973). Bearing cancer. *British Journal of Medical Psychology, 46,* 105–113.

Hirsch, H. V. B., & Spinelli, D. N. (1971). Modification of the distribution of receptive field orientation in cats by selective visual exposure during development. *Experimental Brain Research, 13,* 509–527.

Hitchcock, P. F., & Hickey, T. L. (1980). Ocular dominance columns: Evidence for their presence in humans. *Brain Research, 182,* 176–179.

Hodgkin, A. L. (1964). *The conduction of the nervous impulse.* Springfield, IL: Thomas.

Hodgkin, A. L., & Katz, B. (1949). The effect of sodium ions on the electrical activity of the giant axon of the squid. *Journal of Physiology* (London), *108,* 37–77.

Hoffman, L. R. (1965). Group problem solving. In L. Berkowitz (Ed.), *Advances in experimental social psychology* (Vol. 2). New York: Academic Press.

Hoffman, L. R., & Maier, N. R. F. (1964). Valence in the adoption of solutions by problem-solving groups: Concept, method, and results. *Journal of Abnormal and Social Psychology, 69,* 264–271.

Holden, C. (1980). Twins reunited. *Science 80, 1,* 54–59.

Holden, C. (1982). NAS backs cautious use of ability tests. *Science, 215,* 950.

Hollander, E. P. (1985). Leadership and power. In G. Lindzey & E. Aronson (Eds.), *Handbook of social psychology* (Vol. 1). New York: Random House.

Hollander, E. P., & Julian, J. W. (1969). Leadership. In E. F. Borgatta (Ed.), *Social psychology: Readings and perspectives.* Chicago: Rand McNally.

Hollis, K. (1984). The biological function of Pavlovian conditioning: The best defense is a good offense. *J. Exp. Psych.: Animal Behavior Processes, 10*(4), 413–425.

Holmes, T. H., & Masuda, M. (1967). Life changes and illness susceptibility. In B. S. Dohrenwend & B. P. Dohrenwend (Eds.), *Stressful life events: Their nature and effects.* New York: Wiley.

Holmes, T. H., & Rahe, R. H. (1967). The social readjustment rating scale. *Journal of Psychosomatic Research, 11,* 213–218.

Honzik, M. P., MacFarlane, J. W., & Allen, I. (1948). The stability of mental test performance between two and eighteen years. *Journal of Experimental Education, 17,* 309–324.

Horne, J. A., & Osterberg, O. (1977). Individual differences in human circadian rhythms. *Biological Psychology, 5,* 179–190.

Horney, K. (1942). *Self-analysis.* New York: Norton.

Hosobuchi, Y., Adams, J. E., & Linchitz, R. (1977). Pain relief by electrical stimulation of the central grey matter in humans and its reversal by naloxone. *Science, 197,* 183–186.

Hovland, C. I., Janis, I. L., & Kelley, H. H. (1953). *Communication and persuasion.* New Haven, CT: Yale University Press.

Hovland, C. I., & Sears, R. R. (1940). Minor studies of aggression. VI. Correlations of lynchings with economic indices. *Journal of Psychology, 9,* 301–310.

Hovland, C. I., & Weiss, W. (1951). The influence of source credibility on communication effectiveness. *Public Opinion Quarterly, 15,* 635–650.

Hrusheskey, W. J. M. (1985). Circadian timing of cancer chemotherapy. *Science, 228,* 73–75.

Hubel, D. H., & Wiesel, T. N. (1959). Receptive fields of single neurons in the cat's striate cortex. *Journal of Physiology* (London), *148,* 574–591.

Hubel, D. H., & Wiesel, T. N. (1962). Receptive fields, binocular interaction and functional architecture in the cat's visual cortex. *Journal of Physiology* (London), *160,* 106–154.

Hubel, D. H., & Wiesel, T. N. (1965). Receptive fields and functional architecture in two non-striate visual areas (18 and 19) of the cat. *Journal of Neurophysiology, 28,* 229–289.

Hubel, D. H., & Wiesel, T. N. (1979, September). Brain mechanisms of vision. *Scientific American.*

Hubel, D. H., Wiesel, T. N., & Stryker, M. P. (1978). Anatomical demonstration of orientation columns in macaque monkeys. *Journal of Comparative Neurology, 177,* 361–380.

Hughes, J., Smith, T. W., Kosterlitz, H. W., Fothergill, L. A., Morgan, B. A., & Morris, H. R. (1975). Identification of two related pentapeptides from the brain with potent opiate agonist activity. *Nature* (London), *258,* 577–579.

Hull, C. I. (1943). *Principles of behavior: An introduction to behavior theory.* New York: Appleton-Century-Crofts.

Hull, C. I. (1952). *A behavior system: An introduction to behavior theory theory concerning the individual organism.* New Haven, CT: Yale University Press.

Hunt, L. G. (1982). Growth of substance use and misuse: Some speculations and data. In N. E. Zinberg & W. M. Harding (Eds.), *Control over intoxicant use.* New York: Human Sciences Press.

Hunt, M. (1974). *Sexual behavior in the 1970's.* Chicago: Playboy Press.

Hurvich, I. M., & Jameson, D. (1974). Opponent processes as a model of neural organization. *American Psychologist, 29,* 88–102.

I

Imber, S. D., Pilkonis, P. A., & Glanz, L. (1983). Outcome studies in psychotherapy. In C. E. Walker (Ed.), *Handbook of clinical psychology.* Homewood, IL: Dorsey.

Imperato-McGinley, J., et al. (1974). Steroid 5 alpha reductase deficiency in man: An inherited form of male pseudohermaphroditism. *Science, 186,* 1213–1215.

Insko, C. A., & Robinson, J. E. (1967). Belief similarity versus race as determinants of reactions to Negroes by southern white adolescents: A further test of Rokeach's theory. *Journal of Personality and Social Psychology, 7,* 216–221.

Issacson, R. L., & Pribram, K. H. (Eds.). (1975). *The hippocampus* (Vol. 2). New York: Plenum Press.

J

Jacobs, R. C., & Campbell, D. T. (1961). The perpetuation of an arbitrary tradition through several generations of a laboratory microculture. *Journal of Abnormal and Social Psychology, 62,* 649–658.

James, W. (1950). *The principles of psychology.* New York: Dover. (Original work published 1890.)

James, W. H. (1971). The distribution of coitus within the human intermenstruum. *Journal of Biosocial Science, 3,* 159–171.

Janis, I. L. (1982). *Victims of groupthink: A psychological study of foreign-policy decisions and fiascoes* (2nd ed.). Boston: Houghton Mifflin.

Janis, I. L., & Mann, L. (1977). *Decision making: A psychological analysis of conflict, choice and commitment.* New York: Free Press.

Jenkins, W. O. (1947). The tactual discrimination of shapes for coding aircraft-type controls. In P. M. Fitts (Ed.), *Psychological research in equipment design* (Research Report 19). Army Air Force, Aviation Psychology Program.

Jessor, R., & Jessor, S. L. (1976). *Problem behavior and psychosocial development: A longitudinal study of youth.* New York: Academic Press.

Johnson, E. S. (1971). Objective identification of strategy on a selection concept learning task. *Journal of Experimental Psychology Monograph, 90*(1), 167–196.

Johnson, E. S. (1978). Validation of concept-learning strategies. *Journal of Experimental Psychology: General, 107,* 237–266.

Johnson-Laird, P. N. (1983). *Mental models: Towards a cognitive science of language, inference, and consciousness.* Cambridge, MA: Harvard University Press.

Jones, E. (1963). *The life and work of Sigmund Freud.* Garden City, NY: Doubleday.

Jones, M. C., & Mussen, P. H. (1958). Self-conceptions, motivations, and interpersonal attitudes of early- and late-maturing girls. *Child Development, 29,* 491–501.

Jones, S. E., & Aiello, J. R. (1973). Proxemic behavior of black and white first-, third-, and fifth-grade children. *Journal of Personality and Social Psychology, 25,* 21–27.

K

Kabanoff, B. (1983). Work and non-work: A review of models, methods, and findings. *Psychological Bulletin.*

Kales, A., & Kales, J. D. (1984). *Evaluation and treatment of insomnia.* New York: Oxford University Press.

Kandel, E. R. (1976). *The cellular basis of behavior.* San Francisco: W. H. Freeman.

Kantner, J. F., & Zelnik, M. (1973). Contraception and pregnancy: Experience of young unmarried women in the United States. *Family Planning Perspectives, 5,* 21–35.

Kantowitz, B. H. (1984). Information-processing theory. In R. J. Corsini (Ed.), *Encyclopedia of psychology.* New York: John Wiley & Sons.

Kaplan, B. (1973). *EEG biofeedback and epilepsy.* Paper presented at the meeting of the American Psychological Association, Montreal.

Kaplan, H. S. (1974). *The new sex therapy.* New York: Brunner/Mazel.

Kaplan, H. S. (1979). *Disorders of sexual desire.* New York: Brunner/Mazel.

Kaplan, R. M. (1982). Nader's raid on the testing industry: Is it in the best interest of the consumer? *American Psychologist, 37,* 15–23.

Kastenbaum, R. (1967). Multiple perspectives on a geriatric "Death Valley." *Community Mental Health Journal, 3,* 21–29.

Kelley, H. H. (1973). The processes of causal attribution. *American Psychologist, 28,* 107–128.

Kelley, H. H., Condry, J. C., Dahlke, A. E., & Hill, A. H. (1965). Collective behavior in a simulated panic situation. *Journal of Experimental Social Psychology, 1,* 20–54.

Kellogg, W. N., & Kellogg, L. A. (1933). *The ape and the child.* New York: Whittlesey.

Kelman, H. C. (1958). Compliance, identification, and internalization: Three processes of attitude change. *Journal of Conflict Resolution, 2,* 51–60.

Kendall, P. C., & Kriss, M. R. (1983). Cognitive-behavioral interventions. In C. E. Walker (Ed.), *Handbook of clinical psychology.* Homewood, IL: Dorsey.

Kennedy, S. T., Scheirer, J., & Rogers, A. (1984). The price of success: Our monocultural science. *American Psychologist, 39*(9), 996–997.

Kerckhoff, A. C., Back, K. W., & Miller, N. (1965). Sociometric patterns in hysterical contagion. *Sociometry, 28,* 2–15.

Kerckhoff, A. C., & Davis, K. E. (1962). Value consensus and need complementarity in mate selection. *American Sociological Review, 27,* 295–303.

Kessler, K. A., & Waletzky, J. P. (1981). Clinical use of the antipsychotics. *American Journal of Psychiatry, 138,* 202–209.

Key, W. B. (1973). *Subliminal seduction.* Englewood Cliffs, NJ: Prentice-Hall.

Keynes, R. D. (1951). The ionic movements during nervous activity. *Journal of Physiology* (London), *114,* 119–150.

Kidder, L. H., & Stewart, V. M. (1975). *The psychology of intergroup relations: Conflict and consciousness.* New York: McGraw-Hill.

Kilham, W., & Mann, L. (1974). Level of destructive obedience as a function of transmitter and executant roles in the Milgram obedience paradigm. *Journal of Personality and Social Psychology, 29,* 696–702.

Kimura, D. (1961). Cerebral dominance and the perception of verbal stimuli. *Canadian Journal of Psychology, 15,* 166–171.

King, F. L., & Kimura, D. (1972). Left-ear superiority in dichotic perception of vocal nonverbal sounds. *Canadian Journal of Psychology, 26,* 111–116.

Kinsey, A. C., Pomeroy, W. B., Martin, O. E., & Gebhard, P. H. (1953). *Sexual behavior in the human female.* Philadelphia: Saunders.

Kintsch, W. (1977). *Memory and cognition* (2nd ed.) New York: John Wiley.

Kintsch, W., & Keenan, J. M. (1973). Reading rate as a function of the number of propositions in the base structure of sentences. *Cognitive Psychology, 5,* 257–274.

Kinzel, A. F. (1971, January 28). Body-buffer zones in violent prisoners. *New Society,* pp. 149–150.

Kirk-Smith, M., et al. (1978). *Res. Commun. Psychol. Psychiat. Behav., 3,* 379.

Kissel, S. (1965). Stress-reducing properties of social stimuli. *Journal of Personality and Social Psychology, 2,* 378–384.

Klein, A. L. (1976). Changes in leadership appraisal as a function of the stress of a simulated panic situation. *Journal of Personality and Social Psychology, 34,* 1143–1154.

Kleinmuntz, B., & Szucko, J. J. (1984a). A field study of the fallibility of polygraphic lie detection. *Nature, 308,* 449–450.

Kleinmuntz, B., & Szucko, J. J. (1984b). Lie detection in ancient and modern times. *American Psychologist, 39*(7), 766–776.

Klineberg, O. (1938). Emotional expression in Chinese literature. *Journal of Abnormal and Social Psychology, 33,* 517–520.

Klineberg, O. (1971). Black and white in international perspective. *American Psychologist, 26,* 119–128.

Klopfer, P. H. (1958). Influence of social interaction on learning rates in birds. *Science, 128,* 903–904.

Knox, R. E., & Safford, R. K. (1976). Group caution at the racetrack. *Journal of Experimental Social Psychology, 12,* 317–324.

Knudsen, E. I. (1981, December). The hearing of the barn owl. *Scientific American, 245,* 112–125.

Koegler, R. R., & Brill, N. Q. (1967). *Treatment of psychiatric outpatients.* New York: Appleton-Century-Crofts.

Kogan, N., & Wallach, M. A. (1964). *Risk taking: A study in cognition and personality.* New York: Holt, Rinehart & Winston.

Kohlberg, L. (1976). Moral stages and moralization. The cognitive-developmental approach. In T. Lickona (Ed.), *Moral development and behavior.* New York: Holt, Rinehart and Winston.

Kohler, W. (1925). *The mentality of apes.* New York: Harcourt, Brace.

Kraepelin, E. (1896). *Dementia praecox and paraphrenia.* Edinburgh: Livingston.

Krasner, L. (1982). Behavior therapy and clinical psychology: A historical perspective. In G. T. Wilson & C. M. Franks (Eds.), *Contemporary behavior therapy.* New York: Guilford.

Krasner, L., & Houts, A. C. (1984). A study of the "value" systems of behavioral scientists. *American Psychologist,* 840–850.

Krosnick, J. A., & Judd, C. M. (1982). Transitions in social influence at adolescence: Who induces cigarette smoking? *Developmental Psychology, 18*(3), 359–368.

Kruglanski, A. W. (1969). Incentives in interdependent escape as affecting the degree of group incoordination. *Journal of Experimental Social Psychology, 5,* 454–466.

Kubler-Ross, E. (1969). *On death and dying.* New York: Macmillan.

Kuffler, S. W. (1953). Discharge patterns and functional organization of mammalian retina. *Journal of Neurophysiology, 16,* 37–68.

Kurdek, L. A. (1981). An integrative perspective on children's divorce adjustment. *American Psychologist, 36*(8), 856–866.

L

Lachman, S. J. (1963). A behavioristic rationale for the development of psychosomatic phenomena. *Journal of Psychology, 56,* 239–248.

Lachman, S. J. (1972). *Psychosomatic disorders: A behavioristic interpretation.* New York: Wiley.

Ladd, G. T. (1887). *Elements of physiological psychology.* New York: Scribner.

Lakoff, G. (1972). Hedges: A study in meaning criteria and the logic of fuzzy concepts. *Papers from the eighth regional meeting, Chicago Linguistics Society.* Chicago: University of Chicago Linguistics Department.

Lamb, M. E. (1981). The development of father-infant relationships. In M. E. Lamb (Ed.), *The role of the father in child development* (rev. ed.). New York: Wiley.

Lambert, M. J., & Bergin, A. E. (1983). Therapist characteristics and their contribution to psychotherapy outcome. In C. E. Walker (Ed.), *Handbook of clinical psychology.* Homewood, IL: Dorsey.

Lambert, N. M. (1981). Psychological evidence in *Larry P. v. Wilson Riles:* An evaluation by a witness for the defense. *American Psychologist, 36,* 937–952.

Landy, F. J., & Trumbo, D. A. (1980). *Psychology of work behavior.* Homewood, IL: Dorsey.

Lasswell, H. D., & Casey, R. D. (1946). *Propaganda, communication, and public opinion.* Princeton: Princeton University Press.

Latané, B., & Darley, J. (1970). *The unresponsive bystander: Why doesn't he help?* New York: Appleton.

Latané, B., Williams, K., & Harkins, S. (1979). Many hands make light the work: The causes and consequences of social loafing. *Journal of Personality and Social Psychology, 37,* 822–832.

Laughlin, P. R., & Earley, P. C. (1982). Social combination models, persuasive arguments theory, social comparison theory, and choice shift. *Journal of Personality and Social Psychology, 42,* 273–280.

Laughlin, P. R., Lange, R., & Adamopoulos, J. (1982). Selection strategies for "Mastermind" problems. *Journal of Experimental Psychology: Learning, Memory and Cognition, 8,* 475–483.

Lawler, E. E. (1973). *Motivation in work organizations.* Monterey, CA: Brooks/Cole.

Lawler, E. E., Hackman, J. R., & Kaufman, S. (1973). Effects of job redesign: A field experiment. *Journal of Applied Social Psychology, 3,* 49–62.

Lawler, E. E., & Suttle, J. L. (1972). A causal correlational test of the need hierarchy concept. *Organizational Behavior and Human Performance, 7,* 265–287.

Lazarsfeld, P. F., Berelson, B., & Gaudet, H. (1948). *The people's choice.* New York: Columbia University Press.

Lazarus, A. A. (1981). *Multimodal therapy.* New York: McGraw-Hill.

Lazarus, R. S. (1984). On the primacy of cognition. *American Psychologist, 39*(2), 117–123.

LeBon, G. (1896). *The crowd.* London: Benn.

Leitenberg, H., Agras, W. S., Thomson, L. E., & Wright, D. E. (1968). Feedback in behavior modification: An experimental analysis in two phobic cases. *Journal of Applied Behavior Analysis, 1,* 131–137.

Lenneberg, E. H. (1967). *Biological foundations of language.* New York: Wiley.

Leon, G. R., & Roth, L. (1977). Obesity: Psychological causes, correlations, and speculations. *Psychological Bulletin, 84,* 117–139.

Lerner, M. J. (1980). *The belief in a just world: A fundamental delusion.* New York: Plenum.

Lesser, G. S., Krawitz, R. N., & Packard, R. (1963). Experimental arousal of achievement motivation in adolescent girls. *Journal of Abnormal and Social Psychology, 66,* 59–66.

Levanthal, H. (1980). Toward a comprehensive theory of emotion. In L. Berkowitz (Ed.), *Advances in experimental social psychology* (Vol. 13). New York: Academic Press.

Leventhal, G. S., Michaels, J. W., & Sanford, C. (1972). Inequity and interpersonal conflict: Reward allocation and secrecy about reward as methods of preventing conflict. *Journal of Personality and Social Psychology, 23,* 88–102.

Leventhal, H. (1970). Findings and theory in the study of fear communications. In L. Berkowitz (Ed.), *Advances in experimental social psychology* (Vol. 5). New York: Academic Press.

Lever, J. (1976). Sexual differences in the games children play. *Social Problems, 23,* 478–487.

Levine, C., Kohlberg, L., & Hewer, A. (1985). The current formulation of Kohlberg's theory and a response to critics. *Human Development, 28*(2), 94–100.

Levine, J. D., & Gordon, N. C. (1984). *Nature.*

Levinger, G., & Raush, H. L. (1977). *Close relationships.* Amherst: University of Massachusetts Press.

Levinger, G., & Snoek, J. D. (1972). *Attraction in relationship: A new look at interpersonal attraction.* New York: General Learning Press.

Levinson, D. J., Darrow, C. N., Klein, E. B., Levinson, M. H., & McKee, B. (1978). *The seasons of a man's life.* New York: Alfred A. Knopf.

Levy, L., & Herzog, N. (1974). Effects of population density and crowding on health and social adaptation in the Netherlands. *Journal of Health and Social Behavior, 15,* 228–237.

Lewin, K., Lippitt, R., & White, R. K. (1939). Patterns of aggressive behavior in experimentally created "social climates." *Journal of Social Psychology, 10,* 271–299.

Lewis, E. R., & Narens, P. M. (1985). Do frogs communicate with seismic signals? *Science, 227,* 187–189.

Lewis, S. A., Sloan, J. P., & Jones, S. K. (1978). Paradoxical sleep and depth perception. *Biological Psychology, 6,* 17–25.

Licklider, J. C. R. (1959). Three auditory theories. In I. S. Koch (Ed.), *Psychology: A study of a science* (Vol. 1). New York: McGraw Hill.

Licklider, J. C. R. (1961, March). *Audio warning signals for Air Force weapon systems.* USAF, WADD, TR 60–814.

Lieberson, S., & Silverman, A. R. (1965). The precipitants and underlying conditions of race riots. *American Sociological Review, 30,* 887–898.

Liebeskind, J. C., & Paul, L. A. (1977). Psychological and physiological mechanisms of pain. *Annual Review of Psychology, 28,* 41–60.

Liem, R., & Liem, J. (1979). Social support and stress: Some general issues and their application to the problem of unemployment. In L. Ferman & J. Gordus (Eds.), *Mental health and the economy.* Kalamazoo, MI: Upjohn Institute.

Liem, R., & Rayman, P. (1982). Health and social costs of unemployment: Research and policy considerations. *American Psychologist, 37,* 1116–1123.

Linder, D. E., Cooper, J., & Jones, E. E. (1967). Decision freedom as a determinant of the role of incentive magnitude in attitude change. *Journal of Personality and Social Psychology, 6,* 245–254.

Lindheim, R. (1970). Factors which determine hospital design. In H. M. Proshansky, W. H. Ittelson, & L. G. Rivlin (Eds.), *Environmental psychology: Man and his physical setting.* New York: Holt, Rinehart and Winston.

Linn, R. L. (1982). Admissions testing on trial. *American Psychologist, 37,* 279–291.

Lisk, R. D., Pretlow, R. A., & Friedman, S. (1969). Hormonal stimulation necessary for elicitation of maternal nest building in the mouse (*Mus musculus*). *Animal Behaviour, 17,* 730–737.

Locke, E. A. (1975). Personnel attitudes and motivation. *Annual Review of Psychology, 26,* 457–480.

Loftus, E. F., & Greene, E. (1980). Warning: Even memory for faces may be contagious. *Law & Human Behavior, 4*(4), 323–334.

Loftus, E. F., & Loftus, G. R. (1980). On the permanence of stored information in the human brain. *American Psychologist, 35*(5), 409–420.

London, M., & Bray, D. W. (1980). Ethical issues in testing and evaluation for personnel decisions. *American Psychologist, 35,* 890–901.

London, P. (1970). The rescuers: Motivational hypotheses about Christians who saved Jews from the Nazis. In J. Macaulay & L. Berkowitz (Eds.), *Altruism and helping behavior.* New York: Academic Press.

Lothstein, L. M. (1971). *Personal space in assault-prone male adolescent prisoners.* Doctoral dissertation, Duke University.

Lubin, B. (1983). Group therapy. In I. B. Weiner (Ed.), *Clinical methods in psychology* (2nd ed.). New York: Wiley-Interscience.

Luborsky, L., Chandler, M., Auerbach, A. H., Cohen, J., & Bachrach, H. M. (1971). Factors influencing the outcome of psychotherapy: A review of quantitative research. *Psychological Bulletin, 75,* 145–185.

Luce, G. G. (1970). *Biological rhythms in psychiatry and medicine.* Public Health Service Report, NIH.

Luchins, A. S. (1942). Mechanization in problem-solving: The effect of *Einstellung. Psychological Monographs, 54*(6, Whole No. 248).

Ludel, J. (1978). *Introduction to sensory processes.* San Francisco: Freeman.

Ludwig, A. M., Brandsma, J. M., Wilbur, C. B., Bendfeldt, F., & Jameson, D. H. (1972). The objective study of a multiple personality. *Archives of General Psychiatry, 26,* 298–310.

Lunneborg, C. E., & Lunneborg, P. W. (1969). Architecture school performance predicted from ASAT, intellective, and nonintellective measures. *Journal of Applied Psychology, 53,* 209–213.

Lurie 1981

Lyons, M. J., Faust, I. M., Hemmes, R. B., Buskirk, D. R., Hirsch, J., & Zabriskie, J. B. (1982). A virally induced obesity syndrome in mice. *Science, 216,* 82–85.

M

Maas, J. W. (1975). Biogenic amines and depression. Biochemical and pharmacological separation of two types of depression. *Archives of General Psychiatry, 32,* 1357–1361.

Machungwa, P. D., & Schmitt, N. (1983). Motivation in country. *APPCW, 68,* 31–47.

MacLusky, N. J., & Naftolin, F. (1981). Sexual differentiation of the central nervous system. *Science, 211,* 1294–1302.

MacNeil, M. K., & Sherif, M. (1976). Norm change over subject generations as a function of arbitrariness of prescribed norms. *Journal of Personality and Social Psychology, 34,* 762–773.

Maehr, M. L. (1974). Culture and achievement motivation. *American Psychologist, 29,* 887–896.

Maehr, M. L., & Kleiber, D. A. (1981). The graying of achievement motivation. *American Psychologist, 36,* 787–793.

Maehr, M. L., & Nicholls, J. G. (1980). Culture and achievement motivation: A second look. In N. Warren (Ed.), *Studies in cross cultural psychology* (Vol. 3). New York: Academic Press.

Malamuth, N. M., & Donnerstein, E. I. (1984). *Pornography and sexual aggression.* Orlando, FL: Academic Press.

Malamuth, N., Feshbach, S., & Jaffe, Y. (1977). *Journal of Personality and Social Psychology.*

Malan, D. H. (1976). *The frontier of brief psychotherapy.* New York: Plenum.

Malhotra, M. S., & Sengupta, J. (1965). Carrying of school bags by children. *Ergonomics, 8*(1), 55–60.

Malpass, R. S., & Devine, P. G. (1981). Eyewitness identification: Lineup instructions and the absence of the offender. *Journal of Applied Psychology, 66,* 482–489.

Mandler, G. (1985). *Cognitive psychology: An essay in cognitive science.* Hillsdale, NJ: Lawrence Erlbaum.

Mann, J. (1973). *Time-limited psychotherapy.* Cambridge, MA: Harvard University Press.

Mann, L., Newton, J. W., & Innes, J. M. (1982). A test between deindividuation and emergent norm theories of crowd aggression. *Journal of Personality and Social Psychology, 42,* 260–272.

Mantell, D. M. (1971). The potential for violence in Germany. *Journal of Social Issues, 27*(4), 101–112.

Marcia, J. E. (1976). Identity six years after: A follow-up study. *Journal of Youth and Adolescence, 5,* 145–160.

Marks, D., & Kammann, R. (1980). *The psychology of the psychic.* Buffalo, NY: Prometheus Books.

Marks, W. B., Dobelle, W. H., & MacNichol, E. F. (1964). Visual pigments of single primate cones. *Science, 143,* 1181–1183.

Marler, P., & Hamilton, W. (1966). *Mechanisms of animal behavior.* New York: Wiley.

Marshall, J. E., & Heslin, R. (1975). Boys and girls together: Sexual composition and the effect of density and group size on cohesiveness. *Journal of Personality and Social Psychology, 31,* 952–961.

Martin, G. B., & Clark, R. D. (1982). Distress crying in neonates: Species and peer specificity. *Developmental Psychology, 18*(1), 3–9.

Maslow, A. H. (1941). Deprivation, threat, and frustration. *Psychological Review, 48,* 364–366.

Maslow, A. H. (1954). *Motivation and personality.* New York: Harper and Row.

Masters, W. H., & Johnson, V. E. (1976). Principles of the new sex therapy. *American Journal of Psychiatry, 133,* 548–554.

Matarazzo, J. (1983). Computerized psychological testing. *Science.*

Matas, L., Arend, R. A., & Sroufe, L. A. (1978). Continuity in adaptation: Quality of attachment and later competence. *Child Development, 49,* 547–556.

Matson, J. L., Kazdin, A. E., & Esveldt-Dawson, K. (1980). Training interpersonal skills among mentally retarded and socially dysfunctional children. *Behaviour Research and Therapy, 18,* 419–427.

Maurer, D., & Salapatek, P. (1976). Developmental changes in the scanning of faces by young infants. *Child Development, 47,* 523–527.

Mausner, B. (1954). The effect of prior reinforcement on the interaction of observer pairs. *Journal of Abnormal and Social Psychology, 49,* 65–68.

Mayo, E. (1945). *The social problems of an industrial civilization.* Cambridge, MA: Harvard University, School of Business Administration.

McCall, R. B. (1985). The confluence model and theory. *Child Development, 56*(1), 217–218.

McClelland, D. C., Atkinson, J. W., Clark, R. A., & Lowell, E. I. (1953). *The achievement motive.* New York: Appleton-Century-Crofts.

McClelland, D. C., & Winter, D. (1969). *Motivating economic achievement.* New York: Free Press. (Paper edition 1971.)

McGuire, W. J. (1969). The nature of attitudes and attitude change. In G. Lindzey & E. Aronson (Eds.), *Handbook of social psychology.* Reading, MA: Addison-Wesley.

McKenna, R. J. (1972). Some effects of anxiety level and food cues on the eating behavior of obese and normal subjects: A comparison of the Schachterian and psychosomatic conceptions. *Journal of Personality and Social Psychology, 22,* 311–319.

McKenzie, R. E., Ehrisman, W. J., Montgomery, P. S., & Barnes, R. H. (1974). The treatment of headache by means of electroencephalographic biofeedback. *Headache, 13,* 164–172.

McKoon, G., Ratcliff, R., & Dell, G. S. (1985). The role of semantic information in episodic retrieval. *Journal of Experimental Psychology: Learning, Memory, and Cognition, 11*(4), 742–751.

McNeill, D. (1970). The development of language. In P. H. Mussen (Ed.), *Carmichael's manual of child psychology* (3rd ed.). New York: Wiley.

Meade, R. D. (1967). An experimental study of leadership in India. *Journal of Social Psychology, 72,* 35–43.

Mebert, C. J., & Michel, G. F. (1980). Handedness in artists. In J. Herron (Ed.), *Neuropsychology of left-handedness.* New York: Academic Press.

Meehl, P. E. (1950). On the circularity of the law of effect. *Psychological Bulletin, 47,* 52–75.

Meichenbaum, D. H. (1977). *Cognitive behavior modification.* New York: Plenum.

Meichenbaum, D. H., & Cameron, R. (1982). Cognitive-behavior therapy. In G. T. Wilson & C. M. Franks (Eds.), *Contemporary behavior therapy.* New York: Guilford.

Melzack, R., & Wall, P. D. (1965). Pain mechanisms: A new theory. *Science, 150,* 971–979.

Menzel, E. M. (1978). Cognitive mapping in chimpanzees. In S. H. Hulse, H. Fowler, & W. K. Honig (Eds.), *Cognitive processes in animal behavior.* Hillsdale, NJ: Erlbaum.

Menzel, E. W. (1973). Chimpanzee spatial memory organization. *Science, 182,* 943–945.

Messick, S. (1980). Test validity and the ethics of assessment. *American Psychologist, 35,* 1012–1027.

Meyners, R., & Wooster, C. (1979). *Sexual style: Facing and making choices about sex.* New York: Harcourt Brace Jovanovitch.

Milgram, S. (1961). Nationality and conformity. *Scientific American, 205*(6), 45–51.

Milgram, S. (1974). *Obedience to authority.* New York: Harper.

Milgram, S., & Toch, H. (1969). Collective behavior: Crowds and social movements. In G. Lindzey & E. Aronson (Eds.), *Handbook of social psychology* (Vol. 4). Reading, MA: Addison-Wesley.

Miller, G. A. (1956). The magical number seven, plus or minus two: Some limits on our capacity to process information. *Psychological Review, 63,* 81–97.

Miller, N. E. (1941). The frustration-aggression hypothesis. *Psychological Review, 48,* 337–342.

Miller, R. R., & Springer, A. D. (1973). Amnesia consolidation and retrieval. *Psychological Review, 80,* 69–70.

Milner, B. (1970). Memory and the temporal regions of the brain. In K. H. Pribram & D. E. Broadbent (Eds.), *Biology of memory.* New York: Academic Press.

Mineka, S., & Snowdon, C. T. (1978). Inconsistency and possible habituation of CCK induced satiety. *Physiology and Behavior, 21,* 65–72.

Mintz, A. (1951). Non-adaptive group behavior. *Journal of Abnormal and Social Psychology, 46,* 150–159.

Minuchin, S., Rosman, B., & Baker, L. (1978). *Psychosomatic families: Anorexia nervosa in context.* Cambridge, MA: Harvard University Press.

Mischel, W. (1979). On the interface of cognition and personality: Beyond the person-situation debate. *American Psychologist, 34,* 740–754.

Moe, J. L., Nacoste, R. W., & Insko, C. A. (1981). Belief versus race as determinants of discrimination: A study of southern adolescents in 1966 and 1979. *Journal of Personality and Social Psychology, 41,* 1031–1050.

Moltz, H., Lubin, M., Leon, M., & Numan, M. (1970). Hormonal induction of maternal behavior in the ovariectomized nulliparous rat. *Physiology and Behavior, 5,* 1373–1377.

Money, J., & Ehrhardt, A. A. (1972). *Man and woman, boy and girl.* Baltimore: Johns Hopkins Press.

Montgomery, R. L., Hinkle, S. W., & Enzie, R. F. (1976). Arbitrary norms and social change in high- and low-authoritarian societies. *Journal of Personality and Social Psychology, 33,* 698–708.

Moore, T. W. (1975). Exclusive early mothering and its alternatives: The outcomes to adolescence. *Scandinavian Journal of Psychology, 16,* 255–272.

Moran, J., & Desimone, R. (1985). Selective attention gates visual processing in the extrastriate cortex. *Science, 229,* 782–784.

Moray, N. (1959). Attention in dichotic listening: Affective cues and the influence of instructions. *Quarterly Journal of Experimental Psychology, 11,* 56–60.

Moray, N., Bates, A., & Barnett, I. (1965). Experiments on the four-eared man. *Journal of the Acoustical Society of America, 38,* 196–201.

Morell, P., & Norton, W. T. (1980, May). Myelin. *Scientific American,* 74–89.

Morris, W. N., Worchel, S., Bois, J. L., Pearson, J. A., Rountree, C. A., Samaha, G. M., Wachtler, J., & Wright, S. L. (1976). Collective coping with stress: Group reactions to fear, anxiety and ambiguity. *Journal of Personality and Social Psychology, 33,* 674–679.

Moscovici, S. (1974). Social influence: I. Conformity and social control. In C. Nemeth (Ed.), *Social psychology.* Chicago: Rand McNally.

Moscovici, S., Lage, E., & Naffrechoux, M. (1969). Influence of a consistent minority on the responses of a majority in a color perception task. *Sociometry, 32,* 365–380.

Moyer, K. E. (1976). *The psychobiology of aggression.* New York: Harper & Row.

Mummendey, A., & Mummendey, H. D. (1983). Aggressive behavior of soccer players as social interaction. In J. H. Goldstein (Ed.), *Sports violence.* New York: Springer-Verlag.

Munroe, R. L., & Munroe, R. H. (1972). Population density and affective relationships in three East African societies. *Journal of Social Psychology, 88,* 15–20.

Murray, H. A., et al. (1938). *Explorations in personality.* New York: Oxford.

Mussen, P. H., & Jones, M. C. (1957). Self-conceptions, motivations, and interpersonal attitudes of late- and early-maturing boys. *Child Development, 28,* 243–256.

N

Nahemow, L., & Lawton, M. P. (1975). Similarity and propinquity in friendship formation. *Journal of Personality and Social Psychology, 32,* 205–213.

Nathan, P. E. (1983). Failures in prevention. *American Psychologist, 38,* 459–467.

Nathan, P. E. (1984). The worksite as a setting for health promotion and positive lifestyle change. In N. E. Miller, J. D. Matarazzo, J. A. Herd, & S. M. Weiss (Eds.), *Behavioral health: A handbook of health enhancement and disease prevention.* New York: John Wiley & Sons.

National Coalition on TV Violence. (1983). *NCTV Newsletter.*

National Institute on Alcohol Abuse and Alcoholism. (1981). *Fourth special report to the U.S. Congress on alcohol and health.* Washington, DC: U.S. Government Printing Office.

Neary, R. S., & Zuckerman, M. (1976). Sensation seeking: Trait and state anxiety and the electrodermal orienting response. *Psychophysiology, 13,* 205–211.

Neimark, E. D. (1975). Intellectual development during adolescence. In F. D. Horowitz (Ed.), *Review of child development research* (Vol. 4). Chicago: University of Chicago Press.

Nelson, K. E. (1978). *Children's language* (Vol. 1). New York: Gardner Press.

Neugarten, B. L. (1968). *Middle age and aging.* Chicago: University of Chicago Press.

Neugarten, B. L. (1970). Dynamics of transition from middle age to old age: Adaptation and the life cycle. *Journal of Geriatric Psychiatry, 4,* 71–87.

Neugarten, B. L. (1971, December). Grow old along with me! The best is yet to be. *Psychology Today,* pp. 45–48.

Newcomb, T. M. (1952). Attitude development as a function of reference groups: The Bennington study. In G. Swanson, T. Newcomb, & E. Hartley (Eds.), *Readings in social psychology.* New York: Holt.

Newcomb, T. M. (1956). The prediction of interpersonal attraction. *American Psychologist, 11,* 575–586.

Newcomb, T. M. (1978). The acquaintance process: Looking mainly backward. *Journal of Personality and Social Psychology, 36,* 1075–1083.

Newell, A., & Simon, H. A. (1972). *Human problem solving.* Englewood Cliffs, NJ: Prentice-Hall.

Nicolaus, L. K., Cassel, J. F., Carlson, R. B., & Gustavson, C. R. (1983). Taste-aversion conditioning of crows to control predation on eggs. *Science, 220,* 212–214.

Norman, D. A. (1968). Toward a theory of memory and attention. *Psychological Review, 75,* 522–536.

Norman, D. A. (1969). Memory while shadowing. *Quarterly Journal of Experimental Psychology, 21,* 85–93.

Norman, D. A., & Fisher, D. (1982). Why alphabetic keyboards are not easy to use: Keyboard layout doesn't much matter. *Human Factors, 24*(5), 509–519.

Nuckols, T. E., & Banducci, R. (1974). Knowledge of occupations—is it important in occupational choice? *Journal of Counseling Psychology, 21,* 191–195.

O

O'Neal, E. C. (1971). Influence of future choice importance and arousal upon the halo effect. *Journal of Personality and Social Psychology, 19,* 334–340.

Olds, J. (1958). Self stimulation of the brain. *Science, 127,* 315–323.

Olds, J., & Milner, P. (1954). Positive reinforcement produced by electrical stimulation of septal area and other regions of rat brain. *Journal of Comparative and Physiological Psychology, 47,* 419–427.

Olds, M. E., & Fobes, J. L. (1981). The central basis of motivation: Intracranial self-stimulation studies. *Annual Review of Psychology, 32,* 523–574.

Olton, D. S., & Noonberg, A. R. (1980). *Biofeedback: Clinical applications in behavioral medicine.* Englewood Cliffs, NJ: Prentice-Hall.

Oskamp, S. (1977). *Attitudes and opinions.* Englewood Cliffs, NJ: Prentice-Hall.

Osterberg, G. (1935). Topography of the layer of rods and cones in the human retina. *Acta Ophthalmologica,* Supplement.

Over, R. (1982). Research productivity and impact of male and female psychologists. *American Psychologist, 37*(1), 24–31.

Over, R. (1982). Collaborative research and publication in psychology. *American Psychologist, 37*(9), 996–1001.

Overton, D. (1964). State-dependent or "dissociated" learning produced with pentobarbital. *Journal of Comparative and Physiological Psychology, 57,* 3–12.

P

Palazzoili-Selvini, M., Boscolo, L., Cecchin, G., & Prata, G. (1978). *Paradox and counterparadox: A new model in the therapy of the family in schizophrenic transaction.* New York: Jason Aronson.

Parish, T. S., & Wigle, S. E. (1985). A longitudinal study of the impact of parental divorce on adolescents' evaluations of self and parents. *Adolescence, 20*(77), 239–244.

Pashler, H. (1984). Processing stages in overlapping tasks: Evidence for a central bottleneck. *Journal of Exp. Psych.: Human Perception and Performance, 10*(3), 358–377.

Paul, G. L., & Lentz, R. J. (1977). *Psychosocial treatment of chronic mental patients: Milieu vs. social-learning programs.* Cambridge, MA: Harvard University Press.

Paul, S. M., Hulihan-Giblin, B., & Skolnick, P. (1982). (+)-Amphetamine binding to rat hypothalamus: Relation to anorexic potency of phenylethylamines. *Science, 218,* 487–490.

Pavlov, I. P. (1906). The scientific investigation of the psychical faculties or processes in the higher animals. *Science, 24,* 613–619.

Pavlov, I. P. (1927). *Conditioned reflexes.* London: Clarendon Press.

Penfield, W. (1975). *The mystery of the mind.* Princeton, NJ: Princeton University Press.

Perlman, D., & Cozby, P. C. (1983). *Social psychology.* New York: Holt, Rinehart and Winston.

Perls, F. S. (1969). *Gestalt therapy verbatim.* Lafayette, CA: Real People Press.

Pervin, L. A. (1970). *Personality: Theory, assessment and research.* New York: Wiley.

Peskin, H. (1967). Pubertal onset and ego functioning. *Journal of Abnormal Psychology, 72,* 1–15.

Pessin, J. (1933). The comparative effects of social and mechanical stimulation on memorizing. *American Journal of Psychology, 45,* 263–270.

Peterson, L. R., & Peterson, M. J. (1959). Short-term retention of individual verbal items. *Journal of Experimental Psychology, 58,* 193–198.

Pfaff, D. W. (Ed.). (1985). *Taste, olfaction, and the central nervous system.* New York: Rockefeller University Press.

Pfaffman, C. (1955). Gustatory nerve impulses in rat, cat, and rabbit. *Journal of Neurophysiology, 18,* 429–440.

Pfaffman, C., Frank, M., & Norgren, R. (1979). Neural mechanisms and behavioral aspects of taste. *Annual Review of Psychology, 30,* 283–325.

Piaget, J. (1926). *Language & thought of the child.* London: Routledge & Kegan Paul.

Piaget, J. (1976). *The grasp of consciousness.* Cambridge, MA: Harvard University Press.

Pine, C. J. (1985). Anxiety and eating behavior in obese and nonobese American Indians and white Americans. *Journal of Personality and Social Psychology, 49*(3), 774–780.

Plomin, R., Loehlin, J. C., & DeFries, J. C. (1985). Genetic and environmental components of "environmental" influences. *Developmental Psychology, 21,* 391–402.

Plotkin, W. B. (1979). The alpha experience revisited. *Psychological Bulletin, 86,* 1132–1148.

Polit-O'Hara, D., & Kahn, J. R. (1985). Communication and contraceptive practices in adolescent couples. *Adolescence, 20,* 33–43.

Porter, L. W. (1961). A study of perceived need satisfactions in bottom and middle management jobs. *Journal of Applied Psychology, 45,* 1–10.

Porter, L. W., & Lawler, E. E. (1968). *Managerial attitudes and performance.* Homewood, IL: Irwin.

Powley, T. L. (1977), The ventromedial hypothalamus syndrome, satiety, and a cephalic phase hypothesis. *Psychological Review, 84,* 89–126.

Pratt, J. G. (1973). *ESP research today: A study of developments in parapsychology since 1960.* Metuchen, NJ: Scarecrow Press

Premack, A. J., & Premack, D. (1982). Teaching language to an ape. In W. S-Y. Wang (Ed.), *Human communication: Language & its psychobiological bases.* San Francisco: Freeman.

Premack, D. (1959). Toward empirical behavioral laws: I. Positive reinforcement. *Psychological Review, 66,* 219–33.

Premack, D. (1965). Reinforcement theory. In M. R. Jones (Ed.), *Nebraska Symposium on Motivation: 1965.* Lincoln: University of Nebraska Press.

Premack, D. (1971). Language in chimpanzee? *Science, 172,* 808–872.

Pritchard, R. D., Dunnette, M. D., & Jorgenson, D. O. (1972). Effects of perceptions of equity and inequity on worker performance and satisfaction. *Journal of Applied Psychology Monograph, 56,* 75–94.

Proshansky, H. M., Ittelson, W. H., & Rivlin, L. G. (Eds.). (1970). *Environmental psychology: Man and his physical setting.* New York: Holt, Rinehart, Winston.

Pruitt, D. G. (1971). Conclusions: Toward an understanding of choice shifts in group discussions. *Journal of Personality and Social Psychology, 20,* 495–510.

Q

Quitkin, F., Rifkin, A., Kane, J., Ramos-Lorenzo, J. R., & Klein, D. F. (1978). Prophylactic effect of lithium and imipramine in unipolar and bipolar II patients: A preliminary report. *American Journal of Psychiatry, 135,* 570–572.

R

Raczkowski, D., Kalat, J. W., & Nebes, R. (1974). Reliability and validity of some handedness questionnaire items. *Neuropsychologia, 12,* 43–47.

Ratcliff, R., & McKoon, G. (1982). Speed and accuracy in the processing of false statements about semantic information. *Journal of Experimental Psychology: Learning, Memory and Cognition, 8,* 16–36.

Ray, W. J., & Cole, H. W. (1985). EEG alpha activity reflects attentional demands, and beta activity reflects emotional and cognitive processes. *Science, 228,* 750–752.

Rayman, P., & Bluestone. (1982). *Private and social response to job loss.* Rockville, MD: National Institute of Mental Health. Center for Work and Mental Health.

Razran, G. H. S. (1939). A quantitative study of meaning by a conditioned salivary technique (semantic conditioning). *Science, 90,* 89–90.

Rees, H. D., Brogan, L. L., Entingh, D. J., Dunn, A., Shinkman, P. G., Damstra-Entingh, T., Wilson, J. E., & Glassman, E. (1974). Effect of sensory stimulation on the uptake and incorporation of radioactive lysine into protein of mouse brain and liver. *Brain Research, 68,* 143–156.

Reid, J. E., & Inbau, F. E. (1977). *Truth and deception: The polygraph ("lie detection") technique* (2nd ed.). Baltimore: Williams and Wilkins.

Reitman, J. S. (1971). Mechanisms of forgetting in short term memory. *Cognitive Psychology, 2,* 185–195.

Rescorla, R. A., & Holland, P. C. (1982). Behavioral studies of associative learning in animals. *Annual Review of Psychology, 33,* 265–308.

Reynolds, D. K. (1984). Motivation. In R. J. Corsini (Ed.), *Encyclopedia of psychology* (Vol. 2). New York: Wiley.

Richards, R. A. (1976). A comparison of selected Guilford and Wallach-Kogan creative thinking tests in conjunction with measures of intelligence. *Journal of Creative Behavior, 10,* 151–164.

Riegle, D. W., Jr. (1982). The psychological and social effects of unemployment. *American Psychologist, 37,* 1113–1115.

Rife, D. C. (1940). Handedness, with special reference to twins. *Genetics, 25,* 178–186.

Robbins, M. J., & Meyer, D. R. (1970). Motivational control of retrograde amnesia. *Journal of Experimental Psychology, 84,* 220–225.

Rodieck, R. W., & Stone, J. (1965). Response of cat retinal ganglion cells to moving visual patterns. *Journal of Neurophysiology, 28,* 819–832.

Rodin, J. (1981). Current status of the internal-external hypothesis for obesity: What went wrong? *American Psychologist, 36*(4), 361–372.

Rodin, J., & Slowchower, J. (1976). Externality in the nonobese: The effects of environmental responsiveness on weight. *Journal of Personality and Social Psychology, 29,* 557–565.

Roethlisberger, F. J., & Dickson, W. J. (1939). *Management and the worker.* Cambridge, MA: Harvard University Press.

Roffwarg, H. P., Muzio, J. N., & Dement, W. C. (1966). The ontogenetic development of the sleep-dream cycle in the human. *Science, 152,* 604–619.

Rogers, C. R. (1942). *Counseling and psychotherapy*. Boston: Houghton-Mifflin.

Rogers, C. R. (1961). *On becoming a person*. Boston: Houghton-Mifflin.

Rokeach, M., Smith, P. W., & Evans, R. I. (1960). Two kinds of prejudice or one? In M. Rokeach (Ed.), *The open and closed mind*. New York: Basic Books.

Romano, J. (1977). On the nature of schizophrenia: Changes in the observer as well as the observed (1932–77). *Schizophrenia Bulletin, 3*, 532–559.

Rosch, E. H. (1973). On the internal structure of perceptual and semantic categories. In T. E. Moore (Ed.), *Cognitive development and the acquisition of language*. New York: Academic Press.

Rosch, E. H. (1975). Cognitive representations of semantic categories. *Journal of Experimental Psychology, 104*, 192–233.

Rose, R. M., Bernstein, I. S., & Gordon, T. P. (1975). Consequences of social conflict on plasma testerone levels in Rhesus monkeys. *Psychosomatic Medicine, 37*, 50–61.

Rose, R. M., Bourne, P. G., Poe, R. O., Mougey, E. H., Collins, D. R., & Mason, J. W. (1969). Androgen responses to stress: II. Excretion of testosterone, epitestosterone, androsterone, and etiocholanolone during basic combat training and under attack. *Psychosomatic Medicine, 31*, 418–436.

Rose, S. D., & LeCroy, C. W. (1983). Group therapy: A behavioral and cognitive perspective. In C. E. Walker (Ed.), *Handbook of clinical psychology*. Homewood, IL: Dorsey.

Rosenthal, M. K. (1973). The study of infant-environment interaction: Some comments on trends and methodology. *Journal of Child Psychology and Psychiatry, 14*, 301–317.

Rosenthal, M. K. (1982). Vocal dialogues in the neonatal period. *Developmental Psychology, 18*, 17–21.

Rosenthal, N. E. (1985). *American J. Psychiatry*.

Rosenthal, R. (1963). On the social psychology experiment. *American Scientist, 51*, 268–283.

Rosenthal, R. (1976). *Experimenter effects in behavioral research*. New York: Irvington Publications.

Rosenthal, T. L. (1982). Social learning theory. In G. T. Wilson & C. M. Franks (Eds.), *Contemporary behavior therapy*. New York: Guilford.

Rosenzweig, M. R. (1984). Experience, memory and the brain. *American Psychologist*, 365–376.

Ross, D. M., Ross, S. A., & Evans, T. A. (1971). The modification of extreme social withdrawal by modeling with guided participation. *Journal of Behavior Therapy and Experimental Psychiatry, 2*, 273–280.

Ross, M., Layton, B., Erickson, B., & Schopler, J. (1973). Affect, facial regard, and reactions to crowding. *Journal of Personality and Social Psychology, 28*, 69–76.

Ross, R. T., & Randich, A. (1984). Unconditioned stress-induced analgesia following exposure to brief footshock. *J. Exp. Psych.: Animal Behavior Processes, 10*(2), 127–137.

Routtenberg, A., & Lindy, J. (1965). Effects of the availability of rewarding septal and hypothalamic stimulation on barpressing for food under conditions of deprivation. *Journal of Comparative and Physiological Psychology, 60*, 158–161.

Rowland, N. E., & Antelman, S. M. (1976). Stress-induced hyperphagia and obesity in rats: A possible model for understanding human obesity. *Science, 191*, 310–312.

Rubenstein, C. (1982). Wellness is all: A report on *Psychology Today's* survey of beliefs about health. *Psychology Today, 16*(10), 26–37.

Rubin, Z. (1970). Measurement of romantic love. *Journal of Personality and Social Psychology, 16*, 265–273.

Rude, G. (1964). *The crowd in history*. New York: Wiley.

Rumbaugh, D. M., Gill, T. V., & Von Glasersfeld, E. C. (1973). Reading and sentence completion by a chimpanzee. *Science, 182*, 1468–1472.

Rumelhart, D. E., & Norman, D. A. (1982). Simulating a skilled typist: A study of skilled cognitive-motor performance. *Cognitive Science, 6*, 1–36.

Russek, M. (1975). Current hypotheses in the control of feeding behaviour. In G. J. Morgenson & F. R. Calaresu (Eds.), *Neural integration of physiological mechanisms and behaviour*. Toronto: University of Toronto Press.

Russell, J. A. (1980). A circumplex model of affect. *Journal of Personality and Social Psychology, 39*, 1161–1178.

S

Sachar, E. J., & Baron, M. (1979). The biology of affective disorders. *Annual Review of Neuroscience, 2*, 505–518.

Sagan, C. (1977). *The dragons of Eden: Speculations on the evolution of human intelligence*. New York: Ballantine.

Sagi, A., & Hoffman, M. L. (1976). Empathic distress in the newborn. *Developmental Psychology, 12*, 175–176.

Salapatek, P. (1975). Pattern perception in early infancy. In L. B. Cohen & P. Salapatek (Eds.), *Infant perception: From sensation to cognition* (Vol. 1). New York: Academic Press.

Salmon, V. J., & Geist, S. H. (1943). The effect of androgen upon libido in women. *Journal of Clinical Endocrinology and Metabolism, 3*, 275–288.

Samuel, A. L. (1963). Some studies in machine learning using the game of checkers. In E. A. Feigenbaum & J. Feldman (Eds.), *Computers and thought*. New York: McGraw-Hill.

Sanada, T., & Norbeck, E. (1975). Prophecy continues to fail: A Japanese sect. *Journal of Cross-Cultural Psychology, 6*, 331–345.

Sanchez-Craig, M., & Annis, H. M. (1983). *Initial evaluation of a program for early-stage problem drinkers: Randomization to abstinence and controlled drinking*. Paper presented at the meeting of the American Psychological Association.

Sanders, G. S., & Simmons, W. L. (1983). Use of hypnosis to enhance eyewitness accuracy: Does it work? *Journal of Applied Psychology, 68*, 70–77.

Sanik, M. M., & Stafford, K. (1985). Adolescent's contribution to household production: Male and female differences. *Adolescence, 20*(77), 207–215.

Satz, P. (1972). Pathological left-handedness: An explanatory model. *Cortex, 8*, 121–135.

Satz, P. (1980). Incidence of aphasia in left-handers: A test of some hypothetical models of cerebral speech organization. In J. Herron (Ed.), *Neuropsychology of left-handedness*. New York: Academic Press.

Scarr, S. (1985). Constructing psychology: Making facts and fables for our times. *American Psychologist, 40*, 499–512.

Schachter, S. (1959). *The psychology of affiliation*. Stanford, CA: Stanford University Press.

Schachter, S. (1964). The interaction of cognitive and physiological determinants of emotional state. In L. Berkowitz (Ed.), *Advances in experimental social psychology* (Vol. 1). New York: Academic Press.

Schachter, S. (1971). *Emotion, obesity, and crime*. New York: Academic Press.

Schachter, S. (1982). Recidivism and the self-cure of smoking and obesity. *American Psychologist, 37*, 436–444.

Schachter, S., & Gross, L. (1968). Manipulated time and eating behavior. *Journal of Personality and Social Psychology, 10*, 98–106.

Schachter, S., & Singer, J. E. (1962). Cognitive, social, and physiological determinants of emotional state. *Psychological Review, 69*, 379–399.

Schaie, K. W. (1979). The primary mental abilities in adulthood: An exploration in the development of psychometric intelligence. In P. B. Baltes & O. G. Brim, Jr. (Eds.), *Life span development and behavior*. New York: Academic Press.

Scheibel, M. E., & Scheibel, A. B. (1975). Structural changes in the aging brain. In H. Brody, D. Harman, & J. M. Ordy (Eds.), *Aging* (Vol. 1). New York: Raven Press.

Scherer, S. E. (1974). Proxemic behavior of primary school children as a function of their socioeconomic class and subculture. *Journal of Personality and Social Psychology, 29,* 800–805.

Schifter, D. E., & Ajzen, I. (1985). Intention, perceived control, and weight loss: An application of the theory of planned behavior. *Journal of Personality and Social Psychology, 49*(3), 843–851.

Schildkraut, J. J. (1974). Biogenic amines and affective disorders. *Annual Review of Medicine, 25,* 333–348.

Schildkraut, J. J. (1978). Current status of the catecholamine hypothesis of affective disorders. In M. A. Lipton, A. Di Mascio, & K. F. Killam (Eds.), *Psychopharmacology: A generation of progress.* New York: Raven Press.

Schmidt, F. L., Hunter, J. E., McKenzie, R. C., & Muldrow, T. W. (1979). Impact of valid selection procedures on work-force productivity. *Journal of Applied Psychology, 64,* 609–626.

Schmitt, F. O., Dev, P., & Smith, B. H. (1976). Electrotonic processing of information by brain cells. *Science, 193,* 114–120.

Schneider, S. (1982). The computer in a stop smoking clinic. *Computers in Psychiatry/Psychology, 4*(2), 19–20.

Schneider, W., & Shiffrin, R. M. (1977). Controlled and automatic human information processing. I. Detection, search and attention. *Psychological Review, 84,* 1–66.

Schopler, J., & Stockdale, J. E. (1977). An interference analysis of crowding. *Environmental Psychology and Nonverbal Behavior, 1,* 81–88.

Schwartz, G. M., Izard, C. E., & Ansul, S. E. (1985). The 5 month-old's ability to discriminate facial expressions of emotion. *Infant Behavior and Development, 8*(1), 65–77.

Schwartz, M. (1984). Integrating computer and videotape/videodisc, part I. *Computer in Psychiatry/Psychology, 6,* 7–13.

Sears, R. R. (1977). Sources of life satisfactions of the Terman gifted men. *American Psychologist, 32,* 119–128.

Segall, M. H., Campbell, D. T., & Herskovits, M. J. (1966). *The influence of culture on visual perception.* Indianapolis: Bobbs-Merrill.

Seidenberg, M., & Petitto, L. (1979). Signing behavior in apes: A critical review. *Cognition, 7,* 177–215.

Seligman, M. E. P. (1975). *Helplessness.* San Francisco: Freeman.

Selman, R. L. (1980). *The growth of interpersonal understanding: Developmental and clinical analyses.* New York: Academic Press.

Selye, H. (1977). *The stress of my life.* Toronto: McClelland & Stewart.

Shaner, J. M., Peterson, K. L., & Roscoe, B. (1985). Older adolescent females knowledge of child development norms. *Adolescence, 20*(77), 53–59.

Shaw, M. E. (1964). Communication networks. In L. Berkowitz (Ed.), *Advances in experimental social psychology* (Vol. 1). New York: Academic Press.

Shaw, M. E. (1976). An overview of small group behavior. In J. W. Thibaut, J. T. Spence, & R. C. Carson (Eds.), *Contemporary topics in social psychology.* Morristown, NJ: General Learning Press.

Sheehy, G. (1976). *Passages.* New York: Bantam.

Shepard, R. N. (1967). Recognition memory for words, sentences, and pictures. *Journal of Verbal Learning and Verbal Behavior, 6,* 156–163.

Sherif, M. (1936). *The psychology of social norms.* New York: Harper.

Sherif, M., Harvey, O. J., White, B. J., Hood, W. R., & Sherif, C. W. (1961). *Intergroup conflict and cooperation: The Robber's Cave experiment.* Norman: University of Oklahoma Press.

Shiffrin, R. M. (1970). Forgetting: Trace erosion or retrieval failure? *Science, 168,* 1601–1603.

Shotland, R. L., & Heinold, W. D. (1985). Bystander response to arterial bleeding: Helping skills, the decision-making process, and differentiating the helping response. *JPSP, 49,* 347–356.

Sibatani, A. (1980, December). The Japanese brain. *Science 80,* pp. 21–28.

Siddle, D. A., Morish, R. B., White, K. D., & Mangen, G. L. (1969). Relation of visual sensitivity to extraversion. *Journal of Experimental Research in Personality, 3,* 264–267.

Sidtis, J. J. (1984). Music, pitch perception, and the mechanisms of cortical hearing. In M. S. Gazzaniga (Ed.), *Handbook of cognitive neuroscience.* New York: Plenum Press.

Siegel, S., Hinson, R. E., Krank, M. D., & McCully, J. (1982). Heroin "overdose" death: Contribution of drug-associated environmental cues. *Science, 216,* 436–437.

Silveira, J. (1971). *Incubation: The effect of interruption timing and length on problem solution and quality of problem processing.* Unpublished doctoral dissertation, University of Oregon.

Simmel, G. (1955). *Conflict and the web of group affiliations.* Glencoe, IL: Free Press.

Simner, M. L. (1971). Newborn's response to the cry of another infant. *Developmental Psychology, 5,* 136–150.

Simpson, I. H. (1967). Patterns of socialization into professions: The case of student nurses. *Sociological Inquiry, 37,* 47–53.

Sirigano, S. W., & Lackman, M. E. (1985). Personality change during the transition to parenthood: The role of perceived infant temperament. *Developmental Psychology, 21,* 558–567.

Sitaram, N., Weingartner, H., & Gillin, J. C. (1978). Human serial learning: Enhancement with arecholine and choline and impairment with scopolamine. *Science, 201,* 274–276.

Skinner, B. F. (1938). *The behavior of organisms.* New York: Appleton-Century-Crofts.

Skinner, B. F. (1948). Superstition in the pigeon. *J. Experimental Psychology, 38,* 168–172.

Skinner, B. F. (1953). *Science and human behavior.* New York: MacMillan.

Skinner, B. F. (1957). *Verbal behavior.* New York: Appleton-Century-Crofts.

Skinner, B. F. (1974). *About behaviorism.* New York: Knopf.

Sleight, R. B. (1948). The effect of instrument dial shape on legibility. *J. Applied Psychology, 32,* 170–188.

Sloan, L. R. (1979). The function and impact of sports for fans. In J. H. Goldstein (Ed.), *Sports, games, and play.* Hillsdale, NJ: Lawrence Erlbaum (Wiley).

Sloane, M., & Blake, R. (1984). Selective adaptation of monocular and binocular neurons in human vision. *Journal of Exp. Psych.: Human Perception and Performance, 10*(3), 406–412.

Sloane, R. B., Staples, F. R., Cristol, A. H., Yorkston, N. J., & Whipple, K. (1975). *Psychotherapy versus behavior therapy.* Cambridge, MA: Harvard University Press.

Slobin, D. I. (1971, May). *Cognitive prerequisites for the development of grammar.* Paper presented at the meeting of the Southeastern Conference on Linguistics, University of Maryland.

Slobin, D. I. (1979). *Psycholinguistics* (2nd ed.). Glenview, IL: Scott, Foresman.

Smart, R. G., & Blair, N. L. (1978). Test-retest reliability and validity information for a high school drug use questionnaire. *Drug and Alcohol Dependence, 3,* 265–271.

Smith, C. R., Williams, L., & Willis, R. H. (1967). Race, sex, and belief as determinants of friendship acceptance. *Journal of Personality and Social Psychology, 5,* 127–137.

Smith, E. E., Shoben, E. J., & Rips, L. J. (1974). Structure and process in semantic memory: A featural model for semantic decisions. *Psychological Review, 81,* 214–241.

Smith, G. P., & Gibbs, J. (1976). Cholescystokinin and satiety: Theoretic and therapeutic implications. In D. Novin, W. Wyrwicka, & G. Bray (Eds.), *Hunger: Basic mechanisms and clinical implications.* New York: Raven.

Snarey, J. R. (1985). Cross-cultural universality of social-moral development: A critical review of Kohlbergian research. *Psychological Bulletin, 97*(2), 202–232.

Snarey, J. R., Reimer, J., & Kohlberg, L. (1985). Development of social-moral reasoning among kibbutz adolescents: A longitudinal cross-cultural study. *Developmental Psychology, 21,* 3–17.

Snyder, M., & DeBono, K. G. (1985). Appeals to image and claims about quality: Understanding the psychology of advertising. *JPSP, 49,* 586–597.

Society today. (1971). Del Mar, CA: CRM Books.

Solomon, R. L. (1980). The opponent process theory of acquired motivation. *American Psychologist, 35,* 691–712.

Solomon, R. L., & Corbit, J. D. (1974). An opponent process theory of motivation: I. Temporal dynamics of affect. *Psychological Review, 81,* 119–145.

Sommer, R. (1959). Studies in personal space. *Sociometry, 22,* 247–260.

Sommer, R. (1967). Small group ecology. *Psychological Bulletin, 67,* 145–152.

Sonderegger, T. B. (1970). Intracranial stimulation and maternal behavior. *Proceedings of the Annual Convention of the American Psychological Association, 5*(Pt. 1), 245–246.

Sorensen, R. C. (1973). *Adolescent sexuality in contemporary America.* New York: World Publishing Co.

Spear, N. E. (1979). Experimental analysis of infantile amnesia. In J. F. Kihlstrom & F. J. Evans (Eds.), *Functional disorders of memory.* Hillsdale, NJ: Erlbaum Associates.

Spence, J. T. (1985). Achievement American style: The rewards and costs of individualism. *American Psychologist, 40,* 1285–1295.

Spence, K. W. (1956). *Behavior theory and conditioning.* New Haven, CT: Yale University Press.

Sperling, G. (1960). The information available in brief visual presentations. *Psychological Monographs, 74,* 1–29.

Sperry, R. W. (1974). Lateral specialization in the surgically separated hemispheres. In F. O. Schmitt & F. G. Worden (Eds.), *The neurosciences: Third study program.* Cambridge, MA: MIT Press.

Sperry, R. W. (1982). Some effects of disconnecting the cerebral hemispheres. *Science, 217,* 1223–1226.

Spinetta, J. J., & Rigler, D. (1977). The child-abusing parent: A psychological review. In R. Kalmar (Ed.), *Child abuse: Perspectives on diagnosis, treatment and prevention.* Dubuque, IA: Kendall/Hunt.

Spitz, C. J., Gold, A. R., & Adams, D. B. (1975). Cognitive and hormonal factors affecting coital frequency. *Archives of Sexual Behavior, 4,* 249–264.

Sroufe, L. A. (1985). Attachment classification from the perspective of infant care-giver relationships and infant temperament. *Child Development, 56*(1), 1–14.

Staats, A. W. (1971). Linguistic-mentalistic theory versus an explanatory S-R learning theory of language development. In D. Slobin (Ed.), *The ontogenesis of grammar.* New York: Academic Press.

Stacks, J. F. (1983). Plain vanilla, but very good. *Time, 122*(2), 44–45.

Stanley, J. C. (1976). Identifying and nurturing the intellectually gifted. *Gifted Child Quarterly, 20*(1), 66–75.

Stapp, J., Tucker, A. M., & VandenBos, G. R. (1985). Census of psychological personnel: 1983. *American Psychologist, 40,* 1317–1351.

Steele, B. F., & Pollock. (1968). A psychiatric study of parents who abuse infants and small children. In R. E. Helfer & C. H. Kempe (Eds.), *The battered child.* Chicago: University of Chicago Press.

Steiner, I. D. (1972). *Group process and productivity.* New York: Academic Press.

Stelmack, R. M., & Campbell, K. B. (1974). Extraversion and auditory sensitivity to high and low frequency. *Perceptual and Motor Skills, 38,* 875–879.

Steptoe, A. (1981). *Psychological factors in cardiovascular disorders.* New York: Academic Press.

Stern, P. C. (1976). Effect of incentives and education on resource conservation decisions in a simulated commons dilemma. *Journal of Personality and Social Psychology, 34,* 1285–1292.

Sternberg, R. J. (1985). Implicit theories of intelligence, creativity, and wisdom. *Journal of Personality and Social Psychology, 49*(3), 607–627.

Sternberg, R. J., & Grajek, S. (1984). The nature of love. *JPSP, 47,* 312–329.

Sternberg, S. (1966). High-speed scanning in human memory. *Science, 153,* 652–654.

Sternberg, S. (1967). Two operations in character-recognition: Some evidence from reaction-time measurements. *Perception and Psychophysics, 2,* 45–53.

Sternberg, S. (1969). Mental processes revealed by reaction-time experiments. *American Scientist, 57,* 421–457.

Stevens, D. P., & Truss, C. V. (1985). Stability and change in adult personality over 12 and 20 years. *Developmental Psychology, 21,* 568–584.

Stogdill, R. M. (1948). Personal factors associated with leadership: A survey of the literature. *Journal of Psychology, 25,* 35–71.

Stokols, D. (1972). On the distinction between density and crowding: Some implications for future research. *Psychological Review, 79,* 275–277.

Stoner, J. A. F. (1961). *A comparison of individual and group decisions involving risk.* Unpublished master's thesis, Massachusetts Institute of Technology.

Stout, R. L. (1974). Modeling and the Michigan experimental simulation supervisor: An overview and some prospects. *Behavior Research Methods & Instrumentation, 6*(2), 121–123.

Straus, M. A., Gelles, R. J., & Steinmetz, S. K. (1979). *Behind closed doors.* Garden City, NY: Doubleday.

Streissguth, A. P., Landesman-Dwyer, S., Martin, J. C., & Smith, D. W. (1980). Teratogenic effects of alcohol in humans and laboratory animals. *Science, 209,* 353–361.

Stricker, E. M. (1980). Thirst and sodium appetite after colloid treatment in rats: Effects of sodium deprivation. *Journal of Comparative and Physiological Psychology.*

Strube, M. J., Miles, M. E., & Finch, W. H. (1981). The social facilitation of a simple task: Field tests of alternative explanations. *Personality and Social Psychology Bulletin, 7,* 701–707.

Suls, J. M., & Miller, R. L. (1977). *Social comparison processes.* New York: Wiley.

Suomi, S. J., & Harlow, H. F. (1972). Social rehabilitation of isolate-reared monkeys. *Developmental Psychology, 6,* 487–496.

Super, D. E. (1980). A life-span, life-space, approach to career development. *Journal of Vocational Behavior, 13,* 282–298.

Super, D. E. (1985). Coming of age in Middletown. *American Psychologist, 40*(4), 405–414.

Swanson, J. M., & Kinsbourne, M. (1976). Stimulant-related state-dependent learning in hyperactive children. *Science, 192,* 1354–1357.

T

Takahashi, J. S., & Zatz, M. (1982). Regulation of circadian rhythmicity. *Science, 217,* 1104–1111.

Tanner, I. (1976). *The gift of grief.* New York: Hawthorne Books.

Targ, R., & Puthoff, H. (1977). *Mind-reach.* New York: Delacorte Press.

Taylor, F. W. (1911). *Scientific management.* New York: Harper.

Terborg, J. R., Castore, C., & DeNinno, J. A. (1976). A longitudinal field investigation of the impact of group composition on group performance and cohesion. *Journal of Personality and Social Psychology, 34,* 782–790.

Terman, L. M. (1925). *Genetic studies of genius: Mental and physical traits of a thousand gifted children* (Vol. 1). Stanford, CA: Stanford University Press.

Terrace, H. S. (1985). In the beginning was the "name." *American Psychologist, 40*(9), 1011–1028.

Terrace, H. S., Petitto, L. A., Sanders, D. L., & Bever, T. G. (1979). Can an ape create a sentence? *Science, 206,* 891–902.

Tetlock, P. E. (1979). Identifying victims of groupthink from public statements of decision makers. *Journal of Personality and Social Psychology, 37,* 1314–1324.

Thibaut, J. W., & Kelley, H. H. (1959). *The social psychology of groups.* New York: Wiley.

Thibaut, J. W., & Kelley, H. H. (1978). *Interpersonal relations.* New York: Wiley.

Thomas, L. (1974). *Lives of a cell: Notes of a biology watcher.* New York: Viking Press.

Thompson, R. F., Patterson, M. M., & Berger, T. W. (1978). Associative learning in the mammalian nervous system. In T. J. Teyler (Ed.), *Brain and learning.* Stamford, CT: Greylock Publishers.

Thorndike, E. L. (1931). *Human learning.* New York: Century.

Thorndike, E. L., et al. (1928). *Adult learning.* New York: Macmillan.

Thornton, G. C., III, & Zorich, S. (1980). Training to improve observer accuracy. *Journal of Applied Psychology, 65,* 351–354.

Thurstone, L. L. (1938). Primary mental abilities. *Psychometric Monographs,* No. 1.

Tilley, A. J., & Empson, J. A. C. (1978). REM sleep and memory consolidation. *Biological Psychology, 6,* 293–300.

Tinbergen, N. (1951). *The study of instinct.* Oxford: Oxford University Press.

Tizard, B. (1974). *Early childhood education—A review discussion of current research in Britain.* Windsor, England: NFER.

Tolman, C. W., & Wilson, G. T. (1965). Social feeding in domestic chicks. *Animal Behavior, 13,* 134–142.

Tolman, E. C. (1932). *Purposive behavior in animals and men.* New York: Appleton.

Tolman, E. C., & Honzik, C. H. (1930). Insight in rats. *Univ. Calif. Publ. Psychol., 4,* 215–232.

Tomkins, S. S. (1981a). The role of facial response in the experience of emotion: A reply to Tourangeau and Ellsworth. *Journal of Personality and Social Psychology, 40,* 355–357.

Tomkins, S. S. (1981b). The quest for primary motives: Biography and autobiography of an idea. *Journal of Personality and Social Psychology, 41,* 306–329.

Tornatsky, L. G., & Solomon, T. (with T. Bikson, R. Cole, L. Friedman, J. Hage, C. A. Kiesler, O. Larsen, D. Menzel, S. D. Nelson, L. Sechrest, D. Stokes, & G. Zaltman). (1982). Contributions of social science to innovation and productivity. *American Psychologist, 37,* 737–746.

Torrance, E. P. (1969). Originality of imagery in identifying creative talent in music. *Gifted Child Quarterly, 13,* 3–8.

Tourangeau, R., & Ellsworth, P. C. (1979). The role of facial response in the experience of emotion. *Journal of Personality and Social Psychology, 37,* 1519–1531.

Trick, R. W. (1985). Communicating emotion: The role of prosodic features. *Psychological Bulletin, 97*(3), 412–429.

Triplett, N. (1897). The dynamogenic factors in peacemaking and competition. *American Journal of Psychology, 9,* 507–533.

True, R. M. (1949). Experimental control in hypnotic age regression. *Science, 110,* 583–584.

Tsunoda, T. (1971). Differences of the cerebral dominance of vowel sounds among different languages. *Journal of Auditory Research, 11,* 305–314.

Tucker, J., & Friedman, S. T. (1972). Population density and group size. *American Journal of Sociology, 77,* 742–749.

Tulving, E. (1972). Episodic and semantic memory. In E. Tulving & W. Donaldson (Eds.), *Organization of memory.* New York: Academic Press.

Tulving, E. (1985). How many memory systems are there? *American Psychologist, 40*(4), 385–398.

Tulving, E., & Pearlstone, Z. (1966). Availability versus accessibility of information in memory for words. *Journal of Verbal Learning and Verbal Behavior, 5,* 381–391.

Turkington, C. (1984, January). The growing use, and abuse, of computer testing. *APA Monitor,* p. 7.

Turnbull, C. (1961). Some observations regarding the experiences and behavior of the Bambuti pygmies. *American Journal of Psychology, 74,* 304–308.

Turner, R. H., & Killian, L. M. (1972). *Collective behavior* (3rd ed.). Englewood Cliffs, NJ: Prentice-Hall.

Tversky, B. (1973). Encoding processes in recognition and recall. *Cognitive Psychology, 5,* 275–287.

Tyerman, A., & Spencer, C. (1983). A critical test of the Sherifs' Robber's Cave experiments: Intergroup competition and cooperation between groups of well-acquainted individuals. *Small Group Behavior, 14,* 515–531.

U

Udry, J. R., & Morris, N. M. (1968). Distribution of coitus in the menstrual cycle. *Nature, 220,* 593–596.

V

Vaillant, G. E. (1977). *Adaptation to life.* Boston: Little, Brown.

Vaillant, G. E., & Milofsky, E. S. (1982). The etiology of alcoholism: A prospective viewpoint. *American Psychologist, 37,* 494–503.

Vallone, R. P., Ross, L., & Lepper, M. R. (1985). The hostile media phenomenon: Biased perception and perceptions of media bias in coverage of the Beirut massacre. *Journal of Personality and Social Psychology, 49,* 557–569.

VanDyke, C., & Byck, R. (1982). Cocaine. *Scientific American, 246*(3), 108–119.

Veroff, J., Atkinson, J. W., Feld, S. C., & Gurin, G. (1960). The use of thematic apperception to assess motivation in a nationwide interview study. *Psychological Monographs, 74*(12, Whole No. 499).

Vincent, K. (1982a). The development of a fully automated inkblot test: The Holtzman Content Analysis Technique. *Computers in Psychiatry/Psychology, 4*(2), 15–17.

Vincent, K. (1982b). Validation of the interpretive schema for a fully automated inkblot test: The Holtzman Content Analysis Technique. *Computers in Psychiatry/Psychology, 4*(4), 16–17.

von Bekesy, G. (1949). The vibration of the cochlear partition in anatomical preparations in the models of the inner ear. *Journal of the Acoustical Society of America, 21,* 235–245.

Vroom, V. H. (1964). *Work and motivation.* New York: Wiley.

W

Wagman, M. (1982a). Solving dilemmas by computer or counselor. *Psychological Reports, 50,* 127–135.

Wagman, M. (1982b). A computer method for solving dilemmas. *Psychological Reports, 50,* 291–298.

Wagner, R. K., & Sternberg, R. J. (1985). Practical intelligence in real-world pursuits: The role of tacit knowledge. *Journal of Personality and Social Psychology, 49*(2), 436–458.

Wahba, M. A., & Bridwell, L. B. (1976). Maslow reconsidered: A review of research on the need hierarchy theory. *Organizational Behavior and Human Performance, 15,* 212–240.

Wald, G. (1968). The molecular basis of visual excitation. *Nature* (London), *219,* 800–807.

Waldfogel, S. (1948). The frequency and affective character of childhood memories. *Psychological Monographs, 62* (Whole No. 291).

Walk, R. D., & Gibson, E. J. A. (1961). Comparative and analytic study of visual depth perception. *Psychological Monographs, 75*(15, Whole No. 519).

Wallace, P. (1974). Complex environments: Effects on brain development. *Science, 185,* 1035–1037.

Wallace, P. (1977). Individual discrimination of humans by odor. *Physiology and Behavior, 19,* 577–579.

Wallach, H., Newman, E. G., & Rosenzweig, M. R. (1949). The precedence effect in sound localization. *American Journal of Psychology, 62,* 315–336.

Wallach, M. A., Kogan, N., & Bem, D. J. (1964). Diffusion of responsibility and level of risk taking in groups. *Journal of Abnormal and Social Psychology, 68,* 263–274.

Wallerstein, J. S., & Kelly, J. B. (1980). *Surviving the break-up: How children and parents cope with divorce.* New York: Basic Books.

Walster, E., Aronson, E., & Abrahams, D. (1966). On increasing the persuasiveness of a low prestige communicator. *Journal of Experimental Social Psychology, 2,* 325–342.

Walster, E., & Walster, G. W. (1978). *A new look at love.* Reading, MA: Addison-Wesley.

Walster, E., Walster, G. W., & Berscheid, E. (1978). *Equity: Theory and research.* Boston: Allyn & Bacon.

Waterman, A. S., & Goldman, J. A. (1976). A longitudinal study of ego identity development at a liberal arts college. *Journal of Youth and Adolescence, 5,* 361–369.

Waterman, W. S. (1982). Identity development from adolescence to adulthood: An extension of theory and a review of research. *Developmental Psychology, 18*(3), 341–358.

Watson, J. B. (1913). Psychology as the behaviorist views it. *Psychological Review, 20,* 158–177.

Watson, J. B., & Rayner, R. (1920). Conditioned emotional reactions. *Journal of Experimental Psychology, 3,* 1–14.

Weary, G. (1980). Examination of affect and egotism as mediators of bias in causal attributions. *Journal of Personality and Social Psychology, 38,* 348–357.

Webb, W. B. (1975). *Sleep: The gentle tyrant.* Englewood Cliffs, NJ: Prentice-Hall.

Webb, W. B., & Cartwright, R. D. (1978). Sleep and dreams. *Annual Review of Psychology, 29,* 223–252.

Weber, M. (1957). *The theory of social and economic organizations* (A. M. Henderson & T. Parsons, Trans.). New York: Free Press.

Wechsler, D. (1939). *The measurement of adult intelligence.* Baltimore: Williams and Wilkins.

Weick, K. E., Bougon, M. G., & Maruyama, G. (1976). The equity context. *Organizational Behavior and Human Performance, 15,* 32–65.

Weindruch, R., & Walford, R. L. (1982). Dietary restriction in mice beginning at 1 year of age: Effect on life-span and spontaneous cancer incidence. *Science, 215,* 1415–1417.

Weiner, I. B., & Bordin, E. S. (1983). Individual psychotherapy. In I. B. Weiner (Ed.), *Clinical methods in psychology* (2nd ed.). New York: Wiley-Interscience.

Weiss, B. (1981). Food colors and behavior. *Science, 212,* 578–579.

Welgan, P. R. (1974). Learned control of gastric acid secretions in ulcer patients. *Psychosomatic Medicine, 36,* 411–419.

Wexler, D. A., & Rice, L. N. (Eds.). (1974). *Innovations in client-centered therapy.* New York: Wiley-Interscience.

White, B. C., Lincoln, C. A., Pearce, N. W., Reeb, R., & Vaida, C. (1980). Anxiety and muscle tension as consequences of caffeine withdrawal. *Science, 209,* 1547–1548.

Whitten, W. K., & Bronson, F. H. (1970). The role of pheromones in mammalian reproduction. In J. W. Johnston, D. G. Moulton, & A. Turk (Eds.), *Advances in chemoreception* (Vol. 1). New York: Appleton-Century-Crofts.

Whorf, B. L. (1956). *Language, thought and reality* (J. B. Carroll, Ed.). Cambridge: MIT Press.

Williams, M. D. (1976). *Retrieval from very long-term memory.* Unpublished doctoral dissertation, University of California, San Diego.

Wilson, G. T. (1982). Adult disorders. In G. T. Wilson & C. M. Franks (Eds.), *Contemporary behavior therapy.* New York: Guilford.

Winch, R. F. (1958). *Mate selection.* New York: Harper.

Winick, M., & Rosso, P. (1975). Malnutrition and central nervous system development. In J. W. Prescott, M. S. Read, & D. B. Coursin (Eds.), *Brain function and malnutrition.* New York: Wiley.

Winston, P. H. (1984). *Artificial intelligence* (2nd ed.). Reading, MA: Addison-Wesley.

Witelson, S. F. (1985). The brain connection: The corpus callosum is larger in left-handers. *Science, 229,* 665–668.

Wolpe, J. (1952). Experimental neuroses as learning behavior. *British Journal of Psychology, 43,* 243–268.

Wolpe, J. (1958). *Psychotherapy by reciprocal inhibition.* Stanford, CA: Stanford University Press.

Wolpe, J. (1969). *The practice of behavior therapy.* New York: Pergamon Press.

Wood, J. V., Taylor, S. E., & Lichtman, R. R. (1985). Social comparison in adjustment to breast cancer. *JPSP, 49,* 1169–1183.

Y

Yang, R. K., Zweig, A. R., Douthitt, T. C., & Federman, E. J. (1976). Successive relationships between maternal attitudes during pregnancy, analgesic medication during labor and delivery, and newborn behavior. *Developmental Psychology, 12,* 6–14.

Yerkes, R. M., & Dodson, J. D. (1908). The relation of strength of stimulus to rapidity of habit-formation. *Journal of Comparative Neurology, 18,* 459–482.

Z

Zaidel, E. (1975). A technique for presenting lateralized visual input with prolonged exposure. *Vision Research, 15,* 283–289.

Zajonc, R. B. (1976). Family configuration and intelligence. *Science, 192,* 227–236.

Zajonc, R. B. (1980). Feeling and thinking: Preferences need no inferences. *American Psychologist, 35,* 151–175.

Zajonc, R. B. (1984). On the primacy of affect. *American Psychologist, 39*(2), 117–123.

Zajonc, R. B., & Bargh, J. (1980). Birth order, family size, and decline of SAT scores. *American Psychologist, 35,* 662–668.

Zajonc, R. B., & Markus, G. B. (1975). Birth order and intellectual development. *Psychological Review, 82,* 74–88.

Zaleska, M. (1978). Some experimental results: Majority influence on group decisions. In H. Brandstatter, J. H. Davis, & H. Schuler (Eds.), *Dynamics of group decisions.* Beverly Hills, CA: Sage.

Zillmann, D. (1971). Excitation transfer in communication-mediated aggressive behavior. *Journal of Experimental Social Psychology, 7,* 419–434.

Zillmann, D. (1979). *Hostility and aggression.* New York: Halsted Press.

Zimbardo, P. (1979). *Psychology and life* (10th ed.). Glenview, IL: Scott, Foresman and Co.

Zimbardo, P. G. (1969). The human choice: Individuation, reason and order versus deindividuation, impulse and chaos. In W. J. Arnold & D. Levine (Eds.), *Nebraska symposium on motivation* (Vol. 17). Lincoln, NE: University of Nebraska Press.

Zimbardo, P. G., Andersen, S. M., & Kabat, L. G. (1981). Induced hearing deficit generates experimental paranoia. *Science, 212,* 1529–1531.

Zimmerman, B., & Smith, D. (1978). *Careers in health: The professionals give you the inside picture about their jobs.* Boston: Beacon Press.

Zinberg, N. E., & Harding, W. M. (1982). Control and intoxicant use: A theoretical and practical overview. In N. E. Zinberg & W. M. Harding (Eds.), *Control over intoxicant use.* New York: Human Sciences Press.

Zucker, I., Rusak, B., & King, R. G. (1976). Neural bases for circadian rhythms in rodent behavior. In A. H. Riesen & R. F. Thompson (Eds.), *Advances in psychobiology* (Vol. 3). New York: Wiley-Interscience.

Zuckerman, M., Klorman, R., Larrance, D. T., & Spiegel, N. H. (1981). Facial, autonomic, and subjective components of emotion: The facial feedback hypothesis vs. the externalizer-internalizer distinction. *Journal of Personality and Social Psychology, 41,* 929–944.

Zuckerman, M. (1979). *Sensation seeking: Beyond the optimal level of arousal.* Hillsdale, NJ: Lawrence Erlbaum Associates.

credits

Photos

Part opener 1, 2, 4, 5: © Jean-Claude Lejeune;
Part opener 3: © Ron Byers.

Chapter 1

1.1: courtesy Patricia Wallace; **1.2:** © Robert
Eckert/EKM-Nepenthe; **1.4:** courtesy National
Library of Medicine; **1.5:** courtesy National
Library of Medicine; **1.6:** The Bettmann Archive;
1.7: The Bettmann Archive; **1.8:** © Christopher S.
Johnson/Stock, Boston.

Chapter 2

2.1a,b: courtesy National Library of Medicine;
2.2: © Ed Reschke; **2.8:** courtesy Technicare.

Chapter 3

3.4: © James Shaffer; **3.7:** The Bettmann Archive;
3.8: courtesy Dr. Ann Pytkowicz Streissguth/
University of Washington.

Chapter 4

4.7: © James Shaffer; **4.9:** © H. Armstrong
Roberts; **4.12a,b:** © Bob Coyle; **4.17:** © Jean-
Claude Lejeune.

Chapter 5

5.1: Smithsonian Institution National
Anthropological Archives; **5.10:** courtesy B. F.
Skinner; **5.11:** courtesy Albert Bandura.

Chapter 6

6.8: © James Shaffer.

Chapter 7

7.3: © Emil Fray; **7.4:** © Susan Kuklin; **7.13:**
Culver Pictures, Inc.

Chapter 8

8.4: courtesy Philip Teitelbaum; **8.7:(left to right)**
© Steve Takatsuno, © Bob Coyle, © Richard L.
Good.

Chapter 9

9.2: courtesy March of Dimes; **9.4a,b:** © Landrum
Shettles, **c,d,** © Steve Takatsuno; **9.6:** © William
Vandivert; **9.7:** courtesy Harlow Primate Lab,
University of Wisconsin.

Chapter 10

10.3: © Steve Takatsuno; **10.5:(all)** Culver
Pictures, Inc.

Chapter 11

11.1: The Bettmann Archive; **11.3:** The Bettmann
Archive; **11.4:** courtesy National Library of
Medicine.

Chapter 12

12.3: © Steve Takatsuno; **12.4:** The Bettmann
Archive; **12.5:** © Jean-Claude Lejeune.

Chapter 13

13.3: © Jean-Claude Lejeune.

Chapter 14

14.1: © James Shaffer; **14.3:** © Steve Takatsuno.

Chapter 15

15.1: © Jean-Claude Lejeune; **15.2:** United Press
Photo.

Chapter 16

16.4: © Jean-Claude Lejeune.

Figures

Chapter 2

Figure 2.3 From Groves, Philip M., and Kurt
Schlesinger, *Introduction to Biological
Psychology,* 2nd ed. © 1979, 1982 Wm. C. Brown
Publishers, Dubuque, Iowa. All Rights Reserved.
Reprinted by permission.
Figure 2.4 From Johnson, Leland G., *Biology.*
© 1983 Wm. C. Brown Publishers, Dubuque,
Iowa. All Rights Reserved. Reprinted by
permission.
Figure 2.5 From Schlesinger, Kurt, and Philip
M. Groves, et al., *Psychology: A Dynamic
Science.* © 1976 Wm. C. Brown Publishers,
Dubuque, Iowa. All Rights Reserved. Reprinted
by permission.
Figure 2.7 From Hole, John W., Jr., *Human
Anatomy and Physiology,* 3rd ed. © 1978, 1981,
1984 Wm. C. Brown Publishers, Dubuque, Iowa.
All Rights Reserved. Reprinted by permission.
Figure 2.9 (part a) From Hole, John W., Jr.,
Human Anatomy and Physiology, 3rd ed. © 1978,
1981, 1984 Wm. C. Brown Publishers, Dubuque,
Iowa. All Rights Reserved. Reprinted by
permission.
Figure 2.9 (part b) From Johnson, Leland G.,
Biology. © 1983 Wm. C. Brown Publishers,
Dubuque, Iowa. All Rights Reserved. Reprinted
by permission.
Figure 2.10 Reprinted with permission of
MacMillan Publishing Company from *The
Cerebral Cortex of Man* by Wilder Penfield and
Theodore Rasmussen. Copyright 1950 by
MacMillan Publishing Company, renewed in 1978
by Theodore Rasmussen.
Figure 2.11 From Lahey, Benjamin B.,
Psychology: An Introduction, 2nd ed. © 1983,
1986 Wm. C. Brown Publishers, Dubuque, Iowa.
All Rights Reserved. Reprinted by permission.
Figure 2.12 From Hole, John W., *Human
Anatomy and Physiology,* 3rd ed. © 1978, 1981,
1984 Wm. C. Brown Publishers, Dubuque, Iowa.
All Rights Reserved. Reprinted by permission.

name index

subject index